compose ▪ design ▪ advocate

a rhetoric for integrating written, visual, and oral communication

Anne Frances Wysocki ▪ Dennis A. Lynch

PEARSON
Longman

New York Boston San Francisco
London Toronto Sydney Tokyo Singapore Madrid
Mexico City Munich Paris Cape Town Hong Kong Montreal

Senior Acquisitions Editor: Lynn M. Huddon
Senior Marketing Manager: Sandra McGuire
Development Editor: Leslie Taggart
Senior Supplements Editor: Donna Campion
Media Supplements Editor: Jenna Egan
Production Coordinator: Virginia Riker
Text Design, and Electronic Page Makeup: Anne Frances Wysocki
Cover Design Manager: Wendy Ann Fredericks
Cover Designer: Anne Frances Wysocki
Cover Illustration/Photo: Anne Frances Wysocki
Photo Researcher: Photosearch, Inc.
Manufacturing Buyer: Lucy Hebard
Printer and Binder: RR Donnelley, Willard, Inc.
Cover Printer: The Leigh Press, Inc.

For permission to use copyrighted material, grateful acknowledgment is made to the
copyright holders on pp 533–537, which are hereby made part of this copyright page.

Library of Congress Cataloging-in-Publication Data

Wysocki, Anne Frances,
    Compose, design, advocate/Anne Frances Wysocki,
  Dennis A. Lynch — 1st ed.
            p. cm.
    ISBN 0-321-11778-6
  1. Rhetoric.   2. Written communication.   3. Oral communication.
  4. Visual communication.   I. Lynch, Dennis A. 1955-   II. Title.

P301.W97 2005
808—dc22   2005030057

Visit us at www.ablongman.com

ISBN 0-321-11778-6

2 3 4 5 6 7 8 9 10—DOW—08 07 06

purposes of this book

This book presents an approach to communication intended to help you determine the most effective strategies, arrangements, and media to use in different contexts.

By giving you a systematic approach for analyzing situations in which you must produce different kinds of documents and presentations, and by giving you concepts and vocabulary that will help you make thoughtful choices in presenting visual, oral, and written communication, we hope to help you gain more confidence and fluency in communication.

In addition, because we see communication as being about building relationships among people, and because we see thoughtful and careful communication as being central to active and engaged citizenship, we present our approach to communication with a focus on civic advocacy. We hope to support you in gaining a thoughtful and strong presence in the organizations and practices that help shape the country and communities we share and nurture together.

the conceptual shape
of this book

This book is shaped by a system of amplification: we start off small and general (represented by the smallest circle in the picture to the left), and then we add to—amplify—that beginning in each of the successive sections so that by the end you'll have a detailed and rich sense of composing effective pieces of communication.

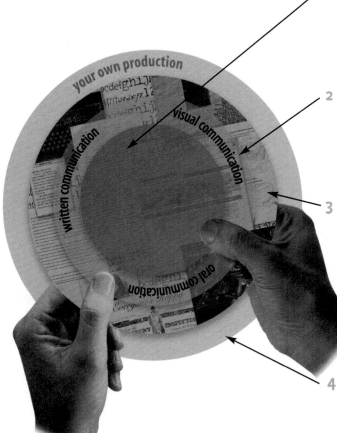

1 designing compositions rhetorically

This book's first section develops a process—using a series of specific steps—to help you think through situations in which you need to communicate with others. You'll see how to develop design plans for different kinds of communication, using a construction set of concepts, vocabulary, and approaches to help you make specific and detailed choices about the communication you are composing.

2 producing compositions

This section starts with a chapter on advocacy, on thinking and talking about how we choose to be productive in our actions in the world. There is a chapter on how to conduct productive, engaged research in support of advocacy. Finally, there are chapters to help you learn more about the vocabulary, concepts, and methods for working with written, visual, and oral communication.

3 analyzing the compositions of others

This section contains examples of many kinds of communication (some of which are on the book's website, *www.ablongman.com/wysocki*). The examples—posters, essays, comics—will help you in several ways. First, they demonstrate conventions we've learned to expect in different kinds of communication; when you need to produce a specific kind of communication, you can refer to the examples to help you think about how to meet your audience's expectations. Second, we use the examples to demonstrate how to analyze different kinds of communication; doing such analysis of texts that are effective (or not) with their intended audiences helps you learn more about strategies and approaches for making your own communication stronger.

4 your own production

You are on your own here. This is where you use the resources of *compose ▪ design ▪ advocate* and your analyses of the texts of others to produce your own texts for the communication contexts that matter to you.

compose ▪ design ▪ advocate

brief contents

detailed contents

compose ▪ design ▪ advocate

compose ▪ design ▪ advocate

contents

acknowledgments

The names of those who helped us become who we are as teachers of rhetoric and composition make a long list, and it is a list that gives us much pleasure in reading. We are forced to put the names in some order because this is writing, but we hope that those whose names follow here know our gratitude for their generosity, spirit, and example: Arthur Quinn, Marilyn Cooper, Diana George, Nancy Grimm, Dickie Selfe, Cindy Selfe, Stephen Jukuri, Jeff Walker, Kathy Yancey, Doug Hesse, Chris Anson, Linda Brodkey, Richard Miller, John Schilb, John Trimber, Mary Hocks, Sharon Hillis, Bruce Beiderwell, Randy Woodland, Jeanne Gunner, Jennifer Bradley, Sonja Maasik, John Gage, Joe Harris, Martha Diepenbrock, Bruce Saito, Amy Sedivy, Ann Savage, Hubert Dreyfus, and Czeslaw Milosz.

This book has its seeds in a course we developed with others at Michigan Technological University. Those in the Rhetoric and Technical Communication graduate program at MTU whose commitment to teaching were invaluable in how this book took shape include Julia Jasken, Cyndi Weber, Patti Sotirin, Randy Freisinger, Kristin Arola, Matt Hill, and Karen Springsteen. We wish to thank Julia Jasken, in particular, for the dedication she showed to classrooms and programs that thoughtfully engage students.

The project of *compose • design • advocate* took longer than any of us imagined. For their intelligence about how people learn to compose but also for their humored patience and many cheering phone calls, we thank Lynn Huddon and Leslie Taggart. Everyone who helped with the production on this book—Virginia Riker, Wendy Ann Fredericks—showed considerable grace and generosity given how this book was not produced following the, um, usual process.

Finally, this book would not be what it is without the thoughtful, helpful, and encouraging feedback of its many reviewers. We give them heartfelt thanks for the valuable time they have given us.

Danielle Nicole DeVoss, Michigan State University

Stephanie L. Dowdle, Salt Lake Community College

Carolyn Handa, Southern Illinois University, Edwardsville

H. Brooke Hessler, Oklahoma City University

Karla Saari Kitalong, University of Central Florida

Marshall Kitchens, Oakland University

Rita Malenczyk, Eastern Connecticut State University

Randall McClure, Minnesota State University

Deborah L. Church Miller, University of Georgia

Martin Mundell, Washington State University

Donna Niday, Iowa State University

Bridget Ruetenik, Penn State University

David R. Russell, Iowa State University

Robert Schwegler, University of Rhode Island

Kirk Swenson, Paradise Valley Community College

Pamela Takayoshi, Kent State University

Summer Smith Taylor, Clemson University

Deborah Coxwell Teague, Florida State University

Steven T. Varela, University of Texas at El Paso

Cynthia Walker, Faulkner University

Patricia Webb, Arizona State University

introduction

Take a few minutes to write about each of these words: *composing, designing, advocating*. What do you think when you hear these words? What experiences or pictures come to mind? What do you think you are getting into with this book that has *compose* ▪ *design* ▪ *advocate* as its title—and what would be the best possible outcome for you from using this book?

In the next few pages, we explain how we use these terms, why we titled the book as we did, and what we hope you will learn from working through the chapters that follow.

composing

People compose music, and they compose salads, and they compose themselves.

If someone describes you as "composed," it is generally a compliment: it means you are calm and collected and at ease, well put together.

"To compose," that is, is to bring pieces together into a whole.

COMPOSING TO THINK, COMPOSING TO COMMUNICATE

But there is more . . .

Since the late 1800s there has been strong academic interest in teaching writing. Those who study the discipline of composition are interested in how people write and in using what they learn to help others write more easily, confidently, and self-awarely.

For example, compositionists have observed that people sometimes write for themselves, to make sense out of what they see around them and experience. This is using writing to think, to work out ideas to shape our thinking into memories and ideas we want to hold on to. This is writing that appears in journals, or on scraps of paper: it is not usually meant for others to read, and often others will have trouble understanding it because the writer will use names of people or places without explanation or will have a kind of personal shorthand for referring to events and thoughts.

People also write to communicate. This kind of writing may start with someone doing some personal writing to work out her or his ideas, but for other people to be able to read this writing it has to be modified. The writing has to be shaped so that other people can follow its logical structure. Names and places have to be explained. Transitions between parts of the writing have to be written into the piece so that readers can see the connections between ideas. And some parts of the writing may need to be expanded and others deleted so that readers can understand what the writer wants to emphasize.

College composition classes are often about helping people make the transition from personal writing to writing for others. In composition classes people learn to observe their own writing practices so that they understand why they sometimes have trouble writing and how they can change what they are doing to improve their writing. They learn to get clearer about what they want to say by thinking, writing, and talking with others. And they learn how to work through multiple drafts of writing: they put their ideas to be more "readable" into an initial arrangement on the page, get the feedback from others, and then rearrange their ideas in response to the feedback.

compose ▪ design ▪ advocate

COMPOSING SOCIALLY

Compositionists also have observed that writing is always social: writing doesn't exist in a vacuum but instead connects people in particular times and places—and so writing is itself connected to and shaped by its time and place. This means that pieces of writing can't simply be picked up and understood by just anyone no matter where they are or when they are reading.

Think, for example, how hard archaeologists in past centuries have had to work to decipher texts they found deep in dusty tombs and caves and forests. This deciphering is not simply about figuring out what words in our language correspond to particular unknown shapes on papyrus or rock; people who decipher texts can only make sense of a text if they also can figure out who wrote the text and when, for whom, and for what purpose. That is, the decipherers can only learn to read such texts if they learn something about the daily lives of the people who produced the text, if they think about the text as woven into a whole web of social practices.

When we say writing is social we mean that it comes out of and fits back into this web of practices. As thinking and as communication, writing shapes people's ideas about what is possible and about what we ought to do as individuals and as groups and about the relations we might have with ourselves and each other.

COMPOSITION AND RHETORIC

The discipline of composition has always been closely tied to the practices of rhetoric, an approach to speaking that first developed in ancient Greece. Rhetoricians in Greece, Rome, the Mediterranean area and Europe, and the United States have, over centuries, developed systematic processes for speakers and, eventually, writers to compose texts; these processes ask composers to think about the particular times and places in which particular people—audiences—will encounter the spoken or written text being produced. These processes also help composers consider what textual strategies and arrangements will best help the composers persuade audiences to consider matters in the way the composer hopes.

composing and this book

Words matter to us. We are all too aware, from spats we have had with others and times we have wanted to disappear into corners because our talk hurt someone else or ourselves, of the power of words to affect others. We have seen political speeches that motivate audiences to action, and we have listened to the carefully crafted arguments that shape jury trials. We have giggled and felt unsettled over love letters and have worked hard to write letters that will let our parents know how much we appreciate what they have put up with—and taught us. We have been knocked into silence by hearing strangers respond enthusiastically and thoughtfully to articles we've written. We've gotten much pleasure from words, and taken much pleasure in arranging them.

The traditions of composition and rhetoric have helped us—and many others—approach writing and speaking situations systematically and thoughtfully, with an awareness of the responsibilities of our words and of the power we have to shape situations around us when we shape our words to fit them. These traditions have helped us, also, to take pleasure and satisfaction from shaping our words to please or move others.

Through this book, we hope to help you become a stronger communicator through drawing on what the disciplines of composition and rhetoric bring to communication.

designing

In addition to what we've written on these pages in the Introduction, here's another reason why we use "designing" in this book: when we think of "designing something" we don't usually think of writing a paper, poem, or report, but when we are writing—or when we are having trouble writing—it can provide a fresh viewpoint to think of writing as "designing." Designing brings to mind drawing plans and making (and remaking) models—using our hands to put things together—and sometimes our problems with writing are caused by being too much stuck in our heads.

Just as words matter to us, so do the other objects we can make to communicate: we've been moved to sweet tears by photographic collages of shared times that friends have made us when we've moved away, and we've been moved to make angry but informative posters in response to television news coverage that graphically depicts working conditions in factories in our state.

In recent years, changes in technologies—especially the digital—have made it easier for people to produce documents that are more visually active than was generally possible when the printing press and the typewriter were the technologies for producing documents. When you used a typewriter, you could only use the typeface that was built into the typewriter, in its one size; you could change the color of the type by changing the typewriter ribbon, but you certainly couldn't (and probably didn't even think about) producing curvy lines of words. With a computer, you can have wavy lines of type, in multiple colors and sizes, and you can produce pages with photographs or drawings. If you are producing pages for the computer screen, you can use animation, sound, or video and you can make your pages interactive, so that things happen when others move the mouse.

COMPOSITION AND DESIGN

Because of these changes in communication technologies, compositionists have over the last years been broadening their notion of composition. They've been working to broaden their thinking about words to include thinking about photographs and typography and color, and about how pages and screens on which alphabetic characters are mixed with drawings (for example) make sense to others.

Because compositionists have done this thinking, they have started to draw on design practices.

Compositionists are often drawn first to graphic design, because this is a field that mixes words (which have been given careful typographic treatment in terms of typeface, size, weight, color, and so on) and photographs or drawings. But in addition to graphic design there is industrial design, product design, interior design, information design, clothing design, experience design, and interface design; people design theater sets and costumes as well as wheelchairs and doorknobs and bridges and buildings and cities and neighborhoods.

Two concerns link all these different categories of design, as the different areas of design have developed since the early part of the twentieth century: designers are concerned with how people use things, and they are concerned that what they design is engaging and, very frequently, that it improves people's lives.

compose ▪ design ▪ advocate

Design, therefore, is similar to composition and rhetoric in several ways: both are concerned with audiences and with how audiences respond to what we make . . .

. . . BUT DESIGN ALSO DIFFERS FROM COMPOSITION AND RHETORIC:

- **Design is a more physically material process than composition and rhetoric.** Composition and rhetoric have been concerned with words, and hence with what people long thought you could do only with words: communicate abstract ideas. People who write usually don't think about the paper they use or the shapes and colors of the words they make; those things just aren't considered to contribute any meaning to what a writer is communicating.

  Designers, on the other hand, think about how people will see and hold and use what they make, or (in the case of architects) how people will move around inside and out of what they make. Designers think about how the size of what they make will relate to the sizes of people's bodies, and about how people with different abilities and ages will be able to use what they make; they think about whether the materials they use are cost-effective or save energy. Designers work to ensure that every part of what they make contributes to the overall purpose of their products.

- **Design has a stronger tradition of creativity than composition and rhetoric.** Since its beginnings centuries ago, rhetoric has had as one of its parts the process of "invention," in which a speaker or writer works to develop multiple strategies for approaching an audience in order to figure out which strategy is most effective—but this process often gets lost in how writing is taught. Design, on the other hand, has as part of its process long periods of time during which designers brainstorm and generate and mull over and have fun with multiple approaches to a design problem. Often designers don't know what they'll be producing, exactly: they'll know the purpose of what they need to make, and the audience and context— but they'll spend time thinking about the different kinds of objects, using different media, they could make, and how they can approach the process in order to develop something that will engage users and be highly functional. Designers have developed myriad approaches to enhancing and engaging their creative faculties.

- **Design has a stronger tradition of testing its productions.** Although compositionists encourage writers to go through multiple drafts of a piece of writing, and to get feedback from others in order to make the piece as effective as possible, the focus is often on how well an audience can read the writing or on the clarity of the arguments, and writers often wait until a piece is pretty much worked out before they give it to others for feedback. In design fields, people making things will often show their idea sketches to others and get feedback while a product is still a concept; designers will often, at every step of their development process, watch people use what they make to see if it works. There is even an approach called "Participatory Design": starting with the conceptual work of developing a product or process, designers make sure the intended users take part in discussions about how the product will be used, and why . . .

> "Design takes the results of past production as the resource for new shaping, and for remaking. Design is the action of setting an agenda for future aims, and of finding means and resources for carrying it out."
>
> —Gunther Kress

- Finally, because of the emphases design puts on materiality, creativity, and testing, designers tend to think hard about how what they make will go on to function in the world, shaping and changing the lives of others.

If you have read this far and thought that what we've written about composition and design shows the two approaches to communication to be not all that different, you are right: *the differences between design and composition (we believe) tend to be not so much hard differences as they are differences in levels of abstraction.*

Writers, like designers, think carefully about how their inventions will go on to function in the world, changing and shaping the lives of others, and they work to be creative, and they watch to see how others respond to what they make—but writers rarely think in concrete, day-to-day imaginings about their audiences and how their audiences will use what they make. They rarely think about what they make as being useful and as needing to fit into people's day-to-day lives, in the way that can openers and drills are and do.

designing and this book

We bring together composition and design—the practices of industrial and interface and product and information and graphic design as well as of architecture—because we think:

- Design's emphasis on the material conditions of production and consumption can help communicators think in new and stimulating and usefully concrete ways about how what they make fits into and can affect people's day-to-day lives and futures—as Gunther Kress, an educational theorist, argues in words like those to the left.

- Design's approaches to the visual and physical aspects of texts can help writers move from being fluid with words to being fluid with words, typefaces, colors, photographs, charts, drawings, animations, sizes and shapes of papers and screens, environments . . .

- Design's approaches to creativity—in terms of both technique and media—can help writers expand from thinking about text-on-paper as their only possible product. Design's approaches can help writers think about different media for developing a multitude of possible responses to the contexts in which they are working and the audiences for whom they are composing, in order, finally, to design what is most effective and fitting, what can shape the best futures.

compose ▪ design ▪ advocate

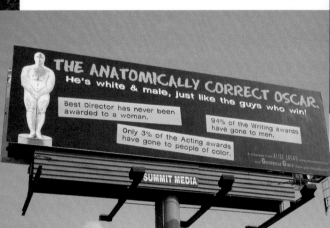

The Open-It tool has a blade, hook, and poking end for opening food.

We've been writing abstractly . . . but if you are interested in where you can see design in the way we are describing it, look around . . .

Look at buildings . . .

Look, for example, at the work of Samuel Mockbee (who, sadly, died at the very end of 2001) and his colleagues and students in the Rural Studio at Auburn University. In the College of Architecture, Design, and Construction at Auburn, students are challenged to experiment with inexpensive or free materials to construct useful homes and community buildings for people living in the poor rural areas of Alabama. The Yancey Chapel, shown above, is made, in part, from donated car tires and from slate the students carried from a nearby creek.

To learn and see more:
www.ruralstudio.com

Look at billboards, posters, and flyers . . .

The Guerrilla Girls are a New York City–based group started in 1985 in response to the museum exhibition "An International Survey of Painting and Sculpture." Although the title suggests that the exhibition included all kinds of art and artists, only 13 of the 169 artists represented were women and all the artists were white and from Europe or the United States. A number of women artists came together to research the situation, and—as a result of working together—founded the Guerrilla Girls, who work to publicize the treatment of people of color and women in the arts. The Guerrilla Girls stay anonymous: when they appear in public, they wear gorilla costumes. They present well-researched arguments about how the art world discriminates, and they present their work in eye-catching ways, like the billboard above.

To learn and see more:
www.guerrillagirls.com

Look at what's in your kitchen . . .

The yellow tool above right helps older people open food packaging. If you are under 60, you may shake your head at the need for something like this, but "as many as 7 percent of elders in the United States 65 years and older and 12 percent 75 and older need help preparing meals and have increasing physical impairments that prevent them from being able to open food containers." The tool was developed by students in an occupational therapy course, who observed during fieldwork the troubles elders have in opening food cans or the food packages that many receive as part of meal delivery services. The students interviewed elders about what they needed, developed a prototype, tested and refined what they made, and found funding to get the tool made and distributed.

To learn and see more: http://cpmcnet.columbia.edu/news/in-vivo/Vol1_Iss10_may29_02/index.html

advocating

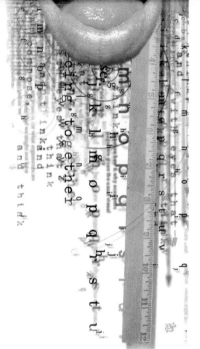

WHY "ADVOCATE"?

Composition and design both emphasize that any communication you make—a piece of writing, a webpage, a house—comes out of and fits (sometimes better, sometimes worse) into the society around it. Any piece of communication, that is, draws on patterns and arrangements that already exist for making meaning (imagine people trying to make sense out of a paper written in a language you made up). Any communication also modifies and reshapes those patterns and arrangements for the context and audience at hand, and then is read by people whose thinking or behaviors will be affected.

Because every piece of communication is a social act in the way we have just described, every piece advocates a view or position on the world in which we live.

Now obviously some pieces of communication do this more directly and self-awarely than others, and the composers of some pieces of communication work to cause direct, explicit, and large changes as a result of what they do:

If you walk up to a friend and ask to borrow money for a movie, and your friend agrees, you have for better or worse changed your relationship—made a dent in the world. Perhaps the change is slight, but still it is a change—and so it will be useful for you to think of the words you spoke not just as "having meaning" but as having "done something."

But if you start thinking of your communication as doing something, then you can start thinking about how much and what you can do. The musician Bono of U2, for example, has been going around and asking people for money, too, but he has been meeting with heads of state of prosperous countries, asking them not to require the poorer countries of the world to repay the immense debts they have racked up as a result of development loans from the prosperous countries. That debt, Bono argues after much research, keeps the poorer countries of the world from being able to use their resources to help their own people because they have to direct all their resource development to paying off the loans.

May I borrow $10, please?

Would your country be willing to help the causes of world peace and prosperity by forgiving the debt of third world countries?

compose ▪ design ▪ advocate

When we consider oral, written, and visual communication in this book, we always treat composing and designing as actions that DO something in and to the world.

The word "advocate" might sound to you like "activist"—and you might not see yourself as an activist. That's fine. What is important is that you recognize the power you have as a result of the communications you compose and design—a power that exists because of what communication simply is—and that you take responsibility for the effects of your communication.

By working through this book we hope you gain in abilities to think about the communications that help you achieve what matters to you in the world. We hope you strengthen your insights about the effects different communication strategies, arrangements, and media have on others.

Bono's actions probably feel out of our grasp (he is, after all, able to see heads of state because of his fame and its concomitant power). You also may not agree with his assessment of the world's economic situation. But Bono's work shows that he is aware his communications do something, and that he has thought about what he is capable of doing with his communication.

If you think about your communications as doing something instead of as words or pages that just exist, then you can begin to appreciate the power you have to build the relationships with and between others that you think should shape our world. You can begin to think about how you can build and shape and participate productively within the families, communities, civic and public service organizations, and political structures that are your life.

It is because of the possibilities of understanding communication as advocacy in the ways we've described that we've written this book.

The photograph above shows Bono meeting in 1999 with Pope John Paul II to discuss a worldwide campaign to cancel the debt owed by poor countries to rich countries. Bono went to this meeting with economists, charity workers, and other musicians. During the meeting, the Pope said, "The Catholic Church looks at the situation with great concern . . . because she has a moral vision of what the good of individuals and of the human family demands. She has consistently taught that there is a 'social mortgage' on all private property, a concept which today must also be applied to 'intellectual property' and to 'knowledge.' The law of profit alone cannot be applied to that which is essential for the fight against hunger, disease and poverty."

Think about how Bono prepared for this meeting: he brought a book of Irish poetry for the Pope (because such formal meetings often include giving a gift), he had facts and figures to back up his arguments about the debt of poor countries, and he did not dress as for a concert. Why did Bono and those with whom he is working think it would be worthwhile for them to meet with the Pope?

In this book we believe that:

COMPOSING + DESIGNING + ADVOCATING = WRITTEN, VISUAL, AND ORAL COMMUNICATION THAT WORKS IN SPECIFIC CONTEXTS FOR SPECIFIC AUDIENCES

COMPOSING +

the helpful approach of considering writing as thinking and as communication

a systematic approach to thinking about communication, based on a rhetorical model

awareness of audience

awareness of the social nature of communication

a rich approach to working and making sense with words

DESIGNING +

attention to the material aspects of communication

being creative with communication

testing what one produces

focusing on the actual day-to-day use of what one produces

a rich approach to working and making sense with the visual and material aspects of communication

ADVOCATING =

that communication not only means things but does things

WRITTEN, VISUAL, AND ORAL COMMUNICATION THAT WORKS IN SPECIFIC CONTEXTS FOR SPECIFIC AUDIENCES

We have brought together approaches, concepts, and vocabularies from composition and design, and woven them together through their attentions to the socially situated nature of communication, to help you become a stronger communicator.

As you will see in the following chapters, we propose a "rhetorically designed process" for helping you determine the most effective strategies, arrangements, and media to use in different communication contexts.

compose ▪ design ▪ advocate

getting
started

We've composed this book to help you become a stronger communicator. Because communication can occur in so many different media—buildings, videos, webpages, brochures, essays, speeches, quick conversations—we want to give you an approach to communicating that helps you move comfortably among various media. We want to help you make smart decisions about the meaning-building strategies available to you with all the different media so that you can produce engaging and strong communication that is appropriate for its situation.

To the right are actions you can take to prepare yourself for the work of this book. The actions ask you to reflect on who you already are as a communicator and what you already know about communicating with others.

All of us learn best when we can connect what is new to what we already know and when we have a clear sense of how what we are learning can help us achieve our particular goals and desires. By reflecting on your communications, by being attentive to what you already know, you set yourself up to be responsible for your own learning and to learn what will be most useful to you.

YOUR ABILITIES AS A COMMUNICATOR

What do you consider your strengths as a communicator? Do you speak well with others? Are you known as the family listener? Do all your friends want you to make flyers for concerts or webpages for them because you're good with visual arrangement? Are you comfortable with writing? Are you funny? Do you like to think at length about current issues? Are you happiest or most focused when you are composing song lyrics? **List, on a piece of paper, anything at all that gives you pleasure or satisfaction when you communicate, in any medium, in any context.**

Now list areas where you see you could be stronger in your communicative abilities. Again, think across media and contexts and audiences, and list ways you could be a more confident communicator. On what would you like to focus as you move through the chapters of this book?

Keep your lists with you and add to them as you work through this book and as you build different kinds of communication with others. If you want to be a communicator whose ideas stay with and move others, it is important to know the strengths on which you can draw as well as the aspects you can make stronger.

WHAT MAKES GOOD COMMUNICATION?

In a small group with two or three others, come up with as many criteria as you can for what characterizes "a good communicator."

Second, consolidate the lists, on a blackboard or large piece of paper.

Then, as a group, categorize the different criteria. Do these criteria only work for specifically oral, written, or visual communication—or a combination? For example, "grammatically correct" might fit into both written and oral communication, while "attentive to audience" would probably fit into all three. Because our schooling has tended to emphasize written communication, you might want to attribute a characteristic just to written communication, but consider, for example, "clarity": this might seem to be appropriate for just written—or perhaps written and oral—communication, but can a photograph or a page layout have clarity? Does clear writing matter if the layout of a page confuses a viewer?

Finally, build a checklist of your criteria. Keep hold of your checklist as you move through this book. Use the checklist to help you as you are producing your own communications—and see if there are more criteria you want to add or shift around the categories.

compose ▪ design ▪ advocate

HOW YOU HAVE BEEN SHAPED AS A COMMUNICATOR

Produce a text that shows how you have been shaped as a communicator. Make something that you can show to others, using any mix of photographs, drawings, alphabetic text, or any other material that will help others see what influenced you in becoming the communicator you are.

Think about how you characterize yourself as a talker or writer or listener or photographer or artist or musician or software developer . . . Then think about growing up, being in school, working, your personal life. In all that you have experienced, what situations or events have had the most effect in making you the communicator you are?

Once you have built your text, show it to others. First, show it without talking, and have the others tell you what they understand about what you have made, and why; listen to how they are making sense out of what you made, and how they are linking the pieces of your text to try to make a whole. Then explain your process to the others, why you chose to show what you did (and how you showed it), and what effect you hoped the text would have on others.

To the right and on the next pages are examples of texts people have made in response to this activity.

But I liked math and science

Kari Haapala made this text to represent how she felt torn while she was growing up. She didn't know any women who did the things she liked, and felt that she couldn't talk with other girls about the things she cared about—but she also felt that because she wasn't male, she didn't know how to act and talk with people who did do the things she liked.

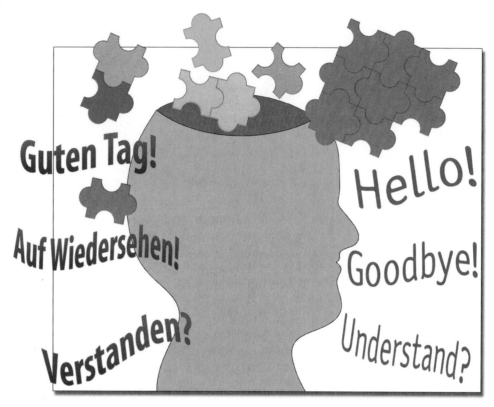

Connie Gherna's poster (the original is cut-out pieces of paper on posterboard) is about how, when she traveled to Germany (her first trip outside the United States), she learned that the pieces of communication don't always fit together the way you'd like.

As you look at this poster, think about why Connie might have chosen to have the head pointing in the direction it does, and why she chose the words, and the colors for the words, that she did. Why do you think she made the head look as though it is open at the top? These are all design choices that contribute to how you understand what Connie has made.

a short narrative about his literacy background, from Michael Dyson:

From the very beginning I was bathed in the ethos of linguistic appreciation. My mother talked to us and read to us. And then I went to church; the church is a very important narrative community for me, very powerful—not only in terms of the norms it mediates in regard to the stances one should take politically and spiritually, but simply because of the resplendent resonances that were there in terms of language: hearing the power of articulations of black preachers, hearing the linguistic innovations of black singers, hearing the rhetorical dexterity of a revivalist who came to town to try to paint the picture of God dying on a cross and the differences that death made, not simply telling us about a theology of atonement, not simply talking to us (in dry, arcane, academized, theological language) about the dispensation of God. They wanted to paint a picture; they wanted us to feel it, to feel the kind of existential and ontological density of linguistic specificity.

compose ▪ design ▪ advocate

a short narrative about her literacy background, from Dawn Powell:

. . . I had my own good reasons for running away the next time, when I was eleven. We were on a farm with a new stepmother who didn't know what to do with us so she put us outdoors after breakfast and locked all the doors. But we couldn't go in the barn because she said it would bother the horses. We couldn't play in the orchard, because we'd spoil the fruit. We couldn't go for a walk because we'd wear out our shoes. We couldn't sing our songs because the racket would keep the hens from laying. We couldn't read our old schoolbooks because we'd dirty them. However, unknown to her, we had discovered a pile of brown ledgers and colored pencils in a burned old cabin in the fields. My sister drew pictures and I wrote poems and stories. I must have knocked off a hundred poems and a dozen historical novels all involving brave Colonial maidens and rich, titled Redcoats. Since our creative labors made no noise, we were happily undiscovered for a good fortnight.

Then one day the ledgers vanished from their hiding place under the kitchen porch.

"No use looking," our stepmother called out from the other side of the locked screen porch. "I burned all that trash you were writing."

So I ran away.

Charles Hoffmayer's poster shows how his family read to him when he was little and how he felt comfortable communicating in his family. When he started school, however, he felt like an outsider—and so he stopped communicating. His grandmother then taught him how to take photographs, and he learned how to communicate through his pictures, which helped him regain his confidence in communicating.

When you look at this poster, what do you see first? How do your eyes move over the poster? Why do you think Charles has arranged his pictures from top to bottom and left to right, and used the colored borders he has? How would this poster be different if it had on it, in words, the story we wrote in the preceding paragraph?

A literacy narrative by Naia Suszek, a student:

MORE THAN JOURNALISM

The best writing experience I ever had was being editor of the high school yearbook. Before the yearbook most of what I wrote were formal papers for English or science classes. They weren't much more than long, elaborate ramblings presented in a fashion as to babble on for three to five pages. Neither creativity nor opinions were usually allowed.

Following such straight-edge rules set by my teachers was just not my style. The yearbook provided me with the opportunity to create my own style, not only in the form of writing, but in the presentation of information. My main objective was not only to do this for myself but to teach and guide others to do it as well. Perhaps this was my greatest obstacle: at the time I was not the best communicator and lived by the ordinance of, "It is better to do something yourself than to watch someone else screw it up for you."

I had fallen into the position of yearbook editor completely by accident. I was asked to look at and try to fix one of the computers in the English department. I then told the teacher I could help her set up the yearbook program.

Being the inconspicuous computer nerd that I was, I didn't find the software all that difficult to use: it was similar to some of the graphics programs I knew. But I soon learned that very few others were as computer savvy as I was. Trying to teach others is not as easy a task as I thought. Patience and good communication, virtues I often lack, are the keys to success.

I also realized that although everyone on my yearbook staff spoke English, we by no means understood the same language. I learned the necessity of being able to convey ideas to someone who does not understand you.

Not Just a Book, an Experience

There are many different types of people in this world, and I can say from experience, they all have different perspectives. Some are artistic, and some are practical, and the world would not be happy if either were absent. For example, take an architect and an engineer. If the world were full of engineers it would be a dull, drab place full of square buildings, efficient yet quite boring. However, if the world were full of architects we would have beautiful spectacular buildings, but they would not be safe to go into. My job was to create a happy medium between the two. This was not easy.

The goal of a yearbook is to create a lasting image of that year. A yearbook is a collection of stories, facts, a calendar of events, and, of course, pictures. Every page tells its story of what happened in a particular program. However, a yearbook story is more compressed than anything I had ever written. How can you sum up a year in a short paragraph? How can you describe a picture in two sentences? Can you create a headline to grab a person's attention?

Teaching people how to write a yearbook story may have been one of the more challenging obstacles, especially because I was just learning myself. I believe the only way to write something of good quality is to be interested in what you write. What better way than to recruit people participating in the focused club or sport? This way they were interested in what they were writing about—but they also knew what was going on in the pictures and the proper terminology.

Another thing I stressed among my yearbook staff was perfection. Not only in properly representing their assigned group, but in correctness of grammar and the spelling of names. It is not only students who look at the yearbook but their parents and present and potential advertisers. In my opinion, if you are going to put something out into the public, it should look and be professional because that piece of work represents you and your work ethic.

If every page in the yearbook were the same it would be boring. Another dilemma I encountered was how to make a page grab someone's attention. This was very difficult to explain to the practical-minded people, but in this case I paired them with the artistic types. Doing is learning, right?

Through my experience of communicating orally, by teaching and learning, I, with the aid of my staff, created a piece of visual art.

compose ▪ design ▪ advocate

SECTION 1

designing

compositions

rhetorically

Throughout this book you'll see "argument."

In common use as well as in the specialized studies of rhetoric, "argument" has acquired different meanings over time. We want to be clear about those meanings— and how we use the word in this book—so that you'll understand our uses of it.

everyday notions of argument

When you hear that someone was arguing with someone else, you probably picture two people (but perhaps more) face to face (if not in each other's face), and perhaps raised voices. This view of argument is of an often acrimonious event, when people vent their opinions and try to downplay—if not tear apart—the others' opinions.

"Argument" might also suggest debates to you, when two sides face off over an issue. Each side tries to present, before an audience, logical reasons for or against a position on the issue, hoping their words— their reasons made visible—will cause others to take on their position.

For the purposes of this book, we want to take from those two notions of argument only that **argument occurs when people hold differing ideas, opinions, or beliefs and when they agree to make visible their reasons for holding their ideas, opinions, or beliefs.**

specialized notions of argument

Rhetoricians sometimes use a very formal definition of argument: they'll say that a speech or a piece of writing is an argument if and only if it presents premises, in logical order, in support of a stated conclusion.

For the purposes of this book, we won't hold such a narrow definition—but we do draw on one aspect of it: we will sometimes speak of formal (and informal) argument. Sometimes we identify an argument based on its structure, or form: sometimes, when you want to be particularly overt about your intentions, you will want to use logical structures to support a position you'd like others to consider.

argument in this book

We all encounter situations every day where we need to make decisions with others or encourage others to act with us. This happens between individuals, when we decide what video to rent with a friend or how to proceed with a partner on a class project. This happens in groups, when a sorority plans a fund-raiser or the delegates to a state political convention decide which candidate to support.

Decisionmaking happens among people who know each other, but you can also be asked to make decisions or take action by strangers, such as when you hear radio commentary about what music is hot, read editorials about affirmative action, or watch sitcoms in which a character learns being thin and pretty does not bring happiness.

In such situations, those who speak, write, or otherwise make their positions visible might use formal argument—which is why there are sections of this book to help you analyze and use formal argumentative strategies. But there is a range of other strategies (including decisions about what media to use) available when we want to shift someone's attention, or help clarify what others are thinking—as we discuss in this book.

Notice, too, that in addition to emphasizing how arguments draw on strategies ranging from formal written or oral structures to the visible arrangements possible in a television production, we have been describing argument not as an event when you try to change someone's ideas 180 degrees. Instead, in this book we consider the overall purposes of argument to be presenting our positions to others in some kind of shape or arrangement so that others can see (or hear) and consider them. Only rarely do our words or other communications completely change someone's mind or cause them to storm out of the room determined to do something; most often, we might only strengthen or weaken their adherence to a belief, or we might move them closer to or further away from a possible action.

When we use "argument" in this book then, we generally want you to have in mind a piece of communication whose purpose is to direct and shape an audience's attentions in particular ways.

compose ▪ design ▪ advocate

formal argument is called "formal" because it uses logical "forms of argument," structures of organization that (generally) have explicit statements of premise and conclusion. "Formal" does not mean that the context in which the argument occurs is formal (like a prom)—just that the argument uses particular logical structures to present premises in support of a stated conclusion.

informal argument can simply be about directing someone's attention in a new or different direction, or showing them a new possible position that they hadn't considered before, or shifting their values—without explicit statement of premises and conclusions.

In this book we most often talk about informal arguments—but we treat all arguments as existing along a continuum because the different types are not mutually exclusive. Sometimes informal arguments will contain small formal argumentative structures, and sometimes a formal argument will start with an appeal to your emotions.

■ **Write informally:** What is your own definition of "argument"? In what ways does your definition align with—and differ from—ours?

■ **Discuss with others:** Look at the list below. Do you consider each example to be an "argument" as we've defined it—or not? If you think an example is not argument, can you imagine conditions under which it would be?

- a public-service TV piece against marijuana use
- a circus performance
- wearing blue jeans to school
- a flyer on the wall about an upcoming fundraising event
- refusing to buy clothing made in sweatshops
- a radio interview with a political candidate
- a spring break trip to build a Habitat for Humanity house
- a brochure about an energy-efficient car
- a book about growing up in Detroit
- going to a church retreat
- voting
- a song about voting
- a tattoo
- shaving your head

SETTING UP CONDITIONS THAT MAKE ARGUMENT (AND SO ADVOCACY) POSSIBLE

Arguments—formal or informal—are only possible when there is disagreement. We don't often argue about the color of the sky on a sunny day or whether humans need to eat to stay alive. We argue when we believe that there are differing ways to understand a situation or to act, and that by presenting our positions to each other we can work out the best understanding or action in the situation.

Similarly, there is little point in argument when there is no possibility of changing a situation. We don't often argue about how workable wings can be added to the human body—and we can't argue if we are in a political situation where disagreement brings imprisonment or worse.

These conditions tell us that when we value argument we value the individual right to hold and discuss opinions. They tell us we believe that the back and forth of argument can help us determine how to proceed in different situations.

We believe, therefore, that making arguments about what matters to you—being an advocate for what matters to you—only makes sense if you respect other people's rights to argue and advocate. This means you also should respect their actual efforts to argue and advocate, even when their choices are not ones you would have made.

Let's face the hard cases for not arguing in this way. Here are ten reasons people frequently give for plugging their ears when those with whom they disagree talk:

10 If it seems that they are not going to change their minds, it seems unfair for you to have to consider their opinions.

9 To show any doubt about the rightness or righteousness of your position is to show weakness and so make yourself vulnerable to attack from your opponents (or enemies).

8 To show any doubt about the rightness (or righteousness) of your position is morally wrong because moral values are clear and absolute, not up for debate or even questioning.

7 You don't want to find yourself persuaded to ideas you think are dangerous.

6 Not listening seems like an effective strategy: if you refuse to listen to others, you force them into a position where they have to give in more to you than you do to them.

5 You have tried to understand their point of view and just can't make sense of it.

4 They talk funny.

3 It takes too long to listen carefully to others and things don't get done.

2 If they have power over you they won't listen to you.

1 If you have the power over them, why should you listen? What does it get you?

Consider the social relations underlying the attitudes implied in those statements. Would it be worth living in a world where everyone held those statements as beliefs? To believe, for example, that you don't need to listen to others if you are in power is not the stuff of democracy, which (we hope) continues to be a value worth holding.

Or look at the statement that if you refuse to listen to others, you force them into a position where they have to give in more to you than you do to them. This statement implies, perhaps, a more defensible world because the statement is practical and, indeed, strategic. The statement might even seem in line with much that is to follow in this book for, as you'll see, we advocate an approach to communication where you locate your purpose and context, take note of your audience, and plan strategies. But we'll argue that you can plan acts of communication using the concepts of purpose, audience, and context in ways that build or strengthen communities and social relations, not cut them down.

Looking carefully at the contexts in which you communicate involves in part looking at how acts of communication are embedded in what is already going on. If the social relations in which you are embedded are unavoidably cut-throat, then planning what you say and how you say it in order to force others into a corner, no matter how it makes them feel in the long run, may make the best sense to you. But in that case, you should face the fact that you do not have a viable long-run vision. All you are doing is running a short-term game, the future (and respectful relations) be damned.

Most social and community contexts for participation and advocacy assume the value of working with others productively. A further assumption is that how we move forward—what we do next—affects the contexts we are in for better or for worse. You size up a situation, you act, and your action influences the situation, so that the next time you size up the situation, you have had a hand in shaping it. If you accept this assumption that how you communicate echoes back into the contexts in which you are communicating, then—and this is our argument—**when you choose to communicate, you become responsible for the ongoing health of the contexts within which you communicate.** Put otherwise, **any serious discussion of argument leads us back to how we want to live and what we want to do to and in the world. Argument is an important, nonviolent way to advocate.**

The lawyer, philosopher, and rhetorician Chaim Perelman and his co-author, Lucie Olbrechts-Tyteca, in their book *The New Rhetoric: A Treatise on Argumentation*, asked what conditions make argument possible; if you assume (as we do here) the value of serious communication and argumentation. Their answer is long, and it is a list. And as we claim in other places in this book, lists can tell a story, a story you sometimes have to search for. To the right is our telling of their list of **the conditions that make argument possible.**

CONDITIONS THAT MAKE ARGUMENT POSSIBLE

Anyone making an argument must:
- have an audience to address.
- share a common language with the audience.
- make contact of some kind with the audience, through spoken or written words or visual means.
- have a sincere interest in gaining the adherence of the audience.
- have a certain modesty about his or her beliefs, not holding them beyond question or discussion.
- be concerned about the audience and be interested in their state of mind.

In their turn, audiences must:
- be willing not only to listen but to try to understand.
- be committed to the argument, to its subject and its outcome.
- recognize how institutions like schools, churches, clubs, and so on both enable and inhibit how arguments happen.
- be willing to accept another's point of view, if only for the time of the argument.

Both the person making an argument and the audience must:
- recognize and accept that they may emerge from the argument changed.

the responsibilities of engaging in argument with others

■ **Discuss and then write informally for a few minutes:** When people write letters to the editor of a local newspaper or call in to a radio talk show, what are their responsibilities to their audiences and community? What about for someone who is creating a personal blog*? What are their responsibilities to audiences and community? Talk with others about their views on these issues, to gain a wider sense of how your communications fit into the larger networks of communication in which we all live and move, and then write down your general observations about how you want to think about your responsibilities as you communicate with others.

* **"blog" is short for "weblog." These are personal, diaristic webpages. For examples, see www.blogger.com. There are also blogs generated by communities; see citystories.com for examples of people using online resources to build a sense of place.**

A process for argument . . .
The process we describe in the first chapter is one we believe helps you make argument possible and engaging to those you want to listen to you.

compose ■ *design* ■ *advocate*

a rhetorical process
for designing compositions

A year ago, Dennis (one of the composers of this book) had a conversation with someone who had been in a class with him a few years before; we'll call the man "Walter." What Walter described to Dennis was a fairly funny (and also fairly embarrassing) communication failure—the kind of failure we've all experienced at one time or another. We'd all also probably like to forget such failures—but, even though we can be made uncomfortable by admitting our failures, in reflecting on them we can learn how to communicate better in future situations.

And so on the next few pages we start our book with Walter's story (after a little necessary background information) because, in reflecting on it later with Dennis, Walter figured out what had gone wrong and what he could have done differently.

In Walter's reflection are the seeds of the process we lay out in this book, a process that we think can help you be a better communicator—whether you have a speech to give, a website to make, or a research paper to write.

so, first, the background to Walter's story

On our campus students can take part in the "Enterprise Program." The Enterprise Program solicits tasks or problems from business, government, or local community groups and then forms a team of students (with a faculty adviser) whose job it is to perform the task or solve the problem. Some of the teams work on design competitions, such as "Fast Car" or "Fast Truck," in which they use their engineering knowledge to develop highly efficient (and fast) vehicles. What all the teams have in common is that they must work together on a large project, learn how to organize and plan the steps of such a project, develop a time-frame for completion, make a business plan for expenses, and prepare a project logo, letterhead, and marketing plan. Throughout the project they must communicate with each other, with suppliers, with the sponsoring organization or national competition organizations, with the rest of the campus, and with their advisers.

One day Dennis (who was Director of the Writing Programs on our campus and hence often called upon to help out all across campus when people want to learn about writing) met with a room full of people involved with the Enterprise Program (students, team leaders, advisers, and administrators of the program) to discuss how they could better learn to compose all the memos, plans, reports, and other documents they needed to produce. After the meeting, Walter came up to Dennis and told him the following story.

WALTER'S STORY

You were always telling us that communication affects how people get along . . . I have a story that'll make you laugh. I'm the team leader for the Fast Car project, and a few weeks ago we met—all guys, so far—and decided we needed more (or at least some!) women on the project. So we set up a meeting with the campus group Society of Women Engineers to pitch our project to them and get some to join us. But it didn't quite work out.

We all showed up at the meeting and began talking about Fast Car and how much fun it is, and then one of the women asked "Why do you want women to join?" And we said, "Well, there are lots of things you can help out with: we need people to take minutes at meetings and write memos to the adviser, secretarial-type stuff, and you might enjoy that."

Well, the reaction was icy. We tried to explain we did not mean that is all they could do, but it was too late. Did we blow it! No one joined. So we are back to square one! I guess we need to work on our communication skills, hey? Ha!

As you read about what we learned from talking with Walter, keep in mind a communication situation of your own that you wish had gone differently. Ask yourself the same questions Walter should have asked, to see what you could have done differently.

compose ▪ design ▪ advocate

What we learned

After Walter told his story, Dennis talked with him and another member of the Fast Car team who had been at the unsuccessful meeting. They talked about what exactly went wrong, and it was clear that they sensed what had gone wrong but could not put it into words. It was a good conversation, and they were glad they talked with Dennis because until he began asking them what went wrong, they thought they understood but then realized they didn't completely—at least not completely enough to prevent doing something similar again.

They knew they shouldn't have said the thing about needing secretaries. But they hadn't thought much beyond that.

Here is what Dennis, Walter, and Walter's friend came up with together as they talked:

1

Their biggest overall problem was **lack of specific purpose:** they hadn't given themselves time to think through carefully what they were doing and why.

They had thought that what they were doing was a no-brainer. After all, they knew their general purpose: they wanted more women in their group. They knew that they therefore needed to communicate with women about joining their group, and so they set up a meeting with the Society of Women Engineers (SWE) so they could describe their project.

They didn't think they needed a more detailed and specific statement of purpose to guide them in the meeting; it never occurred to them to make a plan for how to proceed in the meeting.

They should have asked: **Why are we communicating? What do we want to achieve here?**

2

They hadn't thought at all about **their audience,** women who are interested in a meeting about a Fast Car project. Because they hadn't thought about what might motivate women to want to work on such a project, they hadn't anticipated that someone might ask, "Why do you want more women on your team?" If they had thought about—and talked to—women who were studying to be engineers, and learned about their passions to design, build, and fix engines and computers and other equipment, Walter's group might have had a better sense of how to describe their project to this audience in order to interest them.

Instead, because they hadn't done this work, they ended up responding as though they thought women would be useful only as secretaries—which isn't what they really thought. But those were the first words out of their mouths, to their embarrassment.

Once they said these things it was too late. The women from SWE were hurt, offended, and angry that their fellow students saw them through such limited and limiting categories.

They should have asked: **Given who they are, what will our audience expect from our communication?**

3

They hadn't thought about **the larger context** of their meeting with their audience.

First, if they had learned about what it's like to be a woman in a career dominated by men, or to be on a campus (like ours) where men outnumber women 3 to 1, they would have had an even better sense of how most effectively to address their audience in the particular place and time of the meeting they called.

Second, they had called the meeting, so it was their responsibility to run the meeting and to anticipate as much as possible what might go on.

They should have asked: **How will the place and time of our communication affect its outcome?**

4

Because they hadn't thought about their purpose, audience, or the context of their communicative situation, they hadn't thought about what kinds of **communication strategies** would help them appeal effectively to the members of SWE.

If they had learned how women in engineering often feel that many men do not think women capable of doing engineering work (which is, after all, the message the Fast Car group sent when they said that the women could help with the secretarial work of the project), the group might have realized that they would show their seriousness and respect for the women by acknowledging how women are often treated in engineering.

They should have asked: **What are the strategies that will help us achieve our ends?**

5

They hadn't thought about **the medium of communication** they were using.

They were making an oral presentation, and so they should have considered what audiences often expect from such presentations. It's not unusual for someone giving an oral presentation to have supporting visual information: the Fast Car group could have brought slides of their work, which would have given their audience a concrete sense of the work they could do on the project.

Most importantly for the Fast Car group, however, is that audiences for oral presentations very frequently expect to ask questions and discuss the presentation with the presenters. Had the group thought about this, they could have discussed the kinds of questions they might be asked—and they might have then been prepared to thoughtfully and respectfully respond to the question of why they wanted women in their group.

They should have asked: **What do audiences tend to expect about the medium we're using? Are we using the best possible medium?**

They hadn't thought about **the order in which they would arrange and combine their communication strategies** in order to build the most persuasive presentation.

Imagine, for example, the kind of reception SWE would have given the Fast Car group if the group had started their presentation by acknowledging the problems women engineers face on our campus and in the larger world. (They would probably also have to acknowledge that others might think they wanted more women involved just because they wanted more dates—and they could laugh about this and say, "Well, that might be a small part of it." Their honesty and humor would deflect some of the criticism they ought to know would be lying in wait for them.) They could have then argued that the Fast Car project was a way for the women, by being involved, to demonstrate how competent they were in areas traditionally thought to be male.

They should have asked: **How will our audience respond to the order in which we present our arguments? Is there a better order than the one we have for achieving what we want?**

Finally, Walter and his group hadn't **tested their communication.**

They went into the meeting with SWE cold. Imagine how much more successful the meeting could have been if the group had rehearsed a bit with some people who were both friends and members of their intended audience, and had gotten feedback in time to make changes.

They should have **tried out their presentation with some members of their intended audience, to see how the friends responded—before they tried it for real and found it didn't work.**

And, absolutely finally, we discussed the long-term consequences of their mistakes in the presentation, **and about how communication creates relationships among composers of communication and their audiences.**

Walter and his friend hadn't been able to figure out why they just couldn't back up in the meeting with SWE and correct their mistakes right then and there.

After some discussion, they realized that whenever we offend a person, it takes time for that person to overcome the offense. We have to let the person work through her or his feelings, and we have to show (and not just tell) the person that we understand our mistake and are willing to learn from it. That takes time. That can't happen in a few minutes, even if we want it to.

We began with Walter's story—and his and our reflections upon it—because it allows us to give you a concrete introductory description of **the composing (and analyzing) process we develop in this book.**

We think that learning this process, seeing it at work in the communication of others, and practicing it yourself will help you improve your own abilities to communicate.

What we present on the next few pages is an overview of the process and steps. In the coming chapters, we describe the steps in more detail, with examples, so that you can start applying them.

If the steps do not yet make sense to you in this introduction, don't worry: it takes a bit of concrete practice with the process and steps to start to feel confident and fluid with them. (And it is a communication strategy to present a process in outline first and then later give the details: this can help an audience get a good preliminary grasp of what is being discussed.)

Once you start working with the steps, they become pleasurable because you will be more comfortable and fluid in communicating with others.

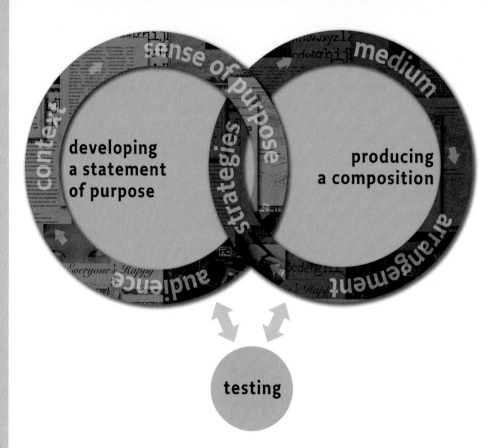

AN OVERVIEW OF THE PROCESS WE PRESENT IN THIS BOOK

If you look at what Walter and his friend discussed with Dennis (it was a long conversation; Walter and his friend were motivated by just how embarrassed they were by what had happened), then the diagram above names the steps they decided—afterward—would have helped them communicate more effectively with their audience of women engineers.

The diagram to the left shows things to keep in mind about the process:

- The process contains three categories: a **statement of purpose, production**, and **testing.**

- Two of the categories can be divided into further steps: there are steps to help you achieve a statement of purpose, and there are steps to help you in the production of the actual communication (whether this is a one-time speech you make or an article you write for many others).

- **The steps do not have to be followed in order.** Sometimes when you need to communicate with others you will know immediately what medium (for example) is appropriate and why, and then will need to do the kinds of thinking asked in all the other steps. Generally, however, you start by working out a statement of purpose, because you can use a solid statement of purpose to make appropriate and effective decisions about the details of production.

- Wherever you start in the process, **you still need to perform each of the steps** to produce effective, thoughtful communication.

THE PROCESS IS RHETORICAL . . .

You've perhaps heard the term "mere rhetoric," as though rhetoric is what people do when they use fancy language to try to cover over poor arguments. But rhetoric more formally names an approach to language use that goes back to the fourth century BCE in Greece, to the time just before and while the philosophers Plato and Aristotle were doing the work that would so shape European thought for centuries. Aristotle wrote a treatise called *On Rhetoric*, which people who study rhetoric still read and use.

When we say that the process we present to you is rhetorical, we draw on the sense of rhetoric that speakers in Greece meant so long ago. Rhetoric grew out of the particular cultural and historical situations of the then city-state Athens, as democratic forms of government were being shaped and as male land-owning citizens were expected—and wanted—to take part in the public conversations that decided how the city was run. Because so much depended on the conversations people had, especially on speeches that citizens made to assemblies, some men started trying to systematize their thinking about how speeches worked.

Those who thought, talked, and wrote about the workings of speeches thought about how speechmakers achieved their ends. That is, how did speechmakers persuade their audiences to do or think certain things? Why did audiences trust some speechmakers and not others? How did speechmakers use emotion to move audiences? How did they arrange the parts of their speeches to have the effects they wanted? What characteristics of their audiences did speechmakers keep in mind as they were working out the particular arrangements of their speeches?

This attention to the relations among speechmaker, audience, and text shapes what we do in this book: we are interested in persuasion, in how you—as you make a text—think about your audience and the kinds of effects you hope to achieve with them. Our rhetorical approach has differences from the original Greek approach (we apply our approach to any situation in which you need to address an audience, and not just speechmaking, and we are working at a time when audiences and situations are more diverse than they were in the city-state of Athens), but **our approach holds on to the core of rhetoric, that you think about how you, as a text's maker, establish relations with an audience through how you shape and deliver your text.**

As we wrote in the preface, we draw in this book on design practices.

The process for developing communication that we have laid out emphasizes (as you will see in the pages to come) the material aspects of communication: as you are asked to think about audience and context, medium and strategies, you will find yourself being asked to consider the physicality of what you are making, and how it will fit into the hands of others or be apparent to their eyes or how your voice strikes the ears of your hearers and resonates in the space where you talk.

In the following pages are also lots of activities to help you creatively and broadly consider your purpose and what you produce. You'll be pushed to think beyond your immediate responses. You'll be asked to look at contexts and audiences from many angles. You will be encouraged to imagine and partially develop different kinds of products in different media and using different strategies and arrangements, in order to test the effectiveness of what you produce and to think about the ways different products can shape different futures.

And you will test what you produce. While your communications still have the shapes of clouds in your head, you can see how others respond. As you continue to give your ideas more concrete shape and substance, you'll watch how others read and react (and laugh or get angry or jump up to go do something . . .) so that you can revise.

You'll also learn something about making meaning with all the materials you use in production. You'll be asked to consider why you are using the particular paper on which you've printed some writing and why you've chosen the margins and type sizes and faces you have. You'll learn about our culture's conventions for arranging elements on a page (and how to experiment with those conventions when your purpose warrants it). You'll learn about color and about how we tend to "read" photographs. You'll learn about how you can use your body gestures and postures and voice in a speech as part of your purpose.

In all of this, rhetoric and design work hand in hand: you will be asked to say, to the best of your abilities, how every choice you have made in your production of a piece of communication contributes to the purpose of the communication.

Communication

as we approach it in this book

is about making things

that establish solid relations

with other people,

about making things

that build community.

We want

to make things

that help ourselves and others

see situations in new and

productive ways.

☐ If you are interested in learning more about the history of rhetoric—or about rhetoric in general—see the resources for chapter 1 at www.ablongman.com/wysocki

thinking through production

■ Several pages ago, before the analysis of what went wrong with the Fast Car group's attempt to appeal to women, we asked you to think of a communication situation you wish had turned out differently—and to keep that situation in mind as you read through the description of the rhetorical process. Write a page or two in which you apply each of the seven steps on the preceding pages to your situation, and describe what you would have done for each of the steps. Then describe how you would have approached the communication situation differently, had you done that analysis. How might things have ended up differently?

■ Imagine that when you arrived on campus for the first time, you were assigned a dorm room and roommate. Your initial impression of your roommate was not good—the person seemed too worried about your having people over, about personal space, and about time alone—but you figured the relationship would work out over time. After 4 weeks, however, it's not any better—it's worse. Your roommate keeps leaving you nasty little notes about your dirty laundry and taste in music. You've decided to make a last-ditch effort and write your roommate a letter explaining your problems with the situation and what you see as the alternatives. Use the numbered steps in the rhetorical process to plan and produce the letter.

■ Imagine you are on the membership committee for your church, skateboarding club, sorority, or fraternity—or any other organization close to your heart. Your organization has decided it needs to increase its membership. You've volunteered to help with this project, but as of now no one is settled on how to proceed. The group members have tossed around ideas for a brochure, for making "cold calls," for putting together an information table for an upcoming community open house, and for ads in the local paper. Use the steps outlined in the rhetorical process to help you decide what specific purpose you have and how best to go about achieving it.

▢ There are more "Thinking through Production" activities in the online chapter 1 resources at www.ablongman.com/wysocki

compose ▪ design ▪ advocate

laying out a design plan

In this chapter, we amplify the categories and steps of the rhetorical process from chapter 1. In this chapter, you shape a general sense of purpose, audience, and context into a full statement of purpose; you plan strategies, media, arrangements, and testing to make your communication as effective as possible.

Developing communication rhetorically is a recursive process, circling back and around on itself as you discover more closely the what and how of your communication. For example, imagine you are helping the head of training at a hospital develop a calendar to advertise upcoming educational events—and so you start off thinking you'll just print out an 8 1/2" by 11" paper to post on bulletin boards. But when you observe your audience and the context in which they work—people constantly busy with patients and records, with little attention for what's posted on the walls, keeping lots of notes in day planners they carry with them—you realize that printing a calendar to fit into the day planners is going to be a more effective approach. So even though we go step-by-step in this chapter, in real life the process will never be so straight.

You can use this chapter in two ways: read it for a general sense of how to proceed in some communicative situation in the future, or apply these steps to any specific situation you now need to address.

sense of purpose statement of purpose

With this step, you want to move from a general sense of why you are in some communicative situation to a more specific sense. The more specific you can be about your purpose for communicating, the more easily you will be able to decide among different possible strategies (for example) to use in producing your communication, because your purpose helps you judge which strategies help you achieve the particular ends you have in mind.

Do not worry if you cannot make your sense of purpose immediately concrete. When you start with this step, do what you can, and then move on to exploring your ideas about audience and context; in the exploring, you will gain new insights into your purpose. (Which also means that you do not do any of these steps just once, if you can at all help it: moving back and forth among the steps and revisiting them helps you fine-tune your overall statement of purpose.)

And, finally, this is important: **If you do not have a clear purpose for communicating, then there is no reason to communicate.**

To develop a more concrete sense of purpose, ask yourself the questions below. Write down your answers: you need to be able to come back to your ideas to see how you can change or add to them after you think about your audience and context.

- **What is your motivation in this communication situation?**
  In other words, why are you communicating? What do you hope to achieve by building the piece of communication you are approaching?
  It might be that you are thinking about this question because you have to write a paper for a class, which is an external motivation. You will do your best work if you are motivated from within: if you have to put time into building communication, work to find reasons that matter to you. Your own curiosity about a topic is enough, but also think about building communication that helps you make connections with others, or that helps you learn something new.

- **What do you hope your audience will do or feel or think after they have experienced the communication you will produce?**
  Do you want more people to vote, or do you want your audience to know more about the situation in Iraq, or do you want others to understand how your relationship with your grandparents, aunts, and uncles was critical to who you are today? Do you want your teacher to be dazzled by the thoughtful, critical, hard work you have done? Do you want people to stop driving cars and ride bikes more, or do you want them to be better at doing mathematical word puzzles?

  Do you want to educate others, or entertain, or inform, or some mix?

  The more specific you can be here about how you want your audience to respond to the communication you are building, the more easily you will be able to shape your communication toward those ends.

compose ▪ design ▪ advocate

- **If there is some event or situation that got you wanting to communicate with others, describe it in as much detail as possible.**

  Sometimes we are motivated to write by seeing something happen to others, or by reading something with which we agree—or disagree—strongly. Because this is motivation, it is important for you to recognize this, so that you can be sure to help your audience understand where you are coming from; they will be more likely then to understand your reasons for communicating what and how you do, and when audiences understand your reasons, they are generally able to make better judgments about your communication.

- **What would be the best possible outcome of the communication?**

  If you can imagine exactly what you would like to happen, then you can use what you imagine to guide and encourage you as you work.

- **What would be the worst possible outcome?**

  Knowing what failure looks like can help you figure out strategies for avoiding it.

- **How will your communication change the situation in which you make the communication?**

  That is, is your purpose worthwhile? When you picture the best possible outcome for the communication you are building, are you imagining effects that are worth striving to achieve? If not, perhaps you should rethink what you are contemplating.

APPLYING SENSE OF PURPOSE

The situations described below might seem obvious to you, but in working out a sense of purpose you will clarify what it is you want to achieve—which will help you in thinking about audience and context in the next pages.

1 Imagine you've just found out your application to study abroad for a semester has been turned down by the committee that makes such decisions. You are thinking about appealing the decision. Use the questions above to write down your sense of purpose in making the appeal.

2 A class you want to take is full, and you are planning to talk with the professor to try to get in. Use the questions above to write down your sense of purpose in talking with the professor.

your responsibilities

■ As you work out your purpose in communicating, your responsibilities are to yourself, to the people with whom you'll be communicating, and to everyone around you:

① To yourself, you are responsible for finding reasons to communicate that help you further your understandings of others and of communicating in general. There is no reason to do this work if you are not learning, if you are not gaining in competence and confidence in moving through and improving the world.

② To those with whom you are communicating, you are responsible for finding purposes that are worth their time and attentions and that show that you care about the matters that lie between you.

③ To everyone else . . . Because communication is what binds us together and helps build—for better or worse—our communities, you are responsible for finding communicative purposes that respond to what is needed around you, that contribute usefully to the networks in which we all live.

audience ▶ statement of purpose

The first time you work out the characteristics of your audience, it might take some time, but this is a process that becomes easier over time, and will almost become second nature the more you do it.

To particularize and concretize your sense of audience, you can do this:

1 **Generate a list of audience characteristics.** (The detailed pages on audience in chapter 3 can help you do this.) The idea here is to generate as full a list as you can of any and all characteristics shared by your intended audience. As you produce your communication, what may seem the oddest characteristics can sometimes suggest to you highly useful and persuasive strategies or arrangements.

There are many categories of characteristics you can think through to generate your list. Think of your audience's attitudes, beliefs, and habits. Think of their backgrounds, how and where they grew up. Think of material qualities like age, race, gender, sexual orientation, and able-bodiedness.

2 **Imagine your audience at the moment they encounter the communication you make,** no matter what you're making. (Try imagining using different media for your communication, to get the widest sense of the conditions under which your audience can respond.) What attitudes or moods are they likely to be in, and why? What might they be thinking? Why should they be interested in your communication? Why might they be disinterested, or hostile?

Add all your observations to the list you've made.

3 **Filter your lists: Which characteristics are most relevant to the purpose you have so far developed?** Cross out—tentatively—any characteristics that you can't see as shaping your audience one way or another toward what you hope to achieve.

If your purpose, as you've stated it so far, is to persuade women to join the "Fast Car" project (to use an example from the Introduction), then you know that your audience is women: but it will also be important that you recognize that the women might be curious but also a bit apprehensive, given that they are being addressed by men on a primarily male campus and about a project that had in the past included almost exclusively men. The women might also be tired, if you are going to meet with them at night, or late in the semester.

The idea is not to shorten your lists as much as possible, but rather to develop as complex and rich an idea of your audience as you can. By thinking of your audience complexly, you will treat them as the complex people they are.

compose ▪ design ▪ advocate

APPLYING AUDIENCE

In the preceding section on sense of purpose, we asked you to write down your sense of purpose for two different situations, one in which you are appealing a decision about studying abroad, the other in which you are trying to get into a closed class. For both those situations, use the three steps on the previous page to write descriptions of your two different audiences.

Sometimes, when you do initial thinking about audience, you learn that you need to learn more; if this is the case here, write down what more you need to learn, and how you might go about learning it. For example, ask others in your class what they know about these kinds of audiences on your campus; others may have experienced similar situations and have useful knowledge to share.

your responsibilities

- You are responsible for respecting your audiences as people who think and have good reasons for believing what they do.

- In order to make good on your responsibility to your audience, you need to listen carefully to what other people have to say about the piece of communication you are building. It is sometimes hard to hear critical feedback about what we produce, but it is important to acknowledge that others have good ideas about how you can strengthen what you make.

- You need to take seriously that any piece of communication you make—written, visual, oral, or any mix—affects other people. Take seriously that you can move other people, for good or otherwise.

context

statement of purpose

If you are in control over the time and place of the communication you are building, it is useful to go through the parts of this step to think about when and where might be most conducive to achieving the results you seek.

As you work toward an effective piece of communication consider:

THE OCCASION OF THE COMMUNICATION

Just when will the communication take place?

Is there a specific occasion that motivates the communication, such as a funeral where you've been asked to give the elegy or a presentation you must make at a conference about research you've been doing? Do you have to imagine the occasion because you won't be there, such as when someone comes to a website you've made, or when your teacher reads a paper you've written, or your father receives the birthday card you've sent him?

Can you picture the time of day or year? Does it matter to your audience the time at which they'll be receiving your communication? (For example, are you giving a class oral presentation last out of a group of five or at night, so that your listeners are likely to be tired and having a little trouble being attentive? Are you developing a fund-raising campaign for a nonprofit around Christmas time, when people are likely to be a little more generous?)

THE PLACE OF THE COMMUNICATION

Where, exactly, will the communication take place? Will you be there?

Will your audience be in a temple, mosque, or church? And, if so, is it a large, formal, and imposing structure, or an informal, comfortable place? How will this shape the attitudes and expectations of your audience, as well as your comfort or level of nerves?

Will your audience be sitting in uncomfortable folding chairs, or in rows of desks? Will your audience be sitting at home, comfortable at their personal desks (or likely to doze in an armchair)?

Or will your audience see your posters up on a wall where everyone else is hanging their posters, too, so that you need yours to be a different color or size—or else taped to the sidewalk or some other place where others will be more likely to see it?

compose ▪ design ▪ advocate

THE BROADER CONTEXT OF THE COMMUNICATION

How do time and place shape your audience's expectations? It's probably obvious that an audience at a funeral in a Gothic cathedral has different expectations than an audience for a business presentation, but nonetheless it's worth asking *why*.

For us, Gothic cathedrals are not new—but the people who built them saw them as grand engineering marvels and signs of a community's willingness to put in years and tremendous resources to construct a concrete representation of their belief in a God up above. Some of this sense has carried down to us, in part because of how our bodies feel in the large, light, airy spaces of cathedrals but also in part because, whether or not we attend such cathedrals, we have seen them and heard about them. Also, they are, simply, churches; many have grown up in communities where churches are valued as holy spaces.

Most business meetings do not take place in holy spaces. Instead, such spaces are usually functional, and we have probably grown up associating business with getting things done, with moving quickly and getting to the point.

Asking about the spaces in which we communicate, and about the perceptions of time we attach to those spaces, gives us a better sense of audience expectations.

You'll be most successful with context if you visualize the moment of communication. The more real you make this moment beforehand, the more you'll be able to develop strategies for approaching your audience and determine what media work best. The more real this moment is for you, the more you'll be able to think about what might most please or engage your audience.

Notice how context and audience overlap, as (for example) when you present a paper late on a panel or late in the day when your audience is tired and needs you to be more energetic and humorous than you might otherwise be. Because of this, revisit your description of your audience after you work through this section on context so that you can add any important characteristics you might have missed.

APPLYING CONTEXT

In the sections on sense of purpose and audience, we asked you to consider two different situations, one in which you are appealing a decision about studying abroad, the other in which you are trying to get into a closed class. For both situations, describe the occasion of the communication you'll be making, its place, and its broader context of how and where decisions are made in schools. As with audience, if you find you need more information, describe what you need to learn and how you can learn it. You can ask others about their experiences in similar contexts on your campus.

your responsibilities

- If you have choices about where to communicate, be sure your audience will be comfortable, can hear you, and, when possible, can see and interact with you.

- The spaces within which we work with one another help or hinder our efforts to communicate effectively, so you will want to think about how you arrange such spaces. Is there room to move around? Is there plenty of elbow room? Are people isolated from one another? Lighting? Temperature?

- Context is more than just physical space, however. Contexts of communication also include what has led up to this point in time—people's histories as well as events that are happening around you (outside your building, or on the day before) and that may be relevant to you or members of your audience.

- Pay attention to the institutional context of your work as well. Do you have more authority than those you are speaking to, or less, and how will that affect what you can or cannot say and do? And how will your words—spoken with institutional force—affect whom you are speaking to?

statement of purpose

With this step you will pull together what you have been writing and thinking about in the past three steps—Sense of Purpose, Audience, and Context—into a **statement of purpose**.

A statement of purpose is clearer and more concrete than a sense of purpose, and it explains your purpose by referring to audience and context. A statement of purpose should be detailed and specific enough to guide you through the next steps of choosing a medium or mix of media, deciding on strategies, and then arranging, producing, and testing what you compose. A final statement of purpose is usually about a half-page in length, depending on how concise you are.

TO COMPOSE A STATEMENT OF PURPOSE

1 Look at what you have written about your sense of purpose, audience, and context and write one- to two-sentence summaries of each.

2 Write a one-sentence explanation of the relations among your purpose, audience, and context of communication. Use this as a draft of your statement of purpose.

3 Look at the statement of purpose you just wrote and ask these questions:

- Does this statement of purpose show how your purpose is tied to characteristics of the audience you want to communicate with and the shared context you are working in?

- Does this statement of purpose make clear what the best possible outcome would be for your effort to communicate?

- Does this statement of purpose make clear the main things that could go wrong with your attempt to accomplish your purpose?

- Does this statement of purpose describe your responsibilities to other people as you move forward with this project?

Revise your statement of purpose to address your answers to the previous four questions.

Renee, from one of our classes, composed a statement of purpose to help her through a sticky but not unusual situation. Renee's sense of purpose, audience, and context are:

purpose *I want to convince the Dean of Students that I should be allowed a late drop from the English class I'm failing. (It's my first semester, and Chemistry is harder than I thought, so I'm putting all my time into it—and not enough time into English. If I drop English then maybe I can get a better-than-passing grade in Chemistry.)*

audience *My audience is the Dean of Students, who will demand strong reasons for my request—and will be reluctant to grant it—because the school has been tightening up on late drops.*

context *The Dean will be in her office when she receives my request, and because there's only one month until the semester ends, everyone—including her—is probably pretty harried and rushed.*

■ This is Renee's one-sentence explanation of how her purpose, audience, and context of communication tie together:

I want to persuade a harried and reluctant Dean of Students that my circumstances warrant me being given a late drop in English.

■ After asking herself the questions on the bottom of page 40, Renee realized she hadn't considered the possible negative outcomes of her request: she hadn't thought about what might make the Dean of Students turn down her request. Here is Renee's revised **statement of purpose:**

I want to persuade a harried and reluctant Dean of Students that my circumstances warrant a late drop in English. I don't want her to think I'm only grade-grubbing so that she turns down my request; instead, I want her to see I'm making the request because I'm serious about doing well and I learned a lot this semester about needing to manage my time.

By doing this revision, Renee sets herself up well to move into thinking about the next category of this rhetorical process—production—and its steps of figuring out strategies, a medium, and arrangement. As we move through these steps, you'll see how Renee carried out her thinking, ending in a letter to the Dean.

APPLYING STATEMENT OF PURPOSE

In the preceding sections you've described sense of purpose, audience, and context for two different situations. Use the model of Renee's statement of purpose to write a statement of purpose for each of the two situations.

your responsibilities

■ Since your statement of purpose connects your sense of purpose to your specific audience and context, you are responsible for making sure that the connections leave room for your audience to respond, if they need to. Be careful not to subsume the audience to the context and treat people like rocks or the ground you walk on.

■ Try to use your statement of purpose to clarify for yourself how what matters to you connects with what matters to other people, given the context you share.

strategies ▶ production

This step is really a mindset you need to get into: you need to start looking at everything you do, say, or put in your communication as a strategy for helping you achieve your statement of purpose. **A strategy is any part of your communication that you can change in order to better achieve your purpose.**

In an essay, for example, strategies include the title, size of title, color of title, typeface of title, size of paper, color of paper, first word, placement of first word, second word, tone or mood set by first and second words, use of photographs, and so on.
To come up with strategies for your communication, you need to:

1 Generate a lot of different possible strategies.

2 Use your statement of purpose to help you decide which strategies are most appropriate for your rhetorical situation.

To generate strategies, first think about an overall strategy. If, for example, you were going before the city council to propose a new traffic light in your town (a light you think they probably don't want), you might consider basing your argument on statistics about accidents at that stoplight, or you might consider basing your argument on the stories of people who have been injured in those accidents—or maybe both statistics and stories together. After considering such large-scale strategies, generate possible smaller scale strategies: you could use overheads or handouts for the statistics, you could use a serious and formal tone of voice or a conversational tone of voice, you might lighten the seriousness with a little humor, you might wear a suit or casual clothes, and so on.

To decide among strategies, always ask which help you better achieve your statement of purpose. If, in the example about going before the city council, your statement of purpose helped you see that your audience is composed of people who are balancing budgets at the same time that they want to improve the quality of life in your city, then statistics about the cost of the car accidents, compared with statistics about the lower cost of the traffic light, will probably be more persuasive than only stories from accident victims.

Note that both medium and arrangement—the next two production steps we'll examine—can be looked at themselves as large-scale strategies. We separate out medium and arrangement as strategies because they help you make large-scale decisions about the shape of the communication you produce.

compose ▪ design ▪ advocate

EXAMPLE: HOW RENEE THOUGHT THROUGH HER STRATEGIES . . .

On page 41, you read Renee's statement of purpose—

> *I want to persuade a harried and reluctant Dean of Students that my circumstances warrant a late drop in English. I don't want her to think I'm only grade-grubbing so that she turns down my request; instead, I want her to see I'm making the request because I'm serious about doing well and I learned a lot this semester about needing to manage my time.*

—which helped Renee think about how to approach the Dean strategically; here is what Renee wrote as she brainstormed about strategies for this communication:

> *I am serious about this—I didn't mess up because I was lazy or not trying . . . I really want to do well in school, especially my science classes, so I can get into med school. If I can persuade the Dean I've really been trying, and really have learned a lesson from what happened, then maybe she'll be more sympathetic. So my main strategy has got to focus on how I've learned, and how I'll do better . . . But what's going to make her see that I'm not just trying to make up for laziness? What will make her see that I've learned and I'm serious? Maybe if I can get my English teacher to put in a word for me because he keeps telling me he knows I could do better if I put in the time and focus. My adviser might help, too. Or maybe if I promise to sign up for time-management or study-skills workshops . . . I'm going to have to present this very carefully, too: I've got to approach her in a polished and serious way . . . and it would probably help if I let her know that I know she's busy and that I am making a special request . . .*

Out of this thinking-on-paper Renee pulled the following strategies:

1 *My overall strategy is to focus on my serious reasons for making the request: I have learned some very useful things about time management and the difficulty of college, and I do want to use them to do even better in the next semesters so I can eventually make it into med school.*

2 *To support my overall strategy, I am going to demonstrate that I am serious by getting support from my teacher and/or adviser, and by signing up for workshops.*

APPLYING STRATEGIES

Use the statements of purpose you wrote for the study abroad situation and for the situation of wanting to get into a closed class to develop strategies for the situations.

your responsibilities

- Admit it when you do not have all the proof you need, and do not fudge your proof.

- Be sure you are using the kind of proof and standards that your context calls for. Some contexts call for logical proof and an airtight case, some call for the words of an expert, some call for concrete examples, and some call for evidence of passion (a sign that you really care).

- Take account of the ideas and positions held by your audience or others who have written or talked about what you are discussing.

- Give appropriate attribution for any words, pictures, or other materials you use that have been made by others.

- Keep in mind the particularities and needs of your audience as you choose strategies. For example, be sure you use a larger typeface if you are designing for older people or children.

medium ► production

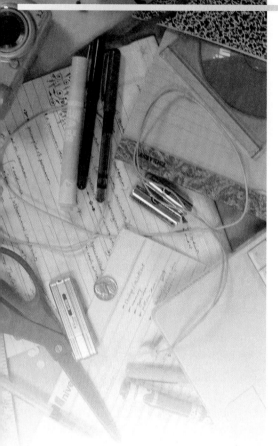

Will your piece of communication be a poster, a webpage, a Flash animation, an essay, a brochure, an editorial, a video clip, a blog, a performance, a report, an illustrated shoe, or . . .? What medium is appropriate for your purpose, audience, and context?

Choosing a medium involves both creativity and common sense.
CREATIVITY asks you to set aside or add to your first ideas. Sometimes the first idea we have about a medium is useful—but sometimes what comes to mind first is the "usual" solution that might not be most effective. If you think about media that are unexpected or unusual in your context—but appropriate—you might think up new and highly useful strategies to achieve your purpose. (For example, turning in a late paper gift-wrapped might just earn a little slack from a teacher, or least some sympathetic laughter—but such a move requires careful judgment: you have to know your audience well!)

  COMMON SENSE tells you the kinds of media people most often use in similar contexts and with similar purposes, and the kinds of media your audience probably expects to see. Common sense reminds you to consider what is practical, too: for instance, do you really have enough time and money—and competence—to make a music video, one your teacher will accept in place of a written term paper?

Because you want to make communication that engages people and helps you achieve your purpose, it is generally a good idea to begin with creativity and then to judge your cool ideas with a healthy dose of common sense.

To figure out the best medium or media for achieving your statement of purpose:

1 **Brainstorm different media you can use.** The more possible media you can think of, the more likely you are to come up with something that will appeal to your audience most effectively and appropriately.

2 **Imagine each medium or media in use,** in the context of your context and audience and overall strategies. By imagining the media in use by your audience in context, and by thinking about how you can shape your overall strategies through your possible media, you'll be able to decide which to use.

3 **Think practically.** Which media can you handle in terms of time, resources, and experience? What will the medium/media demand of you?

compose ▪ design ▪ advocate

EXAMPLE: HOW RENEE FIGURED OUT HER MEDIA . . .

Renee is the student trying to persuade the Dean of Students to give her a late drop in her English class. She's decided that her main strategies are to convince the Dean that she's learned from her hard semester, and that the late drop will help her do better.

Renee knows that she can send the Dean an e-mail making her request, that she can send a letter, or that she can make an appointment to see the Dean. She could also send flowers to the Dean with the request written on an attached card.

Because she is trying to show that she is serious about the request and her schooling, Renee decides to send a letter and make an appointment. She thinks that an e-mail is just too informal for her purpose and that flowers might make her look just a little too goofy or like she was trying to bribe the Dean. But she figures that if she drops a letter by the Dean's office, and sets up an appointment to see the Dean at the same time, she'll look like someone who is committed to her work and serious enough to make sure her case gets heard. (Renee also thinks she'd be a little too nervous to present her case to the Dean only in a face-to-face meeting; if the Dean has seen a well-crafted letter first, then Renee won't have to say too much, but will only need to answer the Dean's questions. Renee also hopes that the Dean is someone who finds it harder to turn someone down in person.)

Renee also figures she needs to write a formal letter, rather than a quick note to the Dean—so she'll need some good paper and access to a computer (and software with a spell checker) and a good printer, as well as access to some sample formal letters (which she can get out of the handbook for her English class).

APPLYING MEDIUM

Use the statements of purpose you wrote for the study abroad situation and for the situation of wanting to get into a closed class to help you determine media you could use in these situations.

AND

Take an upcoming assignment you have in another class (a paper, report, or presentation, for example), and use the questions on page 41 to come up with several unexpected but appropriate media you could use to satisfy the assignment's requirements.

your responsibilities

■ Keep in mind that all the members of your audience need to have access to the communication medium you are using. Keep your eye on who is included—and who is excluded—by the medium you choose. Not everyone has easy access to computers, or to high-speed Internet connections.

■ Keep in mind also the resources required to produce the medium you are using, and try to waste as little as possible during production. (And do think about how people will use what you make: flyers to put under windshield wipers might help you advertise an event, but most people will pull them off their cars and drop them on the ground.)

■ If you are using a medium that takes up a lot of resources, ask yourself if you are using your medium to its fullest potential to justify your choice.

■ Since choice of medium is also a choice of strategy, think about whether you are using the medium in ways familiar to you and your audience, or, when appropriate, whether you are challenging yourself and your audience by pushing the boundaries of the medium.

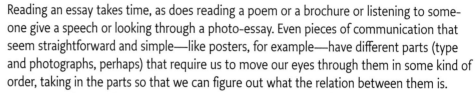

arrangement ▸ production

Reading an essay takes time, as does reading a poem or a brochure or listening to someone give a speech or looking through a photo-essay. Even pieces of communication that seem straightforward and simple—like posters, for example—have different parts (type and photographs, perhaps) that require us to move our eyes through them in some kind of order, taking in the parts so that we can figure out what the relation between them is.

Because almost all pieces of communication require an audience to move through them in time, the different parts of the communication have to be arranged. They have to be put in some order—and that order can be arranged to be more or less persuasive, more or less tied to your statement of purpose.

There are usually several kinds of arrangement or structure going on at the same time in any piece of communication. In a piece of writing, for example, you'll be thinking about the arrangements of words in an individual sentence, but you'll also be thinking about how to order your different paragraphs in order to achieve your purpose. If you are producing a photo-essay, you'll similarly be thinking about the arrangement—and resulting effects on an audience—of the elements within each photograph, but then you'll also be thinking about how to arrange the photographs together on a page or across multiple pages in order to move your audience in the ways you want.

Finding the most effective arrangement strategies for your purpose requires you to . . .

1 **List the parts of your communication.** In order to figure out what arrangement to use, you need to know what you're arranging. If you have worked out a statement of purpose, and thought about strategies and medium, then along the way you'll have developed a sense of the different possible parts to the communication you are building.

2 **Brainstorm different possibilities.** Every medium has associated with it many possible arrangement alternatives to choose among, invent for the occasion, or transform to fit your needs. In chapters 7–13—the chapters of examples of different kinds of communication—we discuss the kinds of arrangements that are tied to different media.

3 **Ask which possibilities best support your purpose and overall strategies.**

compose ▪ design ▪ advocate

EXAMPLE: HOW RENEE FIGURED OUT HER ARRANGEMENT . . .

From thinking about strategies and media, Renee knows she will write a formal letter to the Dean. She also knows she needs to approach the Dean carefully, given how late it is in the semester and how the school is trying to give fewer late drops—and how stressed the Dean must be at this time in the semester.

Renee also knows, from developing her statement of purpose and thinking about production, that she needs to address the following matters in her letter:

- a clear and concise statement of her request: that she wants a late drop
- what she has learned about time and college from the experience of her first semester—and how she is going to take a workshop to help her with the challenges she's faced
- her reasons for wanting the late drop
- the situation that led to her wanting a late drop
- the support her English teacher and adviser will give her (after talks with them) in seeking the late drop
- the Dean's harried and busy state of mind

Because the Dean's state of mind is not directly related—but still important—to her purpose, Renee decides it shouldn't be the center of her letter; it should come at the beginning or end—or maybe in both places, so that Renee can show her appreciation for the Dean's personal attention.

The most important thing is the request for a late drop—but before that, Renee thinks she should probably explain the context of her request. She'll explain who she is and what happened in her semester, and then she'll ask for the drop, followed by her reasons, backed up by her commitment to taking a workshop and the support of her teacher and adviser.

APPLYING ARRANGEMENT

Use the statements of purpose you wrote for the study abroad situation and for the situation of wanting to get into a closed class to help you think about arrangements you could use for the different media you've described.

your responsibilities

- Try always to think of arrangements not as lifeless things but as structured, social arrangements, that is, as relationships between people. Arrangements arrange the pieces in a composition, but they also arrange our needs, expectations, hopes, and desires. Take seriously the needs, expectations, hopes, and desires of those who read your writing or use what you design.

- Keep in mind that the conventions of different kinds of arrangements imply values, ways of seeing and feeling, and preferred ways of living. Think of the choice of arrangement as a moral choice.

- Make sure you arrange your composition so that it is accessible to everyone who may be in your audience. Consider ways of integrating multiple, alternative arrangements for complex audiences within the overall composition.

production

If you have worked through all the preceding steps, then you are ready to take on the material production of your communication, to start mucking around intentfully with your chosen media, making your chosen arrangements and strategies visible or touchable.

With some media—like written essays or posters or brochures—you may have already produced some parts or drafts of your communication. With others—such as a video—you may have stayed at a conceptual level throughout all the preceding steps, not taking any footage until you had worked out a clear plan of what you need.

Now it is time to start building a complete piece of communication. (Be sure to look at the next pages on testing—you do not want to have a completed piece that you have not checked at various stages with your intended audience, to see if you are on the right track toward building an effective piece.)

This is where you have to be attentive to **practical technical details.** If you are making a full-color brochure, for example, you need to know or learn about bleeds and dpi and lpi and cmyk inks—these production details strongly affect the quality of what you make. Every medium has different technical requirements, which will be affected by your various strategies and arrangements. There are books on printing processes, as there are books on video and website development; there are also people who will be willing to help you figure out how to most effectively produce the object that is your piece of communication. **The best thing you can do is ask lots of questions:** if you *are* printing a color brochure, for example, there will be someone at the print shop who can respond to the question, "What details do I need to be careful about as I make this brochure so that it prints well?"

compose ▪ design ▪ advocate

Sometimes, however, you will already be familiar with the materials of your production.

RENEE'S PRODUCTION

Here is the letter Renee sent to the Dean of Students. The letter may not look like much, but it required careful attention to produce. Renee typed it on good white paper and spell-checked it (and had it read—tested—by friends and a helpful teacher). You might be pleased to know that Renee's letter (along with the support of her English teacher) helped her get the late drop for which she was hoping.

Box 3639
Calumet University
Calumet, MD 21400

November 18, 2003

Dean Gloria Meldrum
Dean of Students
Calumet University
Calumet, MD 21400

Dear Dean Meldrum,

I know it is a busy time of the semester, so I appreciate the attention you are giving me.

I am a first-year student, finishing up my first semester. I've learned some hard lessons about time and college work since I've come to the university—which is why I am asking you for a late drop in my English class (ENG 1000, section 22, taught by Professor Davidson).

I am failing English because I have been putting all my time into my Chemistry class. I want to go to medical school eventually, and so Chemistry is very important. I know that English is important, too, but I always used to do so well in it in high school that I thought it would be easy here and that I could get caught up if I got behind. I've learned otherwise.

I have signed up for two of the Learning Center's workshops—one on time management and one on study skills, for next semester—so that I can get a better handle on doing well in college. I've also spoken with Professor Davidson about taking the English class over again, which he thinks is a good idea. Professor Davidson supports me in my request for a late drop, because he thinks I can do really well in the class—if I am able to be more focused and on top of the work. He has said he will call you about this, if you think that would help you make a decision about my request.

I hope you can see that I am serious about my schoolwork, and want to have a good record for getting into medical school. I am trying to fix a bad start, so I hope you will grant my request.

I will make an appointment to see you when I drop off this letter, so that we can talk about my situation more if that would be useful.

Thank you very much for considering my request. I look forward to talking with you.

Sincerely,

Renee Saari

your responsibilities

- Treat those with whom you work, especially those helping you with production, as ends in themselves, not as means to your ends.

- Attend to the smallest details in the production process, by asking how this or that detail might seriously affect someone else. The smallest details can have large effects on people's lives.

APPLYING PRODUCTION

Sketch out the practical and material details of the communications you would produce for appealing the decision about your application to study abroad, and for trying to get into the closed class. Would you need to learn anything new for these productions?

testing

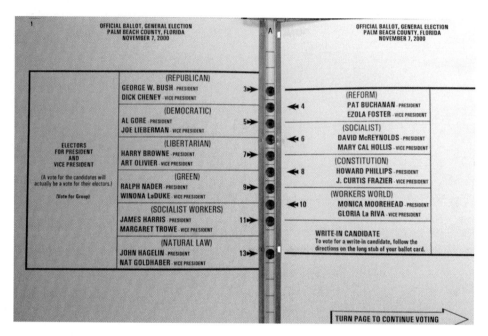

OFFICIAL BALLOT, GENERAL ELECTION
PALM BEACH COUNTY, FLORIDA
NOVEMBER 7, 2000

How can you tell if your piece of communication is successful? How will you know if you achieve what you set out in your statement of purpose? You can wait until your piece of communication is completely and absolutely done—after you have put in hours and hours of work—and then you can see how your audience responds. But what if you find out—as did the designers of the butterfly ballot used in Florida in the 2000 presidential elections—that your design doesn't work and in fact fails miserably, when it is too late to make any changes?

This is why many designers use testing from the very beginning of their design process. They develop a thorough and thought-out statement of purpose, and then—before they start any production—they give the statement of purpose to their intended audience for feedback. They'll use the feedback to reshape the statement of purpose and to guide them through the steps leading to production. And then, before they start actual production, they'll show a design plan—outlining medium, strategies, and arrangement—to their audience, to get feedback and to learn about any changes that might help them.

> **"**The butterfly ballot simply points out what happens when you neglect human psychology. The ballot was designed by well-meaning amateurs who never considered testing the resulting ballots (and probably didn't know how to do such a test). The ballot machinery was designed to save money, not to maximize accuracy.
>
> Is the design done by non-designers? Yes. But most designers would do worse. Designers learn about esthetics. They seldom learn about human psychology. They seldom learn about the need to do iterative design with a repeated cycle of watching people at work, determining requirements, doing a rough prototype, testing the prototype, then refining the design by watching, predetermining requirements, doing a new prototype, and retesting. The cycle can be done in one day.**"**

Don Norman, usability expert, quoted in "Back Talk," an interview with Steven Heller, *PRINT*, 55:2 (March/April 2001): 40D-40E, 167.

compose ▪ design ▪ advocate

There is an area of design called *Participatory Design*, which started in Scandinavia during the 1980s. Designers who use this approach involve their intended audience in the design process from the very beginning and throughout the whole process of design. These designers recognize that audiences are smart, have opinions, and need to be able to use—well and efficiently, and even maybe with pleasure—what the designers are producing. *Participatory design* has been used primarily in the design of processes—like how an assembly line is structured—and of software, but it is a concept that can be highly useful in composing communication: *if you involve your audience in designing your communication, you are much more likely to build a piece that the audience responds to well—and so you are much more likely to build a piece of communication that achieves your purposes.*

To involve your audience in your composing processes, so that you test what you are producing in order to make it as effective as possible:

- Think about how you can gather together people from your intended audience to go over your statement of purpose and give you feedback, before you start producing your communication.

- Make plans for testing during the steps leading to production. This will save you time (and perhaps expenses) in the long run, because you'll find out early in the process how to adjust your medium and strategies before you're fully committed to them.

HOW RENEE TESTED HER LETTER . . .

After she planned it out, Renee talked about her letter with her English teacher, who thought her ideas were solid and made sense. She asked him to read a draft, and he helped her with her grammar and tone of voice, so that they would be more formal—but not too stiff. She had two friends who are attentive to detail read the letter and check it for spelling and grammar before she finally took it to the Dean of Students' office.

APPLYING TESTING

How would you test your production for appealing the decision about your application to study abroad? How would you test your production for trying to get into the closed class?

your responsibilities

- Testing is a moral act. The mere fact of testing shows others that you do not presume to know everything, to be able to see every consequence of your choices, or to anticipate every way someone might respond to what you've made or composed. *Testing shows that you trust and care about the judgment, ideas, and concerns of others.*

- Remember that to test something is to ask other people how it works for them. As is the case with attending to your audience, good testing requires carefully listening—and not being so attached to your own work that you can't hear what others think.

- Testing is a way of being responsible to yourself. Getting feedback to a draft for a class essay or a brochure for a non-profit organization will help you produce work that makes you proud, that helps you gain more confidence, and that therefore helps you become a better, more effective communicator in general. (And if, like most, you are nervous about giving speeches, testing out parts of your speech will help you be less nervous when you really have to give it.)

A SAMPLE DESIGN PLAN

These are the materials that were developed through the design plan described here.

Sometimes, as with Renee's letter, you needn't develop a formal design plan. Other times, however, when you are producing a more complex piece of communication—one that has many parts or is long—or when you are producing a piece that has important consequences for you (like a final class project on which most of your grade hangs or an application to graduate school) you will want to get a design plan down on paper. **The more you articulate for yourself on paper the steps of the rhetorical process (which is all that a design plan really is), the better you are preparing yourself to smoothly and with the least stress produce an effective piece of communication.**

A design plan lays out, on paper,

- your statement of purpose
- a description of your overall strategies, with justifications based on your statement of purpose
- your choice of medium or media, with justifications based on your statement of purpose
- your ideas about arrangement, with justifications based on your statement of purpose
- a description of how you will produce the communication
- a plan for testing the communication at all stages of production

Generally, your audience never sees your design plan, so you needn't make it anything fancy or grammatical—you just need to be able to read and work with it. The ideas in the last sentence, of course, all go out the window if, in the course of working through this book, your teacher asks you for a sample design plan or if (as in the example we are about to give) you need to produce a design plan for a client.

You should also think of design plans as ever and always provisional. They help you get started and help you with the specific directions of a project—but sometimes, as you are deep into production, something just isn't working out. You won't need to start over, but you do need to revisit your design plan. If you get stuck or confused in a project, come back to your design plan: look again at your statement of purpose, to see if it hasn't shifted as you more concretely produce whatever it is you are producing. If you need to fine-tune your statement of purpose, as you gain a more concrete sense of audience or production, it's no big deal—and if you shift your statement of purpose, you probably need to adjust your strategies or arrangements or media.

DESIGNING FOR THE GOVERNMENT: A SAMPLE DESIGN PLAN

Several years ago, Anne (one of the designers and composers of this book) was asked to develop some educational curriculum for the Corporation for National Service, a government agency that runs programs for those who want to be of service in this country. The AmeriCorps*National Civilian Community Corps (or NCCC) had been in existence for a year, and the people running this program wanted to have a strong educational component to the program.

Those running NCCC recognized the program was different from many service programs, and so they arranged for Anne to visit the program's sites and talk with the people involved. They also wanted, before Anne produced the materials, a description and justification for what Anne would do; they wanted, in other words, a design plan. In what follows, we describe how Anne went about developing that plan.

The NCCC is a residential service program: people between 18 and 24 commit to a year of service, during which they live on a decommissioned military base, traveling out to work on projects like tutoring, building trails in national parks, organizing immunizations in rural communities, helping communities rebuild after hurricanes, and so on. Corpsmembers work in teams, and each team has a team leader. Those who established the NCCC hoped that, in the course of their service, corpsmembers (who receive a stipend at the end of their service) would learn to use the tools for trailbuilding or the skills necessary for tutoring kindergarten children. They also hoped, however, that corpsmembers would learn about the contexts of their service: they would learn (for example) why schools in poorer communities have fewer resources than others and so were in need of regular tutors, or how the National Park Service came to be. The team leaders, often not much older than corpsmembers and rarely having formal teaching backgrounds, were to shape this learning to fit their teams, with the assistance of full-time trained education staff on each campus.

As Anne visited NCCC campuses, she interviewed corpsmembers, team leaders, education staff, and administrators. She gained an overall sense of the program—like the description we just gave you—but she also got to know corpsmembers and team leaders personally. She saw the conditions in which they lived (you would probably recognize the dorm life), and the conditions under which they worked. She learned that there was formal time set aside each week for classroom work, but often that project schedules were messy and varied—and that teams often lived off campus for several weeks if (for example) they were working in a desert park several hours away to put in new latrines or trails. She saw the vans in which the teams traveled, and the cafeterias in which they ate.

Anne first wrote out her descriptions of audience, context, and purpose, little of which she would have had if she had not talked directly with her audience.

audience My audience is the team leaders, who will be teaching, and—through them—the corpsmembers. The team leaders are of all ages (starting at 24) and educational backgrounds. Some are doing this work for the money, but most believe in the service goals of the NCCC (it's not as though anyone is going to get rich doing this). The team leaders have different commitments to education, but they are all smart and tough—and they have to be flexible in what they do. They are (for the most part) enthusiastic, idealistic, and energetic. The corpsmembers are similar, just younger, generally, or less experienced.

context The materials I develop will be used all over the place. Teams might be on campus in a classroom, but they might just as well be out camping or in a van. Sometimes teams will set aside an hour or two for education, but often the education will be on the run, quick discussions.

purpose These materials are to help team leaders help corpsmembers think of their service broadly. The materials are to help corpsmembers think about how their service shapes the larger communities in which we all live. The materials somehow have to address all the different kinds of service teams are doing, but the materials also have to help team leaders, who might have no prior teaching experience, lead these teaching sessions.

Here is the statement of purpose that came out of her research into her audience, context, and purpose:

I want to help busy but enthusiastic and knowledgeable (in different areas) team leaders become enthusiastic shapers of experiential learning for corpsmembers—in all different kinds of contexts that do not include desks or tables.

By doing this writing, Anne could see that she couldn't just produce a binder of materials that described step-by-step things teachers could do in classrooms—although that was the image of materials that the people who hired her had (vaguely) in mind. Because her audience was constantly on the move and involved in all different kinds of work, she saw that she would have to develop very flexible—and portable—materials. Here is a shortened version of the document—a design plan—that she sent to the people who hired her at the Corporation for National Service.

The design plan was approved, and production began. Notice how the plan describes the media—small, colorful printed booklets—and general strategies for arrangement (that the materials would be presented as booklets rather than in one big binder is an aspect of arrangement) into the various topics. The plan also describes some strategies—the overall tone and look of the booklets—as well as a plan for testing the materials through review by those who would be using the materials.

DESIGN PLAN
Service-learning materials for AmeriCorps* National Civilian Community Corps

NCCC team leaders come from a wide variety of education and work backgrounds—and will be helping corpsmembers learn the technical skills for doing their different service projects as well as the historical and geographic contexts that give meaning to their service. Teams will often be traveling and rarely in classrooms; they'll be living out of their backpacks and vans.

To help team leaders teach in these circumstances—and to teach with enthusiasm and drawing on their abilities—I propose that the educational materials I develop be a series of 12, small, back-pocket-sized booklets (packaged together in a zip-loc bag that can travel easily in a backpack) that cover a range of topics:

- **A "Cycle of Questions" booklets**
  These are 4 booklets—an Introduction and then a booklet each for before, during, and after a service project—that describe a process of questioning team leaders and corpsmembers go through with the project, in order to help them structure and learn—through a systematic use of questions—from their service.
- **Booklets for each of the four service areas in which the NCCC works**
  These booklets (named Education, Environment, Human Needs, and Public Safety) contain resources (odd questions, videos to rent, books to read) for team leaders to use on projects in the different service areas, to enhance and spark the team's learning.
- **Booklets on being an effective Team Leader**
  These booklets are:
  - On Being a Team Leader
  - On Facilitating Service-Learning
  - On Asking Questions
  - On Setting Goals & Reaching Them

By being separated into booklets, the materials will look less daunting than a big heavy binder. Seeing the different booklets and their topics will also help team leaders conceptualize the different areas of education they can address—and will help them see that education can be informal as well as formal, and can be relaxed, without always needing formal lesson plans.

These materials will also have colorful covers so that they are attractive. They will be written in an informal tone, and use lots of informal hand-drawn clip art, so that they will be friendly and inviting. Team leaders ought to feel that they can pick up any of the booklets at any time and flip through, picking up directions and suggestions—but the materials will also provide serious and rich educational support.

TESTING: As each booklet is initially completed, it will be reviewed and tested in the field by a small group of team leaders and education staff at each campus. Staff at Corporation headquarters will also review the booklets.

thinking through production

■ Choose a project assignment you know is upcoming in a class, or a communication task you've taken on for a church group or sorority or fraternity or other organization to which you belong. Take 30 minutes to apply the rhetorical process to the assignment or task—and then write up a short design plan. How is your plan different from your very first thoughts about how you were going to proceed?

□ There are more "Thinking Through Production" activities in the online chapter 2 resources at www.ablongman.com/wysocki

■ How is the rhetorical process we've laid out here—the process of developing a statement of purpose, figuring out the details of production, and planning for testing—different from how you usually compose communication? What in the process do you think will be most useful to you, given your strengths and weaknesses as a communicator? What in the process can you see giving you trouble? What in the process do you think will give you the most chances for being creative as you communicate with others?

■ The process we've described is not one that people in school usually think of using for school assignments such as research papers or essays. Often, those assignments seem too circumscribed for you to have many rhetorical choices: for example, you probably usually expect research papers and essays to be on 8½" by 11" white paper, in black ink, in a single typeface (with maybe some bold type for section heads); such papers sometimes use photographs, charts, or graphs to support their arguments. Choose a research paper or essay you've had to write for a class (in high school or college) and use the rhetorical process to develop a design plan for the assignment as though there were no restrictions on the media or arrangements you could use. (You'll have to reconceive your teacher's expectations and the context more loosely than usual.) Write a description of how you would change what you produced for the original assignment, and why—and describe how the new piece of communication would help you relate differently with your audience.

Woody Pirtle works at Pentagram Design in New York, an extremely well-known and influential design firm. Pirtle says this about how he comes up with ideas:

"I try to be very calculating in the way I approach a problem. It is never just intuitive. The very first thing I do is learn as much as I can. Then I sit down and try to make something happen—I could do this, I could do that. If I know I am not getting anywhere, I get away from the job for a while. I go to a bookstore, turn on the news, take a shower. Then I try to think what subject or element I have not considered, which might offer another avenue . . . .

"There are times when I get really stuck, and need outside input. So I speak to someone about it. I am amazed how often a person who is uninvolved will come at the problem from a completely different direction."

developing
a (more complex)
statement of purpose

Chapters 3 and 4 repeat the same set of steps for a rhetorical process of communication that we described in chapter 2, but in chapter 2 you worked through the steps for the first time and in a fairly basic way. In chapters 3 and 4, we assume you have a basic familiarity with the steps, and as we move through them again this time we bring out details and complexities. For instance, in chapter 2, we pointed out that if you don't have a clear purpose for communicating, there's no reason to communicate. In chapter 3 we consider, among other things, the possibility of having conflicting purposes for communicating, or what we might call "layers of purpose."

You can use chapters 3 and 4 as we recommend you use chapter 2: you can read these chapters to get a general sense of how you might proceed in some communicative situation in the future, or you can apply these steps to any specific situation you now need to address.

Chapters 3 and 4, however, help you develop a rich and concrete design plan—for complex communication contexts—by helping you think through a considerable range of details that can affect how and why you make the communication choices you do. You can also drop into these two chapters when you need to think in more detail about any one aspect of the rhetorical process we've been describing.

thinking through production

Yes, these pages may look out of order here, since every other chapter *ends* with pages like these—but chapters 3 and 4 are a little different from the others, and we think it will be most useful to you if you work through these two chapters while having a project in mind.

With a project in mind, you will read our suggestions and descriptions through the particularities of your project, which will make what we write here less abstract to you. You'll read (we hope) while considering how you can enrich your sense of purpose and how you are thinking about audience and purpose; you'll read looking for strategies and ideas for arrangements and media.

To help you with a project, here are suggestions:

1 Collect examples of brochures and handouts meant to influence the behavior of people your age. For example, look at your campus or local health department for print materials meant to teach about sexual health, alcohol or drug use, or eating. Identify what you think the materials are supposed to teach, and then test the materials with their intended audience to see how effective they are. (This is using testing as a kind of research— and the section on testing in chapter 4 can help you.)

Based on what you learn from your testing, use the sections of this chapter and chapter 4 to help you develop a statement of purpose and then a design plan (including a testing plan) for materials you think will work more effectively. (You needn't be constrained by a print medium: your testing may suggest that it will be more effective for you to produce a video or a game-show type event.)

Produce your communication.

What in your design and development process do you think was most useful to you?

2 Choose a topic that matters to you and that you'd like to teach others. Use the sections in this chapter to help you develop a design plan for producing a short piece of communication for teaching about this topic to children, and then to develop a design plan for teaching this topic to adults your age. How do the design plans differ? Why?

compose ▪ design ▪ advocate

3 Find a short text of some kind—an editorial, a cartoon, a webpage—that you don't think is as effective as it could be. Use the resources of this chapter and chapter 4 to develop a design plan for a revised text, paying particular attention to the statement of purpose. Re-produce the text, and test both its and the original's effectiveness with its intended audience. Write up your observations about the effectiveness of your redesign: what did you learn from the redesign that might help you develop communication in the future?

4 Develop a design plan (including a testing plan) for a board game intended to help parents and their children talk relaxedly and learn—while playing—about drug use. This is a complex audience situation, so carefully consider why parents and their children would want to play—and also consider how your game would engage both parents and children in the playing. You'll also need to consider the complex role of drugs (including alcohol and medicinal drugs) in our lives, so you'll need to do research into this area.

Produce the game, with the testing you planned.

How effective is the game? What qualities make it effective—and what would you change, and why would you change it?

What do you learn from this production that you want to remember for future productions?

5 Use the resources of this chapter, chapter 4, and chapter 6 to help you write an academic research paper.

You'll need a topic—an issue about which you'd like to learn more.

Because the medium of academic research papers is fairly well constrained (white paper with black ink), you won't need to worry about medium. You also won't need to work out some of your strategies, because academic research papers ask you to have a fairly formal voice and to develop certain kinds of logical support for your arguments.

Once you have your research paper, work back through the resources of this chapter to develop an alternative approach to your arguments. You can shape your work toward a non-academic audience, using any media and strategies that fit with how you rethink your purpose.

❑ There are more "Thinking Through Production" activities in the online chapter 3 resources at www.ablongman.com/wysocki

FIRST . . .
something more about design and communication . . .

The *New London Group*, educators who are interested in how to make education more responsive to our lives in these fast-changing times, have recommended that those who teach literacies think of what they do as teaching **design,** and specifically as teaching **the design of social futures:**

> The notion of design connects powerfully to the sort of creative intelligence the best practitioners need in order to be able continually to redesign their activities in the very act of practice. It connects as well to the idea that learning and productivity are the results of the designs (the structures) of complex systems of people, environments, technology, beliefs, and texts. (p. 20)
>
> (The New London Group, "A Pedagogy of Multiliteracies." In *Multiliteracies: Literacy Learning and the Design of Social Futures*. Eds. Bill Cope and Mary Kalantzis. London: Routledge, 2000.)

We talked in the Introduction about how we use "design" in communication—and it includes this notion of **designing futures.** Because we see composing for others as advocating for change (whether in an attitude others have toward an issue or in a new bike path or a dropping of third-world debt) then we believe that when you compose you are designing different relationships people will have with each other and their worlds. When you compose to do something, you are, that is, designing futures.

SECOND . . .
about argument, design, and communication . . .

Arguing is a social activity. The aim of most arguing is to affect people somehow, through shaping their experience, influencing their attitudes, inviting them to consider an issue with you, or changing their minds. Rarely, though, do you ever completely change someone's mind with an argument (and it is when we want to change people's minds completely that we most often have tooth-and-nail shouting matches). Instead, most arguments are about shifting someone's *level* of belief in or adherence to a position or attitude: through argument, we most often strengthen or weaken people's beliefs or desires. If we think of argument and communication as being about designing futures, then what argument can achieve is to give people ideas about what the future could be if their attitudes or beliefs were to shift somewhat.

WORKING WITH MORE COMPLEX COMMUNICATIONS

and working toward designing arguments and futures . . .

Before we go into detail about sense of purpose, context, audience, strategies, arrangements, media, production, and testing, there's a distinction we want to make. This distinction will help you think about where you are at any point in producing communication, and will help you be attentive to and learn about the processes that are most comfortable for you in producing texts. This distinction is between . . .

COMPOSING FOR COMMUNICATION, AND COMPOSING TO LEARN

In Section 3, you'll see a lot of texts: posters, photographs, calls to war and to entertainment, instructions, interviews, "traditional" and "experimental" essays, comic-book arguments. Although a lot of features differentiate these texts, one thing unites them: they are all communication.

Another way to put it, however, is to say that each of the examples has been composed by people thinking about their work rhetorically, as texts with a purpose in a context for a particular audience. And that is the kind of communication, obviously, we want you to consider producing—with the help of the resources in chapters 3 and 4.

But it is possible also to speak about private writing or speaking or drawing or painting, the production of texts not meant for the eyes of others. This can be making things to express to ourselves or record what we think or feel at any one time, in diaries or journals or artists' notebooks. (If you have not seen *The Journey Is the Destination: The Journals of Dan Elder*, the photographic/writing journals of a young journalist who was killed covering a war in Africa, get them from your library. Or look up *Everyday Matters* by Danny Gregory.)

Such private productions can also help us learn about what matters personally to us or what our own opinions are at any one time. Sometimes it takes writing or sketching our ideas to see them, to see how they connect and where they lead—and so to see if we want to adhere to the ideas and their consequences.

This notion of composing to learn should matter to you if you care about communicating. Private production can live on its own—in notebooks and diaries, and on scraps of paper—but it is also material that can be shaped into communication with others. There is no text in this book—our own writing and arrangements or the examples from others—that does not have its origins in jotted notes on scraps of paper or a sketch in a journal. There is no example in this book that did not start out in someone's quiet, personal musing about an idea.

When we wish to communicate with others, we always start out writing or sketching to ourselves, alone, not worrying about others. We stumble in this writing or drawing, and maybe use quick handwriting that only we can read. Or maybe we type, using shorthand expressions we but no one else will know. We wander if we write, not caring about grammar or English teachers with red pens. We make mistakes—who cares? We go down blind alleys, we find lovely expressions or neat ways to diagram an idea, we drift.

And then we look back over what we've written or sketched—or sometimes something hits us as we work. Sometimes just the act of writing or sketching and following an idea to its consequences leads us to a fresh angle.

Only after we have found something in our words and pictures that matters to us do we start thinking about how we might shape what we've made so that others can understand our cares and ideas, too. We produce to learn, for ourselves, and then we decide if and what we want to produce for communication.

What follows is a description of how you can go about communicating with yourself (and perhaps with others) to begin a communication project. We describe approaches you can use for any communication project, no matter the medium you finally choose. Eventually, you will have to turn to the different chapters of the next section for specific help in working with written, oral, or visual communication, but on the next pages is help to get you there.

You've been given an assignment to write a paper, or you have taken on a project to design communication to help a nonprofit organization increase its appeal to older people, so:

HOW DO YOU COMPOSE?

In previous chapters we've given you the framework of the rhetorical design process, and we're about to fill in the framework more—but creating communication is not a linear process, and sometimes (especially when you are working on communications that have some complexity in their context or audience or purpose) it can be hard to know how to start thinking in depth about what you are taking on. Sure, we tell you to think about your audience (for example), and to think about as many features as you can of that audience—but how do you think *usefully*? How do you make connections between audience and context and purpose? This is where composing-for-yourself comes in.

FIRST **MAKE TIME FOR THINKING . . .**

No matter what the situation is in which you need to produce communication, it is very rare that you can just sit down and make the thing. Before you do anything else you need to set aside time to think.

Few people plan time for thinking. We plan time for buying food, for exercising, for writing, for studying, for hanging out with friends. But having a quiet time and place set aside for nothing but thinking is necessary if you are to produce communications that satisfy you and that are effective. We do speak from experience here.

The amount of time you devote to percolating, to composing for yourself and to thinking, depends on the project and how practiced you are in developing ideas—the more you do this (and the more you attend to your own processes of developing ideas in order to see which work best for you), the easier and often the quicker it becomes. The amount of time should be proportional to the project: the bigger and/or more important the project, the more careful thinking you want to put into it. The more the project matters to you, the more you want to give it solid beginnings.

SECOND FIND STRATEGIES THAT HELP YOU THINK . . .

How do you start thinking about what you need to do with a project? How do you find ideas, a purpose, and strategies? There are many possible approaches to generating ideas and possible directions.

compose ▪ design ▪ advocate

- **Freewrite.** Sit down with paper and a pen or at a computer and just write about your project for 5 or 10 or 15 minutes. Do not stop, do not correct grammar, do not think about the writing—just let yourself write. The idea is to see what comes out, not to criticize it as you are going. (If you freewrite on a computer, try turning off the monitor so you can't see what you write; this will keep you from worrying about grammar or spelling and instead will keep you just generating ideas—the whole point.)

- **Brainstorm.** Write down any word or phrase that comes to mind about your project, and then write down any word or phrase that comes to mind in response to the first. Keep going as long as you can—but challenge yourself by setting a goal of 50 or 100 ideas. Brainstorming only works if you are not judgmental. Sometimes you'll come up with something that is just plain goofy or silly or dangerous and you'll know immediately that it won't work, but it may suggest to you something else that will work as long as you don't cut yourself off by thinking about how useless the idea is. (Brainstorming is an activity that is fun and often highly productive when done in a group of 2–4.)

- **Draw a picture.** Sketch out what you have in mind. Sometimes making your ideas into a picture opens up new ideas and directions. Try drawing a picture of

your audience when and where they'll encounter what you make. Try drawing a picture of what your audience will look like *after* they've read what you've made. This will help you make your audience—and your purpose—more concrete, and so will help you (when you turn to it) make your statement of purpose more detailed and useful.

- **Collect photographs and pieces of words that suggest possible directions to you.** Go through old magazines or newspapers, or copy photographs off the web (as long as you are using them just for yourself, you needn't worry about copyright infringement). Look for photographs and printed titles that suggest *anything* to you about your topic—or that you simply like. After you have a number, look to see what they have (or don't) in common. The act of collecting is important, because—when you see something that looks to be about your topic—you have to ask yourself how and why it connects, and so you have to define better what it is you are about. Don't stop with one object; the more photographs or phrases, the more ideas you'll generate and the more potential you'll have for finding a new, interesting, and fruitful line of approach.

- **Do some preliminary research.** If you are working on a research paper, this is absolutely necessary. We talk more about research in other chapters, in the

context of developing a research paper for a class. The idea at this point is to skim with an open mind, just looking for ideas and possible directions: how have others approached your topic, what directions have they followed, and what do titles of articles or other materials suggest? Let yourself be led along, jumpily, waiting for something that catches your eyes and interests.

But even if you aren't composing a research paper, look for things people have made that relate to your sense of purpose so far. If you know you need to produce something that will help draw young people to a new after-school program, see what materials you can collect or examine that have done this before: brochures, videos, printed balloons, and so on. The more ideas you let yourself run into, the more likely one (or possibly more) will strike you as a potential direction to follow and modify.

- **Read poetry.** Sometimes, looking into another genre of writing, especially one as expressive as poetry, can help you see connections and directions other people have followed. Because poetry is often more emotionally full than some other types of writing, and because a lot of poetry uses concrete descriptions or metaphors, looking to poetry for ideas can help you find a way to make your topic concrete and real.

- **Go to the movies or listen to music with your sense of purpose in mind.** Go to a movie (or rent a video), and watch it while trying to connect it somehow to your sense of purpose. Or listen to your favorite music while making the same effort. The effort to do this—often a stretch—can lead you to odd ideas, but also to new ways to connect audience and purpose or context, or to some new ideas about media or arrangement.

- **Generate questions.** In the beginning of chapter 6 (the chapter on doing research) we present a scheme for asking particular kinds of questions for developing a research question. Use this scheme to help you spin out as many questions as you can about your purpose. In the process of letting your mind move freely within the general guidance of the questions, you can have one of those *eureka* moments of discovering a direction.

- **Go walking.** The long quotation to the right is from the German-British writer W. G. Sebald, who wrote fiction about how lives and events (both big and small) overlap in small, easy-to-miss ways. Sebald describes making finds while walking. His finds aren't random, but—because he was thinking about an issue while walking—he looked at what was around him through the frame of his thinking and his searching, and that helped him see how he could make con-

nections between odd finds and the ideas moving in his mind.

We know that what we recommend might sound loopy—if not feeble—but the important thing is to find strategies that allow you to think comfortably, widely, and without pressure about your project. When you are starting up a project, you simply want to generate ideas, and often this happens best when you are being loose and a little wacky; later you will judge the ideas you have generated and shape them.

THIRD KEEP WORKING TOWARD A STATEMENT OF PURPOSE AND A DESIGN PLAN

You've brainstormed or freewritten or drawn pictures . . . then what? How do you know you have anything useful? *Keep coming back to your sense of purpose and the audience and context for the communication you are developing, and to the medium, strategies, and arrangements you might use.* Freewrite about context or find pictures of the context; brainstorm or read poetry about your purpose—then try to develop a statement of purpose and later a design plan, as we described in chapter 2 and in more detail here.

Keep going back and forth between the thought-encouraging strategies we've described in these two pages and articulating a statement of purpose and a design plan. You'll know you have a useful statement of purpose and a design plan when you find yourself concretely visualizing

"But then, as you walk along, you find things. I think that's the advantage of walking. It's just one of the reasons I do a lot. You find things by the wayside or you buy a brochure written by a local historian which is in a tiny little museum somewhere, and which you would never find in London. And in that you find odd details that lead you somewhere else, and so it's a form of unsystematic searching, which, of course, for an academic, is far from orthodoxy, because we're meant to do things systematically."

—**W. G. Sebald**

Waste time

compose ▪ design ▪ advocate

some aspect of the thing you're going to produce, whether what you visualize is how your first paragraph is going to sound, the overall structure of the piece, or a particular photograph to use on the inside of a brochure.

FOURTH RECOGNIZE THAT COMMUNICATION RARELY DEVELOPS IN A STRAIGHT LINE

You may be four pages into a five-page paper and think, sadly, "Nope, this isn't quite working . . ."—and you'll need to come back to the thought-generating strategies we've described here. Or you may just need to do several different kinds of producing-to-learn to develop a good statement of purpose. This is just how communication works: never in a straight line.

☐ In the online chapter 3 resources (at www.ablongman.com/wysocki) there are links to tools to help you get started with the initial steps of composing, through generating and mapping ideas.

How do you know when you're ready to move from composing-to-learn to composing-to-communicate?

When you have a statement of purpose that feels to you like a solid ground for moving forward, you are ready to start producing for the eyes (or ears) of others. When you have a statement of purpose that gives you good ground for choosing a medium or specific strategies or a particular arrangement, you are ready to move into the chapters in Section 2, so that you can find strategies and arrangements that are appropriate to the medium you are using. Also be sure to look through the examples in Section 3 for ideas about strategies and arrangements, and do collect for yourself other examples that you think do well what you want to accomplish.

Composing-to-learn doesn't happen once and then go away when you are producing communication for others . . .

Producing any piece of communication is not a straight-line process. Producing communication is a recursive process: it circles back and repeats itself.

You may find yourself (for example) writing a paper for a class and getting to a point where you thought you'd give a certain kind of supporting example. But, once you have the other writing pretty well in place, you can see that your example just doesn't work. Go back to brainstorming or freewriting or picture-making or -collecting to find another example. Give yourself time to wander purposefully but loosely through possibilities—something will come up.

Every person who produces communication—writers, graphic designers, those who write the words the President speaks in formal situations—understands about the recursivity of production. Needing to stop and find another approach is not a sign of failure or of loss of creativity or imagination or intelligence. Instead, it is a sign that the communication matters to you and that you are producing something where all the parts fit together and work to a purpose. It is a sign that what you are producing is more likely to have the effects you desire because all the parts work.

Where "composing-to-learn" comes from, and how it's useful

"Composing-to-learn" is an awkward phrase, we admit. It is a modification of the phrase "writing to learn," which (together with "writing to communicate") comes out of studies done by people who observe and learn about writing processes.

One of the first observations such researchers made is that people sometimes write for themselves and sometimes they write for others. You might be thinking, "Well, duh"—but this distinction is highly useful. In the early stages of learning to write, it seems plenty to try to get sentences and paragraphs to say what we want, to have them show our thoughts back to us. It is an additional complexity to think about how to shape words and paragraphs so that others can follow our ideas, especially when we begin to develop complex arguments. This is precisely the problem Walter had, way back in chapter 1 of this book: he hadn't learned how to think about shaping communication for others.

When you are aware of the distinction, you can observe your own production processes—not only if you are writing but also for any kind of communication for production—to see if you are still trying to work out ideas for yourself or if you are ready to start shaping communication for others. You can also see when you need to step back from shaping ideas for others to work through your own ideas.

Using composing-to-learn in other ways

Composing-to-learn needn't be something you do just to get started developing ideas and a statement of purpose for a big project. This kind of producing can be extremely useful in helping you study or work out various other situations.

When you are studying for a biology exam, for example, stop every 10 or 15 minutes to jot down what you are learning. Just summarize informally the main ideas or a process you are trying to learn. This will help you see if you indeed understand.

If you are reading a book or article that flummoxes you, jot down ideas about what is going on. For example, when we (Anne and Dennis) were working on the essay chapter of this book, the way we came up with the rhetorical analyses we offer is by jotting observations in the margins of the essays. Then, in not-too-careful and quick writing, we'd try to pull those observations together. When we could easily come up with three or four sentences that hung together, we knew we were on the right track.

Sometimes teachers use writing to learn to help students in their classes. If you've ever been in a class where a teacher asks you to write down questions about a lecture and then collects them and responds to them, she is using your writing to check that people are learning what she thinks important. A teacher might ask you to start class by writing a one-sentence summary of a reading from the night before, to check whether you understand. Teachers can ask you to write down one thing that is working for you in a class and one thing that isn't, or to describe what you'd change about a paper you just handed in: all these are ways teachers use writing to learn to help you—and them—see how a class is going and how your learning is developing.

When you write in a diary or journal about a friendship that is struggling or a work situation that has become dicey, you are writing to learn. It may seem too organizational or scientific to put a name on something so personal, close, and emotional—but writing like this is thinking on paper. It is one way to figure out what's going wrong (or right) and how to make things better.

MOVING ON TO THE RHETORICAL PROCESS . . .

In the rest of this chapter are pages devoted to each of the parts of the rhetorical process. These pages contain concrete ideas and suggestions to help you think through communication situations and support you in moving toward final production. You will hit moments of frustration because your situation is your own, but the ideas we offer can suggest directions for solving challenges.

sense of purpose

One way of summarizing the questions we laid out in chapter 2 about sense of purpose is that they ask you to think about *where you are now* and *where you would like to be in the future*. That is, a sense of purpose is what starts you toward "**designing possible futures.**" To design futures, look at where you—and your communities—are now; then imagine how you and your communities could be different. Take the sense of purpose that such thinking gives you and use the resources of this chapter to make the future you envision concretely desirable to your audience through the communication you build.

The future you envision needn't be a full-scale, fully worked-out city, country, or universe. You can think about different possible futures for your church or place of work or neighborhood—changes like bike paths or recycling or fair access to resources or Sunday afternoon potluck dinners—and then work to compose communications to engage others with your imaginings.

THINKING IN MORE DETAIL ABOUT YOUR SENSE OF PURPOSE . . .

1 in terms of now: complex motivations
In chapter 2, we asked you, simply, as though you were a method actor, what your motivation is in taking on the communication you are designing. Sometimes your motivation *will* be simple—"I've been assigned a paper"—but it can be more complex—"I want to build a webpage to teach others about neuropathic diseases because my father was just diagnosed and there's nothing available except in complex medical jargon and there's no way to communicate supportively with others whose family members have this diagnosis."

When you have complex motivations, try to separate out the different parts of your motivation so that you can consider what this means for the audience you want to address and what kinds of media and strategies to use, and so on.

For example, Martin Luther King, Jr. wrote a now famous letter—"Letter from Birmingham Jail"—to eight clergymen explaining his participation in civil disobedience. As he composed the letter he realized he had to be mindful that the letter would eventually make its way into the world and be read by more people than the original clergymen. Dr. King thus had to make sure he

spoke the language of the clergymen and connected his purpose to as many of their beliefs and values as he could, and yet he also had to keep in mind that arguments that might be effective with the clergymen might not be effective with others. In this case, Dr. King had to keep straight the different motivations behind speaking to the two audiences, and he had to make sure that his purposes in each case were not in conflict, or conflicted as little as possible.

Look at the motivation we described for the website about neuropathic diseases. There's strong and empathetic motivation in the desire to connect with and help others—but this also means the person building the website will need to be careful not to be too personal, not to make the website all about her experiences if she is to make others comfortable in coming there.

2 in terms of now: when the motivation isn't yours
When you're asked to give a presentation or write a memo at work or for an organization where you're volunteering, the motivation for communication comes from outside you, and you must communicate not only for yourself but for someone else. In such circumstances, you need to be clear about differences between your values and those of the institution. You need to be

clear to yourself that you can communicate the values of the institution without qualification, or you need to find strategies for showing, in the communication, where you differ, without undercutting the purpose of the communication. You need to be willing to go through all the steps of this rhetorical process with integrity both to yourself and to the people who have entrusted you with communicating. If you cannot, back out.

in terms of the future: how will you live up to your motivation?

It's easy to convince yourself that you know what you want and that you can go ahead, paying no attention to hidden complexities in the context that, were they heeded, would change your sense of purpose.

Our actions have short- and long-term consequences, and it is easy to lose sight of one or the other—and to have our efforts then tangle. Look at Dr. King's situation: in the short term he wanted the clergymen to understand how his civil resistance and desire to speak truth to power flowed from his religion, but he realized that in the long term his thoughts and actions needed to be answerable to a broader public, especially (in this case) to a white middle-class public who felt threatened by his actions. As you consider what you want to achieve with your communication, ask:

- Are my short- and long-term aims in harmony?

- Am I in a position to ask of my audience what I am asking of them? Do I have the proper authority, or have I built up the proper trust with them?

- Do I want to draw attention to myself and my cause at this time?

in terms of the future: when the motivation isn't yours

We talked above about outside motivation when you communicate for someone else. But motivation can come from outside in another way, as when you are assigned a class paper. Sometimes you'll want to write such papers, sometimes not. And when you don't, this is how the future enters: if you cannot find internal motivation for writing, you plan yourself a lousy future. You're planning frustration, boredom, or time you hurry through. If you can find a larger motivation for communicating—learning about written structures, perhaps, or trying out a creative approach—you'll make a much better future for yourself.

in terms of the future: does it help to break your purpose into different parts?

When you plan communications, think incrementally about achieving the future you want. That is, you might break down what you want to happen into steps and in each case ask, *Is this step worthwhile? Is it worth striving for? Can I achieve this?*

This process may also help you discover strategies that get overlooked when you are focused on the big picture. You may need to think about making multiple or smaller communications rather than one big one.

audience

In chapter 2, we asked you to generate as long a list as you could of audience characteristics; we also asked you to imagine your audience at the moment they encounter the communication you make, and to sort out from your lists those audience characteristics relevant to your purpose and context. The idea was to develop a picture of your audience that will guide all your other decisions in building some piece of communication.

As a result, we are hoping you will see how audiences are not one-dimensional and that they generally do not want to be treated that way. The women with whom Walter spoke in the story we told back in chapter 1 did not want to be pictured as secretaries. You probably do not like it when you are treated only as a student or as a young person who doesn't know anything or hasn't experienced anything in the world. You can probably remember times you were angered when someone spoke to you as though you were *only* a simple-minded stoner or metal-head or teenager or hair-club member. We are all more complex than any title or epithet can convey—and when we acknowledge that complexity in the ways we treat people, we shape better relations among us all.

Nor is any audience just three-dimensional: we are at least four-dimensional, because we live in time. We all exist as bodies with histories, and we have particular identities, allegiances, roles, memberships, and commitments that have developed and shifted over time. All these qualities contribute to how we read, understand each other when we are talking, and look at all the paper and computer screens around us.

What follows is intended to help you think in some detail about the people you'll address any time you need to communicate.

TO BEGIN: Complex and Shifting Audience Characteristics

First, go through the list to the right and think or discuss with others how these characteristics—when made concrete in a particular person of a particular age, and so on—generally impinge on communication. Also use the list to help you start thinking about the particular audience(s) you are addressing in any particular situation.

Consider an audience's

- ❑ age
- ❑ gender
- ❑ ethnicity
- ❑ level of education
- ❑ able-bodiedness
- ❑ sexual orientation
- ❑ class
- ❑ upbringing
- ❑ place of living
- ❑ place of work
- ❑ emotional states (will they be tired, angry, receptive . . .?)
- ❑ past experience with the topic/issue/matter
- ❑ learned habits (how they have learned to look at the topic/issue/matter)
- ❑ values/beliefs/commitments relative to the topic/issue/matter
- ❑ possible questions about the topic/issue/matter
- ❑ self-identity: the kinds of relations we see ourselves as having with others (mother ± unemployed ± daughter ± Republican ± leftist ± rich ± boss ± worker ± student ± teacher ± friend ± poor ± ambitious ± ??)

But that list is just a beginning . . .

The list complicates how we often judge people by age and gender. When, in addition to thinking of these, we think about the values audiences hold and their emotional states (because of a national crisis or a personal achievement) or the relationships that matter to them, we are more likely to think in ways that help us address them respectfully. In turn, that helps us develop a good relation with them.

There are also other ways you can think more deeply about the people with whom you communicate, whether you are thinking about communicating in day-to-day or more formal ways. Designers, for example, often spend considerable time thinking in as many ways as they can about their audiences, because doing so helps them conceive of their audiences as concretely and complexly as possible—and hence helps them design what is as engaging, delighting, functional, and effective as possible.

THINK ABOUT HOW . . .

the people in your audience have lives in which things happen . . .

The next time you walk through a crowded space—a cafeteria or an airport, for example—*look at the people around you and imagine what their days have been like leading up to the moment you see them.* You can't know for sure, obviously, but notice how your thinking about someone changes when you look at the person while thinking he or she just came out of a diffi-cult interview on which a career depends, or has been up all night helping a friend who's had a death in the family, or is just leaving on a well-deserved vacation.

When thinking about your audience, think of them not as an "audience" but as people who are free to move about the plane, who bite off more than they can chew, who get tangled up in blue . . . you get the idea. This makes them less formidable than when they seem like a faceless list of characteristics, but also helps you think about them generously and humanely.

(Some designers, when they are developing software or furniture or tools, make up imaginary people who might use what they are making. The designers give these imaginary people names, ages, occupations—all the characteristics in our list above. Then the designers work as hard as they can to keep these imaginary people in mind as they design. Such designers also bring in real people to test their products during the design and production processes, but—since it is often impossible to have "real" audience members present through every moment of the process—the designers work hard to make their intended audience members as concrete as possible.)

THINK ABOUT HOW . . .

you have preexisting institutional relationships with your audience . . .

Imagine you are writing a paper for a teacher you hardly know (big stretch, eh?).

If the teacher thinks of you as a "mere student" and so does not expect much from you, but you want the teacher to see you as knowing more than the typical student about the topic at hand, what can you do? How can you design this relationship so that the teacher doesn't see you as "just another student"?

Look at this hypothetical situation from the other angle. Being a teacher in a classroom sets certain limits on how you can relate to students. As teacher, you have a certain authority and the students are (mostly) predisposed to acquiesce to that authority. What can you do if you do not want students just to fall in line but rather want them to be responsible for their own learning? You may want to change the way you use your authority by giving students a range of choices and responsibilities, or by setting up small group discussions so that you are not always the center. Even so, when teachers do things like that, they can still undermine all their efforts by referring to students (for example) as "my" students. The possessive "my" can imply a certain paternalism that re-positions students as children and thus undercuts a teacher's effort to get students to take more responsibility for the classroom and their educations. It is so easy to fall back into old habits, especially around the roles we are all asked to take up in the various institutions where we live, work, and play.

These two examples show that, often when we communicate with others, we do so within already existing institutional relations with others. In addition to school, we go to church, we work in offices and fast-food outlets and chainstores and auto repair shops and web design studios. We live in families of different configurations and within different civic organizations and administrations. Each of these institutions gives us different titles or names—brother, employee, head fry cook, niece, citizen, deputy chief—and titles or names have meaning only relative to other people and *their* titles and names. You cannot be a father without a child, you cannot be a head fry cook without an assistant (otherwise you are just "fry cook"), you cannot be an employee without a boss, you cannot be a citizen without there being many other citizens.

Any time you communicate within such institutional frameworks, you need to keep the particularities of the relationships in mind. How do others see you because of who you are within the institution, and how do you see them? What expectations of behavior do people have about you—and you about them—because of your roles or titles or names? How might these expectations shape what you can say or write or show?

And do you need to step outside the relationships or call attention to them in order to achieve what you hope? Teachers can do this in classrooms when they ask students to talk about how they experience being students and when they then suggest how the teacher can change classroom structures or practices—such as grading policies or seating arrangements—so that students feel more responsible in the class.

Put otherwise, the fact that you have a preexisting relationship with your audience does not need to hamstring your efforts to communicate. By thinking about your role and what your audience knows about you as part of the context of communication, it becomes tied to your sense of purpose and thus becomes a part of what you need to strategize about.

4 THINK ABOUT HOW . . .

you often have primary and secondary audiences . . .

In a complicated world, what you want to accomplish can get complicated.

For example, the U.S. *Declaration of Independence* has layers of purposes addressed to more than one audience. It was a declaration to the King of England that the authors—representatives of the people of the 13 original states—believed they had the right to break away from England and form a sovereign nation. But for the Declaration to do all the writers intended it to do, they had to think about several other audiences as well: the people of England and not just the King, foreign governments with whom the colonies had been doing business and who would be worried about trading with "radical" people, and future generations of Americans who might look back and wonder why the break with England was made. Neglecting any of these other audiences would not only have made the *Declaration of Independence* less complex than it needed to be, but it would have excluded from consideration people who were being affected by the actions being declared. (The *Declaration of Independence* is reproduced in chapter 7, so you can see for yourself how it addresses its primary and secondary audiences.)

Other texts can have multiple—primary and secondary—audiences. For example, you might be helping a domestic abuse shelter publicize its hotline, and, in working through this communication situation, you and the people at the shelter decide to put informative flyers about the hotline in restaurant and campus restrooms. But rather than just put the name and phone number of the hotline on the flyer in order to reach people who are abused, you also describe all the different actions that count as domestic abuse, in order to help others figure out whether they are in abusive relationships or perpetuating abuse.

Thinking long and hard about how your communication might have multiple audiences—sometimes hidden from view—is a good way to ensure that what you say is as complicated as it needs to be. It is also a good way to keep your eye on who you are including and who you are excluding (perhaps accidentally) by what you are saying or how you are saying it.

5

THINK ABOUT HOW . . .

your audience is only ever your intended audience . . .

When you think about your audience, you can never possibly address every audience perfectly—precisely because people are complex. There is simply no way to compose communications that take into consideration every concern or feature of every member of your audience at the moment you communicate with them—even when you are speaking directly with them.

It is important, then, to keep in mind a distinction between your real audience and the audience you imagine as you prepare to communicate. The distinction between real and intended audiences is important to remember in all modes of communication: as you plan and communicate you are living in the space between what you think, imagine, and believe about your audience and who they actually are and how they actually respond.

It can be humbling to remember that at the end of the day, after all the planning in the world, the moment the words leave your mouth (or the paper gets turned in), your communication is out of your hands.

Even though we can never be certain we have anticipated our audience's reactions correctly, we still must try. In the final analysis our audiences are both real and intended, both imagined and actual, and we have a hand in how our relationship to them plays out.

6

THINK ABOUT HOW . . .

audiences step into the characteristics you imagine them to have . . .

At the beginning of this section on audience we asked you to remember when you felt someone addressed you as though you were only a student or only a young person. We asked you to recall such memories because they are most often unpleasant.

But also recall when someone said something complimentary to you, or introduced you as "the smartest person I know" or "the funniest person" or "my best friend." Remember how you probably felt a bit of a glow, and felt more capable and at ease.

Now extend such personal memories into how you—and other communicators—address audiences.

The distinction between real and intended audience is important precisely because the ways we talk to each other can have effects on how we feel about ourselves and behave. This should remind us that we are responsible for how we imagine—or construct—our audiences, for how we position them, and whom we include and exclude in the process. When we address audiences, we are asking them—for the time we are addressing them—to step into the characteristics we imagine they have. If we imagine those characteristics to be less than respectful, audiences either must take on those characteristics or actively resist them. If we imagine them in positive ways, they will generally respond likewise.

As you think about your audience, then, do keep in mind how your decisions shape who you ask them to be and how you ask them to act.

☐ There are additional materials to help you think about audience in the online chapter 3 resources at www.ablongman.com/wysocki

ANALYZING
audiences

■ **Discuss with others:** Adam DeConinck is a physics major. Here is his description of his audience and purpose as he was preparing to write a paper on space travel for his class:

"The audience for this paper is a person who has given little thought to the space program, but also probably sees no outstanding reason why he or she should be paying for it—in other words, nearly everyone. This is the type of person I hope to persuade to support the space program in general and in particular to support the idea of human spaceflight. This leads to two general ideas I have to keep in mind throughout my writing: first, I need to show that the space program as a whole is a benefit to society and, second, why sending humans into space is a valuable part of that project. At the end of my paper, my readers should not be asking themselves, 'Sure, that's great, but why not just send robots?'"

How does Adam's description connect his audience with his purpose? What more about his audience could Adam learn to help him achieve his purpose?

■ **Write informally:** List the people with whom you have relationships shaped by the institutions within which you live and work. As you develop your list, don't forget your religion, your job, your school, hospitals, civil institutions like the police and the Department of Motor Vehicles, your family, the military—any institution through which you have contact with others. For each person you list, describe how your relationship shapes how you communicate.

■ **Discuss with others:** Sometimes when you write papers for a class you're told to consider your classmates as your audience—and yet you know you have to write to your teacher, too, since it is the teacher who really judges your writing. In such a situation, how do you think through these primary and secondary audiences? Who is primary to you—the teacher or the students? How do you address them?

Similarly, you might in some classes produce communication for a client, with the communication aimed at still another group of people: for example, you might produce a poster—aimed at attracting young people to an after-school program—for a local nonprofit. The client has to approve the project—and it will be graded by the class teacher. What can you do to work with these primary and secondary audiences?

context

In chapter 2 we asked you to consider

❏ **the occasion of your communication.**
Is there an event motivating the communication, such as a presentation you've been asked to give children about effects of pollution on frogs, or a toast you've been asked to give at a wedding? What is the time—of the day, week, year—of your communication, and how is it likely to affect audience response?

❏ **the place of your communication.**
What are the characteristics of the place where the audience will be when they receive the communication from you?

Figuring out the specific event, time, and place is generally pretty easy. Determining other factors that might weigh on your communication can be difficult: it's hard to decide how broad your context is—but you can always benefit from thinking broadly.

When you compose, use the following suggestions to think broadly about the contexts in which you work; list any ideas about your context that come as you read. You can always shorten a long list, but the longer the list, the more ideas you'll be able to generate about strategies, and the more the communication you produce is likely to fit its particular time and place.

ALSO THINK ABOUT . . .

1 . . . how audiences perceive the time of communication

When you argue with a friend over which movie to see, you might understand the temporal context for the discussion to be just this one evening but your friend may include a string of similar past disagreements in which your choice always won. Or you might have been asked to give that presentation about the effects of pollution on frogs to a fourth-grade class. For you, this is a special 20 minutes; for the children, you are just part of every day's science hour.

These are examples of how you and your audience might perceive the time of communication differently. Keep in mind that how each of you understands this aspect of context affects how your audience attends to the communication.

2 . . . how YOU fit into the time of communication

You may think stand-up comedians talk off the top of their heads, but they practice their different routines repeatedly; they can then draw on and mix routines to respond to different audiences: they practice to be spontaneous and relaxed. So an important part of considering context is to consider the time *you* need to prepare sufficiently.

There's another aspect of time and context to consider. Many movie distributors, for example, would not release action films until well after September 11, 2001, which shows how contexts *do* depend on time. Ask yourself, then, if your context is right for your purpose and audience. Events can change a context because they can change what an audience is thinking or feeling or where you meet them: keep asking if the time is right to make your arguments.

3 . . . how audiences perceive the place of communication

Have you ever gone to a religious service for a religion not yours? How did you feel the first day of college, in your first class? Being in a place we know well or in an unfamiliar place affects how at ease we are, and hence how well we listen to others. Often, people in new circumstances are too distracted by just figuring out where they are to see posters on a wall or hear a speaker. Sometimes people are uncomfortable in places they know well (perhaps something bad happened there), and sometimes they are relaxed. If you can learn about an audience's general response to the place of communication, you can better shape your communication to work in the particular situation.

compose ▪ design ▪ advocate

4 **. . . the contexts of bodies in space**

In chapter 2 we asked you to visualize the contexts of your communications and how they might affect how people receive your productions. For instance, if you make an oral presentation, how do you ensure your audience sees and hears you comfortably? Such decisions depend on your purpose, of course: it could be the case that to achieve your purpose you *want* your audience to feel odd, cold, or uncomfortable so they will be slightly off balance. Sleazy people know that sleazy actions put other people at disadvantage in communication contexts; these are actions like having an interviewee sit in a chair lower than the interviewer's, shaking someone's hand limply, or speaking a little too softly for someone to hear. Unethical communicators take these actions when they want to make audiences feel weak or powerless. *But you can also help audiences feel comfortable and strong.* You can ask them (even in a brochure) to sit if they are standing or take some deep breaths to relax. You can tell jokes. You can take care that a booklet you make has large enough type for their young or old eyes.

5 **. . . institutional contexts**

In addition to the physical dimensions of contexts, attend to the institutional dimensions. We talked about this in the section on audience, about how audiences understand themselves through our institutions: families, religions, businesses and workplaces, and so on.

The contexts in which you communicate—in classrooms, church halls, bank meeting rooms—might call to audience's minds some institutional relations more than others. When you give a speech in class, your audience sees you primarily as another student, an equal—but were you to present at a high school, students there would probably see you as a cool, older college person. If you are brought into a business or school to give a workshop about a topic you know well, your audience will see you as an authority, deserving (at least initially) of respect for your knowledge—just as you do not generally question the authority of the people who write the textbooks you are assigned.

The institutional relations audiences have with one another also affect how they respond to communications. If you give a speech to family groups and only talk to the adults, they will notice that you ignore the children. Similarly, if someone in your class makes a comment during discussion and you ignore it and instead address only the teacher, other students can think of you as a snob or only out for a good grade.

Being alert to institutional contexts can help you think about whom to include as your audience and how to address them.

ANALYZING
context

- **Write informally:** Imagine you've been asked to give a speech to a group of 50 older people to teach what you learned about Indian art during your studies in Bombay. Sketch out—design—a space that would be the most conducive to their comfortable and attentive learning.

- **Write informally:** Consider an assignment on which you are now working for another class. Sketch out—design—the time and place in which you think that class's instructor would most generously respond to your work. How can you suggest that space and time through how you produce the assignment?

statement of purpose

In chapter 2, we asked you to compose a statement of purpose that explains the connections among your sense of purpose, your audience, and your communication context. In the previous sections of this chapter we have encouraged you to look more complexly at those aspects of communication. A result should be that, as your understanding of purpose, audience, and context becomes more complex, your statement of purpose likewise will become more complex. For instance, since complex contexts sometimes mean that we have to juggle several purposes with respect to several different audiences, your statement of purpose will need to explain not only the relations between purpose, audience, and context, but the relations between different purposes and audiences.

composing a more complex statement of purpose

The steps in composing a statement of purpose are the same as they were in chapter 2—with some additions. In addition to the questions we listed for step 3 on pages 34–35, add the following questions:

- Does this statement of purpose explain the relations between my main purpose and any secondary or subpurposes I may have?

- Does this statement of purpose reflect and respect the complexities of my audience? Does it take into account primary and secondary audiences?

- Is this a purpose everyone could share, or is it peculiar to my own interests or my social position?

- Is this a purpose I would want others to have?

- Is this purpose puerile, petulant, or petty? Am I base, brutish, or blind for having this purpose? Or is my purpose one that—when I achieve it—will help me feel proud and a useful member of the community I address?

re-composing a more complex statement of purpose

We hope you are seeing that even your statement of purpose is a strategy. How you state your purpose, how you represent your audience to yourself and to themselves, and how you envision your contexts are all strategic choices that shape how you think about and how you produce your communication—and will shape how your audience responds.

statements of purpose

■ **Discuss with others:** It is often useful to stop and tinker with a statement of purpose, to see how—by changing parts of it—your overall picture of your task changes. Below is a statement of purpose for a research project being undertaken by Stephanie Hill (a sociology major). Read through the statement of purpose, and then with a partner discuss the questions that follow.

> Men in their late teens and twenties are my audience. I want them to learn just how much body-image is a problem for women because of how men look at women. I know most men think this isn't really a problem, and that eating disorders are just personal issues for individual women. But I want men to be thinking about their sisters and girlfriends (and even potential daughters), and about how they probably don't want these people they care about to be spending so much time thinking about their bodyshapes—even to the point of starving themselves. I want to try to put my readers into the position of women, who see thousands of magazine covers of skinny women on them (or think of all the women on TV!), and about how the repetition of all those skinny women makes women feel . . . and then I want my readers to think about what it's like to have a boyfriend or brother who constantly makes comments about how you look like you've just added a pound . . .

- Change the audience characteristics Stephanie describes. How does this change the overall statement of purpose?

- Stephanie doesn't say much about the context in which her audience will experience her communication. Imagine different contexts in which her audience could encounter her communication: how do the different contexts change your ideas about what media Stephanie could use? How do the different contexts suggest the statement should be modified?

- Imagine Stephanie carrying out her purpose in several different media: how do different media change the context?

- What strategies does this statement of purpose suggest to you?

producing a (more complex) composition

In this chapter we speak generally about the strategies, media, and arrangement you can choose to achieve your statement of purpose. But also look closely at the individual chapters in Section 2 on writing and oral and visual communication for information about strategies—and strategies of medium and arrangement—that are appropriate for those particular modes.

Look at Section 3 for many examples of texts made in different media to see how strategies of all kinds, including arrangement, get used by different authors in different kinds of communication contexts.

CHAPTER 4

(And note that chapters 3 and 4 are separate in order to make the material in them into two more readily graspable sections. By splitting these chapters, we do not want you to think that first you think about audience, purpose, and context, and then you think about strategies, medium, arrangement, and testing. A design plan most often develops in a continual back and forth through all these steps—you need to be prepared to jump about between the steps, in whatever ways your thinking and your particular project catch your imagination.)

strategies

In chapter 2 we defined "strategy" as any part of your communication you can change to better achieve your purpose. We asked you to work toward an overall strategy for your communication project and then to generate smaller scale-strategies that supported your overall strategy and, ultimately, your overall purpose.

In this section, we introduce traditional rhetorical terms that allow us broadly to categorize strategies used in communication. These three terms—*ethos*, *pathos*, and *logos*—allow us to name strategies as being based in the character of the person(s) making an argument, in the emotions being engaged by the argument, or in how the parts of an argument are ordered.

These strategies can be used at the level of sentences or the colors in a photograph, but they can also be used as a base for a whole argument. You can use these terms both to generate arguments and to analyze the arguments of others.

Like any other scheme, that of *ethos-pathos-logos* cannot explain everything about arguments—but it can help you name what is going on in an argument and so can help you think with some control about the strategic choices you use to engage others.

ETHOS, PATHOS, AND LOGOS

Ever since the philosopher Aristotle wrote *The Rhetoric* (which is a set of lecture notes handed down over the years and now translated and printed in book form), people trying to improve their communicative strategies have distinguished among three basic strategies that Aristotle argued appear in all communication: *ethos*, *logos*, and *pathos*. These are Greek terms, and people continue to use the Greek terms because there are no single English words that hold all the same meanings as the Greek ones.

As we explain these terms, you'll see that even though the words look weird, you already know the basic ideas behind them and already have used them in your spoken, written, and visual designs. In this chapter and beyond, we want to help you use these basic strategies more awarely in order to increase their power for you. We'll define the terms and then talk about how you can use these concepts as overall strategies.

ETHOS, or what your audience sees in you

Ethos is how you come across to your audience—how "you" fit into your communication as part of what you are trying to do.

Everything you do or say not only conveys information to your audience, but it sets up a relationship between you and them, and that relationship influences how things go. For instance, if you walk up to a podium and say that on your way to give this speech you showed a lost cat its way home, the story is not just an explanation for why you were late but it also stirs the emotions of cat lovers in your audience and begins to incline them toward you. They begin to see you in a certain furry light, so to speak, and you can build on that.

Communicators create an *ethos* to give them authority to make certain claims, as when Kimberly Wozencraft names her experiences when she writes that:

> Having seen the criminal justice system from several angles, as a police officer, a court bailiff, a defendant, and a prisoner, I am convinced that prison is not the answer to the drug problem, or for that matter to many other white-collar crimes.

Similarly, when Penny Wolfson writes,

> I am at the Grand Union [supermarket] in Dobbs Ferry, New York, with my son, Ansel, who is thirteen years old.

she tells us (without having to say it explicitly) that she has the authority—as a mother—to write in both anguished and happy detail about her son and the debili-

compose ▪ *design* ▪ *advocate*

tating disease with which he contends; she also pulls into her writing (also without having to say it explicitly) all the emotions we share culturally about mothers and sons.

Recognize that, contrary to the two preceding examples, communicators do not have to use "I" to tell us about themselves. The topics they choose, the tone of voice they use, their vocabulary—all these shape how we understand the character of the communicator and hence the quality of attention we give. For example, the words below, from Hans Magnus Enzenberger, tell us nothing directly about him, but they tell us what matters to him, how he thinks, and how he thinks we should be in the world:

> Inconsistency is not the answer to our predicament, but it has its advantages and its attractions. It cannot be preached. It increases our freedom of thought and our freedom of movement. It is fraught with intellectual risks. It also takes a lot of training, but, if you put your mind to it, you may end up not only being less afraid, but even less afraid of being afraid.

Enzenberger says not a word about himself, and yet his words lead you to have a definite opinion about him and his character.

Ethos is in all communications, even when you cannot read or hear the words of the communicator. The photographs by Gueorgui Pinkhassov in chapter 11, for example, ask us to look at Tokyo through the position where the photographer stood with his camera: we see the photographs through his eyes and so through the attitude he had toward Tokyo and its people and places. To analyze *ethos* in these examples, we have to ask what his position is relative to the city, as he shows it to us through the choices he's made in framing, cropping, and arranging the photographs.

Ethos is a basic but complex strategy because so much affects *ethos*: tone of voice, gesture, stories one tells (or does not tell), how one smells, institutional roles, manner of approach, and so on.

PATHOS, or how your audience feels about what you are doing

Pathos is about how you handle emotions and feelings in communication. Do you try to evoke emotions and feelings in your audience, or do you try to present arguments unemotionally (keeping in mind that being unemotional is itself a kind of emotion)? Here Mary Pipher bases her argument on factual events as well as on fear, horror, and sadness:

> I do believe our culture is doing a bad job raising boys. The evidence is in the shocking violence of Paducah, Jonesboro, Cheyenne, and Edinboro [school shootings that preceded Columbine]. It's in our overcrowded prisons and domestic violence shelters. It's in our adult bookstores and white supremacy groups. It's in our Ritalin-controlled elementary schools and alcohol-soaked college campuses.

Notice how Pipher evokes emotion not only through her examples but also through her word choices ("shocking," "overcrowded," "alcohol-soaked") and the quick and repetitive rhythms of her sentences. Try reading Pipher's words aloud, and you ought to be able to hear how the sentences have a kind of urgent rhythm to them, which audiences will pick up, awarely or not.

A simple way to think about emotion is in terms of cause and effect. What you communicate can cause certain feelings in others, and there are many ways to influence how people feel: if you strike a confident pose you might instill respect in your audience, if you use a vividly photographic example you can shock them, if you tell a story with an unexpected but happy ending you can delight them, if you make an analogy between drinking the local water and drinking poison you can frighten them, and so on. There are more complex ways of thinking about emotion, however.

When you think about feelings and emotions, it is useful to separate *background emotions*, or moods, from more *temporary or target emotions* that you can evoke through the communication you build. The same emotion can operate in either way. Take fear as an example. When we say, "The country is in the grip of fear," we usually mean that we are operating within a "climate of fear"—a background emotion that many of us experience in some part of our days, after we watch the news, say, or hear from a sister serving in the military overseas—that needs to be taken into account by the communicator. Background emotions like this are not something you as a communicator are responsible for causing—they are instead part of the context in which you communicate, and so you need to take them into account (as anyone writing about the events of September 11 must, for example). Fear also can be a target emotion—one you want to create at a specific time and place—as when someone shouts "fire" in a movie theatre (don't try this), or when a strong speaker invites you to resist your fears by saying "The only thing you have to fear is fear itself."

Another more complex way to think about emotion is as a developing pattern or structure. Once you have done something in a communication that encourages someone to feel a certain way, you need to think about what that feeling prepares them for, and how what you do and say next can lead to still other feelings. For instance, fear is closely related to anger (if, while living with your parents, you ever came home way past curfew, you probably experienced how your parents' fear about you turned into relief—and then anger—when you returned). A communicator who evokes fear in an audience can then easily shift that fear into anger; this is often a strategy used by governments that want to go to war against another country, for example.

Here is an example of a writer, Charles Simic, using *pathos* to develop a pattern—and an argument—about how mundane and practical details of life necessarily entwine with what is horrible, sometimes blindingly:

One day in Yugoslavia, just after [World War II], we made a class trip to the town War Museum. At the entrance we found a battered German tank which delighted us. Inside the museum one could look at a few rifles, hand grenades, and uniforms, but not much else. Most of the space was taken up by photographs. These we were urged to examine. One saw people hanged and people about to be hanged; people on the tips of their toes. The executioners stood around smoking. There were piles of corpses everywhere. Some were naked. Men and women with their genitals showing. That made some kid laugh.

Then we saw a man having his throat cut. The killer sat on the man's chest with a knife in his hand. He seemed pleased to be photographed. The victim's eyes I don't remember. A few men stood around gawking. There were clouds in the sky.

There were always clouds, as well as blades of grass, tree stumps, bushes and rocks no one was paying any attention to. At times the earth was covered with snow. A miserable, teeth-chattering January morning and someone making someone's life even more miserable. Or the rain would be falling. A small hard rain that would wash the blood off the hands immediately, that would make one of the killers catch a bad cold. I imagined him sitting that night with his feet in a bucket of hot water and sipping tea.

Whatever you feel or think about the man with a cold depends completely on what Simic has described before. Look at the way in which Simic builds emotion, moving from class trip to tank to horror, and then seemingly giving us a breath with the mention of clouds and grass and trees—only to use that pause to show how horror occurs amid daily breathing.

As the preceding passage shows, *pathos*, like *ethos* and *logos*, develops over time, and in that development we see the intertwining of all three of the basic strategies. Over time, an audience's emotional responses are the result of what you have said (*logos*) and how you have come across (*ethos*), and yet how you come across in turn is influenced by the emotions being stirred (*pathos*) and the argument being made (*logos*). The audience is always feeling something, but what you say and do can redirect their mood and build a set of emotional responses that influences in turn how the audience hears your words.

LOGOS, or the reason and structure in arguments

You have seen the Greek word *logos* a lot in your life, usually attached to another Greek word such as "bio" (life) or "psyche" (spirit or mind). *Logos* is not the plural of "logo"; instead, for the ancient Greeks, *logos* meant word, structure, reason, thought, language, and argument—and so "biology" is the study of life, while "psychology" is the study of our internal mental workings. Our word "logic" derives from *logos*. As a basic category of strategy, it includes all the strategies connected with the structure of an argument (including arrangement) as well as the kinds of reasoning you choose to use. Look at this passage, written by David Halberstam, about

compose ▪ design ▪ advocate

the aftermath of the events of September 11, 2001:

> This, then, is the ultimate challenge to us as a society, far more difficult and complicated than the one that followed Pearl Harbor; Pearl Harbor had the ability not merely to unify the country—as this attack has—but also to sustain that unity for as long as was required. The phrase we used in those days, lest we forget, was "for the duration." The September 11 assault is infinitely more insidious, and it strikes a nation that after a half century of relentless affluence is quite different—much more materialistic, with a significantly more abbreviated and fragmented attention span. The responses the attack inspired at different levels of our society are quite complicated and in some ways terribly revealing: contrast, if you will, the selfless behavior of those magnificent New York firefighters, rushing into the inferno of the Twin Towers to save strangers, with that of the stock-market players, architects of the greatest one-week drop in the stock market since the depression.

Halberstam's words cannot help but evoke emotions because they are about September 11, and we certainly make judgments about his character based on what and how he writes, but his main strategy here is *logos*, using primarily the structure of comparison. Halberstam makes comparisons between Pearl Harbor and September 11, in order to raise questions about who we are and how we respond now. He makes comparisons between firefighters and stockbrokers to raise questions about how different groups understand and enact their social responsibilities.

Facts and numbers (like statistics) are also strategies of *logos*. These are strategies Barbara Ehrenreich uses to argue about the causes of breast cancer:

> Like everyone else in the breast cancer world, ...feminists want a cure, but they even more ardently demand to know the cause or causes of the disease without which we will never have any means of prevention. "Bad" genes of the inherited variety are thought to account for fewer than 10 percent of breast cancers, and only 30 percent of women diagnosed with breast cancer have any known risk factor (such as delaying childbearing or the late onset of menopause) at all. Bad lifestyle choices like a fatty diet have, after brief popularity with the medical profession, been largely ruled out. Hence suspicion should focus on environmental carcinogens, the feminists argue, such as plastics, pesticides (DDT and PCBs, for example, though banned in this country, are still used in many Third World sources of the produce we eat), and the industrial runoff in our ground water. No carcinogen has been linked definitely to human breast cancer yet, but many have been found to cause the disease in mice, and the inexorable increase of the disease in industrialized nations—about 1 percent a year between the 1950s and the 1960s—further hints at environmental factors, as does the fact that women migrants to industrialized countries quickly develop the same breast cancer rates as those who are native born.

Facts and numbers carry persuasive weight in our scientifically minded culture—which is why when we or others use them, we need to be alert to how they can be presented for different emphasis.

As with the other strategies, *logos* is not restricted to arguments made with words. The photographs by Josef Koudelka in the chapter on documentary photographs ask us to consider industrialization's effects on a landscape by presenting three similarly arranged photographs. Look at the photographs: the repetition of the long horizontal arrangement asks us to read the photographs as though they flow into each other, making one long barren scene. Koudelka is therefore relying heavily on *logos* in how he has arranged his photographs.

It is important to keep in mind that presenting yourself as a logical person in an argument is not about *logos*; presenting yourself as a logical person is about your *ethos*, how you present yourself to your audience. *Logos* is simply about the structures and arrangements you choose as you build an argument, both in terms of overall and smaller scale structures.

Some kinds of *logos* are appropriate only to writing or only to speaking or only to visual communication—we discuss those in the chapters on each of the modes.

choosing *ethos, pathos,* or *logos* as an overall strategy

A helpful way to think about an overall strategy to choose in a piece of communication you're developing is to choose *ethos, pathos,* or *logos* as your guiding term. That is, does it make the most sense for your overall guiding strategy to be that of putting emphasis on your character and qualities, on the emotional connections you can build with an audience, or on the structure of the piece?

In chapter 2, we imagined a situation in which you make a presentation to the city council in favor of a traffic light at a dangerous intersection. We suggested there that you could argue by using the stories of people who had been hurt in traffic accidents in the intersection; this would be to choose *pathos* as your overall strategy. You could argue from statistics about the money accidents at that intersection cost the city, and this would be to choose *logos* as your overall strategy. In chapter 2, we also described how the choice comes down to knowing your audience: a city council concerned about budgets is more likely to be persuaded by an argument based in *logos* than in *pathos*.

If you choose *ethos*, *logos*, or *pathos* as your overall strategy, keep in mind that you still have to address the other two strategies, shaping them in support of the overall guiding strategy. In this book, for example, the divisions of sections and chapters and our writing whose purpose is to help you learn about the thoughtful use of rhetoric show that our overall strategy is *logos*. Imagine then the effect if we developed an *ethos* that was silly or arrogant or plodding. Instead, we have tried to sound authoritative to you in our writing, so that you will take our points seriously. We want you to understand us as thoughtful, enthusiastic,

and concerned about your abilities as a communicator, to establish a relationship with you that invites you to consider these matters as seriously and with as much sense of possibility as we do. As for *pathos*, given that our overall strategy is *logos*, we could not very well write to evoke emotions of disgust, fear, or anger. Instead, we've tried to write with a broad range of examples and with some humor, so that perhaps your intellectual curiosity will be piqued by what you can learn.

Here are other ways that choosing an overall strategy shapes how you use the other two. In chapter 13, there is an editorial in favor of affirmative action and an editorial against. Both use *logos* as their primary strategy, listing reasons why their readers should be for or against affirmative action and responding to criticisms others might raise. The first editorial is written by a man who benefited from affirmative action, and from the first sentence he identifies himself in this way, telling how he grew up poor and only went to college because he could take advantage of "minority outreach programs." Only after constructing an *ethos* that (he hopes) gives him the authority to speak from personal experience—and perhaps arousing in his readers the emotion of compassion—does he turn to his main logical points. In the second editorial, the two writers tell us nothing about themselves; instead, they start their writing with claims about the effects of affirmative action and then give

support for their claims. To be persuasive about an issue that is so emotionally charged in this country, they cannot sound motivated by self-interest or anger in trying to deny benefits to others—and so they try to develop an *ethos* that sounds impartial, and they avoid strategies that will arouse much emotion. They use long words that slow down the rhythm of their writing, making it sound unemotional. Their sentences rarely describe individual people taking specific actions but instead often have abstract nouns as their grammatical subject, making the problem seem less emotional because less tied to real people.

Almost all the examples in the chapter on posters use the primary strategy of *pathos*, drawing us in by evoking romance or horror or by making a direct visual appeal to patriotism. But all these posters have to be arranged visually so that we can see and make sense of the emotional appeals, and so *logos* is at work. It may seem that there is no *ethos* in posters, because the person who designed the poster isn't ever present in it—but there are several ways viewers get a sense of *ethos*. When we look at the examples from wartime, we see that whoever designed the poster is trying to cause certain actions to happen, and we understand their choice of action to indicate something about their character. We also judge the production qualities of a poster as a sign of *ethos*: just as we make judgments about writers based on how they've used spelling and grammar, we make judgments about anyone who produces communication based on the quality of attention they give to their production and how knowledgeably they've used their materials.

Remember that, although pieces of communication will have *ethos*, *pathos*, or *logos* as an overall strategy, they are always also shaped by the remaining two substrategies. Attend to this both as you analyze and produce communications. Note, too, how the *ethos, pathos,* or *logos* in a communication builds over time, over the course of the whole communication.

using *ethos, pathos,* or *logos* as small-scale strategies

The overall sense a reader, viewer, or listener has of *ethos*, *pathos*, or *logos* in any piece of communication is built up from all the different ways these strategies are used in the various elements that make up the whole composition.

In the chapters on written, oral, and visual modes of communication, and in the chapters of examples of many different kinds of texts, we will point out how *ethos, pathos,* or *logos* are made present in many different small ways appropriate to the different modes.

▢ In the online chapter 4 resources (at www.ablongman.com/wysocki) there are links to more information on rhetorical terminology and strategies.

ANALYZING
ethos, pathos, and logos

■ **Write to learn:** To understand *ethos*, *pathos*, and *logos* in communication using words, try restating the words to achieve different results. Look, for example, at the paragraph below about the 1994 U.S. crime bill. The paragraph was written by Bruce Shapiro, who along with several others that year had been stabbed, almost to death, by a "socially marginal neighborhood character" who believed his mother had been killed.

> In early autumn I read the entire text of the crime bill—all 412 pages. What I found was perhaps obvious, yet under the circumstances compelling: not a single one of those 412 pages would have protected me or Anna or Martin or any of the others from our assailant. Not the enhanced prison terms, not the three-strikes-you're-out requirements, not the summary deportations of criminal aliens.

We would say that Shapiro is working to construct an *ethos* that is dispassionate and informed (look at what he's read), and deserving of readers' sympathies because of what he's undergone—but it's an *ethos* that might also gain persuasive strength for readers because they might expect him to want revenge for his injuries or tougher laws; instead he is making an argument, based on painful personal experience, that tougher laws would have made no difference. There seems to be little *pathos*: Shapiro applies no judgmental adjectives to his "assailant" (and look at the relative neutrality of that noun); there does seem to be emotion in the quick repetitive rhythms of the last sentence. There is an implied formal argument, which is a particular use of *logos*; that argument might be stated like this:

> The crime bill is useful if it prevents crimes.
>
> The crime bill would not have prevented the attack on Shapiro and others.
>
> The crime bill is therefore not useful.

You may not agree with the premises of this argument (or you might state them differently based on your reading), but something like this *logos* is at work in Shapiro's paragraph.

Rewrite Shapiro's paragraph to make him sound angry or vengeful. Increase the emotion by changing nouns, adding adjectives, or making all the sentences choppy and harsh. Take out the implied formal argument—or make it more obvious.

Give your revised paragraph to others. How do your changes shape how others read and respond?

medium

In chapter 2, we said that choosing a medium involves both creativity and common sense. In this chapter, we don't just amplify that message but twist it a little in an effort to encourage you to be more creative than common-sensical. We live in a time when the media we have at our disposal are dissolving, reconstituting, and morphing into new shapes and combinations, and it behooves us all to pay attention to the media around us and the opportunities they present to communicate ever more effectively.

CHOOSING WHICH MEDIUM OR MEDIA TO USE . . .

1 **Is it appropriate to use a medium or media with which your audience is familiar or that is expected in the context?** That is, does your context suggest you will be most persuasive if you stick with a medium your audience knows well? For a class research assignment, for example, it will generally make sense to turn in a printed, double-spaced report on white 8 1/2" by 11" paper, printed in black ink. If you are asked to give a eulogy at a friend's funeral, most mourners would think it inappropriate if you brought your guitar and amps and played a black metal anthem. If you are trying to persuade an audience to vote for your candidate because she has good economic policies, you are probably going to be most effective making a poster that's easy to read and states facts. Chances are that audiences expecting political information will have trouble understanding a lyric poem about her economic policy—even if the poem contains all the facts. How audiences attend to communication is shaped by their expectations of the context and purpose of the communication—and an odd or unfamiliar medium can distract or upset them and so get in the way of you achieving your purpose. Thinking about the kind of communication your audience might expect in a given context can help you think about the medium to use.

2 **Is it appropriate to use a medium or media with which your audience is *unfamiliar* or that is *unexpected* in the context?** Suppose you are writing a research paper on the Scott expedition to the South Pole in the early twentieth century, and—as you learn about the explorers' diets—you come to understand that your purpose is to argue that a better diet might have saved the expedition. To call attention to and support your arguments, it might make sense to turn in your paper with an attached ball of oatmeal and lard (which is what the explorers ate for months on end), with a note asking your teacher to have a taste to better understand why you think the explorers were undernourished. (And, of course, you probably have a good sense of your audience in this case, of which teachers will be receptive to such argumentative choices.) If you are asked to give a eulogy for a member of a metal band, then playing a black metal anthem (especially one she wrote) might be

compose ▪ design ▪ advocate

unexpected, but probably not inappropriate. If you're going to a poetry slam and wish to highlight the economic policies of a political candidate, then a poem about those policies will probably be unexpected but not unwelcome given the context—and your creativity (and, we hope, facility with poetic rhythms) might catch the audience's attentions as a regular speech or poster wouldn't. This last example is similar to President Clinton's interview on MTV when he was first campaigning for president: MTV was an unexpected medium for a presidential candidate, but it brought him in contact with voters who otherwise might not have been able to talk with him so directly, and it led to an increase in the voting of people under 20. If you want to use an unexpected or unfamiliar medium, it needs to fit with and strongly support your statement of purpose.

3 **How do you figure out a medium that might be unexpected but that works in the context?** At the end of chapter 2, we described a set of learning materials that Anne (one of the authors of this book) made for the National Civilian Community Corps. The materials were unexpected, in that most previous materials used in the Corps had been in big binders; Anne made a series of small, colorful booklets in a plastic bag—but what led Anne to make such materials was the research that led to her state-ment of purpose. In the course of figuring out who the audience was and how they needed to use the materials, people talked about how they'd like to have something they could carry with them to work, something small and easy to get to. It was Anne's audience who suggested the medium; Anne just had to listen.

You can also come up with unexpected but appropriate media through a kind of brainstorming. Go to a mall and wander, looking at and listing all the things that people make for each other to communicate: greeting cards, board games, stuffed animals, documentaries on audio cassettes or CDs, hands-on museum displays, fancily covered books, candy bar wrappers, skits, balloons, noisemakers, fold-out photo albums, and on and on. Go to a bookstore and look at the different ways magazines and books are put together (look especially at children's books). Look at books and magazines about design. Such varied looking can suggest to you new media for carrying out your purpose, but do test your ideas with audience members (by describing to them what you are considering) before you go into production.

4 **How do you choose a medium that is responsible to your audience and context and purpose as well as to the environment and your pocketbook?** It would be fun to design a full-color brochure for the nonprofit organization where you volunteer, but do they have the budget? When you are deciding among media, consider:

- *How many of this piece of communication are needed?*

- *How much will each piece cost? Do I—or the people for whom I am doing this work—have the money to produce as many as we need? (If you are going to a print shop, the people at the shop can give you an estimate for the costs of reproduction.)*

- *What resources are required by the medium? Can I use recycled paper or soy-based inks? Can I make the piece so that it uses fewer resources?*

- *Does the intended audience have access to the medium? Can they access computers, for example, or computers that can handle memory-intensive animations?*

- *Is what I am making a size and shape that my audience will be able to use?*

- *Will my audience understand how to use the medium? Will I need to include instructions, or is it part of my purpose that they have to struggle a bit to understand what I make?*

- *If I need multiple copies of the communication, is it easy and inexpensive to reproduce (on a regular copy machine) or does each piece require a lot of direct hands-on manipulation and expensive materials?*

Talking directly with people is just about as close as we can get; the intimacy of the situation will depend on how well we know the audience and how many people there are.

Unexpected media (fortune cookies are our example here), because they will generally seem informal to an audience, will tend to feel like a gesture from someone known or comfortable.

Handwritten letters feel very intimate; letters delivered directly to us can feel like a gesture of closeness.

Photographs of people we know will always be intimate communications; photographs of people in general will pull us in because of our connected sense of bodily experience.

Comics, because they carry with them both the sense of hand-drawn production and illustrations of people, will feel close and informal.

Recordings of voices, film, or photographs seem one step removed from our actually being there.

Printed documents—because there is no visual presence of messy bodies in them and only a reduced sense of voice—can seem to audiences to set you at a distance. Printed interviews and personal essays—because they will have printed representations of individual voices—will seem closer than opinion pieces and editorials, which usually have voice but also formal argumentative structures and the desire to address groups of people. Academic articles—because they are supposed to be objective—can feel farthest away from audiences.

5 **What kind of relationship—of closeness or distance, intimacy or objectivity—do you want to establish with your audience through the medium or media you choose?** The graphic above shows some typical media in use today—media you might be in a position to produce—and how close an audience tends to feel, conventionally, toward the maker of the media. Some media—your voice or a hand-written letter—can give your audience a fairly direct sense of you: they will feel that the communication between you is per-

sonal and perhaps even intimate. Printed texts tend to feel more distant, and certain printed texts, such as academic articles are, by conventional design, produced to feel distant and consequently (their authors hope) more objective.

As you are considering which media to choose, think about the sense of nearness and presence—or distance and objectivity—you want to have with an audience. There are other strategies for producing a sense of nearness or distance, as we describe in the section on strategies and in the chapters on strate-

gies specific to written, oral, and visual communication. But the medium or media you choose—because of the conventional attitudes audiences tend to carry about them—matter very much in the relationship you establish with your audience.

In Section 3 are examples of writers who try to break some of these conventions by, for example, writing essays that try to mix a sense of the public and the private, to have both objectivity and intimacy. See, for example, "Red Shoes" by Susan Griffin.

compose ▪ design ▪ advocate

6 **Can you, responsibly, make an effective production with the medium you're considering?** Do you know enough, for example, about the technical aspects of four-color print production to make a full-color brochure? Do you have sufficient access to equipment for making a broadcast-quality public service announcement? While you are working on a project, if it seems that the best medium to use is one with which you have little familiarity, your decision to go ahead will depend on the whole context: if you are producing a piece of communication within a class, and your teacher is willing to let you try a new medium, then you are all set. But if, for example, you are working with a nonprofit organization and they ask you to produce a newsletter or four-color brochure for them (or you all agree that this is what they need) and you've never had experience with such productions, tell them. Since they are paying for the production of the piece, they need to be able to make the decision whether to proceed.

ralph nader / public

■ **Write informally:** Over the course of a week, list every medium (or mix of media) you use, consume, produce, or encounter. Which of these media are within—or could be within, with a little effort, creativity, or time—your capabilities to use?

■ **Write informally:** To the left are two pieces of communication that use unexpected media.

The top photograph is of the Lucent Technologies Center for Arts Education in Newark, New Jersey; the building doesn't have a sign—it *is* the sign, describing all that goes on inside. (Paula Scher, of Pentagram, in New York City, is the designer of the words.)

The second photograph is of a skateboard deck, designed by Mike Mills of the Directors Bureau (which has offices in Los Angeles and New York City). Why is it unusual to see Ralph Nader on a skateboard?

Try to re-create the statements of purpose for these two objects that would encourage the designers to come up with these uses of media.

arrangement

In chapter 2, we asked you to consider how arrangement contributes to the overall effectiveness of any communication. Here we discuss in more detail some general strategies of arrangement you can use to achieve your purpose. Turn to Section 2 to learn more about strategies specific to written, oral, and visual communication. Section 3 has examples of arrangements in many media.

When you are trying to figure out how to arrange the pieces of your argument, or looking for an arrangement that might suggest ideas about how you could argue, look through these suggestions and examples. See if you can mentally work out how to use several of these different structures as overall strategies of arrangement, in order to consider what might help you best connect with your audience. Also think about how these strategies of arrangement can be used at the sentence or illustration level, to add interest to the details of your productions.

ARRANGEMENTS THAT MOVE

If communication is about "designing possible futures" (as we described in chapter 3) then it is about showing your audience how some set of conditions could be different and better. One way, then, to understand how the arrangement of a communication needs to function is to move an audience imaginatively from where they are now into the future conditions you—and they—think best. That is, you can arrange your piece so that what the audience experiences first is what they know now, ideas or images with which they are familiar or comfortable. Then, step by step, you move them into the unknown or unfamiliar— hoping, generally, that each step builds upon the previous one so that the audience never feels any huge or unknown or unexpected gaps or feels that any step will take them in a direction they think is wrong or frightening or ill-considered. You want the audience to be able to follow your reasons and reasoning and to be able to judge your points from your perspective.

Another way to think about arrangement is that what you create is always a progression: there is always some change for your audience from the point where they first enter your piece to where they leave.

small to big

In a "small to big" structure, you are showing your audience how something small they accept or understand can lead to bigger consequences that they may—or may not—want. There is a classic proverb that uses this kind of arrangement:

> For want of a nail the shoe was lost,
> For want of a shoe the horse was lost,
> For want of a horse the rider was lost,
> For want of a rider the battle was lost,
> For want of a battle the kingdom was lost,
> And all for the want of a horseshoe nail.

People have used some version of this proverb since at least the fourteenth century to argue—by analogy—that we ought to attend to small details because they can lead to big consequences. If you do an online search for "for want of a nail," you can find examples of this proverb and its arrangement of small to big used in car ads, history books, and computer programming examples.

In chapter 14, the essay "Higher Education" offers an example of "small to big" structuring in a multi-page piece of writing. "Higher Education" is about a black man who comes to a small, all white, Mennonite town as a basketball coach and, after an initial awkward period, winds up having a strong effect on the town, its people, and

compose ▪ design ▪ advocate

its children—an effect the author, Gary Smith, calls a "miracle." The essay is an argument, in other words, about how one "small" human can have big effects.

Here is a description, from Cullen Murphy, of how small to big can be used to arrange whole books: a writer, Murphy says, can take

> something seemingly unremarkable (a kind of food, an article of dress, a body part) and from it derives a larger world of meaning. In the mid-1970s the historian and John Adams biographer Page Smith and the biologist Charles Daniel published *The Chicken Book*, a conceptual vivisection of *Gallus domesticus*, and a tour de force. A decade and a half later the engineer Henry Petroski devoted an entire volume to the pencil. Last year the architect Witold Rybczynski produced *One Good Turn*, a history of the screwdriver and the screw.

big to small

You've probably heard the slogan, "Think globally, act locally." This is condensed argument of the "big to small" variety: "Think globally" precedes "act locally" and directs our attention to the larger perspective first before focusing our attentions on the small, the local, the place where our actions stand the best chance of doing good and echoing back out to the big.

Here is another example of big to small from the humor newspaper *The Onion*:

U.S. Dept. of Retro Warns: "We May Be Running Out Of Past"

Washington, DC—At a press conference Friday, U.S. Retro Secretary Anson Williams warned of an imminent "national retro crisis," cautioning that "if current levels of U.S. retro consumption are allowed to continue unchecked, we may run out of past by as early as 2005."

At first this may not seem like an example of "big to small," but the humor works by taking something big—the past in its entirety—and making it seem small—something we could run out of. Humor often disguises argument, too, and this is the case here. The article pokes fun at our love of "retro" trends through two exaggerations—the idea that we might go so far as to have a "U.S. Retro Secretary" and the idea that we crave retro so much we might run out of a past to which we can return.

With this kind of structure, you can also show your audience how something big they accept may have hidden in it smaller consequences they may or may not want to accept. In chapter 13's "Who would call warrior 'squaw'?," E. J. Montini writes about a Native American servicewoman, Army Pfc. Lori Piestewa, killed in the Iraqi war; Montini observes that in all the public writing and talking about her death no one called her "squaw." He argues that if it is inappropriate to use the term in the most careful and respectful circumstances, then it must also be inappropriate to use the term in less formal circumstances, such as when we name streets or mountains.

best case to worst case (or worst case to best case)

These arrangements work along a continuum: you start at one end of a situation and show how what you propose moves the situation to or toward the other. You can use these arrangements to argue that things are good now but will get bad if x happens or that things are bad now but will get better if x happens. This arrangement is used in many political arguments: it can be used, for example, to argue why we should adapt (or not) a proposed policy or law.

When you move from best case to worst case, you can instill a sense of decline that may leave your audience feeling nostalgic . . . remember the good old days? You also might create in your audience a motivation to stop the decline, as when you say, "The neighborhood is going down hill," or "The world is going to hell in a handbasket."

Imagine that we get our community organization up and running, and it inspires other more skeptical people in the community to join or support us; or imagine that we get our community organization up and running and nothing happens, and after a while we lose the energy behind the idea; or imagine that we get our community organization up and running, and it scares those who are against us and causes them to take action against us. What then?

A variation on best to worst is good to better: "If you think this is good, it only gets better."

before and after

You might remember this question from a past presidential campaign, "Are you better off now than you were four years ago?" The question is a short "before and after" argument: it asks us to look at previous circumstances, compare them to where we are now—after some set of events, such as the presidential tenure we had just experienced—and to then judge whether our circumstances have improved or worsened. If circumstances are better, this is an argument for keeping things as they are; if not, this is an argument for change.

When Dan Kindlon and Michael Thompson write the introduction to their book *Raising Cain: Protecting the Emotional Lives of Boys*, they include this short argument:

> . . . unless we give him a viable alternative, today's angry young man is destined to become tomorrow's lonely and embittered middle-aged man.

They are looking from the present into the future, showing us the "before" of angry young men and the "after" of the miserably middle-aged. If we accept this relationship, then we will agree with these two writers that we need to do something now about the emotional education of boys.

At least two pieces of writing in this book use the arrangement of "before and after": the opinion piece "Walking the Line" and the essay "A Partly Cloudy Patriot." Once you read them, you will see why the two authors, Turner and Vowell, would choose a "before and after" structure. Their subject is the events of September 11, 2001, and it is now hard to approach all the many complex issues involved in the subject without using "before and after" as a strategy for helping us compare how things are now with how they were before. As both authors point out, we heard over and over again on television and radio talk shows that "things will never be the same"—but these two writers ask us to compare now with then, and they make their particular arguments based on how they encourage us to understand the comparison.

We described above how the essay "Higher Education" in chapter 14 uses a "small to big" structure. Entwined with that structure—showing how you can lay some kinds of arrangements over others—is also the structure of "before and after." "Higher Education" describes the town before the Coach came, and then afterward; it needs to have this arrangement in order to help us feel the aftereffects of this encounter between a town and one man.

For now, here's a final small example. One of our favorite singers, Patsy Cline, sang the song "She's Got You," which contains the lyric, "I've got your picture, she's got you." There is an implied "before" in these words, a time when the singer had a sweetie, but now, after some changes, sweetie is with someone else, and the singer ruefully suggests in this lyric that "before" (when she had more than just a photograph to hold) was much better than the present handful of Kodak.

near to far

We arrange an argument "near to far," like small to big (or big to small), when we want to put a person or event in a particular context. We start close up and move away (as filmmakers use tracking shots) to get the bigger picture. We use this arrangement in order to put what is close into a larger context, showing how it carries much more weight than we might otherwise have thought; we can also use it when we want to make what is near feel even nearer, more delicate, valuable, and in need of our care and attentions.

An example of the first kind is in an article by Stephen Katz titled "The Ethics of Expediency: Classical Rhetoric, Technology, and the Holocaust." In this article, Katz puts a simple memo in front of us—an example of technical or business communication—examines it as a piece of writing, and concludes that it is well written, clear, and efficient. Then he moves the memo further away from us in time and moral purpose by talking about how the memo was written by a Nazi bureaucrat and provided instructions for how to turn trucks into mobile gas chambers and what that fact tells us about the relation of technical writing to ethics.

An example of the second kind is the movie *The Wizard of Oz*, which starts at home in Kansas and takes Dorothy (and us) far, far away—so that, after our experiences there, we're happy to be back at home amid the chickens, scarecrows, and the little dog, too.

I WANT YOU
FOR U.S.ARMY
NEAREST RECRUITING STATION

far to near
This arrangement helps tame what seems foreign or dangerous or weird. Look at the "I want you!" poster, and all its variations (which you can see in chapter 10). One strategy at work in all of these is "personification": putting an abstract idea—patriotism or our country, for example—into the guise of a person. This makes the abstract idea more concrete to us, and so less scary or amorphous or hard to attach ourselves to. But notice how, also, once the idea is personified, the person in these posters gestures to us, as though to pull us in even closer. In all these posters, going to war—a terrifying and horrible action even when justified—is changed from something we'd like to keep at a distance into something (the designers hope) closer, more friendly, and acceptable.

Similarly, some of the examples in chapter 15—where we show different comics—bring what is strange nearer to us. In "The Veil," for example, Marjane Satrapi shows us how it was for her to live in Iran during its revolutionary period: by using the medium of comics, and engaging readers with her relaxed drawings of a small girl and her family, she brings closer to her readers what it was like to grow up in a place and a time few others in the world know.

ARRANGEMENTS THAT DON'T (SEEM) TO MOVE

Some arrangements seem to be about staying in one place, such as lists or arguments not to change conditions, or visual compositions that stay on one page or screen. But such arrangements can really be about moving audiences—maybe from an imagined future they don't want back to a fine present—when they are shaped for context and audience.

lists

Chances that an American adult can't identify the source of the phrase "life, liberty, and the pursuit of happiness": 7 in 10

Amount spent [in 1998] by Mount Vernon's directors to give George Washington's reputation "more sizzle": $3,000,000

Percentage of Americans who describe "barbecue" as the aroma that best describes America: 39

(*Harper's Magazine*, July 1999, p. 17)

We may think lists exist only to help us buy food, but sometimes we make lists to compare two objects or possibilities (which you might have done in deciding which college to attend or which stereo system to buy), and sometimes lists can be argumentative, as with the above example.

If you wanted to argue that Americans are shallow and don't know much about their own history, you could simply make that statement and then give examples. In this list, however, there is no statement of the argument's conclusion: instead, you are given the examples and left (or encouraged) to draw your own conclusion. The examples start with something we all know to be serious—words from the *Declaration of Independence*, words that name the fundamental values upon which the framers of the *Declaration* based all their other arguments; the example points out that almost three-quarters of Americans don't know the words' origins. The second example seems to show that our values have shifted, if someone is willing to spend $3 million to upgrade George Washington's reputation—and if George Washington's reputation needs upgrading in the first place (and why do you think the list writers used "sizzle" [placed in quotation marks to show that it is a word used by the people spending this money] instead of "upgrade" or "improve"?). The third example is similarly banal: the people questioned didn't name "the smell of hay being harvested in the Great Plains" or "the quiet scent of the voting booth" as aromas describing America. Naming such an aroma is an odd thing to do, certainly, and we do not know if the people who chose "barbecue" had other choices, but we do know that "barbecue" is a word with connotations less glorious than "life, liberty, and the pursuit of happiness."

This list is an argument because it is intended to move you. It is to take you from a place of not thinking about our values to thinking more about what we value now, the words we use to name our values, and how we spend our money. Notice how important the order of the list items is in making such an argument: how would this argument be changed if the list items were arranged in the opposite order?

In the middle of the *Declaration of Independence* (which you can read in chapter 5) is a long list of grievances against the then King of England. The list is long—so long that it can overwhelm with the "proof" it offers: if a reader accepts one of the listed items as reason for the 13 states to declare independence, then the continual addition of more items keeps adding to the necessity of the declaration, and so increases the likelihood the reader will accept the overall argument of the *Declaration*.

In addition, the list moves from most egregious to least egregious offense by the king, and it also moves from the offense closest to home to the offense farthest way from home (or with effects felt farthest away). These various arrangements all help move a reader from what is close or known or easiest to accept to what is less familiar but equally, if not more, important in supporting the overall argument.

Lists can thus be an important argumentative strategy of arrangement—but they do have to be arranged in some order.

comparison

Kate Winslet was the female lead, the figurehead and a very fetching cabin companion, in what is history's most successful film, *Titanic*. But, of course, Mark Hamill was the lead in the *Star Wars* trilogy.

Film critic David Thomson published those words in 2002, before the *Lord of the Rings* trilogy replaced *Titanic* in the realms of success—but that doesn't undo the effect of how he compares Kate Winslet with Mark Hamill. Thomson doesn't explicitly state the terms of his comparison, but he is arguing that even though Kate Winslet might seem to have an amazing career ahead of her, we only need look to the example of Mark Hamill, who once seemed similarly poised (following a blockbuster film) for a life of large film success.

Comparison asks us to see similarity between two (or more) people, situations, or events, so that we can judge the one by the conditions of the other.

juxtaposition

When I was a soldier, I was often struck, as by a paradox, that at the very moment artillery was pounding somewhere, somewhere else men and women in soft clothing were touching glasses and carrying on flirtations; and that after and before this moment, but in this place, the peaceful pursuit of human purposes would go innocently forward, that families would picnic where men were killed.

Those words are part of an argument Arthur C. Danto makes, that there has not yet been sufficient investigation into tensions in the Civil War—between the romantic view many had of war and soldiering and the vulnerability of soldiers to the deadly weapons of the time—with the result that our memory of the war is inappropriate. The juxtaposition above,

between fighting and the daily lives lived elsewhere or before or after, embodies both the forgetfulness and the tension Danto describes.

Juxtapositions are like comparisons in that they ask us to compare two situations—but juxtapositions hold two very different situations or conditions before our attentions so that we can feel the jangly and often disturbing differences.

arguments for not changing current conditions

Suppose your partner wants to move to another town—and you don't. As you and your partner go back and forth, trying to persuade each other, your argument will be for staying put—and so it may seem that your argument is one that goes nowhere. But it's only the conclusion of the argument (one you hope your partner accepts) that stays put; the argument itself has to move. One arrangement for such an argument is to start by describing all the good things about your lives now, with the jobs, opportunities, and friends you now have, and to contrast that with the possible future you imagine in the other place. That is, you could paint a picture of an alternate future, one dependent on moving, and describe why that future will probably be worse than staying put. You'd obviously have to address your partner's particular concerns about staying, but moving into a possible alternate future—and not liking it—is a way of moving back to where you are now.

compose ▪ design ▪ advocate

But I liked math and science

single page or screen visual arguments
We discuss visual argument in chapter 9, but we'll note here that some visual arguments don't appear to move because they are on a single screen or page. In the example above, from earlier in this book, you probably see the drawings first, since they are big and at the top, and then the words; you probably also understand that the words are spoken by the girl in the middle, since she is big and central. You probably notice, with a little looking, that there are males on one side and females on the other, and that the men are shown being active, doing work outside the house, while the women are shown doing what is often considered traditional women's work. Your understanding of this poster depends completely on its arrangement; the arrangement implies other possible arrangements, and so it takes you from the present—from this particular arrangement—to the future of possible change.

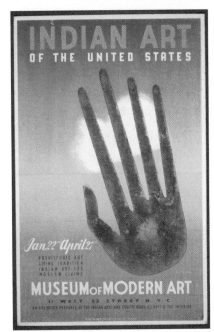

arguments that seem to repeat the same thing
Rarely do we use repetition in the same way a small child can, when he repeats, endlessly, "I want ice cream. I want ice cream. I want ice cream . . ." (The strategy here might really be that of exhausting your audience into acquiescence.) Instead, repetition in most adult arguments will be more subtle because there will be slight variations in what is repeated, so that the weight of the argument is in the slight (or sometimes not so slight) differences.

Look at the two posters above. Through what they repeat and don't repeat, what sense do they ask you to take on about the art—and artmakers—that are the subject of the publicized exhibition? What relations do they posit between art and landscape?

The lyrics below from the Dave Matthews Band song "Don't Drink the Water" use slight variations of repetition to build a tight, closed description of awfulness, a way of arguing (using cause and effect) that this is what results (according to the whole song) when we think we can run others out of our town or country:

Cause you're all dead now
I live with my justice
I live with my greedy need
I live with no mercy
I live with my frenzied feeding
I live with my hatred
I live with my jealousy
I live with the notion
That I don't need anyone but me
Don't drink the water
There's blood in the water.

The photographs above come from Josef Kudelka's exhibition *The Black Triangle: The Foothills of the Ore Mountains* (there are larger reproductions in chapter 11). All the exhibition photographs have a panoramic format, contain no people, and are in black and white. Even though Kudelka has positioned the camera so that sometimes you look at the ground and sometimes at the horizon, and so that sometimes there are obvious indications of human involvement (the train and car signs) and sometimes less obvious (the ridges in the water in the top photograph) the repetitions of format ask us to look in a certain way: What overall sense of this landscape do you develop through Kudelka's repetitions?

▲ ▲

OTHER ARRANGEMENTS

Later chapters focusing on written, oral, and visual communication suggest arrangements peculiar to those particular modes—although a creative approach to arrangement is to rework a strategy that only seems to fit writing (for example) into a visual composition and vice versa.

Look also to Section 3 of this book, where there are many examples of different communications: mine those examples for arrangements you can use.

■ **Discussing with others:** In a small group, look through a stack of recent popular magazines. Try to identify in the advertisements any of the arrangements we've described in this chapter. Sometimes the arrangements will be in words, sometimes in photographs or drawings—and sometimes in how words and photographs play off each other.

■ **Discussing with others:** With a partner, come up with a name for the arrangement strategy at work in the *Leviathan* comic on page 511. Can you name it from the list we've given you here, or do you need to come up with your own name?

■ **Discussing with others:** How would you characterize the overall arrangement strategy of this book?

■ **Writing informally:** How would you characterize the overall arrangement strategy of the last paper you wrote?

compose ▪ design ▪ advocate

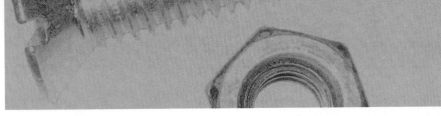

production

The preceding steps in this rhetorical process of design are primarily conceptual: they ask you to think, ponder, and imagine. With production, you get more physical. With production your body is involved—your hands, arms, eyes, ears, and perhaps noses, mouths, and legs. With production you intentionally use material objects such as paper, ink, light on glass (pixels shining onto the glass of a monitor), voices, glue, string, food, fabric, the space of a theater, radio waves, and so on.

With this step, you need to attend carefully to how you integrate physical objects into your process, because what you produce—all the details of its arrangements and media and other strategies—now becomes available to your audience. They can now really touch, see, and hear what you make. This is it.

As you produce, the materials with which you work can suggest yet new strategies to you, or you may find out that the medium or media you've chosen don't quite have the flexibility to do what you are planning. So you need to approach production openly, keeping the following considerations in mind.

■ **Gather your materials as you move through the other steps of the rhetorical design process.** Once you've got a sense of the medium or media you're going to use, start gathering the materials you'll need in order to produce. You want to do this both so that you are prepared to produce when you need to, but also so that you can work with your materials a bit ahead of time to make sure you can do what you need to. This leads to the next consideration . . .

■ **If you are trying a new medium or media, or if you are designing a relatively complex production, make mockups.** By making mockups of your project, you can learn to work with your materials fluently so that your final production is as carefully, appropriately, and effectively articulated as possible. You can also test mockups with your intended audience (see the next pages about testing), to make sure that your production—once it is physically available to audiences—achieves its purposes. When you make mockups, you do not need to produce your piece completely; instead, develop just enough so that audiences can respond.

■ **As you are producing, be open to what you discover.** As we mentioned earlier, it will often happen that—as you produce—your work with materials can suggest new strategies. When you see the color of some video you've shot, for example, you might realize that tinting it will better support your purpose. Or when printing out a draft of a paper you might see that changing the widths of some paragraphs will put more visual emphasis on them and hence on the important arguments in them.

■ **Be attentive to the details of your production.** Do not produce hurriedly or without thinking about your materials. There are potentials in your materials that you can only discover by looking or touching attentively, asking yourself how you can have all the details of your production support your purpose. Thinking about word choice in your writing (consider the differences between describing people as "underpaid" instead of "poverty stricken" in shaping how an audience perceives such people and their power in the world) is similar to deciding whether to use bright blue or sky-blue for the background color of a website or whether to produce a text that is coffee table- or hand-size. In addition, it is your attention to the details of a production—whether those details be spelling, how cleanly cut the edges of a card are, or the varied tones of voice you use—that indicate to audiences the care you give the communication and hence the seriousness with which they should approach it.

- **Plan plenty of time for production.** Because production isn't often considered a part of the "real" work of making communications, we often don't leave much time for it. We print out papers at the last minute, don't leave time to practice (test) oral presentations, or get files for brochures to the printer at the last minute. But a lot can happen when you don't leave enough time. If you print your papers in a lab (as happens on our campus), many others can be trying to print at the same time, and paper or toner sometimes runs out late at night when no one can get the keys for the supply cabinet. If you write out a speech and make some handouts but never practice, you might find yourself fumbling with your overheads in front of your audience while trying to speak sentences that work better on paper than in voice—none of which helps you establish a persuasive *ethos*. Not making enough time for production keeps you from testing your production but also keeps you from being able to take advantage of the persuasive potential in

the materials you are using, which you can't discover until you really start working with your materials (and remember that your voice is a material, too!) in producing your communication.

- **Enjoy yourself, darn it.** You are representing yourself to the world through what you make. In the process of production you're deciding how you want others to see and understand you through what you make: show your pride, your intelligence, your humor, your liveliness, your. . . . You know what it is about you that matters to you. What you make is something you get to look at, too, to see yourself, to see if you want to be the person you've produced through and in your communication.

ANALYZING
production

- **Discuss with others:** Bring to class a textbook that you think *doesn't* help you learn—or a textbook that does. Analyze how the book's production supports your judgment. For example, did the designers of the book choose thin paper so that you are distracted by what's printed on the other side, or did they use as little paper as possible so that the pages are crammed? Or are the pages designed with clear organization so you can easily see how the ideas relate? How has the book been produced to be a pleasing and engaging experience—or was production even considered in how the book helps you in your learning?

- **Discuss with others:** Compare how different music is produced. Consider how garage bands—without much equipment—often want to sound rough and edgy, while pop music is often produced to sound smooth and untied to the messiness of daily life. What other examples are there of how different kinds of music take advantage of production to create their effects? What can you use from your observations about music and production in working with other media?

compose ▪ design ▪ advocate

testing

You probably already test formal communications you make, although you may not think of what you do as testing. But if we define testing as "taking action to check the effectiveness of a piece of communication before its final production," then you have tested your writing in any English class where your classmates read drafts of your papers. In such circumstances, it might have felt to you that you, rather than your paper, were being tested. A more useful and perhaps less stress-producing way to think of this process is as testing your writing to see if others read it as you hoped they would, to see if others understood your points and were open to considering them.

You can do such testing with any piece of communication, to help you make it as effective as it can be. Keep in mind that testing is not about just being sure that people can read what you produce; instead, when you test, it demonstrates that you care enough about your audience to listen to them—and so testing shapes how you relate to them and how they relate to you. You test to see whether your most important arguments are coming through, are being heard, are connecting with others.

WHAT TO TEST

When you are developing communication, you have to decide what sorts of feedback from others—and hence what aspects of the communication to test—will help you best determine how well you are achieving your purposes. There are no hard and fast rules for this, and no single approach to testing, because different communications *are* different and because your own composing processes will have you approaching design differently from others.

As you are deciding which aspects of communication to test, and when, keep the following considerations in mind:

❑ Before you start producing a composition, before you commit to material so that you won't want to revise, you can learn a lot—and make big and helpful changes in your plans—by checking **your statement of purpose** with people whose communication abilities you respect, or with your intended audience.

❑ After you have **your design plan**—outlining your major strategies, arrangements, media, and timeline in light of your statement of purpose—ask others (especially some who are in your intended audience) to read the plan and respond. As with testing your statement of purpose, such testing helps you think concretely about your communication before you start production and major revision becomes less easy.

❑ As you are considering a particular medium to use, you can observe how people from your intended audience use **similar samples of the medium** (website for nonprofit organization? brochure for school program? board game for teaching science concepts?). Observing, you can see the typical patterns of use and thinking with which your audience approaches the medium; this will tell you what they expect from the medium, so that you can both meet and perhaps sometimes break their expectations, depending on your purposes. This will also indicate whether the medium you are considering is appropriate for your context and audience.

❑ If you are planning a fairly complex communication, then before you produce it you can test **mockups** of it. If your final communication is a complex website, you can test whether people understand its structure by linking together a series of pages in the way you are planning for the final site: put just a name and a short description of content on each page, and then observe members of your audience moving through the pages and ask them if they understand why the pages are linked in the order they are. If you are writing a long research paper, you can test an outline of it with your teacher.

❑ As you are producing your communication, you can test **parts of the communication.** You can build just the first page of a website to test if your audience responds as you hope to the design. You can ask others to read the introductory paragraph to your paper to see how they respond. You can show the photographs you are considering for a brochure to your audience to see how they respond.

❑ You can test **the whole communication.** If you have done the previous testing we've described, chances are any changes suggested by testing at this stage will be minor.

Just what you test depends on the complexity and importance of what you are designing and how much time you have. Chances are, for example, that you aren't going to have time to test a one-page response paper for a class (except to have someone else proofread; see the very next column of text for our thoughts on this). But for anything more complex, for anything on which rests a major grade or the reputation of a nonprofit or your job, be sure to make time to incorporate testing— as much as you can do—into your design process.

WHAT NOT TO TEST

well, at least what not to test until last . . .
Yes, you want to be sure any piece of communication is "mechanically" appropriate for its purpose, audience, and context. For a class paper, you want to be sure the paper has the expected-by-your-teacher level of grammar and spelling. For a website for a nonprofit, you want all the links to work. But these are, really, minor things: you can ask someone else to double-check your grammar and spelling or the links as the last test on your project, and these are qualities you can fix relatively quickly.

We aren't saying that these qualities of a text aren't important, because they are: if the mechanics of a piece of communication don't function as the audience expects, they will frustrate an audience's understanding of the heart of your arguments. But you can and should test and adjust the mechanics *only after everything else is in place.*

If, in testing, you fixate on these qualities instead of what is most central to your arguments, then you are going to miss chances to design and produce a text that is as strong as possible. Besides, when you are writing a paper or developing a website, the grammar, spelling, and links are the aspects of the communication that change most, and that change up until the end; there is no point in testing or fixing them until you are sure all the other material aspects of what you produce are stable.

WHEN TO TEST

Do not wait until you have a completed composition to test it. You will be too invested in what you have built to be willing to make large changes and you might not have time to make changes, anyway. In such circumstances you will also be less willing to listen carefully to what your audience tells you about your composition.

Instead, because we recommend that you test plans for what you are designing as well as pieces of what you are designing, we recommend that you start testing communications early—and often.

You do not want to spend all your time testing, obviously, because then you would never finish the communication you are building—but you do want to plan several different tests, at different times in your process.

At the beginning, test your statement of purpose and design and production plans. Once you have tested and revised those various plans, you can retest, or you can test mockups or parts of the communication.

As you will see in the next section on "How to Test," testing does not have to be hugely time-consuming—and the difference between testing and not testing can be the difference between a composition that engages its audience and one that falls flat.

compose ▪ design ▪ advocate

HOW TO TEST

There are many, many different kinds of tests for seeing how your compositions are working. You can observe people using texts, you can ask people to fill out feedback sheets, you can ask people to mark up your compositions. But before we discuss these, we want to make a distinction about *how* you carry out testing: **you can think of your audience as adversaries or you can think of them as participants in your design process.**

You can think of your audience as less smart than you or as people you have to change without them realizing it. Think back to the pages on strategies in this section, where we asked you what relations you want to build with your audience through your compositions: if you think of your audience in these denigrating ways, you will not take their testing feedback seriously, you will not benefit from their responses, and your final composition will encourage adversarial and disrespectful relations.

On the other hand, if you think of your audience as participants in the design process then you are more likely to think of them respectfully and carefully. Because you are making compositions that shape the relations we have with each other, you can engage your audiences in helping you test—in helping you, in effect, design—your projects so that they are as effective and respectful as possible.

By thinking of your audience as participants in the design process, you can also think of your compositions not just as things you make, not just as things that reflect who you are all by yourself. Instead, thinking of your audience as participants in the process can help you see that what you produce is always larger than just you: if your productions have effects—and have the effects you want—it will be because they engage and embody the values of your time and place. If they are effective, it is because they are able to take part in our ongoing conversations about what matters to us, and in ways that show audiences they matter and are respected.

As you decide what testing strategies to use, figure out how to keep your audience participating in the process.

TESTING STRATEGIES

The very first testing strategy is simply to do testing; the next is to decide to involve your intended audience in the process as full participants.

Here are other strategies to use for testing any production:

■ **To test a statement of purpose or a design plan,** simply sit down with people from your intended audience and let them read what you have. Ask if they have any questions. Ask if what you've planned makes sense to them. Ask specific focused questions about the parts of your plan: *Does my purpose seem sound to you? Do my main strategies seem to you appropriate for my purpose? Do you think the medium I'm planning supports my purpose?* Be sure to ask if they have any suggestions for changes or additions that would help. You can give them a feedback sheet for written responses (there are samples on pages 104 and 220), which you should probably do if there are more than three or four people helping you, but the most important thing is for you to listen carefully.

■ **To test a medium you are considering,** collect samples of the medium that communicate something like what you intend. Then ask members of your intended audience to look through the samples and to speak out loud as they look through or write, in response to the following questions: *What do you think is the overall purpose of this piece? What are the main strategies the designers of this piece have used to achieve their purpose? Do you think this piece is effective—and why, or why not? Do you think this medium is appropriate for this purpose?*

■ **To test a mock-up,** first build a mock-up that will focus your audience's attentions on what you want to test (such as the navigation of a website, the outline of a paper, or the overall look of a brochure). Then describe to your audience your overall purpose (or give them your statement of purpose or design plan), and tell them what is important for them to focus on as they look at the mock-up. (Be sure you make it clear to them that they are looking at a mock-up.) Ask them questions—for spoken or written feedback—about how well the mock-up helps you achieve your specific purpose for testing.

- **To test parts of your communication,** show your audience your design plan so they understand the context of your full piece. Then show them the parts of your communication you are testing, and ask whether they think what you are showing them supports your purpose—and how. Also ask if they have suggestions for changing what you are showing them to better support your purpose.

- **To test your whole communication,** you might ask your audience to look carefully through the communication; then ask them to tell you what they think the purpose is and the strongest strategies supporting your purpose. If they can't determine your purpose or they describe something other than what you planned, this indicates you need to make major revisions. If they identify your purpose pretty closely and identify your major strategies, ask if they have any suggestions for strengthening the communication, given your purpose.

HOW TO RESPOND TO TEST FEEDBACK

Listening to input and feedback can be hard, especially when you have put a lot of time into what you are testing. The responses you collect to testing can feel like criticism—but they shouldn't. You are asking people not to tell you whether your work is good or bad, but how it works in its context and how you can make it better.

The purpose of testing is to help you compose the most effective communications possible. If you are someone who is sensitive to feedback, keep that in mind as you go through the responses you get.

HOW TO HELP OTHERS IN THEIR TESTING

When you test the communications of others, it is of no use to the composer to say "I like this!" or "This sucks!" Instead, give a response that says "Given your purpose (which I understand to be [fill in the blank here]), I think the strengths of this piece are . . . And I think this piece would be stronger if . . ." Give specific examples, pointing to specific parts of the plan or communication. The more detail you can give, the more helpful your responses will be, whether you are speaking or writing them. (And as you think about receiving feedback from others, imagine how much easier and more helpful it will be to hear feedback in these ways.)

WHAT TESTING IS NOT

Testing is not market research. Market research—performed by advertising agencies, many movie producers, and many political campaigns—is not about designing possible futures: it is instead about asking people what they care about now, to see how one can reinforce and build on what people already know. Market research is making decisions **about** audiences.

Testing is instead about helping you design futures **with** your audiences by involving them in direct decisionmaking about your communication.

compose ▪ design ▪ advocate

KINDS OF TESTS

Here are descriptions and a sample of tests that help you get various feedback. Modify these tests as you need for your own projects—and remember that you need to use tests with at least several different people if you are to get feedback that isn't idiosyncratically connected to just one person. But do test your plans and productions with people from your audience.

Observational tests

When you watch others use a piece of communication to see if they *can* use it, you are conducting an observational test. For example, if you've written instructions for your parents to help them record on their VCR, you would watch to make sure they could use the instructions and successfully record *The Daily Show* (for example). In this case, when you watch them, you wouldn't want to speak: you'd just watch, to see if they could get by on their own. By watching, you might see where they run into trouble (*if* they do)—but you might also need to talk with them afterward to find out if they had any trouble with particular aspects of the instructions.

When you observe people using more complex texts, or in more formal situations, you'll want to take notes as you observe, recording the actions people take. You will probably also want to talk with them afterward. In such cases it's a good idea to have prepared questions to ask, such as "Where did you get lost?" or "What parts of the

communication were most helpful to you?" You might also want to give them a questionnaire, because some people will write more than they will speak, and because writing encourages a different kind of reflection and so different responses.

Watch for where your audience repeatedly had troubles, as well as for where they felt they moved easily. Knowing what works well for them can indicate strategies you can apply to the not-yet-working parts.

Think-aloud tests

With think-alouds, you ask someone to describe what they are thinking *as* they work through a website, for example, or a piece of print. Think-alouds are observational tests with a twist: tell those you're observing that they should speak aloud *anything* they think as they move through the communication. Because this is a bit odd for people, help by suggesting comments that will help you understand their responses to the text, comments like "Hmm, I really don't understand this phrase" or "I'm looking for an index but there doesn't seem to be one in this book" or "This green looks like bad soup." But, as you suggest such comments, remind them that they should comment about anything in the text that stands out to them. If you are having people do a think-aloud with a piece of your writing, you can ask them to stop after each of your sentences, to tell you what they understand and what they think will come next. This will help you hear

if others are understanding the fine details of your writing, such as the construction of your sentences; this will also help you hear if others are catching the larger concerns of your writing, such as how you move from paragraph to paragraph or how you construct your overall argument.

You can use sound-recording equipment to hold on to their comments, or you can take written notes.

As with observational testing, look for patterns in the feedback: Where did your audience repeatedly have troubles and where were they at ease?

Read-aloud tests

Read-aloud tests are a way to test writing, and are most useful for finding small-scale, sentence-level bumps. You can do these tests yourself or have others help you. If you do them yourself, read aloud a piece of writing on which you're working. Often in the reading you'll stumble over awkward words—or change words and phrases to smooth them out. If you do this, you almost need to split your brain: one part has to read what it thinks it sees, the other has to look at what's really on the page.

If someone else reads your paper, follow along with your own printed copy. Underline or highlight any places where the other person stumbles or changes your words. Sometimes a reader will correct your grammar without noticing it as they read: you need to be reading and listening to catch this.

HERE IS A FORM DEVELOPED BY PEOPLE IN A CLASS to test the effectiveness and overall quality of books they were designing and producing to teach scientific concepts. At each stage of developing the book, they gave their plan or mock-up to someone else, along with this form, for feedback. The form focuses on the qualities of the book the people in class thought were most important for their purposes.

TESTING YOUR BOOK

quality	does this perfectly/ beautifully	does this better than expected	does this	does this, sort of	doesn't do this yet	N/A	comments
The book…							
is visually appealing.							
is effectively interactive for its audience and purpose (as *Experience Design* defines it, "interactivity is a process of continual action and reaction between two parties" and involves "feedback, control, creativity, adaptivity, productivity, communications…)" (142).							
is organized to support the learning that the audience is supposed to do by using the book.							
teaches what it sets out to teach.							
is usable & sturdy.							
is constructed with a quality appropriate for its audience.							
The information in the book…							
has an appropriate tone for its audience.							
is formatted appropriately for the audience.							
has an overall design tied to what the book is trying to teach.							
is written in a polished and grammatical fashion.							
has visuals (photographs, illustrations, etc.) that are of appropriate quality for the audience & context.							
Overall, the book…							
shows careful and attentive production.							
is appropriately creative.							
stimulates audience thinking (by encouraging them toward new thinking on a topic or looking at something familiar in a new way).							

Please indicate here any specific actions you think the book's maker can take in order to improve the book in the areas where the book is not perfect.

compose ▪ design ▪ advocate

ANALYZING
testing

- **Informal writing and sketching:**
  You've been asked to design a T-shirt
  for elementary students that sends the
  message that smoking is unhealthy.
  Develop three different approaches for
  testing the effectiveness of your
  designs. Don't forget to consider when
  in the design process you would do the
  testing.

- **Discuss with others:** Imagine you are
  producing a board game intended to
  help parents and their children talk
  relaxedly and learn—while playing—
  about drug use. What about this game
  will you need to test, to be sure it is
  effective?

- **Informal writing:** Develop an
  approach for testing your own writing
  that helps you focus on and learn
  about what matters most to you in
  your writing.

- **Informal writing:** Design testing
  strategies for another class you are
  taking, strategies that would help you
  see how well you were comprehending
  the material. Be creative: consider
  multiple choice tests, but also think of
  how you could demonstrate your
  learning through a portfolio of your
  work, or through teaching others, or . . .

design plans

At the end of chapter 2 we showed you a design plan for a particular communication project. To see another, look in chapter 6, for a research paper design plan, a plan that takes into consideration sense of purpose, audience, context, strategies, arrangement, media, and testing—as the one to the right does.

It may seem that we are asking you to do a lot with a design plan, but keep in mind:

- Design plans get easier as you go on. The steps become second nature, and what is most important is considering them.

- Design plans are never final. They change as you go along, and there is no way to figure out ahead of time every single detail of a production. Their purpose is to help you think richly about all the rhetorical potential available to you as you communicate with others so that what you produce will be as effective as possible. Before you start producing a project, try to have a design plan in which you've considered all the steps—but know that you will modify and adjust your plan as you produce and work through the concrete details of production.

Design plan for a poster by Justin Foley

Atheists lead a life very similar to any person who believes in God. It is not until you dive deep into their thoughts and emotions that you see the difference. This difference is painful—to me, at least—and it segregates us from our Christian counterparts. Christians can say they will see their loved ones when they die, and that their loved ones are in a better place. Atheists like me do not have this privilege, and it makes me grieve. This is what I would like to show in my poster.

Christians in the United States are my audience for this poster, and I want to increase the sympathy and understanding they have for atheists. I want them to understand that being an atheist isn't a choice but is just something that happens: I didn't try to become an atheist, but I just can't make myself believe in God—even though I'd like to have the confidence toward what happens after death as my Christian friends do.

Even though I have sometimes gotten angry at how some Christians I know yell at me or continually try to tell me what to do—even though I tell them nothing has worked—I don't think it will be useful if my poster is angry. I do want my poster to center on emotion, though: I would like for my audience to feel compassion for atheists like me.

Because this is about emotion, I think it makes sense for me to make my poster black and white. I want the poster to be about ideas, too, so black and white is probably better for that. I want to keep it stark and strong, so that the strength of the emotion comes through.

I'm going to need some words—just a few—to make it clear to my audience what I'd like to happen. I think if I use words that address them directly, it will help pull them in because it will be more like I am talking directly with them.

I have an idea for someone looking up at a church, sadly, to show the longing I feel—I hope that such a picture together with my words will evoke the emotions that will ask my audience to be understanding toward people like me.

compose ▪ design ▪ advocate

ANALYZING
design plans

- **Informal writing:** Find two or three websites *you* consider to be cool or intriguing. To help you learn about producing your own coolness or intrigue, put together (in retrospect) the design plan for each site. Describe your initial sense of the purpose, audience, and context of each site, and use that to develop a statement of purpose. Then describe carefully the medium, strategies, and arrangement of the site, and combine those descriptions with the statement of purpose to develop the design plan. What do the plans you've developed have in common? How do they differ? Where in the design plans do you find what makes the sites cool or intriguing?

- **Informal writing:** Choose two or three examples of other kinds of communication that matter to you and that you think are examples worth emulating. Analyze these examples as you did the websites, above, to write down their design plans. Such analysis helps you see the details that go into communication that moves or engages you—so that you can then attend to a similar level of detail in what you produce.

- **Discuss with others:** Here is the poster Justin Foley produced after writing the design plan on the opposite page. Discuss how the poster asks you to think about the person shown, in relation to the church steeple. Also discuss how the words address the audience: try imagining different words about the same issue to see how different words put the audience in differing positions relative to the person in the poster and the argument of the poster.

  Notice that Justin does not describe using "ATHEISM" in his design plan. Do you think how Justin places the word in his poster supports or undermines the purposes he describes in his plan?

I did not choose not to believe in God. In fact I wish I could.

ATHEISM

If you would like to help an atheist, listen and be kind.

**if you are thinking about using
unconventional strategies or media . . .**

When you use strategies that your audience doesn't expect in your context, you very well might need to address directly that you are doing this—audiences can otherwise be confused or hostile or dismissive. Unexpected media and other strategies can disorient audiences. As a result, they might think you don't care about them, or that you just don't know what you are doing. But if you let them know, in one way or another (if this fits your overall purpose), that you know what you're doing and why, then they might be more receptive. In other words, you need to ask them to be generous toward your text.

There's a complementary converse to this situation: if you want audiences to approach your texts generously (even if your texts aren't unconventional), then it is probably a good idea for you to be generous in your approach to texts made by others. If we want there to be a wider range of texts and strategies available to us, so that we can have a wider range of arguments to use and express ourselves within, then we need to cultivate a more generous approach to texts that do not fit our immediate expectations of what texts ought to be.

ABOUT SECTION 2 . . .

Because we hope that during your life you will make communications for a broad range of audiences in a broad range of contexts, there is no one, linear, fill-in-the-blanks approach we can give you for producing texts. We couldn't do that even if this book were only about academic writing or comic strip production. You can, with careful observation, make lists of the features of certain kinds of texts (like academic essays or horror films)—but producing texts is never a matter of then just building something that has all the apparent features of other texts of its kind.

Frankenstein's monster apparently had all the features of a human being—a head, arms, legs, the ability to speak—but they still didn't fit together to make a happy human. The book *Frankenstein* can be read as an argument about what happens when you make something out of context: Doctor Frankenstein attempts to build a human who is not born in the usual way and who does not grow up in the usual way with a family or other experienced adults to care for and guide him into the complexities of living with and caring for others. And effective communication is like that: only when you develop it with careful thinking about its audience, context, and purpose can you make something that doesn't just look like an academic research essay (for example) but that also functions successfully as an academic research essay.

In this section, then, we offer you, first, some further thinking about two particular contexts for communication and then, second, some further thinking about three major modes of communication: the written, oral, and visual. We offer this section to you to help you when you are in the midst of production, when in specific contexts you need to make choices about the strategies that will help you build the relations you want with your audiences.

compose ▪ design ▪ advocate

about
advocacy and argument

Sometimes we think of advocacy as something that just wells up inside, regardless of where and when we are. Passion certainly strengthens advocacy, but effective advocacy is also about finding out what is worth caring about in the situations around us—and about figuring out how to design changes that will help us achieve the future we believe ought to be. This chapter then is about contexts of advocacy: there are readings about others who think strategically—or not—about advocacy, and there are many questions about what constitutes advocacy, for whom and when. We hope to support you in thinking more about your potentials to advocate through argument, to help you strengthen what you already do.

In the *Declaration of Independence*, Thomas Jefferson included the "pursuit of happiness" as one of our unalienable rights. "Pursuit" implies that happiness is something we have to seek actively. But is the pursuit something we do as individuals, as citizens, or as some combination of both? What are our responsibilities in and to this country that grounds itself on a belief in our ability to pursue (if not reach) happiness?

Our first questions to you in this chapter, then, are these: *How is your happiness bound up with the happiness of others— friends, family, and fellow citizens? How is it bound up with the health of your communities? What is the happiness that you pursue—and does advocacy have any part therein?*

becoming an advocate

In the introduction we spoke of advocacy: "*When we consider oral, written, and visual communication in this book, we always treat composing and designing as actions that DO something in and to the world.*" Every time you communicate with others you shape your relations with them. If you speak, your tone of voice indicates the respect or friendship you have (or don't have) for them, and so strengthens how you feel toward each other. You've probably realized someone likes you (or not) through the person's way of speaking to you and word choice.

Communications also show what communicators value. When you ask a friend to go to a basketball game or to help out with a Saturday car wash raising money for "Big Brothers, Big Sisters," you tell what you value in the world without explicitly stating your beliefs and concerns. You start a ripple effect around you because your actions ask others to accept that what you do is worth doing. Similarly, communications aimed at multiple people tell us what the communicators value and how they think the world should be. This is often easiest to see in communications *not* aimed at us, because in communications aimed at us the values just seem so normal and accepted that they can be invisible. But look at TV shows, newspapers, and radio programs: when

people speak about or show you certain topics, they are choosing and so emphasizing those topics over all others. Chances are your local newspaper has some kind of regular section about the stock market but not about blue- or pink-collar work. Look at magazines on a supermarket checkout line: what values are repeated in what is shown on the covers? What isn't shown? The values underlying how all these communications are designed and what they choose to emphasize all shape your sense of what is important, of what is worth doing—or not.

To talk about argument, and so to talk about advocacy, is to talk about how we can and should live our lives. It is to talk about what we should do as communities and as individuals. *What position do you want to have in the world? What do you want the world to be?* To answer these questions is to become an advocate for what matters to you. It is to start shaping the world in ways you—having grown up in your local and national communities— believe will better your communities.

ANALYZING
being an advocate

■ **Write informally:** Make a list of
- qualities you have that make you proud and could be useful in the communities around you.
- everything you are able to do that might be useful to others.
- ways you've already participated in your communities.
- situations in local communities or at your school that need changing for the better.

■ **Interview** an older friend or relative. Ask them about their understanding of advocacy. Ask them also about when and how they've participated in public or civic life and why they've chosen the actions they have.

■ **Discuss with others:** Throughout this book we've been arguing that all arguments—because they advocate particular positions on issues or ways of seeing the world, because they do something in the world—are advocacy. Is it possible to make the converse claim, that all advocacy is argument?

compose ▪ design ▪ advocate

who changes and who benefits when you advocate?

We often think of advocacy as a one-way street. You do something, and it affects others, and that's that.

The actions of advocacy, however, move in multiple directions, often coming back to us or moving off in other directions.

Precisely because the arguments involved in advocacy shape the attitudes of others and show what we value—and because we are talking about a process involving people—our arguments often have much more than a single effect. When we advocate, we enter the complex web of human conversation and work, which means we open ourselves to the actions and thinking of others. It is therefore not always or even often possible to know who changes and who benefits when you advocate. What is certain is that you are wrong if you think only you are giving and others are benefitting.

Situation 1 to the right is probably how a lot of people look at taking action. Situation 2 is a more accurate description of what can happen.

For these reasons, humility, openness to surprise, and generosity are often the best attitudes to have in approaching the arguments that make advocacy possible.

1 makes a workbook to help children develop their literacy skills through learning about recycling

2 makes a workbook to help children develop their literacy skills through learning about recycling

by helping with the workbook, children's confidence and pleasure in their literacy abilities increases

children develop a school recycling program

by watching children use his book and listening to their feedback, learns that they already have literacies, tied to community contexts—and revises the book to build off what the children already know

children think he's cool and want to be like him, making a big end-of-the-year goodbye card

his enthusiasm for the project pulls others into working at the school

working at an inner-city school, becomes overwhelmed by seeing how many children grow up without health care, or parents whose work schedules allow them to be there when children come home...

he thinks the children are cool and decides to be a teacher

the time that advocacy requires

Some advocacy is short-lived: you write a letter to the editor, a few friends make positive comments after they read it, and then someone you don't know writes a semi-critical response. You don't know how many people will read your letter and mull over your ideas and take some specific action as a result. But after you've written the letter you can forget about it with few if any consequences.

Some advocacy requires a longer, engaged commitment. Sometimes, as with the example on the previous page about the recycling workbook, a project—to be truly effective—will require you to put in focused and extended time. We know people who have been involved in such projects, and we have been involved with some ourselves. Only by developing an ongoing and sustained relationship with your audience—and including them in the design process—can you ever produce communication that works respectfully and appropriately.

Anne once designed math lessons for an educational program in South Central Los Angeles. Only over a period of months, by spending time with people in the program, did she learn where best to start, with math lessons that drew on people's experiences. She helped them write lessons for each other. The experience taught her how important confidence is to learning, and how learning is most effective when it grows out of what people already know. By being involved in designing the lessons, the people in the program were more committed to the results, and learned more than just math—although they did learn that, too. By being involved for an extended period of time, Anne learned how to be a better communicator—she also learned how different can be the lives of people who live only a few miles apart.

Perhaps this is something you'll need to learn on your own, but if you ever decide to take on a communication project with an audience you do not know or know well, plan in extra time. Plan time for activities that will help you get to know each other, such as social activities and activities of working together. These might not have much to do with your direct purpose but they will have a lot to do with the ultimate success of what you produce—and of the relations you strengthen and improve in the world.

▢ In the online chapter 5 resources (at www.ablongman.com/wysocki) there are links to websites that connect people with nonprofit organizations of all kinds.

compose ▪ *design* ▪ *advocate*

styles of advocacy

If you look through the examples in Section 3 with an eye on argument and advocacy, you may be surprised at how much argument and advocacy you find there—and not because we stacked the deck but because argument and advocacy permeate our communications with others, even where we least expect it (as in the selections in the comics chapter). What you will also find in those examples is a wide range of styles of advocacy. By "styles of advocacy" we mean the particular relation one has to the subjects of one's advocacy, how much effort one puts in and of what kind, and what kinds of relationships one develops with others in the course of one's advocacy.

Here and on the pages that follow are pages from a website and an article from a magazine. The website pages describe people who, for at least a time, make advocacy their life. The article focuses on a woman who has taken on a particular life of advocacy; the article also discusses the people with whom she works.

As you read the webpages and article, compare how these different people have decided to do what they do.

THE "AVODAH" WEBSITE

"AVODAH" means "service" in Hebrew, and the screenshots of the webpages that follow are from the website of an organization that supports young Jewish people in living a year of service in inner cities.

As you read the parts of the website we have included here, consider how religious affiliations, practices, and beliefs can shape advocacy. What relations toward others do religious affiliations, practices, and beliefs often encourage, and how do those relations shape advocacy?

"AFTER SEATTLE: ANARCHISTS GET ORGANIZED"

In this article that was originally published in the *New Yorker* magazine, writer William Finnegan profiles activist Juliette Beck.

How different is Beck's advocacy from that of the AVODAH alumni? What differences do you see in the relations between Beck and the people with whom she does her advocacy work and between the AVODAH alumni and their colleagues? Between Beck and the people she believes she is helping and between the AVODAH alumni and the people they believe they are helping? How do you think the differing organizational structures in which they work shape their advocacy?

How do these different relations and organizational structures shape the kind of advocacy and the actions and activities the different people profiled on the next pages take on?

This is the opening screen to the AVODAH website.

What adjectives would you apply to this webpage, in terms of the overall feeling it seems to be trying to create? What in the design of the webpage—in terms of both writing and visual elements—suggests those adjectives to you? Why do you think the designers of this site would make such choices in arrangement and other strategies?

compose ▪ design ▪ advocate

HISTORY & MISSION | ABOUT US | JOIN AVODAH | ALUMNI COMMUNITY | SUPPORT AVODAH | TEACHINGS & LINKS

AVODAH's commitment to social justice, community-building and Jewish life.

register to vote
your vote matters

ABOUT THE PROGRAM · HISTORY · MISSION

DONATE NOW THROUGH **Network** for **Good**

Exciting News
AVODAH named one of the most creative and effective Jewish organizations.

History and Mission

AVODAH: The Jewish Service Corps integrates work for social change, Jewish learning and community building. It provides an opportunity for young Jews to live out and deepen their commitments to Jewish life and social change through a year of work in low-income communities in New York City and Washington, D.C. After participants complete this intense one-year program, the AVODAH Alumni Community supports and encourages alumni in their continued work for social change.

AVODAH changes the lives of people in poverty by joining with them to improve their neighborhoods and their access to opportunity. Engagement in this sort of work changes our participants' lives as well. AVODAH offers a Jewish framework for that transformation, welcoming Jews of every background into a pluralistic, multi-denominational program.

ABOUT THE PROGRAM

Each year, AVODAH recruits Jews in their 20s from across North America to spend a year **working on urban poverty issues** as full-time employees in local non-profit organizations. During their year of service, participants live and **study together**, forming a **community** of people making a connection between social activism and Jewish life.

At the program's current size-with **33 participants** in two cities-our corps members help bring housing, education and other basic services to some 10,000 people each year, and save the organizations for which they work a total of more than half a million dollars in staffing costs.

HISTORY

AVODAH was founded by its Executive Director, David Rosenn, and a group of activists and educators from across the spectrum of the American Jewish community. Some were religious; others not. Some worked in the nonprofit world; others were educators or rabbis or graduate students. They were united by the sense that there was a disconnect between their involvement in Jewish life and their commitment to working for social change. Dedicated to the notion of "AVODAH" - a Hebrew word which encompasses spiritual, communal and work-related "service" -- they joined forces to create the first and only Jewish service corps.

AVODAH was developed as an opportunity for people to integrate Judaism and social activism in ways that nourish their ideals and provide them with the capacity for stronger, enduring activism.

From the beginning, its founders and board have envisioned AVODAH's expansion into a national program. Launched in New York in 1998 with one house of nine participants, the program doubled within a few years. In 2002, AVODAH began a new program in Washington, D.C. which quickly grew from nine participants to fifteen. The Washington program is just the first in what we hope will be a number of regional sites, part of a growing national Jewish service corps with programs in multiple cities.

AVODAH has also recently expanded to include-in response to alumni requests-a formal Alumni Community, through which former participants can continue making connections between their social activism and their Jewish lives, and with one another. To read more about our Alumni Community, **click here.**

This page from the AVODAH website describes the program. What values might a person hold to be engaged by these descriptions? What hopes and desires might a person hold to be engaged by these descriptions?

This webpage (spread over these two pages of our book) describes people who have taken part in the AVODAH program, and includes their own words about their year in AVODAH.

Do the people who took part in a year of service with AVODAH share any qualities? Does their service appear to change them?

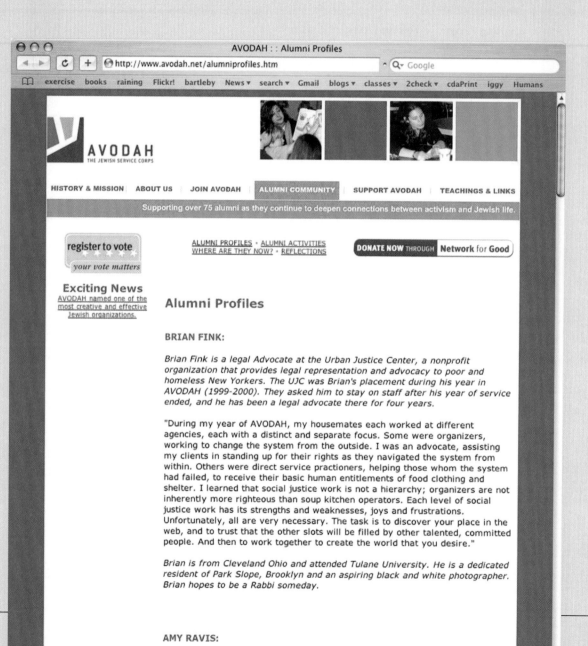

AVODAH : : Alumni Profiles

http://www.avodah.net/alumniprofiles.htm

Q▾ Google

exercise   books   raining   Flickr!   bartleby   News ▾   search ▾   Gmail   blogs ▾   classes ▾   2check ▾   cdaPrint   iggy   Humans

AVODAH
THE JEWISH SERVICE CORPS

HISTORY & MISSION | ABOUT US | JOIN AVODAH | ALUMNI COMMUNITY | SUPPORT AVODAH | TEACHINGS & LINKS

Supporting over 75 alumni as they continue to deepen connections between activism and Jewish life.

register to vote
★ ★ ★ ★ ★
your vote matters

ALUMNI PROFILES · ALUMNI ACTIVITIES
WHERE ARE THEY NOW? · REFLECTIONS

DONATE NOW THROUGH   Network for Good

Exciting News
AVODAH named one of the
most creative and effective
Jewish organizations.

Alumni Profiles

BRIAN FINK:

Brian Fink is a legal Advocate at the Urban Justice Center, a nonprofit organization that provides legal representation and advocacy to poor and homeless New Yorkers. The UJC was Brian's placement during his year in AVODAH (1999-2000). They asked him to stay on staff after his year of service ended, and he has been a legal advocate there for four years.

"During my year of AVODAH, my housemates each worked at different agencies, each with a distinct and separate focus. Some were organizers, working to change the system from the outside. I was an advocate, assisting my clients in standing up for their rights as they navigated the system from within. Others were direct service practicioners, helping those whom the system had failed, to receive their basic human entitlements of food clothing and shelter. I learned that social justice work is not a hierarchy; organizers are not inherently more righteous than soup kitchen operators. Each level of social justice work has its strengths and weaknesses, joys and frustrations. Unfortunately, all are very necessary. The task is to discover your place in the web, and to trust that the other slots will be filled by other talented, committed people. And then to work together to create the world that you desire."

Brian is from Cleveland Ohio and attended Tulane University. He is a dedicated resident of Park Slope, Brooklyn and an aspiring black and white photographer. Brian hopes to be a Rabbi someday.

AMY RAVIS:

Amy Ravis, a community organizer and social worker, currently works at Columbia/Barnard Hillel as the Director of the Tzedek/social justice Program. Amy worked at Genesis - a Domestic Violence Shelter through Jewish Board of

AMY RAVIS:

Amy Ravis, a community organizer and social worker, currently works at Columbia/Barnard Hillel as the Director of the Tzedek/social justice Program. Amy worked at Genesis - a Domestic Violence Shelter through Jewish Board of Family & Children's Services while in AVODAH (1999- 2000). Throughout the year, she worked as the Housing Specialist and case manager, providing advocacy and support to survivors of domestic violence.

"When I first heard about AVODAH - a program that explores both Judaism and justice, but more importantly the connections that exist between the two - from the Director of my Hillel at the University of Kansas, I knew immediately that AVODAH was just what I had been searching for. AVODAH has given me the tools necessary to build a foundation on which my life's passion has grown. AVODAH taught me the importance of making lasting, real and systemic change. AVODAH has provided me with an ever-growing community, support and resources. AVODAH has served as a constant source of inspiration and connection to others who are passionate about making serious change informed and connected to their Jewish identity."

A native of Kansas City, Amy moved to New York four years ago to be a part of AVODAH: The Jewish Service Corps. Amy recently completed a Masters degree at the Hunter College School of Social Work.

MARK GOODMAN:

Mark worked at Talbot Perkins Children's Services, a foster care agency, during his year in Avodah (1999-2000), where he managed their mentoring program for youth in foster care.

"I always knew that Judaism commanded us to a mission of radically transforming our world into a more just and righteous place. But the nuts and bolts of how and why were inaccessible, and there was no community of people for me to learn from and contribute to. AVODAH is all these things."

Mark Goodman is a student in the Conservative movement's Ziegler School of Rabbinic Studies, at the University of Judaism in Los Angeles, CA. He is currently spending his 3rd year (of a 5 year program) in Jerusalem at the Schechter Institute for Jewish Studies and working with survivors of terrorism.

ABBY MAIER:

Abby Maier, AVODAH 2002-2003, worked as a Youth Advocate at her placement, N Street Village, a center for homeless women and low income families in Washington, DC. She was responsible for coordinating children's activities for the families living at N Street, connecting them with services in the city, and teaching in the addiction recovery program.

"AVODAH facilitated the collaboration of faith, working for justice, trying to understand poverty, looking for community... all of these things I had been trying to figure out on my own. My year with AVODAH put it all in one place. It was an incredible year of work and reflection that also put me in the middle of the unique Jewish community I had been searching for."

Abby is from Cleveland, Ohio and graduated from the College of Wooster in 2001. She has decided to stay in Washington D.C. where she is working with residents of an Alzheimer's home.

TOP OF PAGE

NATIONAL OFFICE • 443 PARK AVE. SOUTH • 11TH FLOOR • NY, NY 10016 • (212) 545-7759 • INFO@AVODAH.NET

AFTER SEATTLE:
Anarchists get organized.
by William Finnegan

For Juliette Beck, it began with the story of the Ittu Oromo, Ethiopian nomads whose lives were destroyed, in vast numbers, by a dam—a hydroelectric project sponsored by the World Bank. Beck was a sophomore at Berkeley, taking a class in international rural development. The daughter of an orthopedic surgeon, she had gone to college planning to do premed, but environmental science caught her interest, and the story of the Ittu Oromo precipitated a change of major. Beck was a brilliant student—"One of these new Renaissance people, so smart they could be almost anything," a former professor of hers recalls. She was intellectually insatiable, and her eagerness to understand the dynamics of economic development propelled her into several academic fields, notably the dry, dizzying politics of international finance and trade. By her junior year, she was teaching a class on the North American Free Trade Agreement. "It was one of the most popular student-led classes we've had," her professor says. "I understand it's been cloned on other campuses."

Beck had found her strange grand passion—international trade rules—at an auspicious time. Besides the popularity of her class, there were the events last November in Seattle, where fifty thousand demonstrators shut down a major meeting of the World Trade Organization. Beck, who is twenty-seven, was a key organizer of the Seattle protests.

"The Spirit of Seattle," she says, crinkling her eyes and grinning blissfully. "Your body just tingled with hope, to be around so many people so committed to making a better world." Beck says things like "tingled with hope" and "making a better world" with no hint of selfconsciousness, and in the next breath will launch into a critique of the Multilateral Agreement on Investment, a set of international trade rules that she and other activists have fought against for the last several years. (The M.A.I. would limit the rights of national governments to regulate currency speculation or set policies regarding investment.) This odd fusion of hardheaded policy analysis and utopian idealism has an exhilarating edge, which may account for some of Beck's habitual high spirits.

Almost six feet tall, she retains, to a striking degree, both the coltishness of adolescence and the open-faced, all-American social style of the Girl Scout and high-school athlete (volleyball, tennis, basketball) she was. Zooming around the scruffy, loft-style offices of Global Exchange, the human-rights organization in San Francisco where she works, she seems conspicuously lacking the self-decor of the other young activists around the place—piercings, tattoos, dreadlocks. It may be that she's simply been too busy to get herself properly tatted up. While we were talking in her office on a recent evening, she tried to deal simultaneously with me and with a significant fraction of the seven hundred e-mail messages that had piled up in her inbox—reading, forwarding, filing, trashing, replying, sighing, grumbling, erupting in laughter. She was determined, she said, to have an empty inbox before she left, in a few days' time, for Washington, D.C., even if it meant pulling consecutive all-nighters.

"Where I grew up, in suburban San Diego, it was so strange," she said. "Politics didn't exist. The only political gesture I ever saw there was during the Gulf War. People drove around waving American flags from the backs of pickups. That was it. When we were teenagers, the consumerism was overwhelming. If you didn't wear Guess jeans, you didn't exist. When I got to Berkeley, I was just like a sponge. At one point, I realized that, in my entire education, having gone through good public schools, advanced-placement programs, and all that, I had never learned anything about the American labor movement.

compose ▪ design ▪ advocate

Nothing. I don't think I ever heard the term 'collective bargaining' inside a classroom. No wonder we were all so apolitical!"

After college, Beck went to work as an environmental engineer for a small Bay Area firm. The pay was good, and the work was interesting, but she found herself spending most of her time competing with other firms for contracts. "It made me realize I didn't want to be doing work that was all about money." So she made the downward financial leap into the non-profit sector (and was recently forced to move from chic, expensive San Francisco to cheaper, inconvenient Oakland, where she lives in a group house with no living room). It's a step she says she's never regretted. "I think a lot of people in my generation—not a majority, maybe, but a lot—feel this void," she told me. "We feel like capitalism and buying things are just not fulfilling. Period." She became an organizer for Public Citizen, Ralph Nader's consumer group, which was campaigning, along with labor unions and other allies, to stop the Clinton Administration's effort to get renewed "fast track" authority to negotiate trade agreements with limited congressional oversight. (The problem with such authority, according to its opponents, is its bias, in practice, in favor of industry.) The campaign was successful—the first major defeat in Congress for trade advocates in sixty years. "That was a great victory," Beck said happily. "We defeated some of the most powerful forces on the planet."

Those powerful forces, once they had recovered from the shock, responded with a public-relations offensive. William Daley, the Secretary of Commerce, embarked on a National Trade Education Tour, meant to persuade the American people of the wisdom of free trade. Daley was met by protesters at every stop. In Los Angeles, Beck helped coordinate his unofficial reception. "We just dogged him." Longshoremen refused to cooperate with the Secretary, she said, for what she called "a photo op at the docks." She went on, "They said, 'No way, come down to our headquarters and we'll have an honest discussion on trade.' He said no. These fat cats only want to talk on their terms. Even the kids at a high school in Long Beach where Daley spoke asked him tough questions. We really caused that tour to flop. Daley had a bus full of C.E.O.s and flacks from the Business Roundtable, but a lot of bigwigs flaked when they saw how hokey the whole thing was." Six corporate leaders, including the chairmen of Boeing and A.T. & T., had in fact appeared with Daley at the tour's kickoff, then made themselves scarce when it began to smell of disaster.

Beck's delight in such disasters is wicked and shameless. I recalled a news story she had circulated by e-mail a few weeks before. The story was about Michel Camdessus, the managing director of the International Monetary Fund, getting hit in the face by a fruit-and-cream pie just before he gave a farewell speech to mark his retirement. Beck's cover note exulted, "The head of I.M.F. got his just desserts this weekend—a parting pie shot!"

Beck likes to call the I.M.F., the W.T.O., and the World Bank "the iron triangle of corporate rule." In her view, these institutions—their leaders, clients, political allies, and, above all, true bosses, multinational corporations—are frog-marching humanity, along with the rest of the planet, into a toxic, money-maddened, repressive future. And she intends to persuade the rest of us not to go quietly.

In her office at Global Exchange, still crashing through the underbrush of her inbox, she suddenly pulled up short. "Oh, check this out," she said, and pointed to her computer screen. "Have you seen this?"

I had. It was a report prepared by Burson-Marsteller, the Washington publicity firm, which had been leaked and was making the electronic rounds. It was titled "Guide to the Seattle Meltdown: A Compendium of Activists at the W.T.O. Ministerial." Burson-Marsteller's cover letter began, "Dear [Corporate Client]," and characterized the report "not so much as a retrospective on the past, but as an alarming window on the future." The report offered profiles of dozens of groups that had participated in the Seattle protests—from the Anarchist Action Collective to Consumers International to the A.F.L.-C.I.O.—naming leaders, giving website addresses, and including brief descriptions, usually lifted from the literature of the groups

themselves. The cover letter mentioned possible "significant short-term ramifications for the business community" because of the "perceived success of these groups in disrupting Seattle" and, more portentously, warned of "the potential ability of the emerging coalition of these groups to seriously impact broader, longer-term corporate interests."

Burson-Marsteller was at least trying to reckon with what had been revealed in Seattle. The press, the Seattle authorities, the Clinton Administration, the W.T.O., and many other interested parties had largely been ignorant of the popular movement being built around them. Suddenly challenged, everyone had scrambled to respond, some (the police) attacking the protesters, others (Bill Clinton) rhetorically embracing them (while his negotiators continued to pursue in private the controversial policies he was renouncing in public), but all basically hoping that the problem—this nightmare of an aroused, mysteriously well-organized citizenry—would just go away. Burson-Marsteller knew better. Its "compendium" had even picked up on demonstrations being planned for April against the World Bank and the I.M.F. during meetings in Washington, D.C. This was before anything about those demonstrations had appeared in what movement activists insist on calling the corporate press.

I say "movement activists" because nobody has yet figured out what to call them.

Sympathetic observers refer to them as "the Seattle coalition," but this title reflects little of the movement's international scope. In the United States, the movement is dramatically—even, one could say, deliberately—lacking in national leaders. It is largely coordinated on-line. I picked Juliette Beck almost at random as a bright thread to follow through this roiling fabric of rising, mostly youthful American resistance to corporate-led globalization.

Global free trade promotes global economic growth. It creates jobs, makes companies more competitive, and lowers prices for consumers. It also provides poor countries, through infusions of foreign capital and technology, with the chance to develop economically and, by spreading prosperity, creates the conditions in which democracy and respect for human rights may flourish.

This is the animating vision of the Clinton Administration, and it is a view widely shared by political leaders, economic decision-makers, and opinion-makers throughout the West. It is also accepted, at least in its outlines, by many important figures in business and government in Third World countries, where it is known as "the Washington consensus."

Critics of this consensus dispute most, if not all, of its claims. Growth, they argue, can be wasteful, destructive, unjust. The jobs created by globalization are often less sustaining and secure than the livelihoods abolished by it. Weak economies abruptly integrated into the global system do not become stronger, or develop a sustainable base; they just become more dependent, more vulnerable to the ructions of ultravolatile, deregulated international capital. In many countries, the benefits of economic growth are so unequally distributed that they intensify social and political tensions, leading to increased repression rather than to greater democracy. To the hoary trope that a rising tide lifts all boats, critics of corporate-led globalization retort that in this case it lifts only yachts.

Nearly everyone, though, on both sides of the globalization debate, accepts that the process creates winners and losers. And it is globalization's losers and potential losers—and all those with doubts about the wisdom of unchecked, unequal growth—who propel the backlash that found such vivid expression in Seattle. One odd aspect of that backlash is the ideological opposites it contains. American right-wing isolationists of the Patrick Buchanan variety are as hostile to the international bodies that promote economic globalization as they are to the United Nations. In Britain, unreconstructed Tories continue to loathe and oppose the European Union, a prime mover of globalization. Meanwhile, young British anarchists also hate the E.U., and the bulk of the Seattle coalition is being drawn from the American liberal and radical Left.

The booming popularity of the movement on college campuses is another odd aspect of its makeup, since American college graduates are unlikely to find themselves, even in the

short term, on the losing side of the great globalization ledger. And yet students, whether fired up by their coursework, like Beck, or simply sensing that this is where the subcultural action is now, have been turning out in surprising numbers for mass "teach-ins" on the W.T.O., the I.M.F., and the World Bank—even eagerly swallowing solid doses of the economic history and international financial arcana that come unavoidably with these topics.

Kevin Danaher, a co-founder of Global Exchange, sees nothing incongruous about young people getting excited about the dismal science. "Economics and politics have been kept falsely separate, traditionally," he says. "We're just trying to drag capital-investment decision-making out into the public realm. That's the terrain of struggle now. The anti-apartheid divestment campaign set the precedent."

Danaher, who in a doctoral dissertation examined the political economy of United States policy toward South Africa, was one of the leaders of the American divestment campaign. Since that campaign's contribution to ending apartheid and bringing democracy to South Africa can scarcely be overstated, his bullishness about the prospects for democratizing the rules of the new global economy may be understandable. He talks, somewhat messianically, about replacing the "money cycle" with the "life cycle," but then puts his ideas to the test by running a bustling non-profit business. Global Exchange, besides its human-rights research and activism—it has mounted corporate-accountability campaigns, targeting Nike, the Gap, and, starting this month, Starbucks for their international labor practices—operates two stores in the Bay Area, plus an on-line store, selling crafts and coffee and other goods bought directly, on demonstrably fair terms, from small producers in poor countries; it also offers "reality tours" of such countries as Cuba, Haiti, and Iran to high-disposable-income travellers not yet ready for cruise ships.

Addressing young audiences, Danaher—who is forty-nine, has a shaved head and a white goatee, and retains enough of the speech patterns of a working class New Jersey youth to carry off the most populist harangue—makes a crossgenerational pitch. He acknowledges the difficulty of understanding what it is that an institution like the World Bank even does, but then urges people to educate themselves and, in recent speeches, to come to Washington in April. "It's going to be Woodstock times ten," he told one college class, pulling out the stops. "I was at Woodstock, I was at Seattle, and Seattle changed my butt."

The World Bank lends money to the governments of poor countries. It was founded, along with the International Monetary Fund, after the Second World War to help finance the reconstruction of Europe. When the Marshall Plan usurped its original purpose, the Bank had to reinvent itself, shifting its focus to Asia, Africa, and Latin America, where the elimination of poverty became its declared mission. This was the first in a long series of institutional costume changes. Today, the Bank, which is headquartered in Washington, D.C., has more than ten thousand employees, a hundred and eighty member states, and offices in sixty-seven of those countries, and lends nearly thirty billion dollars a year. It ventures into fields far beyond its original mandate, including conflict resolution—demobilizing troops in Uganda, clearing land mines in Bosnia. The I.M.F., whose founding purpose was to make short-term loans to stabilize currencies, has similarly had to shapeshift with the times. Also headquartered in Washington, it now makes long-term loans as well and tries to manage the economies of many of its poorer member states.

Both institutions have always been dominated by the world's rich countries, particularly the United States. During the Cold War, this meant that loans were often granted on a crudely political basis. Indeed, the World Bank's first loan—two hundred and fifty million dollars to France, in 1947—was withheld until the French government purged its Cabinet of Communists. In the Third World, friendly dictators were propped up by loans. Robert McNamara, after presiding over the Vietnam War, became president of the World Bank in 1968, and he expanded its operations aggressively, pushing poor countries to transform their economies by promoting industrialized agriculture and export production.

There were fundamental problems with this development model. By the time McNamara retired, in 1981, his legacy consisted largely of failed megaprojects, populations no longer able to feed themselves, devastated forests and watersheds, and a sea of hopeless debt. Bank officials have consistently vowed to improve this record, to start funding projects that benefit not only big business and Third World elites but also the world's poor.

Accordingly, projects with non-governmental organizations and other "civil society" groups, along with efforts to promote access to health care and education, have increased. But Bank contracts are worth millions, and multinational corporations have remained major beneficiaries. In 1995, Lawrence Summers, then an under-secretary at the Treasury Department—he is now its Secretary—told Congress that for each dollar the American government contributed to the World Bank, American corporations received $1.35 in procurement contracts. One of the Bank's major proposals at the moment is for the development of oilfields in Chad, in central Africa, and the construction of an oil pipeline running more than six hundred miles to the coast at Cameroon. The environmental impact of this pipeline is predicted by many to be dire, the benefits to the people in the area minimal. The big winners will, in all likelihood, be the Bank's major partners in the project—Exxon Mobil and Chevron.

More onerous than ill-advised projects, however, for the people of the global South has been the crushing accumulation of debt by their governments. This debt now totals more than two trillion dollars, and servicing it—simply paying the interest—has become the single largest budget item for scores of poor countries. About twenty years ago, the World Bank and the I.M.F. began attaching stricter conditions to the loans they made to debtor countries to help them avoid outright default. More than ninety countries have now been subjected to I.M.F.-imposed austerity schemes, also known as structural-adjustment programs. Typically, these force a nation to cut spending in health, education, and welfare programs; reduce or eliminate food, energy, and transport subsidies; devalue its local currency; raise interest rates to attract foreign capital; privatize state property; and lower barriers to foreign ownership of local industries, land, and assets.

This is where the World Trade Organization comes in—or, rather, where its agenda dovetails with the work of the Bank and the I.M.F. All three institutions have always sought to increase world trade. (The W.T.O. is the successor to the General Agreement on Tariffs and Trade, which began in 1947 and was folded into the W.T.O. in 1995.) But the W.T.O. is the spearhead of the present surge toward economic globalization. It is a huge bureaucracy that makes binding rules intended to remove obstacles to the expansion of commercial activity among the hundred and thirty-five countries that constitute its membership. This means, in practice, an incremental transfer of power from local and national governments (the bodies likely to erect such obstacles) to the W.T.O., which acts as a trade court, hearing, behind closed doors, disputes among members accusing one another of creating barriers to trade. These "barriers" may be health, safety, or environmental laws, and a W.T.O. ruling takes precedence over all other international agreements. A country found to be impeding trade must change the offending law or suffer harsh sanctions. The effect is to deregulate international commerce, freeing the largest corporations—which, measured as economic entities, already dwarf most of the world's countries—to enter any market, extract any resource, without constraint by citizenries. Speaking anonymously, a former W.T.O. official recently told the Financial Times, "This is the place where governments collude in private against their domestic pressure groups."

There is, in other words, little mystery about why the W.T.O. and its partners in free-trade promotion, the World Bank and the I.M.F., have become the protest targets of choice for environmentalists, labor unions, economic nationalists, small farmers and small-business people, and their allies. Trade rules among countries are obviously needed. The question is whom those rules will benefit, whose rights they will protect.

The fifty thousand people who took to the streets of Seattle chanting "No new round—

turn around!" had clearly decided that the W.T.O. was not on their side when it came to steering the direction of global trade. But even that might be too broad a statement—for the coalition that gathered there was wildly diverse, its collective critique nothing if not eclectic. Many of its members would probably not agree, for instance, that trade rules are "obviously" needed. That's my view, but the movement against corporate-led globalization contains many people who accept fewer rules of the capitalist game than I do.

The Direct Action Network (DAN) probably belongs in the deeply anti-capitalist category. But the group is less than a year old and extremely loosely structured, so its ideology isn't easy to get a fix on. What does seem certain is that the shutdown (or "meltdown," as Burson-Marsteller has it) of the Seattle Ministerial would never have happened without the emergence and furious efforts of the Direct Action Network.

Juliette Beck was present at DAN's creation. Late last spring, a young organizer named David Solnit, who was well known in the movement for his dedication and ingenuity, and for his giant homemade puppets— Solnit's allegorical figures have appeared in demonstrations from coast to coast— approached Beck with a plan to shut down the Seattle meeting. Dozens of groups, including the A.F.L.-C.I.O. and Global Trade Watch, a leading branch of Nader's Public Citizen, were already planning for Seattle. But no one was talking shutdown. Solnit thought it

could be done, and he figured that Global Exchange could help. Beck and Kevin Danaher called in the Rainforest Action Network and a Berkeley-based group called the Ruckus Society, which specializes in nonviolent guerrilla action, and DAN was hatched.

Solnit was the dynamo but not the leader. "DAN is lots of lieutenants, no generals," Danaher says. The word went out, largely over the Internet, about DAN's plans, and dozens of groups and countless individuals expressed interest. The DAN coalition developed along what is known as the "affinity-group model." Affinity groups are small, semi-independent units, pledged to coalition goals, tactics, and principles—including, in DAN's case, nonviolent action—but free to make their own plans. Members look out for one another during protests, and some have designated roles: medic, legal support (avoids arrest), "spoke" (confers with other affinity groups through affinity "clusters"), "action elf" (looks after food, water, and people's spirits). Thousands signed up for training, and for "camps" organized by the Ruckus Society, where they could learn not only the techniques of classic civil disobedience but specialized skills like urban rappelling (for hanging banners on buildings), forming human blockades, and how to "lock down" in groups (arms linked through specially constructed plastic tubes). Solnit coordinated a road show that toured the West in the months before the W.T.O. Ministerial, presenting music and speakers and street theatre, urging people to get involved and come to Seattle.

They came, of course, and the combination of strict civil-disobedience discipline (the only way that the lines around the hotels and meeting places and across key intersections could have held, preventing W.T.O. delegates from gathering) and polymorphous protest (dancers on vans, hundreds of children dressed as sea turtles and monarch butterflies, Korean priests in white robes playing flutes and drums to protest genetically modified food) could never have been centrally planned.

The affinity-group model proved extremely effective in dealing with police actions. Downtown Seattle had been divided by a DAN "spokescouncil" into thirteen sectors, with an affinity cluster responsible for each sector. There were also flying squads—mobile affinity groups that could quickly take the place of groups that had been arrested or beaten or gassed from the positions they were trying to hold. The structure was flexible, and tactically powerful, and the police, trying to clear the streets, resorted to increasingly brutal methods, firing concussion grenades, mashing pepper spray into the eyes of protesters, shooting rubber bullets into bodies at short range. By the afternoon of November 30th (the first day of the meeting), the police had run low on ammunition, and that evening the mayor of Seattle called out the National Guard.

There were hundreds of arrests. Beck, who was teargassed on a line blocking the entrance to the convention center, had credentials, through Global Exchange, to enter the theatre where the W.T.O. was supposed to be having its opening session. She went inside, found a few delegates milling, and an open microphone. She and Danaher and Medea Benjamin—another co-founder of Global Exchange—took the stage, uninvited, and suggested that delegates join them in a discussion. The interlopers were hustled off the stage. Beck elected not to go quietly. Marshals put her in a pain hold—her arm twisted behind her back—and dragged her through the theatre. A news camera recorded the event. "Then CNN kept showing it, over and over, them carrying me off, whenever they talked about the arrests," she says. "My claim to fame. Except I wasn't arrested! They just threw me out."

Ironically, the only protesters not following the nonviolence guidelines—a hundred or so "black bloc" anarchists, who started smashing shopwindows—were hardly bothered by the police. The black-bloc crews, whose graffiti and occasional "communiques" run to nihilist slogans ("Civilization Is Collapsing—Let's Give It a Push!"), were masked, well organized, young and fleet of foot, and armed with crowbars and acid-filled eggs. The police in their heavy riot gear could not have caught them if they'd tried. The targeted shops belonged to big corporations: Nike, the Gap, Fidelity Investments, Starbucks, Levi's, Planet Hollywood. Still other protesters chanted "Shame! Shame!" Some even tried to stop the attacks. There were scuffles, and suggestions that the

black blocs contained police agents provocateurs—hence the masks. Medea Benjamin, who had helped produce the original expose of Nike's sweatshops in Asia, found herself in the absurd position of siding with protesters who were defending a Niketown. And her fear (shared by many) that a few broken windows might snatch away the headlines in the national press proved justified.

The political spectrum represented in the protests was improbably wide, ranging from, on the right, James Hoffa's Teamsters and the A.F.L.-C.I.O. (who fielded tens of thousands of members for a march) to, on the left, a dozen or more anarchist factions (the black blocs were a rowdy minority within a generally less aggressive minority), including the ancient Industrial Workers of the World. All these groups had found, if not a common cause, at least a common foe. Some unlikely alliances were cemented. The United Steelworkers union and Earth First!, for example, had a common enemy in the Maxxam Corporation, which logs old-growth forests and owns steel mills, and the two groups are currently working together to end a bitter lockout at a Kaiser Aluminum plant in Tacoma.

Inside the besieged W.T.O. Ministerial, there was a rebellion among countries from the global South, which raised the possibility of another, truly formidable alliance with some of the forces out in the streets. The leaders of the poorer countries, though often depicted as pawns of the major powers, content to

offer their countries' workers to the world market at the lowest possible wages—and to pollute their air and water and strip-mine their natural resources, in exchange for their own commissions on the innumerable deals that come with corporate globalization—in reality have to answer, in many cases, to complex constituencies at home, many of whom are alarmed about their own economic recolonization. In Seattle, delegations from Africa, Asia, the Caribbean, and Latin America—rattled by the total disruption of the Ministerial's schedule, and furious about being excluded from key meetings held privately by the rich countries—issued statements announcing their refusal to sign "agreements" produced at such meetings. In the end, no agreements were signed, no new round launched, and the Ministerial finished in disarray. This insurgency was often depicted in the American press as a refusal by the representatives of the poor countries to accept higher labor and environmental standards being imposed on them by the West, but that was not the gist of the revolt, which ran deeper and echoed the fundamental questions being asked outside in the streets about the mandate of the W.T.O.

"Coalition-building is hard," Juliette Beck said. "There's no doubt about it. But it's what we do." We were sitting in a deserted cafe in some sort of Latino community center one Sunday night in Berkeley, sipping beers. "At Global Exchange, we try to think of campaigns that will appeal to the average Joe on

compose ▪ design ▪ advocate

the street. We're really not interested in just organizing other leftists. Big corporations are a great target, because they do things that hurt virtually everybody. My dad, who's very right-wing, but libertarian, hates corporations. The H.M.O.s have practically ruined his medical practice, mainly because he insists on spending as much time with his patients as he thinks they need. After Seattle, he read a column by the economist Robert Kuttner, and suddenly, he said, he got what we're trying to do. Kuttner apparently explained that corporations just naturally grab all the power they can, and when they've grabbed too much there has to be a backlash. That's what led, a hundred years ago, to trust-busting and federal regulation after the robber barons did their thing, and that's what's causing this movement now. It was nice to hear my dad say that."

Across the street was a cafe/bookshop/community center, this one run by an anarchist collective (we were, remember, in Berkeley) called Long Haul Infoshop, which distributes a radical journal called *Slingshot*. In a special W.T.O. edition, *Slingshot* had derided Global Exchange and "other despicable examples of the corporate left"; another column slammed Medea Benjamin for her defense of Nike. I asked Beck about the attacks from the left. She sighed. "Yeah, there's been a lot of fallout. A lot of people believe property destruction isn't violence. But that wasn't really the issue in Seattle. The issue was what message, what images, we were sending out

to the world. There's always going to be disagreement. When it comes to these institutions—the W.T.O., the I.M.F., the World Bank—we have reformists and abolitionists. If we're talking about the World Bank, I, for instance, am an abolitionist."

I asked Beck if she considered herself an anarchist.

She shrugged, as if the question were obtuse.

DAN seemed, at a glance, to be an anarchist organization, or at least organized on anarchist principles, I said.

"Sure," Beck said, still looking nonplussed. Finally, she said, "Well, I definitely respect anarchist ways of organizing. I guess I'm still learning what it means to be an anarchist. But the real question is: Can this anarchist model that's working so well now for organizing protests be applied on an international scale to create the democratic decision-making structures that we need to eliminate poverty?"

I took this opportunity to float a theory, somewhat grander and iffier than Kuttner's, about the historical forces that cause anarchism to flourish. Anarchism, I said, first arose in Europe as a response to the disruptions of peasant and artisanal life caused by industrialization and the rapid concentration of power among new business elites. After a good long fight, anarchism basically lost out to socialism as an organizing vision among workers—and lost again, after a heady late run, in Republican Spain, to Communism (which then lost to fascism). But anarchism was obviously enjoy-

ing some kind of small-time comeback, and, if today's Information Revolution was even half as significant as both its critics and its cheerleaders like to claim—the most important economic development since the Industrial Revolution, and so on—then perhaps the time was ripening, socialism having been disgraced as an alternative to capitalism, for another great wave of anarchist protest against this latest, alarmingly swift amassing of power in the hands of a few hundred billionaires. Did Beck know that the term "direct action" was used by anarcho-syndicalists in France at the turn of the last century?

She did. She also knew, it seemed, that anarchism has become wildly popular among Latin American students who are fed up with what they call neoliberalismo (their term for corporate-led globalization) but disenchanted, also, with the traditional left. And she knew that the students who went on strike and took over the National University in Mexico City for nine months recently were mostly anarchists. But did I know (I didn't) that it had been a structural-adjustment edict from the World Bank that led the Mexican government to raise student fees, which sparked the strike and the takeover?

Beck drained her beer. DAN, whatever its historical analogues, had been thriving since its triumph in Seattle, she said. The network was now directing most of its considerable energies toward the April action in Washington, D.C., which people were calling "A16," for April 16th, the day the I.M.F. planned to meet.

She was going to Washington herself in a couple of days, and then joining a road show, which would start making its way up the East Coast, beating the drums for the big event.

"I Am Funkier Than You," the bumper sticker said, and it was almost certainly true. But the Mango Affinity Group, as the road-show crew had taken to calling themselves, had scored this big, extremely grubby van free from a woman in Virginia simply by asking for a vehicle on the A16 E-mail list serve, so they were not complaining. Liz Guy, an efficient DAN stalwart usually known as Sprout, had pulled together both the crew—eight or nine activists, aged nineteen to thirty-two, including Juliette Beck—and a tight, three-week, show-a-day itinerary that ran from Florida to Montreal before looping back to Washington. I found them in St. Petersburg, bivouacked under a shade tree on the campus of Eckerd College, working on a song.

Beck introduced me. They were a sweet-voiced, ragamuffin group, drawn from Connecticut, Atlanta, Seattle (Sprout), and the mountains of British Columbia. This afternoon was going to be their first performance together, and, judging from the situation as showtime approached and they began lugging their gear into a low-roofed, brutally air-conditioned hall, somebody had blown the publicity. There was virtually no one around except their hosts—two young DAN guys, Peter and Josh, who were hopefully laying out anarchist and vegan pamphlets and books on

a table. Peter and Josh, embarrassed, said they had just returned from a Ruckus Society camp. Evidently, they had left arrangements in the wrong hands. "Let's do a skate-by, see where people are," one of them said, and both jumped on skateboards and shot off.

"Woodstock times ten," Kevin Danaher had said. Pure hooey, I now thought. In truth, A16 did not have going for it many of the things that had converged so resoundingly in Seattle. The planning for the protest was far more rushed. The W.T.O.'s Seattle Ministerial had been, moreover, a momentous gathering, meant to kick off a so-called Millennial Round, whereas the World Bank/I.M.F. spring meetings were strictly routine, and scheduled to be brief. Big labor, finally, had no special interest in the World Bank and the I.M.F., and the A.F.L.-C.I.O., while endorsing the A16 protest, had decided to concentrate its energies this political season on preventing the permanent normalization of United States trade relations with China. A demonstration by union members to press these issues was scheduled to take place in Washington on April 12th. And it wasn't the only event threatening to disperse attention from A16. There was a big protest planned for April 9th, also in Washington, organized by a movement called Jubilee 2000, to demand debt cancellation for the poorest countries.

The hope, of course, was that all these protests would produce some sort of anti-globalization synergy that might just culminate, on A16, in the type of massive turnout

that would certainly be needed to have any chance of shutting down the World Bank and the I.M.F. meetings. On the Internet, as always, anything looked possible. Caravans were being organized all over the country, reconnaissance was being conducted on "targets" in Washington, anti-capitalist revolutionary blocs were breaking away from the DAN-centered action with furious objections to mealymouthed talk of "fair trade" and alleged "collaboration with the enemy at large"—to, that is, meetings being held by organizers with the D.C. police to try to prevent bloodshed. (In fact, the D.C. police had gone to Seattle to observe the demonstrations, and had spent a million dollars on new riot gear for A16.) Beck had told me, back in San Francisco, "I get so tired of the Internet and e-mail. We couldn't do this work without it, but, really, it's not organizing. There's nothing like face to face."

Now in Florida, Beck, perhaps getting desperate for some F2F, approached two young women who had wandered into the frigid hall, possibly just to get out of the afternoon heat, and started regaling them with a spiel about how the World Bank and the I.M.F. are "partners in crime." The young women, who wore tank tops and looked as if they belonged on a beach somewhere, nodded politely but said nothing. In the background, Damon, a tall, dark-skinned, curly-haired musician from British Columbia, strummed a guitar, and the rest of the Mango Affinity Group busied themselves making posters denouncing exploitation.

compose ▪ design ▪ advocate

Blessedly, between the skate-by and Damon's guitar, people began to trickle into the hall. Soon there was an audience of thirty or so, and the show began. Damon disappeared inside a towering, black-suited puppet with a huge papier-mache head, sloping skull, and cigar stuck between his lips, Beck slapped a "World Bank/I.M.F." sign on his chest, and he began to roar, "You are all under my power!" The crowd laughed, and he roared, "It's not funny, it's true!" They laughed harder. A political skit followed, with a series of fresh-faced young women getting thrashed by an I.M.F. henchman for demanding health and safety standards, then put to work in a Gap sweatshop. "Right to Organize" also got pounded. Afterward, Beck led a teach-in called Globalization 101, with pop quizzes on the meaning of various trade and finance acronyms, and Hershey's Kisses tossed to those who got the answers right. One middle-aged trio—Eckerd faculty, from the look of them—seemed well versed on the topic. Then the Mango members introduced themselves individually—Leigh, from an "intentional community" in Atlanta, Ricardo, from a Canadian "solar-powered cooperative" where people grew much of their own food. Sprout took the opportunity to encourage people to form affinity groups, explaining what they were and how they worked.

I was struck by Sprout's poise. Talking to dozens of strangers, she somehow made her presentation seem like an intimate conversation, with pauses, eye contact, murmurs back and forth, little encouraging interjections ("Awesome!" "Cool!") when she felt she'd been understood. Twenty-five, physically small, and dressed with utter simplicity—loose shirt, cargo pants, no shoes—she achieved, with no theatricality, an effect of tremendous presence. It occurred to me that Sprout, with her neighborly voice and unerring choice of words, could easily be very successful in a completely different arena. On another sort of road show, for instance—the sort that dot-com startups mount, touring and performing for investors and analysts, before taking their companies public. The same was true for Beck. And both women came from cities (Seattle, San Francisco) that were crawling with rich dot-commers more or less their age. What was it that made them choose this raggedy, low-status, activist's path instead? While the rest of the country obsessed over its stock portfolio, these brainy young people were working killer hours for little, if any, pay—quixotically trying, as they sometimes put it, to globalize the world from below.

Next on the program was a rousing folk song, with Damon on guitar and Sage, his regular bandmate from B.C., on drums. Their vocal harmonies sounded fairly polished. Then Sprout produced a viola, slipping without fanfare into the tune, and began improvising fiddle breaks of steadily increasing warmth and precision. I caught Beck's eye. Who was this woman? Beck could not stop grinning. The Mango group then ruined the soaring mood, as far as I was concerned, by leading the crowd in some mortifyingly corny chants—"Ain't no power like the power of the people, cuz the power of the people don't stop!"

Beck asked for a show of hands. How many people thought they might go to Washington for A16? Fifteen or twenty hands shot up, including those of the two women in tank tops. I was amazed that they had even stayed for the show. A signup sheet was circulated.

Next came nonviolence training, for which ten or twelve people stuck around. Leigh and Sprout led the training, which lasted into the evening and included a lot of "role-playing"—people pretending to be protesters, police, I.M.F. officials, workers trying to get to work. There were drills in quick decision-making among affinity groups: shall we stay locked down or move when threatened with arrest and felony charges? Group dynamics were dissected after each scene. Sprout demonstrated unthreatening body language. Hand signals for swift, clear communication were suggested. Peter and Josh, the two local DAN guys, joined in the training, and it was soon obvious that they had a lot of experience. Peter, who was wiry, bushy-bearded, and soft-spoken, firmly refused to be bullied by some of the bigger, more aggressive men in the group. It became clear that effective nonviolent protest needed a cool head, and that bluster wasn't helpful. Toward the end of the evening, Leigh presented a list of things to bring to an action. Most were common-sense items like food, water, and herbal remedies for tear gas. The rationale for others was less self-evident. Maxi pads?

Leigh and Sprout glanced at one another. "If the cops start using chemical warfare, some women start bleeding very heavily," Leigh said. There was a brief, shocked silence. "They're good as bandages, too," she added.

What about gas masks?

"They can become targets," Josh said. "In Seattle, the cops tried to tear them off, and if they couldn't reach them they fired rubber bullets, or wooden bullets, or these wooden dowel rods they had, at the masks. Some people got a lot of glass in their faces. Masks can be dangerous."

The trainees stared.

"One thing that's good to have is big toenail clippers," Peter said cheerfully. "Put 'em in your pocket, and if you're arrested, and just left in a cell or a paddy wagon, somebody can fish them out of your pocket and cut off your cuffs with 'em. They use cheap plastic cuffs when they arrest a lot of people, and if they leave you sitting for ten or fifteen hours it's a lot more comfortable if your hands aren't tied behind you."

Ten or fifteen hours?

"It happens. It happened to me in Seattle."

It had happened to Sprout, too—seventeen hours in an unheated cell alone, doing jumping jacks to try to stay warm.

The tone of the gathering was entirely sober now. Somebody asked about carrying I.D. during an action.

"It depends whether you want to practice jail solidarity," Beck said. "That's something you need to decide with your affinity group."

None of the trainees knew what jail solidarity was.

"Noncooperation with the system," they were told. It might be widely used in Washington—to clog the jails and courts and try to force mass dismissals of charges.

But the details of jail solidarity could wait for another session, Beck said. It was late. People were tired. DAN would be offering more nonviolence training locally in the weeks ahead, and everybody going to Washington for A16 should get as much training as possible.

We stayed that night with Peter and Josh. They lived in a mobile home near a strip mall in Clearwater. People slept on couches and chairs and on the floor, in the van, on a back porch, and on a tiny plywood dock on a fetid canal behind the trailer. I tried to sleep on the dock, but mosquitoes kept me awake. There was a full moon, and low, cotton-puff clouds streaming across it at an unusual speed. The clouds were glowing a sort of radioactive mauve from all the strip-mall lights.

At some point, the mosquitoes woke Beck, who was also on the dock. Out of the darkness, a restless voice: "We need a name. For the movement as a whole. Anti-Corporate Globalization isn't good enough. What do you think of Global Citizen Movement?"

I thought it needed work.

Beck started talking about plans she had for disrupting the Democratic Party's national Convention this summer, in Los Angeles. She mentioned a Millennium Youth March.

"You're thinking big."

"That's my job."

I wanted to know what would happen in Washington on A16.

"Me, too," she said, and I thought I heard her sigh. "For now, crowd-building is the main thing. That's why I'm really glad I'm on this road show. I kind of feel like I should be in D.C., walking the site, doing messaging, doing logistics, but I'm going to stay with this as long as I can."

"Messaging" meant press releases, banners, slogans—even sound bites for protesters to give to reporters, should the opportunity arise. I had begun to think that for the American public effective messaging about the I.M.F. and the World Bank was a hopeless task. In Nigeria and Venezuela, yes, everybody knew and had strong opinions about structural adjustment and I.M.F. debt. That was never going to be true in this country. People might turn out in large numbers, for many different reasons, on A16, but it would basically be Americans expressing solidarity with people in poor countries who are on the receiving end of bad policies. That wasn't a formula for real political leverage. The plight of, say, the Ittu Oromo would never move more than a few faraway hearts. In the great shakeout of economic globalization, most Americans probably believe, not unreasonably, that they will be among the revolution's winners. As for the big goal—democratizing

compose ▪ *design* ▪ *advocate*

international decision-making, in order to eliminate poverty—it seemed to me impossibly abstract.

I was loathe to tell Beck that. While she seemed quite dauntless, her identification with her work seemed, at the same time, perilously deep. She once told me that she thought it was significant that she had been born in 1973, the same year that Richard Nixon allowed the dollar to float—"and the I.M.F. should have been allowed to die!" On another occasion, she'd said, "I really feel lucky to be doing this work. When I started studying the World Bank in college, I couldn't believe how evil it was, even while it's supposedly all about fighting poverty. I thought, you know, it would really be an honor to dedicate my life to fighting this evil institution. And that's all we're asking people to do: help us drag these institutions out into the sunlight of public scrutiny, where they belong. They'll shrivel up like Dracula!"

While I tried to doze, Beck reminded me that the World Bank and I.M.F. had pressured Haiti to freeze its minimum wage, that NAFTA was a failure from beginning to end—details available if I needed them—and that the United States Supreme Court was hearing a crucial case, which I should watch closely when I got back to New York. It seemed that the federal government was trying to stop the Commonwealth of Massachusetts from boycotting companies that did business in Burma, which uses forced labor.

At dawn, finally agreeing that sleep was hopeless, Beck and I took a canoe that was tied to the dock and paddled off down the stinking canal, gliding past the battered, moldy back doors of mobile homes. It was a Sunday morning. Everybody in the trailers seemed to be asleep—probably dreaming about their stock portfolios. The mangroves on the banks slowly closed over our heads. We tried to push through. There seemed to be wider, brighter water ahead. Beck was happy to keep going, but I was in the bow, catching spider webs with my face. In the end, we turned back.

The Mango Affinity Group held a morning meeting on the little dock. While trying to decide who would be responsible for grocery shopping, they started goofing on the hand signals developed by DAN for anarchist consensus decision-making, cracking each other up. Beck was supposed to be guiding the discussion-facilitating, they called it—but she had the giggles, too. Group morale seemed high.

Bushy-bearded Peter came out of the trailer, yawning and stretching. He started filling a plastic bag with grapefruit from a low, gnarled dwarf of a tree. The fruit looked awful, with upper halves all blackened as if by grime falling from the sky, but Peter assured me they were fine. I cut one open. It was the best grapefruit I had ever tasted.

Inside the trailer, there was a small room devoted to Josh and Peter's book and periodical distribution business. They had a dense, nondoctrinaire selection, with sections on Organizing, Anarchism/Social Theory, Animal Liberation, Punk, Direct Action, Media, Globalization, Feminism/Sexuality, and Youth Oppression/Radical Education. They had ten Noam Chomsky titles, lots of Emma Goldman, a guide to "understanding and attacking mainstream media," arguments against compulsory schooling, even a collection of Digger tracts (seventeenth-century free-love proto-anarchists). Josh and Peter's catalogue included an introduction that traced their own political development from 1996, when "we were straightedge as fuck," to more recent days, when "our distro grew greener and more anarchistic."

Elsewhere in the trailer, somebody had put on a Delta blues tape. Out in the living room, I found Josh sprawled on a couch. He was a quiet guy, in his early twenties, with sparse blond muttonchops and small blue eyes. He was wearing a baseball cap and talking to a glum-looking young woman with an elaborately pierced nose. I started asking Josh about himself. He wasn't a student, he said pleasantly. He had realized he could learn more outside school. He didn't have a job. "But I need to get one, just to make money. The problem is, I'm really too busy to work."

Through a window, I could see the Mango Affinity Group loading up the van. Beck and Sprout, the lanky, tireless trade wonk and the barefoot fiddler, had their heads bent together over a map. Today, the road show went to Gainesville. Tomorrow, Valdosta, Georgia.

ANALYZING
styles of advocacy

■ **Discuss with others:** What values do the people described in "After Seattle" share with those described on the AVODAH website? What are their differences?

■ **Discuss with others:** Do you think the people described on the AVODAH website would consider their work to be "advocacy"? Why—or why not?

■ **Discuss with others:** Why do you think those who designed the AVODAH website chose the particular Alumni profiles that they did? What strategies—visual and verbal—have shaped the design of these webpages in order to persuade others to get involved?

■ **Discuss with others:** What do you understand to be Finnegan's purposes in writing "After Seattle"? What sort of person do you think would read his article most sympathetically?

■ **Discuss with others:** Chapter 15 of this book contains an excerpt from the book *Persepolis*, by Marjane Satrapi. Satrapi is an Iranian woman who grew up during the Islamic Revolution in the late 1970s. Although she does not state it explicitly, Satrapi is advocating an attitude toward a certain group of people in Iran; she is also advocating parental attitudes toward children and the rights of women. How does Satrapi use the particular strategies of comics to advocate? How does her style of advocacy compare with that of the young woman described in "After Seattle"?

■ **Research and write:** Find other service organizations that, like the AVODAH organization, are based in religious belief; also find similar webpages for sectarian service organizations or service organizations that bring together different faiths. Write a short paper that analyzes how the rhetorical appeals of the sites that draw on religious beliefs differ from the appeals of the sectarian sites. What kinds of rhetorical strategies can webpage designers or writers use when they can assume an audience shares a set of core beliefs?

being an advocate, being a citizen, and being a critic

"THE PARTLY CLOUDY PATRIOT"

On the next pages is an essay written by Sarah Vowell, who lives in New York, publishes smart and humorous essays about contemporary life in American, and is a contributing editor to public radio's *This American Life*. As a contributing editor, she not only provides oral stories and essays to the show, but is partially responsible for its production. She communicates on different levels with her audiences, in other words.

The essay "The Partly Cloudy Patriot" is from a collection of essays that address a wide range of topics—visiting Civil War sites, being poor in California, *Buffy the Vampire Slayer*, political and other kinds of nerds, and George W. Bush's inauguration. In this essay, Vowell starts by talking about her response to the Mel Gibson movie *The Patriot* as a way of thinking through what it means to be a patriot. She moves on to talk about the events of September 11, 2001, with the same end in mind. As her title indicates, she has an ambivalent relation to the idea of patriotism—not that she is against it, but she wants to know what others think it means to be patriotic and if she agrees with their style of patriotism.

In this essay, Vowell speaks in a personal tone, drawing on her own experiences, and so it may seem that if she is advocating something, it is focused around herself. It might seem she is engaged in a style of selfish advocacy. Selfish advocacy—advocacy based in personal experiences, personal grievances, themselves based in public arrangement—is not necessarily a bad thing. We all need to find out what matters to us, to draw on our experience of suffering, to connect with others who share similar ideas about what might make society better. There is a fine line between knowing what is right, however, as Vowell argues, and seeing yourself on a journey of discovery with others.

Much had happened in and to the U.S. after September 11, 2001, even by the time Vowell wrote this essay, and she clearly feels the need to do something to influence the direction people are moving.

As you read, look for what Vowell is advocating for us all.

The Partly Cloudy Patriot
by Sarah Vowell

In the summer of 2000, I went to see the Mel Gibson blockbuster *The Patriot*. I enjoyed that movie. Watching a story line like that is always a relief. Of course the British must be expelled, just as the Confederates must surrender, Hitler must be crushed, and yee-haw when the Red Sea swallows those slave-mongering Egyptians. There were editorials about *The Patriot*, the kind that always accompany any historical film, written by professors who insist things nobody cares about, like Salieri wasn't that bad a sort or the fact that Roman gladiators maybe didn't have Australian accents. A little anachronism is part of the fun, and I don't mind if in real life General Cornwallis never lost a battle in the South as he does rather gloriously in the film. Isn't art supposed to improve on life?

Personally, I think there was more than enough historical accuracy in *The Patriot* to keep the spoilsports happy. Because I'm part spoilsport on my father's side, and I felt nagged with quandaries every few minutes during the nearly three-hour film. American history is a quagmire, and the more one knows, the quaggier the mire gets. If you're paying attention during *The Patriot* and you know your history and you have a stake in that history, not to mention a conscience, the movie is not an entirely cartoonish march to glory. For example, Mel Gibson's character, Benjamin Martin, is conflicted. He doesn't want to fight the British because he still feels bad about chopping up some Cherokee into little pieces during the French and Indian War. Since I'm a part-Cherokee person myself, Gibson lost a little of the sympathy I'd stored up for him because he'd been underrated in *Conspiracy Theory*. And did I mention his character lives in South Carolina? So by the end of the movie, you look at the youngest Mel junior bundled in his mother's arms and think, Mel just risked his life so that that kid's kids can rape their slaves and vote to be the first state to secede from the Union.

The Patriot did confirm that I owe George Washington an apology. I always liked George fine, though I dismissed him as a mere soldier. I prefer the pen to the sword, so I've always been more of a Jeffersonhead. The words of the Declaration of Independence are so right and true that it seems like its poetry alone would have knocked King George III in the head. Like, he would have read this beloved passage, "We hold these truths to be self-evident, that all Men are created equal, that they are endowed by their Creator with certain unalienable Rights—that among these are Life, Liberty and the pursuit of Happiness," and thought the notion so just, and yet still so wonderfully whimsical, that he would have dethroned himself on the spot. But no, it took a grueling, six-year-long war to make independence a fact.

I rarely remember this. In my ninety-five-cent copy of the Declaration of Independence and the Constitution, the two documents are separated by only a blank half page. I forget that there are eleven years between them, eleven years of war and the whole Articles of Confederation debacle. In my head, the two documents are like the A side and B side of the greatest single ever released that was recorded in one great drunken night, but no, there's a lot of bleeding life between them. Dead boys and dead Indians and Valley Forge.

Anyway, *The Patriot*. The best part of seeing it was standing in line for tickets. I remember how jarring it was to hear my fellow moviegoers say that word. "Two for *The Patriot* please." "One for *The Patriot* at 5:30." For years, I called it the P word, because it tended to make nice people flinch. For the better part of the 1990s, it seemed like the only Americans who publicly described themselves as patriots were scary militia types hiding out in the backwoods of Michigan and Montana, cleaning their guns. One of the few Americans still celebrating Patriot's Day—a nearly forgotten holiday on April 19 commemorating the Revolutionary War's first shots at Lexington and Concord—did so in 1995 by murdering 168 people in the federal building in Oklahoma City. In fact, the same week I saw *The Patriot*, I was out with some friends for dessert. When I asked a fellow named Andy why he had chosen a cupcake with a little American flag stuck in the frosting, I expected him to say that he was in a patriotic mood, but he didn't. He said that he was "feeling jingoistic."

Well, that was a long time ago. As I write this, it's December 2001 in New York City. The only words one hears more often than variations on patriot are "in the wake of," "in the aftermath of," and "since the events of September 11." We also use the word *we* more. Patriotism as a word and deed has made a comeback. At Halloween, costume shops did a brisk business in Uncle Sam and Betsy Ross getups. Teen pop bombshell Britney Spears took a breather during her live telecast from Vegas's MGM Grand to sit on a piano bench with her belly ring glinting in the spotlight and talk about "how proud I am of our nation right now." Chinese textile factories are working overtime to fill the consumer demand for American flags.

Immediately after the attack, seeing the flag all over the place was moving, endearing. So when the newspaper I subscribe to published a full-page, full color flag to clip out and hang in the window, how come I couldn't? It took me a while to figure out why I guiltily slid the flag into the recycling bin instead of taping it up. The meaning had changed; or let's say it changed back. In the first day or two the flags were plastered everywhere, seeing them was heartening because they indicated that we're all in this sorrow together. The flags were purely emotional. Once we went to war, once the president announced that we were going to retaliate against the "evildoers," then the flag again represented what it usually represents, the government. I think that's when the flags started making me nervous. The true American patriot is by definition skeptical of the government. Skepticism of the government was actually one of the platforms the current figurehead of the government ran on. How many times in the campaign did President Bush proclaim of his opponent, the then vice president, "He trusts the federal government and I trust the people"? This deep suspicion of Washington is one of the most American emotions an American can have. So by the beginning of October, the ubiquity of the flag came to feel like peer pressure to always stand behind policies one might not necessarily agree with. And, like any normal citizen, I prefer to make up my mind about the issues of the day on a case by case basis at 3:00 A.M. when I wake up from my *Nightline*-inspired nightmares.

One Independence Day, when I was in college, I was living in a house with other students on a street that happened to be one of the main roads leading to the football stadium where the town's official Fourth of July fireworks festivities would be held. I looked out the window and noticed a little American flag stabbed into my yard. Then I walked outside and saw that all the yards in front of all the houses on the street had little flags waving above the grass. The flags, according to a tag, were underwritten by a local real estate agency and the Veterans of Foreign Wars. I marched into the house, yanked out the phone book, found the real estate office in the yellow pages, and phoned them up immediately, demanding that they come and take their fucking flag off my lawn, screaming into the phone, "The whole point of that goddamn flag is that people don't stick flags in my yard without asking me!" I felt like Jimmy Stewart in *Mr. Smith Goes to Washington*, but with profanity. A few minutes later, an elderly gentleman in a VFW cap, who probably lost his best friend liberating France or something, pulled up in a big car, grabbed the flag, and rolled his eyes as I stared at him through the window. Then I felt dramatic and dumb. Still, sometimes I think the true American flag has always been that one with the snake hissing "Don't Tread on Me."

The week of the attack on the World Trade Center and the Pentagon, I watched TV news all day and slept with the radio on. I found myself flipping channels hoping to see the FBI handcuff a terrorist on camera. What did happen, a lot, was that citizens or politicians or journalists would mentioned that they wonder what it will be like for Americans now to live with the constant threat of random, sudden death. I know a little about what that's like. I did grow up during the Cold War. Maybe it says something about my level of cheer that I found this notion comforting, to remember that all those years I was sure the world might blow up at any second, I somehow managed to graduate from high school and do my laundry and see Smokey Robinson live.

Things were bad in New York. I stopped being able to tell whether my eyes were teary all the time from grief or from the dirty, smoky wind. Just when it seemed as if the dust had started to settle, then came the anthrax. I was on the phone with a friend who works in Rockefeller Center, and he had to hang up to be evacuated because a contaminated envelope had infected a person in the building; an hour later, another friend in another building was sitting at his desk eating his lunch and men in sealed plastic disease-control space suits walked through his office, taking samples. Once delivering the mail became life-threatening, pedestrians trudging past the main post office on Eighth Avenue bowed their heads a little as they read the credo chiseled on the

façade, "Neither snow, nor rain, nor heat, nor gloom of night stays these couriers from the swift completion of their appointed rounds."

During another war, across the river, in Newark, a writer turned soldier named Thomas Paine sat down by a campfire in September 1776 and wrote, "These are the times that try men's souls. The summer soldier and the sunshine patriot will, in this crisis, shrink from the service of their country; but he that stands it now, deserves the love and thanks of man and woman." In September and October, I liked to read that before I pulled the rubberband off the newspaper to find out what was being done to my country and what my country was doing back. I liked the black and white of Paine's words. I know I'm no sunshine patriot. I wasn't shrinking, though, honestly; the most important service we mere mortal citizens were called upon to perform was to spend money, so I dutifully paid for Korean dinners and a new living room lamp. But still I longed for the morning that I could open up the paper and the only people in it who would irk me would be dead suicide bombers and retreating totalitarians on the other side of the world. Because that would be the morning I pulled the flag out of the recycling bin and taped it up in the window. And while I could shake my fists for sure at the terrorist on page one, buried domestic items could still make my

stomach hurt—school prayer partisans taking advantage of the grief of children to circumvent the separation of church and state; the White House press secretary condemning a late-night talk show host for making a questionable remark about the U.S. military: "The reminder is to all Americans, that they need to watch what they say, watch what they do, and that this is not a time for remarks like that." Those are the sorts of never-ending qualms that have turned me into the partly cloudy patriot I long not to be.

When Paine wrote his pamphlet, which came to be called "The American Crisis," winter was coming, Washington's armies were in retreat, the Revolution was floundering. His words inspired soldiers and civilians alike to buck up and endure the war so that someday "not a place upon earth might be so happy as America."

Thing is, it worked. The British got kicked out. The trees got cleared. Time passed, laws passed and, five student loans later, I made a nice little life for myself. I can feel it with every passing year, how I'm that much farther away from the sacrifices of the cast-off Indians and Okie farmers I descend from. As recently as fifty years ago my grandmother was picking cotton with bleeding fingers. I think about her all the time while I'm getting overpaid to sit at a computer, eat Chinese takeout, and think things up in my pajamas. The half century separating my fingers, which are moisturized with cucumber lotion and type eighty words per minute, and her bloody digits is an ordinary Land of Opportunity parable, and don't think I don't appreciate it. I'm keenly aware of all the ways my life is easier and lighter, how lucky I am to have the time and energy to contemplate the truly important things— Bill Murray in *Groundhog Day*, the baked Alaska at Sardi's, the Dean Martin Christmas record, my growing collection of souvenir snow globes. After all, what is happiness without cheap thrills? Reminds me of that passage in Philip Roth's novel *American Pastoral* when the middle-aged, prosperous grandson of immigrants marvels that his own daughter loathes the country enough to try to blow it up:

> Hate America? Why, he lived in America the way he lived inside his own skin. All the pleasures of his younger years were American pleasures, all that success and happiness had been American, and he need no longer keep his mouth shut about it just to defuse her ignorant hatred. The loneliness he would feel if he had to live in another country. Yes, everything that gave meaning to his accomplishments had been American. Everything he loved was here.

A few weeks after the United States started bombing Afghanistan and the Taliban were in retreat, I turned on the TV news and watched grinning Afghans in the streets of Kabul, allowed to play music for the first time in years. I pull a brain muscle when I try to fathom the rationale for outlawing all music all the time—not certain genres of music, not music with offensive lyrics played by the corrupters of youth, but any form of organized sound. Under Taliban rule, my whole life as an educated (well, at a state school), working woman with CD storage problems would have been null and void. I don't know what's more ridiculous, that people like that would deny a person like me the ability to earn a living using skills and knowledge I learned in school, or that they would deny me my unalienable right to chop garlic in time with the B-52s' "Rock Lobster" as I cook dinner.

A few years back, a war correspondent friend of mine gave a speech about Bosnia to an international relations department at a famous Midwestern university. I went with him. After he finished, a group of hangers-on, all men except for me, stuck around to debate the finer points of the former Yugoslavia. The conversation was very detailed, including references to specific mayors of specific Croatian villages. It was like record collector geek talk, only about Bosnia. They were the record collectors of Bosnia. So they went on denouncing the various idiotic nationalist causes of various splinter groups, blaming nationalism itself for the genocidal war. And of course a racist nationalism is to blame. But the more they ranted, the more uncomfortable I became. They, many of them immigrants themselves, considered patriotic allegiance to be a sin, a divisive, villainous drive leading to exclusion, hate and murder. I, theretofore silent, spoke up. This is what I said. I said that the idea of Memphis, Tennessee, not to mention looking down at it, made me go all soft. Because I looked down at Memphis, Tennessee, and thought of all my heroes who had walked its streets. I thought of Sun Records, of the producer Sam Phillips. Sam Phillips, who once described the sort of person he recorded as "a person who had dreamed, and dreamed, and dreamed." A person like Elvis Presley, his funny bass player Bill Black, his guitarist Scotty Moore (we have the same birthday, he and I). Jerry Lee Lewis. Carl Perkins. Hello, I'm Johnny Cash. I told the Bosnian record collectors that when I thought of the records of these Memphis men, when I looked out the window at the Mississippi mud and felt their names moistening my tongue what I felt, what I was proud to feel, was patriotic. I noticed one man staring at me. He said he was born in some something-istan I hadn't heard of. Now that my globe is permanently turned to that part of the world, I realize he was talking about Tajikistan, the country bordering Afghanistan. The man from Tajikistan looked at me in the eye and delivered the following warning.

"Those," he said, of my accolades for

Elvis and friends, "are the seeds of war."

I laughed and told him not to step on my blue suede shoes, but I got the feeling he wasn't joking.

Before September 11, the national events that have made the deepest impressions on me are, in chronological order: the 1976 Bicentennial, the Iran hostage crisis, Iran-Contra, the Los Angeles riots, the impeachment trial of President Clinton, and the 2000 presidential election. From those events, I learned the following: that the Declaration of Independence is full of truth and beauty; that some people in other parts of the world hate us because we're Americans; what a shredder is; that the rage for justice is so fierce people will set fire to their own neighborhoods when they don't get it; that Republicans hate Bill Clinton; and that the ideal of one man, one vote doesn't always come true. (In the U.S. Commission on Civil Rights' report "Voting Irregularities in Florida During the 2000 Presidential Election," the testimony of Dr. Frederick Shotz of Broward County especially sticks out. A handicapped voter in a wheelchair, Dr. Shotz "had to use his upper body to lift himself up to get up the steps in order for him to access his polling place. Once he was inside the polling place, he was not given a wheelchair accessible polling booth. Once again, he had to use his arms to lift himself up to see the ballot and, while balancing on his arms, simultane-ously attempt to cast his ballot.")

Looking over my list, I can't help but notice that only one of my formative experiences, the Bicentennial, came with balloons and cake. Being a little kid that year, visiting the Freedom Train with its dramat-ically lit facsimile of the Declaration, learn-ing that I lived in the greatest, most fair and wise and lovely place on earth, made a big impression on me. I think it's one of the reasons I'm so fond of President Lin-coln. Because he stared down the crap. More than anyone in the history of the country, he faced up to our most troubling contradiction—that a nation born in free-dom would permit the enslavement of human beings—and never once stopped believing in the Declaration of Indepen-dence's ideals, never stopped trying to make them come true.

On a Sunday night in November, I walked up to the New York Public Library to see the Emancipation Proclamation. On loan from the National Archives, the docu-ment was in town for three days. They put it in a glass case in a small, dark room. Being alone with old pieces of paper and one guard in an alcove at the library was nice and quiet. I stared at Abraham Lin-coln's signature for a long time. I stood there, thinking what one is supposed to think: This is the paper he held in his hands and there is the ink that came from his pen, and when the ink dried the slaves were freed. Except look at the date, Janu-ary 1, 1863. The words wouldn't come true for a couple of years, which, I'm guessing, is a long time when another person owns your body. But I love how Lincoln dated the document, noting that it was signed "in the year of our Lord, one thousand eight hundred and sixty-three, and of the Independence of the United States of America the eighty-seventh." Fourscore and seven years before, is the wonderfully arrogant implication, something as mirac-ulous as the virgin birth happened on this earth, and the calendar should reflect that.

The Emancipation Proclamation is a per-fect American artifact to me—a good deed that made a lot of other Americans mad enough to kill. I think that's why the Civil War is my favorite American metaphor. I'm so much more comfortable when we're bickering with each other than when we have to link arms and fight a common enemy. But right after September 11, the TV was full of unity. Congressmen, political enemies from both houses of Congress, from both sides of the aisle, stood together on the Capitol steps and sang "God Bless America." At the end of the memorial service at the National Cathedral, President and Mrs. Carter chat-ted like old friends with President and Mrs. Ford. Rudolph Giuliani, the mayor of New York, kissed his former opponent Senator Hillary Clinton on the cheek as the New York congressional delegation toured the World Trade Center disaster area.

compose ▪ design ▪ advocate

In September, people across the country and all over the world—including, bless them, the Canadians, and they are born sick of us—were singing the American national anthem. And when I heard their voices I couldn't help but remember the last time I had sung that song. I was one of hundreds of people standing in the mud on the Washington Mall on January 20 at the inauguration of George W. Bush. Everyone standing there in the cold rain had very strong feelings. It was either/or. Either you beamed through the ceremony with smiles of joy, or you wept through it all with tears of rage. I admit, I was one of the people there who needed a hankie when it was over. At the end of the ceremony, it was time to sing the national anthem. Some of the dissenters refused to join in. Such was their anger at the country at that moment they couldn't find it in their hearts to sing. But I was standing there next to my friend Jack, and Jack and I put our hands over our hearts and sang that song loud. Because we love our country too. Because we wouldn't have been standing there, wouldn't have driven down to Washington just to burst into tears if we didn't care so very, very much about how this country is run.

When the anthem ended—land of the free, home of the brave—Jack and I walked to the other end of the Mall to the Lincoln Memorial to read Lincoln's Second Inaugural Address, the speech Lincoln gave at the end of the Civil War about how "we must bind up the nation's wounds." It seems so quaint to me now, after September, after CNN started doing hourly live remotes from St. Vincent's, my neighborhood hospital, that I would conceive of a wound as being peeved about who got to be president.

My ideal picture of citizenship will always be an argument, not a sing-along. I did not get it out of a civics textbook either. I got it from my parents. My mom and dad disagree with me about almost everything. I do not share their religion or their political affiliation. I get on their nerves sometimes. But, and this is the most important thing they taught me, so what? We love each other. My parents and I have been through so much and known each other for so long, share so many in-jokes and memories, our differences of opinion on everything from gun control to Robin Williams movies hardly matter at all. Plus, our disagreements make us appreciate the things we have in common all the more. When I call Republican Senator Orrin Hatch's office to say that I admire something he said about stem cell research, I am my parents' daughter. Because they have always enjoyed playing up the things we do have in common, like Dolly Parton, ibuprofen. Maybe sometimes, in quiet moments of reflection, my mom would prefer that I not burn eternally in the flames of hell when I die, but otherwise she wants me to follow my own heart.

I will say that, in September, atheism was a lonely creed. Not because atheists have no god to turn to, but because everyone else forgot about us. At a televised interfaith memorial service at Yankee Stadium on September 23, Muslim, Christian, Jewish, Sikh, and Hindu clerics spoke to their fellow worshipers. Placido Domingo sang "Ave Maria" for the mayor. I waited in vain for someone like me to stand up and say that the only thing those of us who don't believe in god have to believe in is other people and that New York City is the best place there ever was for a godless person to practice her moral code. I think it has something to do with the crowded sidewalks and subways. Walking to and from the hardware store requires the push and pull of selfishness and selflessness, taking turns between getting out of someone's way and them getting out of yours, waiting for a dog to move, helping a stroller up steps, protecting the eyes from runaway umbrellas. Walking in New York is a battle of the wills, a balance of aggression and kindness. I'm not saying it's always easy. The occasional "Watch where you're going, bitch" can, I admit, put a crimp in one's day. But I believe all that choreography has made me a better person. The other day, in the subway at 5:30, I was crammed into my sweaty, crabby fellow citizens, and I kept whispering under my breath "we the people, we the people" over and over again, reminding myself we're all in this together and they had as much right—exactly as much right—as I to be in the muggy underground on their way to wherever they were on their way to.

Once, headed uptown on the 9 train, I noticed a sign posted by the Manhattan Transit Authority advising subway riders who might become ill in the train. The sign asked that the suddenly infirm inform another passenger or get out at the next stop and approach the stationmaster. Do not, repeat, do not pull the emergency brake, the sign said, as this will only delay aid. Which was all very logical, but for the following proclamation at the bottom of the sign, something along the lines of "If you are sick, you will not be left alone." This strikes me as not only kind, not only comforting, but the very epitome of civilization, good government, i.e., the crux of the societal impulse. Banding together, pooling our taxes, not just making trains, not just making trains that move underground, not just making trains that move underground with surprising efficiency at a fair price—but posting on said trains a notification of such surprising compassion and thoughtfulness, I found myself scanning the faces of my fellow passengers, hoping for fainting, obvious fevers, at the very least a sneeze so that I might offer a tissue.

ANALYZING
being partly cloudy . . .

- **Discuss with others:** Why do you think Vowell starts the essay with her discussion of the movie? What do we learn about how she thinks from her discussion of the movie, and how does that set us up for the rest of her essay?

- **Discuss with others:** Vowell moves from talking about the movie to talking about the attacks on the World Trade Center and the Pentagon on September 11, 2001. In the first two paragraphs of this part of her essay, how does she approach the events of that day and their aftermath? What is the issue she addresses in those paragraphs?

- **Discuss with others:** Vowell tells us she went to George W. Bush's inauguration and was patriotically moved. Look at the details of the story. How does what she tells us affect our view of her?

- **Discuss with others:** If Vowell's view of patriotism is "partly cloudy," does that mean she does not have a clear understanding of what patriotism is?

- **Write informally:** Vowell ends her essay talking about a sign she read in the New York subway instructing people how they might help a fellow passenger who's sick. Why might she end an essay on patriotism with this story?

- **Write informally:** Toward the end of the essay (and several times) Vowell says that her "ideal picture of citizenship will always be an argument," and yet in the last few pages she implies that kindness toward strangers is connected to patriotism in some way. Is this a contradiction? Assuming it is not a contradiction in her eyes, explain how she might reconcile these two ideas.

thinking through production

- Develop a design plan and then produce a kit of materials that elementary school children can use to understand and to get started being advocates, active citizens engaged with the issues that matter to them.

- Research the organizations on, connected to, or near your campus that provide opportunities for civic involvement and being an advocate. Put together an annotated list of the organizations that someone new to campus could use to decide where to get involved. Produce the annotated list as a website, extended brochure, or small booklet.

- The readings and website in this chapter discuss the ideas of citizenship, success, and freedom—sometimes overtly, sometimes implicitly.

  Pick one of those three ideas, and look for how it is discussed or used as a guiding value through the readings and the website. Write a paragraph summary of what is said about the idea in the readings and website. Do summarize; try to keep your own opinions out of this writing.

  Break into groups based on the idea you want to discuss further and talk about your response to how citizenship, success, or freedom was discussed in the reading: with what do you agree, what do you find lacking, and what you find just plain wrong?

  Also discuss what role you see visual, oral, and written communication playing in the creation/promotion/continuation/suppression of the idea in our daily lives. Report back to class.

  Use what you learned to design a visual explanation of Citizenship, Success, or Freedom. (Consider a poster, flyer, comic, drawing, painting, photomontage, photo-essay, video . . .).

- Research the life of someone no longer living whom you and others consider to be a strong advocate. Design, produce, and test a memorial to that person and her or his work.

  Be creative with "memorial." Research memorials: look at statues on your campus and in your town, but also look at television shows that honor individuals, encyclopedia entries, bulletin boards, websites, and so on. What media will help you best engage others with the life and work of the person you research—and also persuade them to take up advocacy themselves?

- There are more "Thinking Through Production" activities in the online chapter 5 resources at www.ablongman.com/wysocki

PRODUCING A USEFUL PIECE OF COMMUNICATION FOR A NON-PROFIT ORGANIZATION

These steps describe one way you can use research and the rhetorical process of design to produce communication for a nonprofit group. This sort of project can be particularly effective if you work with others from your class in small teams; a whole class can take on this project, dividing the research and recommending different communications possibilities to the organization.

1   Contact a non profit group whose work you respect. Explain to them the process you are undertaking, to be sure they are willing to work with you—and that they need you to do the work described below.

2   To gain background for designing communications that best support the group, research their purpose and history. You can do this work through reading materials produced by the group, and/or through interviewing directors, employees, or volunteers. (Use pages 256–258 of this book to help you prepare for interviews, and be sure you check with the group's director(s), to let them know your purposes in doing the interviews and to be sure it is okay.) Look for a mission statement in the group's materials. Also look online and in the library for anything that people outside the group have written about the group. (If the group is well established, there might also be information about them in local library archives.)

3   To know how the group has represented itself in the past, and to see where and how they might communicate more effectively, collect the group's brochures, flyers, or posters; explore their website. Depending on the group, you might be able to find speeches made by people within the group. Any communications produced by or about the group will help you.

4   If you can, interview people served by the group who are the audience for the communications you have collected. Ask questions that help you understand how the audience members respond to the communications.

5   Analyze all the information you have collected through your research, with the goal of making recommendations to the group about how they could improve the communications they already have or perhaps could open up new directions for communication. This is rhetorical analysis you are doing—examining communication in light of its audience, purpose, and context—so use pages 320–326 of this book to help you do your analysis.

6   Write a formal research paper—for your class, alone or in a small team—in which you use your analysis as a basis for recommending specific new communication the group could use. (For example, you could recommend that the group add to its website a section specifically addressing teenagers or that they produce a brochure better explaining their application process.)

7   Use feedback you receive to your paper to prepare a short (10–15 minute) oral presentation, with supporting visual materials, for the director and/or other pertinent members of the group. In the oral presentation, make your recommendations for how the group can improve its communications. Use chapter 8 on oral communication to help you prepare your presentation, and present a full design plan (as we describe in chapters 2–4).

8   At your oral presentation, ask for feedback to help you strengthen your proposal. Unless you have interviewed and worked with the audience for the communications you recommend, the group's director or other workers are in the best position to help you refine how you are addressing that audience.

9   If the group approves what you recommend, produce the communication you have designed.

compose ▪ design ▪ advocate

researching for advocacy and argument

You do research in order to get yourself into a new position, to discover different views on a subject, or to learn about new and different possibilities for doing what needs to be done.

In chapters 3 and 4, we mentioned that as you plan your communication with others, you need to learn more about—to research—your purpose, your context, your audience, and the range of strategies and media available to you. We also talked about specific kinds of research, connected with advocacy work or with work you are doing in other classes. And of course there are still other kinds of research. Every time you decide what movie to go see, plan a trip to another country, or get ready to take the DMV test—any time you look for information or resources to help you make decisions—you do research.

In this chapter we write mostly about the contexts of academic research projects—the kinds you will be asked to do in college—and the products such research leads to: papers and reports. The research you do in school can be as simple as performing an online keyword search and checking out the results, or it can be as involved as designing and carrying out a laboratory experiment whose results will fill in a gap in existing knowledge. Often, however, the contexts of classroom research can seem vague—to whom are you writing, and why?—and so in this chapter we try to make those contexts more concrete and intriguing.

research, argument, and advocacy

A large part of advocacy happens through research. It can be through research that you learn of the issues or organizations to which you want to devote time and energy. But anytime you decide to make something happen through the texts you produce—whether those texts be print, online, or spoken—you need to have solid support for what you advocate. You need to be able to communicate accurately about what has happened in the past or about what is happening now if others are to take seriously any recommendations you make for change. You can only communicate accurately—and so you can only responsibly represent others—if you have done research, if you have learned to the best of your abilities all that you can about a situation or issue.

It is by doing research that you come to understand how others have stood in the past—and so it is by doing research that you can learn positions you can take or possibly make in the world.

what research is

Consider "research" as "re-search": emphasize the root meaning "research" as *searching again*. It might even be better if we had—or invented—a word that meant "deep search" because when you research you acknowledge that you do not know everything you need in a given context. You research, that is, when you need more depth in an area or when you need expert knowledge about what something is, what happened, how something works, what others have said or done. You research in order to add depth to what is already known about something.

You might think that research is only about going to the library or looking online for what others have written. That is certainly a part of research. But when you want to add depth to what you—and others—already know, your purpose should guide you: the library might be necessary, but so might an informal interview or taking photographs. When you interview or take photographs to figure out or support your arguments about an event or organization, you are just as much researching as when you read an encyclopedia.

ARGUMENTATIVE RESEARCH PAPERS
You ought to be able to tell from what we've written on these pages that the approach to research we offer is aimed at helping you develop an argument for taking a particular position on a topic. You will need to make judgments, and give reasons for the judgments.

the ethics of being a researcher

The word "ethics" is connected to the word "ethos" (a strategy we introduced in chapter 4 and discuss throughout this book). Both words are connected to an ancient Greek word meaning "dwelling." As we said above, when you research you are adding depth to what is already known. But another way to look at what you do when you research is that with new knowledge you strengthen your ties to other people because knowing more about what something is, about what happened, or about how something works changes how you go about living with other people. Knowledge has effects—practical and moral—on yourself and other people.

Given what we've been saying about ethics, it should be clear that each step in this chapter has an ethical dimension. For instance, you need to make sure that what you say you discovered is accurate (see the section on "Evaluating your sources"). You need to tell the truth about what you discover. You need to use your research results responsibly. You need to respect your sources and your readers. And you need to adopt an ethical attitude as a researcher, which means being open to what the research shows you and being willing to change your position if you cannot support it through the research you do. This also means treating beliefs and positions like hypotheses, not like unassailable truths.

Put otherwise, research may feel like something you do alone in a dark library late at night away from the others—and that may be part of research—but that does not mean research is private. **Research is social action.** Through our research we build stronger shared foundations with others and our communities.

MOTIVATIONS FOR RESEARCH

Motivations to do research come from inside and outside. Are you going to the library for government documents because your supervisor asked you to write a report that requires examining the current governmental policies and laws? Or are you going to city hall to look for when and how often a piece of land has changed hands because your neighborhood community group wants to buy land for a park? Have you just discovered you like jazz music and want to learn more about where it comes from and how its sounds have changed over time—or do you have a class research project?

If the motivation to research does not feel like your own, then figure out how to get yourself excited about it. It may be enough motivation—if you are working for a grade—to aim for a good one. But you will do even better work—both for yourself and others—if you develop your own excitement. Do not stop researching possible topics until you shape one that helps you learn what matters to you, that sets you up to build communications that do what you value.

ANALYZING research

■ **Write informally, then discuss:** Describe what you already know about research and write down in a list all the research you've already done—in school, at work, at home, and elsewhere.

Combine your lists with another person and then put the items of your lists into categories that show many different kinds of research you've done.

Describe problems you've run into in the past doing research.

Describe successes you've had with research.

■ **Write informally:** Choose any of the examples from the chapters of opinion pieces, interviews, or essays, or choose one of the longer comics examples. What sort of research did the people who composed the example do? How do you see their research reflected in what they produced? How does their research help persuade you (or not) to read and consider the arguments being made?

designing rhetorical research

To the right are steps you can use to complete a research project. As with any process—but especially with research—these steps look neat on paper but are less so in reality. Sometimes you have to start over when a line of research leads you nowhere or when you simply cannot find anything interesting or motivating. Sometimes you have a purpose in mind but then when you get into the nitty-gritty of writing you find that you have to change your purpose, do more research, and start writing all over again.

Modify this process to make it your own—or develop your own. Pay attention to the actions and ways of thinking (or productively procrastinating) that help you most in developing communications that achieve what matters to you.

In academic writing, the process is one of continually trying to state your overall argument—your purpose—in as clear and precise a manner as possible. You need to be able to state your purpose to yourself, so that you can decide what research you need to do and how to choose among different possible writing strategies. You need to be able to state the purpose clearly in your writing, too, in order to shape an introduction, body, and conclusion to a paper that others will read thoughtfully and with understanding.

In what follows, we suggest approaches to help you keep focused on the goals of academic writing, which certainly include getting a good grade but which also include making careful, supported arguments for positions you want others to consider respectfully.

1 Develop an initial question about what you want to find out.

2 Use your question to help you figure out what you need to research and learn to write your paper.

3 Carry out your research.

4 Use the research to help develop and test a design plan.

5 Produce and test your communication.

compose ▪ *design* ▪ *advocate*

1
a research project
developing an initial question

DEVELOPING A QUESTION TO ANSWER THROUGH RESEARCH

One way to develop a statement of purpose for a research paper is to get very clear about the question you want to answer through your research. Combining this question with audience and context can help you develop a solid statement of purpose that will help you figure out how to proceed creatively with your research.

Research can really begin with a research question, a question that motivates you to do the research and gives you direction, a question that opens up a complex subject and shows you what you need to do to research your subject successfully, a question that links you to what interests other people.

Research questions evolve as you do the research. Questions lead to other questions, and early answers sometimes lead to new and revised questions.

The question you develop will vary depending on the kind of research you do. You may be doing "friendly" research, for instance, tracing a family genealogy, which calls for an eye for detail rather than a critical eye. But you may also be researching what happened in Palestine in 1948, and that requires a critical eye because there are conflicting accounts of events.

One scheme for developing questions
People who study critical thinking have devised a scheme for questions to help you figure out directions you need to go; this scheme is based on how lawyers have learned to focus the point they are arguing. This schema says that you can ask:

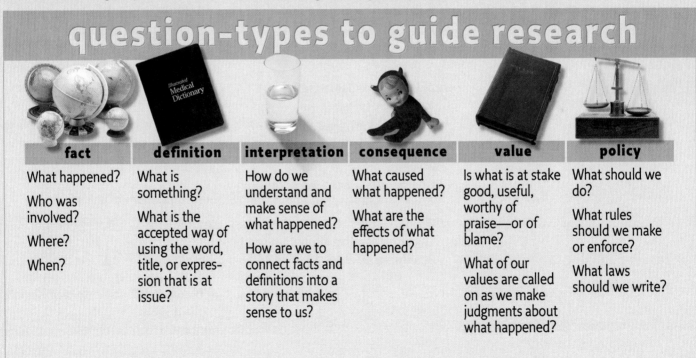

question-types to guide research

fact	definition	interpretation	consequence	value	policy
What happened? Who was involved? Where? When?	What is something? What is the accepted way of using the word, title, or expression that is at issue?	How do we understand and make sense of what happened? How are we to connect facts and definitions into a story that makes sense to us?	What caused what happened? What are the effects of what happened?	Is what is at stake good, useful, worthy of praise—or of blame? What of our values are called on as we make judgments about what happened?	What should we do? What rules should we make or enforce? What laws should we write?

How others have used this scheme to develop questions

Your immediate purpose in writing a research paper is to demonstrate to your teacher that you can (or can learn to) write such a paper—but you need to develop for yourself a stronger purpose, one that intrigues you. This is where you can use the question-generating scheme we just described, to get yourself interested by finding a question that matters to you.

In a class that Anne taught, Andrew Rajala, a mechanical engineering major, started working toward a research paper by jotting down his initial sense of purpose: he wanted to get others thinking about the loss of manufacturing jobs in the United States. Andrew was interested in this question because his family has been involved in manufacturing for several generations. Here are the kinds of questions that such an initial sense of purpose can generate.

Here are **questions of fact** about the loss of manufacturing jobs in the U.S.:

- How many jobs have been lost?
- Are the jobs being lost in one area of the country or all areas?
- Is the rate of job loss increasing or decreasing?
- Are the jobs simply disappearing, or are they going elsewhere?
- Who makes the decisions that end in job loss?

Here are **questions of definition:**

- What counts as a "manufacturing job"?
- Are manufacturing jobs different in any way from other kinds of jobs in this country?
- What has to happen for a job to be counted as being "lost" in the U.S.?

Here are **questions of interpretation:**

- What causes job losses in the manufacturing sector in the U.S.?
- Why should people care about job loss?
- Is job loss useful in any way to the companies that move their jobs to other countries?
- Is there any way that job loss can be useful to the U.S.?

Here are **questions of consequence:**

- Aside from the loss of a paycheck, what are other consequences of an individual losing a job?
- What are the concrete effects of job loss, besides someone losing a job?
- Who in a community is affected by the loss of one job?
- How is the country's economy overall affected by job loss?
- Do our actions as individuals in this country contribute to job loss in any way?

Here are **questions of value:**

- Why should we value keeping manufacturing jobs in the U.S.?
- What values lie underneath the willingness of companies to lay off workers?
- What values lie underneath the willingness of companies to move jobs elsewhere?
- What kinds of values would we have to change as individuals and as a country to keep jobs in the U.S.?

Here are **questions of policy:**

- What legal policies encourage companies to move manufacturing jobs out of the U.S.?
- What kinds of legal policies would encourage companies to keep jobs in the U.S.?

compose ▪ design ▪ advocate

TURNING GENERAL QUESTIONING INTO A PRELIMINARY RESEARCH QUESTION

By looking at which questions interested him the most, Andrew could see that he was interested in the effects of job loss on individuals and their families, but also on what we can each do as individual citizens and as a country to stop job loss.

He pulled his concerns into one general research question to help him get his thinking started:

> What is causing manufacturing job loss in the United States, who is affected by it, and what can the average person do about it?

You can see that Andrew has pulled together an overall question that is a combination of a question of interpretation, a question of consequence, and a question of policy. This is perfectly fine—and the overall question (as you will see in steps 2 and 3) helps Andrew focus the matter of his paper so that he knows what he needs to find out if he is going to develop some sort of answer to the question. The other questions listed on the previous page don't disappear now; in addition to the research question above, Andrew can use the other questions to be sure he is finding out enough—as you'll see in step 2.

ANALYZING
research questions

■ **Discuss and write with others:** With a partner, use the questions of fact, definition, interpretation, consequence, value, and policy we just described to develop preliminary research questions about the following topics:

- the decline in the frog population around the world
- the military draft in the U.S.
- why women earn less money on average than men in the U.S.
- music downloading
- the drinking age in the U.S.
- religious affiliations in the U.S. over the last century

Use the questions you generate to develop and write down a preliminary research question for each topic.

Compare your question with that of others in class. Discuss what interests you in the potential research—and what doesn't—and why. How can you modify the question to make it as interesting to you—and to your identified audience—as possible?

■ **Write and discuss with others:** Choose a topic that interests you, and write down as many questions as you can about it using the questions of fact, definition, interpretation, consequence, value, and policy.

Exchange your list of questions with others in class. How many questions can you add to the lists of others? Make this trade with two or three other people so that you get a wide range of questions.

Based on the questions you generate and that your classmates contribute, develop a potential research question. Show your questions to others, and get their feedback on how effective they think your approach is going to be.

■ **Write and discuss with others:** Imagine studying the organization Mothers Against Drunk Driving (or another organization you know) in your economics class, your history class, and your composition class. With a partner, come up with questions about the organization using the questions of fact, definition, interpretation, consequence, value, and policy scheme we just described.

Compare your questions with others in class and decide which have the most research potential for the different classes we listed above: which look to you like they might lead to interesting results in each area—and why?

a research project
using the questions to determine what you need to research

THE OBVIOUS RESEARCH INTO THE TOPIC

Andrew's question—

What is causing manufacturing job loss in the United States, who is affected by it, and what can the average person do about it?

—indicates several obvious issues Andrew needs to research. He needs to find out about:

- the causes of job loss in this country
- the effects on people of job loss in this country
- the actions individuals can take

It may seem ridiculously silly to lay out such obvious matters, but in doing research **it is important to be as obvious as possible**. The best research papers are the papers in which writers make absolutely clear what they are arguing—to themselves as well as to their readers.

Writers who can say to themselves exactly what it is they need to know to answer their question—and who can stay focused on what they asked, with room for discovery of cool additional information to carry the research into deeper and more intriguing questions and directions—set themselves up to write the papers teachers like: focused and well-supported.

NOT SO OBVIOUS RESEARCH: RESEARCHING YOUR AUDIENCE

Research is only worth doing if you learn something from it—and research papers are only worth writing if your audience learns something as well. Because each of us reads or watches differing amounts of news from different sources and is interested in different topics, you cannot count on your audience for a class research paper—the other people in your class—knowing anything, or even caring, about the question you are asking.

How do you learn what they know and care about? You ask them. You can do this formally, by asking your audience to fill in a written survey sheet through which you ask what they know about your topic and what aspects of it matter to them. You can also do this through informal conversations. Sitting down with a group of others to chat about your topic can be a relaxing way to learn quite a lot about how others think. You can also use your topic as a ground for conversation with friends over lunch or dinner—anyone who could be in your class can help you learn how others think about your topic and consequently how you can shape your writing so that others can be persuaded to care about your topic as you do.

NOT SO OBVIOUS RESEARCH INTO THE TOPIC

After you research your audience's knowledge and attitudes toward your topic, you are in a position to figure out what you need to research in addition to the obvious directions suggested by your research question. For example, by chatting informally about his topic with others in class, Andrew learned that were he only to research the three directions indicated by his research question, he would not have all the information he needed. By looking through the whole list of questions he generated on his way to generating a research question, and asking if any touch on what his audience thinks and believes, Andrew understands that he also needs to:

- Research how many jobs have been lost, and where, and whether the trend of job loss looks like it will continue, in order to persuade his classmates that this topic could affect them when they graduate.

- Research how job loss happens, in order to be able to explain to his readers what it is they can do to keep job loss from happening.

- Research what about manufacturing jobs should make them matter to those in his audience.

compose ▪ design ▪ advocate

3 a research project
carrying out your research

STAGES OF RESEARCH

You have a research question, and you've learned what your audience does or does not know and does or does not care about relative to your question. It is time to research what others—experts, opinion writers, people who have experienced something relative to your topic—know or think about the topic. As you pursue your research, keep in mind that there are two stages of researching, stages that don't relate in an orderly manner.

1 You research with an open mind to learn more, to see if there are other positions on your topic that matter to you or other possible arguments. Maybe as you research broadly and look into topics you narrow your question or shift its focus.

2 When you feel that your position is focused, you research to find specific support to make your argument.

The first stage needs to come first, but it may sound as though you then move automatically into the second stage and that's it. But often you will think you have a solid position on your topic, but as you research you'll realize that your position changes—and you need to learn more through stepping back into the first stage.

When you are in the first stage, you read just to take in general information, to let your thoughts move back and forth through facts, ideas, and positions put forward by others, to get a sense of a position you yourself want to take; for example, as Andrew does his initial research, he is just simply looking to see who is affected by job loss and how it happens. As he reads this way, he can keep asking himself what he thinks, and what other opinions are persuading him, and why.

When you know your position, you can look quickly through sources, seeking only the specific support you need.

If you know what stage you are in as you research, you know what attitude you need to take toward reading and looking.

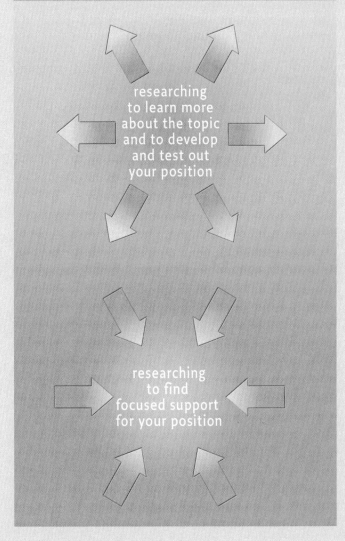

stages in research

researching to learn more about the topic and to develop and test out your position

researching to find focused support for your position

WHAT TO RESEARCH?

Once you have the questions you need to research, you can start thinking about where to research.

We assume you've had to write research papers before and that you understand that you need to find sources that you will cite in your paper in support of your arguments. We offer you an approach for thinking about what sorts of sources will be most useful to you depending on the directions your research is taking.

Instead of just taking your questions and plugging them straight into Google (which we will discuss as an approach), there are other approaches that can help you more reliably find trustworthy, appropriate sources.

The categories into which your questions fit can indicate where to research:

what to research

fact	definition	interpretation	consequence	value	policy
statistics	dictionaries	editorials	statistics	organizational mission statements	governmental decisions
"hard" news sources	disciplinary dictionaries	opinion pieces	historical accounts	results of votes	organizational policy statements & decisions
government or organizational documents		partisan news sources	photographs of the aftermath of events	surveys & polls	business records
first-hand accounts (interviews, autobiographies)		stories	the items in the "interpretation" column	position statements	trial decisions
photographs of events		artwork: movies, novels, short stories		the items in the "interpretation" column	
trial transcripts		position statements			
surveys & polls		biographies			
government archives					
atlases & encyclopedias					

This chart is not all encompassing, and some may disagree over exactly where some of these items fit—but nonetheless this chart can get you started doing your research in useful directions.

compose ▪ design ▪ advocate

USING THE "WHAT TO RESEARCH" CHART TO THINK ABOUT WHERE TO LOOK

As we indicated in step 1, Andrew's question—

> What is causing manufacturing job loss in the United States, who is affected by it, and what can the average person do about it?

—is a combination of a question of interpretation, a question of consequence, and a question of policy.

To help him think in more depth about his question and find support that will help him produce a persuasive paper, the "What to Research" chart helps Andrew see that he can search for useful information by looking for and in the kinds of sources listed under "interpretation," "consequence," and "policy" in the chart; furthermore, the additional questions Andrew saw that he needed to ask—from the work he did in step 2—require him to ask questions of fact (how many jobs are being lost) as well as of interpretation (how job loss happens and why his audience should care about manufacturing job loss).

CHOOSING THE KINDS OF SOURCES TO PURSUE

Eliminating possibilities

It may look to you, from the lists, as though you are going to have to do hours and hours of looking in order to peruse all the kinds of sources that can help you think in more detail about your question. But your question can also help you eliminate some kinds of sources.

Andrew needs facts to persuade his audience that manufacturing job loss is indeed happening in numbers that ought to concern them, and that this is an ongoing condition. As he looks down the list of kinds of sources to seek, he can see that statistics—probably from governmental sources—will be most useful to him. He doesn't need to look in encyclopedias or atlases for that kind of information, and first-hand accounts—although they could show some of the factual consequences of job loss—will not help him make the case that manufacturing job loss is happening to too many people now.

Thinking creatively about possibilities

As Andrew looks over the lists, however, and thinks about first-hand accounts, he thinks that such accounts could help add *pathos* to his argument: by seeing how job loss affects individuals, Andrew's audience might have a better feeling for the consequences of job loss—and might see how it could affect them, too.

ANALYZING
what you need to research

■ **Write and discuss with others:** With a partner, look at the preliminary research questions below; decide what kinds of questions they are (fact, definition, interpretation, consequence, value, policy—or some combination). Make a list of the kinds of sources someone who was asking these questions should turn to for research assistance:

- In what countries do men and women earn close to the same amounts of average pay? What social and working conditions encourage such equitable pay?
- How are television shows rated? How do the ratings affect the kinds of shows that appear?
- How are environmental decisions made about Antarctica?
- What factors led to the popularity of spoken word poetry and poetry slams in past years?
- How is "gun control" different from "gun rights"?
- What causes mad cow disease? How does mad cow disease move into humans? Are current laws about meat production sufficient to keep us safe?
- Is it a good idea to allow young children to play video games?

where to research

in the library

books   the stacks   maps

microfiche   encyclopedias

journals

databases

reference materials

newspapers   government webpages

government documents   organizational webpages

national organizations

business organizations   events

nonprofits   local government

international organizations

governmental groups   clubs & social organizations

community-based organizations

faith-based organizations

private organizations   local organizations

meetings

in organizations

online

search engines

blogs

social networking tools

personal memories

stories

interviews

visible living patterns

in neighborhoods

WHERE TO RESEARCH?

Ah, we know that your first impetus is to sit at your desk and Google some keywords tied to your research. We all do this—there are good reasons and good ways to do this. And we'll discuss this shortly. But keep in mind that when you want to do thorough, creative, persuasive research you need to stretch a bit.

In the illustration above we've listed places for carrying out research—and what you can find in those places, which overlap.

On the next pages we step through when and how to take advantage of all the research resources listed above.

USING THE LIBRARY

You probably know how to walk into your school or local library and use the online catalog to look for books that have something to do with your topic. And this is one way to take advantage of the library.

But if you really want to take advantage of the library's riches, and until you yourself are a reference librarian, it is a good idea to ask a reference librarian at your library for help in carrying out your research. Reference librarians know specific resources and directions to follow—and they therefore can save you a lot of time and help you find solid, useful support for your research.

preparing to get help from a reference librarian

A research question sets you up to get great help from a reference librarian. For example, Andrew can use his question and his knowledge about what he needs to research to ask a librarian for specific help; he can say:

- "Hi, I need to find some statistics about how many manufacturing jobs have been lost in the U.S. in the past 10 years. What are the best places you can suggest for finding that information?"

- "I have some ideas about what's causing recent manufacturing job loss in the U.S.—but do you know any sources that are more likely than others to have opinion pieces on this?"

- "What sort of government sources or business reports would help me understand how companies make decisions about layoffs in the manufacturing industry?"

By preparing questions that combine his research question with the kind of sources that will help him answer the question, Andrew gives his reference librarian information that will help the librarian more easily and quickly pick out of the wide range of sources in the library those that will be most directly useful.

The reference librarian may point you to shelved books or journals, or may help you in searching online databases of journal and magazine articles, abstracts, and newspapers. The reference librarian *will* help you find sources you wouldn't otherwise.

semi-focused research in the library that encourages creative thinking

Use the library's catalog to get the names and locations of several books relating to your topic. Find the books, look through them to see if there is anything in them that might be useful—and then look at the books on the shelves right around the books you found. Because library books are organized by topic, the books on the shelves near the ones to which the catalog pointed you might be useful, too—and might be just enough off topic to suggest alternate approaches or a more fruitful direction for your questioning. (You can also do this in bookstores.)

ANALYZING
researching in the library

■ **Write and discuss with others:** With a partner, develop questions to ask a research librarian for each of the following preliminary research questions:

- In what countries do men and women earn close to the same amounts of average pay? What social and working conditions encourage such equitable pay?

- How are television shows rated? How do the ratings affect the kinds of shows that appear?

- How are environmental decisions made about Antarctica?

- What factors led to the popularity of spoken word poetry and poetry slams in past years?

- How is "gun control" different from "gun rights"?

- What causes mad cow disease? How does mad cow disease move into humans? Are current laws about meat production sufficient to keep us safe?

- Is it a good idea to allow young children to play video games?

RESEARCHING ONLINE

Chances are you have a favorite search engine you use for all sorts of different searches. To use a search engine most effectively for preparing for a research paper, however, you need to be both focused and broadly creative.

Coming up with useful terms for a keyword search

You'd think that all Andrew would have to do is enter "manufacturing job loss" into a search engine. And that could indeed turn up several thousand hits. But would you want several thousand hits to explore?

Given that Andrew knows the kinds of questions he needs to ask, here are ways he can focus his searching so that he is more likely to get fewer but more helpful responses:

- "manufacturing job loss U.S." will ensure the only information that comes up is about the particular country with which Andrew is concerned for this paper.
- "manufacturing job loss U.S. statistics" is more likely to help Andrew find the supporting numbers he needs—just as "manufacturing job loss U.S. causes" is more likely to help with finding causes.
- "manufacturing job loss U.S. policies" gets at the last part of Andrew's research question. "manufacturing job loss U.S. government policies" focuses the search even more.

When search terms don't yield useful results

Sometimes your search terms get you no or unhelpful results—which may be disheartening but which also means you just need to try other terms. In addition, research that gets you the most interesting and persuasive supporting information—and that encourages you to think in appropriate depth about your topic—doesn't stop with one set of search terms.

To develop other search terms, try this:

- Write down the words for your search that seem most obvious to you (in Andrew's case, that would be "manufacturing," "job," and "loss")—and then list as many synonyms or related words as possible. For "job" Andrew could write "work," "career," and "employment"; for "loss," there is "decline," "decrease," and "disappearance." For "manufacturing" Andrew could use "fabrication" or "production"—but there should also be online information about the various specific kinds of manufacturing jobs that are being lost, such as in the shoe and clothing industries, in computer and telecommunications equipment, and so on. By trying different combinations of these terms, Andrew is likely to find a wide array of information—much of which ought to be helpful.

ANALYZING
online research

■ **Write and discuss with others:** For each of the preliminary research questions below, work with a partner to develop search terms you could use in an online search:

- In what countries do men and women earn close to the same amounts of average pay? What social and working conditions encourage such equitable pay?

- How are television shows rated? How do the ratings affect the kinds of shows that appear?

- How are environmental decisions made about Antarctica?

- What factors led to the popularity of spoken word poetry and poetry slams in past years?

- How is "gun control" different from "gun rights"?

- What causes mad cow disease? How does mad cow disease move into humans? Are current laws about meat production sufficient to keep us safe?

- Is it a good idea to allow young children to play video games?

☐ In the online chapter 6 resources (at www.ablongman.com/wysocki) are links to online research tools that can help you look in places you might not find through the usual search engines.

RESEARCHING (IN) ORGANIZATIONS

Sometimes your research question indicates you need to look into an organization as part of your research (as when your initial question is "How did the National Rifle Association become so powerful?" or "Why did Mothers Against Drunk Driving work to change the drinking age in 1984?"). Sometimes, as happened to Andrew when he stumbled upon a mention of the National Association of Manufacturers in an article, you'll find an organization that ought to be useful to you in your research.

Most organizations now have websites, where you can find information, but—nonetheless—sometimes you might need to telephone or write to an organization.

What to research in organizations

Here is a checklist of things you might need to learn about an organization. You may not need to look into everything on the list, given your purpose, but it is always better to know a little too much about the organization rather than too little.

❑ history
❑ founding documents
❑ mission statement
❑ legal status
❑ structure
❑ leadership
❑ membership
❑ decision-making processes
❑ finances
❑ tax status
❑ promotional materials/publicity
❑ role in the community
❑ ways it is perceived by others
❑ adversaries & rival organizations
❑ affiliated organizations
❑ events sponsored
❑ projects undertaken
❑ past successes and failures
❑ vision for the future

Don't forget to look outside the organization to what has been said and written about the organization, and especially to talk to and listen to people affected by what the organization does.

Also, remember as you research organizations that most often they want others to have a positive view of them—which means that some materials may present only a positive view of the organization.

Finding information in organizations

When Andrew found mention of the National Association of Manufacturers, he realized the organization might have not only statistics about manufacturing jobs but also opinion pieces on what causes job loss. Andrew checked their website and read the organization's mission statement—which told him the particular bias of the organization toward this topic (as we'll discuss more in the next pages). With that in mind, he knows that he must present this information carefully—but he does find useful statistics about why companies are moving their jobs out of the U.S.

RESEARCHING IN COMMUNITIES AND NEIGHBORHOODS

Your decision to research in a community or neighborhood depends on your research question. For example, about an hour from our university is a town that until very recently was dependent on a factory; when the factory closed, everyone working there lost their jobs, of course—and had Andrew time and a car, and a way to get an introduction to people still living in the town, going there to interview people would have helped him learn directly who is affected by job loss.

Researching in communities and neighborhoods can mean researching in local government, but it often means talking with people. People who have lived in a community for a long time can tell you about the history of the community or about their perspective on the effects of past events. Most anyone can tell you about the effects of present events or laws.

Look to chapter 8 for information on what to do to carry out helpful and respectful interviews with people.

Things to look out for

When you move into and through a community or neighborhood for the purposes of researching, the most important thing you need to think about is how your actions affect others. As you approach people, the way you approach them positions them and you in specific ways. You set up a relationship of a certain kind, and you want to make sure you are paying attention to that relationship. If you walk up to someone on the street and say, "Hey, I want to study you!" (we know this is too obvious, but it makes the point) you not only come out of the blue and so potentially disorient the person, but you position yourself as the one doing the studying and the person as an object of study. It might seem normal to you. It might seem normal to the other person. But it also might make that person feel weird.

Think about how you can talk with others so that they are participants in your research rather than distant objects of study.

In addition, be sure those you interview know exactly what your research is, and that they give you permission to record their words (either through taking notes or using a recorder of some kind) as well as to use their words or any photographs or other objects that support your work.

ANALYZING
researching in neighborhoods

■ **Write and discuss with others:** With a partner, decide which of the research questions below could be well supported by interviewing community members as research. How could you rephrase the questions—or reshape their purpose—so that interviewing would be useful?

- How has religious affiliation in the U.S. changed in the past century?

- Why did many men move to Canada to avoid the draft during the Vietnam War?

- How is music downloading affecting musicians?

- How does high school education shape the kinds of careers graduates decide to pursue?

- How do most families pay for the college education of their children?

Based on your judgments about the value of interviewing community members for the above research questions, what sorts of questions—about fact, definition, interpretation, consequence, value, policy, or some combination—seem to you the kinds of questions that best benefit from such interviews?

EVALUATING RESEARCH

How do you know if your sources will be appropriately persuasive, if your audience will accept them as reliable? Do the quotations you wish to make (whether of someone else's words, a photograph, a chart or graph) support your argument—while offering no extraneous information that might distract your readers from your argument? The chart below can help you start evaluating your sources.

evaluating research

fact

Would most everyone in your audience judge the facts to come from an objective and authoritative source?

Is it important that your audience judges the facts to come from an objective and authoritative source?

Is the fact appropriately timely? (How old can your facts be for an audience to find them still relevant?)

definition

Have you used a dictionary or source that your audience will accept as an authority?

Have you checked multiple dictionaries to be sure you are not using an idiosyncratic definition?

Can you use the whole definition and not some small and misleading aspect of it?

interpretation

Does the person you are quoting have the proper experience and knowledge to give a reliable interpretation?

Does the source making the interpretation you are quoting make the interpretation based on a limited view of events or from a wider perspective?

What beliefs or perspectives shape the interpretation? How can you address those beliefs or perspective in your writing?

consequence

Does the source you are quoting have the proper authority, experience, or knowledge to argue believably about the consequences being presented?

What beliefs or perspectives shape the the source's judgment of the consequences? How can you address those beliefs or perspective in your writing?

Does the source give an accounting of a limited or a wide range of consequences?

value

What gives this source the authority or position to argue for the values claimed? Why should your audience trust this source?

Using what criteria has the source you are quoting made the value judgments you wish to cite? Do you need to make these criteria explicit in your arguments, in order to persuade your audience?

policy

Have you gotten your statements of policy from the government or organizational sources where the policy originated—or from a similarly authoritative source?

Questions to ask of all sources

- Might others interpret your sources differently than you do? If you ask others how they understand a source that you consider to be very important, you'll find out whether others interpret the source differently than you do—and hence you'll find out whether you can use the source to support the arguments you want to make.

- Does your range of sources offer a fair view of the topic, offering multiple positions?

- Have you used the source with integrity? On movie posters, you sometimes see quotations of movie reviews—and there's no easy way to know whether the poster's claim that someone called the film " . . . brilliant!" isn't taken from the phrase, "This film is almost brilliant in its stupidity!" Once an audience finds out that a communicator has used a source in this way, they lose all trust in that person.

No source is perfect everywhere

When we stress to you the importance of evaluating your sources, we are not saying, "Hey, only trust the sources your parents, teachers, the experts, etc., say are valid sources." All our perspectives are limited, and there are sources out there you don't know about and we don't know about that—once found, listened to, and thought about—might give you a fresh outlook. The point is to always cast a wider net than you are used to casting and than you think you need to cast in any given context. You never know how what you catch might change your story—and complicate your research project.

The other point is, once you catch your sources, think seriously about where they came from and how you use them. Just because you like the sound of your source's voice doesn't mean the facts, definitions, interpretations, consequences, values, and policies found in your source are sound or fair.

☐ In the online chapter 6 resources (at www.ablongman.com/wysocki) are links to online tools to help you keep track of the research you do.

KEEPING TRACK OF SOURCES

Everyone we know who writes papers that cite sources has experienced finishing a paper, checking the sources, realizing some are missing—and then having trouble finding them. This is particularly distressing when people are working on long projects that rely on tens and hundreds of sources. There is nothing like thinking you are finished—and then understanding you have to spend two more days retracing a source.

As you move back and forth between the two stages of research, working toward your final focused paper, it may seem that the first stage—while you're reading broadly, looking for ideas—doesn't require you to keep track of sources. But keep track of any source that seems that it might be useful to you in any way.

Get in the habit of keeping a file in which you record as many of the following bits of information about the source as you can as you research:

- the author
- the title of the book or article
- the publisher
- the place (city, state, country) where the source was published
- the year of publication
- the URL
- a page number for a quote you want to use
- the name of the journal or magazine in which the source was published

compose ▪ design ▪ advocate

a research project
using your research to develop and test a design plan

Remember from chapters 2 and 3 that a statement of purpose pulls together your sense of purpose with thoughts about your audience in the particular context in which you are communicating—and then a design plan uses the statement of purpose to help a communicator think about what strategies to use.

Writing a statement of purpose and then a design plan is an informal way to start organizing your thinking, to see if your questions and research are holding together. Because statements of purpose and design plans are writing meant to move you toward another piece of writing, they don't need to be particularly polished—they just need to be your thinking in print.

When you are working on a research paper, your sense of purpose is encapsulated in your preliminary research question. If you have followed the steps we have outlined in this chapter, you will have arrived at this step—step 4—having researched your audience and gotten a better sense of what sorts of sources, evidence, and examples you need to use to persuade your audience.

To the right is Andrew's design plan, which continues on to the next page. We don't show you Andrew's statement of purpose because it is embedded in this design plan.

A design plan for my research paper
Andrew Rajala

My topic is the loss of manufacturing jobs in the United States, and I want to know why we are losing jobs and who is affected by this job loss—and what any of us can do about it.

My audience is students who are attending this school and also those who are involved in manufacturing. Students here ought to be concerned with this topic because many are probably hoping to work in the manufacturing industry some day—but if the industry no longer exists in this country then there may be no jobs. This concern is shared by people who already have jobs in the manufacturing industry.

There is another concern that many members of these two audiences most likely have. That concern is for the people they care about, their families and friends, as well as their communities. I've learned from my research that job loss not only affects the individuals who lose the jobs but can devastate families and whole communities because families lose benefits and money that would be spent to keep the community vibrant. I'm going to need to find a way to make this possibility be more real to people in class so that they think this only happens to others.

Because when I talked with people in class I learned that many of them have heard about manufacturing job loss but don't know the extent of it, I've looked into how many jobs have been lost, and found some really scary statistics. I've found out why jobs have gone other places, too, and most of the evidence points to the high price of doing business in this country versus others. Because most everyone in class values money, they are going to be torn about this, I think; they'll understand why companies leave but still probably want to find a way to keep jobs here.

Because my topic seems kind of distant to my audience, I think I need to start my paper in a way that will make job loss seem more real—so I think that I am going to start my paper with *pathos*. I have a story about the loss of a manufacturing job and how it affects a family. Another way that I could start would be to tell a story about a town whose main employer was a manufacturing facility—until it shut down—and then to tell about what happened when the facility shut down. Either of these two options will initially grab my audience's attention and bring into play their emotions. This will bring this particular issue close to home by showing what can really happen due to the loss of manufacturing jobs.

After such an introduction I will back up these stories with cold hard facts and statistics. By adding in numbers this will make the argument harder to deny, especially to students at this university, because they tend to believe numbers.

The next thing I want to do is try to make the link between a struggling manufacturing sector and an unhealthy economy. This might be tough because my audience probably won't want to read through an economics lecture in my paper. But I do want to make a connection between buying products made in the United States and saving manufacturing jobs here. This last part of my paper really ought to hit home with my audience because most of them are or will be involved in the manufacturing industry in one way or another.

Because this is a research paper—and because I am no expert—I can't hope to develop an expert *ethos*. Instead, I hope that the facts and figures I've found will show my readers that I've done enough that they will trust me. I also think my concern with this topic, which I show in my using stories about people, will help people understand why I write.

By the end of reading my paper, I want my audience to think to themselves that this country has a serious problem with the loss of manufacturing jobs but that there is something they can do about it. I want them to feel that their present or future job may be in peril—so they should do something now. Another thing that I want my audience to consider seriously is the fact that paying a little extra money to buy U.S.-made products can help to stop and maybe even reverse the loss of jobs.

ANALYZING
a design plan for a research paper

■ **Discuss with others:** How does Andrew use his knowledge about his audience to make preliminary decisions about how he will shape his paper? See if you can link the strategies he mentions with the way he is thinking about arranging his argument.

■ **Write:** Imagine Andrew was going to present this argument as a speech to a small group of people rather than as a paper. Rewrite his design plan for such a change in medium. Be sure to consider how Andrew's relation with his audience will change as you consider how his strategies might change.

■ **Discuss with others:** How persuasive do you think Andrew's paper is going to be? Why? How could he strengthen his argument? What other sorts of sources do you think might help him at this point?

responding to a design plan for a research paper

■ **Discuss with others:** To the right is one person's response to Andrew's design plan. With a partner, discuss whether you think this response will be helpful to Andrew, and why.

Develop a short list of qualities of feedback that you think help others. Consider tone of voice and how to address the person receiving the feedback, as well as the detail of observation and how the observation attends to the purpose of the design plan.

■ **Write:** Write a short note to Andrew, telling him what you think is strongest about his plan and what you think could be stronger. You very likely fit into the audience he describes, so tell him if you think the plan looks to result in a paper that will persuade you—and why or why not. Be sure to give reasons for any judgments or suggestions you make.

Response to Andrew's design plan
Stephanie Hill

It sounds to me as though you have thought pretty well about how to engage your audience by starting with a real-life story about how people's lives get messed up when they lose a job. Because your audience is people like us who usually don't need to worry about jobs and families, it might be a little hard to tell a story that will be real to us. If you know someone at Tech whose family and community have been affected by manufacturing job loss, it might be interesting to start with that.

Following up on the strategy of beginning with *pathos* by pulling in the *logos* of facts and figures makes sense to me. I think that starting with a compelling story prepares us to read facts and figures with more connection to real life experience, and so makes the facts and figures seem less abstract. And, no, I don't want to read an "economics lecture."

This gives me an idea about an arrangement that maybe would work.

Since it sounds as though the story you are going to tell is a story that spins out from job loss hurting one person to effects on that individual's family and then on to their community (and then even out to state or country?), it might be compelling to your audience if your paper was in sections. The first section could start with a story about the individual's job loss, and then tell the facts and figures about the economic and other effects on the individual. Then you could tell the next part of the story, about the effects on that person's family, and then give facts and figures about the family. Then tell the story about the community, then give facts and figures about the community, and so on. That way, you could help your audience understand even more, perhaps, how the effects of job loss spiral out and have big effects. Such a structure would also keep the *pathos* wound up with the logos. That might work with the people around here.

It also seems to me that ending with actions we can take is important. I always feel like nothing I do makes much difference, so I hope you can help. Maybe you need to tell us about why jobs are being lost? If we know why, then we would know something we could do. Buying American is important, and showing people the effects of paying just a little bit more seems really useful.

A FIRST DRAFT
On the next pages is Andrew's first draft of his research paper, followed by comments he received to his draft (keep in mind that developing a draft and getting feedback from others is a form of testing), followed by his final version (with which he included all his sources).

Manufacturing job loss
research paper draft
Andrew Rajala

Throughout the country you can hear people say things like, "I lost my job after 17 years and it's like losing a leg. I feel worthless and don't want to leave the house. I don't want people to know I'm out of work." Statements and stories like this are all too common in the United States today. There's Joe, for example, a former worker in a plant that manufactured school buses in a small town in Iowa. Joe took a job with the bus manufacturer right out of high school because he thought that kids will always go to school—so there will always be a need for school buses. Then one day, ten years later, Joe was told that the plant was closing and he would be out of a job. Joe never thought this would happen in his little town in Iowa. Joe had become one of the statistics and that made him scared.

The manufacturing sector makes up more than 10 percent of the total workforce in the United States but throughout the country jobs have been lost at an alarming rate. In fact, since the year 2000 the United States has lost nearly 2.7 million manufacturing jobs, but this trend isn't just in the past. In the past month of June alone, according to the Bureau of Labor Statistics, the United States lost another 11,000 manufacturing jobs.

The reasons for this loss of jobs are varied. One reason is that it is cheaper to move a plant to a foreign country. This might be cheaper because of a few things. One reason it might be cheaper is because the labor costs in foreign countries, especially third world countries, are so much lower. Labor costs are lower because the countries have a lower standard of living and the companies don't have to pay for insurance or benefits like they usually do in the United States. For example, in 2002, the Ford Motor Company spent an estimated $2.7 billion on healthcare and drug charges for its employees, retirees, and dependents; something that is very unlikely for a firm in a third world country. The labor costs are not the only thing that drives up the cost of doing business. There are also countries where the environmental restrictions are more lax so in some cases it is cheaper to use a more hazardous but cheaper method of production. Another reason is that many of these countries don't have a legal system that could hurt the manufacturers. On average it costs manufacturers 22% more to produce products in the United States than in any other country, including third world countries. Another reason that manufacturing jobs are being lost is innovation. This happens when a new process or machine is developed that cuts down on the need for more people. While this does not account for a large percent of total job loss it is still important. Another reason for this job loss is the fact that some companies just can't keep up with their competitors. These competitors may be either foreign companies with cheaper labor or they may be domestic companies with better processes or machines and/or working with smaller profit margins.

Many of these workers that have lost their jobs are not alone in life. Many of them have families that were completely or partially supported by the manufacturing job that they held. So when it is said that workers have to do with less, that is only part of the story.

Back in Iowa, Joe struggles to find a way to let his wife and family know that he has lost his job. He knew that with his paycheck gone it would be very difficult. Before Joe lost his job their family was already living on a tight budget. With his job gone, they would lose the benefits that had come with the paycheck like healthcare and a future pension. Even with an unemployment check there was no way that they could get through this ordeal unscathed. Joe knew that this loss would have a lasting effect on him and his family.

According to the U.S. Census Bureau, in September of 2003 there were 4.6 million people in this country without health insurance. Now I'm not saying that all of this is the fault of manufacturing job loss, but it can show you how many families that it affects.

Many of these jobs pay more than most others. In California, for example, where they have lost well over 250,000 manufacturing jobs between 1998 and 2002, most of the jobs lost paid over 50% more than the average job in California. This means that the jobs that are being lost are fairly high-paying jobs and if the workers are lucky enough and can replace their jobs they will most likely have to settle for a lot less than they were used to.

Joe's community hurts, too.

Many people refer to manufacturing jobs as something like a "job multiplier." Manufacturing jobs are thought of as this because they tend to affect other economic sectors that are in the general area. This happens because these jobs are usually high paying jobs and when you have more money you can spend more. In California, the loss of 250,000 jobs resulted in an overall loss of $98 billion in revenue. That is money that could have been spent in the communities where workers live.

In that little town in Iowa, the bus manufacturing plant had been the largest employer in the county. When it closed down it had a ripple effect throughout the community. Many of the smaller companies that supported the bus manufacturer now had no one to supply to, and many of the stores in town now tried to sell their goods to people who had no money to spare. This ripple continued to spread. With many companies shutting down, the county lost a lot of tax revenue, which meant that there was less money to go around for the same number of programs.

There are ways that you can help to stop the loss of manufacturing jobs. As a consumer you can seek out products that were made in the United States. Some of these products cost a little more than those made overseas, but that little extra cost will help those companies remain in the United States and keep jobs here. Another very important way that you as a citizen of the United States can help the manufacturing sector is to vote for officials who favor manufacturing jobs. It is not hard to find out if a candidate is opposed to or in favor of legislation that protects manufacturers.

There have been people who have tried to help. For example, in the U.S. Senate several bills have been introduced that would give tax incentives to companies staying in the United States. Two of these bills are the Job Protection Act of 2003 and the Save American Manufacturing Act of 2003. Both of these bills have sought protection for U.S. manufacturers that have remained in this country and that may need a little boost to help them compete with foreign firms.

The loss of manufacturing jobs has had a devastating effect on the country as a whole. Countless numbers of people have been adversely affected by these losses. In this paper, you read a story about a man named Joe, his family, and his small town. This story was developed from a number of reports and various stories and personal experiences. It was developed to give you a different perspective on this issue. I believe that it shows a side of the situation that is not often told. There are people out there like Joe and his family and there are things you can do to help them.

ANALYZING
revision in research paper

■ **Discuss with others:** You've just read Andrew's first draft of his research paper, after you've followed its development from his preliminary research question and through his research and statement of purpose and design plan—and you are about to read his final draft.

- How does Andrew's draft match the expectations you have about his paper through seeing it develop? Is there anything you didn't expect in his paper, or is everything just as you imagined? What changes or shifts or observations in Andrew's thinking about his topic—as he carried out his research—led to what you notice?

- To the right is some feedback Andrew received from another person in class. What of the feedback did Andrew listen to, and what did he not? Why do you think he made the choices he did? How would his final paper be different if he had followed some of the other suggestions?

- As you read Andrew's final paper, starting in two pages, work with a partner to circle anything you notice that is different from the first draft. With a partner, discuss why you think Andrew made the changes he did. How did the changes he made contribute to strengthening the overall effect of his paper?

Everyone in class read drafts from several other people, and then each wrote a response to one of the drafts, using these questions to guide the response:

- Keeping in mind what you believe to be the writer's purpose, how does the order of the paper support that purpose?

- Why do you think the writer's strategies (keep *ethos*, *pathos*, and *logos* in mind) support—or could more strongly support—that purpose?

- How persuasive is the research supporting the arguments of the paper? What other kinds of research or sources do you think would help make this argument more persuasive?

To the right is feedback Andrew received from someone else in class, a philosophy major.

Response to Andrew's draft

Jessika Lamsey

Hi Andrew—

I like your draft so far: I can follow it pretty well. Several things stick out for me, though. Here's my suggestions for two kinds of things you could do.

First, I think you could play with the arrangement of your arguments still some more. You've got a start on ordering your argument through telling the story of Joe. The story you use could provide the structure for the other information you have: because the story moves from personal to public, and from small to big, that could also be a way to arrange all the facts and figures you have. As the paper is arranged now, the facts and figures can feel sort of randomly placed to me. In the beginning, you talk about the reasons for job loss, which turns my attention away from Joe to global manufacturing conditions. I lose focus with that, sorry.

Maybe you could give facts and figures about the effects on individuals in the beginning, and then build up the numbers as you move through the story? Do you think it might make sense not to explain the causes of the job loss until the end, when your readers (me) will want to understand it more because they've seen its effects?

Second, I am a little messed up in your overall argument. Now, it seems that what you are trying to build to at the end of the writing is persuading us to buy American and to vote for candidates who support keeping manufacturing jobs here.

But, when you get to that point in your paper, I think you need to say more about what's involved in buying American and voting. I think you need to say just how much more money this means people will have to pay. My Dad was talking last week about how a lot of foreign cars are a lot cheaper. I'm not sure he's right, but I know people who think like him. So I don't think you can just mention quickly that it costs just a little bit more. Maybe you need to give some examples of actual products and cost? If you could make us think about exactly where our money goes when we buy something? Teach us a little bit about how to figure out where something has been made. That would help me. You could do the same thing with voting for candidates: how can I know how a candidate will really do work to keep jobs here? And what sorts of things could happen at state and national levels to keep jobs here? Knowing that would help me understand better how to vote.

And I'm wondering if it would help you make your case more if you did more research into how companies use their money. You say that companies argue that they need to take jobs overseas because they can't afford to keep them here because of wages and health costs. How do I know if this is true? Can companies really not survive if they have to pay health costs and wages here? Because if it is, you might need to be arguing for companies to change from valuing money/profits to valuing money/profits and a good life for their employees.

One story of manufacturing job loss

Andrew Rajala

Throughout this country you can hear people say things like, "I lost my job after 17 years and it's like losing a leg. I feel worthless and don't want to leave the house. I don't want people to know I'm out of work" (Anonymous). Statements and stories like this are all too common in the United States today. Take for example the story of Joe, a former worker in a plant that manufactured school buses in a small town in Iowa. Joe took a job with the bus manufacturer right out of high school because he thought that kids will always need to go to school—so there will always be a need for school buses. Joe also thought that all he had to do was put in his years and retire with a pension. Then one day, ten years later, Joe was told that the plant was closing and he would be out of a job. Joe never thought that something like this would happen in his little town in Iowa. Joe had become one of the statistics and that made him scared.

Joe has a right to be scared—because the statistics depict a truly scary sight. The manufacturing sector in the United States makes up more than 10 percent of the total workforce (or about 12 million workers)(Bureau of Labor Statistics), but throughout the country jobs have been lost at an alarming rate. In fact, since the year 2000, the United States has lost nearly 2.7 million manufacturing jobs (Bivens), but this trend isn't just in the past. In the month of June alone, according to the Bureau of Labor Statistics, the United States lost another 11,000 manufacturing jobs.

If someone says workers simply have to make do with less when they lose their jobs, that is telling only part of the story. The rest of the story shows what happens to the people involved in the manufacturing process when this process is halted—but the story also shows what you can do about it.

Joe struggles to find a way to let his wife and family know he lost his job. He knew that with his paycheck gone it would be very difficult. Before Joe lost his job his family was already on a very tight budget. With his job gone they would lose the benefits that had come with his paycheck, like healthcare and Joe's pension. Even with an unemployment check there was no way they could get through this ordeal unscathed. Joe knew this loss would have a lasting effect on his family.

Many of the workers who lose their jobs are not alone in life. Many of them have families that are completely or partially supported by the manufacturing job held by someone in the family.

compose ▪ design ▪ advocate

Joe's job had been a good one. Many jobs like Joe's pay more than others. In California, for example, where they have lost well over 250,000 manufacturing jobs between 1998 and 2002, most of the jobs paid over 50% more than the average job in the state ("Study"). This means that the jobs being lost are fairly high-paying jobs and if the workers are lucky enough and can replace their job, they will most likely have to settle for a job that pays a lot less.

The amount of money is not the only reason that losing a job is hurting these families. Many manufacturing jobs also come with benefits like healthcare. According to the U.S. Census Bureau, in September of 2003 there were 43.6 million people without health insurance in this country (Bergman); with every manufacturing job lost this already staggering number grows. I'm not saying that all this is the fault of manufacturing job loss alone, but it gives us a sense of just how many families are affected.

In Joe's little town, the bus manufacturing plant had been the largest employer in the county. When it closed down it had a ripple effect throughout the community. Many of the smaller companies that supported the bus manufacturer now had no one to supply to, and many of the stores in town now tried to sell their goods to people who had no money to spare. This ripple continued to spread, causing more layoffs in other companies and more people out of work. With many companies shutting down, the county lost a lot of tax revenue, which meant that there was less money to go around for the same number of programs.

Many people refer to manufacturing jobs as "job multipliers" because manufacturing jobs tend to affect other economic sectors. This happens because manufacturing jobs are usually high-paying jobs and when you have more money you can spend more. In California, the loss of 250,000 jobs resulted in the state losing over $98 billion in revenue. That is money that could have been spent in the communities where workers live.

The reasons for this serious situation in Joe's town and all the other places like it are varied. One large reason is that it is cheaper to move a plant to a foreign country, because it is cheaper for companies to do business elsewhere. For example, labor costs in foreign countries, especially third world countries, are so much lower. Labor costs are lower because the countries have a lower standard of living and the companies don't have to pay for insurance or benefits like they usually do in the United States. For example,

Notice how Andrew has cited a source just about any time he has given statistics in his paper. Are there other places where you think he should include sources?

in 2002, the Ford Motor Company spent an estimated $2.7 billion on health-care and drug charges for its employees, retirees, and dependents ("Ford")—such benefits are very unlikely for a firm in a third world country. The labor costs are not the only thing that drives up the cost of doing business in the United States. There are other countries where the environmental restrictions are more lax than here, so in some cases it is cheaper to use a more hazardous but cheaper method of production. In addition, many of these countries don't have a legal system that could hurt the manufacturers. On average it costs manufacturers 22% more to produce products in the United States than in any other country, including third world countries (Leonard).

Another reason that manufacturing jobs are being lost is innovation. This happens when a new process or machine is developed that cuts down on the need for more people. While this does not account for a large percent of total job loss it is still important. Finally, some companies just can't keep up with their competitors. These competitors may be either foreign companies with cheaper labor or they may be domestic companies with better processes or machines and/or working with smaller profit margins.

There are ways that you can help stop the loss of manufacturing jobs in the United States. As a consumer you can seek out products that are made in the United States. In order to find out if the product you want to buy is manufactured in the United States, look at its original packaging: it will say where the product was made. Many products manufactured in the United States will have a sticker that says, "Made in the U.S.A." Some of these products cost a little more than those made overseas, but that little extra cost will help those companies remain in the United States and keep jobs here. Another very important way that you as a citizen of the United States can help the manufacturing sector is to vote for officials who favor manufacturing jobs. It is not hard to find out if a candidate is opposed to or in favor of legislation that protects manufacturers.

There have been people who have tried to help. For example, in the U.S. Senate several bills have been introduced that would give tax incentives to companies staying in the United States. Two of these bills are the Job Protection Act of 2003 and the Save American Manufacturing Act of 2003 ("Trade, Manufacturing, and U.S. Jobs"). Both of these bills have sought protection for U.S. manufacturers that have remained in this country and that may need a little boost to help them overcome the 22% higher manufacturing cost of staying in the United States; to help them compete with foreign firms these bills reduce the amount of taxes U.S. manufacturers pay and eliminate tax breaks for shipping jobs overseas.

The loss of manufacturing jobs has had a devastating effect on the country as a whole. Countless numbers of people have been adversely affected by these losses. In this paper, you read a story about a man named Joe, his family, and his small town. This story was developed from a number of reports and various stories and personal experiences. It was developed to give you a different perspective on this issue. I believe that it shows a side of the situation that is not often told. There are people out there like Joe and his family and there are things you can do to help them.

WORKS CITED

Duffy, Susanna. "I've lost my job!" *BellaOnline: The Voice of Women*. 10 Oct. 2004 < http://www.bellaonline.com/articles/art17165.asp > .

Bergman, Mike. "Numbers of Americans With and Without Health Insurance Rise, Census Bureau Reports." *United States Department of Commerce News*. 30 Sept. 2003 U.S. Census Bureau. 12 Oct. 2004 < http://www.census.gov/PressRelease/www/2003/cb03-154.html > .

Bivens, Josh. "Shifting Blame for Manufacturing Job Loss, Effect of Rising Trade Deficit Shouldn't Be Ignored." *The Economic Policy Institute*. 8 Apr. 2004. 28 Sept. 2004 < http://www.epinet.org/content.cfm/ briefingpapers_bp149 > .

Bureau of Labor Statistics. *United States Department of Labor*. 28 Sept. 2004 < http://www.bls.gov > .

"Ford: Healthcare Fee May Drive Us Offshore." *The Taunton Gazette*. 20 July 2004. 1 Dec. 2004 < http://www.tauntongazette.com/site/news.cfm?newsid = 12413280&BRD = 1711&PAG = 740&dept_id = 226963&rfi = 6 > .

Leonard, Jeremy A. "How Structural Costs Imposed on U.S. Manufacturers Harm Workers and Threaten Competitiveness." *National Association of Manufacturers*. Dec. 2003. 1 Dec. 2004 < http://www.nam.org/s_nam/bin.asp?CID = 201715&DID = 227525&DOC = FILE.PDF > .

"Study: Loss of Manufacturing Jobs Worse than Thought." *Sacramento Business Journal*. 23 Feb. 2004. 12 Oct. 2004 < http:sanantonio. bizjournals.com/sacramento/stories/2004/02/23/daily26.html > .

Andrew used the MLA style for listing his sources in his "Works Cited." There are other styles, such as APA, ACS, AIP, and CMS; these styles are discipline-specific, and if you go on to write research papers as part of your post-undergraduate life, you will need to learn the style appropriate to your discipline. For a writing class, the preferred styles tend to be MLA (the style supported by the Modern Language Association) or the CMS (Chicago Manual of Style).

Check with your teacher about which you should use in your own papers.

☐ Look in the online chapter 6 resources (at www.ablongman.com/wysocki) for links to websites that explain these forms of documentation fully. There are also links to websites that will help you generate the citations you need from the information you record about your sources.

"Trade, Manufacturing, and U.S. Jobs." On-line Office of United States Senator Fritz Hollings of South Carolina. 3 March 2004. 12 Oct. 2004 < http://hollings.senate.gov/inthenews_trade.html > .

QUALITIES YOU CAN CONSIDER IN TESTING A RESEARCH PAPER

The same reason makes writing pleasurable, challenging, or a pain for different people: that reason is that there are a tremendous number of details that go into producing a polished piece of writing.

At the end of chapter 6 we offer one possible rubric, which we have used in a writing class, to show how writers can choose the qualities on which they want to focus as they compose for a particular audience, purpose, and context. **But to the right (and going on to the next page) is a long list of the many other qualities that can characterize polished writing;** it can help you gain in confidence as a writer if you choose only a specific set of these on which to focus at any one time; move on to another set when you believe you are comfortable with the first set. (Notice too that some items might contradict others: some qualities apply only to certain kinds of writing, depending on audience, purpose, and context.)

QUALITIES OF POLISHED RESEARCH WRITING

❏ The writing is focused on one main argument.

❏ Any supporting arguments do indeed support the main argument.

❏ The argument is understandable to its audience.

❏ The argument is worth making: it focuses around a topic or controversy that matters to its audience.

❏ The writing shows that the writer has tried to demonstrate to the audience that the topic matters to the audience.

❏ The writing acknowledges and discusses multiple sides to the issue being discussed.

❏ There is an appropriate level of support —such as examples (which can include personal experience), facts and/or figures, illustrations or photographs, charts and/or graphics—to support the argument being made.

❏ The writing shows that the writer has made an effort to find appropriate and interesting sources.

❏ Sources are appropriately cited in the body of the paper.

❏ Any sections of the paper that appear to come from other sources show the source.

❏ All used sources are appropriately cited at the end of the paper, using one of the accepted citation styles.

❏ Any graphics used are clear and easy to understand.

❏ Any graphics used are appropriate to the argument.

❏ All graphics are treated appropriately as sources.

❏ Readers will easily understand why the paragraphs are ordered as they are.

❏ The writer has supplied transitions between each paragraph or section so that readers will understand why one paragraph moves into the next.

❏ Readers will be able to read the sentences easily because the grammar and spelling have been carefully checked.

❏ The grammar and spelling are rhetorically appropriate.

❏ The writing has a neat and easy-to-read appearance.

❏ The writing has an introduction that appropriately brings readers into the argument.

❏ The writing is as long as it needs to be to make its argument fully.

continued on the next page . . .

- At its conclusion, the writing sums up its argument in a manner that the audience both will understand and is likely to remember.
- The writing has a consistent *ethos* (if this is appropriate to the purpose of the paper).
- The *ethos* is appropriate to the purpose of the paper.
- The writing doesn't ramble, whine, or shout at its audience (unless rambling, whining, and shouting are appropriate to the purpose).
- The writing demonstrates that the writer has an appropriate level of authority and/or knowledge to write on this topic.
- The writer pays attention to the emotions of the audience.
- The writing shows that the writer respects the audience's intelligence and ability to think.
- The writing shows that the writer has tried to make the writing interesting to readers.

- **Write with others:** With two or three others, go through the qualities we've listed for polished research writing: categorize them as best you can as qualities that connect to *ethos*, *pathos*, or *logos*—or come up with another categorization scheme.
- **Write for yourself:** Choose among the items in the list of qualities of polished writing to develop a set of the five or six qualities from which you believe you could most benefit in your next writing assignment. How will you go about learning what you need in order to strengthen your abilities in those areas?
- **Discuss with others:** Pick five items on the list, and work to imagine contexts in which the *opposite* of each item would be appropriate.
- **Discuss with others:** What have we left off the list?

thinking through production

■ Well . . . what did you expect here? The first suggested project has to be to write a research paper on a topic that matters to you, using the steps we've laid out in this chapter.

With everyone in class, choose among the qualities of strong research writing to develop rubrics for giving feedback to each other on your research questions, on your statements of purpose, on your design plans, and on your drafts and final paper.

Keep a journal on your process as you design and produce your paper. What will you do differently next time? What gave you pleasure? What didn't?

■ Use the steps in chapters 2–4 to plan and produce a research scavenger hunt that gets students into your campus library and using as broad a range of its various resources as possible.

As a class, develop a set of criteria for judging the creativity and effectiveness of the scavenger hunt.

■ Use the steps in chapters 2–4 to plan and produce guidelines for high school school students to help them judge the authority and credibility of websites to use in support of research.

■ At the end of chapter 5, the chapter on advocacy, there is a step-by-step description of using your communication and research abilities to assist a nonprofit organization in its work.

■ Research does not always have to end in a paper: on the next page are suggestions for "creative" research projects.

▢ There are more "Thinking Through Production" activities in the online chapter 6 resources at www.ablongman.com/wysocki

ALTERNATIVE RESEARCH PROJECTS

In the previous section we gave you possible steps for producing an argumentative academic research paper, one that most teachers would recognize. There are other possible approaches to research; use the following ideas as suggestions:

■ **Produce an annotated visual timeline on an aspect of communication that has changed over time.** You could research how public spaces have changed over time, from the ancient Greek agora through the Roman forum and medieval and early American public squares to shopping malls; collect photographs or illustrations of these spaces (and more), and put them on paper or online with written explanations, to produce an argument about how the nature of public space has changed depending on governmental, economic, or technological structures. To produce such a timeline, you would do your research (with help from this chapter), produce a design plan (using chapters 2, 3, and 4), and use the chapters on documentary photographs and visual communication to help you choose your illustrations and design your arrangements.

■ **Build a "museum" about a communication medium.** Choose a particular medium—brochures, postcards, newsletters, flyers, website magazines—and collect as many examples of it as you can. Build a "museum" display

(which could be online) with explanatory signs: the signs should help your audience understand how you think the examples were produced—with different strategies and arrangements—to engage different kinds of audiences.

■ **Make a video about public communication practices on your campus.** Shoot video of the ways people on your campus communicate about social or political events. Out of the clips you collect, make an arrangement (with a voiceover or explanatory titles) that argues how public communication on your campus could be more effective or engaging.

■ **Demonstrate research in an unexpected medium.** Make your own series of postcards by using a digital camera and whatever software you have or by using a conventional camera and writing on the back of your pictures: use the postcards to document and build an argument about (for example) how people use clothing styles to communicate the group to which they belong. Produce a website that uses sound recordings of interviews with older and younger people in your community to argue how communication between people has changed as communication technologies change. (These are suggestions about how you can use research to build arguments in media where people might not expect to see them.)

■ **Write a new chapter for this book by researching a kind of communication that we've not included.** Each chapter in Section 3 discusses a particular kind of communication, such as posters, documentary photography, opinion pieces, illustration sets, and so on. Choose a kind of communication we haven't discussed (webpages for colleges, posters about movie Westerns, academic articles, billboards . . .), and use the chapters in Section 3 as a model to produce your own chapter. Research the communication you choose, develop a design plan, and then produce a chapter that helps others learn how to analyze and produce that kind of communication.

☐ The online chapter 6 resources (at www.ablongman.com/wysocki) contain links to research projects composed digitally. These online research projects look very different from academic research papers, but are composed to do much of the same work as academic research papers. Use them as examples to turn your research into an online project.

This section is about production, and about how you produce your own communications using written, visual, or oral modes—or some combination. The chapters of this section get concrete about conventions and possibilities of written, spoken, and visual production and how you can use them.

what differentiates these modes of communication

	SENSES ADDRESSED	AMOUNT OF ABSTRACTION	CONTACT WITH AUDIENCE

Note, however, that we can write so that our words can evoke a sense of a speaking voice, so that readers can "imagine" their ears are being addressed, too.

In human history, writing is the last mode of communication to be developed. It requires us to understand that marks made on some surface (clay, tortoise shells, stone, paper) can be arranged to represent things or sounds or ideas.

Because writing addresses, generally, only our eyes through these abstracted marks, we can write in ways that direct our attentions away from the things and events and people of day-to-day life; we can write so that we direct readers' attentions to abstractions only, if we choose.

Because writing is put on some surface, it is portable: it can be carried to other places—and to other times. Writing need not be seen by anyone close to the writer.

Writers can thus have no direct physical contact with their audiences, and audiences must imagine writers through how they present themselves through their words.

In writing, then, writers and audiences can be (but needn't be) distant from each other in time and in space.

When we use the telephone or devices that record voices and sounds, then ears only are addressed.

Generally, when we speak we use words—and so speaking can be about abstract ideas just as much as writing can be. But speaking is always attached to a voice, and voices cannot be separated from bodies. When we hear another speak, even if we cannot see the person, we always imagine—alertly or not—a particular person who has a gender, an age, a country, and, often, a race; we imagine the person's character (the person's level of seriousness, humor, amount of education, generosity). Speaking will thus generally seem more attached to concrete bodily existence than writing.

Speaking can be the most direct and intimate of the modes of communication: speakers and listeners can be inches apart and—if a voice is not recorded or amplified—speakers and listeners must always be physically close together. Speakers and listeners in these conditions can see (and perhaps smell and touch) each other; they can respond directly to each other.

When voices are recorded, the sense of bodies communicating stays (as we note to the left), but the ability to respond back-and-forth goes away. Telephones hold on to our ability to respond back-and-forth, but without the intimacy of physical closeness.

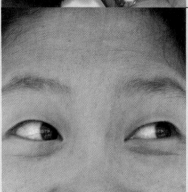

If we use photographs or drawings to create visual communication, then we almost always have to show particular people or things in particular places at particular times of day—which makes these kinds of visual communication seem very much tied to bodies and day-to-day existence and not very abstract. But there are the possibilities of abstract painting or design, for example, which can be about emotion or intellectual connections; the designs of page layout—which needn't use photographs—can also suggest abstract ideas and values such as geometric order or hierarchy. But is visual communication capable of the extended development of abstract ideas, as writing and speaking are?

Like writing, visual communication is on a surface such as paper or a movie or television or computer screen—and so, like writing, visual communication tends to be a means for recording ideas and arguments for people who are at a distance (in space or time) from those who make the communication.

compose ▪ design ▪ advocate

This chart compares qualities of written, spoken, and visual communication. We've put this chart here, before the chapters on the individual modes, to encourage you to think about what the modes have in common and how they differ. This can help you in deciding which mode—and hence, ultimately, which medium—to use in some communication context. You can also use this chart to help you think about when and why to combine modes.

FORMAL EDUCATION NEEDED	**PERMANENCE**	**FORMALITY & LENGTH OF TEXTS**	

How many years have you been in school learning to write? First you learned to make the shapes of the alphabet, and you learned how to arrange those shapes into words, and to read the words of others—and then things got complex, with grammar and writing structures that allow you to say much more and different than "What I did during my summer vacation." There are some kinds of writing with which you are now probably comfortable—e-mail and instant messaging, lists, short notes, certain kinds of essays—and possibly you have written short stories or novels or research reports.

Because writing is marks on a surface, writing is as permanent as its surface.

But the permanence of writing depends also on people being able to read the writing. If the people who speak a language disappear, then our abilities to understand the language—and all its nuances and cultural weight and possibilities of expression that shape the world differently from ours—disappear even though marks on paper or stone or bone remain.

Because of where and when we have all grown up, writing has seemed to us the mode (generally) for the most formal contexts of communication, when we want to be most serious and/or when we want to record what matters to us individually and culturally.

Through schooling, we now probably have more familiarity with longer written texts than with longer texts in other modes—although outside of school many people have used more time to watch an individual movie or play a computer game than to read any individual book.

It's possible that you've never received formal education in speaking. Those who raised you taught you to speak (though they might not have thought of it as "teaching") and you learned by paying attention to others (though you were probably too young to remember). You also learn to speak now, whenever you enter a new group that has its own ways of speaking. Because we can learn to speak just by being around others, you may feel you need no formal education in it—you do it all the time already. It is for contexts like public speaking, and for alert group communication (for example), that learning about how speaking works and how you can modify your speaking for different contexts is useful.

Words spoken between people drift off into the air—unless someone records the words. The words can be recorded in memory (which usually means that the words will be recorded not exactly as they were spoken but as the listener or speaker remembers them) or they can be recorded now onto all kinds of surfaces, in which case, they are as permanent as the surface and as the language in which they are spoken.

Speaking can be used in very formal contexts—presidential addresses, funeral orations—but speaking also can seem the most informal mode because it can seem so effortless when we are in comfortable contexts. Often, writing seems more formal and serious simply because it requires the effort of putting words onto paper.

When we make informal speeches, they can be a few minutes long. Audiences are no longer familiar with the abilities to listen to three-hour speeches, which were common in the nineteenth century, for example, but we can attend to speeches of an hour and longer movies.

Do you remember as a child being shown pictures of objects and hearing their names repeated? Perhaps you're now helping your children learn this way, which carves the world into conceptual categories so that we see the world through those categories. So we do learn to see because we have to learn what our culture considers worth seeing—it's just that this doesn't happen formally.

Just because you can see doesn't mean you can produce effective visual communication. In our time and place, producing effective visual communication might not be as valued as writing, but in other times learning to draw (for example) was considered a necessary part of any "educated" person's upbringing.

Visual communication is as permanent as anything else recorded on a surface—although photographs and drawings may seem to be expressive even if the language of those who made the photographs or drawings disappears. Photographs and drawings only make sense in their full temporal and locational contexts: we might see that a carving from centuries ago represents a deer—but was the deer seen by its makers as food or a god?

We tend now to see visual communication in informal personal situations (photo albums, home movies) and in informal public situations (films, advertising)—although visual communication is a part of more formal situations, if you count as visual communication (for example) President Bush's decision to wear the uniform of the military group he addresses. We also use visual recording devices now to hold on to what matters to us—such as presidential speeches and family scrapbooks.

Visual communication now can be short one-page or one-screen pieces; it can be multi-page photo-documentaries; it can be long epic films.

thinking through production

- List all the different ways you've used (or been asked to use) writing to learn in school. Which ways have been most useful to you? Why? Are there ways you can use these approaches in other contexts?

- Annotate the chart on the preceding two pages: mark any places where our observations fit well with your observations and places where you think we've made mistakes. Do you have other examples to offer from your experiences with written, oral, and visual communication that support (or not) what we've claimed about each of these modes?

- How do digital communications—like instant messaging, MOOs and MUDs, or e-mail—fit into the chart on the preceding two pages? Do they? On separate paper or using any other technology to which you have access, make a fourth row for the chart for these kinds of communication. What picture should you use to represent digital communication? What text should you write in the various columns? Do you think these kinds of communication deserve to be called a separate mode and should be studied separately?

- Many kinds of communications mix the modes we discuss on the previous two pages: films, computer games, home pages, and newspapers (for example) are each mixes of two or all three of the modes we've described. Choose one of these kinds of mixed-mode media, and on separate paper or using any other technology to which you have access, make an additional row for the chart: use the categories of the chart ("Senses Addressed," "Amount of Abstraction," and so on), to analyze the medium by describing how the medium you've chosen can be described in terms of that quality. What does this tell you about the kinds of communication situations in which your medium might be most effective?

compose • design • advocate

about written modes of communication

You've started a project and decided (by working your sense of purpose, audience, and context into a sharp statement of purpose as we describe in chapters 2, 3, 4) that your project either needs to involve only written communication or needs to contain some writing . . .

This chapter is about how you develop initial ideas about what to write into the appropriate kind of writing for your context and audience. We offer suggestions about writing processes here, and we offer arrangement strategies (both large and small scale) that are specifically appropriate for written texts.

We focus also in this chapter on writing academic essays because you are probably being asked to produce such texts in the class for which you are using this book—but we also discuss other kinds of writing you will probably encounter in other contexts.

the pleasures of writing

finding your own

Anne (one of the composers of this book) hates a blank page and hates having to come up with initial ideas and words—but once she has some words on paper she loves revising, moving words and paragraphs and sections around; she delights in the possibilities of arrangement in writing (and in page design) and in how arrangement (and transitions) can suck people into reading and being carried along. Anne likes well-structured final products best of all, especially when they are finished. Dennis (the other composer of this book) hates having to move out of reading and thinking: he generates page after page (after page) of notes and ideas and possibilities because he likes following out the potentials of ideas, seeing where they lead. But he too likes writing when it is done, finished, shaped, and in its audience's hands.

The pleasures of writing come from many places: positive past experiences with writing, being caught up in an important or exciting project that happens to involve writing, or having developed a feel for the look and sound of words and the effects written words can have with others. The pleasures of writing also come at different times in one's life, and at different times in the writing process itself, as we described above for ourselves. Some people learn to love writing at an early age because they love reading or because they like to put down on paper—hold on to—everything that happens to them. Other people come around to writing later in life, having circled around it wearily until circumstances pushed them into it. And still others embrace writing only intermittently, now enjoying turning a stuffy memo into a joke, later dreading having to write a job application letter. Likewise, some people love the early stages of writing when the blank page feels as open as the open range and full of possibility, whereas others (like Anne) dread this stage, feeling paralyzed by such vast openness, longing instead for structure and direction, and wishing instead they already had a first draft to work on.

You need to find your own pleasures in writing if it is to give you power in the world. Recognize that pleasure often comes in hindsight, after you are done: there is nothing like success or happy responses from others to make a hard process seem pleasant and worthwhile in memory.

If you are one of those people who was told by a teacher sometime earlier in your life that you can't write, don't despair—get angry. Writing can be hard, and in some contexts we do better than in others. There are many different kinds of writing, and one

compose ▪ design ▪ advocate

way may provide a more pleasant opening to you than another. But writing is something you can learn to do with pleasure precisely because you can learn to do it. Being a competent writer is not something that comes with birth: it comes with practice, with reading and responding, with doing, with finding yourself in it.

And here is perhaps where some of the deepest potential pleasures of writing come in: writing is one way of making your ideas and positions visible to others—and to yourself. When you are thinking through an issue or problem through writing and producing writing for others, you are figuring out where you stand: you are, in effect, producing the position you take up. You are not taking that position whole cloth from elsewhere, but reworking ideas and opinions and words of others into something that holds together (at least for a while) for you. You are creating yourself into relations with others, producing positions you've wrestled into shape.

When you have a finished and polished piece of work in front of you, you get the pleasure of completion. But you also get to see someone you constructed in the writing, and you get to decide if you respect that person and that person's relation with the world—or not. You construct who you are in your writing.

how writing grows out of and in response to and sustains other writing

When one is writing, one is literally writing into and writing from, and those poles of writing into and writing from— inscribing and re-inscribing—situate the writer in a kind of interpretive and performative moment that allows the writer to be the mediator, to mediate between these two poles of invention.

—Eric Michael Dyson

Good writing requires good reading because writing grows out of and responds to other writing in myriad ways. Nearly every example of writing in this book testifies to this. Thomas Jefferson, for instance, used the phrase "life, liberty, and the pursuit of happiness" in the *Declaration of Independence*—but he borrowed (today we would say "sampled") the phrase from the British philosopher John Locke, who in his own political writing had used the phrase "life, liberty, and the pursuit of property." Jefferson didn't mention Locke in the *Declaration of Independence* because he assumed anyone reading the document would recognize the echo of Locke's words. Over two hundred years later, Sarah Vowell (in an essay in chapter 5) quotes her favorite passage from the *Declaration of Independence*, including "life, liberty, and the pursuit of happiness," in order to make the point that Jefferson's writing in the *Dec-laration* is strong and beautiful—and resonates for us still. From Locke, to Jefferson, to Vowell, writing grows, responds, and sustains other writing.

Even what seems like everyday, unimportant writing—a letter sent home or an e-mail message to a friend—has its roots in other people's writing. Your letter sent home may have been occasioned by a letter received from home, but if not, the mere fact that it is a letter means it has ties to the history of letter writing and to letter writing as a genre. You knew how to write a letter or e-mail because you had seen and read many letters or e-mails before. You understand the letter thing. Indeed, it might feel weird to put it this way, but as you wrote that letter to your parents your hand was being invisibly guided by a multitude of hands extending back thousands of years across hundreds of cultures—all ghosts writing letters. To be familiar with a written genre like letter writing is to have built into our perception certain expectations based on past experience with the genre. And as you write, you add to and shift and change the ways letters—or essays or e-mails or comics—are written, sustaining for others these ways of sharing.

ARGUING FOR FREEDOM: STARTING WITH AN IMPORTANT PIECE OF WRITING—*The Declaration of Independence*

To the right is a later draft of Thomas Jefferson's work on the *Declaration of Independence*. This draft should give you some idea of the kind of work that went into producing this document that declared Britain's restless and edgy American colonies to be independent of British rule.

Farther to the right is a printed version of the *Declaration*, from (as you can tell from the yellowed pages and also perhaps from the style of typography) an older book.

We've included this text here because we've discussed it in chapter 3 and will discuss it more in this chapter. We figure that—if you haven't read the *Declaration of Independence* before—you should. It is a carefully crafted production and one that matters to the United States and to what we consider this country to be about.

This is a text that did—and ought to continue doing—something. This text shows the value of using words precisely and carefully to make an argument. It shows how texts always draw on what precedes them (as Jefferson here drew on the words of the British philosopher John Locke, when Jefferson came up with the phrase "life, liberty, and the pursuit of happiness.)"

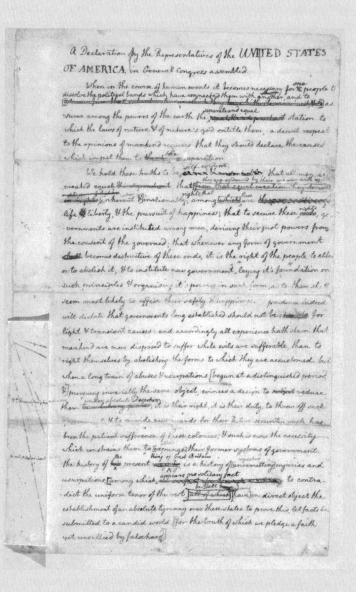

compose ▪ design ▪ advocate

4

INDEPENDENCE, CONFEDERATION, AND MAKING THE CONSTITUTION

13. THE DECLARATION OF INDEPENDENCE—1776

"The job that Tom Paine had begun in *Common Sense* Jefferson intended to finish in the Declaration of Independence." Such is the view expressed by John C. Miller in his *Origins of the American Revolution*. Though a Resolution of Independence had been approved by the Continental Congress on July 2, 1776, it is the Declaration of Independence of July 4, 1776, which is considered the formal justification of the separation from England. The committee appointed to draft the Declaration was composed of Thomas Jefferson, John Adams, Benjamin Franklin, Robert R. Livingston, and Roger Sherman. Jefferson made the first draft, and was the principal author of the Declaration. As is evident from the document, he realized that it was the tie with the king that remained to be broken in the minds of many Americans.

Locke's influence on the document is apparent. For a good discussion, see Carl Becker, *The Declaration of Independence*. Jefferson's own account of the making of the Declaration may be seen in Volume 1 of *The Writings of Thomas Jefferson*, Andrew A. Lipscomb, editor-in-chief. The text used below is taken from *Revised Statutes of the United States*, Second Edition (Washington: Government Printing Office, 1878).

THE DECLARATION OF INDEPENDENCE—1776

In Congress, July 4, 1776.

The unanimous Declaration of the thirteen united States of America,
When in the Course of human events, it becomes necessary for one people to dissolve the political bands which have connected them with another, and to assume among the Powers of the earth, the separate and equal station to which the Laws of Nature and of Nature's God entitle them, a decent respect to the opinions of mankind requires that they should declare the causes which impel them to the separation.

We hold these truths to be self-evident, that all men are created equal, that they are endowed by their Creator with certain unalienable Rights, that among these are Life, Liberty and the pursuit of Happiness. That to

As you work through this chapter, keep referring back to this text. Look, for example, at the *ethos* its writers constructed, and at the logical structure of its parts. Look at how it tries to shape our emotions loftily and with integrity—but do notice how it works to shape our emotions.

Although this text now sounds (and looks) old-fashioned, it describes who we are as citizens of the United States—and who we want to be.

secure these rights, Governments are instituted among Men, deriving their just powers from the consent of the governed, That whenever any Form of Government becomes destructive of these ends, it is the Right of the People to alter or to abolish it, and to institute new Government, laying its foundation on such principles and organizing its powers in such form, as to them shall seem most likely to effect their Safety and Happiness. Prudence, indeed, will dictate that Governments long established should not be changed for light and transient causes; and accordingly all experience hath shown, that mankind are more disposed to suffer, while evils are sufferable, than to right themselves by abolishing the forms to which they are accustomed. But when a long train of abuses and usurpations, pursuing invariably the same Object evinces a design to reduce them under absolute Despotism, it is their right, it is their duty, to throw off such Government, and to provide new Guards for their future security.—Such has been the patient sufferance of these Colonies; and such is now the necessity which constrains them to alter their former Systems of Government. The history of the present King of Great Britain is a history of repeated injuries and usurpations, all having in direct object the establishment of an absolute Tyranny over these States. To prove this, let Facts be submitted to a candid world.

He has refused his Assent to Laws, the most wholesome and necessary for the public good.

He has forbidden his Governors to pass Laws of immediate and pressing importance, unless suspended in their operation till his Assent should be obtained; and when so suspended, he has utterly neglected to attend to them.

He has refused to pass other Laws for the accommodation of large districts of people, unless those people would relinquish the right of Representation in the Legislature, a right inestimable to them and formidable to tyrants only.

He has called together legislative bodies at places unusual, uncomfortable, and distant from the depository of their Public Records, for the sole purpose of fatiguing them into compliance with his measures.

He has dissolved Representative Houses repeatedly, for opposing with manly firmness his invasions on the rights of the people.

He has refused for a long time, after such dissolutions, to cause others to be elected; whereby the Legislative Powers, incapable of Annihilation, have returned to the People at large for their exercise; the State remaining in the mean time exposed to all the dangers of invasion from without, and convulsions within.

He has endeavoured to prevent the population of these States; for that purpose obstructing the Laws for Naturalization of Foreigners; refusing to pass others to encourage their migration hither, and raising the conditions of new Appropriations of Lands.

He has obstructed the Administration of Justice, by refusing his Assent to Laws for establishing Judiciary Powers.

He has made Judges dependent on his Will alone, for the tenure of their offices, and the amount and payment of their salaries.

He has erected a multitude of New Offices, and sent hither swarms of Officers to harass our People, and eat out their substance.

He has kept among us, in times of peace, Standing Armies without the Consent of our legislature.

He has affected to render the Military independent of and superior to the Civil Power.

He has combined with others to subject us to a jurisdiction foreign to our constitution, and unacknowledged by our laws; giving his Assent to their acts of pretended Legislation:

For quartering large bodies of armed troops among us:

For protecting them, by a mock Trial, from Punishment for any Murders which they should commit on the Inhabitants of these States:

For cutting off our Trade with all parts of the world:

For imposing taxes on us without our Consent:

For depriving us in many cases, of the benefits of Trial by Jury:

For transporting us beyond Seas to be tried for pretended offences:

For abolishing the free System of English Laws in a neighbouring Province, establishing therein an Arbitrary government, and enlarging its Boundaries so as to render it at once an example and fit instrument for introducing the same absolute rule into these Colonies:

For taking away our Charters, abolishing our most valuable Laws, and altering fundamentally the Forms of our Government:

For suspending our own Legislature, and declaring themselves invested with Power to legislate for us in all cases whatsoever.

He has abdicated Government here, by declaring us out of his Protection and waging War against us.

He has plundered our seas, ravaged our Coasts, burnt our towns, and destroyed the lives of our people.

He is at this time transporting large armies of foreign mercenaries to compleat the works of death, desolation and tyranny, already begun with circumstances of Cruelty & perfidy scarcely paralleled in the most barbarous ages, and totally unworthy the Head of a civilized nation.

He has constrained our fellow Citizens taken Captive on the high Seas to bear Arms against their Country, to become the executioners of their friends and Brethren, or to fall themselves by their Hands.

He has excited domestic insurrections amongst us, and has endeavoured to bring on the inhabitants of our frontiers, the merciless Indian Savages, whose known rule of warfare, is an undistinguished destruction of all ages, sexes and conditions.

In every stage of these Oppressions We have Petitioned for Redress in the most humble terms: Our repeated Petitions have been answered only by repeated injury. A Prince, whose character is thus marked by every act which may define a Tyrant, is unfit to be the ruler of a free People.

Nor have We been wanting in attention to our Brittish brethren. We have warned them from time to time of attempts by their legislature to extend an unwarrantable jurisdiction over us. We have reminded them of the circumstances of our emigration and settlement here. We have appealed to their native justice and magnanimity, and we have conjured them by the ties of our common kindred to disavow these usurpations, which, would inevitably interrupt our connections and correspondence They too have been deaf to the voice of justice and of consanguinity. We must, therefore, acquiesce in the necessity, which denounces our Separation, and hold them, as we hold the rest of mankind, Enemies in War, in Peace Friends.

We, therefore, the Representatives of the united States of America, in General Congress, Assembled, appealing to the Supreme Judge of the world for the rectitude of our intentions, do, in the Name, and by Authority of the good People of these Colonies, solemnly publish and declare, That these United Colonies are, and of Right ought to be Free and Independent States; that they are Absolved from all Allegiance to the British Crown, and that all political connection between them and the State of Great Britain, is and ought to be totally dissolved; and that as Free and Independent States, they have full Power to levy War, conclude Peace, contract Alliances, establish Commerce, and to do all other Acts and Things which Independent States may of right do. And for the support of this Declaration, with a firm reliance on the Protection of Divine Providence, we mutually pledge to each other our Lives, our Fortunes and our sacred Honor.

JOHN HANCOCK.

New Hampshire.

JOSIAH BARTLETT,
Wm. WHIPPLE,   MATTHEW THORNTON.

Massachusetts Bay.

SAML. ADAMS,   ROBT. TREAT PAINE,
JOHN ADAMS,   ELBRIDGE GERRY.

Rhode Island.

STEP. HOPKINS,   WILLIAM ELLERY.

Connecticut.

ROGER SHERMAN,   Wm. WILLIAMS,
SAM'EL HUNTINGTON,   OLIVER WOLCOTT.

New York.

WM. FLOYD,   FRANS. LEWIS,
PHIL. LIVINGSTON,   LEWIS MORRIS.

New Jersey.

RICHD. STOCKTON,   JOHN HART,
JNO. WITHERSPOON,   ABRA. CLARK.
FRAS. HOPKINSON,

Pennsylvania.

ROBT. MORRIS,   JAS. SMITH,
BENJAMIN RUSH,   GEO. TAYLOR,
BENJA. FRANKLIN,   JAMES WILSON,
JOHN MORTON,   GEO. ROSS.
GEO. CLYMER,

Delaware.

CAESAR RODNEY,   THO. M'KEAN.
GEO. READ,

Maryland.

SAMUEL CHASE,   CHARLES CARROLL
Wm. PACA,   of Carrollton.
THOS. STONE,

Virginia.

GEORGE WYTHE,   THOS. NELSON, jr.,
RICHARD HENRY LEE,   FRANCIS LIGHTFOOT LEE,
TH. JEFFERSON,   CARTER BRAXTON.
BENJA. HARRISON,

North Carolina.

Wm. HOOPER,   JOHN PENN.
JOSEPH HEWES,

South Carolina.

EDWARD RUTLEDGE,   THOMAS LYNCH, Junr.,
THOS. HEYWARD, Junr.,   ARTHUR MIDDLETON.

Georgia.

BUTTON GWINNETT,   GEO. WALTON.
LYMAN HALL,

14. ARTICLES OF CONFEDERATION—1781

The Second Continental Congress, which had assembled in May, 1775, found it necessary to assume authority in order to direct action against the British government. The government under the Second Continental Congress, the first government of the United States of America, has been called a "benevolent tyranny." In order to set up a stable, authorized government, delegates to the Second Continental Congress drafted the Articles of Confederation and submitted them to the several states in 1777. John Dickinson, of Pennsylvania, was chairman of the committee appointed by the congress to draft the Articles. This committee had the benefit of discussions and plans which had been before the colonial leaders in preceding years, such as The Albany Plan of Union which had been worked out by Benjamin Franklin in 1754.

In March, 1781, after all thirteen states had ratified the Articles of Confederation, the second government of the United States of America, the government under these Articles, began to function. This government lasted until 1789, when the third government, the

the contexts, audiences, and purposes of writing

writing contexts

The contexts for writing are strange when compared with those of speaking. Speakers imagine themselves standing before an audience, and they plan for that—and once the occasion to speak arrives, the context is clear: it is the time, space, and relations of being there, face to face, speaking. When writers write, however, they imagine someone else reading—and then never (or hardly ever) have a chance to sit and watch another quietly (or not) read the writing.

In writing, then, there is a gap between production and delivery that allows for all sorts of oddness. The act of speaking to an audience unites production and delivery; the act of writing does not. There can be long stretches of time and many miles between the scene of writing and the scene of reading. Something written can be dispersed, like seeds in the wind, and end up in odd or unlikely places, read by unknown, unexpected readers.

Sometimes you'll know the context in which your writing is received—as when you can picture your mother reading your letter in her favorite chair—but most times you have to give your best guess. You have to write with a picture in mind of a reader reading in some particular place and time.

There are several approaches that can help you work with this odd but fruitful state of affairs.

You can imagine the best possible place and time for a reader to read your words. Picture the lounge chair on the sunny blue vacation beach overarched by gently swaying palm trees, or picture the rocking chair, cat, and cocoa in front of the glowing fireplace, a light snow out the dark windows. These contexts might give you a sense of a gentle, responsive reader . . .

But do also picture the harder contexts, the swaying clang of subway cars after work, the cramped dorm rooms and blasting mp3s at 2 a.m., your teacher's dining room table covered with the 20 or 35 other papers to be read and responded to by tomorrow. These contexts give you a sense of the distraction and worries with which readers sometimes read.

We ask you to imagine these contexts not to frighten you, but to encourage you to think instead about the ability you have to address such contexts with your writing. Because writing is read by one person at a time, part of this peculiar context is the potential all writers have to shape their words for other individuals at this moment of eye-meeting-page (or screen).

You may have a good sense of context, given your particular writing, and you can work with that. But when you don't, when you can only imagine someone in some vague somewhere and -when, think about how your words can shape the context. How can you shape your words to slow down (or speed up) time? How can you shape your words to ask the subway rider to imagine a more comfortable ride—or that beach and palm tree?

You can use your writing, in other words, to build a word-shaped context, one into which you can invite your readers. Always.

compose ▪ *design* ▪ *advocate*

writing audiences

Audiences for writing—readers—have obvious and not so obvious differences from the audiences of speaking. From the perspective of the writer, the reader is an abstraction, a ghost-like presence hovering around the production of the writing. The reader to whom writers write is all-important, and yet often writers rarely meet many or most of their readers. And if one takes oneself to be writing to future generations, as Jefferson did, in part, when writing the *Declaration of Independence*, then a writer never meets his audience. Jefferson, for example, relied on his imagination and knowledge of people around him to understand his audience—the possible future readers of our *Declaration*.

It thus requires a concerted act of imagination to "see" your audience when they are not physically present, and it requires practice to see clearly what is relevant in and about your audience to the writing task at hand. The same is true when you are planning a talk, but the difference is that when you give a talk, you plan and then finally come face to face with your audience. Not so with writing.

In the last 50 years, some theorists have made much of writing's odd independence: once words are on paper, they can pass from hand to hand, and so it is hard to imagine or control who the reader really will be. For some writers, this could become a reason not to think at all about readers: after all, why worry about what you can't control? But we wouldn't have written this book if we didn't think effective writing comes out of trying to connect with audiences through knowing them as much as you can—even though you cannot ever know them thoroughly or completely, and even though you cannot possibly know them all. (And we couldn't have written this book without long and late talks about and with people in college classes hoping—we hope—to strengthen what they know and do about communicating with others.)

And if readers are always hard for writers to know, the reverse holds true for readers: for a reader, the author also is a ghostly presence, a voice half heard behind the words read silently or sounded out in the reader's own voice. The reader reaches out imaginatively to the writer in ways similar to the ways the writer reaches out imaginatively to the reader. Again, this could become cause to give up on ever understanding one another through writing. How can I ever really know what a writer was trying to say—or do—with a piece of writing? We still think it is important for readers to try to understand—based on the many clues that the strategies used tell us—what the writer's purpose is or was. This is why we stress "rhetorical analysis" in this book. Rhetorical analysis is a way of searching for what the author/speaker/designer/composer is trying to do with a particular piece of communication (while admitting the difficulties involved). By doing such analysis, you strengthen your sense of how you, as a writer, can reach through your words to the audiences you engage.

So you can talk with potential audience members before and while you write, and after, testing your ideas and how they take shape in the words you do finally place on a page. You'll never know your audiences completely, and you most often will have to imagine them during those moments when it is just you and the keyboard or pen trying to make words—but it is those acts of imagination informed by discussion, listening, and respecting that will best help you make decisions about what words to use.

writing purposes

Why did Thomas Jefferson and the signers of the *Declaration of Independence* decide the declaration should be in writing? Why did Jack Turner decide that his concerns about the way people—citizens, politicians, and the media—are responding to 9/11 should be a written magazine article?* Why did Clarissa T. Sligh, a photographer, decide the story of her role in the civil rights movement would best be told in a written essay?**

The obvious answer to the questions above is that these people are writers, so they decided to write. All that means, though, is that writers look for purposes that lend themselves to writing, or they shape their purposes to the demands of writing. These people, through experience and reflection, have a good sense of what writing can (and can't) do—and so they are able to take a purpose, consider its related contexts and audiences, and figure out that writing is the best strategy in the situation. Or they are able to figure out how to shape the purpose to writing.

---

* See chapter 13.
** See chapter 14.

But what kinds of purpose lend themselves to writing?

Purposes that are effectively addressed by writing involve

- *passing along large amounts of information.*
- *detailed descriptions of things, people, or events, fictional or non.*
- *making a complex argument that has many steps and tries to answer many possible objections.*

Sometimes—especially these days when the choices of media, new media, or multimedia are so available—people who are thinking about writing something have to ask themselves seriously if what they are trying to accomplish can best be accomplished through writing.

As you work, attend to how your approach is supported by writing—and, as with all communication—continually ask how you can modify and play in order to build communication that reaches out to others and fulfills your purposes.

compose ▪ design ▪ advocate

ethos, *logos*, and *pathos* as writing strategies

Each mode and medium has its own distinctive ways of embodying *ethos*, *logos*, and *pathos* as strategies to accomplish a purpose. Basically all that writing has to work with is the arrangement of words and the chosen graphic medium you use. Put in that simple way, the potential richness and complexity of writing can be surprising: how many ways there are to establish relations with a reader, to structure an argument, and to influence the tight braid of emotion and judgment.

The main point we make about *ethos* in writing is that, as with speaking and visual communication, the way you come across in writing is through the myriad of choices you make and how they reflect on you. Unlike speaking, though, writing cannot shape *ethos* through physical presence—the gestures, tone of voice, manner of dress, way of carrying yourself—of the person speaking. *Ethos* in writing relies on a more restricted range of choices. But that said, it always amazes us how numerous and complex is that range.

The main point we make in this chapter about *logos* in writing is that *logos* spreads across writing in three ways: We find *logos* in the overarching arrangement of writing, in smaller pieces of discrete argument that fit together to make the whole, and in the little patterns of words and phrases that shape individual sentences and phrases.

The main point we make about *pathos* in writing is that it is always there, even—or especially—when a writer is trying to hide or avoid it. Writing can seem less emotional that spoken or visual communication because it is simply abstract shapes on a page. And in the cultures that have developed out of western Europe (like the United States), we have a tradition of treating writing as the most objective, formal, rational, controlled, assessable, reliable, durable, explicit, and honest mode of communication. But writing is always shaped by emotions of one kind or another, always shaped by an individual or group with particular understandings of our world. Like speaking and visual communication, writing can only convey a limited view to others because it cannot possibly detail the experiences of breathing, smelling, moving, swimming, singing, or being on the street. (And it's not as though we ourselves can ever attend to every sense and action around us even when we're not trying to communicate about it with others.)

It is worth questioning, then, always, what attitudes writing asks us to take toward emotion, both through how writers evoke and so teach us about particular emotions, and through the ways kinds of writing treat emotion when they try to avoid or suppress it.

ethos in writing

In chapter 4, we introduced you to *ethos*: *ethos* is "the face you put on" for your audience.

You already know, simply from living with others, and perhaps without thinking much about it, how to shape yourself, your clothing, your actions, and your words so that you fit into a Friday night party, Sunday's church bench, Monday morning's classroom, or Wednesday afternoon's job. In each of these places you speak a little differently—just as you do when you address your mother, your minister, a childhood friend, a child . . . A challenge when you write is to translate this knowledge of "real world" strategies like clothing and tone of voice into words on a page or screen.

As with living day-to-day with others, you undoubtedly already do this work when you write. Without too much thinking you choose different ways to present yourself when you chat online, when you write job application letters, and when you compose research papers. If you study the writing of others, however, looking for how they construct themselves through words, you can expand your repertoire of strategies for engaging with others through how you—as a writer—come through.

Look back at the *Declaration of Independence*, for example. The overall purpose of that document is to argue to the world why the "united States of America" (to use Jefferson's capitalization) should be free from the rule of England's king. This is a daunting purpose and audience, for sure—but if we were to give it to you to write for homework, you could probably make some quick and easy decisions. *Logos* would probably be your choice for a main strategy, to demonstrate the high motivations of careful thought rather than rage or disgruntlement. Look how one approach to *pathos* then immediately arises: you know you need to appeal to what we consider to be "higher" emotions or values, such as freedom, liberty, and honor, rather than to the emotions that can make us seem small, crabbed, and selfishly pissed-off to others. What then of *ethos*? The *ethos* of the *Declaration* is constructed as a reflection of the *logos* and *pathos*. The *ethos* is a rational, balanced, enlightened *ethos*, as reflected in the logical structure of the document and its careful avoidance of emotional tones. The *ethos* borrows authority, as we said earlier, from the British philosopher John Locke, by echoing his words. And the calm, steady enumeration of grievances that make up the body of the document never gets shrill, and it provides more evidence that the author and those signing the docu-ment are not acting in haste. In short, the relation of the authors to their purposes largely determines the qualities we find in this *ethos*, this relation of writer (and signers) to readers.

For another example (or two): the *ethos* we find in Clarissa T. Sligh's essay "The Plaintiff Speaks" and the *ethos* we find in Marjane Satrapi's autobiographical comic later in this book share an important feature. In each case the writer's purpose is to present a struggle going on within herself, a struggle determined by the particular times and places of her growing up, and so the two writers have to filter their arguments through their experiences, their roles, and the struggles into which they were born—and so for each of them *ethos* is fore-grounded as it cannot be in the *Declaration of Independence*. If you look to their writing, you'll see you get a strong sense of them as individuals through their written tones of voice, individual words they choose, what they tell us about their lives and in what order, and so on.

As with Sligh and Satrapi, the times and places in which we live—because they shape contexts, purposes, and audiences—necessarily impinge on how readers perceive writers. For instance, Gary Smith and Julian Dibbell are white European-American

compose ▪ design ▪ advocate

men who each tell a story (in chapter 14) about African-American men. In our time and place, this is a delicate writerly task, for—as Sligh argues in her piece—when we represent others, especially others who have tremendously different experiences than ours, we risk making those others invisible by covering them over with *our* perceptions, *our* understandings, *our* words. In other words, sometimes we don't (or can't?) really write about those others: we write about ourselves and how we— not they—understand and experience what's going on. Do Smith and Turner show any evidence of self-consciousness about being white in their writing? How do they represent their own selves through their words and try to persuade readers that their writing isn't the erasing of others?

We won't answer those questions, because responses to those questions are probably going to be different for different readers—so look to those essays to see the strategies Smith and Dibble use to represent themselves. See if you think Smith and Dibble are able to persuade you through their *ethoi** that they can represent others fairly—and compare your responses to people whose skin color is different from yours: in our writing we all must at different times represent others, and it is important to learn strategies for representing ourselves with integrity and care so that we can represent others similarly.

factors contributing to *ethos*

Obviously, from what we have said above, many factors contribute to *ethos*. Small matters like word choice and diction can contribute. Larger matters like choice of example can contribute. If the writer becomes part of the writing, as we see in Sligh's case, then anything we learn about her (what she experienced, how she responded to what she experienced) can contribute. Also, prior knowledge of the person can contribute: Jack Turner, the author of a piece from *Outside* magazine that we use in chapter 13, is probably well known to the readers of *Outside* as someone who cares, and writes extensively, about the environment.

As you read through this book and its examples, look for other textual features that contribute to a written *ethos*—to your relationship to your readers and how they see and respond to you.

* The plural form of *ethos* is *ethoi*, a holdover from the word's origin in the ancient Greek way of making plural forms of words.

ANALYZING
ethos

■ **Discuss with others:** With a partner, look at Smith's "Higher Education" and Dibbell's "A Marketable Wonder" (in chapter 14) and describe the ways the authors come across in each case. Are there any noticeable differences? Does one use a strategy that affects *ethos* that the other does not? If so, can you make sense of why?

■ **Write with others:** In small groups, produce two different short letters to your college president requesting a walkway over a busy, dangerous street running through campus. (This is a concern on our campus; substitute a concern you have on your campus if you wish.) In both cases, make your *ethos* the most important part of the letter, because you are someone directly affected by the situation you are addressing. In one letter, be playful, be the epitome of the partying student; in the other letter, write as the student who is pale from library work. Do not be afraid to exaggerate your *ethos* in these letters; you want to experiment with pushing things, to see the kinds of results you get. Share the letters with others, and ask what they think of the character written into the letters.

building *ethos* in introductions to written compositions

We include this section here, after examining *ethos*, because *ethos* as a strategy is closely related to the introductions of written pieces, just as *logos* (as you will see) is closely related to the body of a piece of writing and *pathos* is closely related to conclusions. Of course, *ethos*, *logos*, and *pathos* are strategies that cut across an entire piece of writing, but they have a special emphasis in the parts mentioned.

Introductions are where readers and writers meet for the first time. Who you are as a writer and how you come across stands out as especially significant and worthy of attention when meeting and greeting—as with all first impressions.

STRATEGIES FOR INTRODUCTIONS

Cornel West, an African-American philosopher, uses a story to start his book *Race Matters* (which argues that race matters in our country, still). West tells us about a day he finished his work at Princeton University, where he teaches. Princeton is in New Jersey, relatively close to Manhattan, so he and his wife drove there for appointments they each had. He took her to her appointment, parked their car in a lot, and tried to get a taxi to his appointment. His appointment was with a photographer who was shooting the cover of *Race Matters*, and so

he was dressed in a nice suit (we can turn the book over and look at him on the cover smiling in his suit, which adds to the effect of his story). He then tells us that he stood on a busy street where he knew there would be many taxis, and he watched as empty taxi after empty taxi passed by, refusing to pick him up. The tenth taxi stopped instead for—as he describes her—a "well-dressed smiling female fellow citizen of European decent." Stepping into the taxi, she said to him, "This is really ridiculous, is it not?" He finally had to take the subway and was late to his appointment, but he chose not to mention all this to the photographer because he did not want to dwell on it, preferring instead to have an enjoyable time. The fact that he did not dwell on it did not mean he was not angry. As we learn, this is not the first time this has happened to him: this is a regular occurrence for black men on streets in the United States.

This is one way to begin a piece of writing—with a story. In this case the story is mostly about West, himself. How do you imagine it sets up the subject of his book, *Race Matters*? How does it set West up to address his subject? What relations does he establish with his readers?

Another way to begin writing is with a quotation. We started this chapter with a quotation from Annie Dillard because she

likes to write about writing and does so (we think) in lively detail. Our use is thus a version of show-and-tell, showing our position on writing through using the words of someone else, and so allowing us—and our *ethos*—to emerge from her authority.

Another way to start writing—and to start building your connection with your audience—is to direct a reader's attentions immediately to the subject at hand, without stories or quotations.

Gary Smith's essay in chapter 14 begins, "This is a story about a man, and a place where magic happened." Smith turns our attentions away from himself (the essay is not about him, after all) and to his topic—but we get a sense of a writer who thinks he has something intriguing to tell us, who wants to engage us in this story. So even though he never uses "I" in this essay, and starts right away directing our attentions elsewhere, we have an immediate sense of some qualities attached to this writer, qualities that shape our sense of how we trust him and respond to his words.

Clarissa Sligh's essay begins, "I was a teenager when I first saw this group of photographs and the article that they appeared with, on June 1, 1956, in the *Washington Post and Times Herald*, the major daily

compose ▪ design ▪ advocate

newspaper in the Washington D.C. area." Opposite these words are the photographs she discusses, and her words tell us where she lived, and she tells us that she is looking back on her past. That fact, combined with the generally unemotional tone of the words, indicate that personal reflection is at work here—and personal reflection is often quiet and slow. But at the same time Sligh's words indicate that events larger than the personal are at work, through her mention of a major newspaper. With one opening sentence, Sligh has immediately pulled us into a major thread of her essay—how personal and public lives entwine—and given us a sense of an *ethos* that is thoughtfully in between, thinking things through.

One way, generally, **not** to start a piece of writing is with what writing teachers call the "In the beginning" start. Every teacher of writing has received a class assignment that begins, "In the beginning, humans invented fire . . ." or "From the dawn of time, people have always worn shoes . . .": the paper could be arguing against gun control or for expanding the U.S.'s connection with the UN, but whoever wrote it clearly had trouble finding an opening into the argument. If you ever find yourself tempted to begin in this way, step back and ask yourself if this kind of beginning really is appropriate to your purpose. If not, go over the list of possibilities here for inspiration,

or read other writers. Take a look at the section on revision later in this chapter: perhaps you are having trouble beginning because you still need to figure out your purpose, or figure it out better.

There are many other ways to begin a piece of writing than what we've described:

- Make a strong, bold statement ("The Case against Affirmative Action" in chapter 13 does this).
- Fill in background knowledge readers need to understand what is to come.
- Give readers an image that will stick with them ("How to Look at the Periodic Table" in chapter 14 does this).

ANALYZING
written introductions

■ **Discuss with others:** With a partner, compare the introductions to Sligh's essay (chapter 14), Turner's opinion piece (chapter 13), and Elkins' essay (chapter 14). What similarities and differences do you see? Do the differences seem related to the kind of writing (essay, opinion piece)?

■ **Write with others:** With two partners, rewrite the introductions to "The Case for Affirmative Action" and "The Case against Affirmative Action" (in chapter 13). Try to write the introductions as though the authors of the second piece were writing the first piece, and vice versa: that is, imagine that the two men writing against affirmative action were to write the pro piece, and vice versa. Look at the strategies the writers use in each piece to construct their *ethoi*, and then apply those strategies to the introduction of the opposing piece.

■ **Discuss and write with others:** Below are introductions to research papers written by students like you. With a partner, discuss the following aspects of each of the introductions:

- Which introductions do you like best, and why?

- Describe the *ethos* that the writer is starting to develop in each introduction. Does the *ethos* seem trustworthy, knowledgeable, interesting, or . . .? How does each writer construct the *ethos* you describe? What word choices, tone of address, and kinds of examples help build the *ethos* you describe?

- What sorts of different relationships do these writers establish with you, their readers? Do you feel respected, trusted, hectored, or . . .?

- What do you expect the paper following the introduction to be about?

Based on your observations, draw up a list of characteristics of effective written introductions.

Customers listlessly drift through the fluorescent-lit aisles of any well-populated department store, pausing to contemplate whether or not their need for the latest television technology is greater than the latest mass-produced pop record. Smiling, interested faces can be seen all around, as people shop and blissfully choose the most fulfilling expenditures for their hard-earned currency. In the background, a smooth cocktail-jazz rendition of Nirvana's seminal "Rape Me" goes mostly unnoticed much in the way that Americans can just tune out television commercials. And even as they make their way toward the check-out lanes, a war is being quietly waged through the spacious, aesthetically pleasing expanses of the store. A war fought for control of customers' thoughts, moods, and behaviors. This war is a subtle, almost silent conflict between the subconscious minds of the shoppers and that inoffensive Nirvana song. (Jacob Loisel)

"The long arm of the law" is a clichéd and widely known phrase, but very representative of the law. The law tells you how fast to drive, when you can drink, how much you have to pay the government, and whom you can marry: the law impacts almost every aspect of your life. When the law has such a long arm it may become brittle and prone to breaking. In fact, there is such a major fracture, and it's called the Tort System. (Chad Wahlquist)

There are many women who work as firefighters, law enforcement professionals, and soldiers and who protect our country every day. I would like to show that these women are necessary for the everyday functions and protection of our country. Some women may feel that they would like to pursue these occupations, but that they are not capable or would not be accepted in doing these jobs. Although the world is more accepting today than it was in the past, there is still the mindset that women might not be as able as men to perform these kinds of jobs. I hope to show, through facts and examples, why women should be encouraged to reach for their dreams if they are looking to become firefighters, police officers, or military professionals. (Tara Holtslander)

Ray guns. Rocket ships. Household robots, a family vacation to the moon, and an alien standing behind you in line to see the latest *Star Wars* movie. Everyone remembers that old "retro" vision of the future, from watching old episodes of *Star Trek* or *The Jetsons*, or newer parodies like *Futurama* on Cartoon Network. A few decades back, when Neil Armstrong had just taken that "one small step" into the future and it seemed that science and technology could produce new wonders every day, the idea of entering a "Space Age" world didn't seem all that unreasonable. But now, in today's world, we can laugh at Fry and Bender and their bizarre adventures, and think how silly all those old visions were . . .

So what happened? How could this futuristic vision, ridiculous as it may have been, simply vanish despite the spectacular achievements that inspired them? (Adam DeConinck)

The year is 1983 and you are hanging out with some hometown buddies having a good time. Being an eighteen year old is fun, right? You are basically able to do whatever you want now that you're an adult. Sure, you have responsibilities like jury duty or (if you're a guy) you have to register for the military draft; if you don't, you'll be fined by the government. But isn't it nice to enjoy an alcoholic beverage along with those cigarettes you're possibly smoking? Isn't it nice to have all sorts of privileges to go with your newly acquired responsibilities? Unfortunately, it's not going to last. (Chris McNally)

Imagine a desolate place where sheer destruction and pollution have occurred. Forests have been stripped bare, the water has been poisoned, the air makes it hard to breathe, and everything has become an essential wasteland. Would this be a place where you would want to live, raise a family, and work? Is this place the complete opposite of any place you would ever like to be? This mysterious place is soon to be our very own earth, and unless there's a dramatic change in how we live, we are headed on the fast track to turning our precious earth into this ecological wasteland. (Jared Yach)

Maybe you haven't noticed, but our planet looks much different than it did just ten years ago. Fortunately, most of you likely live in an area that has not changed dramatically. Because you are not directly observing some of the changes I'm going to discuss, you may be tempted to think that nothing is changing—and never will. You would be terribly wrong to think this in today's world. It could be the case that a place where you planned to vacation is now underwater, or that the office building where you planned to work is flooded because it was built too close to the ocean. Or maybe the place you thought you might live has a permanent water shortage because the city's reservoir is drying up. Each of these could become a reality for you or someone you know.
(David Steslicki)

logos in writing

You can conceive of *logos* as applying to three levels in writing, as the diagram to the right shows:

1. There's the overall *logos* or structure of the whole piece of writing.

2. There are the various smaller arguments—such as syllogisms or lists—that a writer combines to build into the overall argument.

3. There are logical structures—such as definitions and other word choices—in every single sentence of writing.

1 The Declaration of Independence has the overall structure of a syllogism.

2 Building to that syllogism, the Declaration contains smaller logical structures, such as this list of grievances.

3 The Declaration shows very careful word choice at the sentence level.

compose ▪ design ▪ advocate

logos as overall structure

As you write and revise, the parts of your writing get combined and recombined, which means the overarching structure will change. It is helpful to start with a plan in mind for the overarching structure, even if it changes as you work. Having a plan can be as simple as deciding on one of the following ways of arranging writing, or can involve mixing these various arrangements.

SYLLOGISMS

The composers of the *Declaration of Independence* decided to give it the overall structure of a syllogism, which is the name for a kind of formal logical argument ("formal" here simply means that the argument has a particular arrangement, or form). As you'll find in a few pages when we discuss syllogisms in a bit more depth, syllogisms are most often short arguments—but they can be used as the pattern for the overall argument of a piece of writing, serving like the skeleton of the writing on which is fleshed out the *ethos* and *pathos*.

For now know this: a syllogism has the form of (generally) two statements and a conclusion following from those statements:

> *Socrates is a human.*
> *All humans are mortal.*
> *Therefore Socrates is mortal.*

The example we just gave is old and probably overused, and it doesn't seem to show us much of anything: one particular person is mortal, will die—well, so what else is new? We showed you that example just to show you the form; when the form is filled in with other statements and conclusions, perhaps the point of the form will be more apparent:

> *If bad conditions exist between a ruler and those ruled, then those ruled have the right to declare independence from the ruler.*
> *Those bad conditions currently exist between us and our ruler.*
> *Therefore, we have the right to declare independence.*

This is the overall form of the *Declaration of Independence*. The composers wanted their audience to understand that the audience was hearing from calm, rational, and educated people, people whose decision to seek independence was the outcome of careful reasoning and was the decision of last resort—and using a logical arrangement conveys that.

But it does more.

When you use a logical arrangement like a syllogism, it can be like challenging your audience: it is like saying to them, "Look, if you accept this first premise and this second premise, then here is a logical outcome—you have to accept it." We can believe that logic, when it works formally, is unassailable.

But of course it isn't. The logic holds only if an audience accepts the premises (or if using formal logic is appropriate for the issue at hand), and so—if we decide to use a syllogism as our overall structure—we have to make sure we present our premises thoroughly and in ways that make sense to readers. And that is precisely what the composers of the *Declaration of Independence* did, in listing all the bad conditions that existed as a result of the king's rule—as we discuss next.

Parallel structures, Juxtaposition, Analogy, and Compare-and-Contrast

Both the Griffin and Dibble essays in chapter 14 use similar arrangements. Both essays contain two, entwined stories, between which readers have to make connections. The stories juxtapose different lives and perspectives, inviting readers to see analogies between the stories or to compare and contrast them. Griffin alternates between the two stories throughout her essay, while Dibble separates the two stories into separate sections.

Griffin alternates her two stories as though she were weaving, showing how the events and ways of living that matter to her have been held separate but can be brought together—as her arrangement itself demonstrates. Dibble, meanwhile, seems to want to show us extended similarities between the past and the present, even though technologies have changed: given such a purpose, it then makes sense for him to tell each story at separate length, so that we can make extended and close comparisons.

Narrative

There are narratives—stories—scattered throughout this book. Griffin and Dibble, as we just described, juxtapose stories to support their different purposes. You could argue that Dibble's story of Bishop—the African-American man who first mapped the Mammoth Caves in Kentucky—is not a narrative so much as it is biographical description, and you would have a point. But information can be presented in more or less story-like ways, and we read the part of Dibble's essay that is about Bishop more as a story.

Narratives obviously involve people and events unfolding over time, but the events do not need to be presented in chronological order in order to be a narrative. Gary Smith's essay "Higher Education" (in chapter 14) is an example of this. The story of "Coach" and his changing relationship with the town of Berlin, Ohio, begins after the coach has died and cuts back and forth in time to capture different aspects of the story (how the coach came to be the basketball coach, how his relationship to the town improved, how the coach handled himself, how the town changed, and so on). In a similar way, the story of Griffin's red shoes has a chronology, but is not present-ed in temporal order because she wants to juxtapose it with the larger story about the ways western thought patterns shape and imprison womens' minds.

Stories about other people engage us because we learn how the choices of others shape their lives—and how we might then make similar (or not) choices. Story arrangements work well, then, when our purposes tell us we need to pull audiences in close, encouraging them to reflect on their own actions as they parallel those of others. Narrative structures suggest the possibility of developing more *pathos* in argument, too.

Problem-solution arrangements

Almost any piece of writing can be seen as using a problem-solution format because this arrangement is ubiquitous to our thinking. One example we include in this book is Clarissa Sligh's "The Plaintiff Speaks" (in chapter 14). Sligh shows how the civil rights movement, like so many social movements, embodied painful paradoxes. In this case, the problem was that in order to attract the attention of people in power—white people—blacks had to compromise and often let whites take the lead and the spotlight in the movement. The solution is not so easy to come by, but Sligh's essay—her writing—tries to forge a solution out of the pain of her story by showing us how the events actually unfolded and how we all might consider implications of speaking for others.

compose ▪ design ▪ advocate

smaller arguments to use for building larger arguments

Within the overarching structure of an example of writing are smaller pieces that have their own arrangements. These can be seen as arguments within arguments, or as steps or moves made that take us in different ways toward an end point, a conclusion. Scholars in the West—mostly philosophers and rhetoricians—have for centuries identified, named, and studied these moves, these forms of thought and argument. Whenever you use the relation between your ideas, or the relation between your ideas and what you see, as a way to persuade other people, you are relying on form—on arguments that depend on their particular formal arrangements for their force. When you say, "Hey, I was there, I saw it, and it was wrong," you are arguing formally. Likewise, when you say "Look, there's nobody on this planet who hasn't made a mistake at sometime in their lives, and I live on this planet, so I'm entitled to some mistakes," you are arguing formally.

What follows are a few forms of argument that especially pertain to writing.

THE LOGICAL FORMS OF DEDUCTION AND INDUCTION

Deduction is usually contrasted with *induction*. They are different ways of relating reasons to a conclusion, and they have different forms. It is easiest to see the difference between these forms of argument with examples.

Deduction

Deduction—deductive arguments—are also called "syllogisms"; we discussed them just a few pages ago as structures you can use to shape a whole argument, but you will most often encounter them and find them useful for making shorter arguments within the body of a paper.

A syllogism is an argument that relates a general claim like "There's nobody on this planet who hasn't made a mistake at some time in their lives," to a more specific claim like "I live here" in order to move toward a conclusion like "I ought to be able to make mistakes without being made to feel like I'm the only person who ever has!"

What makes a syllogism a syllogism is its form, which is, generally, this:

All A is B.

All B is C.

Therefore, all A is C.

Often these two forms of argument are worded as "if-then" statements:

If Heather has threatened the United States,

And if people who threaten the United States are potential terrorists,

Then Heather is a potential terrorist.

Or

Modern language classes expose students to other cultures.

Classes that expose students to other cultures prepare students to live in the expanding global economy.

Therefore, modern language classes prepare students to live within the expanding global economy.

You can perhaps imagine these examples, without much modification, supporting larger arguments about what to do about Heather or the sorts of classes that ought to be offered at a university—but often syllogisms are entwined with *ethos* and *pathos*, and need to be unpacked. For example, the following passage, which quotes a woman whose father was murdered when she was nine, contains at least one syllogism; see if you can separate it out:

"A ten-year-old boy was raped and killed by two pedophiles in a suburb of Boston, and it raised a huge rallying cry for the reinstatement of the death penalty in Massachusetts," she says. "What helped defeat it—by one vote—was the testimony of survivors, going as a group before the legislature and urging it not to kill in their name. I met some of those people and for the first time started to sort out my feelings about the politics of murder. There's a whole crowd out there—certain prosecutors and demagogues—that presumes to speak for the survivors in murder cases. They trot us out as the almighty victim and tout the death penalty as our path to 'closure.' But they can't even begin to know what heals us. No one can, till they've been in our shoes and had their soul split open."

We see the following syllogism in the quotation above:

Most prosecutors have not experienced the murder of a loved one.

Not experiencing the murder of a loved one prevents one from knowing what heals the pain of murder.

Most prosecutors cannot know what heals the pain of murder.

This syllogism may seem trivial or obvious when it is finally teased out from the *ethos, pathos,* and facts surrounding it, but it is only by teasing it out that readers can decide whether they want to be persuaded by it or not. Also, imagine that the quotation above had been presented only in its syllogistic form: would it have held your attention as much as the quotation did?

Take away these ideas, then, from our presentation here on syllogisms:

- Syllogisms can be wound up in other strategies, and—when you are a reader—need to be unwound for you to decide if you want to accept them.

- When you are a writer, you will often need to wind *ethos* and *pathos* together with the logos of syllogisms in order for them to be compelling to your readers.

Induction

Induction relates a string of specific statements to a more general statement—to a generalization that is the conclusion you hope others will accept. Here is an example that caught on with philosophers for some reason and has been handed down from generation to generation:

Look, this crow is black!
And this crow is black!
And this crow is black!
And that crow is black!
And that crow over there is black!
so . . .
All crows must be black.

Inductive arguments can also be phrased as "if-then" statements:

If this crow is black, and that crow is black, . . . then all crows must be black.

Here is an example of induction from K. C. Cole's book *First You Build a Cloud, and Other Reflections on Physics as a Way of Life,* a book intended to explain physics to readers wary of its complexities:

What we see depends on what we look for. It also depends on our point of view. A house viewed from an airplane does not look at all the same as a house viewed from its own front door, or from the window of a rapidly passing car. A baby does not recognize a toy viewed from the top as the same toy that looked so very different when seen from the side. A rotating shadow of any three-dimensional object will take on an amazing variety of different shapes. Which is

the "true" perspective? It may be that the only true perspective is the one that insists on a single perspective.

Cole gives three examples of how what we see changes based on the perspective from which we see—and uses those examples to support her conclusion that we ought always to acknowledge multiple perspectives. You ought to be able to picture yourself using similar strategies in your own writing.

...

Deduction and induction are called kinds of *inference:* they are ways of "inferring" a conclusion from reasons or premises. *Premises* are reasons put in the form of statements.

- Deduction lets you infer a conclusion based on the formal relations between the premises (general and specific) and the conclusion.

- Induction lets you infer a conclusion based on the probability that all the (specific) premises add up to the (general) conclusion.

Each form of argument has its weaknesses—which you might expect, given that these are ways to make jumps between one belief and another that might not be safe or honest jumps.

Deduction's problem: *deduction requires us to accept the truth of a general statement in order to lead to a conclusion, but how are we to establish the truth of that statement?*

compose ▪ design ▪ advocate

Induction's problem: *induction requires us to leap from a list of examples to a generalization about those examples, but how do we know when we have enough examples?*

LISTS AND REPETITION

The body of the *Declaration of Independence* has the structure of a list, a list of grievances against King George. The effect of the list in this case is aggregative: as grievance upon grievance builds, the reader of the document should feel what the colonists experienced under King George's rule and finally accept, as just, the decision to break away from England.

The list is so long that it threatens to overshadow the introduction and conclusion and undermine the syllogistic effect of the *Declaration*. When you read the *Declaration* earlier in this chapter, what did you think? Does it overwhelm the intended effect? If not, why not?

Both of the pieces about affirmative action in chapter 13 also have a middle part, or body, structured as a list. In this case the authors use the list arrangement because the issue of affirmative action, like most hotly debated issues, has turned into a long series of arguments and counterarguments. Both sides are aware what the other side has argued and of the impact the arguments have had, and they feel the need to counter those arguments, which leads inexorably to a list. When public deliberation reaches this stage, the media best suited to covering the issue may be broadsheets, brochures, and briefs—anything that lets you make a bulleted list.

But it is also helpful to consider what arrangements—what relations to audience and purpose—might help you break through stalemates of lists of positions stood up against lists of other positions. What strategies can help you bridge a context of such opposition?

ARGUING BY EXAMPLE

The best way to explain this form of argument is to, well, give an example, or, better still, to give several examples. Of course, if we are to be effective explaining this form, we have to know how many examples to offer. How many is not enough? How many is too many? To answer those questions requires a judgment call on our parts, based on our sense of the context and on you, the audience. We don't think you'll need many examples to understand what an example is. But to understand that examples can function in different ways we suspect will require more than one example.

One way examples work is to substantiate a general claim. We will risk boring you by returning to the *Declaration of Independence*. (U.S. citizens ought never to tire of their founding documents, yes?) The examples in the body of the *Declaration* serve to show or substantiate that King George was a lousy ruler for the colonists. James Elkins uses a different sort of example in his essay in chapter 14, when he shows us multiple versions of the periodic table of the elements to support his claim that our ways of understanding the physical world have perhaps been too shaped by that table of the elements hanging in all our high school chemistry classes. (And this shows how visual examples can be used in writing to support claims.)

But there is an important difference between those two examples. In the *Declaration*, the grievances are listed, but they are not explained at any length. Once placed before us, they are pretty much taken at face value. Their nature as grievances seems easily understood. In Elkins's article, however, the examples do not and cannot stand alone. They require his expert analysis of them, his careful explanation of who made them, the circumstances in which they were made, how they were made, and most importantly, how they function to shape our understanding.

This may be the most important decision you make when using examples. How much surrounding explanation do the examples need—and what kind of explanation?

THE FORM OF "CAUSE AND EFFECT"

When you start looking for this kind of argument, you find it everywhere. Western people are obsessed with finding causes. To locate the cause of something is a form of power in our societies because it feels as if, once you have a cause in hand, you are half way to understanding or solving a problem. Here are words from an essay about Willa Cather, a novelist whose *My Antonia* you may have read:

> . . . Cather went off to Lincoln, the home of the University of Nebraska. The following spring, for her English class, she wrote a theme on Thomas Carlyle which so impressed her teacher that, behind her back, he submitted it to Lincoln's foremost newspaper, the *Nebraska State Journal*. One day soon afterward, Cather found herself in print. The effect, she said, was "hypnotic." She was no longer going to be a doctor; she was going to be a writer.

This writing attributes Cather's life change to one event, one cause—neatly explaining how Cather became who she did.

For a different example, look at Susan Griffin's essay in chapter 14: Griffin identifies western ways of thinking (such as causal thinking) as the cause of certain limitations in women's thinking. In chapter 13, in their piece against affirmative action, Sacks and Thiel argue that affirmative action programs cause more racial problems than they solve.

This last example illustrates an important point to remember when studying and using causal arguments: causes vary in kind and degree, and they often must be argued for, because there are few cause-effect relations—especially in the areas of human social, cultural, and political affairs—we readily accept.

ARGUMENTS FROM CONSEQUENCES

Related to causal arguments are arguments from consequences. Causal arguments just assert a causal connection between one thing and another. Arguments from consequences make an evaluation of a slightly different sort. They assert that something should be judged based on the effects it has had, is having, or will have. The main arguments in both the opinion pieces about affirmative action in chapter 13 in this book argue that affirmative action programs should be maintained—or abandoned—because they have had good—or bad—effects. In the latter case, the authors against affirmative action argue not only that affirmative action programs have had bad effects, but that they have had the opposite effects of those they were intended to have. As was the case with examples as a form of argument, arguments from consequences require more or less explanation in order to be effective. It is only a first step to assert that something has had a bad effect; other steps are required to support that idea and to make the connection convincing to an audience.

☐ Look at the online chapter 7 resources at www.ablongman.com/wysocki for links to more information on using formal logical structures in writing.

Look at the online chapter 7 resources at www.ablongman.com/wysocki

ANALYZING
logical forms

■ **Observe:** Pick up any book or magazine at random, and see what logical forms you can identify in the writing. How do the forms support the overall purpose of the writing?

■ **Write creatively:** There are many more forms for arranging the smaller pieces of written arguments. Here are some others:

> Argument from absurdity
> Argument by elimination
> Argument from authority
> Argument from precedent

The names ought to suggest to you how these kinds of arguments function. Make up paragraphs that use these forms.

■ **Write creatively:** Follow the form of the list above—"Argument from" and "Argument by"—and make up your own possible argumentative forms: "argument by headache," for example, or "argument from strength." Then write paragraphs that use these forms.

We hope you can see that, although many forms already exist on which you can draw as you produce writing, you are not limited to what is there. You only need what works appropriately for your context, audience, and purposes.

compose ▪ design ▪ advocate

logos in helping others follow your arguments

We have been writing about *logos* as the arrangements that structure an overall piece of writing and then as forms that structure the paragraphs or series of paragraphs that build the whole. Now we look at *logos* at the level of sentences. First, as the sentences that help readers make connections between paragraph, and then as sentences and phrases on their own.

USING TRANSITIONS IN WRITING TO SIGNAL STRUCTURE TO READERS

Transitions in writing matter, big time. They keep readers oriented to where they are in writing, and help them understand how and why one sentence follows the next. Because transitions are so important, we're going to jump (almost) immediately into asking you to work with them. First, however, here's a list of transitional phrases to help you in the work we're about to ask you to do:

- **To indicate sequence:** first, second, third, next, then, finally, after, afterward, at last, before, currently, during, earlier, immediately, later, meanwhile, now recently, simultaneously, subsequently

- **To show position:** below, beyond, here, in front, in back, nearby

- **To emphasize a point:** even, indeed, in fact, of course, truly, above, adjacent

- **To provide an example:** for example, for instance, namely, specifically, to illustrate

- **To show addition of ideas:** additionally, again, also, and, as well, besides, equally important, further, furthermore, in addition, moreover, then

- **To show similarity:** also, in the same way, just as . . . so too, likewise, similarly

- **To show an exception:** but, however, in spite of, on the one hand...on the other hand, nevertheless, nonetheless, notwithstanding, in contrast, on the contrary, still, yet

- **To show cause and effect:** accordingly, consequently, hence, so, therefore, thus

- **To conclude or repeat:** finally, in a word, in brief, in conclusion, in the end, on the whole, thus, to conclude, to summarize

ANALYZING
transitions

■ **Hands-on analysis:** Take a piece of writing you like because it is easy to follow—any piece of writing that is at least several pages in length—and make a copy of it. Circle (a thick colored pen helps) every transition you see. Use the list to the left to help you identify transition words and phrases, but circle any set of words or phrases that helps you understand what comes next or how one sentence or section connects with what comes before or after.

After you do this, look to see if any patterns emerge. Are there transitions clustered at the beginnings and endings of paragraphs, or in the middles?

Try this with several other pieces of writing. What overall patterns for transitions emerge for you? Can you copy these patterns into your own writing?

logos as word play

Words are resources we've inherited. They let us draw attention to objects or people, show existing connections among people and objects, and suggest connections between objects and people that aren't but should be there. Obviously the more words we have to choose from, the richer we are in resources, but however many you have available to you, you still need to be careful about your choices. Some choices are regional or tied to groups of people, such as *pop* and *soda*, *pan* and *skillet*, *bakery* and *baked goods*, *submarine* and *hoagie*, *dinner* and *supper*. Other choices are situational, such as when you say "What's up?" instead of "What has happened since we last met?"

Put otherwise, words do not just refer to objects and people, they fit (or not) into the contexts of our use: they fit (or not) our expectations, values, beliefs, and habits, and they fit (or not) the roles from which we speak. A classroom teacher may say, "Let's start," but in a courtroom, the words are, "All rise, for the honorable Judge Hortense Johnson."

The humor newspaper *The Onion* often plays with word choice. For example, a recent headline was "Congress Passes Freedom From Information Act," as a way of pointing our attentions—subtly but with humor—to concerns the writers have about some governmental decisions.

TITLES

Titles matter: they are the first thing others see when they come to a piece of writing (or to a movie) and because we assume they clue us about what follows. For the most part, titles are words chosen and arranged on the first page or on the top of the first page. Titles have a certain authority. They can sound solemn, even when they are funny, because, well, because they are titles. They are special words set aside to frame the communication as a whole. Titles can begin the process of getting the audience in the mood, they can make a comment on what is to come, or they can begin the work of arguing by challenging the audience's expectations.

The power of titles is reflected in the following posting to an online discussion list:

On the way home from school today, my friend and I started coming up with alternate titles for "Meet the Deedles," titles that would make us actually WANT to see the movie, based on the premise it sets forth. Some of the titles I remember:

"Beat the Deedles," "Godzilla Meets the Deedles," "Beat The Deedles Into A Mushy Pulp," "Hot Lead, Meet the Deedles," "Sharks Eat the Deedles Alive," "Treat the Deedles . . . To Strychnine," "Watch the Deedles Die A Horrible, Painful Death of Fire and Twisted Steel."

Just thoughts . . .

The Enigma

ANALYZING
titles

■ **Discuss and write with others:** Here are some titles from student papers. Which titles engage you and encourage you to want to read the paper? How do they engage you? What sorts of audiences might be more likely to be engaged? Which titles aren't as interesting—and why? What do you think is going to happen in the body of the paper, based on the title?

With a partner, share your observations, and draw up a list of characteristics of titles that engage their audiences—and titles that don't.

Manufacturing Job Loss

The Quiet War for Freedom of Thought

Working Women and Society's View of Them

Earth: Used and Abused

A Story of Success

Youth of America

I'm 18. Give Me a Drink!

The Dilemma of Tort Reform

Same-sex Marriage

Don't Hurt Fluffy!

Textbooks: The Other College Expense

compose ▪ design ▪ advocate

NAMING

The choice of a name—of how to define a term—can be on the same level as the choice of overall argument to make. Here are some examples:.

"child with Down Syndrome" or "Down Syndrome child"

Michael Bérubé is an English professor married to another professor; they have two children, one of whom has Down syndrome. In a book Bérubé wrote about what he has learned from and about his son, *Life as We Know It: A Father, a Family, and an Exceptional Child*, Bérubé discusses the arguments swirling around what to call children like his son:

> As far as I understand the current status of our language, it's more proper to say "child with Down syndrome" than to say "Down syndrome child," on the grounds that the child should come first. We've even been known to have heated arguments that center entirely on an apostrophe, bickering over whether to say *Down* or *Down's* (the issue here having to with with whether our children should be symantically possessed by J. Langdon Down [who named the syndrome], as if they were DS versions of Jerry's Kids).

These arguments may seem petty, as Bérubé acknowledges, and yet he gives in to them: as a father of a child whose treatment is shaped by how others look at him—which is shaped by the names we use—he understands the delicacies and subtleties of how we approach others through the names we call them.

"undocumented immigrant" or "illegal alien"

In the chapter 10, we quote the historian and scholar George Lipsitz talking about the difference between calling someone an "illegal alien" and calling her or him an "undocumented immigrant." A close look at the differences between these names is telling. Those who prefer "illegal alien" do so because they feel it captures the reality of the situation: the people who are in the country without the proper papers are in the country illegally. They disagree with the use of the term "immigrant," which implies they have come into the country through legal means. Those who prefer "undocumented immigrant" do so because they feel that the term "alien" is mean-spirited and meant to dehumanize the people captured by the term. They feel that the term "undocumented" captures enough of the reality of the status of such people. Notice how each side has a term to vex the other.

"affirmative action" or "racial preferences"

David Sacks and Peter Thiel have an opinion piece, in chapter 13, against affirmative action, and as an argumentative strategy, they use "racial preferences" in place of the more familiar expression "affirmative action." They obviously feel that the former expression is better. What is at stake in this (and other) efforts to rename? Is it just a matter of which name or expression more accurately reflects reality?

ANALYZING names

■ **Discuss with others:** Below are names used to identify positions available to us in this country. Come up with new names that help reframe the debates that often separate—and polarize—those who take up these names.

pro-choice	pro-life
Democrat	Republican
liberal	conservative
homosexual	straight
gun rights	gun control

■ **Discuss with others:** What attitude toward "Muzak" is Jacob Loisel asking his readers to try on—and what strategies does he use to do this—in this research paper extract?

The term "Muzak" describes any music specifically designed to influence behavior and that is played in stores, offices, and other public places. Its name refers to the Muzak Corporation, which was the first company to develop such music and is also the chief supplier to the world. (There are several other competing companies, but none so successful as Muzak.) It's important to differentiate between Muzak and other forms of ambient music that you might hear in stores and workplaces; many stores simply tune in a radio station and play whatever is on. Such radio music is actual music, not engineered to influence customer behavior or mood.

DICTION

Courtrooms, classrooms, the aftermath of disaster, funerals, festivals, parties, births—these are all contexts that can call forth communication from us. And as we've seen, different contexts bring with them different sets of expectations on everyone's part. Often the people involved agree in their expectations; sometimes they don't. At a funeral, most people expect silence, solemnity, and seriousness. They also expect that when someone does speak, the person will speak quietly, but above all, with a certain kind of dignity. To achieve the proper dignity when speaking of the deceased at a funeral is to achieve a certain level of diction: "Randy loved his friends and loved being with them," not (generally), "Randy liked hanging with his buds." Diction is word choice made with an eye toward the particular context in which one is communicating.

Diction is tricky because it is not an exact science, and frankly, it often involves class- and culture-based norms, as the funeral example suggests. What is "proper" in a context? And for whom? And what is at stake if the "correct" level of diction is not achieved? These are questions we all have to struggle with.

Most significant perhaps for us using this book is the level of diction many people expect in college classrooms but especially in college writing. A good place to start is with the distinction between a conversational tone and a formal tone. It is common for students when they first start writing for school to write the way they have always talked, in part because it makes writing a little easier. But teachers often find such writing "sloppy" because when we talk we are not as careful about word choice, phrasing, and punctuation as we are or should be when we write. For many of your teachers, what is at stake is "exactness" of meaning and the proper demonstration of care in your choice of words and expressions. Differences in meaning that are not crucial in a casual setting can become very crucial in a research laboratory, an academic research paper, or a courtroom, for that matter. ("It was about a half a glass or water," instead of "It was a litre of water." "We went home," instead of "We drove Esmerelda's car back to my house at 8:30 p.m.")

ANALYZING diction

■ **Write creatively:** Below are the words someone used in thinking aloud about what to do with an introductory paragraph to a paper. Rewrite these words into a written introduction for a paper—but write two versions: make the first version as though it were shouting rudely at its audience, and then write a second version so that its readers will imagine its writer is wearing a formal suit.

I am, like, interested in how people walk in different cultures and at different times. I've been reading about how, like, men in ancient Greece were supposed to walk with long strides while women were supposed to move in these small dainty steps. I've seen movies of women in Africa carrying heavy jugs of water on their heads, and they look like they are dancing—how do they do that? When I visited India it looked as though people moved gracefully like trees—but tourists like me from the United States looked like we belonged in the Army—we moved so stiffly! I have a Japanese friend who says the same thing about how people walk here. You just think people just learn to walk all the same—I mean, it's just walking!—and instead it looks more and more to me like how you walk reflects some kind of values of where you grow up.

pathos in writing

Pathos in writing is
the stimulating
or *avoiding*
or *managing*
or *directing*
of emotion through your
written arrangements and word
choices.

We believe western culture has (or, rather, certain western societies at certain times have) undervalued emotion—the fact of emotion, the roles emotion plays in our lives, and expressions of emotion. But whatever your upbringing or cultural background, **emotion is always there**. We can't choose to "have" it or not. It surrounds us like space and air, unavoidable, and, more importantly, crucially necessary to a full and prosperous life.

The goals of "life, liberty, and the pursuit of happiness (or property)" would not make sense without emotion—or without thought, for that matter. If you're not sure you agree, that is fine. But as you read through this book, see if you can separate the emotions that move through the writing from the arguments being made.

STIMULATING *PATHOS* THROUGH WRITING

The opinion piece "Native education boosted by presence of elders" (in chapter 13) does not strike us as strongly emotional in its tone. Does it strike you that way? But it does seem infused from start to finish with certain distinct feelings and passions. The author, Robert Baptiste, clearly cares about this issue. He is not just writing a column to fill space. He writes with a gentle but clear feeling of respect for the Native Hawaiian elders who have been going into public schools and teaching children "important lessons" about Hawaiian culture. The evenness of Baptiste's tone is attested to by the fact that there is one moment, really only one that we can see, in which emotion seems to break through. It is when he says, "How dare someone tell our elders they are unqualified?" Notice that he does not begin his writing with this statement, as he could if he wanted to begin boldly, to shock or provoke a response. His emotional statement comes instead in the very middle of the writing, as though we slowly move toward it, and then just as slowly move away from it, letting it be as the honest outburst that it is. (*Is* it an "outburst"? Is that the right word to describe it?)

AVOIDING *PATHOS* IN WRITING

Two pieces of writing we've mentioned in this chapter share the desire to avoid emotion, any connection with emotion, or the expression of emotion—and each for different reasons: these articles are Sacks and Thiel's opinion piece against affirmative action, and Jefferson's *Declaration of Independence*.

Sacks and Thiel's opinion piece against affirmative action presents an argument, or a series of arguments, against affirmative action programs like those operating on the Stanford campus, their alma mater. They know the subject is controversial. They also know that their position can easily be seen as mean-spirited, as wanting to take something away from someone else (though they argue the opposite is true), or as branding some people "undeserving." As a result, Sacks and Thiel try to steer clear of emotion. Ogeltree, the person who wrote the companion opinion piece in favor of affirmative action, seems less concerned to avoid the emotional dimension of the issue. Why do you think this is? Is the issue more personal to Ogeltree than it is to Sacks and Thiel? Can you find any indication in Sacks and Thiels' writing that indicates it may be personal to them too?

MANAGING OR DIRECTING *PATHOS* THROUGH WRITING

We said that Jefferson's *Declaration of Independence* tries to avoid emotion, but really we think the situation is more complex: the *Declaration* is a study in both the avoidance and the inciting of emotion—that is, in the managing and directing of emotion. Here's how to understand it as avoidance: those who signed the declaration wanted to be seen as Enlightenment rationalists, balanced in their judgment and prepared to take on the challenge of inventing a new government. The body of the document, however, is a long list of egregious actions mostly attributed to King George. The emotions weaving through the body of the *Declaration* are rich and complex. They involve fear and anger, frustration and righteousness, and disgust and hope, among others. The line Jefferson walks in the *Declaration* is between rationally justifying the act of declaring independence from England and steeling himself, those signing the Declaration, and the colonists actually to do this brash, bold thing of revolution. In this way, we might say the *Declaration of Independence* appears to be avoiding emotion, but really is about managing and directing it—toward the proper objects: King George and securing independence.

ANALYZING
pathos

■ **Write:** Here are some emotions: joy, resentment, anger, contempt, love, compassion, sympathy, pity, grief, jealousy, pride, envy, hope, terror. Pick one of the emotions (or another you can name) and, for a week, look for examples of that emotion in your daily life, in movies, and in what you read.

Use your examples to respond in a piece of writing to the following questions about your emotion:

- What objects or events tend to evoke the emotion? (For example, jealousy can be evoked by other people who have qualities or possessions we would like to possess ourselves.)
- How is the emotion expressed? What do people say, do, or look like when they are experiencing the emotion?
- In order to experience that emotion, what beliefs must someone hold? (For example, experiencing hope requires us to believe that the situation in which we find ourselves can change.)
- In order to experience that emotion, what values must someone hold? (For example, experiencing grief about the loss of another means that we valued the love or company of the other in some way.)

- What ways of dealing with things— what strategies—does the emotion point us to?
- What kinds of relationships to other people does the emotion set up or suggest?
- What limits do you see being imposed on the emotion and its expression: what, when, who, how, why?

■ **Discuss with others:** Pick one of the editorial and opinion pieces in chapter 13. Identify one or two emotions you believe are evoked by the piece. Describe how the emotions are evoked, but also describe how they relate you as a reader to the people, policies, or events that are the focus of the writing: are you asked to be a judge, or to take on a particular value, or . . . ?

CONCLUSIONS

As we said when we talked about introductions in the section on *ethos*, *pathos* and conclusions traditionally have a special relationship because how an audience/reader is feeling matters especially at the end of an effort to communicate. It is a question of whether you are able to get under the skin of the people to whom you are writing: leave them laughing or leave them crying, or better still, leave them in a more complex emotional state that works with the more complex thinking you hope they'll do.

When you are the end of something, you can either look back over what you have done, look around you at where you have gotten to, or look ahead to what might or should come next. Most written conclusions do a little of each, and they differ in the emphasis they put on one or the other activity.

Strategies for conclusions

The article "The Partly Cloudy Patriot" in chapter 5 is a rumination on the notion of patriotism. The writer, Sarah Vowell, argues that she is uncomfortable with full-blown patriotism, with the kind of idealized patriotism whose single-minded focus can lead to civil strife (as she quotes others who are from countries that have more recently suffered from civil war than ours). Instead, she is a "partly cloudy patriot" who loves her country but wants room for disagreement and argument, argument based on respect and concern for others—and so she ends her essay with an example that sums up all her reasons by demonstrating what she calls "the very epitome of civilization [and] good government." Vowell describes riding on the subway in New York City and seeing a sign that promises riders they will be cared for if they are sick, and, as a result of seeing that sign, she starts looking more closely at the people around her on the train. She ends, then, with an example rooted in *pathos*: the way she has written her conclusion puts us on the train with her, imagining the fellow passengers, imagining individuals who need care. Readers thus finish the essay thinking about patriotism not as an abstract idea but as bound up in relations between us and real breathing others.

❧❧❧❧❧

The essay "Higher Education" (in chapter 14) also ends with an example. The author of "Higher Education," Gary Smith, tells us that after "Coach" died the people of the town of Berlin, Ohio, remembered him not in word only but also in deed. Smith writes for several pages to describe the aftereffects of Coach's having been a loved member of that town because (Smith believes) the things the town did—especially one of Coach's student-athletes moving to a mostly African-American neighborhood to do what Coach did "in reverse"— are like policies, policies for a better life. Of course, the ending to "Higher Education" is much more emotional than the ending to "The Case Against Affirmative Action," as we would expect, or rather, as the readers of each piece of writing would expect.

❧❧❧❧❧

Our favorite strategy for ending is one we stole from someone's paper in one our classes. We call it the abrupt ending: on the last line of the paper it says, "I'm done." Other versions include "The end" and "That's all folks!"

Obviously there are many other ways to end a piece of writing. Here are a few:

- ☛ Make a strong, bold statement.
- ☛ Fill in the last bit of background knowledge readers may need to understand what they have just read.
- ☛ Give readers an image that will stick with them.

Can you think of others?

ANALYZING
written conclusions

■ **Write creatively:** Here are the last paragraphs of the essay "Save the Whales, Screw the Shrimp," by Joy Williams. Analyze this conclusion—its arguments, *ethos*, and *pathos*—by rewriting the paragraphs to drain all the energy out of them and then seeing how others respond.

The ecological crisis cannot be resolved by politics. It cannot be solved by science or technology. It is a crisis caused by culture and character, and a deep change in personal consciousness is needed. Your fundamental attitudes toward the earth have become twisted. You have made only brutal contact with Nature, you cannot comprehend its grace. You must change. Have few desires and simple pleasures. Honor nonhuman life. Control yourself, become more authentic. Live lightly upon the earth and treat it with respect. Redefine the word progress *and dismiss the managers and masters. Grow inwardly and with knowledge become truly wiser. Make connections. Think differently, behave differently. For this is essentially a moral issue we face and moral decisions must be made.*

A **moral issue!** *Okay, this discussion is now toast. A* **moral** *issue . . . And who's this* **we** *now? Who are* **you** *is what I'd like to know. You're not me, anyway. I admit, someone's to blame and something must be done. But I've got to go. It's getting late. That's dusk out there. That is dusk, isn't it? It certainly doesn't look like any dawn I've ever seen. Well, take care.*

■ **Discuss with others:** Individually or in small groups, compare the conclusions of Turner's opinion piece (in chapter 13), Elkins' essay (in chapter 14). What similarities and differences do you see? How are the similarities related to purpose?

■ **Write creatively:** With a partner, rewrite the conclusion to any recent article you've read. Choose one of the strategies we've listed here, or one that you've discovered, and produce as *awkward* a conclusion as you can.

■ **Discuss with others:** Bring to class just the conclusion to a piece of writing you've read on your own. (Type up the conclusion, or make a copy of it.) In class, trade conclusions with someone else. From just the conclusion you've been given, try to re-construct the rest of the writing. Describe the kind of writing (essay? opinion piece? academic writing?), the *ethos* of the writer, and the structure of the piece as best you can in an act of writing archaeology.

compose ▪ design ▪ advocate

the written strategies
of revising, editing, and proofreading

"How appalled I was to learn that, in order to write so much as a sonnet, you need a warehouse. You can easily get so confused writing a thirty-page chapter that in order to make an outline for the second draft, you have to rent a hall. I have often "written" with the mechanical aid of a twenty-foot conference table. You lay your pages along the table's edge and pace out the work. You walk along the rows; you weed bits, move bits, and dig out bits, bent over the rows with full hands like a gardener."

—Annie Dillard

When you put something down on paper, it can be hard to see it in any other way than how it first came out. It just looks so good there printed out on paper—and besides, we are all busy, so it is tempting to mumble, "This is just fine," and just turn it in. Much of the writing you do in college and beyond, though, needs to do complicated work and the only way to ensure your writing does all it needs to do in any given context is to revise, not just edit.

WHAT'S THE DIFFERENCE BETWEEN REVISING AND EDITING?

Alice Horning is a scholar of composition studies who has carefully studied revision of writing. Horner argues that revision takes many forms: it can involve changing an overall plan, changing an approach to the writing task, changing an approach to the audience, changing overall arrangement, changing tone of voice, or changing examples or kinds of evidence.

Revision, in short, can occur in many different ways, on many different levels—but common to them all is that the writer must be willing to make large, sweeping, substantive changes to the first (or even the fifth) version of writing. Often this can mean changing words or dropping paragraphs or whole pages we really like.

Editing, by contrast, is a concern with the surface features of a text. Editing might involve a writer trying to keep tone of voice consistent (when that is desired) throughout a composition, correcting mechanical and typographical errors, or inserting transitional phrases or passages, and so on. Both revision and editing are important, but it is also important not to confuse them and to understand when one or the other is called for. For example, too much editing early on can be a waste of time, if the passages edited are later marked for elimination. What you can learn from this is: **don't worry about grammar, spelling, or other such details until you are in the final stages of polishing writing for its final purposes.** In the early stages of writing, keep yourself focused on figuring out your statement of purpose and the particular strategies that will help you achieve that purpose; don't let your attentions get all fragmented by trying to make your grammar perfect so early on—and, in fact, you'll do a better job of polishing writing if you consider that as a step in the process, **the last step.**

WHY REVISING AND EDITING ARE RHETORICAL

In the introduction to section 2 we distinguished between writing-to-learn and writing-to-communicate. The distinction exists precisely because few people produce, in a first pass, writing that others can understand readily. Revising and editing are parts of any process for producing writing for others precisely because the writing is for others: revising and editing are about making sure your writing makes sense to others. And any time you are concerned about how your writing strikes your readers—any time you are concerned about the effects of your writing—you are being rhetorical.

But there is another dimension to the rhetoricality of revising and editing. You need to revise and edit to the extent that make sense for the context and audience for which you are writing.

When you are writing something that is meant as a quick memo, you want others to be able to read it—but they do not need to appreciate its careful sonorous language. When you are writing something that you want to strike others as professional, you want to be careful that it has no typos or odd grammatical moments. (We've known people who haven't been hired for writing jobs because there was one single typo in their writing samples.)

Revising and editing show that you care about your context and audience.

MORE DISTINCTIONS: REWRITING AND REVISING / EDITING AND PROOFREADING

Rewriting can be the term we use for rethinking an overall project, redefining it, and starting over again, whereas **revision** can be the term we use for staying with one's main idea or core argument by making large-scale deletions and adjustments.

Likewise, **editing** can be the term we use for combing through a finished draft, making relatively small changes in words, phrases, and transitional sentences. **Proofreading** can be the term we use for the very last pass over a piece of writing, when all you need to do (or have time for) is finding mechanical and typographical errors and misspellings.

Many different aspects of the writing context ought to lead to or prompt revision. That is, you know you need to revise when:

- You give your draft to others to read and they can't figure out what your argument, purpose, or audience is.

- You try to summarize each paragraph of your writing, to see that you have built a logical argument, and suddenly you don't have a clue why one paragraph follows another. (This may be a sign that you need to revisit your statement of purpose.)

- You realize that a reader probably won't understand why you moved from one point to the next.

- You discover you are trying to say two things at once and then have to decide if you should say one first then the other, or save one for another paper.

- You discover your last paragraph should be your first, that it would make a really great introduction (with a few changes) because it was not until the end of your first draft that you began to understand clearly what your overall project is.

In order to write well, then, you need to revise or at least always keep open the possibility of large-scale revisions. To keep yourself open to revising often means recognizing and overcoming various built-in resistances to revision, among them the belief that the first draft of a piece of writing is always the best, refusing to imagine how a piece of writing might be changed, and privileging what is actual over what is possible.

If you find yourself resisting revision or being tired of revising, hang in there. It is through struggling that you find your own way through, that you find strategies that work for you. But revising can also be intensely pleasurable, satisfying, and creative work: revision is where you try out different arrangements, different word choices . . . Writing is a way of making your ideas and positions visible to others—and to yourself. Through revising, you get to try out different positions, different possible ways of being.

Here are other tips to help you **revise** your writing:

- Write more than you need or feel you need. The first and second times around, say everything you can at each step of the way. Explain what you are trying to do at each step, and say it in detail. The reason for doing this is that, often, we use shorthand in our writing, making jumps that we understand well—but that someone else might not. If you spell everything out, you are more likely to say things in ways that others can follow. One of the things we have learned from writing is that you can rarely be too explicit in giving your reasons; it is surprising how little others are capable of reading your mind!

- From Marilyn Cooper, a friend of ours who knows how to teach writing: Identify all the "stakeholders" in a given context and plan the changes you need in order to respond responsibly to everyone interested in and affected by what you write. Another version of this: Try to make your main ideas seem strange to you by finding a perspective on those ideas that is different than your own.

- Have a friend (or enemy) read your draft aloud to you slowly and listen for large-scale problems in meaning and coherence.

- Have a friend read your draft and identify two or three specific changes to make.

- Identify the one passage you would keep if you were forced to keep only one. This helps you locate the strongest points in a draft of writing.

There are a lot of ways to **edit and proofread.** Here are several ideas. We encourage you to use more than one.

- If you are writing on a computer with a spell-checker and/or grammar-checker program, the program can help you find misspellings and indicate where your idea of good grammar doesn't match the software designers' ideas—but this, you probably know, is not nearly enough. Sometimes such programs get things wrong. Spelling-checker programs cannot tell when it is appropriate to use *there* rather than *their*, for instance. Also, no program is going to catch problems you might have with the sound or flow of your writing, or the need for a transition between steps. To catch important changes, you need people—your other self, a friend, or colleague—people with ears, eyes, and brains attuned to language.

- You can set aside time for giving full attention to do proofreading yourself.

- You can have a friend or classmate read carefully in the same way, marking places for you to consider and perhaps change.

- You can read your paper aloud to yourself or to a friend listening for places that do not read smoothly and so may need attention. It is good to read slowly and steadily, but not too slowly, of course, or you will not be able to hear the missing transitions, awkward phrasing, or oddly placed words.

- You can silently read your paper backward looking for misspellings. Often when we know what a word is supposed to be, we do not notice it is misspelled. Our eyes trick us. Moving backward through the paper will not help with mechanical or stylistic problems, but professional editors use it to catch hard-to-spot misspellings.

☐ To help you understand the differences among—and better work with—revising, editing, and proofreading, look to the additional materials on these topics linked in the online chapter 7 resources at www.ablongman.com/wysocki

AN EXAMPLE OF REVISION

To the right is the first draft of a letter to the editor, written by Justin Foley, who was taking a class with Anne.

After reading the draft, other people in class who were Christian told Justin that they felt a bit attacked by the draft: he describes Christians as "despising" others and just flatly states in the writing that he does not think they can understand or help him. They could see that his purpose was to encourage others to listen thoughtfully to him, but they didn't think that this writing yet achieved that purpose. They also told him that the first sentence of the draft right away made his *ethos* sound judgmental and angry—and that such an *ethos* would get in the way of their being able to think of the writer as someone to whom they would want to be attentive.

On the next page is Mr. Foley's revision of this draft.

TO THE EDITOR:

Preachers of God really irritate me. Being an atheist, I cannot stand the thought of preaching about god with no viable proof as to if there really is a god. Questions such as, if there is a god then why do so many people suffer around the world? And if God forgives all sins then if I killed somebody and felt bad for it should I still be able to make it into heaven? Although I have many doubts about Christianity and its beliefs I also see that most church-goers are happy that they are part of it. They also have a group of people with whom they feel comfortable and have their religion in common. I understand that working for god can be an unbelievably rewarding thing and that many people experience this if and only if they have faith. This brings me to my point, how can Christians, or any faith for that matter, convert me so that I once again believe in something larger than myself?

Missionaries are very successful at converting people who are in third world countries to the Christian faith, so where are the missionaries in our country? At one time I was a Christian, I did not go to church but I believed in god and I knew if I lived correctly I would have a place in heaven after I died. Now I cannot ascertain how I am supposed to think those thoughts again without tremendous help from persuasive believers in faith.

Christians despise atheists because of their denial of God and the Bible. However I do not believe they understand the state in which atheists are in. Without hard proof or a miracle of some sort, I think it is extremely difficult to escape the atheist belief that there is no god. So how can I start to believe in something that has not shown itself in any way to me? Perhaps trying to go to church and talking with pastors and priests will help. I will try both; however I am doubtful that Christians can help a lost soul named Justin Foley.

Sincerely, Justin Foley

TO THE EDITOR:

Being an atheist is not only painful it is a relentless pain that will not subside. I have the unfortunate luck of not believing in God and I have been both condemned and ignored for my beliefs. I once considered myself religious; I did not attend church, but I believed in God and I knew if I lived correctly I would someday find heaven. However, I have strayed from those former beliefs and have relied on science and facts instead of intuition and faith for my thoughts on religion.

Christian friends of mine have tried to convert me, ceaselessly telling me that I "just" have to believe and have faith. Faith is something I do not have and cannot possess at this time. Other Christians believe we, atheists, are blasphemers who will go to hell because of our refusal to believe in God and the Bible. These latter people do not understand our disposition. I would love to have faith and have a place in heaven where I will see all of my loved ones when I die, but I cannot.

Condemnation and people trying to convert me because of my honest doubt of religion do little to ease the anguish of my beliefs. Christians, Muslims, Jews, Buddhists, Hindus, and countless other religions of the world, please allow atheists to speak with you and ask questions about your religion. Give them space to think and do not berate them with questions or force upon them your beliefs. Listen to them and try to see religion from their perspective. I believe this is the only way for atheists to find the way in any religion. I know I need help and if there is anything I believe can help, support from others, not criticism and hatred, is the key.

Sincerely, Justin Foley

Here is how Mr. Foley revised his original draft. What sort of *ethos* has he created in this writing—and how has he created it? What emotions does he raise in you, as a reader? Do you think he has succeeded in revising his draft so that you listen more closely to his words—and think more about what he asks of his readers?

- **Hands-on revision:** This exercise is productive when you have a solid draft of a paper, and want to check how others are following your arguments.

In your word processor, set up your paper so that there is only one paragraph per page. Print the paper, shuffle the paragraphs, and give them with tape to a friend or classmate. Ask that person to read the pieces and then tape the paper back together in an order that makes sense. (And if your reader can't figure out where some paragraphs go, just leave them out.)

Compare the taped-up result with your original paper.

Did the reader see the same arrangement of paragraphs you did, or is the order different? Which do you like best, and why? Is there anything from the alternative order that you can learn from? For instance, do the differences suggest that you need to clarify the transitions between parts of your paper? Do the differences suggest that some step is missing from the way you present your argument? Do the differences suggest that your introduction (or conclusion) do not yet do what introductions and conclusions are supposed to do?

A NOTE ABOUT THE RHETORICALITY OF GRAMMAR AND SPELLING . . .

An awful lot of us have been subjected to writing educations that treat grammar and spelling religiously, as though somehow grammar and spelling are ineffable, transcendent, and always and everywhere the same. We do not think this.

Let us offer up some examples in support of the claim that grammar (and by extension, spelling) depend on context and audience. Shakespeare, whose plays you very likely have been required to read as an exemplar of pleasurable English, is responsible in his plays for phrases like the "knot intrinsicate of life" and to "lie blist'ring fore the visitating sun." More recently, Mick Jagger sang "I can't get no satisfaction" and Bob Marley sang "Them belly full, but we hungry." And still more recently Missy Elliott sang ███████████████████.

The point is that multiple prepositions, double negatives, "nonstandard" use of pronouns and verbs, and four-letter words have their place. The point is that context and audience expectation are everything. Sometimes grammar has to go out the window to make a strong statement about love or politics in music, and that sometimes—as with some hip-hop—not using what teachers (and other standard bearers) think is proper is precisely the point.

When you are revising, editing, and proofreading, make your choices about grammar and spelling based in terms of your audience and context.

■ **Write creatively:** Change the following sentences to be shorter or clearer or free of grammatical and/or spelling errors. How do your changes modify your original sense of the sentences?

- For thine is the kingdom, and the power, and the glory, forever. Amen.
  —*Matthew 6:13*

- And all the people saw the thunderings, and the lightnings, and the noise of the trumpet, and the mountain smoking.
  —*Exodus 20:18*

- We shall not flag or fail. We shall go on to the end. We shall fight in France, we shall fight on the seas and oceans, we shall fight with growing confidence and growing strength in the air, we shall defend our island, whatever the cost may be, we shall fight on the beaches, we shall fight on the landing grounds, we shall fight in the fields and in the streets, we shall fight in the hills; we shall never surrender.
  —*Winston Churchill*

- Injury, violation, exploitation, annihilation, cannot be wrong in themselves, for life essentially presupposes injury, violation, exploitation, and annihilation.
  —*Friedrich Nietzsche*

testing writing

When you ask others to read your writing before you consider it finished, you are testing your writing. And there are different approaches you can use to help others read your work in more or less useful ways depending on where you are in the writing process. We've described some approaches on previous pages for how you can get assistance with the arrangement of your composition and with editing and proof-reading.

Here are other ways to test your work during different stages of drafts:

- When you complete your very first draft of a piece of writing, give it to someone else to read for feedback, preferably to someone from the audience for whom you are writing—but don't just hand over your writing. Tell the person what you are trying to achieve and why, so that she or he can read knowledgeably. You can write down on a piece of paper the points to which you want your reader to attend, and ask your reader to write comments on this paper.

- Give your writing to someone else, as above—but now ask your reader to summarize each paragraph in a phrase or sentence. Look over the list of sentences and see if the order makes sense—the sense you thought your composition made before this exercise. You can do this yourself, also.

- Give your writing to someone else, as above—but now ask your reader to describe the relation between *ethos*, *pathos*, and *logos* in your writing. You can do this yourself, also.

- Draw a map that shows the arrangement or structure of your composition.

- Design a plan for revising your composition.

A reminder: Before you decide which kind of testing to do, however, take a few minutes yourself to figure out the kind of feedback that will be most useful to you. Freewrite for a few minutes to figure out the kind of help you really need: Do you really just need someone to look over your grammar for you, or are you still working to figure out your main argument?

Self-test for a writing draft

❏ Describe your audience.

❏ What is your purpose?

❏ What is strongest about this draft?

❏ What concerns you most about this draft?

❏ What sort of feedback would be most helpful to you now?

You can use this chart to get feedback on a research paper—If the categories for feedback are helpful to you. Otherwise, modify what's here to work for your context, purpose, and audience. (When you give a chart like this to others, ask them to fill in all the comments explaining how they checked off the paper's qualities: it can help, before you use a chart like this, to discuss what kinds of comments are helpful.)

Testing a research paper	doesn't do/ have this	<>	does this okay	<>	done per- fectly	comments
The introduction to the paper...						
grabs the attention of the reader.						
focuses the topic (that is, it clearly expresses the problem or question with which the paper is concerned).						
The paper's overall argument...						
makes sense.						
can be argued.						
answers the question or problem posed in the introduction.						
The supporting argument(s) of the paper...						
can be easily followed by a reader.						
are ordered to support the overall argument.						
The ending/conclusion of the paper...						
supports the overall argument.						
follows out of the preceding supporting arguments.						
In terms of differing viewpoints, the paper...						
acknowledges that they exist.						
addresses and considers those viewpoints.						
The *ethos* of the paper is...						
appropriate to the argument.						
credible.						
engaging to a reader.						
The paper's sources are...						
credible.						
appropriate for the arguments.						
appropriately documented and cited.						

compose ▪ design ▪ advocate

responding to the writing of others

When you are asked to respond to the writing of someone else:

- **Be sure you know the kind of feedback the writer needs.** Perhaps the writer only needs someone else to make sure the grammar and spelling are correct—but perhaps the writer needs feedback on the order of ideas, in which case correcting spelling is useless because the words you corrected might go away in the revision. If a writer asks you for help with a piece of writing, and does not specify what kind of help—ask (and this can assist the writer in articulating what the writing needs).

- **Do tell writers what you like about their writing, and why.** Writers (like any person) need to know what they do well. When we have a sense of what we do well, it gives us a ground on which we can stand as we start developing our other abilities.

- **Read the writing at least twice before you make any comments.** You might take some notes during a first reading, but use the first reading to get a sense of what the writer is trying to do—then reread to look for the parts in the writing that most support what the writing is trying to do, and for the parts that aren't as supportive.

- **If you are asked to give feedback on the main argument of a piece of writing, say first what you think the main argument is.** You may be seeing a different main argument from what the writer intends, and the writer needs to know; the writer can then reshape the argument to fit the original intention, or can reshape it to pull out what you see. But if you give feedback on a different argument than what the writer intends, the writer will be revising at cross (and confusing) purposes.

- **Give reasons for your comments.** If instead of, "I get lost in this paragraph," you say, "In this paragraph you started out writing about the effects of video game violence on children but then you ended by writing about television cartoons, and I couldn't see what connected those two ideas," you give the writer information useful for revision. (And if you work to articulate feedback in this way, you'll find it easier to look at your own writing just as carefully; teachers of writing often talk about how useful to their own writing it is to have to formulate feedback to people in their classes.)

- **Think about the most useful, respectful feedback you've ever received, and emulate it.** (You might keep a collection of useful feedback, and analyze what makes it useful. This will not only help you give good feedback to others, but will help you develop a stronger eye for reading your own words more critically.)

- **Think about the most useful, respectful feedback you've ever received, and emulate it.** We repeat this advice because how you give feedback determines how others use it—and even if they can use it. You know how it feels to put a lot of time and effort into any production, and then to get it back with only negative comments. You know how it feels when someone simply says about your work "I don't like this," or, worse yet, "This sucks." Giving feedback is not a neutral process—it involves emotions. If you really want to help someone, be positive in your feedback. Say, "I think this could be stronger if . . ." or "It looks to me like you are trying to achieve x, so maybe a more effective way of doing it would be . . ."

thinking through production

- Describe your writing process, what it looks and feels like and the steps you go through in order to produce a piece of writing. Hold on to this. The next time you write something, keep a journal that describes each step as you go through it. Finally, compare and contrast the first account of your writing process with the second account in your journal.

- Take the introduction to a paper on which you are working or have already written and write two more versions of it. In one combine *ethos* and *pathos* by showing your reader the passion you have for your subject (and so try to stir up a similar passion in them). In the other, combine *ethos* and *logos* by establishing your credentials: prove why you are the person to write this composition.

- ☐ There are more "Thinking Through Production" activities in the online chapter 7 resources at www.ablongman.com/wysocki

- On page 190 we asked you to list all the kinds of writing you and others encounter, and to draw up lists of audiences, contexts, and purposes.

  Use your lists as the basis of a report to the local school board about how you think writing should be taught in high school. Develop a design plan for your report, and then produce it—and ask your teacher to test it.

- Write three different, short opinion pieces on an issue that matters to you. Each time you write, pick a new arrangement—a narrative, a problem-solution structure, juxtaposition, whatever makes sense given your purpose—and make it the overarching structure for the piece. How do each of the different structures shape what you are able to argue?

  Give your pieces to others to read. Ask them to figure out your overall structure—and to say which structure seems most effective, and why.

- Research the kinds of writing people produce with the printing press and the kinds of writing people produce for computer screens (writing to be read only on screen, not to be printed out). List the kinds of writing you can do with these different technologies, but also consider the relations these technologies allow composers to set up between themselves and their audiences, as we've been discussing. Consider the contexts in which people read these different kinds of writing. What sorts of similar as well as different purposes can be achieved with these two technologies?

  Do a library and/or online search for "writing technology," "writing technologies," and "history of writing." Read through a range of the materials you find.

  Use your various researching to plan and produce an academic print essay that compares and contrasts the audiences, contexts, and purposes of the two technologies. Use the essay to develop an argument about the differing relations we can establish with each other using these technologies.

compose ▪ *design* ▪ *advocate*

about oral modes of communication

People think speaking well is easy—or they think it's impossible. Often they think it's both. On the one hand, we grow up speaking, so what is there to learn? All you need to do is think for a few minutes about what you want to say and then say it. On the other hand, speaking in front of a group of people and keeping your thoughts straight for longer than a minute feels like too much to ask of any normal human being. It will not surprise you to hear us say that you can learn to be a more comfortable speaker when you approach speaking by thinking about context, audience, and purpose and when you consider some of the specifics of oral communication.

We can't try to cover every aspect of oral communication in this short chapter, but we will get you started thinking about speaking (and listening) and what you can do to improve your oral—and aural—abilities. We cannot possibly cover in depth all the kinds of speech or speaking occasions you may encounter. We do not go into the physiology of speech—how to breathe, the muscular expression of emotion, the chemical causes of speech anxiety—nor do we discuss radio and television broadcasting, or debate, or parliamentary procedure.

But it does make sense for us to offer you a basic vocabulary for understanding speaking situations, to discuss listening, to offer strategies for learning to speak publicly, and to give you tips on delivering a speech. We touch on speech anxiety and ways to deal with it, the ethics of oral communication, and interviewing.

You may not emerge from this chapter and its exercises a seasoned, fully practiced, versatile public speaker—but we do hope you will know more about what goes into a well prepared speaking performance and feel a little more confident in your ability to talk to, and talk with, others.

the pleasures of speaking...

...PUBLICLY AND INTERPERSONALLY

Speaking is something we've been doing since we were little kids. We have such a long and varied and day-to-day history of speaking with others—sometimes marred by some bad experiences—that it is easy to lose sight of the fact that speaking has its distinct and distinctive pleasures.

Speaking well can get things done. A few words in the right ear can work wonders. When we need to step in and speak directly to people, the sense of action—of making something happen—can feel both right and good. Speaking directly to people, in small or large groups, can quickly pull everyone together, especially when there is a sense of urgency to the occasion. Seeing what needs to be done and motivating others to act makes one feel connected and somewhat powerful.

And, then, well, there also are those personal moments when you remember to attend thoughtfully and gently to the one listening to you, when you tilt your head and what you are saying toward that one, and the response is a head tilted back toward you with a soft-spoken "yes"—well, that can be quite satisfying too, no?

We talk to other people because we live in the world with them. Even if, sometimes, we feel it is not worth all the trouble listening to other people and finding the right words to say back to them—be they friend, acquaintance, colleague, or just another person on the street—those should not be the defining moments in our lives together. Talking, telling, speaking, stammering, discussing, conversing, shouting, rapping, schmoozing, whispering, arguing—these are some of the most pleasurable ways we live our daily lives together and remake our worlds.

Let us not overlook the range of possible joys in this basic fact of our existence with others.

- **Write informally:** Remember a time in the past when you had to speak publicly and weren't happy about it. Or visualize an upcoming occasion in which you need to speak before others.

In writing, describe in detail what you could have done or can you do to make the occasion pleasurable. Don't settle for figuring out how to make the occasion tolerable; instead, think hard about what would make the occasion memorable and fulfilling.

We're not asking you to make the occasion "fun": many speaking occasions—such as funerals—cannot ever be fun. But you can make funerals (like other occasions) feel right—thoughtful and comforting, and thus pleasurable and satisfying.

Consider how to make the occasion of which you are thinking pleasurable in that way, pleasurable for yourself and for your listeners.

compose ▪ design ▪ advocate

After thinking about the pleasures of speaking, listening is a good place to begin the study of speaking well because good speaking grows out of good listening. Listening also provides guidance we need to make decisions about what to say and when to say it.

It is safe to say most of us do not listen enough. We think speaking is how to get things done—and so listening can feel only like waiting for our chance to speak. But there is much more to listening than meets the ear, and this is why we talk about listening: to help you start to think about listening as a dynamic part of speaking.

Another reason to attend to listening is that it turns out we all more or less have learned ways to avoid listening without even realizing it—but listening creates a social and ethical bond between people. It provides insight in what matters to the people with whom you want to communicate and thus provides you essential guidance. And it yields material you may want to use in your talk or presentations.

Two important aspects of listening you will want to concentrate on are how to facilitate productive listening in your audiences and how to be a good listener yourself in ways that will make your speaking more successful.

Like seeing, listening is deceptive because it seems easy and obvious. We've been doing it for as long as we can remember, and we think we've learned everything about it we need. It can be helpful, however, to put aside our familiarity with listening and consider the possibility that we do not really know how to listen and that over the years we possibly have learned some bad listening habits we could stand to unlearn.

We don't have time or space to go into everything people have learned by studying listening, but we pass along to you useful distinctions and ideas for changing how we listen in order to make our listening sharper and more effective.

Communication theorists differentiate among various kinds of listening:

Participatory listening and passive listening

Most of us simply hear. We have functioning ears and if we are lucky those ears just do their work. Noises and sounds and voices come to us, without—it seems—us having to do any work. We can let the sounds pass through us, and if we don't pay attention we can miss things and then sometimes we fill in the gaps with assumptions of our own. That is passive listening.

Participatory listening, by contrast, involves paying attention, leaning in, remembering and checking to make sure you remember what was said, thinking about what is being said, and showing you are engaged by nodding and saying "yes" occasionally—even if you disagree. Participatory listening shows that you do consider a conversation or a talk to be an event between people.

Depending on your needs and occasion, you can choose to be an active or a passive listener. Choosing to be an active listener is especially appropriate when you are engaged in conversation with someone who matters to you or when you need to learn or to participate.

Empathetic listening and objective listening

Empathetic listeners want to understand those to whom they're listening. As they listen, they try to imagine what it is like to be in the speaker's position; as they listen they ask what the speaker is feeling and why. Empathetic listening is charitable and supportive. Empathy, though, is hard to do, and sometimes when we think we have understood and empathized with someone, we really have not done so to full effect, as when we are too quick to say, "I feel your pain."

Objective listening tries to stay alert to the context. It balances what someone is saying against the listener's own (and developing) understanding of the speaker's context and purpose, as well as to the perspectives of others.

These two kinds of listening are appropriate in different contexts. The first is useful with friends and others we want to give full support. The second is appropriate in learning situations or when someone is trying to persuade us.

Nonjudgmental listening and critical listening

It is not easy to listen without making judgments or assumptions about what you are hearing, but it is necessary, in some circumstances, to try—such as when you are trying to listen empathetically.

Nonjudgmental listening involves keeping an open mind and is different from objective listening, which involves positioning what you hear against what you already know or can see for yourself.

Critical listening is more like objective listening in that you adopt a questioning attitude toward the speaker. Critical listening goes a step further because when you listen in this way you work hard to detect inaccuracies, biases, and mistakes. Critical listening assumes that people are not fully in control of their prejudices and deep-seated beliefs—and that listening can help us understand what prejudices and beliefs shape a speaker's words.

Surface listening and in-depth listening

Sometimes you just have to take what someone is saying at face value because such acceptance builds trust and demonstrates that you may not know everything. Other times you just have to take what someone is saying at face value because you know that pointing out the hidden or buried arguments underneath the surface will cause too much trouble or will lead a discussion in directions it simply doesn't need to go. This is called "discretion."

Depth listening is useful when you suspect there is a hidden message that the speaker cannot herself see or bring herself to acknowledge or needs you to acknowledge without her having to say it. Sometimes we think everything should be explicit and without secondary hidden messages, but that simply is not possible. Some things are better left unsaid—but still acted upon. In order to act upon them, you need to practice depth listening so that you will know what to do.

ANALYZING
listening

- **Discuss with others:** In small groups discuss differences between "listening" and "hearing." Can you tell by looking at others if they are listening, or if they are hearing? What can you do to help others listen? What can you do to increase the chances you will be heard?

- **Write with others:** In pairs, make a list of the obstacles, habits, and behaviors that get in the way of hearing and listening. When you are listening to someone, what obstacles might prevent you from hearing or listening carefully? Compile the lists in a large group to compare and to check that you've thought as broadly as possible. (As you do this, look around the room to see who is listening and who isn't; when you see someone not attending to the others in class, ask the person why. You can learn more about the decisions people make about listening.)

Together, come up with a list of what you can do to improve your own listening and overcome the obstacles to others listening to you.

preparing a talk: context, audience, purpose

PREPARING A TALK OR SPEECH

Here we step you through how the rhetorical process—of considering context, audience, and purpose—can help you consider and make decisions about what to say. We also discuss the strategies of *ethos*, *logos*, and *pathos* as they apply particularly to speaking.

the contexts in which you speak

The physical and social contexts for any speaking occasion exist before you enter a space or begin talking and will go on after you talk, and so they are like the frames for your talk: careful consideration of these frames for your speaking will help you make the most appropriate choices for effective speaking.

The **physical context** of a speaking occasion is (of course) the actual location of your talk and the time you have for speaking. Once you know or can concretely imagine the situation in which you will be standing you will often know certain actions you will have to take. Will the room be large? You'll need to speak more loudly and perhaps take effort to make the room feel less impersonal for your audience. Will the room be cold? You'll perhaps want to use words and arrangements that suggest warmth or that otherwise distract your audience from the cold. Will the sound be good, or just adequate? Will everyone be able to see you? And how much time do you have: 5 minutes? 10 minutes? 2 hours? This tells you whether the audience will expect talking that is short and to the point or more languid, able to develop ideas in pleasurable detail. Once you know these factors, they can help you think about the appropriate relations you want to shape with your audience, and how you need to prepare yourself and your words.

Social context includes everything that has happened in the world that leads up to your occasion to speak, as well as everything you and your audience anticipate will come after—in part as a result of—your speaking. You cannot be in a situation to give a talk unless you and your audience share something—a concern or interest based on past experience, or alertness to some clear and present danger, or knowledge of impending problems. Such contexts "surround" the room and occasion of your speaking.

CONSIDERING PHYSICAL CONTEXTS

Whether you are being interviewed or you are speaking to the skateboard club on campus, try to visit the room where you'll speak. Get a feel for its lighting, size, furniture arrangement, and where you'll be standing or sitting. If you cannot actually visit, find people who know the space.

When you think about the physical spaces in which you'll speak and how those spaces might shape your interactions with others, keep in mind that when we are together with others we act (even if we are not aware of it) within personal, social, and institutional senses of space. These distinctions remind us that context is more than lighting and temperature, though these matter. As you think about where you'll talk—and how you'll place yourself and move within that space—keep these distinctions in mind both because you can use them and because your audience will understand what you do in terms of them.

Personal space is our skin and the immediate area around our skin. When we are this close to others, space is intimate and sensual, and so very comfortable or uncomfortable. When we are this close to others, we are aware of the possibilities of touch—whether the touching be gentle, tender, and friendly or the opposite. In personal space we can often smell others and be smelled ourselves. Smell, like touch, shapes how we consider and respond to those who are within this space.

In the United States, **social space** is roughly two to seven feet around us. (If you've traveled to other countries, you may have experienced closer social spaces.) Social space is less intimate than personal space, but is still close: it is the space of shared activities, of leaning in together to look at a car engine or shake hands. How we act in social space draws on the special (but perhaps not explicit) training we've had growing up to be sensitive to the proximity of people, actions, and events. Much of communicative interest goes on in this space. It is the space of whispering and significant eye contact. It may include the first row of your audience. You may find yourself talking in a large space: given your purposes, is it appropriate to lean into your audience to create a sense of shared social space?

Institutional space is a term meant to describe how we understand the physical spaces in which we meet and how those spaces shape how we feel and act. For example, think of waiting rooms: they can be warm relaxing places or cold and awkward rooms that make us more uncomfortable and nervous than we already were. Lobbies of movie theaters invite chaotic movement, directed toward the theaters but also directed toward the snack bar where you're encouraged to buy bite-size sweets. Grocery stores are usually designed to move you through in-your-face displays and tempting racks of little packaged goods. The spaces in which we make oral presentations to each other—classrooms, meeting rooms, city council chambers, convention center rooms with daises—are rarely warm, comfortable, or personal spaces, but you can shape that space by how you draw your audience's attentions to or away from the space, by how you ask them to imagine other spaces or by how you move relative to the audience.

We mention these general kinds of dwelling space not because we picture you giving speeches in a movie lobby (though who knows?), but because they are examples of how space influences behavior, including communication. The distinctions among personal, social, and institutional spaces helps keep our thinking about context complex enough to make thoughtful decisions about how to speak with others. By considering these different aspects of space as you plan what to say, you can figure out strategies for shaping the relation you want to build with your audience in order to support your purposes.

Similarly, **our senses of the time** in which we speak shape our—and audience—expectations. You cannot tell a long rambling story in five minutes. Audiences will be unhappy if they've come for an hour and you finish in 15 minutes—unless you give them good reason to understand.

In addition, however, audiences at the end of the day have a different sense of time than at the beginning of the day. Tired audiences are often impatient audiences, wanting to get away, and often will be

compose ▪ design ▪ advocate

more inclined to listen if you acknowledge their state of mind and the time. Rested audiences are generally more generous.

As you plan what to say, then, consider the contexts of both how much time you have and when in the audience's daily rhythms that time comes. This will help you fine-tune your purposes and strategies.

CONSIDERING SOCIAL CONTEXTS

Think back to Walter's story in chapter 1: Walter and his group ran into the trouble they did—in a fairly simple and straightforward communication situation—precisely because they had not considered the social contexts of their speaking. They were speaking to a group of people—women at a technological university—who had already and too many times experienced being treated as less competent than they were. If Walter and his friends had taken time to think through the social contexts in which they were approaching their audience, they would not have tanked.

Perhaps the most important decision to make when you research the social side of context is that of depth: how far back and to what level of detail do you need to look, think, or study in order to be effective— and to approach your work as knowledgeably as required? And how far forward do your conclusions need to look in order to be effective—or fair? This is particularly important when you speak because time in speaking is usually limited—which means time is conspiring against us, pushing us to narrow our view of things ("Just the facts, ma'am)". Planning to speak often is an exercise in resistance: how can I resist the constraints preventing me from getting done what I know needs to get done?

But the more you research the social background of your reasons for speaking— and your audiences' understanding of that background—the more your words will be able to address your audience's specific concerns, and the more you will be able to decide whether you need to continue developing lines of thinking that already exist or you need to strike off in a new direction.

☐ The links to speeches (in written, spoken, and video form) in the online chapter 8 resources at www.ablongman.com/wysocki give you materials to analyze, to help you in thinking about your own oral presentations.

ANALYZING
the contexts of speaking

■ **Discuss with others:** In small groups, pick a current event or controversial topic. Discuss different time frames for the research you might do in preparation to talk with others about this issue. How far back do you need to look, in your research and in what you say? How far forward do you need to look as you consider the consequences of your position or conclusions? Do different time frames change the issue? Do different time frames change how people consider the issue?

considering audiences as you plan

In preparing to give a talk, you need to learn about your audience just as when you are preparing to produce any other communication. The approaches and questions of chapters 1 and 2 are as useful and necessary here as for any communication. When you are preparing to speak, however, there are additional considerations that can be of use.

SPEAKING WITH AND LISTENING TO AUDIENCES

In an article we've included a few pages later in this chapter "Inviting Transformations," the authors point out that any time we open our mouths, we position ourselves to speak **at** people—rather than **with** them. That is, if you initiate the speaking, you tend to see yourself as active and you tend to see those to whom you are speaking as passive. This is the first problem to overcome to be a successful speaking person (as opposed to being just a "talker"). The best way to approach audiences as you begin to speak, then, is to find ways to **listen to them**.

There are at least two ways to listen to audiences. The first is what you do when you prepare to speak: when you research audiences and social contexts, you are in essence listening to your audience. You may be listening to them directly, if you talk to potential audience members to learn what matters to them; you may also be listening indirectly, when you research the background of a situation to learn how audience attitudes have been shaped by historic events (even those of last week). As you prepare to speak, try starting as though you know nothing about your audience, so that you have to build the most fundamental understanding of them, questioning how you know what you think you know. You can uncover assumptions on your part that you might need to work against, or you might find a new way of considering the people with whom you interact so that you work more easily together.

The second way of listening to an audience happens as you settle yourself in to talk with them: as you approach your audiences, see and think of them as whole people, as people who think and feel and have material needs, who care about the world around them and yet can be blind to parts of it, and, above all, as people who listen and speak just as you do.

RESEARCHING AUDIENCES TO ENCOURAGE LISTENING

Because audiences are complex, preparing for the moments when you stand with them to talk isn't something you can do once and then drop. You need to start researching right away, research in stages, and continue up and through your actual talking. (Consider as research what happens while you speak, as you attend to the facial expressions of the people before you, modifying what you say in response to their responses.)

One way to begin researching an audience is with a simple questionnaire you ask potential audience members to take so you can learn about them. (Sometimes people bring brief questionnaires to a talk, hand them out in advance, and glance through them before they are scheduled to speak. Ideally, you would leave yourself more time to think the responses through.) When designing a questionnaire, though, it is important to know what you need to learn, given your purpose and social context: what would Walter from chapter 1 have needed to ask potential audience members in order to find out what would have kept his group from failing in their approach to women on their campus?

Sometimes, even if the questionnaires do not provide useful information that helps you plan your talk, it brings your audience closer to you in concrete ways. They need to be real for you. If you can learn more about their relevant characteristics, habits, tastes, knowledge, skills, and background experiences you are more likely to produce oral strategies that bring audiences to consider what matters to you.

Another way to research people is to interview potential audience members, people like them, people who know them,

compose ▪ design ▪ advocate

or people who are familiar with people like them. This may include reading what someone has written, for instance, about teenage girls, divorced men, or convicted CEOs before you speak to such groups. For more on interviewing, see the later section in this chapter as well as chapter 16 online.

Finally, don't forget you are considering an audience that you will meet face to face—something that rarely happens with essays or posters. Look then especially for information about an audience that pertains to the context and purpose of speaking. Do people who have the characteristics of your audience attend talks often and so are used to giving their aural attentions at some length? Will the room be filled with tension, or will people be tired and in need of a lively talk? Do they know little about your topic, so that support materials—handouts, video, visual aids—might be especially helpful?

A short way of putting all that we've just written: **make your audiences as real and human in your mind as possible**. Perhaps they are a little scarier this way, but then they are also concrete, like the people with whom you live. You know how to talk **with** (rather than **at**) the people directly around you because you know them so well and so complexly; the people in your audience are no different. They are like you, wanting to be respected, wanting to be treated complexly, wanting to be engaged with others.

BEING AN AUDIENCE

If you've ever given a talk and seen in your audience a sullen face, a pouty face, or a frown, you know how hard it can be to ignore. But often you can ignore it: most people do not realize the faces they wear, and were you to ask them what about your speaking upset them so, they'd look at you quizzically and say that on the contrary they were enjoying listening.

Keep this in mind as you speak with others, but also keep this in mind as you listen. If you want to support communication among us all, listen generously and attentively. Smile (at least a little), make your eyes bright, nod: let the speaker know that you are there, paying attention. This is how we build bonds with others. You can still disagree—but disagreement that stands on bonds of respect, generosity, and the willingness to listen and be moved is potentially productive. Disagreement built on the conviction that you are absolutely right and the other without a prayer is what destroys friendships, families, and countries.

ANALYZING audiences

■ Discuss and write with others: In groups of five to seven, draw up lists of your ages, genders, incomes, religions, educational backgrounds, majors, clubs, organizational affiliations, political affiliations, lifestyles, moral commitments, family lives, and so on. You don't need to get deeply personal—but try to get a sense of the characteristics that shape each of you as social beings.

After about 20 minutes, come back together as a large group and pool your results, putting them into any categories you see.

Then pick a topic or issue that is of interest to the class, something you have been reading about or discussing as a class already.

Go back through the various characteristics you've listed and sort out the ones that are most relevant to the issue. Do they all seem potentially relevant? Are there any characteristics you did not mention at first, but that in light of the issue chosen seem relevant now? (For instance, whether you own guns or cars, whether you vote, whether you have cats, and so on.)

preparing a talk:
approaching purposes as you plan

MOVING FROM GENERAL TO SPECIFIC PURPOSES

Often your general purpose is given to you by the speaking occasion. Because you have grown up into particular places and times where certain events always happen according to certain patterns, you can probably easily respond to the following list of speaking occasions with descriptions of a general purpose for each case. Imagine, for example, that you've been asked to toast a couple at their wedding, give a funeral eulogy, speak at someone's 50th birthday party, accept an award at a banquet, make a presentation to co-workers explaining a project, or confront a city council that has made a bad decision for your community. You probably can easily picture yourself, in these contexts, saying something funny and something warmly emotional about the bride and groom, something respectful and heartfelt about the deceased, something funny and respectful about the person who made it to 50, and something humble about yourself and grateful to those who gave you the award; you can probably picture yourself laying out what the project is and asks of each worker in the job situation and speaking formally and with moral strength at the city council.

None of this is really different from other kinds of communication. When you are asked to write a class paper, you know

without too much thought that you want to sound smart, that you want your writing to support your arguments, and that your paper ought to look neat. If you make a brochure for a nonprofit organization, you know that it needs to make the organization sound solid and worthy, that it will have several panels of different information, and that it needs to look professional. All these are general purposes.

In all these cases, you know enough about the general contexts of different communications to have in mind what you can do—generally. You can probably see, though, how articulating these general purposes out loud to yourself can help you think more carefully about what you want to achieve more specifically.

So what you need to do next, once you know general context and general purpose, is to get specific. You need to get specific about your purpose, and you need to think about how your purpose—grounded as it is within the particular mode(s) of your communication—can be worked through and supported by strategies particular to the mode(s) you employ.

To get specific about your purpose in giving any kind of talk, use what we have written in chapters 2 through 4. In chapter 3, we present actions you can take to generate—to invent—ideas about purpose. Look also to chapter 6, the chapter on

researching: there we present questions to help you think about focusing the question that will guide a research paper—but the scheme we give for generating questions can help you focus in on exactly what you want to accomplish by helping you focus on exactly what question(s) you need to address through your speaking.

PURPOSES SPECIFIC TO SPEAKING WITH OTHERS

Once you have a specific purpose, make it even more specific for the occasion of speaking, for being present in a room with others.

When you speak, you can see the faces of others, and judge their reactions—so use this to help you think about what you want to achieve. For example, imagine that you have to make an oral presentation to your sorority or fraternity about how the group has been handling rush: you want to persuade the others that you're losing potential members because the group's rushes have been, ummm, a bit on the boring side. Imagine yourself talking to the group: given your purpose, do you want them to look at you with the devastated faces of people who've come to realize through your talking that they've been lackluster and dull? Or would you rather have them look at you with lights in their eyes, excited about the wonderful possibilities you're creating for them as you talk?

compose ▪ design ▪ advocate

By having a focused sense of your purpose and then visualizing the moment of speaking, you can fine-tune your purpose. In the example about rush above, this would help you understand that your purpose is not really to persuade the group that rush hasn't been working; it is instead to persuade them that rush would be more effective were the group to approach it with a fresher and more creative spirit. The differences between those two ways of wording your purpose may seem subtle, but they are crucial to the success of what you undertake.

On the next pages is a reading—"Inviting Transformation"—which is a chapter from a book by Sonja K. Foss and Karen A. Foss, *Inviting Transformation: Presentational Speaking for a Changing World.*

"Inviting Transformation" asks us to look at the aim and practice of public speaking in a different way than we are used to, not as "persuasion" so much as "inviting transformation." The difference is in the nature and quality of the relationship between the speaker and the audience. Persuasion, some feel, directs the speaker to try to change the audience through her use of words and occasion, whereas a speaker who invites transformation leaves the audience room to move, to make decisions, to play a role in the event of communication.

We have included "Inviting Transformation" at this point in the chapter because it gives you further ways to think about *preparing a talk.* A reading about the aim of speaking and the kind of relationship you strike up with your audience will be most useful as you begin to think about preparing to talk, as you plan how you will go about saying what you have to say.

Inviting Transformation

by Sonja K. Foss and Karen A. Foss

Presentational speaking is an invitation to transformation. Speakers initiate communications with others because they are seeking opportunities for growth and change and because they believe they can offer such opportunities to others. As a result of communication, an audience may accept a speaker's invitation and leave the interaction changed in some way. A speaker, too, may re-think ideas and gain new insights as a result of the interaction that occurs. This notion that presentational speaking is an invitation to transformation, which is crucial to understanding and applying the principles of speaking discussed in the rest of this book, can be clarified by exploring the primary concepts it entails—presentational speaking, transformation, and invitation.

PRESENTATIONAL SPEAKING

When you think about giving a speech or making a presentation, what probably comes to mind is a situation in which one person is standing in front of an audience composed of at least several people and probably more. The speaker does the talking, and any oral participation by the audience, more often than not, is limited to asking questions at the end of the speech. You probably associate this kind of speaking with public settings such as lecture halls, classrooms, senate chambers, courts of law, churches, and campaign rallies. If you suffer from stage fright at all, this is the kind of speaking situation that tends to make you nervous.

In contrast to public speaking is conversation or interpersonal communication, where two or three people talk informally, with everyone participating equally in the interaction. This type of interaction, which most people find comfortable and enjoyable, usually is associated with private places such as homes or offices or perhaps places where private spaces can be created within public spaces, such as restaurants or bars.

Some oral communication cannot easily be put only into one format or the other: it can occur in conversational formats as well as in more formal speech contexts. We have chosen to call this kind of communication presentational speaking, and it is distinguished by two features. The first is that one person has more responsibility for the communication than do the others involved in the interaction. Perhaps that person has been asked by others to share her perspective on a subject, she has an idea she thinks will be useful to her co-workers, or she might be leading a discussion to generate ideas to solve a problem. For whatever reason, she has been given a greater role in the interaction, and other participants will expect more from her than they will from the others involved. Her communication will be somewhat more important than theirs in creating the nature, tenor, and environment of the interaction.

A second feature of this kind of oral communication is that at least one of the individuals involved in the interaction has done some thinking about the message or the ideas to be conveyed prior to the interaction. This person will not always have had a lot of time to prepare, but he will have in mind a goal for speaking, the basic message he wants to convey, and some thoughts about how to present that message.

Presentational speaking is the kind of oral communication with which this book is concerned. It deals with communication in which you have had some prior preparation time. This communication may occur in the format of a public speech, a private conversation, or something in between. It simply involves some kind of presentation—even if it is only a few sentences long and is designed to get discussion started.

Presentational speaking, then, involves a variety of forms. The answers a candidate gives during a job interview constitute presentational speaking; the interviewer in this situation also is engaged in presentational speaking. A coach who gives a pep talk to a wrestling team is giving a presentation, as is the new manager who begins the first meeting of her staff by introducing herself. In all of these situations, one person has primary responsibility for communicating a message thought about ahead of time. When members of a group explore an issue together to figure out what they know and believe about it, they also are engaged in presentational speaking. Although this interaction produces presentations that may contain many of the hesitations, incomplete thoughts, and overlaps of spontaneous conversation, it counts as presentational speaking because the convener of the meeting has thought about the issue, asks others to participate, and assumes responsibility for starting the discussion.

TRANSFORMATION

Transformation means growth or change. It may involve changing your opinion on an issue, gaining information about a subject you did not have before, or adopting a new behavior. Transformation also includes the more subtle kind of change that occurs when you incorporate new information into your systems of thought, allowing you to imagine and generate new ideas. A student at Ohio State University, Sherveen Lotfi, provides a good summary of this kind of transformation, which he hopes his presentations facilitate: "I'm hoping that after the speech is over, the kernels of information represented by the key words will expand in their minds as they did in mine and lead to other images . . . . I try to challenge them to take the next step on their own and to infer additional conclusions based on their own circumstances and understanding."

Transformation happens only through the process of interaction: it cannot occur in isolation. When, for example, you see your position as the only right or correct one and are not willing to consider or to try to understand other positions, transformation is not possible. Neither can it occur when one perspective is privileged over others. Transformation is generated when you share your perspective with others— when it is subject to comparison with other perspectives in a process of discovery, questioning, and rethinking. The transformation that may be engendered in presentational speaking, then, is not the result of the skill or expertise of one speaker. If it occurs, it results from the exchange and interaction to which the speaker's presentation contributes. Your role as speaker is to keep the conversation going—to sustain interaction—so that new ways of thinking and acting are able to emerge.

INVITATION

Invitation is a critical concept in the notion that presentational speaking is an invitation to transformation. Any change that results from presentational speaking is not forced on the audience. Your efforts are directed at enabling transformation—making it possible for those who are interested—not imposing it on those who are not. The speaker's invitation is an offering, an opening, an availability—not an insistence. Some in the audience may choose to accept this invitation; others will not. Your communication may not appear to change thinking and behavior, but you do not and cannot change others. Such changes are the results of decisions by listeners who choose to hear others or to learn from others. Transformation occurs only through the process of self-change generated by interaction with other perspectives.

When you offer an invitation to transformation and do not impose it, you recognize that audience members have had experiences and hold perspectives that are as valuable and legitimate as your own. You view audience members as the authorities on their own lives who hold the beliefs they do and act as they do for reasons that make good sense to them. You respect, then, the integrity and authority of audience members by offering your ideas to them rather than imposing your ideas on them. Sherveen Lotfi uses a metaphor of baking cookies to convey this notion: "Giving a speech is like sharing cookies we've baked with the people around us. They may or may not like them. I hope that the cookies are so tasty that the people who ate them want to go and bake some of their own." Audience members may refuse the invitation—may not take any cookies from the plate that is passed—for any number of legitimate reasons.

Although you cannot force transformation on your audience, what you can do is create, through the communicative options you select, an environment in which others may change if they are inclined to do so. As Sally Miller Gearhart explains, "No one can change an egg into a chicken. If, however, there is the potential in the egg to be a chicken . . . then there is the likelihood that in the right environment (moisture, temperature, the 'external conditions for change') the egg will hatch."

Four external conditions are particularly critical for the creation of an environment in which self-change may take place—safety, value, freedom, and openness. When these conditions are present, self-change is more likely to occur. As you prepare your presentation, you can select communicative options that either facilitate or impede the development of these conditions in your particular speaking situation.

Safety is the condition of feeling free from danger, of feeling secure. Your communication contributes to a feeling of safety when you let audience members know that the ideas and feelings they share with you will be received with respect and care. You also help create a safe environment when you do not hurt, degrade, or belittle your audience members or their beliefs. Providing a means for your audience members to order their world in some way so it seems coherent and makes sense to them is another way to contribute to their feeling of safety. When people feel their sense of order is threatened or challenged, they are more likely to cling to familiar ways of thinking and to be less open to possibilities for change. When you create safety in a speaking situation, audience members trust you, are not fearful of interacting with you, and feel you are working with and not against them.

Value is the acknowledgement that your audience members have intrinsic or immanent worth. You convey that you value your listeners when you allow all participants in the interaction to be heard. But valuing them means more than recognizing their right to participate in the conversation: it involves encouraging their participation—inviting them to share their perspectives with you and listening carefully when they do. When audience members' perspectives vary widely from yours, try to understand them by learning more about the individuals in your audience and trying to discover why they might have developed the perspectives they have. Making the effort to think from the standpoint of your audience members—trying to make vivid in your own mind their perspectives—also is a way of valuing them. When value is created in a speaking situation, audience members feel that you care about them, understand their ideas, and allow them to contribute in significant ways to the interaction.

Freedom, the third condition whose presence in an environment contributes to the possibility of transformation, is the power to choose or decide. You contribute to the creation of a sense of freedom when you create opportunities for others to develop and select their own options from alternatives they themselves have created. Freedom also is developed when you do not place restrictions on the interaction. Participants can bring any and all matters to the interaction for consideration; no subject matter is privileged subject matter, and all presuppositions can be challenged. If audience members do not make the choices you would like them to make, you do not ban their participation from the interaction, halt the interaction, or sever your relationship with them. They are free in the interaction to make their own choices and decisions.

If communication is to create an environment in which transformation may occur, it cannot deliberately exclude any perspectives. In fact, you want to encourage participants in the interaction to incorporate as many perspectives as possible to ensure that the greatest number of ideas is considered. The condition of openness, then, is the fourth characteristic of a potentially transformative environment. It involves genuine curiosity about and a deliberate seeking out of perspectives different from your own or from the standard view. It involves exploring carefully and thoughtfully these other perspectives and approaching the differences they represent with an attitude of appreciation and delight.

With our emphasis on presentational speaking as a means to create the conditions of safety, value, freedom, and openness and thus to invite transformation, we are privileging growth and change. We are suggesting that being open to being changed is desirable and is better than developing a rigid position and coming to a "correct" understanding of a subject and sticking to it. Our primary reason for this focus is that many of the problems facing the world today seem to be the result of people's beliefs that they hold the only right positions, which they try to impose on others. The conflicts among people in the former Yugoslavia, between the pro-choice and anti-abortion forces, and between loggers and environmentalists in the Pacific Northwest, for example, seem to be the result of such rigidity. On a more personal level, misunderstanding, conflicts, and severed relationships are often the result of an unwillingness to yield on positions and a lack of openness to those held by others. We believe understandings are more likely to develop, differences are more likely to be bridged, and creative and imaginative solutions are more likely to be generated when people are open to the possibility of transformation.

Because we have chosen to privilege the opportunity for transformation, the kind of speaking dealt with in this book may look very different from the kinds of speaking with which you are familiar. We are not interested in the kind of speaking that occurs when a speaker intimidates audience members, making them afraid to speak and humiliating them when they do; the environment that results from this type of presentation is not one in which individuals feel safe or valued. We are not interested in the kind of speaking that is designed to showcase the talents of the speaker and to enhance his status or ego; this kind of speaking devalues and is closed to the potential contributions of others involved and is not directed at encouraging an exchange of perspectives. The kind of speaking covered in this book also will not be relevant to those who engage in the kind of competitive speaking where the goal is to overpower others' positions by establishing the superiority of their own. This kind of speaking, again, does not create an environment in which others feel valued and free to hold their own perspectives. Although you may find yourself involved in speaking situations in which such communication occurs, we hope that your familiarity with and skill in using the model presented in this book will enable you to help convert those situations into ones of safety, value, freedom, and openness.

speaking *ethos*, *logos*, and *pathos*

USING *ETHOS*, *LOGOS*, AND *PATHOS* IN SPEAKING

In preparing a speech, you can first approach *ethos*, *logos*, and *pathos* as you do in writing: you can sit alone at a desk looking at a piece of paper considering what *ethos* to project, playing with arrangements and arguments, and shaping sentences to evoke some precise emotion. After you've noodled thusly with writing, you polish it, get feedback, make revisions—and then give it to your intended readers so they can sit alone out of sight to read. *But you have to perform a speech*: you can practice a speech with comfortable friends or with a small group from a class, but eventually there's a moment when you have to stand in front of others and—in real time—perform. When you speak, you construct your *ethos*, *logos*, and *pathos* from all that you do during those moments of being in front of others. The following sections help you think about what you do to construct your *ethos*, *logos*, and *pathos* in the presence of listening, watching others.

ethos as speaking strategy

Ethos just naturally feels a part of speaking. Have you ever developed a crush on someone just from hearing that person's voice on the phone? Rightly or wrongly, we all believe that character resides in voices, that we can tell others' internal strength or seriousness simply from how they speak.

In speaking situations, therefore, *ethos* is simply waiting for you—the speaker—to shape it with your voice and your choices about tone of voice and loudness or softness of voice. Your facial and bodily expressions also matter: audiences can have sympathy for you if you shake from nervousness or they can respect your quiet calm; they can trust your forthright confidence or they can be pulled in by humor.

But *ethos* can also be a more complex part of verbal interactions. In the movie *Bulworth*, the senator played by Warren Beatty becomes disillusioned and suffers a nervous breakdown while visiting his supporters. He begins to deliver his speeches in rap, which is disconcerting because Beatty is (and is playing) an aging white guy. At first his audiences are shocked and don't know how to respond because rap is unexpected and unfamiliar for most political contexts. With a little time, though, as Beatty persists with his political rap speeches (and direct talk), some audiences begin to warm up to him. In addition to his refreshingly direct challenges to the audience, his sincerity wins them over. Once he starts to rap, he does not waver. He looks and feels committed to what he is doing. His *ethos* shifts for his audiences, but the shift doesn't lose his audiences because, finally, Beatty himself is convinced by what he is doing. During the transition, people think he is crazed, but when he completes the transition (into a rapping aging white U.S. senator) many do not see him as crazy, but rather as a refreshingly different candidate who is cutting through the crap and making good sense.

There are several lessons about *ethos* and speaking to groups of people we can take from *Bulworth*. *Ethos* is complex. It "happens" in the interactions of what you

compose ▪ design ▪ advocate

say and do and how others perceive what you say and do. *Ethos* is ethical. We connect ourselves to others through how we come across to them and how they receive us into their lives, and that means there are ethical responsibilities all around, on all sides. And, finally, *ethos* can change within an occasion and from occasion to occasion. We build it, and we can unbuild it and rebuild it. Or we can build it in one direction, and then shift what we have built in a slightly different direction, as we sense and test our audience's response to us. *Ethos* is malleable in writing and visual communication, but especially in speaking, when you are facing others in the moment.

Here are some factors that go into how audiences perceive you:

- *what audiences know about you already*
- *how you dress*
- *how you walk into the room*
- *how you stand*
- *the gestures you make*
- *your tone of voice—and how you vary it*
- *what you say and do not say*
- *how quickly you speak*
- *whether or not you tell jokes*

What does it say to your audience if you do not take off your baseball cap when speaking to them? What does it say to your audience when you say you will talk about jobs in American and forget to discuss globalization and industrial flight to countries that don't expect health benefits and retirement packages for employees? How will your audience respond when you scratch yourself, or show up in a suit?

Sustaining *ethos* throughout oral communication

> "When I began going about by car I got just as angry at the carelessness of pedestrians as I used to be at the recklessness of drivers." —Sigmund Freud

If *ethos* is a relationship between speaker and audience, then, as with all relationships, you need to keep an eye on it the whole time you are with your audience. If you set yourself up as being on the same level with your audience—as just working together, as opposed to you taking the lead—then make sure you do not later slip into ways of talking that imply you know more or better. Sigmund Freud was always aware that much of what he had to say might seem like finger-pointing at his audience, so he often used himself as an example in order to keep a more humble *ethos*. Rather than say, "You probably don't get it that you judge others from a single, limited point of view, and you should think about that," he said the words of the quotation above. He was aware that a relationship with his audience unfolded as he spoke, and that a large part of that relationship depended on himself and how he came across. So he paid steady attention to his place in his communications—and he used the fact of his presence to his advantage.

Building *ethos* in introductions to oral communication . . . or, "How do you do?"

Because communication is a human activity, one of its most conspicuous features is that it unfolds over time. This means that it must begin and must come to an end. And nowhere is this more obvious than when you speak formally with others: you probably wait a bit nervously to get started, but then there is a definite start. Informal conversations can sometimes seem to start out of nowhere and then fade away without any ceremony—but even conversations need to warm up, and good conversations acknowledge the end, with participants smiling and saying how much they enjoyed what happened.

With more formal oral presentations, you may want to ask what general kind of opening would work best for you as you begin building the relationship you desire with your audience. Your beginning is your first impression, and so it is important to think hard and creatively about what sort of introduction will do what matters. Options include beginning with:

- *A brief story, humorous or riveting*
- *A question that grabs your listeners*
- *An unexpected statement or declaration*
- *A long, uncomfortable pause, followed by a strong, short statement or declaration*
- *A quotation delivered with feeling*
- *A greeting*

Here is how writer Virginia Woolf began a talk (titled "A Room of One's Own") she gave at a women's college in the early twentieth century:

> "But, you may say, we asked you to speak about women and fiction—what has that got to do with a room of one's own? I will try to explain."

She seems to begin in the middle of a thought. She also begins by raising what might seem a problem: the announced title of her talk does not obviously fit with the subject she was asked to speak on. (Don't worry, it turns out it did fit very well, and her talk was eventually published as a short book and is read to this day.) Thus Woolf's *ethos* starts in this way: she comes across as always thinking, and she positions her audience almost to eavesdrop on her. Her listeners are dropped midstream into her thoughts as though they are there with her. At the same time, she sends a clear signal that she respects her audience enough to anticipate an important objection that might be troubling them and to reassure them she will "try to explain." There is even a hint of humility hidden in the word "try."

ANALYZING
ethos

■ **Discuss with others:** Another—quite different—example of building *ethos* can be found in the introduction to Franklin Delano Roosevelt's first inaugural speech. In the early years of the Depression, President Roosevelt took office and delivered what became a famous rallying cry to the nation. Below is the first paragraph from that speech. With a small group, discuss the kind of relationship Roosevelt constructs with his audience. How does he come across, and what role does he prepare for his audience early on? What does he promise his audience? What does he ask of his audience?

First Inaugural Address of Franklin D. Roosevelt

Saturday, March 4, 1933

I am certain that my fellow Americans expect that on my induction into the Presidency I will address them with a candor and a decision which the present situation of our Nation impels. This is preeminently the time to speak the truth, the whole truth, frankly and boldly. Nor need we shrink from honestly facing conditions in our country today. This great Nation will endure as it has endured, will revive and will prosper. So, first of all, let me assert my firm belief that the only thing we have to fear is fear itself—nameless, unreasoning, unjustified terror which paralyzes needed efforts to convert retreat into advance. In every dark hour of our national life a leadership of frankness and vigor has met with that understanding and support of the people themselves which is essential to victory. I am convinced that you will again give that support to leadership in these critical days.

■ **Speaking with others:** Plan and deliver three different openings to a speech about a topic with which you are familiar and feel confident you can explain to the class. Try some of the introduction types we've described here—but also find other possibilities by analyzing speeches you see on television or find online.

compose ▪ design ▪ advocate

pathos as speaking strategy

"Speak when you are angry—and you'll make the best speech you'll ever regret."—Anonymous

Like *ethos, pathos* naturally feels a part of speaking. When we hear others speaking, we not only make often unaware judgments about their characters but we also hear and respond—again often unaware-ly—to the emotional content of their voices. In speaking situations, therefore, *pathos* like *ethos* is simply waiting for you—the speaker—to shape it with your voice and your choices about how you say what you say. Audiences are likely to take on your sadness if you speak quietly and with a catch, just as they are likely to take on your joy if you speak gleefully.

So your first decisions to make about *pathos* involve your body and voice—but there are also (of course, of course) other choices.

Pathos can already be there in the thick-ness of your context, needing only to be put into words that direct an audience's attentions and shape the implications of the emotions you evoke.

Part of the pleasure of speaking to and talking with others—whether you admit it or not—is that when speaking it is almost impossible to ignore how emotion is always there, helping us see and blinding us at the same time.

Compare the openings of these two speeches from times of extreme national tragedy for the ways they work to construct and shape the audience's emotions:

Franklin Delano Roosevelt, Broadcast (on radio) from the Oval Room of the White House

December 9, 1941, 10:00 PM

My fellow Americans:

The sudden criminal attacks perpetrated by the Japanese in the Pacific provide the climax of a decade of international immorality.

Powerful and resourceful gangsters have banded together to make war upon the whole human race. Their challenge has now been flung at the United States of America. The Japanese have treacherously violated the longstanding peace between us. Many American soldiers and sailors have been killed by enemy action. American ships have been sunk; American airplanes have been destroyed.

The Congress and the people of the Unit-ed States have accepted that challenge.

Together with other free peoples, we are now fighting to maintain our right to live among our world neighbors in freedom, in common decency, without fear of assault.

I have prepared the full record of our past relations with Japan, and it will be submit-ted to the Congress. It begins with the visit of Commodore Perry to Japan eighty-eight years ago. It ends with the visit of two Japanese emissaries to the Secretary of State last Sunday, an hour after Japanese forces had loosed their bombs and machine guns against our flag, our forces and our citizens.

I can say with utmost confidence that no Americans today or a thousand years hence, need feel anything but pride in our patience and in our efforts through all the years toward achieving a peace in the Pacif-ic which would be fair and honorable to every nation, large or small. And no honest person, today or a thousand years hence, will be able to suppress a sense of indigna-tion and horror at the treachery committed by the military dictators of Japan, under the very shadow of the flag of peace borne by their special envoys in our midst.

George W. Bush, a television address to the nation

September 11, 2001, 8:30 PM

Good evening. Today, our fellow citizens, our way of life, our very freedom came under attack in a series of deliberate and deadly terrorist acts. The victims were in airplanes, or in their offices; secretaries, businessmen and women, military and fed-eral workers; moms and dads, friends and neighbors. Thousands of lives were sudden-ly ended by evil, despicable acts of terror.

The pictures of airplanes flying into build-ings, fires burning, huge structures

collapsing, have filled us with disbelief, terrible sadness, and a quiet, unyielding anger. These acts of mass murder were intended to frighten our nation into chaos and retreat. But they have failed; our country is strong.

A great people has been moved to defend a great nation. Terrorist attacks can shake the foundations of our biggest buildings, but they cannot touch the foundation of America. These acts shattered steel, but they cannot dent the steel of American resolve.

America was targeted for attack because we're the brightest beacon for freedom and opportunity in the world. And no one will keep that light from shining.

Today, our nation saw evil, the very worst of human nature. And we responded with the best of America—with the daring of our rescue workers, with the caring for strangers and neighbors who came to give blood and help in any way they could.

Immediately following the first attack, I implemented our government's emergency response plans. Our military is powerful, and it's prepared. Our emergency teams are working in New York City and Washington, D.C., to help with local rescue efforts.

BUILDING *PATHOS* IN CONCLUSIONS . . . OR "HOW DID YOU DO?"

With more formal oral presentations you may want to ask what general kind of conclusion would work best for you. There are many options for how you can end a talk, including:

- A funny anecdote that captures your main point

- A suggestion for further research or a listing of questions that are still to be answered

- A description of consequences following from your argument

- A summary of what you already said

- An emotionally charged call to join arms and march forward

- A challenge to the audience

Compare the closing remarks from the same two speeches by Roosevelt and Bush whose openings you read above:

Franklin Delano Roosevelt, Broadcast (on radio) from the Oval Room of the White House

December 9, 1941, 10:00 PM

The true goal we seek is far above and beyond the ugly field of battle. When we resort to force, as now we must, we are determined that this force shall be directed toward ultimate good as well as against immediate evil. We Americans are not destroyers—we are builders.

We are now in the midst of a war, not for conquest, not for vengeance, but for a world in which this nation, and all that this nation represents, will be safe for our children. We expect to eliminate the danger from Japan, but it would serve us ill if we accomplished that and found that the rest of the world was dominated by Hitler and Mussolini.

So we are going to win the war and we are going to win the peace that follows.

And in the difficult hours of this day— through dark days that may be yet to come—we will know that the vast majority of the members of the human race are on our side. Many of them are fighting with us. All of them are praying for us. But, in representing our cause, we represent theirs as well—our hope and their hope for liberty under God.

George W. Bush, a television address to the nation

September 11, 2001, 8:30 PM

The search is underway for those who are behind these evil acts. I've directed the full resources of our intelligence and law enforcement communities to find those responsible and to bring them to justice. We will make no distinction between the terrorists who committed these acts and those who harbor them.

I appreciate so very much the members of Congress who have joined me in strongly condemning these attacks. And on behalf of the American people, I thank the many world leaders who have called to offer their condolences and assistance.

America and our friends and allies join with all those who want peace and security in the world, and we stand together to win the war against terrorism. Tonight, I ask for your prayers for all those who grieve, for the children whose worlds have been shattered, for all whose sense of safety and security has been threatened. And I pray they will be comforted by a power greater than any of us, spoken through the ages in Psalm 23: "Even though I walk through the valley of the shadow of death, I fear no evil, for You are with me."

This is a day when all Americans from every walk of life unite in our resolve for justice and peace. America has stood down enemies before, and we will do so this time. None of us will ever forget this day. Yet, we go forward to defend freedom and all that is good and just in our world.

Thank you. Good night, and God bless America.

ANALYZING
pathos

■ **Write:** Circle the words and phrases in the introductions and conclusions of the Roosevelt and Bush speeches that seem designed to strongly affect the listening audience's emotions.

List the specific emotions each speaker names or suggests. List the emotions each speaker tries to make the listening audience feel—or assumes they already feel.

In writing, describe what each speaker does with the emotions the audience is presumed to be experiencing or may be experiencing as a result of what the speaker is saying. Discuss how each speaker builds on emotions over the course of the speech. For instance, if the speaker assumes the audience is angered by the events, what does the speaker do with and about this anger?

Given that both the attack on Pearl Harbor and the attacks on the World Trade Centers and the Pentagon made people both angry and afraid, do the two speakers approach that anger and fear in the same way? What other emotions do they talk about or evoke that might combine, lessen, intensify, or otherwise change the anger and the fear?

■ **Write:** Rewrite the first two paragraphs of each speech in order to evoke more fear, less fear, more anger, less anger—or something other than fear and anger—in the listening audience.

■ **Discuss with others:** Have several different people read aloud the introduction and conclusion of each speech. (Do not try to read them in the same way.) Do you respond differently to hearing these speeches than reading them? Can you hear anything emotionally different about the speeches in the different readings?

logos as speaking strategy

Your *logos* comes across to your audience through the choices you make in structuring your speaking. Structuring your speaking is about the formal arguments you choose to make as well as about the overall method you choose for your presentation and the arrangements you use. Formal arguments in speaking and writing differ in how you deliver them, not in how you conceive of them—so look to the strategies of argument we discuss in chapters 4 and 7 for ideas on what you might argue, and then turn to this chapter for help in speaking the arguments.

METHODS OF PRESENTATION

Looking forward to when you will speak, you need to settle on whether you'll read a prepared speech from typed paper, or talk through a planned speech from talking points (and perhaps 3x5 cards or projected Powerpoint slides). Or you might not have much choice, having been asked to speak extemporaneously—as when you are invited to respond to questions from a group of people about a subject but you do not know the questions in advance.

Each of the above methods presents its own challenges. Reading from a prepared script (or teleprompter) requires you to avoid the stiffness and droning that can accompany reading word after word, sentence after sentence, without feeling or tone changes. Speaking from a set of talking points requires you be familiar with each point and how it leads to the next, so that you don't forget the order and overall structure of the talk you planned.

We have not exhausted the possible methods of presentation here—and we challenge you to be creative in developing methods that balance what your audience knows and expects with what new approaches best serve your purpose. What is important is that your method fit your purpose—and that you are comfortable and at ease with what you choose.

ARRANGING A SPEECH

We have included the reading "Constructing Connections" (which starts in two pages) because it reminds you that, when preparing to speak, it is useful to think that you are constructing connections with your audience through how you order your talk. The most difficult thing to control when talking is the form. Your words have a tendency to pour from your mouth and can wash over an audience without being absorbed. "Constructing Connections" provides a good list of connection strategies or strategies for arranging specifically oral communication. These are ways of connecting the main points in a talk that are mostly familiar to your audience and so will keep them oriented as you move along.

Since audiences are quick to pick up on the arrangement or structure you use—especially if you are sign-posting your connections—don't shift patterns in midstream. Or if you do, you need time to make it work. The shift needs to make sense within your overall purpose—and it needs to make sense to the audience. Normally you stay with one arrangement because of time constraints. Anytime you do something more interesting and complex—and don't get us wrong, we encourage that—you need to take care to make sure those listening are in a position to fully appreciate what you are doing.

LOGOS AS ORAL WORD PLAY: TURNING AN ORAL PHRASE

Word choice and turning a phrase are important when you give a talk, especially a timed talk: what you say needs to be memorable and your structure vivid to your audience so they can hold on to and think about your arguments. We discuss figures of speech in chapters 4 and 7, so you can turn there for inspiration—but do think particularly hard about how you shape words when you speak: in the contexts of speaking, a clever turn of phrase can catch an audience's ears and encourage them to listen more generously. Read the quotations on the next page aloud, then re-state without the repetition of words or phrases that makes them almost musical. How likely are you—or any audience—to remember the different versions?

compose • design • advocate

"The sooner you treat your son like a man, the sooner he will be one."
—John Locke

"How good bad music and bad reasons sound when we march against an enemy!" —Friedrich Nietzsche

"We learn from experience that we never really learn from experience."
—George Bernard Shaw

At the 1984 and 1988 Democratic Conventions, Jesse Jackson gave two much-admired speeches that have been studied by people interested in how language works well. Jackson aimed to cast a wide net of unity over those at the conventions and those watching on TV; at the same time he did not hide some very contentious issues. His theme was common ground.

In 1984 he said, "We must leave the racial battle ground and come to the economic common ground and moral higher ground." In 1988 he said, "Tonight there is a sense of celebration. Because we are moved. Fundamentally moved, from racial battle grounds by law, to economic common ground. Tomorrow we'll challenge to move, to higher ground. Common ground."

Common ground is both his core idea (he includes such variations as "common grave," "common table," "common thread," "common good," "common direction," and "common sense") and a formal verbal mechanism for unifying his argument. The combination of sound and meaning reminded people that spoken language can be both intelligent and pleasurable.

But spoken language can also give signs of not being so intelligent—by the standards of some. This is where grammar comes in. As we wrote about writing, grammar is rhetorical: you need to choose the kind of grammar that will persuade your audience you know what you are talking about, or you need to make it clear that if grammar matters to them you have a good reason for not satisfying their expectations. (Happily for us all, no one can see our spelling when we speak.)

There are contexts in which grammar doesn't matter. You might have heard the Wings song, "Live and Let Die," which intones "In this ever changing world in which we live in." There do not need to be three "in"s in that line—and the last "in" is guaranteed to make people crazy who care about hanging prepositions (which is why this line shows up on every website devoted to funky lyrics)—but did anyone *not* buy the album because of the prepositions? The Doors sang, "Till the stars fall from the sky/For you and I"—"correct" grammar would have killed this lyric with a final non-rhyming "me." Wilco sings, "I assassin down the avenue," substituting a noun for a verb, making English teachers quiver but giving us a very clear picture of how that walk looks. The point is that you can do wonderful things by playing with grammar, especially when you speak (or sing)—as long as you are in contexts in which this is expected—or unexpected but in harmony with your purpose.

"CONSTRUCTING CONNECTIONS"

On the next pages is another chapter—"Constructing Connections"—from Sonja K. Foss and Karen A. Foss's book *Inviting Transformation: Presentational Speaking for a Changing World*.

"Constructing Connections" is a compendium of forms—organizational patterns or arrangements—for speaking and oral presentations. Seeing and naming different ways of organizing your words and ideas gives you choices that will help as you plan talks—and even if you already know what a "causal pattern" is, or a narrative, having them all laid out together brings some back to mind that might have slipped out.

This reading on organizational patterns—overall arrangements for oral presentations—will be most useful as you begin to prepare a talk, as you plan what you will say. But the forms or patterns do not just help prepare a talk, they also play a role in shaping the relationship you as a speaker develop with your audiences. Think of the differences between using a narrative format and using a problem-solution format: the former sets, or can set, a *no nonsense, let's get down to it* tone, while the latter says, *let's take the time to hear the whole story*. Which relationships do you want to build with your audience, given your purpose and context—and the particularities of your audience?

Constructing Connections

by Sonja K. Foss and Karen A. Foss

Constructing connections is the process by which you formulate relationships among the major ideas of your presentation. At this stage, you decide how you will connect the ideas you began to generate in the focusing step. The forms that result are organizational patterns; they are the basic structures in which you issue your invitation to transformation. There are no correct or right organizational patterns that will emerge from your attention to the relationships among your ideas. Let your own style—your personal, unique, characteristic way of constructing connections—guide you. You also will want to take into account any expectations generated by environmental factors for the form of your presentation. The subject you are discussing, your interactional goal, the genre of your presentation (a commencement address or a presentation at a staff meeting, for example), and the characteristics of your audience affect the choices you make in constructing relationships among your ideas.

Constructing relationships may be done in a variety of ways. Two common ways are playing cards and clustering. Playing cards is a technique in which you "play cards" with ideas or pieces of information. You put each idea you have generated or collected on a separate card or slip of paper and lay them out in various possible arrangements until a pattern appears that seems to you to encompass the information in a useful way. Cards that contain information or data that do not fit the emerging schema are discarded.

In clustering, a second approach to connecting your ideas, you start with key concepts and cluster some related concepts, images, and ideas around them. Some of the clustered concepts become the centers of new clusters and being to generate ideas for concepts and images associated with them. At some point in this process, you become aware of an emerging form or organizational pattern that connects your ideas.

Sometimes, you may find that you could use a little help in figuring out how to organize ideas for your presentation. In this case, you might want to turn to fixed forms of arrangement or organizational patterns as sources of possible ideas. These are common or conventional formats that others have considered to be useful ways of connecting ideas and, in fact, you may discover that you naturally tend to use some of them. They should not be regarded as ideal patterns into which you should make your ideas fit, however. These patterns simply may provide you with leads to follow in developing relationships among your ideas. Among these conventional organizational patterns are:

Alphabet. The alphabet can be used as an organizational pattern for a presentation. It involves arranging ideas in alphabetical order: this is the form used to organize this list of organizational patterns. A variation of this pattern is the structuring of a presentation around an acronym such as SAFE to discuss earthquake preparedness. S might stand for securing the environment, A for advance planning, F for family meeting place, and E for emergency supplies.

Category. A category format is suggested by a set of categories that either is relatively standard for your subject or naturally arises from it. The major components, types, questions, functions, or qualities of a subject can be used as its organizational schema. The subject of leadership, for example, readily breaks down into the categories of different models of leadership or the categories of qualities of a good leader; either could be used to organize your ideas.

Causal. A causal organizational pattern is structured around a series of causes or contributing causes that account for some effect. This pattern can be organized either by discussing how certain causal factors will produce a particular effect or by suggesting that a particular set of conditions appears to have been produced by certain causes. In a presentation on the condition of the American educational system, for example, educational consultant David

Boaz spent the first part of his presentation establishing that schools do not work (the effect) and the second part establishing that there is no competition and thus no incentive to improve the school system (the cause).

Circle. In a circle organizational pattern, ideas are structured in a circular progression. One idea is developed, which leads to another, which leads to another, which leads to another, which then leads back to the original idea. You might suggest to your co-workers, for example, that greater cooperation is needed among staff members. To achieve this, you propose that the group come up with some goals for working together, such as being honest with each other. Honesty may contribute to a greater feeling of trust which, in turn, may contribute to an environment in which staff members are more likely to cooperate.

Continuum. A continuum organizational pattern is structured by gradation; objects or ideas are linked by some common quality but differ in grade, level, or degree. Using this pattern, you move from one end of the continuum to the other. You might organize a presentation using a continuum pattern by discussing ideas in the order of, for example, small to large, familiar to unfamiliar, simple to complex, or least expensive to most expensive. For a presentation on absenteeism in a company, you might talk first about the department with the highest rate of absenteeism and end with a discussion of the one with the lowest rate to discover what can be learned about the factors that contribute to absenteeism.

Elimination. An organizational pattern of elimination begins with a discussion of a problem, followed by a discussion of several possible solutions to the problem. The solutions are examined in turn and eliminated until the one preferred remains. In a presentation on the state's budget deficit, for example, you might suggest solutions such as imposing an additional tax on cigarettes, implementing a sales tax, cutting state programs, and raising property taxes. You dismiss the first three solutions for various reasons and devote your presentation to advocating an increase in property taxes.

Location. Ideas are assembled in terms of spatial or geographical relationship in an organizational pattern of location. In a presentation on the closing of military bases in the United States, for example, a speaker could discuss the bases to be closed in geographical order, beginning with the Northeastern part of the United States and moving to the Southeast, the Midwest, the Southwest, and the Northwest.

Metaphor. Metaphor, a comparison between two items, ideas, or experiences, can be used as an organizational pattern that structures a presentation. One example of this use of metaphor is a presentation by Richard R. Kelly, the CEO of Outrigger Hotels Hawaii. He used the metaphor of a cold to organize his ideas on how the company could survive in recessionary times in a presentation entitled "Prospering in '92: How to Avoid a Cold When the World Is Sneezing."

Motivated Sequence. The motivated sequence is a five-step organizational pattern designed to encourage an audience to move from consideration of a problem to adoption of a possible solution:

1 *Attention*: the introduction of the presentation is designed to capture the attention of audience members. In a presentation to high-school students on the sexual transmission of AIDS, for example, a speaker might begin by citing statistics on the number of high-school students who have AIDS and who have died of the disease in the United States.

2 *Need*: In the need step, a problem is described so that the speaker and audience share an understanding of the problem. At this point, the speaker describes the transmission of AIDS through sexual intercourse and suggests there is a need for young people to engage in honest, explicit discussion about sex and sexual practices with their partners.

3 *Satisfaction*: A plan is presented to satisfy the need created. The speaker might suggest various ways young people might initiate talk about sex with their partners.

4 *Visualization*: In visualization, the conditions that will prevail once the plan is implemented are described, encouraging the audience to visualize the results of the proposed plan. The reduced risk of AIDS and more open communication in the relationships would be results the speaker could encourage the audience to visualize.

5 *Action*: The audience is asked to take action or grant approval to the proposed plan—in this case, to use the techniques offered to discuss sex more explicitly and openly with their partners.

Multiple Perspectives. An organizational pattern created around multiple perspectives is one in which an idea is developed or a problem or object analyzed from several different viewpoints. In a presentation at a PTA meeting on how to deal with the drug problem in schools, for example, you might examine the problem from several different perspectives—medical, social, legal, and educational—in order to understand it fully and to generate creative and workable solutions to it.

Narrative. In a narrative organizational pattern, ideas are structured in a story form, using characters, settings, and plots. Communication professor Sally Miller Gearhart's presentation, "Whose Woods These Are," for example, consisted solely of a story that vividly conveyed her ideas about the violence implicit in many forms of communication.

Narrative Progression. The organizational pattern of narrative progression consists of the telling of several stories, one after another, with the speaker following the leads or implications of one story into the next. Photographer Anne Noggle's commencement speech to the Portland School of Art provides an example of narrative progression as an organizational pattern: the presentation consisted of one story after another about her life, loosely connected by the notion that life is a feast.

Perspective by incongruity. Qualities or ideas that usually are seen as opposites or as belonging to different contexts are juxtaposed to create an organizational pattern of perspective by incongruity. This form works particularly well in presentations in which discovery of knowledge is the focus because juxtaposing opposing concepts often generates new perspectives. Feminist theorist Ti-Grace Atkinson, for example, used an organizational pattern of perspective by incongruity in a presentation at Catholic University when she juxtaposed religion and law and judged the Catholic church guilty of a number of crimes.

Problem/no solution. In the organizational pattern of problem/no solution, a problem is developed and its significance is established, but no solution to the problem is suggested by the speaker. A solution is seen as desirable and actually is anticipated, but it either comes as individual audience members draw their own conclusions or through group discussion by those present. Using this organizational pattern, a supervisor might discuss, with the staff, the morale problem in the office and then ask everyone to join in coming up with solutions to it.

Problem/solution. A problem/solution organizational pattern begins with a discussion of a problem and concludes with a suggested solution or solutions. In a presentation to the Central States Communication Association, for example, communication scholar Samuel L. Becker began by establishing as a problem the "loss of our ability—and even apparently of our desire—to work out our disagreements in a thoughtful way, in a way that seeks understanding, a way that brings others in rather than locking them out, a way that builds community instead of destroying it." He then went on to propose that teachers of communication take more responsibility for developing the kinds of discourse needed to deal effectively with social problems.

Rogerian. This organizational pattern, derived from the work of Carl Rogers, is based on the belief that if people feel they

compose ▪ design ▪ advocate

are understood—that their positions are honestly recognized and respected—they will cease to feel threatened. Once threat is removed, listening is no longer an act of self-defense, and people are more likely to consider other perspectives. This pattern begins with a demonstration of understanding of audience members' positions. This means you must discover what your listeners' positions are—either prior to or at the beginning of the presentation—and demonstrate that you really understand and respect them. In the second part of the presentation your own ideas are presented, taking into account what you have learned from the audience.

Space between things. The essence of this organizational pattern is consideration of the opposite or the reverse of what usually is accorded attention or viewed as important. This pattern is particularly useful for generating new vantage points for viewing and understanding a subject. In this approach, you attend to whatever is not typically considered—the time between notes of music or the space between buildings, for example. You might focus, in a presentation on communication between the sexes, on what happens in the spaces between talk—in those silences when neither person is speaking.

Stream of consciousness. Stream of consciousness is an unfocused organizational pattern that does not contain easily identifiable connections among main ideas. It is held together by a central idea, but this idea is not as explicitly stated as it is in other organizational patterns. Careful examination of the presentation, however, usually reveals the system or idea that unites the seemingly irrelevant fragments. Garrison Keillor's monologues on his radio program, "A Prairie Home Companion," are examples of a stream of consciousness organizational pattern. In one monologue, for example, he discussed the sights he would show visitors to Lake Wobegon, Flag Day, a Flag Day celebration in 1958 in which the town created a living flag, gardens, porches, air conditioning, a ritual of greeting people from porches, and the Lunberg family and their sleepwalking habits—in that order.

Time. When the ideas of a presentation are organized according to their temporal relationships, an organizational pattern of time is used. Ideas presented in this form usually are organized chronologically—from past to present or from present to past. In discussing the economic relationship between Japan and the United States, for example, a speaker could show the chronological progression of the relationship and how it has changed over time.

Web. A web organizational pattern revolves around a central or core idea, with other ideas branching out from the core; each branching idea is a reflection and elaboration of the core. In the web form, you begin with the central idea and then explore each idea in turn, returning to the core idea and going out from it until they all have been covered. Judaic studies professor Jacob Neusner's commencement speech at Brown University in 1981 provides an example of this organizational pattern. His core idea was that higher education had failed to prepare students for the outside world. The major ideas he discussed were the faculty's lack of pride in the students' achievements, the high grades earned by students for poor performances, the forgiving world created by professors for the students, and professors' disdain for students. Before Neusner developed each new idea, he reiterated the core idea.

In the connection step to the forming process, you construct the relationships among your major ideas, resulting in an organizational pattern in which the ideas you are generating are presented. Your next task is to elaborate on those ideas.

arrangements for speaking

■ **Discuss with others, and then write:**
Imagine you are having trouble with your roommate, and things have gotten so bad you both agree you need to bring in a third party (a resident assistant, say). You think your roommate has been using your stuff without asking and that she brings her boyfriend around too much. Your roommate thinks you are standoffish and do not act like a real roommate. The plan is for each of you to take five minutes and present your case to the mediator. The mediator then will find a way of reconciling your conflict.

In pairs, discuss the pros and cons for each roommate of each of the organizational patterns described in "Constructing Connections."

Individually, choose a pattern and in writing sketch your presentation to the mediator using it.

compose ▪ design ▪ advocate

A CHECKLIST FOR PREPARING A DESIGN PLAN FOR A TALK

CONTEXT

physical context

❏ Describe the room where you'll present. What characteristics of the room might shape how your audience listens and responds?

❏ How much time do you have for speaking? How does the amount of time constrain what you can say?

❏ What time of day will you be speaking? How might this shape your audience's abilities to listen?

social context

❏ How will intimate space play into your talk? How ought you to address or shape intimate space to help you achieve your purpose?

❏ How will social space play into your talk? How ought you to address or shape social space to help you achieve your purpose?

❏ How will institutional space play into your talk? How will your audience understand the space in which they hear you? How ought you to address or shape intimate space to help you achieve your purpose?

AUDIENCE

❏ After you have researched the room where you'll speak, imagine yourself speaking to your audience in this space. Describe what you'll see.

❏ What approaches can you use to listen to your audience before you speak?

❏ What approaches can you use to listen to your audience as you speak?

PURPOSE

❏ Does the context of your speaking give you a general purpose (as when being asked to toast a couple at their wedding gives you a general idea of what you need to say)?

❏ How do you want the audience to respond as you talk? After you talk?

Use these observations—together with other observations you generate about context, audience, and purpose from chapters 2 and 3—to develop your **statement of purpose**.

STRATEGIES—INCLUDING ARRANGEMENT

ethos

❏ What sort of *ethos* do you want to build through tone of voice, body posture, and so on?

❏ What sort of introduction will start you toward achieving your purpose?

pathos

❏ What sort of emotions can you evoke through tone of voice, body posture, and so on, that will help you achieve your purpose?

❏ What sort of conclusion will leave your audience with the closing thoughts, ideas, or emotions most in support of your purpose?

logos

❏ What method seems most appropriate to your purpose?

❏ What overall arrangements for your talk (look to "Constructing Connections") seem most appropriate to your purpose?

❏ What level of grammar in your speaking will help you achieve the *ethos* you think appropriate for your audience and purpose?

❏ Try to develop one or two memorable phrases for the parts of your talk that you most want your audience to remember and consider later.

Use these observations—together with other observations you generate about strategies from chapters 2 through 4—to develop your **design plan**.

As with any checklist, do not let this one suggest it encompasses everything. It covers a lot and can help you see potentials for communication you might not otherwise—but it is you being attentive in your own ways to your time, place, and others that will help you know how best to proceed in ways that build on and support your own strengths.

preparing (yourself) to talk

the anxieties of public speaking

Speech anxiety hits us all—and there is much useful information out there for dealing with it.

First, know that there are different kinds of speech anxiety.

Some derive from your context: you may be easygoing when you talk with lunchtable friends and you may have no trouble standing up and speaking your mind in a student organization where you know everyone, but you may have more trouble standing up in class and giving a formal or informal presentation because you know you are being graded, or you may have trouble in an interview for a position you really want.

Other kinds of speech anxiety are more personal. You may have had bad experiences in the past or you may have always been unhappy with the idea of getting up in front of people and talking, and you are not about to suddenly feel great about it now, just because, once again, you are being asked to do so.

Second, speech anxiety rears its ugly head in generally recognizable stages:

1 Setting out to speak, you get a jolt of adrenaline and your body tells you to bolt. Your heart races (not unlike being around the one you love), and you might even start breathing funny and notice sweaty palms. You know the routine.

2 Soon thereafter, you become conscious of your feelings—sweaty palms are hard to ignore—but that only exacerbates the problem because it starts a cycle: feeling anxious, being self-conscious about it, getting more anxious . . .

3 And what is worse, once you recognize the reaction you're having, you start talking to yourself about yourself and saying unkind things. You "internalize" the experience and the fact of having reacted that way, and you start telling yourself that this is the kind of person you are. You become a sweaty-palmed person and not just a person with sweaty palms. This sets you up for further, even more intense, negative experi-ences in the future. Isn't it fun to be a human being? Where is Data when we need him? We are, of course, joking about what is a serious matter, but that, it turns out, is one way of dealing with speech anxiety. Try to distance yourself from yourself. Try not to take it as seri-ously as you are taking it. Try to relax.

Third, there are a lot of approaches for working with speech anxiety, and they vary depending on the kind of anxiety you expe-rience, the intensity of your experience, and the extent to which you have entered into a feedback loop of fear and self-depreca-tion. Here is a brief list of coping strategies:

- **Deep breathing.** Take long, slow breaths on a regular basis and really let yourself feel the air moving deeply into your lungs. Stand in a doorway and press your arms against the jambs, slowly, and then with gradually more force. When you stop pressing, concentrate on how your muscles feel. Feel them relax. These are bodily efforts, and they remind us that our mental states are also bodily states.

compose ▪ design ▪ advocate

If you know how to use breathing to relax, and you know how your body feels when you are relaxed, you can more easily re-create these feelings, even when you are about to speak formally.

- Other kinds of **relaxation exercises** also help, such as tensing your feet, relaxing, tensing your calf muscles, relaxing, tensing your thighs, relaxing, and so on, moving up through the muscles in your body. This works best lying down in the dark—but, again, knowing what relaxation feels like can help you be relaxed in many situations.

- **Talk to yourself** about how you are making too big a deal out of this speaking thing. Remind yourself that worrying about having to speak only reinforces the problem. At the very least, remind yourself that at such times you need to strongly stress the positive. Tell yourself you have done many good things in your life—and when you getting ready to give a speech, tell yourself, "I can do this; I can do this . . . !" Remind yourself that what you are experiencing is normal and that lots of people feel the same way in similar circumstances. The odd thing is that feelings like these isolate us just at the moment we most need to feel connected with other people—all the other sweaty-palmed people standing out there waiting their turn to make their mark on the world.

- Sometimes knowing something about **the physiology of speech anxiety** can help because we can think about that instead of about the speech. That is why we described the stages your mind/body goes through, so that anxiety does not take you by surprise but rather seems normal—and manageable. Speech anxiety is an adrenaline rush that sends us into a flight-or-fight response. Adrenaline rushes last about 20 minutes, so if you get anxious just before speaking, the anxiety won't go away quickly. But you can use that extra energy. For instance, research shows that once you start speaking the tension caused by the adrenaline rush seems to lessen. One strategy then is just to plunge into the speech, like swimming in cold water. If you do this, though, it is even more important to make sure you are prepared and know what you want to say.

- **Preparation** is another way to lessen stress levels. If you are stressed about speaking in front of other people so that you put off thinking about it then you will find yourself when the time comes standing in front of others with nothing to say. So remember that preparation, planning, and practice will accustom you both to the idea of speaking in front of other people and to actually speaking. Preparation, planning, and practice give you confidence that you know what you are doing and can pull it off. Practicing also gives you positive feedback because when you practice in front of your goldfish, you are guaranteed a sympathetic audience response.

One last word to those of you who, like us, are a bit nervous about speaking in public: you may or may not think of yourself as a "shy" person, but, in either case, it helps to set yourself small, achievable goals, and this strategy is easy to do over the course of a semester or quarter. For example, if you are nervous about speaking in a class, tell yourself you will say just one thing during each class discussion for the first two weeks—and then do it and relax. Make sure you also have a plan for when you will challenge yourself to move on to two contributions each class, and then three.

Finally, remember that we are all different—and some of us really do have strong apprehensions about speaking before others. You probably already have some sense of this about yourself, and you may need to pull your teacher aside and discuss the matter, and you may want to talk to other professionals on campus who have experience dealing with people on an individual basis. We are in this together. Even when it feels we are alone . . . especially when it feels we are alone.

visualization: preparing to deliver a talk

Visualizing yourself giving a stupendous, knockout speech is a good way to combat speech anxiety, especially if you do it several times in order to let the experience—the feeling of success—sink into your heart and bones.

But anxiety aside, visualizing yourself giving a talk or a speech, or conducting an interview, helps in several other ways. First, it is a form of practice, and practice is essential to working out the kinks and becoming comfortable with the material and the rhythms of delivery. Second, visualizing puts a kind of imprint in the back of your mind that then gets activated as you start to give the real thing and in a sense guides you through it. It is a way of substituting for not having actually given this particular speech, or one like it, before.

Many professionals use visualization techniques to enhance their chances of success. Surgeons visualize an operation the night—or for days—before an important or unfamiliar surgery. Musicians visualize a performance. Sports figures visualize a game or specific moves in a game or event. And teachers visualize classes, setting up class activities, leading class discussion, and so on.

delivery: wording, gestures, smells

In our talk about planning a speech, we described different arrangements and methods of delivery. When you turn to the question of how to **deliver** your speech, an entwined set of questions arises. What voice will you choose for speaking, how will you make the divisions in your talk clear to those listening, how will you use gestures, and how will you hold yourself?

People have studied how to speak, gesture, carry yourself, and dress while performing a speech for thousands of years in the west, going back, we know for sure, at least to 400 B.C.E. in the Mediterranean societies of ancient Greece, Rome, and Asia Minor. What follows grows out of this rich background of experiences.

It is a good rule of thumb to **vary your tone** as you speak (volume, pitch, pace). But if you speak in a monotone out of habit, it will not help matters to vary your tone in a mechanical way. You need to practice varying your tone in conjunction with what you want to say and the effect you want to have. You need to think and talk at the same time, like walking and chewing gum.

How you carry yourself into a room or up to a podium, how you stand up from a table to speak, or how you turn to someone who has just introduced you are all modes of communication. **Your body talks and people listen.** Often your body talks behind your back, if you can picture that,

and then you are not only not in control of your communication, but you may be communicating the very thing you do not want to communicate. Coming out of high school, all Dennis (one of the composers of this book) wanted to do was keep his head low and pass unnoticed—even when he was called upon to speak. These combined acts, speaking and keeping his head low, always struck people as confusing and made it such that he might as well not have spoken at all. If you need to speak, you need to speak, and that becomes the primary force behind decisions you make. You have to face up to that and change the head-hung-low behavior because it's not in step with your overall plans.

What we just said is good advice, generally, in some contexts in the United States. But depending on the culture into which you grew up, **not speaking or being silent can mean different things.** What to Dennis felt like his head hanging low might to someone else feel like a sign of respect. We need to be careful how we read other people's body language, even as we learn to read—and change—our own.

There is too much to say about **bodily movement and communication.** We encourage you to observe, to think about what you see, to talk with others about it, and to read the studies others have done. Stop and think about facial expressions, for instance. They are fascinating in their complexities. You can learn to see more in people's expressions than you currently register. And you can train yourself to better express what you want to express through a smile, a raised eyebrow (look at Hollywood actors), or a taut forehead.

Formal occasions call for a stiff posture, but sometimes you can achieve a good effect by relaxing a little. If the occasion is solemn and you do not have a complicated role to play, getting up stiffly and saying a few words may be just fine. If the occasion is a ritual, you may want to be serious, but not too stiff. Imagine yourself as a second-year college student asked to speak to incoming first-year students; you may want to balance between being official, more knowledgeable, and being cool. Stiff but not too stiff is the stuff of practice.

Finding the appropriate and comfortable expressions, postures, or ways of moving is a slow, experimental process that begins and ends with what you can do, comfortably.

> *A **word to the wise**: there are many verbal mannerisms that force their way into the way we speak in front of others, and when we are nervous they often become exaggerated. Here are some that are generally worth avoiding:* **"ah," "er," "um," "like," "you know," "whatever."**

delivery: using support materials

When you give a speech, consider using support materials such as statistics, examples, pictures, graphs, charts, stories, quotations, or testimony. You might use these materials to support your specific arguments: look to chapters 3, 4, and 7 for help with how to structure such strategies and how to give proper credit for others' words or data. There is also a practical reason for using such materials: audience attention.

When we discussed context above, we encouraged you to think about the time you have to talk. This helps you think about someone in your audience sitting for that time, listening. Even a well-rested, eager audience can only hold on to part of what you say. Research suggests people do not retain everything they hear in a speech. Researchers charted the attention span of audiences over an hour or so, and discovered that retention is sharp initially, wanes after about 10 minutes (unless listeners find ways to resist this tendency), and returns when the audience senses the end. This tells you that in planning a speech you need to keep your audience's bodily attentions in mind: if you want to hold their attentions (especially in a longer speech) then you need to vary how you present your ideas, in line with your purposes.

Once you have gathered appropriate support materials, attend to their use. What will be effective—and ethical? Statistics are often expected and can win the day—but they can cause people to feel lost in a sea of numbers, and nearly everyone agrees they can easily be manipulated. Likewise, charts and graphs can be a breath of fresh air—or they can nastily obscure the issue by presenting misleading information or skewing the issue. Audiences must hear you explain how and why you've used the statistics you do.

Examples and stories are pleasing to audiences, but they have their drawbacks. One example or story, harped on over and over, can be boring but can also present itself as the way things really are and thus can squeeze out other relevant examples and stories. One picture repeatedly pushed at an audience, or just prominently displayed, can dominate people's thinking unfairly. Testimony, often coming as narrative, is vitally important to making a case—but testimony too can be fabricated or one-sided, and so is in and of itself no guarantee of true support.

You can be creative with support materials, bringing in interesting objects to pass around the audience or playing music in the background—but use these materials thoughtfully, purposefully, and with respect for your audience.

interviewing

You can learn about your audience through interviewing, and interviewing is also a useful way to gather information, or supporting material, for the body of a talk.

Interviewing, especially in preparation for giving a talk or speech, is an odd mix of the public and the private. You often sit face to face—body to body—with another person whom you do not know well, and you talk in the same way you might talk with your sister or friend over coffee. And yet it is not intimate in the same way as having coffee with a friend and in fact, since it is "on the record," it is really quite a public thing.

As you plan for an interview, remember that you are looking for specific information, information you can use in shaping your talk or as material for your talk. But also remember that interviewing someone about the subject of your talk gives you an opportunity to try out your ideas and check the response you get.

Interviewing is an essential tool for doing research. Like listening and seeing, it can seem so easy and obvious you hardly need to think about it. Just sit down and start asking questions. In chapter 16, online, we look at professional examples of interviews and ask you to think about how much preparation—research—the interviewers did. Here we will sketch some basic interviewing strategies that should help with your research.

Many of the subjects we address in this textbook, interviewing among them, can themselves be the subject of a book-length study. For more detailed information on interviewing, we recommend Shirley Biagi's *Interviews That Work: A Practical Guide for the Journalist* (Belmont: Wadsworth Publishing Co., 1986). Even though Biagi steers her advice toward journalists, she has much to offer anyone who needs to plan and carry out a successful interview. We have drawn much of what we have to say about interviewing from Biagi.

compose ▪ design ▪ advocate

rules for effective interviews

RULE NO. 1
Prepare your interview.

Interviewing feels and moves like a conversation—which is deceptive. Yes, you should expect and look forward to interviews taking unexpected turns as conversations do, but don't decide that you therefore don't need to plan. What you plan will be useful even as the discussion twists and turns in ways you didn't anticipate, because as it twists away from what you anticipated, at least you can follow it, knowing what it is deviating from. Knowing what you expected to happen helps you understand and hold on to what unexpectedly happened.

To prepare, you need to get really clear about your purpose. What do you want to get out of the interview? Are you looking for specific knowledge, or someone else's particular take on a situation? You then need to work up a line of questioning that will help you achieve your purpose. You need an opening question to set the tone of the interview, a set of questions to follow, and a set of concluding questions. You also want to prepare follow-up questions that you might use at the end of the interview, after the person you have been interviewing turns the tables on you and asks you questions, or in a follow-up session.

Prepare your questions, but also think about the context of the interview: location, possible distractions, length of time

needed, the mood the person may be in, and so on. Attend to what you say through your non-verbal actions like showing up on time or sitting straight and leaning forward to display your interest and concern. You of course want to establish a relaxed atmosphere, but concentrating on what the person is saying to you is crucial.

RULE NO. 2
Interviews are interactive.

After your careful planning and preparation, learning what you can about the person you will interview, thinking about the context of the interview and how that will affect your questioning and the subject's responses, and laying down a smooth line of questions, you need to back away a bit. Put into your plan pauses, questions that invite the person you are interviewing to take over and make suggestions, responses of your own to what the person is saying (without you taking over the conversation).

Of course you are listening carefully and taking notes when appropriate, but attend to what else is going on. Pay attention to the gestures and expressions of the person you're interviewing. If you are in the person's home or office, check out the paintings or posters on the wall, or awards displayed—these can give you topics for "small talk," the kind of conversation that eases relations between people.

What helps interviews be interactive

- Smile. Introduce yourself calmly but enthusiastically.

- Set an agenda early by stating what you want to get out of the interview.

- If possible, establish a shared goal with the person you interview.

- If you are using technical words or special references to people, places, or institutions, make sure that both of you understand these words in the same way: define what you mean when you talk, and ask the person you interview to define any words you might understand differently.

- Give the other person time to answer. It's fine to let pauses go a little longer than when you are talking with friends because the person you are interviewing may need a little time to think. When it seems as though the person you are interviewing has finished speaking in response to your questions, ask if she or he is finished.

- Once you have a sense of the other person's rhythms in speaking, keep the discussion moving. This is especially important in phone interviews.

- Try to sense early on if the person really doesn't want to talk.

- Don't just hang up or walk away from an interview. Make a point of concluding. Ask for a phone number and time where the person can be reached for follow-up questions. Say, "Thank you."

RULE NO. 3
Establish respect and trust as best you can.

Even when an interview is strained and you are seeking information the informant is not willing to give up easily, treat the person as you want to be treated. This is especially hard if the person you are talking to is not treating you the same way. The hard part about being moral is that it is your own responsibility that matters. If someone is not responsible to you in return, you have to let it go. This is important in contexts like interviewing, where all that is at stake is whether you learn what you need to learn. All you can do is be the interviewer you know you should be: open, thoughtful, prepared, critical, and respectful.

RULE NO. 4
End the interview.

With the person you are interviewing, go back over what has been said in order to double-check your grasp of the main points from the interview. If you are taking notes, put away your notebook toward the end and keep listening.

Ask if follow-up questions, perhaps over the phone, are acceptable.

PREPARING QUESTIONS TO ASK

In chapter 6, we distinguish some basic kinds of questions: fact, definition, interpretation, value, and policy. Read about these questions, because when you plan an interview it is useful to know what questions to ask and in what order.

Here is other help for thinking about interview questions you might ask. As you consider possible questions, ask yourself whether the person you are interviewing is qualified or otherwise in the appropriate position to answer what you ask.

- Begin with an open-ended question.

- Concentrate on *how?* and *why?* questions because these lead to fuller answers than yes and no questions.

- Ask the person you are interviewing to define a term.

- Ask questions that invite the interviewee to rank or evaluate something.

- Give an either/or choice in a question when you want to know the interviewee's position on an issue.

- Ask for a chronology of events from the interviewee. This often brings out details to an event that an interviewee might otherwise miss.

- Avoid two-part questions, overly long questions, unfocused questions, clichéd questions, leading questions, yes-no questions, and absolute questions (using qualifiers such as certainly, positively, or absolutely). Such questions do not encourage thoughtful or detailed responses.

When you conduct an interview with another person—a human being!—it is especially important to know in advance what you want from the interview and to explain that up front to the interviewee. If you use a recording device, make sure you ask permission. If you take notes, make sure you ask permission. And since this is research, do your own research into the subject of the interview and the person you are interviewing before planning and conducting the interview.

When you are in the middle of the interview, here are some approaches to help you learn more or be sure you understand:

- Re-state an interviewee's answer to make sure you heard correctly or to invite a qualification.

- Ask the person to expand on a point or enlarge on a specific incident if it will help you better understand what happened.

testing and evaluating oral presentations

Testing and evaluating oral presentations can be awkward, because it can feel so personal: it is you, speaking, being tested and evaluated. But, really, you just have to get over it—and you can help yourself do this by remembering that when you test and evaluate speeches the point is for you to acknowledge what works well and to strengthen what could be more effective. That's all.

But, meanwhile, here are

Ways to address evaluation fairly and humanely.

❑ Make the evaluation criteria as clear as possible.

❑ Come up with the criteria as a class.

❑ Talk through the criteria with those assessing a talk: discuss what they mean and what kinds of responses will be helpful.

❑ Practice applying the criteria with everyone involved and then discuss differences in your responses.

❑ Err on the side of being positive in your responses to one another.

❑ Emphasize verbal feedback over numerical evaluations.

❑ Use a variety of evaluations (self, peer, instructor, written, verbal).

A SPEECH EVALUATION FORM *(which needs room for you to write the requested comments)*

THE INTRODUCTION

How did the introduction capture audience interest? How could it have been stronger?

Describe your understanding of the speech's purpose from what you heard in the introduction.

Describe what you understand the arrangement of the speech to be, based on what you heard in the introduction.

THE BODY

What were the main points you heard?

What evidence was offered to support the main points?

How did the evidence persuade you? How could it have been more concrete or more detailed?

How did the arrangement of the speech support the purpose?

What were the strengths of the language used in the speech?

What suggestions do you have for how the language of the speech could be more engaging?

THE CONCLUSION

How did the conclusion help you remember the purpose of the speech?

How does the conclusion give you a satisfying sense of closure? How might it do this more effectively?

DELIVERY

What were the strongest qualities of voice in support of the purpose and engaging the audience?

How did the postures and gestures contribute to the effectiveness of the speech? How might they be more effective?

How did the speaker's eye contact engage you with the speech?

What was the overall manner of the speaker (enthusiastic? reserved?)—and how did it support the purpose?

How aware were you of the speaker's use of notes?

OVERALL

How could the topic be narrowed or focused to be even more appropriate for the length of time of this speech?

How persuasive to its audience was the speech? How might it be more persuasive?

ethical contexts of speaking—and listening

Earlier in this chapter, there is an article—"Inviting Transformation"—written by Sonja K. Foss and Karen A. Foss, in which Foss and Foss argue that the ethics of the speaking context suggests speakers should try to invite transformation when they speak to an audience, rather than do whatever they can to ensure change in the audience. To reinforce this idea, Foss and Foss urge speakers to resist seeing themselves as the active partner in communication and seeing audiences as passive. Instead, they urge speakers to learn to be better listeners in order to be better speakers, to build better relations with audiences.

Speech communication scholar Karlyn Kohrs Campbell, in her article "Hating Hillary," turns the table on Foss and Foss, in a sense. Campbell argues that the ethics of the speaking context suggest audiences (at times) should acknowledge when speakers are caught in a social double-bind not of their own making, rather than blindly reinforce the double-bind by going along with superficial expectations. In support of her argument, Campbell examined all the speeches given by Hillary Rodham Clinton during the first term of the Clinton presidency in order to consider how effective a speaker Clinton was at that time.

Campbell was particularly interested in Clinton's speeches on health care reform because that was a project on which Clinton worked closely. What Campbell discovered is interesting and complex. She discovered that Clinton's speaking manner was sharp, direct, and at times aggressive. No more so than any other politician, but it turns out, according to Campbell, that women in politics must walk a fine line between being aggressive and strong and coming across as feminine or motherly. Campbell refers to this as a double-bind because women are expected to be both aggressive and not aggressive at the same time—quite a trick.

Campbell concludes that Clinton was not a wholly successful speaker. Clinton tended to ignore the double-bind and speak forthrightly—and as a result many people in her audience responded negatively (in some cases very negatively) to her manly way of speaking and carrying herself. Campbell also concludes, however, that much of the fault for Clinton's lack of success can be laid at the feet of her audience for unselfconsciously, uncritically, and unfairly expecting Clinton to give in to the double-bind and both be and not be the proper woman speaker.

Campbell thus tries to nudge her readers into admitting that they listen to men and women speakers differently, to the unfair advantage of male speakers. We made a related point earlier in this chapter when we urged you to be more self-conscious about how you sit in an audience and how responsive you are to a speaker's efforts. We were raising the question of the ethical responsibilities of audiences, just as Campbell is doing.

In addition, then, to being a careful listener while you are speaking, having integrity in your arguments, and being an attentive audience while you are listening, do consider how attitudes of which you may not always be aware shape how you listen and evaluate. If, while you listen, you find yourself responding negatively, and you can't honestly pin your response to the speech's long-winded phrasing, obvious faulty logic, or mean-spiritedness, then consider whether unspoken assumptions are at play. And even if you think you can point to such faults as we listed, it is sometimes worthwhile (especially in politics or when a speaker comes from a differing background) to consider whether you are judging based on your own attachments rather than on the merits of the speech.

compose ▪ design ▪ advocate

thinking through production

- Using the design process from chapters 2 through 4—and the interview sections in this chapter—plan and conduct an interview about the civic side of their life with an older relative, older friend of the family, or someone you know at school who is at least 10 years older than you. Cover the activities in which they are involved outside of work and home, what they think being a good citizen means, how they divide private and public life, and relevant commitments, attitudes, and beliefs.

  Use the interview as the basis of a five-minute talk you design and then deliver to class about your interviewee's civic life.

- Take this poem from Langston Hughes home with you and read it aloud to yourself at least 10 times. Commit it to heart. Find a way to read it—where to pause, where to change tone, where to put emphasis—that lets it do for a listening audience what Hughes wanted it to do (as you understand it).

  Dreams
  Hold fast to dreams
  For if dreams die
  Life is a broken-winged bird
  That cannot fly

  Hold fast to dreams
  For when dreams go
  Life is a barren field
  Frozen with snow

  Compare different readings in class.

- Remember a time you gave a speech or talk that didn't go as well as you would have liked. Describe how you would redesign the physical context in which you gave that speech so that the audience would have been as comfortable and supportively listening as possible, and also so that you would have been as relaxed and confident as possible.

  What can you take away from your redesign to help you shape the physical contexts in which you speak in the future?

- There are more "Thinking Through Production" activities in the online chapter 8 resources at www.ablongman.com/wysocki

compose ▪ *design* ▪ *advocate*

about
visual modes
of communication

Do you think you need a degree in art or design to include photographs effectively in a research paper or to compose a poster for a fund-raising event?

There is certainly much more to learning to be a professional visual communicator than we present in this chapter. For example, we do not give any history of design, which could give you a sense of how visual conventions have changed over time and place. We do not ask you to spend a semester drawing lettershapes—by hand—so that you have the smart expressiveness that calligraphic work requires. We do not discuss how to prepare a document for printing or how to design interactive online interfaces: both processes can be highly complex and require extensive technical knowledge.

What does make sense for us to offer you, however, are basic but sufficient vocabulary, concepts, and methods to help you start

being as rhetorical with the visual aspects of texts as with the verbal. Almost all the texts you compose—in school or out—require you to make visual choices (even if your only choices are typeface, the size of margins, and alignment). Almost all texts you encounter have been designed to have visual effects on you; you can only respond to those texts analytically if you have vocabulary and concepts to help you see how the texts are working.

We don't intend to make you an expert in this chapter; we do intend to give you resources that will help you move thoughtfully through our visually full and varied environments.

263

the pleasures—and complexities—of visual communication

We often associate seeing with pleasure or delight. Think of how parents look at their children, and how people who are in love look at each other. Think of how enjoyable a walk in the woods is, whether we go to see the bright greens of early spring or the stark soft shapes of an overnight snowfall. These visual pleasures seem easy: we just open our eyes and, automatically and effortlessly, there is the world to linger over with our eyes. Seeing, that is, can seem to be a result only of physiology, a result only of the physical processes of our bodies and unaffected by who we are, where we live, or how we've been raised.

This easiness of seeing appears to extend to the visual texts we make for each other. When we take photographs or videos, or try to capture an "exact likeness" in a drawing, it seems as though we are capturing a bit of reality, so that anyone anywhere ought to understand what the picture is about, without explanation. Think of how first books for children are composed only

of pictures with little or no text, and how we take it as a sign of maturity when a child can read words-only books.

Because seeing and understanding photographs and drawings can seem so effortless, and can be so pleasurable, some people think that visual texts are not as serious as verbal texts, which by comparison appear to require more abstract and conceptual thinking. Because of this, some people look at the increase in visual texts in this country and time—advertising, comic books, music videos, webpages, movies—and think we are becoming less thoughtful and complex people because we spend less time than ever reading texts composed mostly of verbal elements.

In this book, however, we argue that visual texts are complex—and can be as complex and thoughtful as any purely verbal text. If someone thinks they are not, it is in no small part because our educations have encouraged us to have that attitude: we have grown up in places and times that have valued verbal texts as being more serious and worthy of educated attention than other kinds of texts.

But every visual text involves choices—just like every written text. A photograph requires the photographer to frame the

picture, to decide what to emphasize and what not, and whether to use color film, and what level of focus to use, and so on . . . and we can only understand photographs if we have some understanding of the contexts in which they are shown. For example, can you tell whether the expression on the face shown to the left is joyful or pained?

We are not arguing that our understandings of the visual aspects of texts have no connections with how our bodies work. For example, our eyes are of a certain size, they cover a certain angle of vision, and they have a certain range of focus, which changes as we age. Anyone who is designing visual objects must keep these matters in mind as she makes compositions for others: if you are composing a poster, you want to be sure people can see its main elements from a distance, and if you are designing a booklet for older people, you want to use larger-size typefaces and colors that help people see contrast more clearly.

We *are* arguing, however, that—if we don't learn to analyze and understand the complexities of visual texts, and to compose thoughtful, complex visual texts ourselves—then it *can* seem as though we just perceive visual texts naturally and easily . . . and we won't read visual texts critically, as

compose ▪ design ▪ advocate

texts made by people who arrange the elements of their texts in order to achieve specific purposes.

On the following pages, we present strategies for analyzing and composing visual texts, strategies based both on how we see physically and on how we see as participants in our cultures.

"Daniel Simons, a professor of psychology at Harvard, has done a . . . dramatic set of experiments . . . . He and a colleague, Christopher Chabris, recently made a video of two teams of basketball players, one team in white shirts and the other in black, each player in constant motion as two basketballs are passed back and forth. Observers were asked to count the number of passes completed by the members of the white team. After about forty-five seconds of passes, a woman in a gorilla suit walks into the middle of the group, stands in front of the camera, beats her chest vigorously, then walks away. 'Fifty per cent of the people missed the gorilla,' Simon says. 'We got the most striking reactions. We'd ask people, "Did you see anyone walking across the screen?" They'd say no. Anything at all? No. Eventually we'd ask them, "Did you notice the gorilla?" And they'd say, "The what?"' Simon's experiment is one of those psychological studies which are impossible to believe in the abstract: if you look at the video (called 'Gorillas in Our Midst') when you know what's coming, the woman in the gorilla suit is inescapable. How could anyone miss that? But people do. In recent years, there has been much scientific research on the fallibility of memory—on the fact that eyewitnesses, for example, often distort or omit critical details when they recall what they saw. But the new research points to something that is even more troubling: **it isn't just that our memory of what we see is selective; it's that seeing itself is selective.**"

—from "Wrong Turn: How the fight to make America's highways safer went off course." By Malcolm Gladwell. *The New Yorker*, June 11, 2001 (pp. 50–61).

the contexts, purposes, and audiences of visual communication

visible contexts

Like writing and unlike speaking, pieces of visual communication most often go off into the world after you make them and you never or rarely get to see the moment when audiences pass their eyes and their attentions over what you've produced. And so you have to be both imaginative and grabby as you produce communication that is primarily visual: imagine hard that moment when others see what you produce, but get yourself out there hungrily observing how others look at similar productions and find people from your audience who will help you test your productions in the contexts where they'll be seen.

One of the biggest—and most avoidable—failures of visual communication is communication that people can't see because it's been designed all wrong for its context. Have you ever noticed road signs that were impossible to read as you drove by at 60 mph because the signs were detailed and pretty—rather than large and simple? Most failures, however, are the ones you don't see, precisely because they are easy to overlook: the next time you

pass that wall on your campus or those telephone poles plastered with announcements, notice how many announcements you don't notice—and pay attention to how the ones that do grab your eyes do their work. If you ever make posters or flyers, test one (before you print 400) by hanging it in a place where it would be hung, and ask someone you know from your intended audience to walk by: do they even see it? Posters and flyers are seen by people walking by, 5, 6, or 10 feet away: there must be something large, really large, on the paper that can catch their attentions. If you've made something with a single feature that interests them from a distance, they *will* come closer and read the more detailed and smaller information.

For visual communications like signs, posters, and flyers, there's an aspect of context that writings and talks don't have to work with: signs, posters, and flyers are hung in places where they compete with other signs, posters, and flyers. For them to be noticeable, they have to stand out against the background of all the other

texts—this is where you need the principle of contrast, as we discuss it in this chapter. Look to the strategies for creating contrast to help you design communication that others can see.

Other visual communications—or communications that require some visual attentions, like any printed or onscreen piece of communication—will be seen in the same contexts as people reading books or magazines. Go back and look at what we wrote about context in the writing chapter (we like that writing) for encouragement and ideas. Most importantly, research contexts.

Or make contexts. If you have a poster, in what unexpected places can you put it so that people will see it? On the ground? Tucked into visible but uncluttered corners?

Always consider how you can shape the contexts in which your productions are seen.

compose ▪ design ▪ advocate

visible audiences

I am 47 years old as I write this (this is Anne, one of your authors), and my eyes are changing. I am one of those people you see in the aisle at the supermarket trying to read the small type on the sides of vitamins. I move the bottles nearer and farther, and eventually end up quite close—closer than my glasses can handle so I look out from underneath my lenses. I am one of those people you—who are most likely not 47 years old—ought to have in mind when you design visual communication for general or older audiences. If you design type and figure that anyone can read it because you can, I will come after you and find you—if my eyes hold out.

So even though writing and visual communication are the same, in that you rarely see your audiences at the time they engage with your productions—and in that you can read again what we wrote in chapter 7 about considerations specific to audiences encountering written communications for assistance with a lot of visual communication work—there are additional attentions you need to give to your audiences when you design visual communications.

I've already mentioned eyes—and their age-bound abilities—but also consider how different audiences respond to different photographs and drawings. Not too many years ago, a software company producing page layout software put a graphic on screen for while the software opened; the graphic included the symbol at the top left of this page—the circle with perpendicular lines over it—which you might sometimes see if you use page layout applications. When a book or poster or other text is printed on a press in hundreds or thousands of copies, its pages are often printed on paper that is larger than the document's final size, and then trimmed. (This is how we get pages that have photographs that run off the edge of a page: the photograph "bleeds" off the edge of the page as it is designed, and then that bleed is cut away when the page is trimmed to its final size.) The symbol above left is a registration mark: printers use it to ensure that pages are all aligned properly up and down when they go to trim big stacks of the pages.

The point of all this information? Many people who bought the software we've just described complained about the registration mark—because they didn't know what it was. Christians complained that the software company was profaning the cross; non-Christians complained that the software company was trying to force Christianity down their throats. Were these audiences for the software being too sensitive? Were they just stupid?

No.

You can never expect others to know everything you know—just as you hope others do not expect you to know everything they do. Judging what others value is also a dicey proposition: even when you disagree, you probably would like others to respect what you value and not to call your values stupid or not worthy of care. Look back at the list of conditions that make argument possible on page 21—if you want arguments that do indeed engage you with others, you do need to respect their beliefs and values.

Because we cannot often predict the associations others will have with photographs or drawings we use, it is crucial—when you are making decisions about photographs or drawings to use in communication—to test them with your intended audiences. Ask people what associations or ideas come up for them as they look at the photographs or illustrations—or with the colors you're considering. You can learn if audiences think the graphics are too childish for them, incomprehensible—or potentially distracting from your purposes.

As you design and produce visual communications, think of audiences as people with beliefs, values, and opinions you want not to alienate but to engage.

visible purposes

When should you use visual strategies for argument instead of or in addition to written or oral strategies? Whenever it is appropriate to your purpose—and when the visual strategies support your purpose.

Like writing and speaking, visual communications and the purposes they can fulfill are complex and interesting because—as we discuss in Section 3, when we consider examples of many kinds of communication—they draw on what we know about the world because we have bodies and because we grow up into cultures.

■ In our culture, photographs and drawings of people can seem automatically to carry more emotion than writing. When photographs or drawings are of people or events, we respond to how the people look—and we respond because we know or can imagine what it is like to be in the body posture shown. We respond because we can imagine the emotions photographed people feel. Including photographs or drawings in a written composition can thus attach emotions and bodily sensations to the writing—but do be alert to how different audiences can respond in very different ways.

■ When we see photographs and realistic illustrations, we see and assume much more than we often are aware because of our knowledge about people and culture. We make judgements about people's ages and character and relationships, about when and where photographs were taken, and so on. These are good reasons to check how your intended audiences understand any photographs or illustrations you are considering for a composition. These ways we respond to photographs and illustrations also suggest that we can use photographs and illustrations to put audiences in mind of particular times and places, and of the associations they have with those times and places.

■ Often when people say "image" they think only of artistic visual texts like paintings or photographs. But consider technical illustrations, charts and graphs, logos, and so on. Technical illustrations or photographs are designed to show us only the details we need to understand a process or machine. Charts and graphs show us the relations that their composers want us to see among numbers or other data. When they compose logos (the plural of "logo"), designers try to compress into such a single graphic object the values they want audiences to associate with a company. Each of these kinds of visual communication has purposes that can help you with particular communications you produce.

■ When we learn to write, we rarely learn about visual potentials of writing. We do understand differences between handwriting and printed documents: the former seem more personal, and we often make judgments about people based on their handwriting (for example, how do you feel about the letter **i** when the dot above it is a circle or a heart?); printed documents generally seem more formal and professional, and so distanced from us. But what about differences in the typefaces and colors you can use on a page? Like photographs and illustrations, typefaces and color can add emotional associations to a page (and, as with photographs and illustrations, this means you should always test your choices with audiences)—and they also can help with the *logos* of a page, helping readers differentiate levels of argument on a page. A lot of this chapter will help you make such choices.

In this chapter we focus primarily on how you can use visual elements of pages (print or screen) to produce arguments. In chapters 10 and 11 we consider the compositional strategies of posters and photographs; in chapter 15 we look at comics, and how words and drawings or photographs can work together to achieve purposes either alone cannot.

ANALYZING
our visual lives

■ **Observe, then write:** This weekend, over two hours on an afternoon, list **every** object you see that has been visually designed.

Unless you stay in bed with the pillow over your eyes, you won't be able to keep up—but try. The plates, silverware, and glasses in your kitchen might not have any text printed on them, but they still have been designed to appeal to your eyes. Open your medicine cabinet: how many bottles of shampoo, aftershave, or medicine—with visuals designed to catch your eye and instruct you in their use—are there? Walk or drive through town: look at all the signs, the clothes (many with printed slogans) on people you pass, traffic signals, objects in store windows. There are the rows upon rows of magazines, boxes, or bottles in any store (or, now, in many movies), each labeled to catch your attention, to create desire in you.

Back in class, compare your lists with others. How do you go through your day (do you?) not being constantly distracted by all these objects calling to your eyes? How have the objects been designed so that they don't distract or overwhelm—or what strategies have you developed to see

selectively (based on your purposes at hand) so that you aren't continually overwhelmed by all the objects?

■ **Discuss with others:** Bring your favorite or an interesting picture postcard to class. In groups of 2 or 3, look at someone else's postcard—but don't look at the back.

List as much as you can about the photograph on the postcard based just on what you see. When and where do you think the photograph was taken? What can you say about who or what is in the photograph?

After about 5 minutes, share your observations with the whole group. Say why you make the guesses you do about the postcards. (Turn over the postcard to see what information is there—how close were you?)

Were you surprised by how much everyone could say about the postcards? What can you learn from this about how we see and understand photographs?

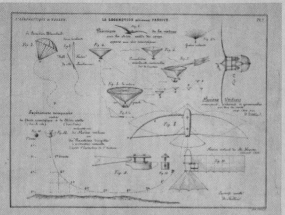

■ **Discuss with others:** The page above and the page below both use drawings to achieve their purposes. When do you think these drawings were made, roughly—and what helps you decide? Describe how the purposes of the pages shape the kinds of drawings used. How are the different drawings shaping audiences' attentions?

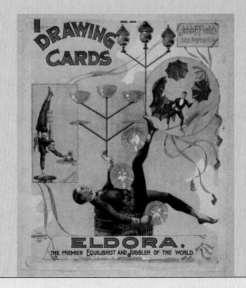

seeing *ethos, pathos,* and *logos*

As with written and oral communication, visual texts have their own particular strategies we can use to compose *ethos, logos,* and *pathos,* strategies that have developed over time and through the shapings of particular cultures. Keep in mind, then, that what we offer you here about *ethos, pathos,* and *logos* in visual arrangements is appropriate for arguments that meet audience expectations in the early twenty-first century United States.

In visual communication—as in the general U.S. approach to how we use space and time—efficiency is now valued. Historians of visual design argue that the rise of efficiency as a value in visual communication paralleled the linked rise of industry and advertising in the twentieth century: as industrialists strove to produce as many objects as possible as quickly as possible, they also needed to produce consumers for those objects. Advertising was born to encourage people to desire things, and to desire them quickly—and visual communication in general therefore took on the values of quickness and directness.

What we present in the sections on the *logos* of arrangement in visual communication, especially, will help you compose layouts whose order supports the efficient communication of information—but keep in mind that *ethos* and *pathos* can also be visually shaped into efficiency. A photograph, for example, can show a person having a single clear emotional response to an event, or can indicate more complex emotional responses. You can visually compose an *ethos* that shows you to be singularly focused on efficiency—or you can compose an *ethos* that shows you to value generosity as well.

Because efficiency has been so highly valued, it can seem not to be a value but instead to be simply how things are and always ought to be. Many books that teach about visual communication teach layout principles as though efficiency—with its concordant layout values of coherence, unity, and a clear hierarchy of informative elements—is the value that should underlie all choices in layout. In the pages that follow, we hope to teach you the ability to use those values well, precisely because they are the values many of your audiences will hold. But as you read through the next pages, keep in mind that there are many other possible values that can go into how you compose *ethos, logos,* and *pathos* on a page or screen.

Because visual communication has such strong ties to advertising, there are many who think that advertising is all that visual communication can do. It doesn't take much looking—whether back in time or in different places in the present—to see examples of visual communication such as stained glass windows, weather charts, biology textbooks, or the pages of Bibles or Korans to see that many other values can shape *ethos, logos,* and *pathos.* We challenge you—both as a composer and as an audience member for the compositions of others—to look for designings of *ethos, logos,* and *pathos* that advocate values such as compassion, respect for complex thinking, diversity, simplicity, and self-awareness.

Precisely because we have grown up into a culture where such values are rarely taught through visual communication, they may look odd to us when we see them made visible. But if we wish to see more such values in our communications, then we ourselves need to make those values visible *and* we need to show generosity toward the designs of others who are trying to make those values present.

☐ If you do not have your own photographs to use in the activities of this chapter, check out the online chapter 9 resources at www.ablongman.com/wysocki

compose ▪ design ▪ advocate

photographing *ethos*

Where are your attentions drawn in the photograph above? How have the elements been arranged so that you notice one element first, and then something else second or third? Is there anything in the photograph that asks you to think about the character of the person who took the photograph?

Photographs tend to direct our attentions to other people and objects, to the "outside" world. In that way, even if they are about family members or intimate events, photographs tend to be more like scientific essays: it is as though they want to show us the world just as it is, without judgment.

How then could there be any ethos?

Along with showing us people or objects in the world, photographs (even those made with cameras that are almost completely automatic) show us a series of decisions made by the photographer. They show us the position the photographer chose for the camera, the exposure time, and the use or not of a flash or filters—and they show us that the photographer thought there was something in the scene worth photographing.

In learning to interpret photographs, then, it is important to acknowledge that such a range of decisions has gone into the photograph, and to ask what that tells us about the photographer and what the photographer wants us to see.

This is particularly important because photographs ask us to become the photographer. Whenever we see a photograph, we see it from the position in which the photographer held or situated the camera. Every photograph asks us to see the world as though we were seeing it through the photographer's lens, as though we were seeing it through the series of judgments the photographer made in setting up the shot. In looking, we need to ask why a photographer wants us to see a particular scene, arranged as it is. What sort of person would look at the world—would make the particular choices about framing and displaying the world—in the way the photograph asks us to look?

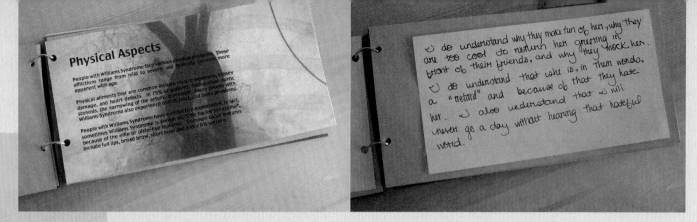

If you find rest or distraction in flipping through TV channels, you can probably tell, almost immediately, whether you've hit an infomercial or a network series. Without thinking, you probably register the difference in production values—in the lighting and in the quality of sound and the set—because you've seen so many different kinds of TV shows that you've learned almost automatically what looks polished and professional and what looks less.

There are two useful-to-understanding-visual-texts qualities in your ability to distinguish between infomercials and other shows. First, you make judgments about the quality of different visual texts all the time, and often without being aware of the judgments. If you want to start producing your own visual texts, or to start being even more alert to how such texts have the effects they do, noticing your existing judgments and tastes about visual texts can help you. The vocabulary and concepts we offer in this book can support you.

Second, the qualities of "polished and professional" are valued in our day and place: as a culture, we often value communicative visual texts if they get to the point efficiently and if they demonstrate that their composers know how to use their materials well. A director who lets a microphone show in a scene or an actor who speaks in a monotone are the stuff of comedy for us. When texts *do* look "polished and professional" we tend to place a certain trust in the makers of the text and hence in the persuasiveness of the text.

Producers of visual texts can use the distinction between what is considered professional and what isn't: precisely because alt bands *want* to look outside the mainstream, posters for their shows are often hand-scrawled and, in comparison to a poster for a Britney Spears concert, they look messy and angry rather than slick and seductive.

In the book from which the pages above come, Karen Koethe wanted to teach others about Williams Syndrome, a genetic condition. She wanted others to understand both the physical and the emotional consequences of the disorder—and so her book alternates hand-written pages with pages of computer-generated typography. The handwritten pages do not look "professional" precisely because they are handwritten, but they are handwritten precisely because the computer-generated pages—while professional looking—do not ask us to consider that the pages were made by a real flesh-and-blood feeling person.

As you analyze and produce visual texts, you need to learn what is generally considered professional looking, in part so that you can decide when nonprofessional strategies are useful.

ANALYZING
visual *ethos*

■ **Observe, then write:** Because "professional" is such a noticed quality in visual texts of our time and place, it is useful for you to be able to say explicitly what qualities make different texts professional or not.

Collect at least 10 samples of a certain kind of visual text. For example, you could collect samples of brochures, flyers for events on your campus, business cards, PowerPoint presentations, or resumes. For each sample, write down any adjectives you would attach to the *ethos* of the composers of the sample. Do you think the composers present themselves and their work professionally? Do they seem friendly and inviting or formal and distant? Do they seem cheerful or neutral? Also, decide which of your samples look most professional and which look less.

Write down the qualities of the different texts that encourage you to make your judgments. As you look and judge, consider how the samples use type, the quality of writing in them, the kind of paper used, any use of color, the size of graphics, what any photographs depict, and so on.

As you work through this chapter, you will learn other terms and concepts to use in adding to your judgments. Your lists of what visual decisions help persuade audiences to see a particular *ethos* in a text can help you analyze visual texts in more detail in the future—but they can also help you if you ever need to produce any of these kinds of texts in the future. Any time you need to produce a kind of text that is new to you—or the first time you are producing a kind of text you've seen many times but have never made yourself—it is useful to collect and analyze a wide range of samples of that kind of text.

seeing *pathos*

pathos in photographs

Obvious *pathos*

When we see people in a photograph, we might identify with them: we understand the situation they are in through our own experiences. When we see happy (or sad or angry) people, we can feel similar emotions because we know the emotions ourselves. It is probably an obvious point to you, but this is why advertisements for cars or cookies show happy rather than perplexed people: the advertisers want you to believe you too will be happy in possession of that car.

Less obvious *pathos*

The two photographs to the right are also composed to evoke emotional response from us. When we see only part of an object, we mentally fill in what isn't shown, which can get us more engaged with the object—especially when it also takes a little time to understand what the photograph is showing us, as in the second picture. A photograph of a storm might invoke memories of being caught in the rain, but it might also invoke the feelings of summer afternoon beauty. The context in which you see such a photograph—printed on a Christmas card or on a postcard from someone's overseas trip—and your specific

cultural background will shape your own specific response.

Neither of the photographs on the right are meant to evoke the emotions of happiness, sadness, anger, or fear, but they do evoke bodily feelings—and therefore can be used rhetorically. To analyze and use the potential *pathos* of photographs, don't be afraid to name the emotions or bodily responses you yourself feel—just be alert to how the different backgrounds of others might lead them to respond differently.

compose ▪ design ▪ advocate

the rhetorical colors of *pathos*

The colors of a photograph or page layout contribute substantially to our emotional responses. Our responses are not random but instead have much to do with what we have learned to associate with different colors. In order to analyze and use color rhetorically, you need not only your cultural knowledge but also some vocabulary. "Color" is analyzed in terms of hue, saturation, and brightness:

In the online chapter 9 resources at www.ablongman.com/wysocki are links to websites that can help you pick sets of compatible colors.

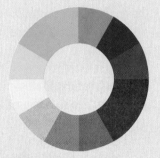

HUE

"Hue" describes what many of us just think of as color: when you name the hue of a color, you are saying whether it is red or blue or yellow. . . . Hues are often represented in a wheel: you can use hues that are next or close to each other on the wheel when you want color schemes that seem harmonious; hues that are opposite have the most contrast. Look, for example, at the 3 samples on page 302: the example on the right stands out because on the color wheel its green hue is separated from the overall blue hues of the other examples.

SATURATION

"Saturation" describes how much of a hue is present in a color. In the illustration above, the colors at the far left are unsaturated; they have no blue in them. As you move to the right in the bar above, the colors become more and more saturated: they have more and more blue in them.

BRIGHTNESS

"Brightness" (sometimes also referred to as "value") describes how light or dark a color is. In the bar above, the color at the extreme left has no brightness; the color at the extreme right is as bright as it can be.

Hue, saturation, and brightness are present in all colors. In the examples to the left, the leftmost color chip is red-hued, with as much saturation and brightness as possible. The color chip in the middle is not very bright, but is still a fairly saturated red hue. The color chip on the right has a hue of blue, is fairly bright, but is not very saturated.

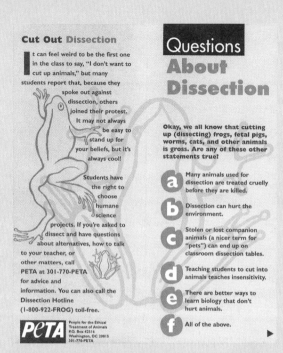

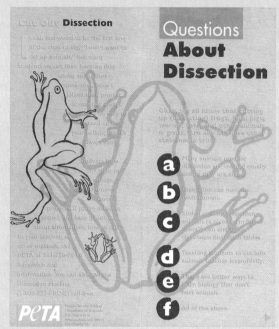

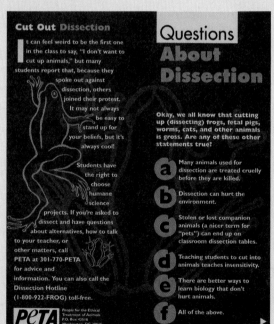

It would seem, then, that the brochure's composers want to address their audience in a nonthreatening and friendly way about the topic—and so the brochure's visual presentation shouldn't "shout" at the audience but should instead "invite" the audience to consider the topic.

The first example uses bright and saturated blue and green. The second uses bright and saturated red and blue. The third uses dark and light purple and a not-very-saturated green. Which use hues that you associate with nature and gentleness? Which use saturation (or lack of saturation) to make it seem as though the colors recede from you (to "pull you in"), and which use such saturated colors that appear almost to "shout" at you? Which use bright colors to keep the brochure light-looking, and which look dark and so more somber and serious? Which do you think uses color appropriately for the brochure's purpose?

Notice that were you just to discuss hue (the green or purple or red of these brochures) you couldn't account for how the colors work fully. You need to consider brightness and saturation together with hue.

ANALYZING THE RHETORICAL EFFECTS OF COLOR

These brochures (of which you can see just one side) are the same, but reproduced in different colors. The purpose of the brochure is to persuade people not to use dissection in biology classes. The composers of this brochure decided to use informal drawings of frogs instead of photographs or thin-lined technical illustrations; they used an informal typeface and kept the brochure fairly open looking. The layout itself is also informal, with large shapes and type that wraps around a frog; it is not rigidly geometric.

compose ▪ design ▪ advocate

■ **Observe, then write:** As you saw with the frog brochures, you can use hue, saturation, and brightness to analyze and produce communications. The "Eat at Bill's" examples below use differing amounts of contrast in hue, saturation, and brightness to create very different effects using all the same elements. Apply one or two adjectives to each of the examples—some adjectives you could use are *hard, soft, inviting, exciting, shouting, cheery, loud, energetic,* *quiet,* and so on. Make a chart like the one to the right, to connect the adjectives with the amount of contrast between the different qualities of color. Because you'll base your decisions on your own associations with color, the chart will be a starting point for deciding how to combine colors to achieve various overall visual effects with audiences who share your general background.

adjective	color qualities
hard	strongest possible contrast in hue and brightness, but similarly saturated

If you were to open your own coffeeshop, which color combination would you use? Why?

When you are analyzing or choosing colors for communication, keep in mind that we have associations with different colors because of our experiences within both the natural world and our cultural worlds—but these associations are not fixed. When we see light blue, for example, we might associate it with a warm summer sky or the glow of winter ice. Black is the color people in the United States associate with death; in some Asian countries, white is the color for mourning. How people understand or respond to colors thus depends on the contexts in which they see the colors.

ANALYZING
color in photography

■ **Write:** Use the discussion of *pathos* in photographs as well as what you've learned about color to write a short rhetorical analysis comparing the emotional effects of the two photographs on this page. First, describe how you respond to the photographs, then describe how you think what is shown in the photographs shapes your response (be sure to mention the kinds of associations you have with what is shown in the photographs); then describe how the colors contribute to your response.

Compare your analysis with others in class: Do you bring the same associations to what is in the photographs as well as to the colors? When you find someone with different responses, work together to figure out how you have come to your different understandings.

■ **Discuss with others:** Discuss our use of color in this textbook. We've tried to differentiate sections and functions of the book through our use of color—color as *logos*—and we've also used color to (we hope) give the book appeal and depth to your eyes and to give it a look that is up-to-date if not even a bit hip—color as *pathos*. How effective do you think our color choices have been for these purposes? What would you change, and why?

■ **Write:** Write a short rhetorical analysis in which you compare the purposes and audiences for the essay "Higher Education" (in chapter 14) and the opinion piece "Walking the Line" (in chapter 13)—and then use your comparison to argue why the photographs in the two pieces have been so differently colored. (You'll need to use the terms of this section to describe the differences in the colors.)

■ **Write:** Choose any poster in this chapter or in the chapter of poster examples, and write a short rhetorical analysis in which you explain how its overall colors (be sure to address hue, saturation, and brightness) support (or not) the purpose of the poster.

compose ▪ design ▪ advocate

seeing *pathos*:
the *pathos* of type

If you are producing visual compositions that use words, then you need to know about **typography.** Typography is the study of how lettershapes—on paper or on screen—work functionally and rhetorically.

In some kinds of visual compositions, such as the papers you write for school, type is not supposed to call any attention to itself: it is not to evoke any emotion or feeling other than that of a calm and even regard for ideas. Such type should rest easily and calmly on the page so that people heed your ideas and not the visible appearance of the letters. And if type can rest this way on the page—so that it almost disappears as you read—this is the result of convention and our bodies. When you are told to turn in double-spaced pages in Times 12 point size, for example, it is because this is a typeface and a size of type that—when double spaced—many people have become accustomed to reading in school papers.

In different visual compositions—brochures, posters, webpages—we have learned to expect that type will evoke more obvious emotion and feeling. We expect to see typefaces that look boisterous, edgy, or loud because they work with the other elements of the composition to create an overall effect in support of some purpose.

If you look at books printed in earlier centuries, you'll see pages that look very different. In old hand-calligraphed manuscripts, pages have large ornate letters. These manuscripts were usually meant to be read aloud, slowly. The purpose of the type wasn't to ease the speed of an individual reading alone and quietly, which is the purpose of much functional typography today.

In order to make effective rhetorical choices with type, you need therefore to know something about the details of type and about its conventional (and not so conventional) uses—which is the purpose of this section as well as the section on thinking about type as a strategy for *logos.*

HOW DOES TYPE EVOKE FEELING AND EMOTIONS?

The curves and straight lines of letters can be arranged to suggest bodies or abstract shapes. Type can be:

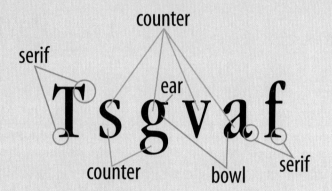

abpxyloABCD

ascenders

descenders

ascender height	
x-height	cap height
descender depth	

counter

serif

ear

Tsgvaf

counter

bowl

serif

Minion

Minion Italic

Minion Semibold

Minion Semibold Italic

Minion Bold

Minion Bold Italic

DESCRIBING LETTERSHAPES

Knowing the names of parts of letters and of the qualities of different typefaces can help you differentiate between typefaces—which can help you then make thoughtful and rhetorical choices.

One really important distinction to be alert to with typefaces is that between **serifed and sans serifed typefaces**. Serifed typefaces have little lines at the ends of the letter strokes; sans serifed have none ("sans" means "without" in French). In the United States, serifed typefaces are considered more formal and easier to read than sans serif typefaces.

STYLES OF TYPE

Typefaces often come in sets, with lettershapes that have the same basic structure but different vertical orientations and visual weights. When you want to compose a page or screen on which the elements look harmonious because they look similar, use the different styles of one typeface.

compose ▪ design ▪ advocate

TYPEFACES

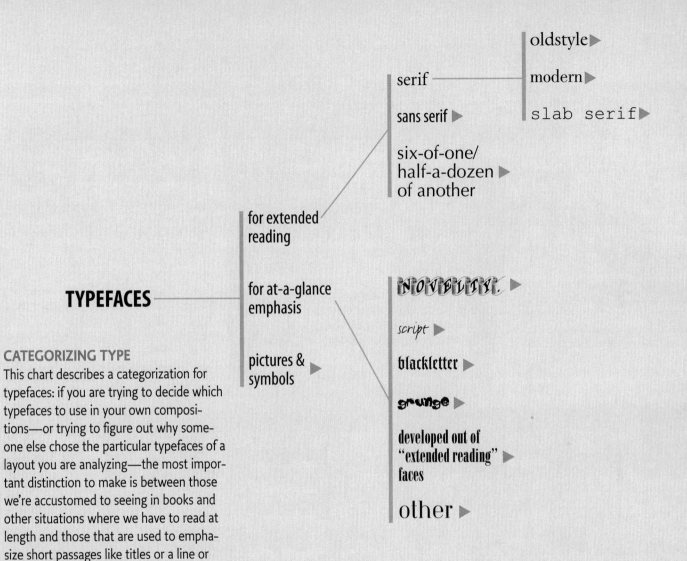

serif ——— oldstyle ▶

modern ▶

slab serif ▶

sans serif ▶

six-of-one/
half-a-dozen ▶
of another

for extended
reading

for at-a-glance
emphasis

NOVELTY ▶

script ▶

blackletter ▶

grunge ▶

pictures &
symbols ▶

developed out of
"extended reading" ▶
faces

other ▶

CATEGORIZING TYPE

This chart describes a categorization for typefaces: if you are trying to decide which typefaces to use in your own composi-tions—or trying to figure out why some-one else chose the particular typefaces of a layout you are analyzing—the most impor-tant distinction to make is between those we're accustomed to seeing in books and other situations where we have to read at length and those that are used to empha-size short passages like titles or a line or two. When you are starting to produce vi-sual communication, divide typefaces into one of these two categories first. (Picture typefaces—as you will see on the next page—are unreadable as lettershapes.)

▶ the arrow means: *look on the next pages to learn more about this category*

TYPEFACES FOR EXTENDED READING

OLDSTYLE

abcdeABCDE   Galliard

abcdeABCDE   Garamond

abcdeABCDE   Janson

abcdeABCDE   Jenson

This category of typeface goes back to the six-teenth century when people were designing type-faces for the relatively-new printing press and were paying attention to creating regularity among the appearances of letters. Oldstyle typefaces always have serifs, and very often wide and rounded let-tershapes. Notice how the serifs at the tops of the letters are usually slanted, and that the strokes are not all the same weight but have some transition from thick to thin. These typefaces look formal.

SANS SERIF

abcdABCD   Avant Garde

abcdeABCDE   Bailey Sans

abcdeABCDE   Helvetica

abcdeABCDE   Officina Sans

Sans serif typefaces were first developed in the late nineteenth century, when type designers wanted typefaces that looked modern and up-to-date, to echo—in how the typefaces looked—the stream-lined mechanical wonders that were filling western factories and streets. Note how the lines in most of these typefaces are all the same weight, and that there is no ornamentation to the letters. These are straightforward-looking typefaces.

MODERN

abcdeABCDE   Bodoni

abcdeABCDE   Fenice

abcdeABCDE   Onyx

"Modern" typefaces were modern in the seven-teenth century, when mechanization picked up its pace and printing technologies supported people's desires for more precision and clarity. New printing technologies allowed type designers to make type-faces with very thin lines. Modern typefaces always have serifs—but their serifs don't slant. Modern typefaces mix very thick and very thin strokes. The contrast between thick and thin can give them a certain elegant feeling.

SIX-OF-ONE

abcdeABCDE   Optima

abcdeABCDE   Poppl-Laudatio

abcdeABCDE   Zapf Humanist

In the "for-extended-reading" category, you will oc-casionally find a typeface that has some features of serifed and sans serifed faces, like the ones above, with mixed weights in their strokes. These faces tend to have an informal feeling about them.

SLAB SERIF

abcdeABCDE   Courier

abcdeABCDE   Lubalin Graph

abcdeABCDE   Officina Serif

In the early nineteenth century, Napoleon invaded Egypt. His army included historians and artists who brought back samples of Egyptian art and writing to France. This started a craze in Europe for all things Egyptian—including typefaces that looked like they came from the Nile area. These typefaces were originally called "Egyptienne." Notice how the serifs are straight slabs with no curves softening how the serif joins the body of the letter. These typefaces often look informal.

PICTURE & SYMBOLS

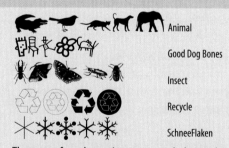

Animal

Good Dog Bones

Insect

Recycle

SchneeFlaken

These typefaces have pictures or symbols attached to the different letter rather than lettershapes. The characters of these typefaces can be used as bullets or paragraph markers or... Be creative with these.

compose ▪ design ▪ advocate

TYPEFACES FOR AT-A-GLANCE EMPHASIS

NOVELTY

ABCDEABCDE	Almonte Snow
ABCDEABCDE	Baby Jeepers
abcdeABCDE	Bailey's Car
(A)(B)(C)(D)(E)	Dialtone
ABCDEABCDE	Elwood
abcdeabcde	Jingopop
ABCDE	Shrapnel

Novelty typefaces are usually kind of cute and lively; you might associate them with circus posters or old-fashioned advertising.

SCRIPT

abcde ABCDE	Avalon
abcdeABCDE	Caflisch
abcde ABCDE	Cezanne
abcdeABCDE	Handwriting
abcdeABCDE	Kidprint
abcdeABCDE	Visigoth

Script faces look as though they were hand-drawn with a pen. Sometimes they look as though they were drawn by someone with a long-practiced hand, and sometimes as though they were drawn by a three-year-old. They can therefore give a feeling of relaxed elegance to a page—or playfulness.

OUT OF EXTENDED READING FACES

abcdeABCDE	Bell Gothic
abcdeABCDE	Bodoni Poster Compressed
abcdeABCDE	Futura Extra Bold
abcdeABCDE	Garamond Bold

Sometimes someone modifies a typeface intended for blocks of extended reading to make the typeface bolder for using as a headline or title or other function. If you use one of these typefaces with the typeface from which it was developed, the look will generally be harmonious because the lettershapes echo each other.

BLACKLETTER

abcdeABCDE	Ancient Bastard Secretary Hand
abcdeABCDE	Ancient Formal Text Hand
abcdeABCDE	Notre Dame

Blackletter typefaces are the ones you now see used in goth settings, but these typefaces go back to the middle ages, to when monks and other scribes used quill pens to write. They can look very formal and elegant on a page, or sometimes dark and oppressive.

GRUNGE

abcde ABCDE	BBQ Cow Moo
AbCDEABCDE	Devotion
abcde ABCDE	Dyslexia
abcdeabcde	Fragile
abcdeABCDE	Industrial Schizophrenic
ABCDEABCDE	Osprey

Grunge faces started appearing alongside grunge music (as you might expect from their name): the typeface and the music share the same quick, hard-edged garage aesthetic.

OTHER

abcde	Bayer Type
ABCDE	Bermuda Squiggle
abcdeABCDE	Journal Text
abcdeABCDE	Katfish

Because typefaces in the "at-a-glance emphasis" category are used in so many different kinds of documents, designers develop new typefaces all the time—and sometimes they don't fit into the other divisions of this category. These typefaces tend to be playful and energetic.

■ **Discuss with others:** Throughout this book we have used primarily one typeface—*Productus*—in its book, semibold, bold, and italic forms. *Productus* is not quite a sans serif typeface (notice how the ends of letters get just a little wider), and its letter are fairly curvy. We chose this typeface because it looked both friendly and hip to us, and because its range of styles have allowed us easily to differentiate between body type and titles. We also decided to use just one typeface (instead of, say, a serifed typeface for the body of the text and a sans serifed face for titles) so that there would be a simple unity across the pages, given how many photographs, illustrations, and other examples we have. Do you think we have achieved what we intended? What would you change?

■ **Practice:** If you have access to a range of typefaces on the computer, you can better learn the possibilities of typefaces (and better learn the typefaces you have) by typing the following list of adjectives into a word processing document; then apply to each word the typeface—and size—that you think best represents the adjective. Type the list again, but now try to give each word a typeface that makes you think the **opposite** of the adjective.

The adjectives:
happy
creepy
ditsy
sad
loud
rich
boring
elegant
angry
gloomy
hard
joyful
edgy

seeing *logos* in the arrangement of elements

"Shaping someone else's attention" is one definition of rhetoric—and this is a highly useful way to think about one aspect of *logos* of visual composition. As the long quotation about the basketball video with the woman in the gorilla suit (on page 265) shows, seeing is about where our attentions are focused: if we are asked to put our visual attentions on one thing, we often miss other things going on.

❑ If you are interested in how these considerations about arrangement apply specifically to websites, see the online chapter 9 resources at www.ablongman.com/wysocki

And so:

When you are making any kind of visual layout, you are working to draw your audience's eyes—and hence their attention and thinking—through your presentation in a certain order, so that they are persuaded by your ordering to take the action or think about the matters or have the experience you're hoping they will. **When you compose visual layouts, you are building an ordered set of elements (alphabetic symbols, photographs, drawings, shapes, and so on) that your audience follows visually—and hence conceptually—to arrive at the points you want to make.**

This all means, then, that your visual compositions must be ordered:

one, your visual compositions generally ought to have a limited number of elements so that your audience is not overwhelmed by detail and can see the point of your composition (think here about how audiences can miss even gorillas when there is a lot going on) . . .

So, first, you need to **consider how much to include**.

two, your visual compositions ought to have a visual hierarchy—a visual path— that indicates to your audience what to look at first, what to look at second, what third, and so on . . .

Second, you need to know how to **create a visual hierarchy through using contrast and sameness.**

three, your visual compositions must look like a set of unified pieces so that your audience understands that the pieces are meant to work together to make one main argument.

Third, you need to **create visual unity through using repetition and alignment.**

 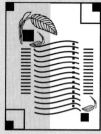

Which of these two layouts is easier on your eyes? Which, that is, feels to your eyes as though all the elements come together into one, simple, unified layout?

We're hoping you agree that the layout on the left—with a limited number of elements and a consequent visual simplicity—requires less effort from eyes and mind: when we look at it, we feel as though our eyes can take it in all at once.

With the layout on the right, however, our eyes feel pulled all over, not quite sure where to stop and focus. It is consequently hard to understand the relationships between the elements of the layout.

Layouts like that on the left are easier for audiences to comprehend because they do not ask much visual effort from an audience. That is why they seem straightforward: an audience can look and easily see what element you want them see first, which second, and which third; there's no need for them to figure out which element you intend to be fourth in their attentions, which fifth, which sixth, which seventh. . . .

Imagine you've brought home a pet rat—and you have a choice of printed instructions to read about caring for the rat. Which of the two rat examples above look like instructions you could read easily and quickly? Which looks like you could find what you needed without much trouble?

The first sample has three elements—a rat, a series of lines (which you might interpret as a block of text), and cheese; the other example has those same elements, plus 8 or 10 or 12 more. . . . The second example might look as though it has more information—but could you find out on it quickly what to do when your rat starts nibbling its way through your books?

As you produce visual compositions, notice that many layouts use a limited number of elements to achieve their purposes. Flip through the examples in this chapter; look at the poster examples in chapter 10; look in magazines. . . .

When you start to produce visual compositions, **limit yourself to three to four elements on a page or screen** (one picture, perhaps, and a title and one block of text) to help you learn how to control the relationships among the elements so you can achieve your purposes straightforwardly; this also shows your audience *your purpose is straightforward*.

- You can have more than three to four elements, but then use the strategies of repetition and proximity (which we discuss in the next pages) to make different elements look closely related. This reduces the apparent number of elements.

- Simple layouts are conventional, in the sense that we see lots in magazines and on television. This means we—like most audiences we will address—are accustomed to not having to do much work in figuring out visual compositions.

creating a visual hierarchy . . .

There are six sets of visual compositions below. For each set, circle the composition that looks to you to have a clear visual path for your eye to follow. That is, in which of the two compositions do you have no question which element you are to look at first, which second, and so on?

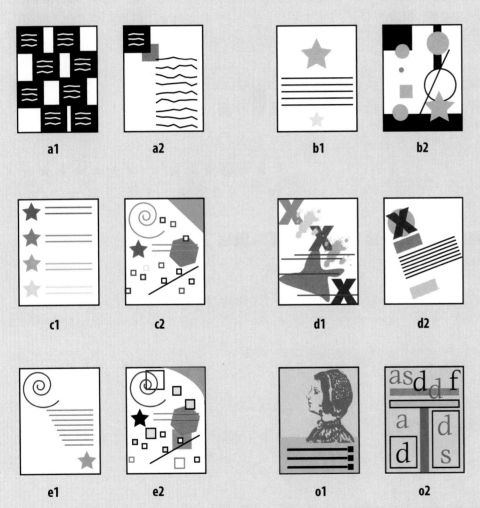

a1   a2   b1   b2

c1   c2   d1   d2

e1   e2   o1   o2

We're guessing you circled a2, b1, c1, d2, e1, and o1. In each of those designs, you should be able to tell which element you are intended to notice first, which second, and so on. In those layouts, in other words, **there is a clear visual hierarchy:** you can see immediately which elements are given most visual weight and which least.

Contrast—a design principle we'll discuss in the next pages—helps one element stand out against a background of repetition, while the repetition helps the elements look like they belong together.

■ *Notice that the element that first draws your attention is usually largest and darkest.* When you are getting started building visual hierarchies, it is easiest to begin by making your contrasts very obvious.

■ *Notice how the elements you are to see first are often in the top left or the top middle.* Because we have learned to read from top to bottom and left to right, the top left of a page is where we are accustomed to start looking or reading. Use that to your advantage when you want to create a clear and unambiguous visual starting point on a page.

■ *Notice how the number of elements helps you see a path:* as we recommended on the preceding pages, limiting yourself to three to four elements when you start to produce visual compositions can help you create compositions that are easy for your audiences to comprehend.

creating a visual hierarchy by using contrast and sameness

Look back over all the example compositions on the previous pages. Notice that, in general, one element (at top left or center) attracts your attention first: this is where your eyes know to start looking at the layout. Creating one element that stands out by contrast is easiest to do if you can think about contrast analytically, if—when you are producing visual compositions—you can describe in words to yourself how you create contrast. The illustrations below ought to help with this: circle the one in each set that has one element that stands out.

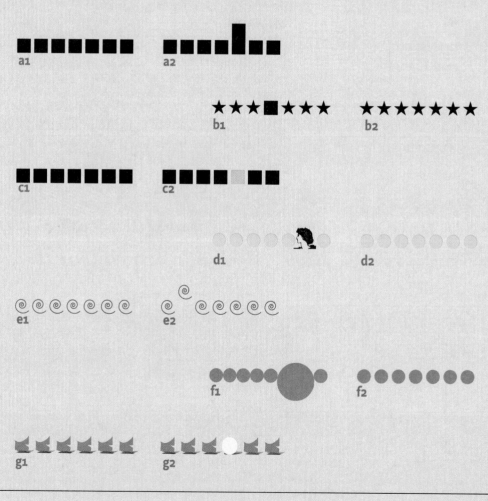

compose ▪ design ▪ advocate

We're guessing you circled a2, b1, c2, d1, e2, f1, and g2. In each of those sets, one element is different from all the others in its set.

That is, in each one of those sets, there is one element that contrasts with all the other elements in the set.

The element contrasted because it had a different size, shape, color, position, or level of abstraction than all the other elements in the set. ("Level of abstraction" refers to what is going on in the "d" set: notice how the abstract shapes create a background against which the more "realistic" face can stand out.)

Contrast helps draw our attention to parts of visual compositions (although contrast isn't a principle for visual composition alone: think of how musical composers play with contrasts of tone or rhythm to create aural interest, and how people composing written works will vary the voice or rhythm or word sound of what they write).

Contrast emphasizes certain parts of a composition, telling us to look there first or to pay particular attention to what has been made to stand out. (Look at how your eyes are drawn to the green letters on this page, which are in a different typeface, size, and color from most of the type.)

When you are composing, and wish to draw your audience's attention to a certain part of your composition, there is a very odd aspect of composition to which you must pay attention:

you can only create contrast when you also create sameness.

Notice how, in the sets of elements on the previous page, one element stands out precisely because all the other elements look alike and are placed similarly.

Elements can only stand out when the things around them blend together, appearing all the same.

This means that when you want to create contrast, you have to be very attentive to creating a background of sameness against which an element can stand out. This means also that you can't make too many things different—or none of them will stand out.

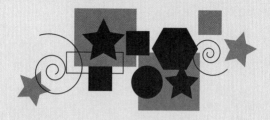

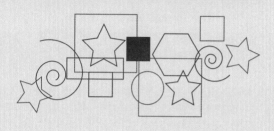

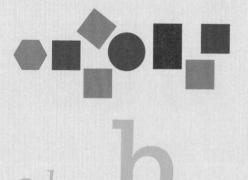

Compare the illustrations on the left with those on the right. The illustrations on the left ought to suggest to you that you cannot create contrast when you try to make everything contrast with everything else.

Note how the change from the illustration on the left to the illustration on the right, while simple, requires you to make one element **VERY** different from the others.

Write down all the strategies you can see at work in the compositions on these three pages for creating contrast with a series of elements—and keep your eyes open for other strategies as you look at visual compositions around you.

Be sure that, as you work on your own compositions, you think consciously about the play of contrast and sameness you are creating.

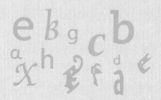

compose ▪ design ▪ advocate

creating visual unity using repetition

We live in a time when unity and coherence are valued: newspapers put similar articles together in sections (world news, entertainment, sports), people like to dress in coordinated outfits, car colors do not vary much, and we expect politicians to appear to base their decisions on a coherent set of values. Just as in those situations, unity and coherence extend to visual compositions. Unity in a visual composition isn't magic: you can design it into your layouts by attending to certain concrete visual principles.

Circle the thumbnail layouts below that look to you as though all the elements are unified and built into a coherent visual composition.

a1

a2

b1

b2

c1

c2

d1

d2

e1

e2

x1

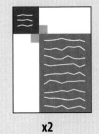
x2

We're guessing that you circled a1, b2, c2, d2, e1, and x2. In each of those layouts, the elements are visually linked with each other.

That is, in each of those thumbnail layouts, each element **repeats** something from the other elements.

Elements can repeat the **size, shape, color, position, alignment, or level of abstraction of other elements**. Notice that these are almost all the same qualities that can be used to create contrast.*

Repetition of the qualities of elements creates visual relationship between the elements. It's like when you meet the sister of a friend and you can tell they are related because their faces look alike. It's also like what you do when you put together an outfit: if you are wearing a shirt with red stripes in it, you might choose to wear red socks or carry a red handbag (depending on your taste in accessories). (Think about how repetition functions in writing or speech-making, too: you show people you are staying on topic by using the same words and phrases and the same tone of voice throughout—except when you then use contrast to emphasize what you want people to remember. You also create a sense of rhythm in writing when you repeat sounds or words of similar length.)

Repetition makes the elements of a layout look like they belong together. Repetition therefore helps layouts look unified—and unified looking layouts do seem to appeal to people's tastes these days.

So repetition serves two purposes in layouts: repetition creates the level of sameness against which some elements can stand out . . .

and it also helps create the sense of unity that helps tie the elements together visually.

*There are many more strategies for creating repetition than are mentioned here. Before you move on in reading these pages, go find a magazine, flip through it, and see if—through observation—you can list at least 10 more strategies for creating repetition.

compose ▪ design ▪ advocate

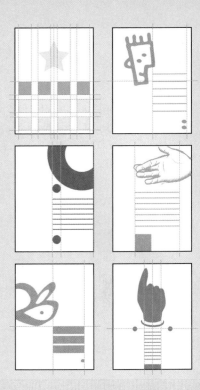

REPEATING ALIGNMENT

Of all the elements you can repeat, alignment often gets overlooked—but alignment is a strategy for creating a unified page. Each of the compositions above left follows the guidelines we've described: each has only a few elements and strong contrast in size and shape against a background of sameness created by repetition of color. Notice, though, how the composition on the right of each pair looks more orderly than the left composition: on the right, each element is aligned with at least one (if not more) other element.

To the right we have added some of the lines to which the elements in these compositions align. Notice how **every element** aligns with at least one other element. Alignment is thus a strategy of *logos*, for creating compositions whose elements have an obvious visual relationship because they all line up with each other.

Here are two kinds of alignment:

■ **"Backbone alignment."** The composition with the star and the one with the pointing blue hand have central alignment. It's as though all the elements hang off a line, like a backbone, in the center of the page. When you choose one line on a page as the backbone, and hang everything off it, you compose layouts with a high degree of unity.

■ **Alignment with the edges of the page.** Notice that the elements in the aligned compositions align not only with each other but also with the edges of the page: everything is positioned vertically or horizontally, and so all the elements of these thumbnail compositions—including the pages they are on—are aligned. You may think, "Well, duh . . . I've been doing this all my life because this is what comes out of the printer," but if you consider this kind of alignment as a choice that you can change then you can use it alertly and purposefully in your visual compositions.

■ **Write:** Here are pages from three books and one website. The first page is from the article "The Plaintiff Speaks," by Clarissa Sligh, which is in chapter 14. The book spread is from *Hiding*, by Mark C. Taylor. The website is 360°, whose overall purpose is to teach about the U.S. prison system. The illuminated page is from a nineteenth-century Qur'an.

Analyze each page as a visual composition. In writing, describe the visual path your eyes follow with each composition, and then describe how the elements of the composition are arranged to create that path. Consider how many elements there are, how contrast and sameness are used to create a starting point for your eyes (or not), and how repetition and alignment work to create visual unity. (What is repeated? What is aligned?)

What visual values do you see at work in the different pages? Is efficiency at work, or standardization, linearity, variety . . . ? The pages are too small for you to tell their specific purposes, but what general purposes do you see in these layouts? If you read only pages that looked like one of these, what general values do you think you'd acquire?

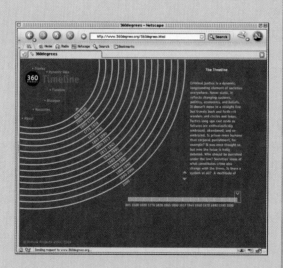

compose ▪ design ▪ advocate

The same strategies for making shapes stand out in a composition apply to typefaces: **there needs to be a background of sameness against which an element (or a few elements) can stand out.**

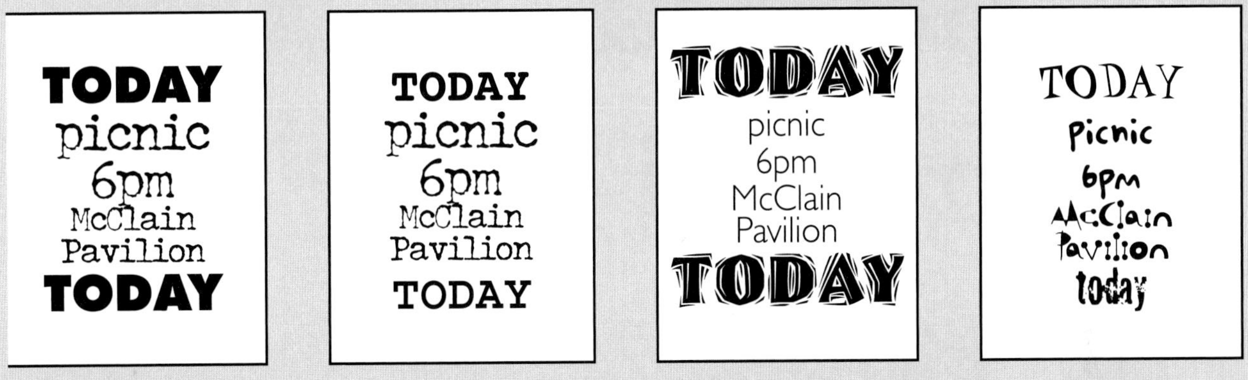

For example, imagine that the above thumbnail sketches of flyers were posted together on a wall: which are most likely to catch your eye? Which help you most clearly see—and differentiate—the information being presented?

Notice how clear differences in size and shape of the letterforms help you more easily see (or not) differences in what the words are conveying. Notice also how differences in color (here, whether a typeface looks black or gray) also help you see and differentiate among the elements of the layouts, so that you can more clearly tell what the flyer is about.

As we've just described, many of the same strategies for creating contrast with shapes apply to typefaces—and we'll write about these on the next pages, as well as about a few additional features of typefaces you can use to help you build contrast (and so clear visual hierarchy) when you are working with type:

CATEGORY

SIZE

SHAPE

POSITION

COLOR

WEIGHT

When you are starting to produce visual compositions and trying to choose and use different typefaces together, you want to choose typefaces that have a lot of strong contrast—and then you want to arrange the typefaces so that the contrast is clear to your audience.

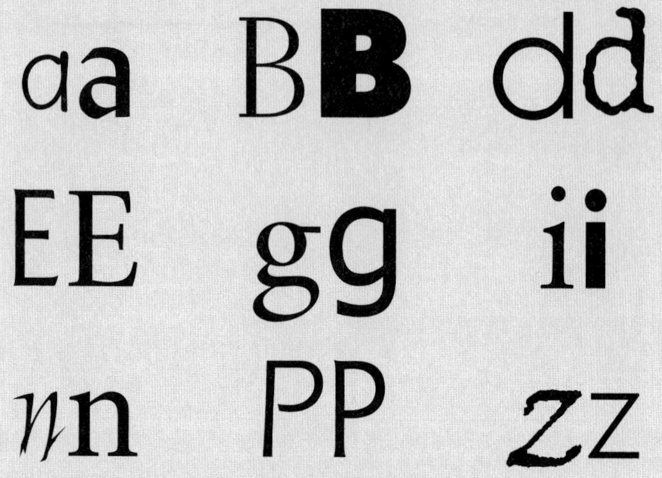

aa BB dd

EE gg ii

nn PP zz

Cc ff

jJ mM

Q rr

how the different CATEGORIES of type can help you choose typefaces with strong contrast

Earlier in this chapter you learned that typefaces can be divided into two large categories: typefaces for extended reading and typefaces for short blocks of text. You learned further breakdowns of those categories, into serif and sans serif and then novelty, grunge, and so on. When you are choosing typefaces for strong contrast, **a handy—but not foolproof—rule of thumb is to choose typefaces from different categories**. That is, you can generally count on a serif and a sans serif contrasting well (*but rarely will the different kinds of serifed typefaces contrast enough for you to be able to use them without some additional work*).

Look at the pairs of typefaces shown above, and circle the ones you think have the most contrast— and then identify the categories of those pairs to see what works for you.

using the SIZE of typeface to create strong contrast among typefaces

Size is probably the most obvious differentiation you can make between different pieces of type. Look at the examples above: in each of the sets of letters, which gives you the clearest contrast?

As with any use of difference in type size, be sure that when you are sizing typefaces you make the contrast clear and bold; it is generally better, as you are starting out, to err on the side of more rather than less contrast. In the beginning, go for bold, rather than subtle: it's easier to learn subtlety after you have the broad moves down.

gg gg gg gG gg

"I have never let my schooling interfere with my education."
—Mark Twain

"I have never let my schooling interfere with my education."
—Mark Twain

"I have never let my schooling interfere with my education."
—Mark Twain

"I have never let my schooling interfere with my education."
—MARK TWAIN

"I have never let my schooling interfere with my education."
—Mark Twain

using the SHAPES of typefaces to create contrast

When you are trying to build strong contrasts between two or more typefaces, look closely at how the shapes of individual letters contrast. This will help you choose typefaces that, on the whole, contrast strongly.

For example, look at the differences in the gs at the top of this page: try to describe (using the names for parts of typefaces on page 281) the differences between the letters in each of the different pairs.

Then look at the phrases from Mark Twain, each of which uses the two letterfaces used in one of the sets at the top: do these seem like strong contrast to you? Can you account for at least some of the contrast by the differences in the shapes of the different letters?

The eight example boxes each contain the quote:

"If men and women are in chains, anywhere in the world, then freedom is endangered everywhere."

— John Fitzgerald Kennedy

arranged in different positions and orientations.

This typeface is Caecilia Light.
This typeface is Caecilia.
This typeface is Caecilia Bold.
This typeface is Caecilia Heavy.

POSITION

Position is about how one piece of type is placed relative to another. In the examples above, notice how position can also involve the direction a piece of type takes. Which of the examples above develop the clearest contrast to your eyes—and why?

Notice how you have to make quite distinct changes in direction for this strategy to be visible.

WEIGHT

If you've chosen typefaces on a computer, you may have noticed that you can sometimes choose Roman (meaning generally that the typeface is a serifed face) or light, bold, or ultra versions of one typeface. Notice, however, that in the example above right there is little contrast between the Light and Roman versions or between the Bold and Heavy versions. If you were to use these typefaces, you would probably want to use the Light and the Bold versions together, or the regular face with the Heavy version.

When you are using different weights of typefaces, be sure the weights are readily visible.

COLOR

Color can mean red, green, blue, puce, lavender, or flesh—but it can also mean the range of grays from white to black.

You can apply different colors to individual letters of words to build contrast, but it is very important—when you are choosing typefaces to use together—to look at the "color" of the whole typeface. Designers do this by comparing paragraphs printed out in different typefaces to see how light (or dark) one typeface looks relative to another; the greater the differences in color between the typefaces as a whole, the more likely the typefaces will contrast well.

compose ▪ design ▪ advocate

Yet I cannot speak your tongue with ease,
No longer from China. Your stories
Stir griefs of dispersion and find
Me in simplicity of kin.
—Shirley Geok-lin Lim

Yet I cannot speak your tongue with ease,
No longer from China. Your stories
Stir griefs of dispersion and find
Me in simplicity of kin.
—Shirley Geok-lin Lim

Yet I cannot speak your tongue with ease,
No longer from China. Your stories
Stir griefs of dispersion and find
Me in simplicity of kin.
—Shirley Geok-lin Lim

Yet I cannot speak your tongue with ease,
No longer from China. Your stories
Stir griefs of dispersion and find
Me in simplicity of kin.
—Shirley Geok-lin Lim

Yet I cannot speak your tongue with ease,
No longer from China. Your stories
Stir griefs of dispersion and find
Me in simplicity of kin.
—Shirley Geok-lin Lim

Yet I cannot speak your tongue with ease,
No longer from China. Your stories
Stir griefs of dispersion and find
Me in simplicity of kin.
—Shirley Geok-lin Lim

Yet I cannot speak your tongue with ease,
No longer from China. Your stories
Stir griefs of dispersion and find
Me in simplicity of kin.
—Shirley Geok-lin Lim

Yet I cannot speak your tongue with ease,
No longer from China. Your stories
Stir griefs of dispersion and find
Me in simplicity of kin.
—Shirley Geok-lin Lim

Yet I cannot speak your tongue with ease,
No longer from China. Your stories
Stir griefs of dispersion and find
Me in simplicity of kin.
—Shirley Geok-lin Lim

Yet I cannot speak your tongue with ease,
No longer from China. Your stories
Stir griefs of dispersion and find
Me in simplicity of kin.
—Shirley Geok-lin Lim

Yet I cannot speak your tongue with ease,
No longer from China. Your stories
Stir griefs of dispersion and find
Me in simplicity of kin.
—Shirley Geok-lin Lim

Notice how different the phrases above look—even though the type is all set in the same size. You can use the color of type not only to choose typefaces that contrast because their color is so different but also to add a light or heavy mood to a visual composition that uses type.

An important note about building contrast with typeface

You might have noticed that when you are building contrast with shapes on a page or screen, you can take two approaches:

First, you can change only one thing about the shapes. For example, if you have a whole set of circles, you can make one of them big—but for this to work, you have to make that shape tremendously bigger for the contrast to be truly visible.

Second, you can change many things about one of the shapes: you can make its shape different (a shape instead of a circle) as well as its size and color and position.

The same holds for working with type:

1 You can build contrast by changing only one aspect of the type with which you are working, such as the color—but you have to make big changes for this to be visible.

2 You can build contrast by being sure the typefaces you choose take advantage of three or more of the ways to build type contrast that we've discussed in this section. If you do this, you are more likely to build effectively contrasting type.

rhetorical type arrangement

■ **Write:** Write a short rhetorical analysis of the visual composition (an informational poster) to the right, using the choices and arrangements of typeface to support your arguments about what the purpose is and who the audience is.

These tips from Women In Media & News (WIMN), a New York-based media-monitoring, training, and advocacy group, can help you make the leap from righteous indignation to effective critique.

how to write a
PROTEST LETTER
by Jennifer L. Pozner

You flip to your local Clear Channel station to find a shock jock "joking" about where kidnappers can most easily buy nylon rope, tarps, and lye for tying up, hiding, and dissolving the bodies of little girls. Reuters run an important international news brief about a Nigerian woman sentenced to death by stoning for an alleged sexual infraction—in its "Oddly Enough" section, where typical headlines include "Unruly Taxi Drivers Sent to Charm School."

When California Democrats Loretta and Linda Sanchez became the first sisters ever to serve together in Congress, the Washington Post devotes 1,766 words in its style section to inform readers about the representatives' preferences regarding housekeeping, hairstyles, and "hootchy shoes." (Number of paragraphs focusing on the congress women's political viewpoints: one.) Nearly a million demonstrators gather in cities across the country to protest impending war on Iraq; America's top print and broadcast news outlets significantly undercount protestors' numbers...again.

So, what else is new? Sexist and biased fare is business as usual for all too many media outlets - but what do you do when hurling household objects at Dan Rather's head just isn't enough?

Be firm but polite Make your case sans insults, rants, and vulgarity. Nothing makes it easier for editors and producers to dismiss your argument than name-calling. Good idea: "Your discussion of the rape survivor's clothing and makeup was irrelevant, irresponsible, and inappropriate. Including those details blames the victim and reinforces dangerous myths about sexual assault." Bad idea: "Your reporter is a woman-hating incarnate of satan!"

Be realistic but optimistic Calling for the New York Times to transform itself into a socialist newspaper will get you nowhere; suggesting that quotes from industry executives be balanced by input from labor and public-interest groups is more likely to be taken seriously.

Choose your battles While we'd all like to see fewer female bods used to sell beer, asking the networks to reject such ads is a waste of time. (A letter-writing campaign to the companies that produce those ads is another matter.) However, its worth the effort to pressure telecom and cable giant Comcast to air the antiwar ads it censored during Bush's State of the Union speech.

Correct the record For example, remind media outlets discussing "partial birth abortion" that this imprecise and inflammatory term doesn't refer to an actual medical procedure but is, rather, a political concept fabricated by conservative groups to decrease public support for abortion rights. Focusing on facts is more persuasive than simply expressing outrage. "Christina Hoff Sommers's quote contained the following inaccuracies..." is better than "Anti-feminists like Christina Hoff Sommers should not be quoted in your newspaper."

Expose biased or distorted framing Look at whose viewpoint is shaping the story. In light of the Bush Administration's assault on affirmative action, for example, Peter Jennings asked on World News Tonight: "President Bush and race: Does he have a strategy to win black support?" Let ABC producers know that you'd rather they investigate the economic, academic, and political implications of the president's agenda for African-Americans than the effects of race policy on Bush's approval rating.

Keep it concise and informative If your goal is publication on the letters page, a couple well-documented paragraphs will always be better received than an emotional three-page manifesto. Sticking to one or two main points will get a busy editor to read through to the end.

Avoid overgeneralization Don't complain that your local paper "never" reports on women's issues or "always" ignores poor people. Even if stories on topics like welfare are infrequent or inaccurate, their very existence will serve as proof to editors that your complaint doesn't apply to their publication.

Address the appropriate person Letters about reportorial objectivity sent to editorial columnists or opinion-page editors will be tossed in the circular file.

Proofread! Nothing peeves an editor faster than typos or bad grammar.

Finally, give 'em credit Positive reinforcement can be as effective as protest. Be constructive whenever possible, and commend outlets when they produce in-depth, bias-free coverage.

Jennifer L. Pozner is WIMN's founder and executive director.

the *logos* of using words and pictures together

In Section 3, in the chapters on posters and documentary photography, we discuss how much people "see" in realistic representations. Anytime, that is, you see a photograph or an illustration* that mimics what you see with your eyes when you just look at the world, you observe it through all the bodily and cultural knowledge you have of the world. When you see a photograph of a person, for example, your mind doesn't just say to you, "Oh yeah, a person," and move on; instead, you are aware of the person's age, ethnicity, and gender, and whether you know someone who looks like that—and your attitude toward the photograph will then be shaped by your general attitude toward a person of that age, ethnicity, gender, and so on. If that photograph is on a page with words, you will then read those words through the attitude you have toward the person in the photograph.

When you are designing communications where you will put words and photographs or illustrations together, think therefore about:

* **"illustration": a nonphotographic representation, such as a drawing or painting**

How our attentions are almost always first directed to photographs or illustrations—and only then to words. In what ways is your audience likely to see a photograph or illustration—and how will that shape how they see all other elements on a page or screen?

The two pictures above are simple—a photograph of a single person with the same single short word—but notice how different their effects are because of the difference in the photographs:

- The woman's posture directs your eyes to the word (this is a "vector of atten-

tion," as we describe in chapter 10), and so encourages a viewer to think there is a relation between the person and the word.

- You probably associate the typeface and color of "oh!"—and perhaps even the word "oh!"—with femininity and youth. So in addition to how the visual arrangement of the photograph and the word help visually unify the composition on the left, these associations help conceptually unify the composition.

How do you make sense of the composition that includes the man?

smell friends

the
pleasures
of
ice
fishing

clothing

When you use words and photographs or illustrations together, there are three ways they can interact:

1

The photograph or illustration "explains" the words. The words, that is, wouldn't make much sense without the photograph or illustration.

For example, does "smell friends" make sense to you as anything other than a very odd command—until you see the words paired with an illustration of dogs? Then, based on your knowledge of how dogs interact, the words probably make perfect sense.

2

Words "explain" the photograph or illustration.

Would you have any idea in the second example of what that triangle on the ice is—an ice fishing tent—if you didn't see the words? Notice also how the words direct your attentions away from the light and clouds to think mostly about the tent.

3

The words and photograph or illustration work together to have a larger effect than either alone has. In the third example, there is not quite as direct a connection between the word and the photograph as in the first two. Instead, you the viewer have to figure out if the word asks you to think of the leaves as clothing for some animal, or asks you to rethink your notion of clothing (as covering) based on the leaves, or both. There is more room for viewer interaction when the connection between word and photograph is not so obvious.

compose ▪ design ▪ advocate

The French theoretician Roland Barthes called 1 and 2 "anchors": the words and pictures tie each other down in the same way an anchor keeps a boat in one place. "Relay" is how Barthes named what is going on with 3, where, as in a relay race, the function of the pairing is to move us along rather than tie us down.

Because our responses to photographs and illustrations depend on our bodily and cultural experiences of the world, there are no hard and fast rules for using words and pictures together. Instead, attend to their rhetorical functioning: how do particular audiences, in particular contexts, respond to particular combinations of words and photographs and illustrations? This is why it is important to test communications you build, so that you can observe and understand how and why people have the responses they do.

For example, Anne once did the caption exercise (the exercise with the woman and phone, on the next page) with a class. After she handed out the photographs, one person said, "Oh, this is easy: people's ideas about women in heels are so limited that the captions will all be about sex." Afterward, when everyone compared their captions (there were many more than we show here), this person acknowledged how wrong she had been. People in class were certainly aware that the photograph shows a woman of a particular age in black heels, but they also were attentive to the phone, her clothing, and her posture.

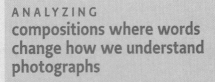

ANALYZING
compositions where words change how we understand photographs

■ **Write:** Write captions under the two photographs above: try to write captions that encourage others to understand the photographs as differently as possible.

Look at the examples on the next page both for ideas and to see just how much the words you use (as well as their typeface and placement) can change how you understand a photograph.

Based on your observations, write a list for yourself of ways in which words (and the ways the words are arranged) can affect your understanding of a photograph. (Lists like this help you think analytically when you need to use words and photographs and illustrations together: you'll remember this list, and be able to come to more effective, thoughtful, and often more quick decisions.)

< Adjust. >

Not tonight, honey.
It's been a rough day.

I always thought Mom would live forever…
I hope Dad's okay; he didn't sound so good.
I wonder how quickly I can get a flight back.
Damn, the last time I talked to her I didn't
tell her I loved her… Damn. And I was mad
because she'd done that thing she always does

a softer world   werewolves@asofterworld.com

There will always
be people taunting me

laughing because
I tower above them,
a giant.

Pointing with fingers that
have never touched a cloud

■ **Discuss with others:** Use the three categories of word and photograph interaction to analyze how the words and photograph play off each other in the comic strip above. If you were to see just the photograph (broken up into the three panels), how do you think you'd respond? If you were to see just the words, how would you respond? What contribution to the overall effect do you think is made by the words-typed-on-paper-scraps? Imagine different typed words; what kinds of words will most change your response to the strip?

strategies for analyzing and producing visual arguments

This chapter has so far been about using the visual elements of texts as parts of arguments.

The writing on creating orderly and unified layouts, for example, is about creating an efficient *logos* in visual layout. The sections on typography and color are in part about the *pathos* of arguments that use those strategies, because different typefaces and different colors draw on associations we have with our bodily and cultural pasts. But typography and color are also about *logos*: in the "Eat at Bill's" samples, for example, different colors create different levels of differentiation—and hence different hierarchies of relationship— among elements. Similarly, different typefaces (as in the "How to Write a Protest Letter" example) help differentiate parts of a layout, indicating to a reader the hierarchical importance of the elements.

All of this is about *ethos*, too: the preceding sections help you understand expectations current audiences in the United States often have about what constitutes an organized, coherent, unified layout. When you create a layout that satisfies those expectations—or that self-awarely bends those expectations—you show your knowledge and professionalism.

In this section, we discuss how to analyze and produce arguments whose primary elements are visual rather than written or oral. Earlier in this book, we described how "argument" can be defined in different ways—and we described why in this book we most often define argument as "a piece of communication designed to shape an audience's attentions in a particular way." We also wrote that sometimes we would discuss more formal kinds of argument, arguments whose arrangements are more explicit. In this section, we consider visual examples that are formally structured to make arguments.

visual analogies

This poster is from 1940s Great Britain, during World War II; as in the United States, so many men were away fighting that factories didn't have enough workers, and conscious efforts were directed at women to encourage them to leave home and go to work constructing war equipment—work that had been traditionally considered inappropriate for women.

This poster can't just show women dressed as industrial workers; in the context in which this poster was produced, to show a woman in industrial garb would have looked weird and unseemly and so probably would have encouraged women *away* from such work. Instead, to show that women in their homes already do the exact same work of factories shows women that they already know and so can do the work of the factory. By showing women in particular postures patching fabric, sewing, and peeling potatoes, and then showing women in almost exactly the same postures working with drafting tools and industrial production equipment, this poster argues that the postures—and hence the abilities and all other qualities needed to do the industrial work—are the same. The argument of this poster isn't "You can do it!"; the argument by analogy is "You are already doing it, so get yourself into the factories!"

An **analogy** is an argumentative form based on the assumption that if two objects or processes are alike in one way, they must be alike in more if not all ways; often people use analogies when they compare something an audience doesn't know well to something they do, to explain the unknown by the known. In this poster, if women can sew, they can make war equipment and work in factories.

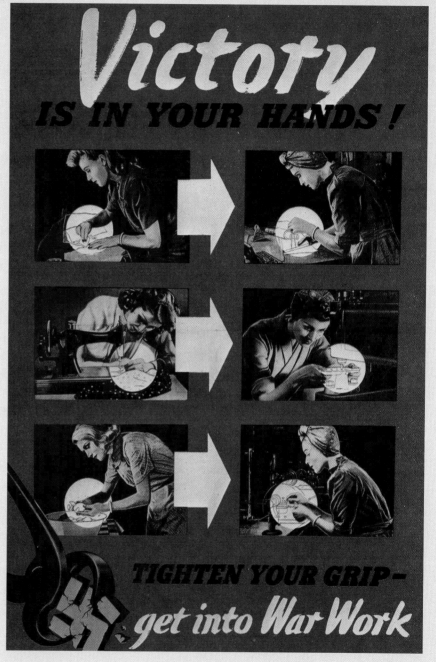

compose ▪ design ▪ advocate

IT'S A TRADITION
WITH US, MISTER!

POS: APR. 11 TO MAY 1 · W · WAR PRODUCTION CO-ORDINATING COMMITTEE

Like the previous poster, this one is from the 1940s, but from the United States. You can probably see how its intention, like the previous example, is to get women into factories and, similarly to the previous example, women are shown doing two different tasks to show that if they can do one, they can do the other. Here, however, the analogy works across time, showing a woman in clothing from the time of the Revolutionary War loading a musket. This poster is using *pathos*—the evocation of the emotion of patriotism—to bring women into the industrial workforce.

In the previous poster, the viewer is directly addressed as "you": women are the audience, and the argument for going to work is aimed directly at them. In the poster to the left, audiences are to understand the words as spoken by women—the "us" of the words—but addressed to men ("Mister!"). So perhaps this poster is addressing two different audiences: women are asked to identify with others across time who have done patriotic work, to give them justification for going to work, while men—husbands, fathers, and brothers who might be resistant to women working—are asked to see industrial work as a patriotic tradition, nothing unusual and in fact justified by the past.

Notice how in these examples visual analogies are used when a composer would like an audience to look (literally and figuratively) differently at a situation. The analogy equates a good someone wants to create (in the future) with a current good, or it equates a situation someone wants to change with another situation an audience will almost automatically understand to be bad so that they will want to change the first situation.

visual accumulation

An exhibition at the Salvador Allende museum in Santiago, Chile, includes pictures of missing prisoners from the era of Gen. Augusto Pinochet.

Helen Hughes for The New York Times

To **accumulate** is to pile up a collection of objects that are similar or the same. This photograph shows an accumulation of photographs that are all the same size and that are mostly in the same format, a closeup of someone's face.

General Augusto Pinochet was president of Chile from 1973–1990; during this time, thousands of people were detained by the military, never to return. In 1998, General Pinochet was arrested under an international warrant issued by a Spanish judge and charged with the crime of torture.

The photograph above, printed in the *New York Times*, shows a 2003 exhibition in Chile of photographs of the missing. The accumulation of so many similar photographs allows the audience to see—literally see—all at once how many people are missing. The audience can see individual faces and think about individuals who are missing, but always as part of the accumulated weight of how many all together are missing. How is this different from reading, "Thousands of people disappeared during General Pinochet's presidency"?

(Notice too how the photograph above has been structured so that you cannot see how high up the wall the photographs go, or how long the walls are. Why do you think the photographer chose this particular framing? To learn about framing as a rhetorical strategy for directing attention, see chapter 11.)

compose ▪ design ▪ advocate

The photograph above is titled "Cell phones #2, Atlanta 2005," and its original size is 44" x 90." The photographer, Chris Jordan, photographs piles of discarded consumer goods ranging from phones (as above) to cell phone chargers, circuit boards, bullet casings, cigarette butts, and cars. (You can see more of his work at www.chrisjordan.com)

Notice how the cropping of this photograph makes it look as though the waves of cell phones extend out endlessly (we discuss cropping more in chapter 11); notice also how the cell phones aren't just piled randomly but do seem almost to be circling in waves about the center.

How often do you see so many cell phones? How often do you see so many *discarded* cell phones?

What might such an accumulation of cell phones, so photographed, tell us about our use of plastic? What might it tell us about our consuming habits?

How would the effect of this visual argument be different if Jordan had photographed and presented each cell phone separately, as in the photograph of the exhibition in the Salvador Allende Museum?

The examples we've examined use accumulation either to make visible and concrete a large number of elements or to make visible a pattern that can then perhaps be broken. In the first and third examples, a number is given emotional weight; in the second, we can see how an individual stands out against a background of sameness. In what sorts of argumentative contexts do you think such strategies will be most effective?

visual symbols

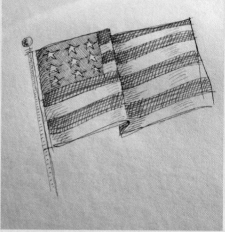

If you've ever let soup sit on the stove bubbling for a while, you've experienced how flavor becomes intensified as the soup condenses. Symbols are like that left-to-bubble soup: it is as though emotions and understandings have been condensed down into a small drawing or an object—the symbol.

Valentine's Day is awash in the symbol of the heart, meant not only to evoke thoughts of love but also (probably more important) the diffuse but usually lovely emotions connected with love.

The flag of the United States—like the flag of any country—is a symbol. In different circumstances it represents the emotions of patriotism or the strength of the country. Its colors represent blood and valor, the stars represent not only the states but all that stars can evoke—aspiration, light, glory. The number of stripes rep-

resents the original 13 states. Even when the flag is represented inaccurately (as above) its power as a symbol still holds, and it can be used to bring people together around common causes or to cause divisiveness as people argue over how they understand allegiance. It is because symbols condense so much emotion and understanding that they can have the power to bring together or to divide.

When you use symbols, recognize then that they will not mean the exact same thing to everyone. Different cultures have different symbols, and the symbols with which we have grown up are usually ones we do not question because they have been such a part of our lives. Often, additional information will help fix the meaning of symbols, as you will see on the next page.

Symbols are linked to what they represent through resemblance (the way the majesty and power of the bald eagle is supposed to represent the majesty and power of the United States) or convention (as the apple is meant to represent temptation). You won't be able to make your own symbols; you can only use the symbols you inherit through living in a particular time and place.

compose • design • advocate

AIDS

PREVENTION

UNIVERSITY OF CALIFORNIA, BERKELEY · STUDENT HEALTH SERVICE

Imagine the poster to the left had no drawing but only said, simply, "Be careful about sex!"

The blandness and lack of force of the imagining ought to give you a sense of how powerful symbols can be. Without having to use any explanation and only a few words, the poster links sex with the temptation of Eve in the Garden of Eden and with devilish evil. It overlays sex with a Biblical history and the loss of paradise. The poster can do this because chances are that if you've grown up in the United States you've learned that an apple and a snake together mean that original temptation.

But also imagine this poster without the words about AIDS. If you saw such a poster on the wall, you'd think about Adam and Eve and the Garden—but you'd be left hanging about purpose: is the poster proselytizing, or being just a pretty illustration of a resonant situation? The addition of "AIDS" gives you the purpose, that the designer wants viewers to see the extreme danger lurking around the red pleasure.

A question to ask about symbols in visual arguments, then, is whether you think the linking of symbol with its purpose is appropriate. Regarding this poster, we can ask whether sex should be linked with the original temptation. Because symbols work without explicit statement of their emotional weight, they can cause us to carry away many more associations and emotions than might really be necessary for the argument to be made. When you compose arguments that use symbols, you need to ask yourself if you are doing too much.

Visual arguments using symbols work because they equate some situation (in this case, AIDS) with a whole set of undescribed emotions and understandings we've learned through growing up in a particular time and place. When you want to bring the weight of an aspect of a culture's beliefs or emotions to bear on an issue, then consider what symbols you can use.

■ **Observe, then write:** Look through magazines and online to find other examples of visual analogy, accumulation, or symbols. Do the examples you find support our descriptions of when these different arrangements seem most effective? See if you can find examples that show other kinds of arguments these arrangements can help build—then write a short paper that argues how these visual arguments work, as we did with the examples in this chapter.

■ **Discuss with others:** Look through writing examples—essays, poems, opinion pieces—to find word examples of analogy, accumulation, and symbol. When these arrangements are built out of words, are the arguments of which they are part similar to or different from visual arguments that use these structures?

■ **Write:** Look at the websites of candidates running for national office or of members of Congress or the administration. You'll find many symbols at work, including (often) the U.S. flag. Write a short rhetorical analysis of one such site, arguing how any symbols used support the overall purposes of the website.

☐ To see more examples of visual arguments, check out the online chapter 9 resources at www.ablongman.com/wysocki

thinking through production

- Using any technologies available to you, produce two to three posters for an upcoming event. Each poster should have exactly the same illustrations or photographs, the same text, and the same layout, but vary the colors. Choose very different color schemes for the posters. Ask your classmates to describe how the colors encourage them to think about the event.

  Record the strategies that seem most effective for the context, audience, and purpose of the poster.

- Use whatever materials and technologies you have available to produce your own visual argument—for any purpose, context, and audience—based on analogy, accumulation, or a symbol. Look again at the examples and our analyses of them to think about the contexts in which these formal arrangements are most effective, in order to decide which to use for the audience and purpose you decide.

- There are more "Thinking Through Production" activities in the online chapter 9 resources at www.ablongman.com/wysocki

- Produce a timeline that presents the changes, over time, in some visual aspect of our lives. You could show how a company's logo has changed since the company began, or how women's dresses or men's pants differ from generation to generation, or how the design of cars or of CD and record covers vary over the decades. *But don't just show pictures of the changes:* annotate them to argue how the changes are in response to other cultural or technological changes.

  You'll need to do various research.* Find examples of the visual artifact you're studying, and research why this visible aspect has changed. Come to your own, supported-with-evidence position on why the changes you see might have occurred.

  When you produce the timeline—using any medium available to you—integrate into your presentation annotations that explain what the visual aspect is, how it changed over time, and why you think it's changed (be sure to take advantage of the layout of your timeline to help you make your argument.)

- Take a short paper you've already produced, and re-produce it twice. Each time, use a very different typeface (you might use a sans serif in one and a grunge face in the other) as well as different spacing between the lines of type. If you have headers in the paper, make them be a very different typeface from the body of the paper. Revise the visual structure of the paper keeping in mind what we've described about using layout rhetorically. Bring your papers to class, and give them to others for reading and response. Compare the responses you receive: do readers appear to give less serious attention to papers printed in typefaces unusual in academic circumstances?

---

* An example of a timeline to help you think about what you might do is in the chapter "Graphic Design in America" in the book *Design/Writing/Research* by Ellen Lupton and J. Abbott Miller, which your library might have or can get for you through interlibrary loan. Also look at these online timelines:

www.motown.com/classicmotown/frameset_2.htmlwww.sciencemag.org/feature/plus/sfg/human/timeline.shtml

www.rom.on.ca/egypt/case/timeline/

www.metmuseum.org/toah/splash.htm

We're supposed to be producing communication, so why are we analyzing & researching the arguments of others?

It would be lovely—because it might make the production of communication very easy—if we didn't have to think about audiences, if we could say or make whatever we felt to express whatever we were thinking or feeling. But communication is precisely about audiences.

We can talk with and understand others because we've grown up together. We know our native languages because other people were around speaking while we were growing up: we heard them and repeated their sounds and they corrected and encouraged us. We also know how to act in certain kinds of communication contexts because we learned—through watching and sometimes through being taught explicitly—what the appropriate moves and actions are. For example, you probably do not talk with your sisters or brothers or friends of your age in the same way you talk with your parents or other adults of their age; you probably talk differently with priests and nuns and reverends and rabbis and mullahs than you do with comfortable friends.

In each of these cases, you've learned—explicitly or not—conventions of behavior for different contexts.

Similarly, different kinds of texts have conventions, too. You know to start a letter with "Dear [insert name here]," and you know to put your name on papers you turn in for assignments.

In the following chapters are examples of many different kinds of texts: posters calling people to war or the movies; documentary photographs of life in Tokyo or of polluted landscapes; instructions for building furniture and for surviving explosions; editorial pieces about affirmative action; essays about the periodic table and an inspiring basketball coach; serious and not-so-serious comic books.

The purpose of all these examples is twofold.

First, we use these examples to point out conventions that exist for certain kinds of media and communication contexts. The examples can be a kind of checklist for you, to which you can refer as you need to produce your own work. In addition, as you become observant about communication conventions, you strengthen your abilities to make communications that meet audience expectations—which means that audiences will be able to be more readily attentive to what you produce. By becoming attentive to conventions, you also become attentive to when and how you can break them so as to be more interesting or more engaging and, ultimately, more persuasive.

Second, we use these examples to demonstrate rhetorical ways of analyzing texts so that you will have more support for doing rhetorical production of texts.

Analyzing texts in this way—thinking about how they work in terms of the audience and context envisioned by the text's creators (which is, in essence, a way to use the rhetorical process of this book backward)—gives you a systematic and organized way to observe communication conventions, strategies, arrangements, and effects. As we wrote in the previous paragraph, by observing how texts work, you yourself gain abilities and ideas for your own work.

PRODUCING AND ANALYZING TEXTS IS A CIRCULAR PROCESS: as you yourself produce texts, working out how to relate audience and context to purpose through your strategies and arrangements, others' texts become more interesting for how they have been produced to achieve their purposes. You'll find yourself wanting to adapt others' strategies and arrangements to your own ends—and you'll find yourself better understanding how documents made by others are trying to shape your responses.

In the next several pages of this section opening, we describe the kinds of examples that we use in the following chapters, and why we chose them. We also describe how to do rhetorical analysis (with pointers to examples of such analysis in later chapters).

Within each of the chapters of analysis of a particular kind of text are suggestions for how you can produce texts of your own— texts like those shown in the chapters as well as analytic texts.

In the preceding section there are chapters focused on the production of written, oral, and visual texts. As you are producing your own texts, be sure to refer to those chapters.

☐ Note also that the website that accompanies this book— www.ablongman.com/wysocki— contains sample speeches you can watch and listen to, as well as a chapter on interviews.

On the next pages is an explanation of why we chose the kinds of examples we did, and what we hope you will learn from each of the particular chapters.

about the

Before we get into particular examples of different media used for communication, and before we talk about how you can analyze the examples, here is a description of the kinds of media we are presenting to you, and why we've chosen them.

POSTERS

Because posters are single pages, they are a straightforward place to begin talking about the *logos* of visual composition. We show you posters from different times and places so that you can see how both time and place—history and culture—affect the visual composition of a text.

DOCUMENTARY PHOTOGRAPHY

Rather than relying on a quick visual hit like posters, documentary photography—multiple photographs building arguments—relies on time (and usually somewhat more complex compositions) to make arguments. This medium builds directly out of posters, but expands the possibilities of strategies for visual argumentation.

INSTRUCTION SETS

This section helps you critique instruction sets so you become more able—and demanding—users of instructions and technologies. Instruction sets help us see how verbal and visual strategies work together. Also, because instruction sets are so tied to helping others, they allow us to analyze an audience to make choices about effective rhetorical strategies.

compose ▪ design ▪ advocate

examples

Op ed writing (whether online or in print) is public writing, striving to change public opinion. The purpose of changing public opinion means that this medium usually involves a more explicit statement of arguments than the previous examples—as well as an emphasis on *ethos* and *pathos* for supporting opinion.

ESSAYS

Essays are the most "writerly" of the examples. Like documentary photography, essays build effects upon effects, and like op ed and interview pieces, essays bring the author's *ethos* into focus. With the rise of new printing and online technologies, writers are experimenting with essays, and so we can raise questions of how and why one would "play" with existing conventions.

COMICS

With this medium, we hope you'll see some of the argumentative potentials that are opening up (primarily because of changes in technologies of publication and distribution) for composers who are competent in both visual and verbal strategies.

INTERVIEWS

Transcribed interviews involve the tricky dynamics of translating speaking into writing, and all interviews require considerable preparation: the list of questions to ask an interviewee is just the beginning. This chapter also allows us to emphasize the ethical responsibilities we have in using the words of others, as in using the work of others.

This chapter is online, at www.ablongman/wysocki

WHAT IS ANALYSIS?

"Analysis" means "taking apart." "Analysis" is to communication what disassembling is to watches or car engines. If your watch or car is broken—or if you want to figure out how it works—you take it apart to look at the parts, to see how the parts are shaped to do something, and to see how they connect into a whole. It helps to remember there are pieces within pieces—that some of the pieces of a watch or car form subgroups with special functions of their own (a carburetor or a watch's winding mechanism). The same is true for communication: speeches, essays, and posters all have carburetors and winding mechanisms.

The steps we describe for analyzing communication follow from this: communication acts or practices communicate something to someone. (And notice how the steps we describe parallel the rhetorical process we described in the earlier chapters of this book: as you analyze, you take into consideration the purpose, audience, context, modes, strategies, and arrangement of the communication you are analyzing.)

Don't worry if the steps don't yet seem concrete—you'll see examples of rhetorical analysis in the examples that follow, and you'll get practice in doing them yourself.

Here are, first, short descriptions of steps you can use to analyze any piece of communication:

STEP 1

What are the piece's purpose, audience, and context? That is, what do you think its maker's statement of purpose is?

Say or write out your initial ideas about who made the object you are analyzing, what their concerns and overall purpose are, with whom they are communicating (or trying to communicate), and what the contexts for the piece's production and reception look to be.

STEP 2

List everything about the piece of communication that seems to you to be a choice, especially regarding arrangement and production.

Look at what stands out in your experience of the piece. As you list all the range of choices open to the piece's maker(s), which ones stand out to you? Why?

STEP 3

How are the choices used strategically?

Go through the list of choices you've made, and try to explain them as choices: Why do you think the author or designer made the particular choices you've identified? How do you think the author or designer hoped the piece's audience would respond to the choice? How do the choices early in the piece prepare the audience for what is to come later?

STEP 4

Test your observations: Are there any anomalies?

Look over your observations from step 3: do they fit with your initial observations about purpose, audience, and context? Look for any choice you've identified that does not seem to fit: how does your understanding of the piece need to change to account for what doesn't fit?

STEP 5

Revise your original statement about the piece.

Use your observations from step 3 and step 4 to revise your original statement about purpose, audience, and context. Try to account for the major strategies you've identified in the piece.

rhetorical analysis

Here are more detailed descriptions for how to proceed with a rhetorical analysis of any piece of communication:

STEP 1

What are the piece's purpose, audience, and context? That is, what do you think its maker's statement of purpose is?

After you read a letter, watch a movie, or stand before an outdoor sculpture, you often sense that you understand what the person who composed the piece wanted you to feel or think about as a response to how she put the piece together. Put this "sensation" of understanding into words. Say aloud or write down what you think the main point is or the main experience you are supposed to have. This statement is a hypothesis, and your analysis from here on out is about testing this hypothesis. (If you do not have a clue what the thing you are reading or looking at is all about, then proceed to step two—start looking at the pieces of the thing you are analyzing and wondering why they are there.)

The steps that follow are about testing and revising your initial sense of what the purpose, audience, and context are for the object you are analyzing.

STEP 2

List everything about the piece of communication that seems to you to be a choice, especially regarding arrangement and production.

When you are reading through an essay, looking at a poster, or listening to your neighbor tell a story about joining the army, certain things tend to stand out: a funky tone of voice, a scary scene in the background, some strange words, or an example that makes you blink. Your attentions might be drawn to a joke, or a lovely photograph of snow in Vermont, or a particular color or word. Gather these observations in your mind or on paper.

If something stands out, it probably is an important choice the author made, and so is a good place to start your analysis. Ask why the author chose the thing that catches your attention.

STEP 3

How are the choices used strategically?

The basic idea behind analyzing any communication is to find out how it works, how the pieces fit together and work with each other to affect the reader or viewer in some way. The way you begin to analyze these pieces is simply to ask what effect you imagine they might have on someone.

Also keep an eye on how the pieces fit together. If the background photo to an advertisement is of a poor U.S. inner-city neighborhood, how does the mood it creates work with the other pieces of the ad? And how does that mood fit with your initial hypothesis?

As you begin to explain why the pieces are there and how they fit together, you will find yourself making further observations, remembering other details of the thing you are analyzing, which will lead to further explanations about what effect these choices have and how they fit—or don't—the overall picture. Don't let this bother you. If you feel you are getting lost in the details, keep going back to what you originally sensed and hold on to what seems most obvious. Then venture out again.

Test your observations: Are there any anomalies?

While looking closely at the parts of the object you are analyzing and asking how they fit together, you may run into pieces that do not seem to fit with your initial sense of what the author is trying to do. Maybe there's a title that does not fit the story, maybe there's an example that goes on for too long, maybe there's a large empty space in the middle, or maybe there's an unexpected interruption in the flow of the story. Looking closely at these pieces—anomalies—and thinking about them often shows you where your initial hypothesis (statement of purpose, etc.) falls short and where you should look for a more complete, more accurate hypothesis. If your other observations have not already forced you to do this, these observations should cause you to revise your earlier statements about the purpose, audience, and context of the piece—that is, they encourage you to move to the next step.

Revise your original statement about the piece.

When you've done this kind of analysis often, you begin to see patterns in your process: for instance, often your initial sense about a text turns out to be based on only a few observations; you did not take in enough detail because it is hard to take it all in at once; what you gained was a partial view of the text; and—often—this partial view is not of the overall effect, but the effect of just a large part of the communication you're analyzing. Keep asking: *if that is only a part of the whole, then what is the whole thing really about?*

It can help to ask these questions:

- *What is the author trying to do? How does the author want the audience to feel or think or experience or . . . ?*

- *Who is the audience? What intrigues or concerns or is a problem for the author about the audience? What characteristics of the audience is the speaker playing to?*

- *What is the context? Is the context historical or imaginary? Are there hidden features of the context (does it pretend to be open to all but in fact excludes some people?)? What is the physical space like within which people will encounter this piece?*

Go back home, and you can start all over again!

(This step isn't listed in the short description of rhetorical analysis, because you come to this step most often when you are analyzing complex pieces of communication like novels, movies, or long speeches that require closer attention.)

Sometimes after the work of the previous steps you have a pretty good idea of what the purpose, audience, and context is for a communication—but something still nags at you. A speech you hear about patriotism might seem simple, for example, but you can't account for why there is so much discussion about spending. You turn off the TV afterward and think about it over the weekend, and then it hits you—the speaker was trying to do two things at once: he wanted you to feel patriotic but also to link patriotism to spending money. Initially, you only saw only the first purpose; the second was a sleeper that only comes to you after you aren't satisfied with your initial analysis and keep pushing on it.

writing up
rhetorical analysis

You might be asked to turn a rhetorical analysis into formal writing (as when you are asked to turn it in for class). Here are approaches for writing a summary of your analysis and for using your analysis to go to the next level of complexity by writing an argument about how the piece(s) you analyzed fit into the larger social and cultural contexts in which we move.

a summary

You know well when you do a class assignment that the writing needs to be more formal than notes and jottings. Teachers generally want to see writing that appears organized (such that it makes sense to a reader why one part follows another) and that has a purpose. *The purpose of a summary of a rhetorical analysis is not simply to give a description of a reading or an advertisement or a poster; a summary of a rhetorical analysis is instead a summary of what you see to be the purpose, context, and audience for the piece, and a listing of the major strategies you believe demonstrate that the piece's author or designer was working toward the purpose, context, and audience you describe.* You can order such a summary by first stating what you see to be the purpose, audience, and context of a piece, and then describing what

you see to be the major strategies and how they support your understanding of purpose, context, and audience.

using your analysis to make
an argument

Rhetorically analyzing individual texts helps you learn about how composers make choices about single texts and about how composers think about audiences; you also learn about yourself as an audience, and how you respond to various strategies (and you can usefully attend to your own responses as you compose).

But no individual piece of communication functions on its own: as you've already experienced, and will read about in other chapters of this book, texts make sense to us because they work in contexts. An author or designer can make strategic choices because our time and place provide us with ranges of choices that different audiences understand. Rappers, for example, choose rhythms that identify their songs as rap, and they rap about subjects that others understand to be appropriate for rap (have you ever heard a rap about vacuuming or writing a rhetorical analysis?).

Because of our social and cultural (not to mention political, economic, religious, and

so on) contexts, texts make the meanings they do for us because we have the experiences we do. Because we experience all the repeated parts of texts (such as the repeated rhythms and topics of rap), texts can teach us, in a very quiet way, what to expect about the larger world and ourselves. We are the people we are because of the things we do over and over every day, such as the ways we tend to respond to and treat others and the actions we think are appropriate or moral—and we learn much of this through watching and experiencing what our families do day in and day out and what we see in all the kinds of media that surround us.

If you analyze a range of similar texts, or a number of texts by one author or designer, you can often see repetitions of strategies—and these repetitions can suggest patterns of thought or behavior that audiences can pick up.

To see different rhetorical analyses that build arguments about how the strategies of different texts might shape us, see the next page; there are also examples in the chapters on essays and opinion pieces.

ATTACK OF THE MONSTER MOVIE POSTER: HOW TO BE A MAN OR A WOMAN IN THE 1950s

a sample rhetorical analysis (that makes an argument) of movie posters, by Leroy Steinbacher for his rhetoric class

Introduction

Why do four horror-movie posters from the 1950s all focus on a scene of attack, involving women? Through a rhetorical analysis of the posters, I argue that the posters place their viewers in positions where they are asked to imagine themselves taking action to save a woman . . . or to do something about a woman causing trouble. The posters ask viewers to become imaginatively involved with the attack scene, which seems like a good strategy for getting people interested in seeing the movies. It also seems to me, however, that getting people involved is also a kind of teaching: it is a way of teaching men and women about their proper roles.

The four posters I analyze were made for these movies:

- *Creature from the Black Lagoon* (1954)
- *Attack of the Crab Monsters* (1957)
- *Attack of the 50 Ft. Woman* (1958)
- *The Wasp Woman* (1959)

These movies were made after World War II and the Korean War. The United States was building in prosperity, and people had time to go to the movies. But people were also uneasy about the world situation: the Cold

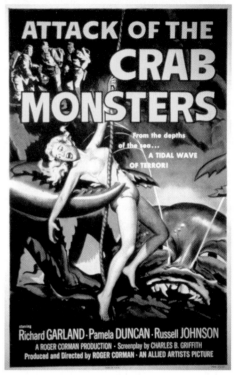

War was beginning, and there were fears of potential nuclear war. There have always been monsters in the stories people tell each other, but in the fifties such stories took on particular urgency because of fears about mutations caused by radiation—mutations that would turn people into fish or insects, or that would make people or animals grow to ungraspable size.

I will analyze each of the posters individually—in the order they were produced—to support my arguments.

About each of the movies

The *Creature from the Black Lagoon* poster has the movie title at the top, large, so that we see it first. What we see next—centered and large—is the creature carrying, underwater, a woman in a skintight bathing suit. The woman doesn't seem injured, and—although she isn't struggling with the creature—her facial expression shows that she isn't happy about being dragged down below the surface of the water, which is made darker (and so scarier) toward the bottom of the poster. At the top left of the poster are two divers—drawn to look like they are farther away—coming toward the

compose ▪ design ▪ advocate

creature and the woman. The divers have a knife and a gun, so we can perhaps assume that they are coming to save the woman. The bottom of the poster shows three scenes from the movie that set up the main scene of the poster: there is a boat sitting calmly in tropical waters, then a scene of a male diver being attacked by the creature, then a scene of the woman clutching a man with a gun. We get the sense that the people have come to this place, been attacked, have tried to protect themselves—and now the woman has been carried off.

Because the main scene of the poster—the woman being carried off—spills off the edges of the poster, the poster makes it look as though we, the audience, are there in the water with the creature. The creature comes toward us with the woman, and because we are closer than the divers at top left, we are in a better position to act. The design of the poster shapes the audience then as another potential rescuer, someone who has come upon this scene and can—probably should—do battle with the monster to save the woman.

The poster for *Attack of the Crab Monsters* has a similar visual composition to the poster for *Creature from the Black Lagoon*. The title is at the top, and directly underneath is another unhappy, unstruggling woman (in another skimpy bathing suit) being carried off by an unnatural being; this poster also shows potential rescuers at the top left. Like the poster for *Creature from the Black Lagoon*, this poster

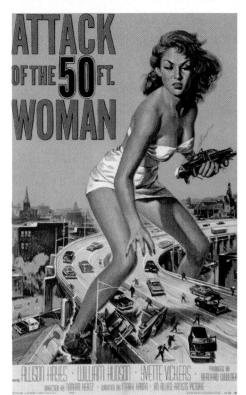

is mostly in dark colors, with the title and the woman's flesh lighter. Also as in the poster for *Creature from the Black Lagoon*, the visual composition of this poster makes the scene of the attack spill off the page, so that we imagine that we are in the scene. The woman is again placed between us and the monster, with the potential rescuers far away: again, the visual composition of the poster designs the audience into the poster, so that we feel we are there, just about to do battle.

Attack of the 50 Ft. Woman turns the tables on the previous two posters. It does not show us an apparently helpless woman being carried away by a monster; instead, *she* is the monster. Although this woman is in a skimpy bathing suit as the others, she is huge and threatening: she straddles a freeway, posed as though caught in the middle of picking up and destroying cars, with a truck that has crashed into her leg smoldering at the lower left—but she apparently isn't hurt. She isn't looking at us; instead, her heavily made up eyes are turned slightly to the side, with lowered lids, as though she's thinking about what to do next; her right arm is poised to pick up another vehicle, her sharply pointed and

another vehicle, her sharply pointed and painted nails like the talons of a huge predator bird. There is a potential rescuer shown in this poster as in the others, but this time the rescuer is a tiny policeman at the lower left of the poster, aiming his gun: given his proportions to the woman, he looks like a feeble, powerless ant.

But we, the audience, are not placed to be feeble in this poster. The poster isn't designed to make us look up at the woman as though she were towering above us, as though we were as tiny as the people in the poster. The poster is instead designed so that we are facing the woman: when we see the poster, it is as though our eyes are at almost the same level as her face, so that we must be almost as big as her. As with the other posters, once again the scene fills the whole space of the poster and spills off the page, so it is as though the whole scene extends around us. Here, then, we are placed to be in the scene, the same size as the woman: once again the audience is visually composed as rescuers—but this time, not rescuers of the woman but rescuers of all the people she is menacing. The designs of this poster again place us to do battle with the monster—it's just a very different kind of monster this time.

The Wasp Woman is also a different kind of monster. A wasp much bigger than a human, but with a woman's face, she menaces a man over a pile of bones and skulls. In the poster for this movie, the title of the movie is again at top, along with "A beautiful woman by day—A lusting queen by night." The wasp's wings are under the title, and lead our eyes down into the huge body. The woman's face has an expression like that of the 50 Ft. Woman: her eyes are heavily made up, but almost closed, as though she is contemplating what to do next with the man in her grip. And once again, the visual composition of the poster places us as though we were in the scene. This time, however, there is no potential rescuer shown in the poster: there is only the audience who is in any position to do battle with the consuming wasp.

conclusion

The visual compositions of the posters all position the audience as potential rescuers. The designers of the posters probably did this so that we would find ourselves imagining ourselves in the movie, being the hero who saves the day: this gets us emotionally involved with the movie before we even see it—and so probably heightens our desire to see the movie, to be able to feel ourselves even more as heroes.

But the heroes—the rescuers—in these movie posters are always shown as men. The audience for these posters—and so for these movies—is therefore asked to imagine themselves as men, even if they are women. If a woman looking at these posters instead tries to identify with the women shown, look at the positions she is allowed to take up: she can either be the passive victim who is carried away by the monster and who must await others to save her, or she can be the destructive monster who must be destroyed.

I don't think horror movies are supposed to be subtle or complex: they are meant to scare us, perhaps to let us experience our fears in the safe environment of the movies so that we can go to our non-movie lives feeling that our fears can be faced. But, unfortunately, what my analysis of these movie posters shows is that the ways men and women are asked to think about themselves aren't subtle and complex, either. Men are asked to think of themselves as heroes and protectors who will do battle with horrors; women get to be passive and weak—but, if they have any power, it is seen as horrible. Men are asked to look at women as needing protection—but if they don't need protection because they are strong, then they are to be destroyed.

These posters are certainly not the only ways that men and women were taught about what their proper behaviors were to be in the United States in the 1950s. But imagine how seeing these posters week after week (there are hundreds more like them!) would contribute to how a teenage boy, for example, would think about himself and about women.

I hope I've shown, through a rhetorical analysis of how these posters visually shape their audiences, how the posters shape the ways men and women were to think about how they were to behave in the world of the 1950s.

compose ▪ design ▪ advocate

thinking through production

■ Choose a kind of text from the list below or come up with another, and then look at no fewer than 10 examples of that kind. Generate a list of characteristics people expect to be in a text that they can recognize as fitting that kind—and get as detailed as possible. If you are looking at texts that involve writing, for example, look at tone of voice, whether the composer uses first or third person to write, their use of logical structures of arrangement, the kind of typefaces used, the use of color, use and placement of photograph or illustration, and so on; use the descriptions of media, strategies, and arrangements in the earlier sections of this book to help you get as detailed as you can.

After you've generated your list of defining characteristics for the kind of text you've chosen, do one or all of the following:

1 Print your list in a format easy for someone else to read but where the kind of text you've analyzed is nowhere given. Give your list to someone else, and have the person try to guess the kind of text from your list.

2 Use your list to produce your own example. For some kinds of texts, you'll have to be creative: you don't, for example, have a budget for making a Hollywood horror film—but you can write up a plotline and storyboards (see the online resources for this chapter at www.ablongman.com/wysocki for information on storyboarding).

3 Make a new chapter for this book, following the model of the other chapters in this book, to teach others how effectively to analyze and compose that kind of text.

possible kinds of texts

Hollywood horror film

office memo for a large company

hip-hop track

popular science magazine article

country-western song

history thesis (check your campus library for copies of theses written in different departments)

romance novel

coffee-table documentary photography book

advertisement for SUV

instruction set for using small electronic devices

store signs

e-mail or instant messaging

sympathy cards

front-page newspaper articles about foreign events

analyzing posters

Throughout the nineteenth century and into the early twentieth, the bare spaces of cities—the sides of buildings as well as specially built kiosks—were covered with posters advertising auction agencies, health remedies, women's wigs, or theatrical performances; the posters might also call people to political meetings or inform them about political decisions.

Posters—large color printed sheets—appeared when they did in cities for several reasons: printing technologies allowed for large color prints, there were for the first time enough people who could read to justify the costs of such publication, and cities had sufficient population massed together that it made sense to publicize ideas, events, and products using posters.

Without public spaces—and a public moving about in those spaces—posters make no sense. Posters were an early kind of mass communication: they were a way for someone who could

afford the costs of printing and who wanted to reach a large audience to reach that audience. For the first time, audiences didn't hear news and information from others in one-to-one conversations or in large meetings. Instead, posters could address many people one at a time in public.

Because posters have been used in public spaces where people are passing by quickly, they are usually designed to be scanned and read quickly. People who make posters consciously design them to get across one idea quickly and easily.

On the next pages, you'll learn something about how the visual elements of a poster are chosen and arranged to catch your attention and hold it long enough for you to understand a poster's purpose. You'll see how posters work both because they attend to how we experience the world through our bodies as well as because they draw on concepts and ideas we already understand because of where and when we live.

HOW WE ANALYZE POSTERS

We start off in this section with this scheme for making sense out of the strategies and arrangements people use when they design posters: Because we can rely on the people with whom we communicate sharing both the experiences that come with having a body (as we'll explain in this chapter) and that come with living in a shared society, we can develop guidelines that allow us to approach the analysis and composition of posters systematically.

We'll use this scheme to analyze the strategies and arrangements used in other media in following chapters, too, so that you can use what you learn about posters for analyzing documentary photography and written essays as well.

As you practice applying this scheme to the examples we've included in this chapter, we'll add to the scheme so that it becomes more detailed and complex and so more useful. Because it is always important to consider what different analytic schemes help you see, and what they miss, we ask you to be attentive to whether the scheme helps you understand as much as possible about the examples we include. We'll be asking if the categories through which the scheme asks you to understand the strategies and arrangements of the examples are appropriate—but that's for later. For now, let's get down to the work of understanding how posters work.

The strategies & arrangements of posters can be used & analyzed rhetorically because they draw on . . .

principles of visual composition

what we already know

what we already know because we have bodies

what we already know because we live in particular times with other people

□ To see more poster examples than are in this chapter—and possibly for help in doing the activities of this chapter— check out the links in the online chapter 10 resources at www.ablongman.com/wysocki

HOW POSTERS WORK:
DRAWING ON WHAT YOU KNOW

In our time, people use public space differently than they did in the nineteenth century, when color posters were first published. Nowadays, in the United States, you probably see posters most often if you live in a large city: the walls put up around construction sites are often plastered with posters for plays, concerts, or political events. On some college campuses, telephone poles and bulletin boards are covered inches thick in letter-size flyers advertising group meetings, band performances, and sorority rushes.

Most people now, however, are most familiar with movie posters, and perhaps with the placards people put on their lawns during political campaigns.

We'll start analyzing posters with the example to the right.

■ What visual aspects of this poster tell you that it is probably for a movie?

■ When do you think the movie publicized by this poster was made? Why do you guess the time period you do?

■ What kind of movie is being publicized here, a comedy or a horror film or a sci-fi film or . . .? What visual aspects of the poster encourage you to make the judgment you do?

Look at how much you knew in order to understand what's going on with this poster.

List all you had to know—about the medium of posters, about the place of movies and movie-going in the United States, about the kinds of pictures used in posters, about genres of movies, and so on—in order to understand what the designers of this poster were hoping to achieve rhetorically with the poster.

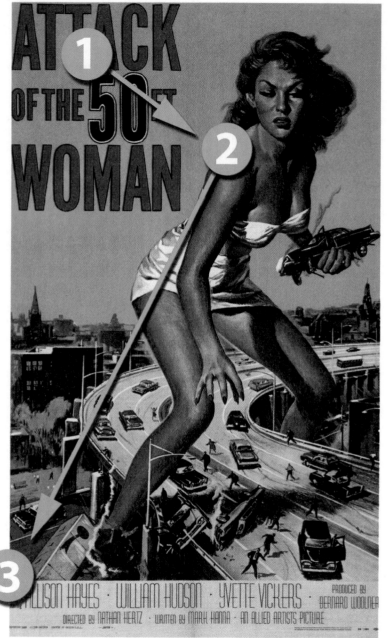

HOW POSTERS WORK: VISUAL COMPOSITION

Like most posters of any kind, this movie poster does not have many elements: there is a title, and then a representational image (a painting in this case, but you've probably also seen posters that use photographs), and then more text—and that is it, so that a viewer can scan the poster quickly and understand its purpose.

Because the elements in the poster for *Attack of the 50 ft. Woman* have been arranged in a logical manner, your eyes probably moved through the poster in the order of the numbers. Here is how the poster's visual composition encourages your eyes to follow that path:

1 Notice how the title is at the top left of the poster— at the spot we expect if we have learned to read in the top-to-bottom, left-to-right motions that English requires. The title is very large relative to the other elements on the page, and it is in a very simple sans serif typeface.

2 The woman has been made much larger than the other elements (so much so that she is much taller than 50 feet!) and placed so that we see her second. Notice, however, that the colors of the poster do not contrast very much, so that the woman doesn't "pop" out of the poster as she would were she (for example) blue-tinted. Notice too how the shape of the woman's body draws you down the page: chances are your eyes move from the title to her face, and then down her right arm to her right leg—which leads your eyes down to the left bottom edge of the poster, where you see a car crash and the remaining typographic information.

3 Finally, at the very bottom of the poster, in an unobtrusively thin typeface, is the information about who is in the movie.

compose ▪ design ▪ advocate

HOW POSTERS WORK:
DRAWING ON WHAT YOU KNOW

Here's a poster for a movie you may have seen.

- Why do you think the poster's designers chose green and black as the main colors? How would the poster be different if it were bright pink and white, or violet and black?

- Why might the designers have chosen to show the people turned with their backs to viewers, with their bodies fading away at bottom—but with their faces turning toward us? What sense of space does this help create in the poster? What sort of emotions does this help create?

- Why might the designers have decided to mix a photographic with a painterly style? Why might the poster not have as much to look at as the poster for *Attack of the 50 ft. Woman*?

- What do the designers of this poster expect their audiences to know about the earlier *Matrix* movies?

- What are all those slanting lines? How do they contribute to your understanding of the poster?

Again, look at how much you already knew in order to understand this poster: you understand about how we use black and a certain shade of green in our culture and how we think about turned bodies, and about illustrations instead of photographs.

The *Matrix Revolutions* poster is publicizing a movie that has some similarities to *Attack of the 50 ft. Woman*: both movies are about situations that (most of us believe) do not happen in real life. Does one poster look scarier to you than the other, or does one look sillier? How do the posters encourage you to think differently about the two movies?

HOW POSTERS WORK:
VISUAL COMPOSITION

We think the poster for *Matrix Revolutions* is composed to direct your eyes something like this:

1. Unlike the poster for *Attack of the 50 ft. Woman,* this poster has no huge words at the top. Instead, we think this poster's center has been designed to catch our eyes first: the poster's main colors divide it in two diagonally; in the middle of the poster, placed on top of that dividing line, are the two people. There are no other people shown in the poster, only text—and so our eyes are probably drawn there first by our interest in people and by their placement.

2. After we see the people, the poster's design suggests two other directions our eyes can follow:

   - There is a line of text at the top of the poster, which gets brighter to the right, ending in a flash of light. The line of the second character's head and up-pointed arm move in the direction of that light. These two features direct our attentions upward.

   - The poster gets lighter at the bottom right, so our eyes will be drawn there. The lines of "rain" all point in that direction—and the movie title is there at the bottom, too.

To our eyes, this poster seems to have been designed to keep our eyes moving back and forth from the top to the bottom, from darkness into light and back again—and the light is on the bottom right, suggesting both the ground but also where the story is moving, since we are used to reading from right to left. If you have seen this movie, how does this movement tie in with what you know about what happens in the movie?

compose ▪ design ▪ advocate

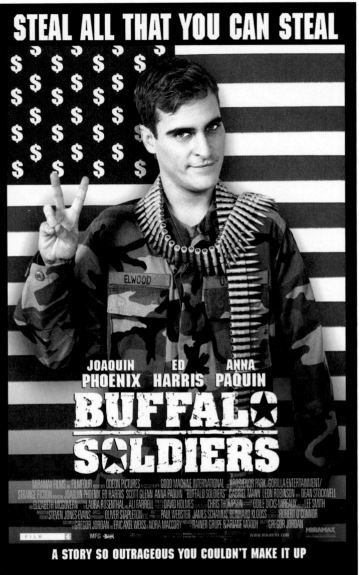

compose ▪ design ▪ advocate

ANALYZING
movie posters from the United States

■ **Write:** On the previous two pages are several movie posters from the United States. Use what you know and what you have read on the preceding pages to write a short paper in which you answer the following questions about the posters:

- When were these different movies made? On what visual evidence or other knowledge do you base your estimates?

- What kinds of movies are being publicized by these posters? What evidence do you use for making your judgment?

- Why do you think the designers of these posters chose the colors they did for the different posters?

- What is the visual path your eye follows through these posters? Why do you think the designers of these posters "ask" you to see the elements of the posters in the order you do?

ANALYZING
poster genres

■ **Write:** From the preceding examples, or finding your own, choose two movie posters for **different** kinds of films. For example, you could choose a poster for a comedy and a poster for a suspense thriller. Analyze the posters' arrangements and what they expect you to understand. What differences do you see in the arrangements? What differences do you see in what the designers of the posters expect you already to know or understand? What do those differences explain about the different effects the designers of the posters wanted to have with their audiences? How do the different strategies used in the posters connect to the different purposes of the posters?

■ **Write:** *(This exercise requires you to be more subtle in your analysis, looking at the fine details of a poster.)* From the preceding examples, or finding your own, choose two posters for the **same** kind of film. Analyze the posters' visual arrangements and what they expect you already to know. What differences do you see? What do those differences explain about the different effects the designers of the posters sought? How do the different strategies used in the posters connect to the different purposes of the posters?

ANALYZING
wartime posters

■ **Discuss with others:** On the next two pages are posters printed during different wars in the United States—and elsewhere. Use what you know and what you have read on the preceding pages to respond to the following questions:

- When do you think these different posters were made? On what visual evidence or other knowledge do you base your estimates?

- From what countries do the different posters come? Try to use visual clues other than language to support your judgments (and know that just because a poster is printed in English doesn't mean it comes from the United States!).

- Why do you think the designers of these posters chose the colors they did for the different posters?

- What is the visual path your eye follows through these posters? Why do you think the designers of these posters "ask" you to see the elements of the posters in the order you do?

wartime posters
from the United States
and elsewhere

compose ▪ *design* ▪ *advocate*

THE VISUAL COMPOSITION OF A WARTIME POSTER

Notice how the various wartime posters use similar—but not the same—strategies of visual composition as the movie posters.

For example, the wartime posters have very few elements, and their elements are arranged to provide viewers a clear visual path from top to bottom.

Notice how with the wartime posters, however, that the first element you see— the element at the top—is a face (or, in one case, a hand) instead of words.

Why do you think the designers of these posters decided to place a face as the first element for you to see?

LOOKING MORE CLOSELY AT THE THINGS WE ALREADY KNOW WHEN WE LOOK AT THESE VISUAL COMPOSITIONS

You undoubtedly know the "I Want You" poster with Uncle Sam. The poster was first designed just as the United States was entering World War I, but it was such an effective poster that not only were more than four million copies printed between 1917 and 1918, but the poster was brought out again during World War II and the representation of Uncle Sam (the poster designer, James Montgomery Flagg, used himself as the model) has been reused in many different ways—as in the examples on the preceding pages.

Uncle Sam's pose in this poster was derived from a British poster. The British poster used an illustration of Lord Kitchener, a military hero in nineteenth-century Britain because of his campaigns in Africa. The illustration of Kitchener pointing directly at the viewer appeared on a magazine cover in 1914, and the British Parliamentary Recruiting Committee (in order to make a poster that would encourage men to enlist) changed the wording to turn the magazine cover into the poster you can see on the first page of examples (it is the yellow example in the top middle).

The success of the Kitchener poster in Britain led to the "I Want You" poster in the United States and then to all the other posters that have appeared since that draw on Uncle Sam's pose. Most of the posters are serious, but some—like the poster for the movie *Buffalo Soldiers* (shown several pages ago)—use the heritage of this poster for other ends.

As with the movie posters, understanding these wartime posters thus requires us to know (awarely or not) many things before we can respond to the posters in the way the posters' designers were hoping.

As we wrote earlier, you can think about what we need to know about posters—as about any visual composition—as fitting into two general categories:

1 what we already know because we have bodies

2 what we already know because we live in particular places and times with other people

compose ▪ design ▪ advocate

WHAT WE KNOW BECAUSE WE HAVE BODIES

The effectiveness of the Uncle Sam poster—and the Kitchener poster on which it was based—depends in large part on how Uncle Sam is positioned to appeal to anyone looking at the poster.

In the full-size poster, Uncle Sam is almost human-size. His body is painted to appear to be close to the front of the poster—as though he were leaning closely toward a viewer—and his facial expression is serious, with his eyes focused a few feet directly in front of the poster. The poster would hang on a wall at almost eye-level, and so—if we were to walk by the poster—it would be hard not to feel that Uncle Sam is looking us directly in the eyes. To those who were caught up in the patriotic fervor prevalent in the United States going into World War I, it would have been hard not to feel emotionally compelled by Uncle Sam's closeness and gestures.

In designing this poster, James Montgomery Flagg thus used his understanding of how the poster would be hung but also, importantly, of how we tend to respond to gestures aimed directly at us (even when they are printed on paper).

We understand some of what is going on in this poster because we know—from our embodied physical experiences—what Uncle Sam's gestures and (perceived) physical closeness indicate.

WHAT WE KNOW BECAUSE WE LIVE IN PARTICULAR PLACES AND TIMES

To analyze the Uncle Sam poster, we need to understand not only the postures of human bodies, but also who Uncle Sam is. Just what do you know about Uncle Sam, and how did you learn it? And what do you have to know to understand why Uncle Sam is dressed in red, white, and blue? Will those colors carry the same emotional weight for someone in (for example) Italy as for a citizen of the United States?

In addition, Uncle Sam is an older white male. How do you think your responses to this poster would change were Uncle Sam Aunt Sam instead? There is one poster on pages 338–339 that has a woman in it, but notice that she is not the same age as Uncle Sam—why do you think that is? How is the appeal built by these posters changed when the person shown in the poster is not older or male? What cultural expectations about gender shape your understanding of the appeal being made in the poster?

Why do you think Uncle Sam is white? What cultural understandings of ethnicity seem to be at work in these posters' representations of people?

We bring our understandings of gender and ethnicity—like class—to making sense of these posters. In addition, what people are wearing as well as our knowledge of what was happening at the time these posters were made certainly shape how we understand them.

ANALYZING
wartime posters

■ Discuss with others: Look at all the posters on the preceding pages and analyze how the body positions of the people represented in the posters are intended to appeal to the poster's audience.

Which posters attempt to pull you closer, and which come out at you? Describe how the body positions, gestures, and facial expressions create these effects—but also describe why you think the posters' designers would make these particular choices. What overall purpose do you think the designers of each poster had, such that they chose the design strategies they did? (These are primarily strategies of *pathos*, as we discussed in chapter 4.)

■ Discuss with others: What do you need to know to understand the different wartime posters? What does this tell you about considerations you need to hold as you design for others?

■ Discuss with others: How would the wartime posters be different, do you think, if they used photographs instead of drawings and paintings? What associations do you have with photographs as opposed to paintings and drawings? How would this change the kind of appeal the posters are making?

Write: To the right is a more recent poster that draws on your knowledge of the Uncle Sam "I Want You" poster. The poster asks its audiences to respond initially to it as they would to the original Uncle Sam poster—but it is also trying to use what audiences already know to encourage them to see a situation differently. This poster is asking you to think differently about the relations between people in the United States who originally came from Europe and people who were already here when the Europeans arrived.

Analyze the poster's visual composition and what you are expected to know about what is in the poster (both in terms of the bodily appeals and the cultural appeals). Use your analysis to think about why the poster designers would choose to use the conventions of the Uncle Sam "I Want You" to make their arguments.

Write a short—two to three page—paper in which you lay out your analysis and use the analysis to support arguments about why you think the poster designers chose to use the conventions of the Uncle Sam poster.

A WRITTEN ANALYSIS OF A POSTER

To the right is what writer George Lipsitz argues about the "Who's the illegal alien?" poster.

Lipsitz's writing is in an academic style that uses terms and expressions common to certain academic disciplines. If you have trouble with some of Lipsitz's sentences, try paraphrasing them in your own words.

Summarize Lipsitz's argument in one or two sentences. Whether or not you agree with what Lipsitz argues about the purpose of the poster, do you agree with Lipsitz's analysis of how the poster's designer—Yolanda M. López—tries to achieve her purpose through her use of the conventions of the Uncle Sam poster?

In this writing, "icon" means a visual representation—some kind of picture—that people come to understand as having a cultural significance. Uncle Sam, for example, is an icon in the United States, giving us a shorthand visual way of indicating emotions of patriotism and the values of tradition.

"Intertextuality" means that a text refers to other kinds of texts—in the case of this poster, it means that this poster refers to the Uncle Sam recruitment posters as well as to the John Wayne movie *The Man Who Shot Liberty Valance*.

Oppositional movements ask people to take risks, to imperil their security in the present in hopes of building a better future. Often it is not sufficient to stress shared cultural signs and symbols, the legacy of past struggles, or the urgency of impending actions. Building insurgent consciousness entails speaking back to power, subverting its authority, and inverting its icons as a means of authorizing oppositional thinking and behavior. Yolanda M. López accomplishes this by subverting and inverting a cluster of nationalist and nativist American icons in her *Who's the Illegal Alien, Pilgrim?*

In a poster designed to defend undocumented immigrants from the dehumanizing phrase "illegal aliens," López presents an indigenous Mexican warrior facing forward and pointing at the viewer in a manner reminiscent of the "Uncle Sam Wants You" recruiting posters that decorated public spaces in the U.S. throughout the twentieth century. The caption plays with a phrase made famous by John Wayne in the film *The Man Who Shot Liberty Valance*, in which he referred repeatedly to the character played by Jimmy Stewart—a newcomer to the West—as "pilgrim." López's poster asks, *Who's the Illegal Alien, Pilgrim?* Her question inverts the moral hierarchy of the discourse about "illegal aliens" by connecting the conquest of lands previously owned by Mexico to the actions of nineteenth century Anglo "illegal aliens" who crossed the border to take Mexican land illegally. The intertextuality of López's poster makes a joke out of the icons of the dominant culture and uses laughter and ridicule to "uncrown power" and build insurgent consciousness. It turns "illegal aliens" into the aggrieved original residents of the region, and appropriates the ideological legitimacy and discursive authority of Uncle Sam and John Wayne for oppositional ends.

—from *Just Another Poster?: Chicano Graphic Arts in California*. Edited by Chon A. Noriega. Santa Barbara, CA: University Art Museum, 2001. pp. 76-77.

- Reread the description of the meeting of the Fast Car team in chapter 1. Given the purpose of the group and their audience, design a poster that will encourage women to come to a meeting. Then write a short paper justifying your design decisions (be sure to justify your decisions about what words to use as well as all your decisions about the visual aspects of your poster).

- Use the conventions of the Uncle Sam recruitment poster to design a poster that presents your position on the draft.

- Use the discussion of typography on pages 279–284 and 295–304 in chapter 9 to analyze how the typography and illustrations of any of the posters in this chapter—or a poster for a current movie or event in your community—work together to create an overall rhetorical effect. If you have access to a scanner or digital camera and image-processing software, scan in the poster and modify its typography or illustrations to see how changes in one or the other change the overall effect.

- Design a poster to interest people on your campus in a nonprofit organization that matters to you. Use the steps in chapters 2 to 4 to develop a design plan; also use the research recommendations in chapter 6 to help you learn as much as you can about the organization so that your poster can be appropriately informative.

  Produce your poster using the technologies you have available to you.

- Redesign one of the posters shown on these pages (or another to which you have access) as an announcement for a webpage. Given the relatively small size of webpages, and the possibilities of creating links to other pages, what changes do you need to make to the original poster to keep its original purpose but to make it work well online? Write a justification of your choices.

- On the following pages are posters from four countries for the Alfred Hitchcock movie, *Vertigo*. There are also questions to help you think about how the visual composition of posters—and what you need to know to understand the posters—changes from country to country. Use the questions to make observations about these single examples from different countries, and use your observations to speculate about what the designers think will appeal to audiences in the different countries. Pick two of the countries to compare, and—in the library or online—find at least five other examples of movie posters for the same (or a similar) genre from the two countries.

  Write a paper comparing the posters from the different countries, using your analysis of all the posters to see if your speculations are supported.

- There are more "Thinking Through Production" activities in the online chapter 10 resources at www.ablongman.com/wysocki

■ Write a rhetorical analysis of the visual compositions of the posters on this page and the next. These questions can guide your analysis:

- What differences do you see between the examples from other countries and the example from the United States?

- Compare the photographs and drawings shown in the different posters. What different senses of the movie do the different photographs and drawings give to an audience?

- What changes in these posters when a designer chooses to use a photograph instead of a drawing, or vice versa?

- In the posters that use photographs, compare the relationship shown between the man and the woman. What do the different posters— with their different relationships—lead audiences to expect about the movie?

- Based on what you know about color and how it works, what do the different color choices in each of the posters indicate to an audience about the movie?

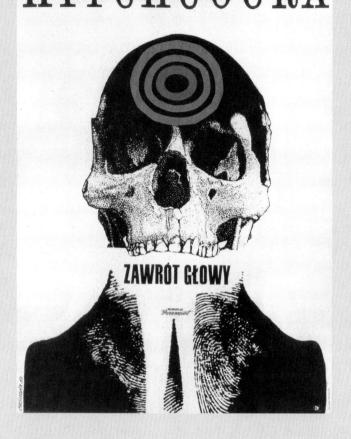

analyzing
documentary photography

Since Aristotle, people have known that light passing through a pinhole could be focused into an image. In the Renaissance, artists fitted lenses into the opening to improve the cast image so they could trace and use it as a base for painting. By the seventeenth century, people had observed that some silver compounds darkened in sunlight, and in the nineteenth century, inventors tried to stop the silver from darkening so they could "capture" an image focused on it. In 1826, in France, Joseph Niépce first "captured" such an image after an eight-hour exposure onto a metal plate; Louis Daguerre built on Niépce's work, so that—in 1839—he announced the "daguerreotype," a kind of photograph made after a few minutes' exposure onto silver-plated copper. A Briton, William Henry Fox Talbot, also announced in 1839 (three weeks after Daguerre) that he had fixed images from a lens—but Talbot's method, which gave rise to the processes of photographic printing used prior to digital photography, used paper instead of metal plates.

Before photography, only artists could "capture" images, requiring time and considerable money; afterward, cities and towns in Europe and the United States filled with photography studios. There were enough people to support these studios (in 1853, approximately three million daguerreotypes were taken in the United States alone) and to encourage studios to sell photographs of other countries and parts of the United States few in cities had seen. Photographers also started going to war (a British photographer recorded the Crimean War in the 1850s, and Mathew Brady's studio recorded the death fields of the U.S. Civil War). In the early twentieth century, photographers started recording social conditions, hoping that others, seeing the lives of the poor, would work toward improvement. All these practices have led to what is now called "documentary photography": photographs that record—document—conditions of a place or time.

HOW WE ANALYZE DOCUMENTARY PHOTOGRAPHY

Photographs do not "capture" reality, as though "reality" were just standing around waiting for someone to make it fit unchanged onto a small piece of paper or a computer screen.

Not only is "reality" at least four dimensional while individual photographs are two dimensional, but every photograph has had someone set up a camera to point in a particular direction; someone has also made decisions about what is included (and how it is arranged) within the space of the lens. The speed of the film and the lens, the capabilities of the lens to focus in closely or at great distances—these all shape the final photograph we see, whether the photograph is shot on film or is digital. Photographers have to decide whether to shoot black-and-white or in color, and—in developing or in digital retouching—have to decide how much to brighten or darken parts of a photograph, and where (perhaps) to crop.

This is a long way of saying that photographs are always rhetorical: they are always about a photographer making decisions about how an audience's attentions will be directed and shaped as the audience looks at a photograph.

Because photographs are rhetorical—are about directing the attentions of an audience just as posters are—we can use the same basic scheme and ideas for analyzing photographs that we used for analyzing

posters (and, with slight modifications, for analyzing other kinds of texts as well, as you will see in upcoming chapters). The strategies we show you in this chapter for analyzing photographs—the strategies of "vectors of attention," "framing," and "cropping"—are also strategies you can use for composing your own photographs, for drawing attention to what you want others to consider and think about; they are also strategies you can apply to drawings and

paintings (when you have finished this chapter, you might go back and use "vectors of attention" and "framing" to analyze the posters of the previous chapter).

☐ To see more examples of documentary photography, explore the links in the online chapter 11 resources at www.ablongman.com/wysocki

---

The strategies & arrangements of photographs can be used & analyzed rhetorically because they draw on . . .

what we already know because we have bodies

what we already know because we live in particular times with other people

which come together to shape our
principles of visual composition

---

compose ▪ design ▪ advocate

HOW PHOTOGRAPHS WORK: DRAWING ON WHAT YOU KNOW

Chances are good you've taken photographs yourself, that you know how to hold and use a camera. You understand—even if you haven't thought about it—how the photographic situation almost always means that there's someone standing behind a camera while facing some situation. And, of course, there's always something or someone being photographed—chances are also great that you've stood in front of a camera yourself sometime.

Until digital photographs, we generally believed that what is in a photograph existed at the time the photograph was taken (although, with considerable effort, photographers using film could always use darkroom techniques to bring together in a photograph what had never been in the same place at the same time in "real" life). We have tended to assume, therefore, that what is in a photograph is tied to a particular time and place, and that we can infer things about what is in a photograph without too much worry.

In fact, when we see photographs, we often infer quite a lot, probably not consciously, just because we know what it is to be in a photograph and what we assume about the photographic situation.

To start analyzing photographs, it's useful to see just how much we infer—and can infer—about almost any photograph.

We'll start analyzing photographs by using the example above.

■ When do you think this photograph was taken—both in year and season? Where might it have been taken—both a specific kind of place but also a general region?

■ What relationships might exist among these people?

■ What sorts of lives do these people live? What kinds of personalities do you imagine these people have?

■ Why do you think this photograph was taken?

Look at how much you were able to infer about this photograph, based on what you know about photographs, the world, and people's lives.

List what helped you make your inferences. Think about what you know about clothing—and how its style can reveal a time period and perhaps someone's class. Think about what you know about the occasions for taking photographs, and about photographic technologies (for example, how the look of this photograph probably helped you date it) and about people's ages and the ways they stand next to each other depending on the relationships they have.

HOW PHOTOGRAPHS WORK:
bodies and visual composition
VECTORS OF ATTENTION

You're probably wondering what all the people in the photograph to the left are looking at—and you've probably already made, as we discussed on the preceding page, a number of assumptions about where these people are and when this photograph was taken, and about the relationships among these people.

This is a fairly dramatic photograph for making the point we want to make here, but all photographs do this: all photographs direct your attentions by the way the people—or objects—in the photograph are arranged.

In this photograph, each person's body is turned to the right, as are the faces. The man is even pointing (and look how he is the tallest person in the photograph, with everyone else arranged around him: like us, you probably assume he is the father of this family, shepherding them carefully on a tour in a city, being responsible for directing their—and our—attentions).

Arrangements in photographs indicate lines of direction for our eyes to follow; these lines of directed attention can be called "vectors of attention" (or just "vectors"), and it is useful to look for them (and even draw them) in a photograph in order to see how the photograph has been arranged and how, therefore, the photographer is trying to direct our attentions, thoughts, and concerns.

Notice how vectors of attention work like the visual paths we described in posters—but note also that vectors of attention work within and across several photographs, not necessarily creating a clear, orderly path for your eye to follow from point of interest to point of interest, as we expect arrangements of words and photographs and/or drawings to do.

compose ▪ design ▪ advocate

You've probably made assumptions about when and where the photographs to the right were taken, and about the relations between the people shown—but notice also how your sense of the particular emotional quality of the relations between the people (and perhaps your sense of the character of the different individuals) probably connects to who is looking where in the photographs, that is, to the vectors of attention arranged in the photographs.

Notice how the assumptions you make about what vectors of attention tell us are based both on what you know because you have a body and also on what you know because you live with others. Because you have a body, you understand where your attentions are directed when you turn your eyes or body in a particular direction or you point or you bend your head in a certain way. Because you live with others in particular places and times, however, it is possible that assumptions you make about photographs of people who live in other places and times might not be (completely?) correct: your understanding of relations between people shown in photographs—based on your understanding of different bodily positions and ways of looking—might not be the same as the people who are in the photographs. They might have been posed by someone outside their culture (as in the case of these photographs), and their sense of relation to others might be based in understandings of religion or family different from yours.

Draw the vectors of attention in these three photographs.

▢ To read an article on how people in different cultures look at photographs differently, look in the online chapter 11 resources at www.ablongman.com/wysocki

■ **Discuss with others:** Because you live with others in a particular time and place, you know something about why you might direct your own attentions in a particular way: you know about relationships between others based on what you have learned about how particular people in your time and place (such as mothers) should or do act toward particular other people (such as children)—but do you think that what you know from your time, place, and experience necessarily or completely applies to the people in the photographs on the previous page? What kinds of judgments can you make about these photographs—and what kinds of judgments should you be careful about?

Based on what we have just written, there are several important things to note here about **how visual composition in general works:** first, it is hard sometimes to separate what we know because we have bodies from what we know because we live with others, and, second, sometimes we can't be sure if what we know because we live with others here and now applies to those who live in different times or places. It is important to keep these limitations in mind as we analyze photographs—or any kind of visual text—so that we do not make assumptions that we cannot support or that lead us in unfruitful or unhelpful directions.

There is something important to note here about vectors, too, and that is about **how vectors involve you (or not) in a photograph.**

Look back at the photographs on all the previous three pages and note how in some photographs some of the vectors of attention come directly out at you and how in other photographs you are not addressed directly by any of the vectors.

How is your sense of a photograph shaped when someone in the photograph is looking directly at you? How about when no one is looking at you?

When a vector of attention is directed toward the audience, it is a way for the photographer to pull you into the scene of the photograph, to build an (often) emotional connection between you and who or what is in the photograph. When the vectors of attention do not include you, you are an onlooker, an outsider, an observer, someone eyeing the relationships shown within the photograph by the vectors of attention among whoever is in the photograph.

Vectors of attention are thus about arrangement—the *logos* of a photograph—but also about emotional connections within the photograph as well as between the photograph and the audience—the *pathos* of the photograph. What the photograph shows certainly affects how you think about and respond to a photograph, but you cannot separate your responses from how the photograph's vectors direct your attentions and connect you to what the photograph represents.

HOW PHOTOGRAPHS WORK:
bodies and visual composition
FRAMING

Vectors are about choices a photographer makes in arranging the elements in a photograph; framing asks us to look at a photographer's choices about what to include (or not) in a photograph as she frames the photograph through a camera's viewfinder.

Take a minute or two to write down your assumptions and thoughts about the photograph above. Then, to see how framing directs our attentions, draw directly on the photograph: you don't need to do anything fancy, but just use a pen to extend out the objects and the head that are cut off by the frame. Try to draw the whole space in which this person is working, based on what you can see . . . then turn the page.

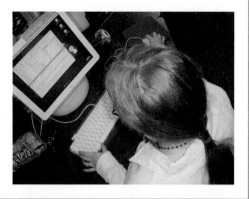

From the one photograph, were you able to guess the kind of space where the woman was working and who was around her? Notice how each of the photographs to the left places her in a different relationship with what is around her, giving you a different sense—were you to have only that photograph to go on—of the space and time.

Because it cuts off what is around a photograph when it is taken, framing focuses your attentions on parts of a situation; you rarely know what else was going on around the photograph.

Another thing to note about framing is how it arranges you as audience in relation to the photograph: you are asked to take on the physical perspective of the photographer relative to what's photographed.

When you are analyzing photographs, notice how close or far away you are placed as viewer. Notice also whether you are placed by the framing to be above or below what is shown or at the same height.

Each of these differences asks you to take up a different relation—intimate or distant—with what is shown, and so shapes how you are likely to respond.

compose ▪ design ▪ advocate

HOW PHOTOGRAPHS WORK:
bodies and visual composition
CROPPING

Vectors are about choices a photographer makes in arranging the elements in a photograph to direct our attention around (and sometimes outside) a photograph; cropping asks us to look at a photographer's choices in focusing our attention on certain aspects of a photograph.

Take a minute or two to write down your assumptions and thoughts about the photograph to the right . . .

. . . then look at the samples on the next page, all of which are simply different ways of cropping the photograph. Pick three or four of the photographs on the next page, and write for a minute or two about what they encourage you to think about generally, or what they encourage you to think about the people in the photograph.

Probably your writing will show that your sense of what each of these photographs is about will shift a fair amount depending on the cropping of the photograph.

Cropping is a very important choice that a photographer makes. For any photograph, it is important to ask what a photographer left out and consequently how she focused your attentions on what she chose to include.

After you look at the cropped photographs, do you see the original photograph in more detail, because you've looked more closely at parts of it? When you are thinking about how a photograph is arranged, try moving pieces of paper over it so that you crop it in different ways and see only parts of it; this can help you not only think about the photograph's cropping but also about how its details work together to make a whole.

And when you look at any photograph, you generally cannot tell whether you are seeing what the photographer saw through his viewfinder or what he cropped from a photograph. In either case, however, pay attention to how the framing or cropping positions you relative to what has been photographed. We pointed this out in our discussion of framing, but it is worth repeating because so much of how we respond to photographs depends on what is shown and the relationship we are asked to take with it.

For example, look at how the close photographs of hands and faces to the left can make you feel closer to the photograph—and so to the people. The cropped photographs can seem more intimate because they place you—as viewer—closer to what is shown.

Go back to the earlier pages of this chapter, and look at how the photographs have been framed or cropped to direct your attentions in particular ways. Draw on the photographs (or do this in your imagination) to think about what isn't included.

COMPLICATING MATTERS: adding time to photographs by making series

Frequently—but not always—photographs can seem to freeze time because they are small enough that it seems your eyes can take them in all at once. Although your eyes do move from element to element—person to person or facial feature to facial feature—and you do need time to look at a photograph, it can seem that the temporality of sequence or moving time is missing from a photograph.

In the rest of this chapter, we'll look at series of photographs; that is, we'll be looking at photographs that people have arranged to be seen together with other photographs, to have a larger or different effect than a single photograph. We could call these series visual essays.

We'll start by looking at a series we have made, to introduce ways of analyzing series of photographs. Then we'll look at several photographic series made by professional photographers.

compose ▪ design ▪ advocate

DOING RHETORICAL ANALYSIS:
Being a family in the United States in the early twentieth century

Here is one possible set of steps—based in the rhetorical process for analysis we described in the opening pages of Section 3—for analyzing the photographic essay on the preceding pages:

1 What do you think the piece's purpose, audience, and context are? Make your best guess—this is just a starting point. (For purpose and context, it's perfectly fine to start with something like, "Teaching people in a composition class to analyze photographic essays," but remember that there is also a title to the essay that indicates the essay is trying to do something more than just teach abstractly about visual essays.)

2 List the choices that you see the makers of this piece to have made. In terms of genre, you know they have chosen to make a photographic essay instead of a written essay or a video, for example. In terms of production and medium, they have chosen to use photographs that they didn't take but that they found (this is a likely inference because the photographs are from the early twentieth century; whoever took the photographs would have to have been minimally in their teens at the time—which would mean the photographer(s) would now be over 100). In terms of strategies and arrangement, use the methods of analy-sis we've laid out earlier in this chapter to say what you can about the photographs both individually and as a group:

- Use what you know (as on page 351) to say what you can about the time and place and people shown in each of the photographs. What are the people doing? What is the occasion of each photograph?

- Analyze the vectors and framing in each photograph to say what you can about how your attentions are directed in the individual photographs.

- What is in common among the photographs, in terms of time and place and people? What is different?

- How do the vectors of attention in the different photographs direct your attention among the photographs *as a group*? What relations are set up between the different photographs? How do the vectors direct your eyes among the photographs? In what order do you see the photographs? Why do you think the essay's composer would have chosen this arrangement, in terms of the purpose you are considering?

- How does the overall arrangement of all the photographs frame them for you as a whole? What other kinds of photographs could have been shown but aren't? What other kinds of people could have been shown but weren't, or what other kinds of familial situations?

3 How are the choices used strategically? Look at the (long) list of observations you've made about the choices the composers of this visual essay made. Why do you think they made the particular choices you've identified? How do you think the author or designer hoped the piece's audience would respond to the choice? How do the choices support your idea about the purpose of this essay?

4 Test your observations: Are there any anomalies? That is, are there choices that don't fit with your idea about the overall purpose of the piece? Do you need to enlarge your sense of purpose?

5 Revise your original statement about the purpose, audience, and context of this essay—that you made in step 1—to account for all the observations you made in steps 3 and 4. Try to account for the strategies you've identified in the piece.

BEING ISOLATED INSIDE THE PICTURE

an informal rhetorical analysis of the visual essay "Being a family in the United States in the early twentieth century"

As I was first looking at this visual essay, I was surprised by the picture of the family working. The pictures on the left are of families doing leisure things—as is the picture on the far right—and I realize that when I think about "family" I just pretty much picture in my head a mother and father and children doing family things together: eating, going on Sunday drives, watching television, or celebrating a holiday of some kind. At first I thought the family in the fourth picture was eating together because they were gathered around a table, but whatever they were eating is kind of strange: when I looked closer, it appeared to me as though they were assembling something, and I thought—given the way the room around them looks, which is not very fancy, with clothes hanging up above and everything pretty cluttered—that they must all have been working, even though the children all look like they are between 4 and 10 years old. Because this picture is so different from the others (it is also the only picture where the family is inside), it makes me wonder if the person who made this essay intended for this photograph to stand out in this way: because the photograph stands out, and makes me realize that I think about families as doing leisure or pleasant things together (and not working) the essay makes me wonder what else I take for granted about families, and what isn't shown here.

For example, I think that families are units to do things together, but in these photographs it's not just that families are doing things together; instead, they are all taking on similar behaviors. In all of the photographs except one (which I'll discuss in a moment), everyone has almost the same expression and is looking in the same direction; all the vectors of attention go to the same place. There is the family looking off into the sky together, the musical family looking at the photographer together, the family concentrating on their work, and the family in the grass all looking back to the left together. The one family that isn't all looking in the same direction appears to me to be the wealthiest family because of the way they are dressed; I am assuming (because the title tells us these photographs are about families) that this photograph shows a grown daughter with her parents. The father is in the middle with his arms around both women, but his head is turned to his wife; the women both look at the camera. The father looks as though he has just said something, and his wife has tilted her head to listen. The two women look almost like mirror-images of each other, like bookends to the father. This is the only family framed as though they are no place, not doing anything, just being for the camera or paying attention to each other—and this is also the only family where anyone has anything like a smile on their faces. One way I guess I could interpret this photograph, based on its differences from all the others, is that because these people are wealthy they do not have to focus together on the same things, that they just get to relax and be who they are without having to concentrate on something together. It's almost as though the other families have to work hard at doing the same things in order to hold together, to survive as families . . . and perhaps just to survive.

I'm also struck by how all the white families are on the left, while the one black family is off to the right but looking back in. The expressions on the different family members in this photograph are thoughtful and serious; I wonder what they would think were they really to find themselves in such a situation. The direction of their eyes asks me to look in the same direction and so I wonder what it would be like to be one of them, and to see all those other white families, and to be so separated. This makes me think again about families in the United States, and how different they are: how is it that we are all in the same place, but so different, as though each of the photographs in the essay contains its own little world, separated from the others. People can look across at each other, but the framing of all the photographs mostly holds them all in place, kind of stiffly.

Perhaps the person who composed this essay was aiming at that: perhaps the person is arguing that families in the early part of last century were separated, cut off from each other, because of having to be families in order to hold on together.

This preliminary analysis leaves me with several questions. Would it be possible to make a visual essay that showed people not being so separated by the boxy edges of the photographs? Would someone who didn't have my suburban background with my family see this differently? What kinds of families aren't included in this essay—and how would that change my sense of families, both then and now?

☐ If you want to experiment with composing your own documentary photograph essays, but do not have access to your own photographs—or want to work with older photographs—check out the links in the online chapter 11 resources at www.ablongman.com/wysocki

adding time to photographs by
making a series over several pages:
an excerpt from Gueorgui
Pinkhassov's *Sightwalk*

Imagine that you travel to a country where the people speak a language that's very different from yours. Sometimes you feel as though you understand what's going on (people take the subway to go to work and then go strolling for relaxation in the evenings afterward) but sometimes what seems familiar isn't quite (you go into a supermarket and think you know how it all works until you get to the checkout, where your purchases get put on a different table and no one bags them—and because no on speaks your language you have to watch to realize that you were supposed to have brought your own bags and bagged your things yourself). At the end of the day, you are exhausted—and exhilarated—by just how inexplicable the place can seem.

Imagine, then, that you wanted to give friends back home a sense of how being in this new place felt to you. You could write a letter, but you could also take photographs.

Gueorgui Pinkhassov was born in Moscow in 1952, and grew up, studied, and worked there for many years before moving to France. In 1996, he was invited to Tokyo—along with other photographers who had never been to that city before—to photograph the city as part of the European Union's Japan Fest. The pictures on the following pages come from Pinkhassov's visit to Tokyo.

As you look and observe what's repeated from photograph to photograph—as you observe, that is, how Pinkhassov is shaping and directing your attention—keep moving back and forth between asking yourself *what?* and asking yourself *how?*

What do you think Pinkhassov's purposes are in both the small arrangements of this sequence (the arrangements within photographs) and in the larger arrangements of the sequence? (*What* stances is he asking you to take as he asks you to look at the photographs? *What* attitudes toward Tokyo—or toward being new to Tokyo—is he shaping?) *How* is the way he has framed and arranged these photographs putting you into positions and stances and attitudes that encourage you to think as he might want you to think about these photographs and about being in Tokyo? (And what does the title of the overall collection of his photographs of Tokyo—*Sightwalk*—suggest about his purposes?)

compose ▪ *design* ▪ *advocate*

ANALYZING

Sightwalk excerpt

■ Discuss with others: Can you look at these photographs and know immediately what they are about and where they were taken? Can you tell easily in what sort of place the photographer was standing when he took the photographs? Why might a photographer choose to show photographs like this?

■ Discuss with others: Why do you think Pinkhassov chose not to include captions with these photographs?

■ Discuss with others: If the only knowledge you had of Tokyo was through these photographs, what would you know about the city?

■ Plan and write: If you were going to document the place where you live for people who had never been there so that they understood how the place looked, what would you photograph— and how would you photograph it? Why?

If you were going to document *the feeling* of living where you do, what would you photograph—and how would you photograph it? Why?

Given the two different purposes of the above photographic projects, develop a design plan for each.

■ Write: Imagine you had been on the trip to Tokyo with Pinkhassov and responded to Tokyo as he had. Write a short letter back home that tries to create through words what Pinkhassov creates with his photographs.

How is your word-description different from his photograph-description?

■ Plan and write: Collect brochures about the place where you live; Chambers of Commerce and Tourist Information offices usually have lots of brochures about local attractions and places to stay and eat. Analyze the brochures: what sense of the place where you live would they give to visitors who had never been there?

Write a short rhetorical analysis of the brochures. Do you think the brochures give visitors fair, accurate, and full senses of where you live? What is left out—and why? What is emphasized— and why? What would a series of brochures need to cover if they were to give someone as full a sense as possible of where you live?

■ Imagine: How would the sense of Tokyo that Pinkhassov gives us be different if the photographs were in a different order? Would the sense be different?

□ On the website for this textbook (www.ablongman.com/wysocki) there is a link to more of Pinkhassov's photographs, including to all of the photographs for *Sightwalk*.

ANOTHER WAY OF ORGANIZING
TIME—AND SPACE . . .
an excerpt from Josef Koudelka's *The
Black Triangle*

Where Germany, Poland, and the Czech Republic come together is a coal belt that people have been mining since the fifteenth century. The coal is soft, and doesn't produce as much heat as hard coal—but it does produce four times the sulfur when it burns. During the twentieth century, people worked tremendous strip mines (or "opencast" mines) in the area because it provided the least expensive local source of heat and power; the ready availability of power attracted many heavy industries to the area. Mountains ringing the area kept the resulting pollution in place.

The photographs on the next pages are Josef Koudelka's document of this triangle of land; the photographs come from an exhibition titled *The Black Triangle: The Foothills of the Ore Mountains*.

Koudelka was born in 1938 in a tiny village in the former Czechoslovakia. He worked for several years as an aeronautical engineer, all the while taking photographs. His first projects involved documenting the lives of the Gypsy communities in Czechoslovakia and Romania. He also published, anonymously and in Western news sources, photographs of the 1968 invasion of Prague by armies of the Warsaw Pact. He left Czechoslovakia in 1970 and gained asylum in England; he became a French citizen in 1987. He returned to the former Czechoslovakia for the first time in 1990, in part to document the Black Triangle, shown in the photographs on the next pages.

Out of the Black Triangle's open-cast mines came 75% of the former Czechoslovakia's brown coal, almost 70% of its electricity, and 80% of its refined oil.

compose ▪ design ▪ advocate

Yearly in the early 1990s these industries released into the air 400,000 metric tons of particulants and 700,000 metric tons of polluting gases. Sulfur. . .

dioxide levels were often almost double what the U.S. Environmental Protection Agency considered the highest acceptable level. Between 1972 and 1989,

compose ▪ design ▪ advocate

o% of the coniferous forests disappeared. Hospitals in the Czech part of the region had 12 times the number of sick children as the national average, and. . .

infant mortality was 40% higher than average. Infant birth weight dropped, as did the average adult life expectancy. At the end of the 1990s, the countries in

compose ▪ design ▪ advocate

...he area began to modernize power plants. By 2000, some air pollutants had been reduced by 90%.

The Black Triangle excerpt

■ Discuss with others: Use these questions to analyze Koudelka's photographs and arrangements:

- Why do you think Koudelka focuses on the place and not people?

- How do the captions underneath the photographs shape your responses to them?

- How would the sequence be different if the photographs were *not* shown as panoramas but were printed in the same proportions as most snapshots?

- Why do you think Koudelka presents these photographs in black and white rather than color?

- Where do these photographs position you as a viewer? Are you set up to feel outside the landscape or down in it?

■ Discuss with others: Imagine the sequence differently arranged—put the last photograph first and the first photograph last, for example. How would that change your understanding of the sequence? Does the sequence ask you to look down initially and then up, with hope, or always to look down at what is wrong?

■ Experiment: Copy the photographs and put different captions under them. Koudelka's captions ask you to think about what has happened in the past and how that is shaping the present; write captions that ask you to think about what *could* happen in this landscape. Try to come up with captions that change the tone of the photographs.

■ Discuss with others: Of his photographs, Koudelka says, "I don't think that Black Triangle is only about environmental issues. . . . In that landscape, you can see how strong Nature is. That it is stronger than man. That it cannot be destroyed."

How do his photographs show this side of nature? If you don't think they do, how would you change the photographs to emphasize the strength of nature?

❑ For a more recent view of the Black Triangle—including photographs— there is a link at the website for this textbook (www.ablongman.com/wysocki) to an online article, "Europe's Black Triangle Turns Green," by Ben Stutz at the National Resources Defense Council website.

There is also a link to more of Josef Koudelka's work—and all the photographs from Black Triangle—at the textbook website.

compose ▪ design ▪ advocate

thinking through production

■ If you have access to a camera and printing, compose your own photographic essay about an issue that matters to you. Your audience and context are your classroom, but consider carefully your purpose: what sorts of attitudes or ideas do you want others in class to take toward what matters to you? Plan out the arrangements of the individual photographs as best you can for your purpose, keeping framing, cropping, and vectors of attention in mind. Also think about how you can arrange the photographs, having in mind the kinds of considerations the photographers in this chapter did. Will you, for example, have photographs that repeat formats or use captions, as Koudelka does? Will you emphasize the viewer's response over what is being seen, as Pinkhassov appears to? (You can also arrange your photographs into an online essay, if you know how to work with digital photographs and webpages.)

Before you produce your essay, write up a design plan in which you use your statement of purpose to justify the choices you make in arranging your essay.

■ If you don't have a camera, use photographs you have from your family or from trips to make a photographic essay—or use photographs you cut from magazines you own. If you have access to the Web, or want to work with photographs from another time or with photographs you probably wouldn't be able to take even if you had a camera, use photographs you can download from government websites. (For the most part, these photographs are fair use, either because they were taken more than 75 years ago [the length of time that copyright now extends] or they were taken in the service of the U.S. government—which cannot copyright photographs or any document. The website for this book—www.ablongman.com/wysocki—has links to different government websites with photographs purposely made available for downloading.)

Look at the photographs available to you, and then compose a design plan and photographic essay as we described above.

■ In chapter 14, the essay "Higher Education" is accompanied by a number of photographs.

Using the analytic tools we introduce in this chapter—framing, cropping, and vectors of attention—analyze the photographs in the essay and the interview. Analyze the photographs both individually and as a collection. Also analyze the words in the essay and the interview: what overall arguments are being made with the words?

Write a rhetorical analysis comparing how photographs and words are played off each other in the essay and in the interview. How can photographs and words be used together to build arguments they can't build on their own? What strategies for using words and photographs together can you describe for your own future use?

□ There are more "Thinking Through Production" activities in the online chapter 11 resources at www.ablongman.com/wysocki

analyzing instruction sets

The purpose of instruction sets seems straightforward: they are to instruct you in doing something. But the purposes—and the contexts—of instruction sets get complex when you start thinking about all that people want or need to learn in the world: there are instructions for learning languages, tying shoes, making dinner, running nuclear power plants, putting out fires, and avoiding terrorist attacks—which is why it is in this chapter you will see the most varied-looking examples.

But perhaps what is most complex and challenging and interesting in instruction sets is their audiences. Whoever is making an instruction set has to decide how to think about and treat their audience in order best to achieve the purpose of the instructions. Should the instructions construe and treat the audience as passive, as people who know nothing and need a lot of simple help in learning whatever the instruction sets are teaching? Or should the audience be addressed by the text as complex and smart people who can, with a little help and suggestion, figure things out for themselves? What does the context suggest about how the audience can and should be treated? What about who the audience is, themselves?

We include instruction sets here for two reasons: first, because they combine words and photographs and drawings in ways that build directly out of posters and documentary photographs, and second, because they allow us to start thinking about how audiences are shaped by a composer's choice of strategies in a text.

The kinds of observations you can make about how instruction sets shape audiences rhetorically will help you as you analyze and make your own texts—of any kind.

■ Take 10 minutes to check your house or apartment: how many instruction sets can you find? Check bottles and boxes in the bathroom and kitchen (and don't forget cookbooks, if you have them). Check magazines you read that are about bodies or beauty. If someone from another planet were to do an archaeology of the instructions in your house, what conclusions might they draw about people surrounded by so many instructions? What sort of lives are shaped by all those instructions?

BEING AN AUDIENCE

In earlier chapters, we've talked as though composers of texts only ever respond to audiences, as though the decisions a composer makes in shaping a text are always in response to who a particular audience is. But the matter of audiences and texts is more fluid and far reaching than that. Composers of texts *do* have particular audiences in mind as they make texts, and they *do* shape texts to fit those audiences—but when a text is finished, whoever picks it up becomes, for the length of time of using a text, the audience. A reader has to step into the behaviors and attitudes that the text's composer has built into the text.

Think about playing a video game. In a game like *Grand Theft Auto*, for example, you cannot play as a poet or as a childcare worker; you can only play within the parameters established by the game, which (in this case) tend to ask audiences to be quick, decisive, and not particularly reflective about their actions: the point is to stay alive in a fast and hard world. *Any* text—no matter the medium or purpose—works similarly: the words or pictures or photographs or the interactions allow or encourage audiences to think or act in certain ways, sometimes subtle, sometimes not so subtle. And for the time you play or read or work with a text, you have to think or act within those parameters.

HOW WE ANALYZE INSTRUCTION SETS . . .

We probably don't need to repeat for you now the scheme we used for analyzing posters and documentary photographs: you probably know that we will proceed here by assuming that instruction sets—like posters and documentary photographs— can be analyzed rhetorically because they draw on *what we know because we have bodies* and *what we know because we live with others in specific places and times*. Because we can all count on people having some common experiences we can develop rules and guidelines that allow us to approach analysis and composition systematically.

In this chapter we proceed as in previous chapters: we start by offering analytic strategies for understanding texts, but we also in this chapter emphasize how audiences can be—to varied extents—shaped by the choices of strategy made by the composer of an instruction set.

Japanese Onomatopoetic Expressions

atsu atsu	Describes something that looks piping hot. Also used to describe a couple who are head over heels in love.
appu appu	Describes someone floundering in water and almost drowning. Also used to describe someone in trouble or difficulty. In deep water.
munya munya	Describes muttering something meaningless. Often used to describe sleep talking.
nyoro nyoro	Describes something long and thin, like a snake, moving along with a wriggling motion
nuku nuku	Describes having a feeling of warmth and comfort. Snugly. Costly.
uki uki	Describes someone who is happy and excited. In a buoyant mood.

page 35

HOW INSTRUCTION SETS WORK: DRAWING ON WHAT YOU KNOW

Imagine you have the purpose of helping English speakers learn Japanese, specifically Japanese onomatopoetic expressions—of which there are a lot. ("Onomatopoetic expressions" are expressions where a word sounds like what it means. In English, for example, the words *murmur*, *clang*, *purr*, *whirl*, *mumble*, *hush*, *squeak*, and *buzz* are onomatopoetic words.)

The page to the left shows one possibility for how you might design a page for a book for such instruction—if your purpose is only to instruct people by showing them a list to memorize. The page makes the words and their definitions clear and easy to read, and it is easy to match a word with its definition.

But what if you think of your purpose—in terms of your audience—a little more intricately and intimately, *based on what we know and have experienced about how we like to learn and how we learn effectively?* What if you think about how most people don't really enjoy memorizing lists, and how it is hard to memorize? What if you think about how learning different languages can be a little nerve wracking for some and that some gentle and inviting friendliness might help?

You might design a book that contains pages like those on our next two pages . . .

These two pages (like the words and definitions on the previous page) come from *An Illustrated Dictionary of Japanese Onomatopoetic Expressions*, published by the *Japan Times* in 1989 with illustrations by Taro Gomi. Notice how there is only one word per page, with a short definition; most of the page is taken up by a soft-edged, hand-drawn illustration. When you see these drawings, what bodily knowledge do they evoke? Is it the knowledge of using rulers to draw and make hard edges, or is it that of a relaxed and amused hand?

We think the book has been designed to charm, to encourage people to wander, stopping here and there, and to associate a drawing with a word. Notice also how the drawings help round out and make the meanings of the words concrete.

The pages do not have the order of a list, although the whole book does. Single-page lists *can* feel rigid, even with typefaces that look hand drawn, as in our made-up example. Instead, on these pages the illustrations rather than the words are made more visually prevalent—although the words and their definitions are certainly easy to find. (The letter in brackets following the words is a guide to pronunciation, explained in the book's introduction.)

A learner could still work through this book systematically, but the appearance of the pages also encourages a learner simply to remember words that stand out, and to remember words by remembering an interesting but friendly illustration.

suya suya [A]

Describes sleeping peacefully. Soundly.

すやすや

やすらかに眠っている様子。もっぱら、
眠る形容に用いる。

sura sura [A]

Describes something proceeding smoothly. Without a hitch. Often used to describe eloquent speech or writing.

すらすら

動作または物事が、よどみなく順調に進むさま。話す、書くなどの形容によく用いる。

Here is how we imagine the statement of purpose for this book might have looked:

Our audience is people learning Japanese. They might be enthusiastic about the language, but they might also be nervous about learning. They'll probably also not think of memorization as being the most pleasant way to learn. So we need to make something friendly and relaxed that will make them feel they are at home and comfortable even if they are in school. We're also teaching them a neat part of the language—words that sound like what they mean—so it probably would be helpful to instruct in some way that helps people almost hear the sound, some way that helps them remember more but that also has some pleasure in it so they'll want to learn.

What this particular set of instructions shows is how the various elements of a set of instructions—what is put on a page, where it is put, how illustrations are made, how much type is used—can shape how an audience approaches a text and how they are asked to act while using the text. The approach of *this* text is obviously not one to use everywhere and in all contexts, but it is a good place to begin thinking about how a composer's strategic choices in designing a text—how *your* choices in designing a text—establish the relationships audiences have with texts.

This set of instructions is from the book *Nomadic Furniture* by James Hennessey and Victor Papanek (New York: Pantheon Books, 1973).

This book uses some similar strategies as *An Illustrated Dictionary of Japanese Onomatopoetic Expressions*: the drawings are quite large, for example, and look hand drawn rather than computer-aided. But there are differences; use these questions to help you do an informal rhetorical accounting for them:

- Given the overall look of these pages and of the words, what would you say the purpose is? "Helping people build inexpensive furniture" is part of the purpose, for sure, but what sort of attitudes toward materials and toward the work of building furniture are being advocated? Look at the words, and specifically at the adjectives being used: *simplest, intelligent, colourful, comfortable, elegant*.

- Look at the tone of voice of the words, which is informal ("It may not be the most comfortable chair in this book . . .") and refers to the authors by nickname ("Vic"). What sorts of relations does this tell you these authors hope to establish with their audience through how they have composed this text?

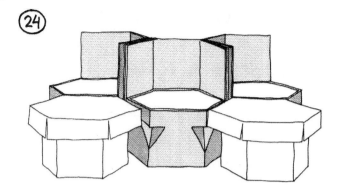

(24)

↰ IN THE MID-SIXTIES, PETER RAACKE DEVELOPED THESE HEXAGONAL SEATING UNITS IN GERMANY. THEY ARE QUITE UNCOMFORTABLE. NONETHELESS WE ARE SHOWING THEM HERE, BECAUSE HEXAGONS ARE AN INTELLIGENT WAY OF "CLOSE~PACKING" SPACE. SO TRY YOUR OWN (& HOPEFULLY COLOURFUL) VARIATIONS OF THE ABOVE.

FOR THIS BOOK, VIC SPECIFICALLY INVENTED THE SIMPLEST POSSIBLE CHAIR THAT COULD BE MADE OF SINGLE~CORRUGATED CARDBOARD, WITHOUT ANY RIVETS, GLUE, FASTENERS OR EVEN TABS. ↘

IT MAY NOT BE THE MOST COMFORTABLE CHAIR IN THIS BOOK, BUT IT IS THE MOST "ELEGANT" IN TERMS OF MATERIAL USE. MOST IMPORTANT → IT IS DINING OR DESK~WORK HEIGHT. NATURALLY IT FOLDS ABSOLUTELY FLAT. HOW TO MAKE IT IS SHOWN ON THE NEXT PAGE.

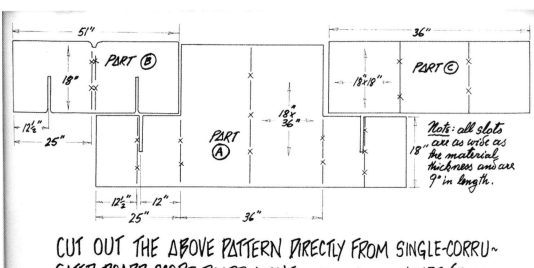

CUT OUT THE ABOVE PATTERN DIRECTLY FROM SINGLE-CORRU-GATED BOARD. SCORE BOARD ALONG —×—×—×— LINES (DON'T CUT ALL THE WAY THROUGH!). FIRST FOLD PART Ⓐ. NOW FOLD PART Ⓑ AND INSERT IN Ⓐ. THE STRUCTURE IS NOW SELF~STABILIZED. NOW FOLD Ⓒ AND JUST LAY IT ON CROSS FORMED BY Ⓐ & Ⓑ. ADD CUSHION.

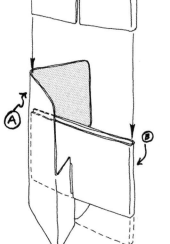

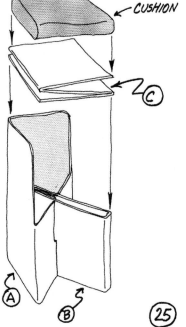

㉕

- Why do you think both the words and the illustrations are hand drawn? Imagine the pages with formal print typography—how would that change the attitude you are being encouraged to take toward this work and furniture?

- Imagine not only that these words and illustrations were produced more formally, but also that the layout was more formal, with the hard left and right edges that can characterize pages of print, and with all the illustrations arranged in numbered order in small boxes. What sort of attitude—creative? distant? precise?—would such a layout encourage you to take toward making furniture?

- Do you think you could follow the instructions for building the chair on page 25? Do the illustrations help you visualize the steps to take? How could you make the steps more complex—or more simple? (How would the steps change your sense of this text were they in a numbered list?)

- Use all your responses to the questions above to draw up the statement of purpose (pulling in your sense of audience and context for these instructions) you think these designers might have used as they were composing this text.

AN INSTRUCTION SET FOR COMMUNICATING WITH OTHERS . . .

These instructions come from the handbook *Arabic Calligraphy: Naskh Script for Beginners*, whose text and calligraphy are by Mustafa Ja'far (New York: McGraw-Hill, 2002).

■ As with the preceding instructions, start your analysis by noting what you think to be this writer's sense of purpose.

■ To deepen that sense of purpose, observe how the words operate here. How is a reader addressed by these words? Do the words command you harshly to do things or do they guide you politely or . . . ?

■ Do these words shape you as someone who can do this work competently or as a goof up? For example, how might this— "Follow these five steps to prepare your first reed pen"—strike a reader, compared to this— "If you follow these steps correctly, steps recommended by experts, you might be able to prepare a decent reed pen." Try rewriting other sentences to see how different constructions of words shape readers to feel more or less able.

Getting started

Today, when it comes to calligraphy tools, we are spoilt for choice. Art shops offer a variety of writing implements, with nibs of steel, glass, nylon fibres, etc, in many different shapes and sizes. But the best tool for Arabic calligraphy was, and still is, the reed pen. It is not only more practical than most of the ready-made pens, but it is cheaper too. It allows you to create a writing implement that suits your own hand posture and writing angle, rather than having to adapt your hand to a ready-made pen. The ideal reed, which grows in swamps and shallow waters, is prepared only when it is completely dry. It is cut with a heavy-duty knife or scalpel.

Follow these five steps to prepare your first reed pen.

Writing angle

Before you tackle the alphabet, test your pen by drawing some diamond-shaped dots. The pen should rest comfortably between the lower knuckles of the thumb and the first finger, as in the illustration. Press the pen diagonally on the paper and pull it in the direction of the arrows. When you manage to draw a diamond-shaped dot with a single short diagonal stroke that means you are holding your pen correctly. If not, try

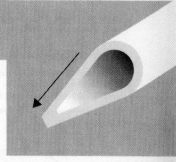

Select a reed stem and cut it to the length of a pen (about 20 cm). The diameter should be around 1cm. If you do not have access to suitable reeds, you can use small bamboo sticks available at garden centres or buy a ready-cut reed pen from an art shop that specializes in calligraphy materials and recut it to the appropriate angle.

Work at the end furthest from any bulge. Hold the reed firmly and cut away a long scoop using a sharp knife or scalpel.

again. Make sure the full width of the slanted nib is touching the paper and that your pen is moving in the direction of the arrows. This is the basic writing angle, but when you begin to copy individual letters or words you will find that a certain amount of pen manipulation is necessary to achieve a pleasing contrast of stroke widths.

Ink and ink jar

Inks suitable for practising include black Indian ink, Rotring black drawing ink, and any calligraphy ink. In order not to flood the pen you need to make an ink jar. Find a small watertight jar or plastic film container. In the past calligraphers placed a small wad of raw-silk fibres inside the jar, but nowadays a small piece of nylon tights or stockings does just as well. Push this into the jar and pour in enough ink to be completely absorbed by the fabric. No excess ink is required, as the source of ink must be the ink-dampened fabric. This prevents overloading the pen and creating unsightly blobs.

Guidelines

To prepare your practice sheet, use a soft pencil to draw the base line (middle line). Then draw the upper and lower lines at equal distances from the base line using the height of the letter *alif* as a guide. In Naskh script the height of *alif* should equal five dots of your pen placed one on top of the other. Use a white fairly smooth matt paper for practising.

Stroke-by-stroke guide

The unique stroke-by-stroke instructions on the following pages show you the best way of writing each letter of the alphabet. Try to write slowly, following the instructions, and moving your pen in the direction of the arrows.

To create the shoulders, make a cut on each side, taking care to create an end with parallel sides. Aim for a nib width of about 4 mm or less.

Place the reed on a hard surface. Make a slit down the middle of the the nib. No slit is required if the width of the nib is less than 4 mm.

Proportions

Proportioned letters like this are designed to help you appreciate the correct shape of each letter. The diagonal-shaped dot represents one full pen width, while the circle indicates half that width. The proportions should serve as a guide only and need not be strictly adhered to.

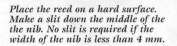

Learning stages

As a beginner, your learning process should be divided into three basic stages, as in this booklet:

1 *Mufradāt* single letters (pages 8-18)
2 *Murakkabāt* joined letters (pages 19-21)
3 *Kalimāt* words (pages 22-25)

You should only move to the next stage when you feel comfortable with the previous one.

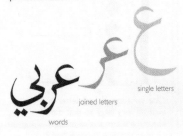

single letters

joined letters

words

Extra effort!

Do not despair if you find these four letters extremely difficult to write. They are indeed considered the most arduous of all the letters, and beginners should give them extra effort.

Cut the nib to an angle of about 45˚. The angle will depend on your hand and you may have to recut the nib to achieve a satisfactory writing angle. Dip the pen in the ink jar and allow it to absorb plenty of ink before you start.

- What values are espoused by the words of these instructions? For example, what is the writer of these words hoping his readers will think about their work when he uses phrases like "unsightly blobs" or "pleasing contrast"? Can you find other expressions that teach value? (And how overtly are these values taught? Does the writer ever say, "I want you to learn to be a neat and elegant calligrapher"?)

- Look at the typefaces that are used, and their alignment. (If you do not have words for talking about these things, look at pages 279–284 and 295–304 in chapter 9.) Is the typeface hard and formal, or soft and informal? How would the columns of type look different if they were fully justified (that is, if their right edge was a straight line just like the left edge)?

- Do the bold headers in the text help you find what you imagine an audience will need to know?

- Look at the words and illustrations together, and their arrangements. Is this a rigid arrangement with everything in well-delimited rows? Just what adjectives would you use to describe this arrangement? What sort of attitude—rigidity? creativity? fear?—toward this calligraphic work does this arrangement as a reader to take on?

- Now focus just on the illustrations in these pages. How would photographs instead of drawings change your sense of these pages? What sort of mood do the drawings encourage? Are they hard or soft drawings? What does this tell you about how the designer of this text was thinking about the audience's state of mind about this work?

- Is there anything else about these pages that stands out to you, that seems important to what the composers of this text were hoping to accomplish?

Stage One: *Mufradāt* single letters

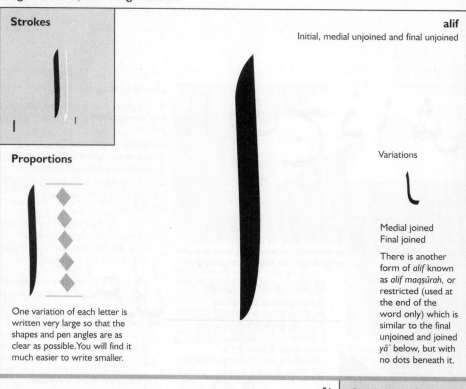

Strokes

Proportions

One variation of each letter is written very large so that the shapes and pen angles are as clear as possible. You will find it much easier to write smaller.

alif
Initial, medial unjoined and final unjoined

Variations

Medial joined
Final joined

There is another form of *alif* known as *alif maqṣūrah*, or restricted (used at the end of the word only) which is similar to the final unjoined and joined *yā'* below, but with no dots beneath it.

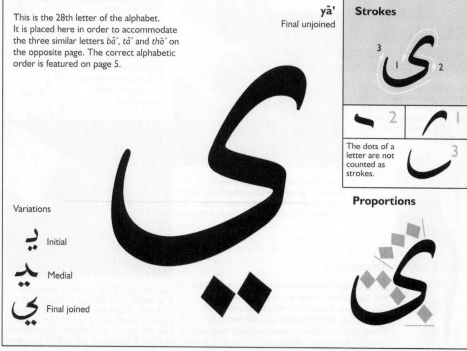

This is the 28th letter of the alphabet. It is placed here in order to accommodate the three similar letters *bā'*, *tā'* and *thā'* on the opposite page. The correct alphabetic order is featured on page 5.

yā'
Final unjoined

Variations

ﻳ Initial

ﻴ Medial

ﻲ Final joined

Strokes

The dots of a letter are not counted as strokes.

Proportions

bā'
Final unjoined

ب

ب ب ب
Final joined Medial Initial

Strokes

2 ب 1

ا

ب

Proportions

◆◆◆◆◆ ◆
ب ◆
◆

tā'
Final unjoined

ت

Variation of the letter:
same as **bā'**, but with two dots above and no dot below

thā'
Final unjoined

ث

Variation of the letter:
same as **bā'**, but with three dots above and no dot below

9
السلسلة التاسعة

We've just asked you a lot of questions, but they ought to help you do this next step:

■ Use all your responses to the questions above to draw up the statement of purpose (pulling in your sense of audience and context for these instructions) you think these composers might have used as they were designing and producing this text.

■ Use the statement of purpose you develop to try to explain why the composers of this text used this medium—a booklet rather than, say, a series of cards or a video—and these arrangements to carry out their purpose.

If you respond to all the various questions we've asked you about these last two instruction sets, you will have done rhetorical analyses of both sets.

ANOTHER INSTRUCTION SET FOR COMMUNICATING WITH OTHERS . . .

Here is another example for helping an audience learn a new way to communicate—in this case, that new kind of communication is the Navy Semaphore Flag Code. *Semaphore* is communication with flags: someone holds a flag in each hand and signals letters of the alphabet by the positions in which the flags are held. Semaphore has been used when people can see each other but are at too far a distance—or there is too much noise—to hear. The Department of Navy Personnel published this device in the 1940s; someone turns the dial (as the instructions say), and the different letters are indicated through cut-out windows.

■ As with the preceding examples, the *basic* purpose of this instruction set is clear: it is to teach people semaphore. But how do you account for this instruction set being an interactive dial device instead of, say, a sheet of paper with all the codes printed on it in a grid?

What ideas about audience—and about the kind of relationship with an instruction set that best helps an audience learn something particular—do you think the designers of this device had as they were working so that they made something that requires the audience to hold it and interact with it?

instruction sets for living with and communicating with others

■ **Discuss with others:** Imagine the *Nomadic Furniture* and *Arabic Calligraphy* instruction sets in other media such as video or webpages or . . . How would a change in media change the relations these instruction sets establish with their audiences?

■ **Writer:** Based on the preceding instruction sets and using whatever vocabulary you have from other chapters of this book and your own experience, make a list of recommendations anyone composing instruction sets ought to keep in mind. Consider the elements we've discussed so far in this chapter: consider the tone of voice you'd recommend in the writing as well as the values you'd encourage; consider the style and kind of illustration (photograph or drawing or . . .); consider the arrangement of elements on a page (or screen . . .); consider the medium to use, and so on.

Use your guidelines to critique other instruction sets. Does your critique show you that you need to add anything more to your guidelines?

■ **Write:** Using the examples of this chapter, and using whatever media you can defend as an appropriate choice, develop a full design plan for an instruction set that would help someone new move as gracefully and comfortably as possible into a situation you know well. For example, how would you help first-year students understand dorm life, or someone who has converted to your religion and church understand the rituals, or a video-gamer-wannabe comprehend the dense levels of play of *your* game? Do any general approaches to audiences and instruction sets develop in your work?

■ **Discuss with others:** Which of the instruction sets in this chapter address you in ways that encourage you to feel smart and competent in what you do? Which address you in other ways? Which address you as a complex being, and which ask you to think of yourself in simple or stark terms? Do these methods of address seem appropriate for their contexts? Do you want to be the people shaped in this way?

INSTRUCTION SETS FOR DANGEROUS CONTEXTS . . .

We hope this never happens: *You walk into your kitchen and the wires at the back of the stove are sparking, and it looks as though the wall might catch fire.* We'd all like to think that we'd be cool and calmly pick up the fire extinguisher that we all keep in the kitchen and that we'd then—without having to read the extinguisher's instructions—put out the fire.

The best way you can prepare yourself for such a situation is to practice using a fire extinguisher (which means you have to buy two—since each is only good for one use—and practice with one while keeping the other for emergencies). But chances are, unfortunately, that you, like us, have never done this—so you are going to have to read the instructions for the extinguisher in order to put out the fire. Do you want the instructions to go into fine detail about just how and why the extinguisher is shaped as it is? Do you want the instructions to have 12 steps? Do you want them to be artistically designed or in the media of an interactive guide wheel like the semaphore instructions? Do you want them to tell you what will happen if you don't get it right?

On the next page are instructions scanned off the box of a fire extinguisher.

It's easy to use a KIDDE fire extinguisher.
Just remember "PASS"
(PULL ▶ AIM ▶ SQUEEZE ▶ SWEEP)

PULL
Pull the pin on the fire extinguisher.

▼

AIM
Aim the fire extinguisher at the base of the fire (standing six feet away from fire).

▼

SQUEEZE
Squeeze the handle of the extinguisher.

▼

SWEEP
Sweep the fire extinguisher left to right while aiming at base of fire.

CAUTION: Contents Under Pressure. Do Not Incinerate.

A FIRE EXTINGUISHER

These instructions are from the fire extinguisher box in our kitchen. There are also instructions on a sheet of paper inside the box as well as instructions printed on the extinguisher itself (as the photograph at the beginning of this chapter shows). The company that made the extinguisher wants to be sure we can find the instructions when we need them.

What attitude do the composers of these instructions hope their audience will have if they encounter fire? We think this attitude is shown by what is in the instructions as well as by what is not.

First, note the color blue, which we can associate with water, calm, pretty days—soothing things. These instructions are not out to excite us any more than we already will be in the context.

We note the "Easy to Use" promise, repeated twice.

We note the photograph of the woman using the extinguisher. She has a calm face and her body posture is calm (notice how we are drawing here on what we know because we have bodies). She is in a neat, clean kitchen, and there are no flames— why do you think that is?

Photographs and illustrations are all carefully aligned, keeping the elements neatly arranged, as though this situation is arrangeable, controllable.

The sequential steps for using the extinguisher are not numbered, but we know they are sequential because of their vertical arrangement and the blue arrows. The steps are also presented as a simple acronym, **PASS—PULL, AIM, SQUEEZE, SWEEP,** suggesting the process is simple and easy to remember. The instructions for the steps are each only one sentence long, again telling us this process is simple.

The photographs of the four steps are taken not in the kitchen shown above but in a neutral background. There is therefore no extraneous detail to distract us from the actions being described, nor is there any flame to frighten us.

The instructions for the fire extinguisher are (we believe) designed to keep us calm and feeling confident if ever we need to use the fire extinguisher. (Notice how it was helpful, even in such a quick analysis, to think about how what we are analyzing could be different: we noticed that there are no flames shown, no extraneous detail—but we could also have imagined that the background color for the instructions were red or that the woman's face shook with fear. Any time you are stuck trying to analyze what a text's composers are trying to achieve, imagine the text with different colors or typography or photographs or . . . You will quickly see how a change in strategy can reveal what composers are trying not to do.) These instructions, with their simple layout and everything simply contained and controlled, are intended to help us believe that fires can be a simple matter and that—if we stay calm and follow instructions—we'll be fine.

compose ▪ design ▪ advocate

Now look at these instructions, in their original language and translated, below. (Remember that Arabic languages—and so the order of illustrations—are written right-to-left.) Are these instructions intended to help you feel calm and collected? These instructions are the front and back of one of the many flyers the U.S. military dropped—in the millions—over Iraq in the lead up and during the war in March 2003.

You may say these flyers do not have the form of instruction: these flyers, after all, do not tell someone how to do something, but rather give a choice with "You Decide." But look how the words and the illustrations play off each other: on the front of the flyer, there is (we are told) the Arabic equivalent of "If" over the illustration of a man shooting artillery at a plane (which we must assume is intended to be read as a U.S. plane); then there is an illustration of the plane firing back at the artillery, with the logical connector "Then" printed over it, as though the firing back necessarily and always will happen if the plane is fired upon. On the back is an illustration of the explosion we are to assume results from the plane's missile hitting the artillery—with no human visible, so that we assume he has been killed—with "You Decide."

If a reader believes this flyer—that U.S. planes will in every case take out enemy artillery—then the decision being offered is between life and death. This instruction set, with its explosion and flames, is intended therefore as an instruction to Iraqis on how to stay alive.

The instructions for using the fire extinguisher are likewise intended to help keep someone alive, through visual strategies of keeping an audience calm. This second set of instructions, on the other hand, is intended to keep people alive (both Iraqis and U.S. military), but now through strategies that are intended to terrify—an illustrated sequence of promised death.

On the next page is another instruction set intended (we think) to persuade us that, if we follow the instructions, if we accept the attitudes offered and implied, we can survive a dangerous situation. These instructions were developed by the U.S. Department of Homeland Security. Analyze these instructions rhetorically to understand how they are intended to persuade us, who they ask us to be, and how we are to think about and act in the face of this kind of danger.

ANOTHER INSTRUCTION SET FOR DANGEROUS CONTEXTS . . .

▓ Why might this site be named "READY.GOV"? Why do you think the name appears at the top, with the government seal? What sort of authority might be being built here? Why the flag, the face?

▓ Why do you think the colors of this instruction set are primarily blues (with a lot of soft blue), with some bits of red, orange, and yellow?

▓ Why do you think there are five steps, instead of two or fifteen? Why are the steps short declarative statements with few descriptive adjectives?

▓ Why might this site use line drawings instead of photographs?

▓ Think back to the layout of the pages from the *Nomadic Furniture* or the *Arabic Calligraphy* instructions, in which the elements on the page are arranged more loosely than on this webpage. This page has its elements arranged in a geometric grid, with everything neatly and linearly ordered. Are explosions—and escaping explosions—neat and orderly events? Why then would the elements of this page be so orderly?

compose ▪ design ▪ advocate

thinking through production

- If you have access to a camera, redo the "If there is an explosion" instruction set using photographs instead of simple drawings. Make two sets: with one, make the photographs as neutral as you can; with the other, make the instructions as frightening as possible. What does doing this tell you about using photographs in such contexts? How do the two versions affect your sense of your ability to respond were you ever to be in an explosion?

- Using whatever media you have available to you, produce an instruction set that is meant to make its audience feel utterly and absolutely helpless, incapable of doing what it is they are supposed to be doing. You could make instructions for tying shoes or composing a rap or making a particular dinner or going on a date or constructing a child's toy. From doing this, can you make recommendations about what you probably never want to do in an instruction set? Can you think of contexts in which it might be appropriate to try to make an audience feel helpless?

- Choose a textbook from any class that you think could better support you in your learning (we hope you don't choose this textbook). Analyze the textbook using all the different kinds of observation we've used here (and you might make other observations beyond the ones we've made, such as where illustrations are placed relative to where they are mentioned in the text, or the size of type, or whether there are useful headers, and so on). Pick several representative pages from the textbook, and redesign the pages so that they encourage you to feel smart and competent. (This is an effective—if somewhat time-hungry—way to study in a course in which you are having trouble. To redesign a text, you have to read it carefully, but—more importantly—the process of taking it apart and putting it back together differently will help you better understand what is going on in the text and will also help you feel more confident with the material because you will feel less powerless in the face of it.)

- The observations you've made in this chapter—about how an instruction set's strategies, arrangements, and media encourage certain thinking and behaviors—are not limited to instruction sets. Choose a communication situation coming up for you in the future (or imagine you are giving a presentation to the local school board recommending that retired people come into elementary schools to read to children, or you are writing a letter to your school newspaper about a current strike by service workers on your campus). How would you like your audience in this situation to think or feel or behave while you are presenting or they are reading? What strategies and arrangements can you take or modify from this chapter to help you be as effective? Write down your statement of purpose, and then write down the strategies you could take from this chapter.

- There are more "Thinking Through Production" activities in the online chapter 12 resources at www.ablongman.com/wysocki

analyzing
editorial & opinion pieces

CHAPTER 13

People have always wanted the news. And with news comes opinions.

Before the invention of the printing press, handwritten newsletters—containing information about events, places, and people—circulated among merchants in Europe, who passed them back and forth as they traveled from market to market. After the invention of the printing press, people published news pamphlets and broadsides (you'll see an eighteenth century example in this chapter), but only irregularly, about particular events. It was in England in the seventeenth century, in London, that regularly published newspapers were first printed.

Newspapers, like posters, thus came to the shape we recognize as a result of technologies and publics. For regularly published newspapers to make sense, there had to be enough people in one place—a city like London, then the largest in the world—and a means of reproduction that was fast, cheap, and reliable enough to print newspapers. (In the mid-nineteenth century presses were developed that could print 10,000 copies of a newspaper in one hour.)

From the beginning of regularly published newspapers, editorials have been a part. "Editorials" are so named because they are written by the editors of newspapers (or magazines); editors are the people responsible not only for the news being correct but for also deciding the approach—conservative? liberal? or . . .?—a newspaper will take. Editorials are meant to represent the opinion of the newspaper and have the authority of the newspaper behind them.

But others contribute their opinions to newspapers and magazines as well—hence "opinion pieces," which often are structured similarly to editorials (which structure we'll discuss in this chapter)—but they are written by individuals who most often claim no authority beyond being a member of a particular community.

And now we have newspapers and magazines—and so editorials and opinion pieces—on the World Wide Web.

HOW WE ANALYZE EDITORIAL AND OPINION PIECES

Because opinions are being expressed—and argued—in this chapter more explicitly than in earlier chapters, prepare to encounter ideas that may not sit well with you. The point of looking at these opinions is not to make up your mind right away whether you agree or disagree, but first to see how these arguments are constructed, and what they ask you to do and whom to become.

Also, recognize that your responses to these essays come because, unlike many of the examples in these chapters, a lot of these editorials and opinions are directed at you: many of the writings in this chapter have a general audience of people living in the early twenty-first century in the United States. You can analyze these writings as though you—and not someone else—are addressed by them, because you are.

THE PURPOSE OF EDITORIAL AND OPINION PIECES , and the consequent general characteristics of editorial and opinion pieces

Editorial and opinion pieces help us communicate with each other about what we ought to do, about what specific actions we ought to take.

This is *writing as deliberation*: we use this writing to deliberate over possible future actions. Such writing is also sometimes *writing as judgment*, asking us to decide whether our actions in the past have been correct.

In such editorial and opinion pieces, we are addressed always as members of some community: we may be addressed as citizens of our village, town, city, county, state, or country; we may be addressed as members of a church or of a civic or advocacy organization. And when we are so addressed, we are most often being addressed by someone who situates her- or himself within the same community, who wants to show us that, given our common goals within our community, there is some action that ought to follow logically out of those goals, given some particular context.

This is public writing, meant to bind us together more strongly, for some length of time, into one of the particular communities in which we circulate so that we will act together.

Because this public writing is most often about trying to persuade others to particular action, this kind of writing usually involves a more explicit statement of arguments than the previous examples. And because this kind of writing requires writers to show that they are in the same kind of community with their readers with the same kinds of concerns, this kind of writing can help us see strategies writers use to present themselves in their writing, in order to persuade us that we can trust them or ought to listen closely.

In this chapter, then, we focus on the following kinds of strategies in composing a text:

- How writers persuade us that we ought to read them attentively and be open to being persuaded by them. In other words, we will be focusing on *ethos* in this chapter, as we described it in chapter 4.

- How writers appeal to our values and beliefs, which can often be a matter of emotion—or *pathos*.

- How writers structure arguments following particular kinds of forms—or the *logos* of these kinds of arguments.

- How writers work to build communities with others through what they write.

compose ▪ design ▪ advocate

THINKING ABOUT EDITORIAL AND
OPINION PIECES through the scheme
we've been using in earlier chapters . . .

How we understand editorial and opinion pieces because we live in particular times and places . . .

Because editorial and opinion pieces are deliberative, as we've described on the preceding page, they ask audiences to act. Writers of such pieces have to persuade their audience that the actions they advocate are worth taking on—which means that these writers must appeal quite directly to the values and beliefs of their audience. Before they write, these writers must therefore pay particular attention to their times and places, to who values or believes what, and why. (If you read editorials in newspapers from even ten years ago, or read editorial in texts from communities different from those with which you are familiar, you might be struck by how values and beliefs shift over even small differences in time and space.)

But editorial and opinion pieces do more than respond to the values and beliefs of a community: they actively shape them. Because those who write editorial and opinion pieces can emphasize only some of the values and beliefs of a community, and because they often connect those values and beliefs together in new ways to argue why their audiences should act in particular ways in a particular time, they can create new values and beliefs or shift relations between values and beliefs. By emphasizing some things over others, they can redefine what a community cares about.

How we understand editorial and opinion pieces because we have bodies . . .

Values and beliefs are ideas, but they are not things we keep in the cool dryness of our minds: as much as they are intellectual constructs, values and beliefs are emotional, too, and they dwell in our hearts and bodies. Values and beliefs result from how and with whom we grew up, and what the people around us think and feel and do. When we discuss values and beliefs about which we care strongly we often have bodily responses: we can shake, forget to breathe or breathe quickly, we can jump up and down, we can sweat, we can yell or become silent.

Editorial and opinion pieces are precisely about what we value and what we believe—and so they appeal to our emotions as well as to our intellects. It is important to be alert, then, to how the examples of this chapter—or any editorial or opinion piece you read—address your emotions as well as your intellect. Because we discuss our emotions much less than our thinking and because we generally know less about how our emotions play out in us and connect up with the emotions of others, we need to attend to how editorial and opinion pieces address us emotionally in order to be sure that we are willing to have our values and beliefs—and our emotions—shaped in the ways that a text asks.

To the left is a broadside (and a small excerpt), which is any publication on a large sheet of paper (generally broadsides were printed on one side only). Broadsides were posted in public places so that many people could see them, and they carried information about meetings or things for sale; they also carried—as in this case—opinion.

In this particular broadside, published November 5, 1799, by Thomas Cooper, the editor of the *Sunbury and Northumberland Gazette* of Pennsylvania, Cooper gives his judgment of then-president John Adams, criticizing him for "a stretch of authority which the Monarch of Great Britain would have shrunk from; and interference without precedent, against law and mercy!"

We found this broadside in the collections of the National Archives of the United States, where it has been stored because it was used as evidence against Mr. Cooper when he was charged by the United States with sedition for his criticism of the president. At his trial, Cooper defended himself on the grounds of the First Amendment's protections of free expression, but—given the political climate of his time—he was found guilty, fined $400, and sent to prison for six months; he was later pardoned by Thomas Jefferson.

To the PUBLIC.

Nor do I see any impropriety in making this request of Mr. Adams: at that time he had just entered into office: he was hardly in the infancy of political mistake: even those who doubted his capacity, thought well of his intentions. He had not at that time given the public to understand that he would bestow no office but under implicit conformity to his political opinions. He had not yet declared that "a republican Government may mean any thing": he had not yet sanctioned the abolition of trial by Jury in the Alien law, or entrenched his public character behind the legal barriers of the Sedition law. Nor were we yet saddled with the expence of a permanent navy, or threatened under his auspices with the existence of a standing army. Our credit was not yet reduced so low as to borrow money at 8 per cent. in

compose ▪ design ▪ advocate

We show you this broadside not only to demonstrate how opinions made public (remember that "publication" simply means to make something public) can have strong consequences but also that those consequences depend on the contexts in which opinions are published. If Cooper had not published his broadside at a time when there was tension in the country—and in the government—over the degree of the government's authority, his broadside might have been seen simply as opinion and not as words meant to incite others to revolution.

Because anyone who publicizes her or his opinions—like all the writers in this chapter—risks the strong responses of others, writers of editorial and opinion pieces put themselves at risk. The risk can simply be nasty or thoughtless responses from others, but it can also be—as for Thomas Cooper—imprisonment. There are several things to note about this risk:

- Writers of editorial and opinion pieces have to attend very carefully to the contexts in which they publish their opinions if they are to be persuasive.

- We readers of editorials and opinion pieces—if we value our own rights to hold our opinions—can help shape the contexts in which opinions appear by insisting on the rights of everyone to opinion, no matter how unpopular.

THE MEDIA AND PUBLICATION OF OPINION PIECES AND EDITORIALS

We also show you Cooper's broadside because it looks different from today's newspapers. We recognize how its columns resemble the columns of today's newspapers, but were you to be able to read it (were this book the size of a poster), you'd see how different the writing is. And were you to travel back in time to see this broadside posted on a building wall in a small town, with people clustered around it, reading, you'd be struck by how differently our media and their methods of publication ask us to read each other's public words.

On some college campuses today there are spots where people speak their minds publicly, and there are traditions of posting news and events on telephone poles and campus bulletin boards—but mostly we get our news alone, with a newspaper and, increasingly, online.

Because so many newspapers now publish online or are archived in online versions for researchers, we use this section (in addition to everything else) to think a bit about how words look on the Web.

We have not magically embedded a working Web browser into the following pages (although people are working on developing digital paper; see www.wired.com/wired/archive/9.04/anoto.html or www.slais.ubc.ca/courses/libr559a/winter2000/resources/epaper.htm)—but we wanted to include editorials that we found online. We made

screenshots of various editorials in order to translate them to print but still keep a flavor of reading online in their original contexts; in so doing, we kept some of the lines from a preceding page on each page, so that you could keep your place.

As you read the "online" texts, think about what it is like to read online (if this is something you do) as compared to reading on paper; ask these questions to help you think about differences and similarities between the context of reading online and the context of reading print material, especially books and magazines:

- How is scrolling through a one-screen online text different from turning the pages of a book?

- How is following links in an online text different from turning a book's pages?

- How is your body positioned differently when you read a newspaper or magazine than when you read or surf online? What effects—if any—do these shifts in body position have on how you read or your relationship to a text?

- Do you think print texts are more "serious" than online texts, or carry more prestige for writers? Why or why not?

There are certainly more questions to ask about differences between reading onscreen or paper, and we do not mean to imply here that these questions work only for editorials.

A few pages back we said we'd discuss how writers persuade us that we ought to read them attentively and be open to being persuaded by them. In the editorial on these two pages (from the newspaper of Iowa State University), we want to focus on how Robert Baptiste, the composer of this piece, presents himself—and is presented to us by the context.

Read the editorial—which is not asking others to take physical action of some kind or another, but it is asking people to judge positively a government's decision to loosen some of its regulations. See if you agree with us on the strategies (described in the following pages) that help shape how we might respond to Baptiste.

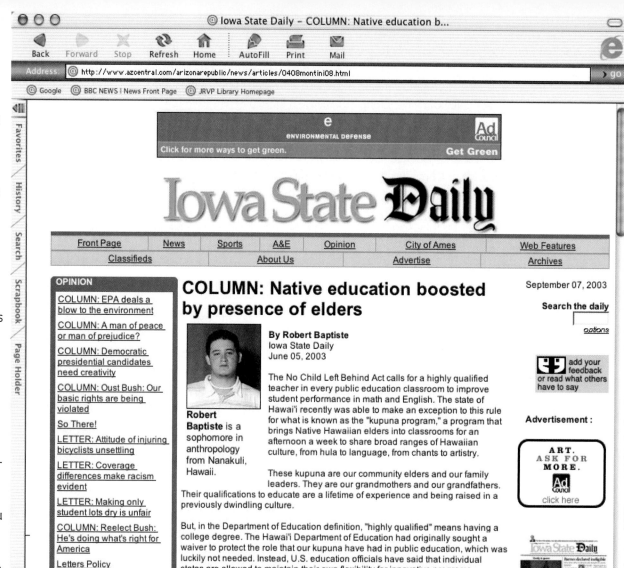

Iowa State Daily

| Front Page | News | Sports | A&E | Opinion | City of Ames | Web Features |

| Classifieds | About Us | Advertise | Archives |

OPINION

COLUMN: EPA deals a blow to the environment

COLUMN: A man of peace or man of prejudice?

COLUMN: Democratic presidential candidates need creativity

COLUMN: Oust Bush: Our basic rights are being violated

So There!

LETTER: Attitude of injuring bicyclists unsettling

LETTER: Coverage differences make racism evident

LETTER: Making only student lots dry is unfair

COLUMN: Reelect Bush: He's doing what's right for America

Letters Policy

COLUMN: Native education boosted by presence of elders

September 07, 2003

Search the daily

options

add your feedback or read what others have to say

Advertisement :

ART.
ASK FOR MORE.
Ad Council
click here

By Robert Baptiste
Iowa State Daily
June 05, 2003

Robert Baptiste is a sophomore in anthropology from Nanakuli, Hawaii.

The No Child Left Behind Act calls for a highly qualified teacher in every public education classroom to improve student performance in math and English. The state of Hawai'i recently was able to make an exception to this rule for what is known as the "kupuna program," a program that brings Native Hawaiian elders into classrooms for an afternoon a week to share broad ranges of Hawaiian culture, from hula to language, from chants to artistry.

These kupuna are our community elders and our family leaders. They are our grandmothers and our grandfathers. Their qualifications to educate are a lifetime of experience and being raised in a previously dwindling culture.

But, in the Department of Education definition, "highly qualified" means having a college degree. The Hawai'i Department of Education had originally sought a waiver to protect the role that our kupuna have had in public education, which was luckily not needed. Instead, U.S. education officials have said that individual states are allowed to maintain their own flexibility for innovative programs. President Bush even says that education is not only a national priority but definitely is a "local responsibility." This is great news to native communities.

In the Native Hawaiian community, kupuna are the ultimate source of knowledge. Not all knowledge is gained through formal education, and it is through our elders that we learn some of the most important life lessons. Our kupuna are irreplaceable, and they are the first and foremost resource for learning and perpetuating our culture.

The U.S. Department of Education letting the State of Hawai'i Superintendent Patricia Hanamo to independently decide on the program's existence is on one

Internet zone

compose ▪ design ▪ advocate

Back　Forward　Stop　Refresh　Home　AutoFill　Print　Mail

Address　@ http://www.azcentral.com/arizonarepublic/news/articles/0408montini08.html　› go

@ Google　@ BBC NEWS | News Front Page　JRVP Library Homepage

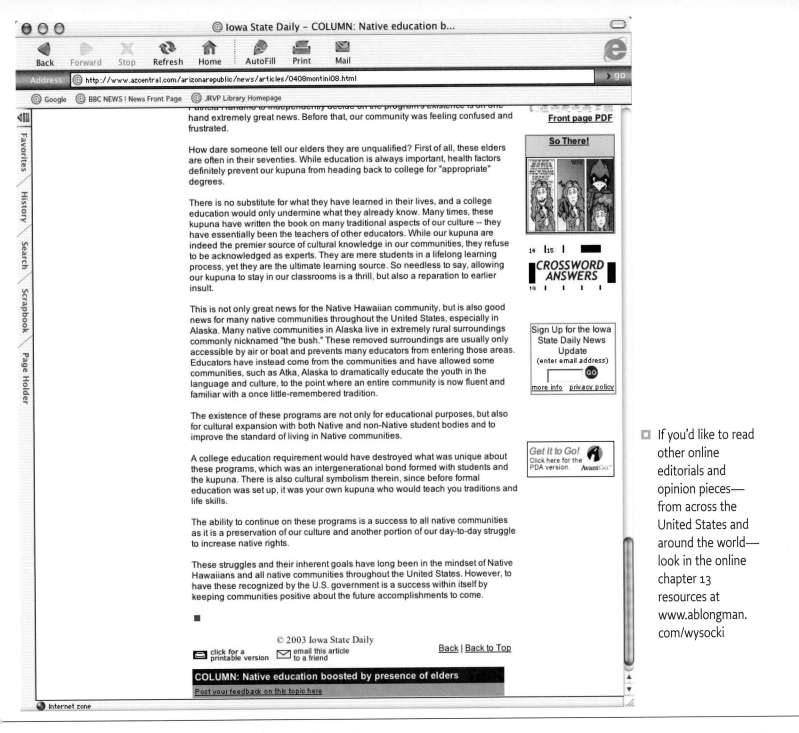

...Patricia Hamamo to independently decide on the program's existence is on one hand extremely great news. Before that, our community was feeling confused and frustrated.

How dare someone tell our elders they are unqualified? First of all, these elders are often in their seventies. While education is always important, health factors definitely prevent our kupuna from heading back to college for "appropriate" degrees.

There is no substitute for what they have learned in their lives, and a college education would only undermine what they already know. Many times, these kupuna have written the book on many traditional aspects of our culture -- they have essentially been the teachers of other educators. While our kupuna are indeed the premier source of cultural knowledge in our communities, they refuse to be acknowledged as experts. They are mere students in a lifelong learning process, yet they are the ultimate learning source. So needless to say, allowing our kupuna to stay in our classrooms is a thrill, but also a reparation to earlier insult.

This is not only great news for the Native Hawaiian community, but is also good news for many native communities throughout the United States, especially in Alaska. Many native communities in Alaska live in extremely rural surroundings commonly nicknamed "the bush." These removed surroundings are usually only accessible by air or boat and prevents many educators from entering those areas. Educators have instead come from the communities and have allowed some communities, such as Atka, Alaska to dramatically educate the youth in the language and culture, to the point where an entire community is now fluent and familiar with a once little-remembered tradition.

The existence of these programs are not only for educational purposes, but also for cultural expansion with both Native and non-Native student bodies and to improve the standard of living in Native communities.

A college education requirement would have destroyed what was unique about these programs, which was an intergenerational bond formed with students and the kupuna. There is also cultural symbolism therein, since before formal education was set up, it was your own kupuna who would teach you traditions and life skills.

The ability to continue on these programs is a success to all native communities as it is a preservation of our culture and another portion of our day-to-day struggle to increase native rights.

These struggles and their inherent goals have long been in the mindset of Native Hawaiians and all native communities throughout the United States. However, to have these recognized by the U.S. government is a success within itself by keeping communities positive about the future accomplishments to come.

■

© 2003 Iowa State Daily

click for a printable version　email this article to a friend　Back | Back to Top

COLUMN: Native education boosted by presence of elders

Post your feedback on this topic here

Internet zone

Front page PDF

So There!

14　|15　|　■■■

CROSSWORD ANSWERS

19　|　|　|　|

Sign Up for the Iowa State Daily News Update
(enter email address)
GO
more info　privacy policy

Get It to Go!
Click here for the PDA version.　AvantGo

□ If you'd like to read other online editorials and opinion pieces— from across the United States and around the world— look in the online chapter 13 resources at www.ablongman. com/wysocki

AN EDITORIAL *ETHOS*, CONTINUED . . .

Here are the major *ethos*-composing strategies we see at work in the "Native education boosted by presence of elders" editorial from the *Iowa State Daily*:

- To be published in a newspaper—whether a campus or a city newspaper—requires that those who run the paper think a writer is proficient enough in words and thoughts to be published. This alone tells us that Baptiste cannot be dismissed immediately.

- Baptiste is from Hawaii (according to the words under his photograph) and he is writing about an issue initially based in Hawaii—so he has some authority to write on this topic. But this really isn't enough. (Are people qualified to speak with total authority about all the affairs of a state just because they are from there?) Baptiste also uses Hawaiian terms (starting in the first paragraph) and he writes about particularities of Hawaiian culture; he also seems to know about the No Child Left Behind Act and the policies and people of the Department of Education. This all suggests that he knows enough about what he's arguing to be worth attending—if we're interested in what he's writing.

- Baptiste shows more than just knowledge: he shows that he is a part of a community of Hawaiians committed to preserving native culture, and he expresses care and concern for the community through his larger argument and through his words about "perpetuating the culture," "improving the standard of living," and "intergenerational bonds"—all of which he discusses positively. Baptiste never explicitly says he is part of this community and culture, but all his words and values point to this conclusion. He is thus not only writing about something he knows, but about a community of which he is part.

- Notice that—even though this editorial is a personal opinion—the word "I" never appears. "We" and "our" are the words Baptiste uses when he discusses his connection with his culture. Baptiste is writing from within a culture, not about someone else's. His use of "we" and "our" not only emphasizes his connection with Hawaiian native culture, but also suggests his reasons for writing are not selfishly limited or motivated.

- Baptiste's words are also gentle and steady. There is no yelling or screaming here, nor is there jumping up and down for joy; the most emotionally strident words in the essay are "How dare someone tell our elders they are unqualified?" Notice how his sentences tend to be longer than the almost-threat we just quoted, so that the writing is given a slower pace than a piece of writing containing all short sentences. This writing strategy helps Baptiste sound carefully thoughtful.

Baptiste's strategies—in the context of being published in this newspaper—construct an *ethos* that is thoughtful, generous, and careful; possesses some degree of authoritative knowledge; and is concerned with the preservation of tradition in education and the bettering of the lives of native peoples.

Whether or not you agree with Baptiste's argument that the government has done a good thing by not requiring native elders to have college degrees, see if you can find other strategies in this writing that are intended to help you develop a positive attitude toward Baptiste. (For example, what effect might it have that he is writing at Iowa State, far away from his home?)

And whether or not you agree, do you find yourself willing to read this argument through, because of how Baptiste presents himself?

strategies for composing *ethos*

If you generalize from the observations on the previous page about how Baptiste composes his *ethos*, you might come up with a list of strategies for composing (and also therefore analyzing) *ethos*:

❏ **The context of the composition.** A writer's publication in a recognized newspaper—or by a recognized publisher—indicates that someone with authority believes that the writer is worth attending. (You then have to ask yourself, as a reader, how much you accept the authority of the publisher.)

❏ **The composer's knowledge of the topic.** How does a composer show that he or she knows the topic? What kind of depth of knowledge does the composer display? (And does the composer appear to be showing off knowledge or, instead, quietly demonstrating through weaving it into the writing that it is there or . . .?)

❏ **The composer's connection to the topic.** Baptiste shows us that he has a personal and deeply felt connection to this topic, which could make him seem motivated solely by self-interest but, in this case, doesn't because (we think) he uses "we" and "our" and also writes about communities that are not directly

his. Looking for the reasons why someone writes a text tells us motivation, and someone's motivation tells us (we all like to think) a lot about him or her.

❏ **The composer's connection to the people affected by the argument.** This is slightly different from the above point, but important. In Baptiste's editorial, his connection to the topic and to the people affected by his argument are similar: he cares about the topic because he is a member of the affected group. Sometimes, though (as seems to be the case in the next editorial on these pages), people argue about groups to which they do not belong (although the group might be seen as belonging within the larger community a writer describes— also something to be alert to in the next editorial).

❏ **The words a composer chooses to present her- or himself.** Baptiste uses "we" and "our" instead of "I" and "my," which in his case shows his identification with his community and that his argument is larger than one man's particular life. As with all the strategies we list here, we cannot say that using "I" will always sound selfish while "we" won't: how these words sound to us always

depends on all the other strategies at work in a composition.

When you are analyzing a composition—or designing one yourself—keep in mind that there are other strategies for self-presentation than just pronoun choice. Look for any words composers use to give you a sense of who they are.

❏ **How a composer addresses the audience.** Baptiste does not address his readers directly—but some composers do (think about how the posters in chapter 10 stare or point at their audiences). In different compositions, this will encourage us to experience different kinds of relations with a text.

❏ **Tone of voice.** Does a composer sound gentle or strident, confused or ambivalent, or absolutely certain? Trust your ears on this when you are trying to decide about tone of voice: read sentences and paragraphs aloud, and name as precisely as you can the sense you get of the composer's tone. Once you name the tone you can start trying to pin down why you hear the tone you do (we pointed to length of sentence previously, but look for word choices and how the composer addresses you).

Read this editorial, and then step through the list of strategies for composing *ethos* from the previous page to help you observe how E.J. Montini, a staff writer for *The Arizona Republic* newspaper, presents himself to his audience in this editorial. (How does his position with the newspaper contribute to his *ethos*?)

(Note also that this editorial is deliberative, in that it argues for specific actions the government of Arizona—which, by implication, means the people of Arizona—ought to take.)

THE ARIZONA REPUBLIC
ONLINE PRINT EDITION

Visit any AJ's Fine Foods

FRONT PAGE · LOCAL · SPORTS · BUSINESS · ARIZONA LIVING · OPINIONS · > azcentral.com

September 7, 2003

Sunday Sections
- A&E
- CareerBuilder
- Travel & Explore
- Viewpoints

Weekly Features
- Food & Drink
- House & Home
- Movie Preview
- Wheels
- Yes

Communities
- Ahwatukee
- Chandler
- Gilbert
- Mesa
- Scottsdale
- Tempe
- North / Central Phoenix
- Northeast Phoenix
- South Phoenix
- Glendale / Peoria
- Southwest Valley
- Sun Cities / Surprise

7-Day Archive
- Sunday
- Monday
- Tuesday
- Wednesday
- Thursday
- Friday
- Saturday

SEARCH THE SITE

All

· Advanced search, tips

NEWS online print edition

SAVE THIS | EMAIL THIS | PRINT THIS | MOST POPULAR | LARGER TYPE | SMALLER TYPE

Who would call warrior 'squaw'?

Here's a chance to right a wrong.

Apr. 8, 2003 12:00 AM

I'm wondering if during her short life Army Pfc. Lori Piestewa was ever referred to as a "squaw." It will never happen now. She has earned that much. Not just for herself, but for every woman like her.

E.J. MONTINI
The Arizona Republic

There have been suggestions over the years to remove the word from parks and public facilities. But these suggestions have failed. Those who like the word point out that in many dictionaries, "squaw" is simply defined as a Native American woman. They say that Indians who find the word offensive are thin-skinned and that non-Indians who believe the word is derogatory are either misinformed liberals or the softheaded victims of an educational system that has replaced historical fact with out-of-control political correctness.

Given that, I'm wondering now if there is anyone out there who would dare to call Pfc. Piestewa, the first Native American servicewoman to die in combat, a "squaw." I have been checking the newspaper headlines and the TV broadcasts for days and I haven't seen it yet.

I have heard Pfc. Piestewa referred to as a "warrior" by her brother and as a "hero" by friends and associates. She also has been described as a good soldier and as a patriot, all of which is true.

But I have not heard anyone call her a "squaw." If the word were not offensive, as so many claim, I would have expected it to be used many times by now.

But it has not been used. And it will not be used. Because those who so confidently and casually informed Native Americans and others that "squaw" is not insulting or defamatory would never use the word to describe this dedicated 23-year-old woman who was killed in Iraq.

On the day that Lori's death was confirmed by the Army a light snow fell in Tuba City, her hometown. According to Hopi beliefs, the soul of a person who has led a good and honorable life returns to Hopi land in the form of precipitation. Lori Piestewa came home that day, but there

breaking news on ▸

azcentral.com

· Overhead runs high at Coyotes Charities
· Palestinian premier resigns
· Bush hopes to win back Iraq support
· McCain legacy on line as court tackles campaign-finance law
· Disneyland accident victim is mourned
· Ex-President Bush adds initials to aircraft carrier
· EU to blacklist Hamas, still hopes peace doable
· Tape surfaces of 9/11 hits on towers
· Family, government clash over child's best interest
· Skakel retrial bid likely as new theory arises
· Clinton says she will block nominee
· Bustamante to redirect election cash
· Suspected priest killer hospitalized
· Longest-serving Florida congressman dies
· S. Carolina prison: Hard times or jobs
· Seafood served with large helping of toxins
· NASA pleased with initial observatory photos
· Opening up on the Web
· High-tech Jesse James
· Separation hailed as future of Taiwanese
· Colombian soldiers kill 25 guerrillas
· Border town in Mexico celebrates Migrant Day
· 4 exiles from Cuba face trial in Panama
· Children of immigrants

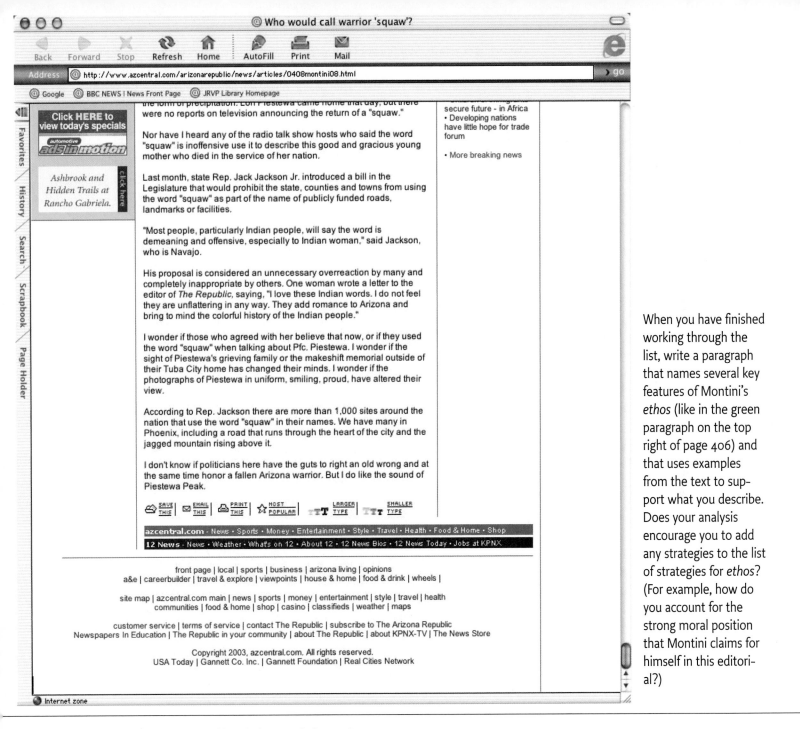

the form of precipitation. Lori Piestewa came home that day, but there were no reports on television announcing the return of a "squaw."

Nor have I heard any of the radio talk show hosts who said the word "squaw" is inoffensive use it to describe this good and gracious young mother who died in the service of her nation.

Last month, state Rep. Jack Jackson Jr. introduced a bill in the Legislature that would prohibit the state, counties and towns from using the word "squaw" as part of the name of publicly funded roads, landmarks or facilities.

"Most people, particularly Indian people, will say the word is demeaning and offensive, especially to Indian woman," said Jackson, who is Navajo.

His proposal is considered an unnecessary overreaction by many and completely inappropriate by others. One woman wrote a letter to the editor of *The Republic*, saying, "I love these Indian words. I do not feel they are unflattering in any way. They add romance to Arizona and bring to mind the colorful history of the Indian people."

I wonder if those who agreed with her believe that now, or if they used the word "squaw" when talking about Pfc. Piestewa. I wonder if the sight of Piestewa's grieving family or the makeshift memorial outside of their Tuba City home has changed their minds. I wonder if the photographs of Piestewa in uniform, smiling, proud, have altered their view.

According to Rep. Jackson there are more than 1,000 sites around the nation that use the word "squaw" in their names. We have many in Phoenix, including a road that runs through the heart of the city and the jagged mountain rising above it.

I don't know if politicians here have the guts to right an old wrong and at the same time honor a fallen Arizona warrior. But I do like the sound of Piestewa Peak.

When you have finished working through the list, write a paragraph that names several key features of Montini's *ethos* (like in the green paragraph on the top right of page 406) and that uses examples from the text to support what you describe. Does your analysis encourage you to add any strategies to the list of strategies for *ethos*? (For example, how do you account for the strong moral position that Montini claims for himself in this editorial?)

FROM *ETHOS* TO ARGUMENT

Ethos is important throughout the previous opinion piece because it serves the overall argument being made. To say how Montini's *ethos* does that, we first have to say what Montini's overall argument is.

Montini's purpose is straightforward: he wants to persuade his readers that Arizona lawmakers should support legislation "that would prohibit state, counties and towns from using the word 'squaw' as part of the name of publicly funded roads, landmarks, or facilities." His reason is that the term is offensive to Native Americans.

Montini has a problem, however, because many people would simply reply that the term isn't offensive. They have, that is, a counterargument to make: the term isn't offensive, and so there's no need for legislation. (Or those same people might agree that the term is indeed offensive, but that the offense is so slight it warrants no attention, much less legislation. Covering the bases in this way in response to an argument can sound contradictory, but is common. Look for examples in the two opinion pieces on affirmative action that follow.)

In order to support his overall argument, then, Montini has to respond to the people who don't think the term is offensive. And recent events provide him the means and context for doing so. A Native American servicewoman, Army Pfc. Lori Piestewa, was killed in Iraq. Her death and the return of her body to her hometown received exten-sive media coverage. Montini noticed—and points out—that no one in the press or whom the press quoted referred to her as "squaw." In all the coverage Piestewa's death received, "squaw" was never used.

By noticing this—and pointing it out—Montini can respond to the counterargument against his claim that the term is offensive. If in the most formal circumstances, when they want to honor a Native American woman, people do not use "squaw," it is an indication that most do not consider the term an honor or respectful. Montini is pointing out a "performative contradiction": people might say "squaw" isn't offensive, but their actions—their performance—show otherwise.

Montini also sees evidence against the secondary claim that if using the term is offensive, it is a small offense: if the offense were small, people would not have been so careful to avoid using the term when describing Lori Piestewa. We could expect to have heard it at least once.

Montini's argument thus rests on his ability to get people to agree that the term "squaw" has not been, nor will it ever be, used to refer to Lori Piestewa, at least in public, because doing so would be wrong—offensive to her memory and to "others like her."

How then does Montini's *ethos* serve this argument?

Imagine if Montini used derogatory names to refer to those with whom he disagrees: he would be contradicting the very argument he wants to make. Instead, because his argument is about how we ought to demonstrate respect for each other through how we speak about each other, his *ethos* has to demonstrate the qualities he advocates.

Here are some details to note about that *ethos*. Montini demonstrates general concern for others by writing about women from a different background than his, and his words about Piestewa are always respectful. He shows he is not just writing off the top of his head by how he refers to others' words and actions; he also says he has been checking newspapers and TV broadcasts "for days" to find information.

Notice, too, the reflective tone of voice he constructs. For example, he says "I'm wondering" or "I wonder," as though he's been thinking things over for a while. His sentences are long but conversational, which—combined with the reflective tone—make his writing sound almost as though he is speaking aloud to himself. It is as though he is asking his audience to join in his thinking with him.

He speaks with disapproval of those "who so confidently and casually informed Native Americans and others that 'squaw' is not insulting"—but that is about as strong as his disapproval gets.

His *ethos* is therefore thoughtful and reflective, strong in its statements of what (he believes) is right but not condemning of others.

compose ▪ design ▪ advocate

■ **Write:** Given Montini's overall argument and counterargument, explain in writing why, so late in his piece, after having explained his opponents' position and after having made his arguments, he feels the need to quote from a letter to the editor opposing the legislation for which Montini is arguing. What problems remain for him, and how does quoting the letter help to solve them?

■ **Discuss with others:** Montini thinks he has observed a contradiction between what his opponents say and what they do, and he takes several opportunities to point this out. Does he need to worry about overdoing his point? What steps does he take to give his opposition room to change their minds gracefully?

■ **Discuss with others:** Describe the similarities in layout between the two preceding online editorials. This may sound like an odd question, but how do you know what on each webpage is the main text? What are the visual clues? What practices or other activities have prepared you to understand how to wade through all the information on these pages to read the editorials?

TWO OPINIONS ON THE SAME ISSUE . . .

As was the case in the opinion pieces we've already examined, *ethos* plays an important role in the two following arguments, one for and one against affirmative action.

Read the two pieces, and then write a paragraph in which you describe the *ethos* in each piece. Ask yourself how a different *ethos* might benefit—or hurt—the different writers. Ask what problems they need to address through their particular constructions of *ethos*.

(As you read, also ask yourself whether the order in which we present the two pieces has any effect on how you read them.)

412

SPECIAL REPORT · AFFIRMATIVE ACTION ON CAMPUS

The Case For Affirmative Action

by Charles J. Ogletree Jr.

MY DREAMS became reality as a result of my Stanford education. My father, who grew up in Birmingham, Ala., and my mother, a native of Little Rock, Ark., never finished high school. They grew up in a segregated South that offered few opportunities and many obstacles for African Americans. I grew up in Merced, Calif., in an environment where many of my peers viewed merely staying alive and getting a job as a successful course in life. But, with a push from my parents, I was determined to be the first in my family to attend college. With help from high school counselors, I discovered Stanford. And thanks to an aggressive minority outreach program by the admissions office, I was given the opportunity of a first-rate education. Without affirmative action, I would never have applied to, and certainly would not have attended, Stanford.

We must keep affirmative action—and keep refining it. It is a small but significant way to compensate victims of slavery, Jim Crow laws, discrimination and immigration restrictions. It is also a means to assure that institutions such as Stanford will celebrate and foster that which they simply cannot avoid: diversity in a democratic society. Affirmative action admissions policies seek to realign the balance of power and opportunity by doing what is, at heart, quite simple: affirmatively including the formerly excluded.

There are critics of affirmative action who claim it is no longer needed, or unfairly discriminates "in reverse" or "stigmatizes" admitted minority students. I disagree.

Those who claim affirmative action is no longer needed believe that the field has been leveled. But they ignore alarming figures. Last year, only 1,455 African Americans received PhDs in the United States. During the same year, 24,608 whites were awardeds PhDs. The truth is that while America has made progress on racial issues, these changes are recent, vulnerable to being reversed and in fact nowhere near completed.

Those who cry "reverse discrimination" base their views almost exclusively on a belief that minority test scores are too low. But they fail to acknowledge that test scores and subsequent performance in college have a correlation that is, to say the least, inexact. When we insist on test scores as an ultimate measure of merit, we exclude, once again, students who have not had access to good public education or to funds that pay for preparatory courses for those tests. We exclude those who, given the opportunity, will display their ability.

Finally, those who would eradicate affirmative action because it "stigmatizes" minorities have two flaws in their argument. Stigma is the product of racist attitudes that still persist today. As a result, killing affirmative action would do little, probably nothing, to ameliorate the stigmatization of minorities. Indeed, one wonders, even for the few whom affirmative action might arguably stigmatize: Would they feel better and achieve more being excluded from a good education entirely? That question ties into the second flaw in the "stigmatization" argument: Opponents rely on the exceptional case, not the rule. (Just as they tend to point to the minuscule number of failures rather than the many

successes.)The majority of minorities strongly favor affirmative action because of the benefits and opportunities it affords.

I was attracted to Stanford precisely because of its affirmative action programs. Here was an institution that clearly recognized that some people enter life with different abilities and opportunities, and that standardized tests were not the only way to judge issues of character, creativity and intellectual promise. When I arrived on campus, I found there was no affirmative action in course selection or grading. I was expected to compete with my peers on an equal basis. I learned that success was not automatic. I got my bachelor's degree in three years and graduated with distinction. I spent my fourth year obtaining my master's degree, and giving serious thought to the next stages of life.

The experiences of many of my minority classmates is a ringing endorsement of affirmative action. Most came from families where the parents had not gone to college, and many were from single-parent households. Moreover, many went on to become successful doctors, lawyers and business leaders, and others are prominent school teachers, public servants and entrepreneurs.

It is my hope that one day we will no longer need affirmative action. As our society becomes more diverse, the need for specific programs aimed at targeted groups will obviously diminish. However, that time has not yet arrived. My two teenage children, who are both college bound, are far better qualified to navigate the educational waters than I was 25 years ago. Despite this laudable progress, they are still judged in everyday life, by race. They are constantly reminded by comments, innuendo and circumstances of their ethnicity precisely because we have not been able

While America has made progress on racial issues, these changes are recent and vulnerable to being reversed.

as a society to overcome the issues of race.

The affirmative action policies promoted by Stanford recognize that, for more than 300 years, African Americans were treated differently because of their race. The important efforts over the course of the past 30 years by government and private institutions have gone a considerable distance in facing up to this history. It will not take 300 years, or even 100 years, to address the sad legacy of our nation's past. We have made a lot of progress. This is no time to turn back. ▣

CHARLES J. OGLETREE JR., '74, MA '75, is a professor at Harvard Law School and a member of the Stanford Board of Trustees.

The Case Against Affirmative Action

by David Sacks and Peter Thiel

FOR THE PAST quarter of a century, Stanford has been discriminating in favor of of racial minorities in admissions, hiring, tenure, contracting and financial aid. But only recently has the University been forced to re-think these policies in the face of an emerging public debate over affirmative action.

We are beginning to see why. Originally conceived as a means to redress discrimination, racial preferences have instead promoted it. And rather than fostering harmony and integration, preferences have divided the campus. In no other area of public life is there a greater disparity between the rhetoric of preferences and the reality.

Take, for instance, the claim that racial preferences help the "disadvantaged." In reality, as the Hoover Institution's Thomas Sowell has observed, preferences primarily benefit minority applicants from middle- and upper-class backgrounds. At the same time, because admissions are a zero-sum game, preferences hurt poor whites and even many Asians (who meet admissions standards in disproportionate numbers). If preferences were truly meant to remedy disadvantage, they would be given on the basis of disadvantage, not on the basis of race.

Another myth is that preferences simply give minority applicants a small "plus." In reality, the average SAT disparity between Stanford's African American and white admittees reached 171 points in 1992, according to data compiled by the Consortium on Financing Higher Education and cited in Richard Herrnstein and Charles Murray's book, *The Bell Curve*.

The fundamental unfairness and arbitrariness of preferences—why should the under-qualified son of a black doctor displace the qualified daughter of a Vietnamese boat refugee?—has led supporters to shift rationales in recent years. Instead of a remedy for disadvantage, many supporters now claim that preferences promote "diversity." This same push for "diversity" also has led Stanford to create racially segregated dormitories, racially segregated freshman orientation programs, racially segregated graduation ceremonies and curricular requirements in race theory and gender studies.

But if "diversity" were really the goal, then preferences would be given on the basis of unusual characteristics, not on the basis of race. The underlying assumption—that only minorities can add certain ideas or perspectives—is offensive not merely because it is untrue but also because it implies that all minorities think a certain way.

What's gone wrong? The basic problem is that a racist past cannot be undone through more racism. Race-conscious programs betray Martin Luther King's dream of a color-blind community, and the heightened racial sensitivity they cause is a source of acrimony and tension instead of healing.

When University officials boast of "looking for racism everywhere," as multicultural educator Greg Ricks did in a 1990 *Stanford Daily* interview, then perhaps the most sensible (and certainly the most predictable) response will be for white students to avoid dealing with such quarrelsome people. In this way, the stress on "diversity" has made interracial interaction strained and superficial; multiculturalism has caused political correctness.

None of this is to deny that there are some people in America who are racist and that there are some features of American life that are legacies of a much more racist past. But racism is not everywhere, and there is very little at a place like Stanford. Certainly, no one has accused Stanford's admissions officers of being racist, so perhaps the real problem with affirmative action is that we are pretending to solve a problem that no longer exists. Moreover, there is a growing sense that if affirmative action has not succeeded in ending discrimination after 25 years of determined implementation, then perhaps it is time to try something else.

Although Stanford's admissions office cannot undo the wrongs of history, its mission is still very important—namely, admitting the best class of students it can find. The sole criterion in finding the members of this class and in defining "merit" should be individual achievement—not just grades and test scores, of course, but a broad range of accomplishments, in athletics, music, student government, drama, school clubs and other extracurricular efforts. But race and ethnicity (or gender or sexual preference) do not have a place on this list; these are traits, not achievements.

Perhaps the most tragic side effect of affirmative action is that very significant achievements of minority students can become compromised. It is often not possible to tell whether a given student genuinely deserved admission to Stanford, or whether he is there by virtue of fitting into some sort of diversity matrix. When people do start to suspect the worst—that preferences have skewed the entire class—they are accused of the very racism that justifies these preferences. It is a strange cure that generates its own disease.

A Stanford without affirmative action will be a Stanford in which the question of who belongs here will no longer need to be answered. It will no longer need to be answered because it will no longer need to be asked, not even *sotto voce*.

> *If, after 25 years, affirmative action has not succeeded in ending discrimination, perhaps it is time to try something else.*

DAVID SACKS (top), '94, *is a law student at the University of Chicago.* PETER THIEL, '89, JD '92, *runs an investment firm. They are co-authors of* The Diversity Myth: "Multiculturalism" and the Politics of Intolerance at Stanford.

ANOTHER POSSIBLE OPINION
Use the list of strategies for composing *ethos* to consider how Sacks and Thiel construct an *ethos* for themselves in this writing.

■ Why do you think the designer(s) of these pages chose the overall colors of the pages?

■ Do you think you would read these opinion pieces any differently if they did not have these photographs on them?

LOOKING AT "THE CASE FOR AFFIRMATIVE ACTION"

The overall argument Ogletree makes for affirmative action policies is an *argument from consequences*. He argues that affirmative action policies have benefited society (have had good consequences, that is) over the past thirty years and will continue to do so—and so we should hold on to them.

Ogletree supports his argument in two main ways: he frames* (begins and ends) the argument with his personal story, a "success" story, about affirmative action, and he offers a number of counterarguments to the arguments his opposition (as he perceives it) has put forth.

Ogletree's story is of a young man born into underprivileged circumstances. His parents never finished high school and grew up in the segregated South with limited opportunities for making their lives. He grew up in Merced, California, an area that provided more obstacles to than opportunities for steering a successful course in life. When he graduated from high school he was able to go to Stanford University because of Stanford's outreach/affirmative action programs and the help he received from his high school counselors. He did well at Stanford, though it was not easy for him. He since has become a successful professor of law at Harvard Law School and is on the Stanford Board of Trustees.

The counterarguments he makes are numerous, as we would expect, given the complexity of this issue and the length of time people have been debating it. Each side has a lot to say. And under such circumstances opinion pieces tend to take the form of lists. For instance, Ogletree counters the argument that affirmative action policies in some places are flawed but that supporters are against making adjustments; he counters the argument that the playing field has become level so that we no longer need affirmative action policies; he counters the argument that affirmative action is inherently bad, unfair, or, "reverse discrimination"; he counters the argument that affirmative action "stigmatizes" those who enjoy its benefits; and he counters the argument that those who support affirmative action do not want "the problem" solved but rather want affirmative action policies to go on forever.

The ways Ogletree argues, or counterargues, are as varied as the arguments he has to address. He uses the language of his opposition ("reverse discrimination" and "stigmatizes") in order to characterize their arguments. He compares the number of African-American students who earned a PhD the previous year to the number of white Americans to do so, in order to suggest that the field may not yet be so level as is claimed by his opposition—and to dispel the fear that large numbers of African-Americans are displacing whites. He challenges his opponents' use of test scores such as SATs to show that those who have entered through affirmative action programs are undeserving. In response to the claim that these policies stigmatize those they are supposed to benefit, he points out that society continues to stigmatize them in worse ways; he suggests that his opponents rely on special cases of minorities who claim they felt stigmatized; he offers his own testimony that he saw affirmative action as an opportunity, not a stigmatization; and he pens a pointed question: "Indeed, one wonders, even for the few whom affirmative action might arguably stigmatize: Would they feel better and achieve more being excluded from a good education entirely?"

Ogletree's writing thus starts and ends with arguments based in *ethos*; in the middle of his list of good consequences is argument based in *logos*.

*Notice how "framing," a concept we introduced in the chapter on documentary photography, can be used for understanding writing, too. In both photography and writing, it is worth thinking about how the composers of arguments draw our attentions to particular events, details, and interpretations out of the whole range of available events, details, and interpretations in the world.

LOOKING AT "THE CASE AGAINST AFFIRMATIVE ACTION"

As in Ogletree's argument for affirmative action, the overall argument Sacks and Thiel make against affirmative action is in part an *argument from consequences*.

Sacks and Thiel argue that affirmative action policies have had bad consequences and that we should discontinue the policies to prevent any further damage. They argue that these policies are inherently unfair.

Sacks and Thiel support their argument in these main ways:

1 They frame (begin and end) their argument with assertions characterizing affirmative action in bad ways.

2 They offer counterarguments to the claim that affirmative action policies have positive effects or the effects they were intended to have.

3 They offer evidence that affirmative action policies have had bad consequences at Stanford.

4 They impugn the motives and character of those who support affirmative action.

Sacks and Thiel offer a range of kinds of argument, mostly aimed at countering the opposition. They make stark challenging statements, such as "Stanford has been discriminating" and "[o]riginally conceived as a means to redress discrimination, racial preferences have instead promoted it." They rename things, such that "affirmative action" becomes "racial preferences" and "political awareness" becomes "political correctness." They use Thomas Sowell from Stanford's Hoover Institution as an authority on who has actually benefited from affirmative action programs. They borrow statistics from the book *The Bell Curve* to show the disparity between Stanford's African-American students' SAT scores and those of Stanford's white students. They argue in the form of rhetorical questions: "Why should the under-qualified son of a black doctor displace the qualified daughter of a Vietnamese boat refugee?"

Perhaps the most pervasive form of argument they make, though, is *causal*. They suggest a causal link between affirmative action policies at Stanford and increased segregation on campus. They suggest a causal link between "race-conscious programs" and the betrayal of Martin Luther King's dream of a color-blind society. They assert a causal link between multiculturalism and political correctness. And they suggest a causal link between Stanford's affirmation action programs and a climate of suspicion on campus that a lot of students have been admitted who do not deserve to be.

opposing opinions

■ **Discuss with others:** How do you characterize the *ethos* Ogletree has constructed in his piece? How do you characterize the *ethos* constructed by Sacks and Thiel? What differences do you see? Try to explain the differences by the kinds of arguments each makes. If Ogletree is appealing—in part—to our sense of justice, fair play, and compassion, what *ethos* will help him? If Sacks and Thiel want to take away policies that have helped some, what sort of *ethos* would get in their way?

■ **Discuss with others:** Both Ogletree and Sacks and Thiel make arguments from consequences. To what consequences does each point? How can they be so opposed in their estimation of the consequences of Stanford's affirmative action programs? What do each of the different writers have to ignore or redescribe in the others' positions to develop the positions they do?

■ **Discuss with others:** Compare the visual presentation of the affirmative action pieces with that of the two earlier editorials. How do the colors, use of white space, and use (or not) of advertisements shape how you read? How do they contribute to the *ethos* and *pathos* you see in the pieces?

■ **Write:** Notice that many differences between the two arguments are based largely on competing perceptions. One position is that the consequences have been good, the other that consequences have been bad. One argues that twenty-five to thirty years of affirmative action policies have been more than enough time to test their effectiveness, the other that twenty-five to thirty years of affirmative action policies have not been enough time for them to correct 300 years of injustices. Those who are admitted through such policies feel stigmatized; those who are admitted through such policies feel grateful. The Stanford campus is torn by racial strife more now than ever before; the Stanford campus has a large number of satisfied and successful African-American students as a result of its policies and is the better for it. Lowering the bar for admission is unfair to those better qualified; once admitted through affirmative action programs, students have to meet the same standards and expectations in their classes as any other student, and the success stories suggest admitting them was fair.

Write a paper in which you argue why you think the perceptions are so divergent. What can be done to address the differences in perception?

AN EDITORIAL that may not seem like an editorial but is, and that uses *ethos* as its key strategy . . .
We've defined editorial and opinion pieces by pointing to their purpose: they aim to persuade us toward some particular judgment or action. The piece on the next pages, from *Outside* magazine, was written in response to the events of September 11, 2001. The piece may not seem like an editorial to you since it (apparently) advocates no action. What it doesn't advocate (we think) is public action; this text instead advocates private action— watch for this as you read, to see if you agree.

Watch closely, also, to see how the writer of the next piece develops his *ethos* over the writing. Does the list of strategies for constructing *ethos* account for all the strategies you see, or do you need to add to the list?

A VERY PERSONAL *ETHOS*

We'll come back to talking about the particular purpose of this writing, but—for now—analyze it as you have earlier editorials, using the list of *ethos* strategies: what sort of *ethos* does Jack Turner compose here, and how?

■ Jack Turner may have suggested the photographs that accompany his writing, but more likely a page designer—having read Turner's piece—chose the photographs and chose how to arrange them together with Turner's words. Into what various frames of mind are such large photographs—of the Teton wilderness in Wyoming—likely to put different readers upon turning to these pages?

Walking the LINE

An ardent defender of wilderness reflects on the solace of the mountains—and reconsiders his long-ago travels in Afghanistan, and a new world of human tragedy

by JACK TURNER

SINCE THE BATHHOUSE near the cabin where I live in Wyoming is closed for the winter, I haul cold water every day from the creek. The water must be heated for bathing and washing dishes, the stove requires wood, the rounds must be split, and the splitting makes you intimate with an eight-pound maul. Few things calm the mind like an hour with an eight-pound maul.

Around me is the ever-changing sky and the Teton Range, the mountains I love most. The rut is in full force. The bulls bugle, the cows answer with their little barks. The pronghorn are gathering for their journey back to the Green River. Geese and eagles are heading south. Three black bears have pestered me for a week; one of them was enthusiastic about pepper spray and kept coming back for more—two canisters' worth. The trout refuse every fly I've ever heard of. A friend got his elk on the first day of the season. It snowed for the first time since June, a storm I call the Winnebago because it sends all the RV folks south for the winter.

If there is fear around me in the wake of the terrorist attacks, it is not so much the fear of bombs or germs as the fear of a collapse of civil order. As a person primed by a diet of Richard Preston's *The Hot Zone* and *The Cobra Event*, and Stephen King's apocalyptic *The Stand*, I bought extra ammo for my sweet-shooting .270 rifle and my grandfather's

Left: "The Tetons and the Snake River" (1942) and, next page, "Cascades in Fern Spring at Dusk" (1961) by Ansel Adams

419

■ Who is the "we" of this paragraph?

■ With whom is Turner contrasting himself when he writes that he goes into the wilderness in response to our national worries? What sort of reader is likely to want to follow him, if not into the wilderness, at least sympathetically into his thinking?

■ Although Turner does not explicitly compare Pakistan and Afghanistan to the United States, then to now, what sort of echoes between the two places and times is Turner establishing for his readers? Why might he be doing this?

12-gauge. Batteries. Extra fuel for the chainsaw. A spare chain.

People have started doing strange things. A friend who traps deer mice with a Havahart trap talked to me about purchasing a 9-millimeter Glock pistol. There were reports of telephone calls from people in cities wanting to know if Jackson Hole was safe. At the stores in Jackson, part of the standard chitchat has become how safe Wyoming seems, especially if you come from a place where the population density is 24,000 people per square mile.

Despite setbacks in Somalia and Vietnam, we have endured and celebrated many victories—World War I, World War II, the Berlin Wall, the demise of the evil empire—but our historical trajectory now seems headed into a worrisome labyrinth. So some people smoke more, some drink more, some decide not to get divorced after all, some start going to church again, some just watch it all happening on television. And some, like me, go into the wilderness.

I'VE ALWAYS GONE into the wild during trying times. When I was a kid, I would hunt and fish near my home in Oceanside, California; later, I'd take long solo trips climbing or on snowshoes into the mountains of Colorado. During the midseventies I spent over a year in northern Pakistan, much of it in the mountains along its border with Afghanistan. I was an unhappy academic in Chicago enduring the remains of a broken marriage, and my home wilderness in Wyoming and Utah seemed insufficient to my needs. When the adventure outfitter Mountain Travel offered me an opportunity to help lead a trek to K2 in Pakistan in June of 1975, I went. Afterward I turned west and spent the rest of the summer traveling in the Hindu Kush, a place I told myself was real wilderness, the kind that could soothe a battered heart.

I visited Hunza. I wandered west from Gilgit to Yasin, then north into the mountains along the Wakhan corridor, the narrow sliver of Afghanistan that leads to the border with China and is adjacent to Tajikistan. Then I walked and rode jeeps south down the Yarkhun and Mastuj Rivers to Chitral, and on to the dreary town of Drosh, and then back up into the mountains to Malakand and by bus to Peshawar. Beyond Drosh the river plunged down a valley into Afghanistan and became the Konar, which in roughly a hundred miles joined the Kabul River near the then-obscure town of Jalalabad.

The land was like Death Valley, but higher. Vast mirages covered the valleys. The passes were sometimes 15,000 feet high, broad saddles veined with ancient trails. The mountains rose another mile or two but were often obscured by dust storms. The only trees in the high mountains were dwarfed birch.

The border with Afghanistan was guarded by soldiers, but their presence back then was merely symbolic. The guard station at the top of the Yarkhun Valley consisted of two men, one horse, a flintlock rifle, and a hand-cranked radio. One of them was reading—somewhat optimistically, I thought—a volume of Rommel's letters. In broken English he railed at us about American support for Israel at a time when "the Jewish

infidels" had invaded Uganda. Uganda? He insisted on it, pointing to his radio. When I reached Islamabad, I learned of the commando raid at Entebbe.

The people inhabiting the villages in the northernmost valleys of Pakistan were farmers, masterly irrigators who were invariably kind and helpful. Some of the older village leaders had been educated at English schools at Srinagar, in Kashmir, before the partition of Pakistan from India in 1947. They wore Harris Tweed coats over their flowing Pakistani clothes, and several smoked English pipes. They hunted with modern British and German rifles. Occasionally they would show off fine markhor horns, a snow leopard skin, or an ancient scimitar.

At their invitation my groups and I often ate yogurt and paper-thin chapatis off silver platters arranged on old carpets spread on lawns beneath mulberry and apricot trees. Their tone was one of interest and amusement that Americans would come so far. For what? Just to look? To find what? Wilderness? They did not know that word. Beauty they understood, but it was faraway, in the cities, the beauty of fine mosques, mosaics, carpets.

And indeed it was not wilderness, it was their home. Much of the land was like what Thoreau, in *The Maine Woods*, called wild pastures, a blank on the map with few roads and little population but lined with trails and munched on by goats for thousands of years. The forests were logged to the point that many valleys looked like they'd been clear-cut. The game, especially predators, had been hunted almost to extinction. Nowhere did I find the carpets of flowers, the crystalline streams, or the concentrations of wildlife I so loved in Wyoming.

When the Soviet Union invaded Afghanistan in 1979, refugees poured over the passes and up the Konar River into Pakistan. Trekking and climbing along the border came to a virtual halt. Eventually, I came home.

A FEW YEARS LATER I SETTLED into guiding for the Moose, Wyoming–based Exum Mountain Guides and was living in a cabin in Grand Teton National Park. It had suffered the same fate as the valleys of the Hindu Kush, although here the damage was limited to a hundred years of grazing. Sheep chewed their way through the Wind Rivers and the west side of the Teton Range; cows did the same in the Escalante, the Gros Ventre, and the east side of the Teton Range. But with the creation of national parks and the Wilderness Act, the land and its diversity, for the most part, had come back.

I became less concerned with the new and novel and more concerned with attaining an intimacy with what was at hand, in my home wilderness. I wanted a haven, my own safe place, thoroughly known and loved, however vast and empty—a place removed, as it were, from human history and its vicissitudes. I thought about my nation's foreign-policy record of oscillation between engagement and escape, commitment and separation, and of my own struggle, of how much, or how little, to engage with the world.

> I wanted a haven, my own safe place, thoroughly known and loved, however vast and empty. And I thought of my own struggle, of how much, or how little, to engage with the world.

I was in search of places that were indifferent to the incessant march of human foible, the unending political squabbles, the putative reality presented each moment by CNN. And yet, I soon discovered, there is no escape. The truth expressed by Muir and Leopold and ecology, by modern physics and Buddhism—that everything is connected—is unrelenting. After the tragedies of September 11, we are almost unbearably conscious that remote forces, of which we are only marginally aware, might suddenly determine our fate, the fate of our families, the fate of our friends. And being far from human tragedy is comforting only if you maintain a rather solipsistic stance toward the well-being of those you love.

When the planes flew into the Pentagon and the World Trade Center, a friend's son was in Kazakhstan working on a thesis in geology; another friend's son was in charge of a Navy SEAL team; another friend was flying from Boston to Montana that morning and was grounded in Michigan. Like virtually everyone else in America, my friends and family live far away—in Washington, D.C., Seattle, California, Utah, Colorado, and Hawaii—and there is no escape for any of us.

Still, I believe that living in a meadow in the Tetons had a certain advantage on that sad day and in the sad days that followed. I have no television and my modem is too slow to run videos, so it wasn't possible for me to watch the interminable replay of footage that feeds our addiction to tragic events. I wanted to shed those images instead of magnifying them; to be informed, not inured. The means to do that was near and known. I went to the wild places I have gone to for 40 years.

I went up the Gros Ventre River and into the wilderness, walking up the stream where I caught my first Wyoming cutthroat many years ago. I said I was looking for hatches, but mainly I was throwing sticks in the creek for my dog and wondering what my heroes, the hermit monks and poets of ancient China, would have done about anthrax and the Taliban. They lived in a time of great strife: a civil war, the suppression of Buddhist monasteries and practice. What did they write about?

> I climb the road to Cold Mountain,
> the road to Cold Mountain that never ends.
> The valleys are long and strewn with stones,
> the streams broad and banked with thick grass.
> Moss is slippery, though no rain has fallen;
> pines sigh, but it isn't the wind.
> Who can break from the snares of the world
> and sit with me among the white clouds?
> —HAN-SHAN

Wang Wei wrote a book he titled *Laughing Lost in the Mountains*. Whenever I get too serious I like to remember that title. I was rather lost myself by the creek in the Gros Ventre when suddenly a shadow passed over me and tore down my little valley faster than any bird could fly, ever. Then the blast, shattering and implacable. As the dim glow of the afterburners disappeared over Lavender Ridge, my wild valley transmuted into a landscape out of *Top Gun*.

The vice-president and his retinue had arrived in Jackson Hole aboard Air Force Two, accompanied by helicopters, squads of Secret Service agents, and jets to patrol the airspace around town. And patrol it they did: around and around all day

and night and all day again. But I still had a slew of other places to go, my collection of havens.

My mate and I went to the Green River Lakes in Bridger-Teton National Forest with our dog, paints, and books. We loaded the canoe and paddled up the first lake, then waded and hauled the canoe up the creek toward the second lake. It was so shallow I was stepping on sculpins. Two men with horses had a camp at the other end of the lake, but they left just after we arrived. We

set up our tent and drank hot toddies on the sandy shore and watched the light fade from the great cliffs surrounding the summit of Square Top. We didn't come home for two days.

And soon I left again. I walked alone up the lower face of Teewinot, the Teton peak that rises just west of my cabin, across the meadow. I followed an old climbers' trail, unsigned, unmarked on the maps. It leads over talus and avalanche debris and onto a broad ridge. I paused at the waterfall just off the trail, a place I always visit. Just a trickle now. Then I climbed into the forest until I reached the first whitebark pines—my favorite trees. I settled there and looked around.

Things have changed since September 11, we've heard it said, again and again. Yes, and we are all obliged to speak and act in this newly dangerous world. But at the same time, I find a measure of relief in the things that haven't changed: the geese that fly south in the autumn, the fir that resists the maul, the winter that has arrived, and the spring to come. I can see a hundred miles of open spaces, mountains and rivers I know and love. The only sound now is the caw of a Clark's nutcracker. ◙

Jack Turner is the author of *Abstract Wild* (1996), a collection of essays, and *Teewinot: A Year in the Teton Range* (2000).

■ What arguments does Turner make that wilderness is not separate from the events of the world?

■ Why do you think Turner tells his readers about where his friends and family were on September 11?

■ Why does Turner make the distinction between "informed" and "inured"?

■ Turner's sentences have remained long, descriptive, and reflective throughout this writing. He started by describing long views of wilderness, and ends by describing long views of wilderness. What sorts of actions do you think he is asking his audience to take on as a result of his various descriptions and other argumentative strategies?

421

Here is an informal rhetorical analysis of "Walking the Line." This analysis makes an argument about how the *ethos* Turner constructs in the piece connects to his overall arguments.

ARGUING FOR A DIFFERENT KIND OF ACTION

Sometimes opinion pieces don't push for direct action. Sometimes they don't seem to make an argument at all. "Walking the Line" might be such a piece because, on its surface, all it does is describe the writer's life and how it influences his thinking about September 11. I think this piece of writing puts forth a strong argument, however, about how we respond to September 11, so let me walk you through it as I see it.

First, let me show why the writer, Jack Turner, might want to write a subtle argument: it has to do with his context. Turner's subject is the aftermath of September 11, a touchy topic now and even more so at the time Turner wrote. If he wants to influence how we are responding to September 11 in any way other than the simple and easy ways sanctioned by the government and the media (from his point of view), then he has to move carefully. Put otherwise, his audience is in a delicate frame of mind, frightened, angry, quick to react, and assaulted daily by media and governmental announcements about the threat of more terror. As a result, this piece can be looked at as a slow negotiation with a wary audience, an audience not exactly prepared to hear what he has to say—or so Turner worries.

The structure of this piece, I believe, is what shows Turner's overall purpose. Through the slow build-up of Turner's story and our possible attraction to the pattern of beliefs, values, and attitudes embedded in that story, we might be moved—persuaded—to consider a different way of responding to September 11 than we have been offered by the government and media. The structure juxtaposes close-up and far-away views of the world around us, in order to suggest we need to find a way of balancing the two.

Turner uses this structure right away. He opens the piece with a few closely described facts about his life: he lives in a cabin in the mountains of Wyoming and heats his own bath water. He then broadens our view of where he is: his words ask us to look beyond the cabin and out into the whole Teton mountain range. He shifts our views again, when he brings up the fears he and his neighbors feel after September 11: they don't fear more attacks, because they are so remote from population centers; they instead fear that panicking city people will flood the mountains. He explains his fear by shifting our perspective again, this time looking back across the wars of the twentieth century, and his feeling that, unlike past times, this time the U.S. seems psychologically ill-equipped to deal with the experience. The argument I see beginning to form questions the contexts within which we are thinking about and responding to the events of September 11 and their aftermath. Will we respond from within the narrow confines of our homes (or cabins) and day-to-day lives, or will we look at those events from multiple

compose ▪ design ▪ advocate

perspectives, including some broader, more global and historical, perspectives?

Turner continues his strategy of writing to shift our perspectives by telling us about his past. After a divorce and other unhappiness, he sought solace in the wilderness—the mountains in Pakistan. Again, Turner's main strategy is to pull us into a visual story and then to add details that slowly build to an argument. Near the end of this section, for instance, Turner emphasizes two details: the mountains in Pakistan where he worked were like moonscapes after centuries of logging and overgrazing and, when he finally left Pakistan, it was because the Soviet Union invaded Afghanistan. In the next section, the story continues in Wyoming, where Turner moved after Pakistan. He notes that the Wyoming mountains suffered from logging and overgrazing in the early twentieth century, but that the establishment of national parks had mostly brought them back. Two subarguments emerge: first, Turner asserts the positive value of balance, either in the moment or over time (by going back and correcting overreactions, as with fixing the overlogging); second, he asserts that his environmental concerns connect to his need to retreat, now and again, in the face of a world full of pain and strife, to retreat and find a balance.

A bit later in the writing, Turner writes that he has always struggled with "how much, or how little, to engage with the world." Then he adds that the same ambivalence he experiences has characterized U.S. foreign policy since the nation's founding. The United States, as a country, has oscillated between isolationist and aggressive foreign policies. Turner could have added that his government's present foreign policy shows little of that ambivalence, but he doesn't. Because he doesn't, this suggests that his argument is not a criticism of U.S. foreign policy. It is instead about how we should think and feel in the aftermath of September 11 more generally. The rest of the piece makes this clear—and clarifies what his argument is.

For example, Turner lists where his friend's sons were when the planes flew into the World Trade Center and the Pentagon and suggests that everyone had similar, personal connections to the tragedy. Suddenly the event itself is a large backdrop to the smaller daily activities of loved ones, instead of the event being placed within a larger cultural and historical context. His overall argument, I think, is not that one perspective on these events trumps all others. The perspective we have when standing in front of our apartment buildings (or cabins) has as many uses as the perspective we gain by remembering the histories behind the events. It is about balance, about walking the line.

But his main argument is not just that having multiple perspectives on an event is healthy, it is that he has his reasons to believe U.S. citizens—their leaders in government and the media—have lost their time-honored balance between preoccupation with daily life and concern for global engagement, by moving too hastily toward the latter. And his main strategy for addressing this has been to use his experience with the wilderness, with nature, to shift our perspective back—or rather around—in order to keep it from calcifying into one set perspective.

The last paragraph turns directly back to September 11. Repeated day after day since then has been the message that everything has changed and that nothing will ever be the same. Turner's response to this captures, in a condensed way, his overall argument. He affirms the message. And then he undercuts it, by asking us to remember all that hasn't changed. His list of things that haven't changed includes snapshots from the first two paragraphs of this piece, chopping wood with a maul and watching birds whose ancestors connect us to the age of dinosaurs. The argument is not that people in the United States are bad. It is not even that how people in the United States and the U.S. government have been reacting to September 11 is wrong. It is just that the reaction may be, or may be becoming, out of balance. He thinks a walk in the woods might help all of us return to walking the line.

"Walking the Line"

- Discuss with others: How do you characterize the *ethos* Turner has constructed in his opinion piece? How does his *ethos* connect with the overall argument?

- Discuss with others: Toward the end of the piece, Turner refers to "hermit monks and poets of ancient China," he quotes eight lines from Han-Shan, and he brings up Wang Wei's *Laughing Lost in the Mountains*. The informal rhetorical analysis on the previous pages doesn't mention any of this. How could you weave these references into the rhetorical analysis, to support its arguments? (Or could you use these references to refute what the analysis claims are the main arguments of "Walking the Line"?)

- Discuss with others: In the short rhetorical analysis of "Walking the Line," the writer suggests that Turner doesn't want to add to the nation's climate of fear following the events of September 11 by describing those events. What emotional relation with those events does it look like Turner is instead trying to construct for his audience?

LEARNING ABOUT *PATHOS* FROM OPINION PIECES

In this chapter we've helped you focus on *ethos*—but we've also asked questions about the *pathos* at work in examples. To focus on *pathos*, look at the opening lines of each of the pieces on affirmative action:

> "My dreams became a reality as a result of my Stanford education."—Ogletree

> "Over the past quarter of a century, Stanford has been discriminating in favor of minorities in admissions, hiring, tenure, contracting, and financial aid." —Sacks and Thiel

Naming emotions is not always easy, in no small part because few of us have had explicit instruction in doing this but also because emotions are tricky. Emotions blend into one another, as anger blends into indignation. And they have underlying dynamics that allow emotions to slide into or become another, as fear can be twisted into anger.

The combinations of fear/indignation and fear/anger are pertinent to the piece by Sacks and Thiel, as even their opening line shows. They want the audience to see Stanford's actions "over a quarter of a century" as wrong and to feel indignant—even angry. As you move through the piece, you can chart the emotions they raise, mostly a steady drumbeat of indignation moving toward anger (look at their word choices: "the fundamental unfairness and arbitrariness" and "the underlying assumption . . . is offensive . . ."). They think affirmative action is wrong, unfair, and offensive and they want us to feel the same way.

Now try to name the emotions captured in Ogletree's opening line. It seems almost like joy or happiness—the pleasure that goes along with one's dreams coming true.

The truly important thing about *pathos*, though, is not that some emotion gets summoned, but what writers do with the emotions they find or elicit in their readers. Both pieces on affirmative action are relatively short, so we would not expect, nor do we get, a complicated weave of emotion. In Sacks and Thiel, as we mentioned above, the indignation voiced in the expression "reverse racism" remains steady as each point in their argument is made, and though their tone of voice does not turn angry—they do not want to appear unreasonable—the steady catalogue of unfairnesses caused in their eyes by affirmative action clearly is intended to stir anger in readers. The other emotion they mix with indignation is, interestingly, frustration. It is a potent and circling combination. The unfairness leads to anger, and the persistence of "failed" programs leads to frustration, which of course can only continue building the anger already present.

The Ogletree piece grows in a different way, as we would expect, given Ogletree's different purposes. The joy of dreams coming true is quickly replaced by a mixture of sadness and respect: sadness at the unfair conditions into which he was born and respect for his parents' hard work and encouragement of him. From there, as his arguments unfold, some guilt creeps in as he reminds people why affirmative action programs were proposed and justified in the first place and that the problems caused by racism have not been solved. Ogletree does not want his readers to feel guilty, though, so as he wraps up his argument, he tries to find a balance between hope for a better future and a continuing recognition of past and present injustices. He begins with a joy he wants his readers to share and to want for others as much as they want it for themselves, and he ends in a similar state of mind.

ethos and pathos, controlling pathos

Editorial and opinion pieces depend on the opinions of individuals—and so when you write such pieces you stand out both in terms of your character and in view of your beliefs and values and how forcefully, thoughtfully, and compellingly you present them to others. In opinion and editorial pieces, then, you can see a clear relation between *ethos* and emotions—*pathos*.

The Baptiste editorial shows a careful use of emotion. As we read the editorial we get a sense that Baptiste really cares about the issue he discusses—and we can see that he is careful not to get too carried away. We might assume that something he senses in his audience is constraining him—telling him to reel in his emotions. Maybe he has learned from prior experiences, but

he realizes that as valid and beautiful as his emotions are, he needs to let them emerge through the story he tells and the argument he makes. He does not want the emotion to overrun the argument.

At this point, it might seem that we are suggesting that *pathos* is something to be controlled, even excluded from faithful stories and valid arguments. But really we think there's no way to exclude emotion from stories or arguments. The trick—the trick Baptiste seems to have learned—is how to work the emotion productively into the stories told and the arguments made. Baptiste knows or senses that in this context, if he rants and raves, he will just be talking to himself or to those few who already share his beliefs and values—and he wants to reach beyond those who already agree with him. So his editorial lets its emotions emerge in a way that makes space for those with different emotional reactions to the issues to connect with his arguments.

What we have just described is an overall emotional strategy. It does not mean that Baptiste was trying to "manipulate" his readers. It means he realized they have their beliefs, values, and emotions, too, and yet he still wants to communicate with them. He knows that if someone pushes their emotions in his face, he will shut them out, and he does not want to shut out the people he wants to reach. So he is careful about how he uses emotion in his writing . . . as you can be in your own writing.

thinking through production

■ Pick a topic that matters to you, and write two versions of an opinion piece on the topic. (For audience and context, plan this opinion piece as though you were writing it for your school paper. After you describe audience and purpose to yourself, use them to help you make decisions about strategies and arrangement.) First, research your topic so that you have facts to support the position you take. Write a version of the opinion piece in which you construct a knowledgeable, thoughtful, appealing *ethos*. Then, using all the same logical arguments and arrangements, write a version in which you construct an unreliable, nonauthoritative, rude, and obnoxious *ethos*. Many people think that *logos* always wins out; producing these two editorials will help you see how *ethos* can very much affect how people take in all the other parts of writing.

☐ There are more "Thinking Through Production" activities in the online chapter 13 resources at www.ablongman.com/wysocki

■ Pick a recent major national or international event that stirred controversy. Find opinion pieces on the event from six or seven newspapers. (If you choose an international event, or a national event of international interest, look at international as well as domestic newspapers. This link gives you access to online newspapers from the United States and around the world: www.refdesk.com/paper.html.)

Analyze the various pieces, considering the following questions for each:

- How would you characterize the *ethos* of the writer(s) in the piece? How do you come to this characterization?

- What is the emotional tone of the piece—and what emotional attitudes are you asked to take toward the event and the people involved? What specific features of the writing suggest this characterization to you?

- How does the ordering of events in the piece ask you to consider what happened? (This is easiest to see when you compare one piece with another.)

- How do you think the writer(s) of the piece think of you, as they write? Are you smart and able to think for yourself, or do you need to be told everything, or . . .? Based on what features of the writing do you make these judgments?

- How do any photographs in the piece shape your understanding?

Write up your analysis into a judgment about what characteristics of an opinion piece make it seem fair (or not) to you.

■ Develop a design plan for an online editorial that you write on a topic that matters to you. As you work out your plan, make choices about the typeface and colors you will use and whether you will include any photographs or other illustrations. How do you think your choices will contribute to the *ethos* and *pathos* readers will see in the piece?

If you have access to and knowledge about making webpages, produce the editorial and test it with various readers to see if your ideas about *ethos* and *pathos* are accurate.

compose ▪ design ▪ advocate

analyzing essays

Essays are short writings that teach us something interesting, useful, or fun—or all three at once. We find them in magazines and journals, collected in books, and, these days, on the Web. The word *essay* goes back at least as far as the sixteenth century when the French writer Michel Montaigne used the French word *essai* (which literally means "to try") to describe his short writings on subjects like "friendship" and "hate." In these short writings, Montaigne used his writing to think through ideas or to understand aspects of his life—like friendship—that are familiar and yet come in many odd forms.

Essays can be more or less argumentative and more or less long. Many thousands have been written, and in them you can find a dizzying range of strategies and arrangements: comparisons, assertions of cause and effect, story telling, logical arguments, accounts of personal experience, historical reconstructions of events, imaginative reconstructions of events, ethnographic studies, facts and figures, interviews, dialogue, self-interrogation, poetry, puns, and pictures.

"Baudelaire wanted to call a collection of his essays on painters 'Painters Who Think.'

This is quintessentially the essayist's point of view: to convert the world and everything in it to a species of thinking. To the reflection of an idea, an assumption— which the essayist unfolds, defends, or excoriates."

Susan Sontag

* Charles Baudelaire was a nineteenth-century French poet and essayist.

Essays, like opinion pieces and academic articles, are highly cultural objects. Unlike drawings and photographs, where using our eyes, and hence our bodily experience of the world, helps us figure out in large measure what is going on, essays require us to have undergone a tremendous amount of overt, particular, and focused instruction. Think about the years you were in classrooms being taught the alphabet and how to read. Think about how you started with simple readers with a lot of pictures and how, over many years, your teachers helped you take on progressively more complex texts, from chapter books to pictureless books.

Through this process you were taught— directly or not—that words are important, and that (in our time and place) being able to express yourself in words is a sign of being cultured or civilized or able to think at all. This is certainly implied in the quotation to the left from Susan Sontag, who herself wrote many essays and novels.

Essays thus carry a lot of cultural weight: they are meant to be popular, such that anyone can (and will want to) read them, but they require you to have had a long and particular training (which is continuing in this book, yes?) in order for you to understand them this way or take any pleasure from them.

Because essays are so tied to culture and to thinking—to notions that thinking is abstract—they can seem far away from bodily experience.

Essays can be about topics that seem very intellectual—on how to think systematically about the elements—but they can also be about very bodily things—on playing basketball and living in a small town. Obviously, we need to have had bodily experiences to understand the pleasures and potentials of basketball, but we also need to have bodies and senses to understand what elements are. So bodily experience is necessary, to some degree or another, in being able to understand particular essays.

But what about understanding essays in general? Where does the pleasure of reading essays come from? We've argued, in the preceding column, that you have to learn this. And some people argue (as you'll see in the last essay of this chapter) that the form of the essay is precisely about learning to turn away from your body, to shift from experiencing your body as a body to experiencing it as a thought or an abstraction. Keep this tension in mind as you read: be alert to how you understand what you read. In these essays, *where is your body? Where is your culture?*

HOW ESSAYS DIFFER FROM OPINION PIECES AND ACADEMIC ARTICLES

Opinion pieces share some qualities with essays: they are generally one person's opinion about a particular topic or event or possible action. But opinion pieces also differ from essays in several ways. Opinion pieces are most often *deliberative*, meaning that they are intended to spur a community to action of some kind or another, with fact and reason; they can also be *judgmental*, in that they look back to the past and argue that an action taken by a community was right or wrong, should be upheld, or should be changed. Opinion pieces are also *public writing*, in that they are aimed at moving community members toward decisions about the community's actions. Essays, on the other hand, tend to be *reflective* and *personal*. They do not try to persuade readers to take particular action in the world but rather to think about and dwell on events or issues. Essays are public insofar as they are published, certainly, but they address readers as individual thinkers and ponderers, not as members of any particular community.

And when it comes to academic articles, essays do not have any specialized audience (except insofar as you are specialized as someone who can read your language and enjoys doing so) or forms specialized for those audiences.

HOW THIS CHAPTER IS STRUCTURED

In addition to offering you a range of examples of the essay, we wish (of course) to continue supporting you in learning to analyze rhetorically. As in earlier chapters, to read rhetorically is to read in such a way that you treat what you are reading as composed deliberately and thoughtfully to direct a reader's attention and build a particular relation with the reader.

We start with an essay by James Elkins on the periodic table of elements. We ask you to read this essay while attending to questions we raise. Then we apply the steps for rhetorical analysis (from the opening pages of this section) to his essay, modeling one way to apply the steps and do a rhetorical analysis of an essay. We show how those steps can be shaped into a rhetorical analysis in a student essay.

When we turn to the second essay, by Gary Smith, we further clarify how to do rhetorical analysis by focusing on the hardest step, the step in which you make observations and ask questions of the communication. This is a difficult step because it is hard to know which observations to make—where to direct our rhetorical attention—and what questions to ask. The questions tend to be of the form "Why did the author do that at precisely that point in the essay?"—but when you are not familiar with doing rhetorical analysis, it is not easy to know which parts of the essay to examine. So we give you tips on generalities to

look for in order to help you get started with your analysis.

By the time we reach the third essay, we back off a bit so you can read the essay—by Julian Dibbell—more on your own. We make a few observations, ask a few questions, and explain why we questioned as we did, to get you started. You will need to complete the job yourself.

The fourth essay is written by a woman who years earlier had been represented by photographs and an article in a newspaper. This essay is about representing others through photographs and writing—and about how it feels to be so represented. Because this essay is based on personal experience, *ethos* is particularly important in how this essay is shaped.

The first four essays are on a range of topics, but the final essay, by Susan Griffin, takes on the essay itself as an event to consider. This might be a hard essay to read: after first looking at it, you could think Griffin is simply weird, but we ask you to consider that she has her reasons, and that her reasons force her to experiment with the form of the essay and what can be considered in an essay precisely because of its form. This essay brings us precisely to the question of whether we understand essays—and ourselves—through bodies or culture and what sort of balance might be useful or might help people who don't like essays or don't see themselves in essays to find strategies for making themselves present in the world of writing.

This is a chapter from James Elkins's book *How to Use Your Eyes*, in which Elkins has sections on looking at "Things Made by Man" and "Things Made by Nature." The sections have chapters on (for example) "How to look at an oil painting," which is followed by "How to look at pavement" (photographs of the cracks in oil paint repeat the cracks shown in photographs of pavement), and chapters on "How to look at the inside of your eye" and "How to look at nothing."

Elkins teaches art history and theory at the School of the Art Institute of Chicago. He has written many books, some very scholarly, some popular, about painting, the workings of sight, words and images, and how we respond to the things we see, art and otherwise. *How to Use Your Eyes* continues in this tradition: it is a popular text with many small chapters, and each of the chapters—like the one shown here—attempt to get the book's audience to use their eyes more carefully and thoughtfully.

As you read, look for strategies Elkins uses—with words and visual examples—to get you to look at and think about the periodic table in ways he thinks you haven't. At the end, we offer a rhetorical analysis of this essay to model how you might do this yourself.

▧ Why do you think Elkins starts his essay by asking his readers—indirectly—to think back to high school? Into what sort of mood or frame of mind do you think he is hoping this will put readers?

16

how to look at

the periodic table

The periodic table of the elements that hangs on the wall of every high school chemistry classroom is not the only periodic table. It is the most succesful of its kind, but the elements can be arranged in many different ways, and even now the periodic table has its rivals. In other words, it doesn't represent some fixed truth about the way things are.

The table arranges the chemical elements into periods (the horizontal rows) and groups (the vertical rows). If you read it left to right, top to bottom, as if it were a page of writing, you will encounter the elements in order from the lightest to the heaviest. The top left number in each cell is the element's atomic number, which is the number of protons in its nucleus and also the number of electrons that orbit the nucleus. If you read any one column from top to bottom, you will encounter elements that have similar chemical properties.

Figure 16.1 is a version of Dmitri Ivanovich Mendeleev's periodic table, the one that has become the standard. It serves many purposes well, but it is also full of drawbacks. Just looking at it, you can see that it has an unsatisfying lack of symmetry. There is a big gap at the top, as if a chunk had been taken out of it. And at the

figure 16.1

The periodic table.

Periodensystem der Elemente

Hauptgruppen

(A reproduction of the German periodic table of the elements, printed sideways, with legend and element data.)

Legend / key (reading sample cell):

Protonenzahl (Ordnungszahl) — 25
Relative Atommasse^1 — 54,94
Elektronegativität (nach Allred u. Rochow) — 1,6
Siedetemperatur in °C — 2032
Schmelztemperatur in °C — 1244
Symbol^2 — Mn
Name — Mangan
Elektronenkonfiguration — [Ar]3d⁵4s²

^{1} Der eingeklammerte Wert bei radioaktiven Elementen ist die Nukleonenzahl (Massenzahl) des Isotops mit der längsten Halbwertszeit

^{2} rot — gasförmig
grün — flüssig   bei STP (0 °C und 1,0 bar)
schwarz: fest
kursiv: alle Isotope radioaktiv

Nebengruppen

Lanthanoide
Actinoide

Elemente 111 – 112 und 114, entdeckt zwischen 1994 – 96 und 1998, sind noch nicht benannt worden.

Walter de Gruyter GmbH & Co. KG, Genthiner Straße 13, D-10785 Berlin, Tel.: 030 / 2 60 05 - 0, Fax: 030 / 2 60 05 - 222, email: wdg-info@deGruyter.de

WDEG

■ How complex is the language Elkins uses to describe the periodic table? Does the writing sound like a college textbook? What does this tell you Elkins is assuming about the kind of education his audience has had?

■ Why might Elkins use a German example of the familiar periodic table?

■ In the writing, Elkins says that this periodic table "has an unsatisfying lack of symmetry," and then he goes on to describe the "big gap at the top" and "elements that couldn't be fitted onto the table." As you read, see if Elkins argues—give reasons—why an asymmetric periodic table should be unsatisfying.

■ This reproduction of the periodic table is printed on its side in Elkins's book. Why do you think the book's designers decided to do this?

■ These pages from Elkins's chapter are arranged in this book just as they are in the original book, where these two illustrations come in between the text. What are the effects on you, as a reader, to come upon these visual examples in the middle of turning the page to continue reading? Do they break your attention to the reading or do they help you see Elkins's points about how "the elements can be arranged in many different ways"?

■ How persuasive would Elkins's claims be, that "the elements can be arranged in many different ways," if he did not include these examples?

figure 16.2

Detail of a portion of the periodic table.

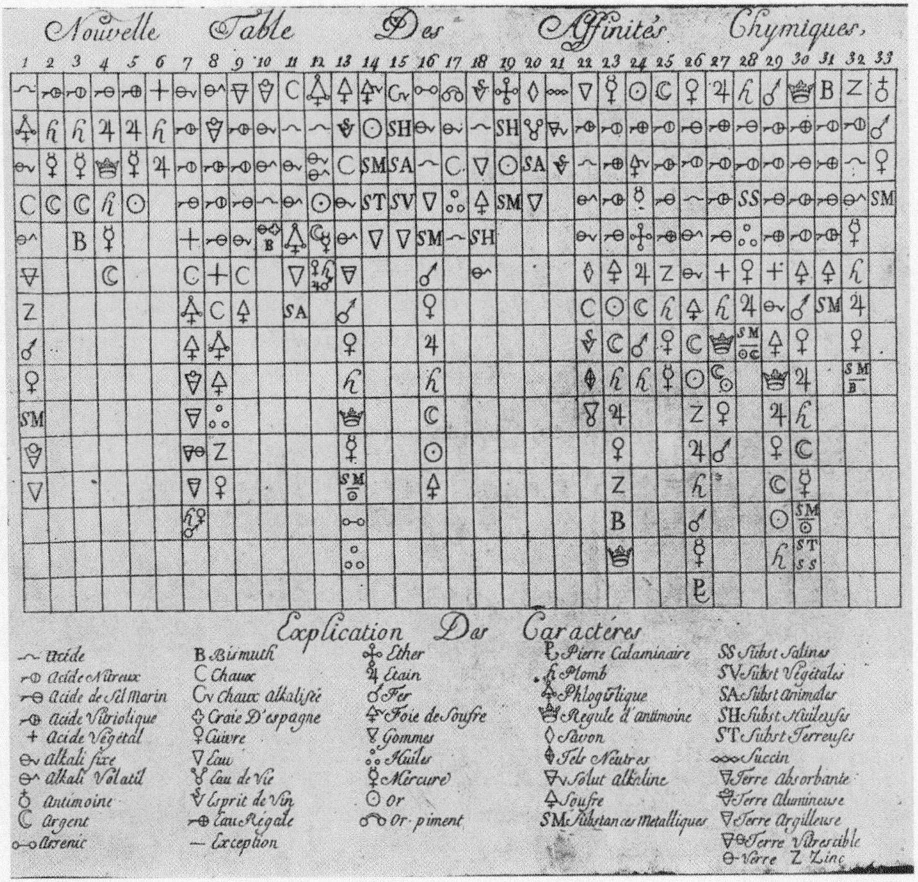

figure 16.3

J. P. de Limbourg, an affinity table of substances and elements.

bottom there are two extra strips of elements that couldn't be fitted onto the table. They would attach along the thick red line toward the lower left. So really the table is not two-dimensional—rather, it is two-dimensional with a flap attached near the bottom.

From a physicist's point of view, the periodic table is only an approximation. A chemist looks at elements for how they behave in test tubes; a physicist looks at them for what they say about the exact arrangements and energies of the electrons in the atoms. When electrons are added to an atom, they can occupy only certain "shells" (orbits) and certain "subshells" within those shells. (That information is given at the lower right of each cell.) A physicist might say the periodic table should really be separated into three blocks, comprised of the left two columns, the middle ten, and the right-hand six. Then each row would represent a single subshell in an atom, and if you were to read left to right across one row of one of the blocks, you would be seeing electrons added, one by one, to a single subshell.

A tremendous amount of information could potentially be added to this simple arrangement. This table distinguishes elements that are ordinarily solid (printed in black) from those that are liquid (green) and gaseous (red), and it notes which are radioactive (white). Each box has a fair amount of information: the key names atomic number, electronegativity, boiling point, melting point, atomic mass, and electron configuration. Yet if this chart were bigger, it would be possible to add much more. Figure 16.2 is a small section from an expanded periodic table with even more detail.

Before modern chemistry and physics, no one had an inkling of such complexities. The forerunners of the periodic table were "affinity tables" (Fig. 16.3). The idea was to list substances across the top and then group other substances underneath them according to how much "affinity" they had—that is, how easily they would combine. This affinity table by J. P. de Limbourg begins with acids at the upper left and runs through a miscellany of substances, including water (denoted by the inverted triangle ∇), soap ($\Diamond$), and various metals. Affinity tables have a logic, since any higher symbol will displace any lower one and combine with the substance given at the head of the column. They were criticized by Antoine Laurent Lavoisier for their lack of any real theory, but it has also been said that they were not intended to exposit any single theory.

In the late eighteenth century, there were a growing number of proposals for tables that would capture some underlying theory. People began to want something

■ Elkins writes that a "physicist might say the periodic table should really be separated into three blocks . . ." Why do you think he chose to write this rather than to quote a physicist?

■ Do you think Elkins's intended audience will grant him enough authority to believe that any physicist would say something like that? How has Elkins built his authority in this chapter? (Consider both his writing and the visual examples he uses.)

figure 16.4

Charles Janet's helicoidal periodic table.

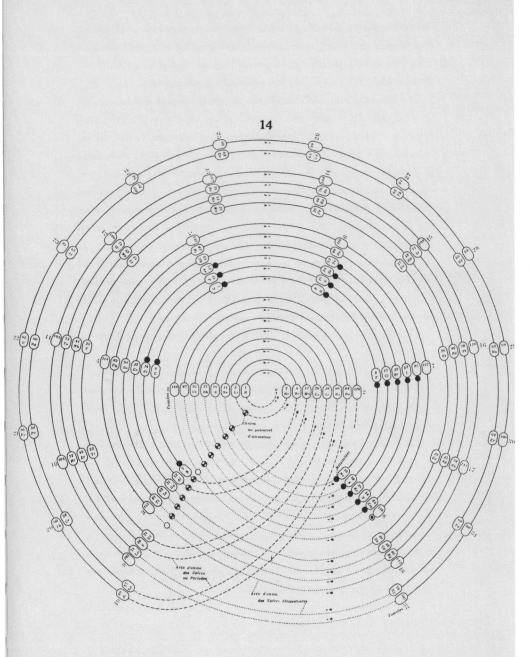

When you see this chart for the first time, coming as it does in Elkins's text before he explains it (on page 124 of his book), what do you think it is? Does it look like any other kind of chart or diagram with which you have experience?

What adjectives would you use to describe this chart? Is it boxy and thick, or light and graceful—or are there other words you would use? Given the adjectives you have chosen, how do you think the arrangements, shapes, and quality of line of this chart ask you to consider the elements? You might be helped to respond by imagining this chart with thicker, heavier lines, or colored rectangular shapes instead of ovals. You can also compare this chart with the more familiar periodic table opposite the first page of Elkins's essay.

In the second full paragraph, Elkins writes that the periodic table shown to the far right "has the virtue of being a single piece instead of a stack of blocks like the familiar periodic table." Why, for Elkins, is this a virtue? What strategies has he used to try to persuade his readers that this is a virtue?

This essay ends with Elkins writing that, ". . . there seems to be an inbuilt notion that something as elemental as the elements should obey some appropriately simple law. It's a hope that animates a great deal of scientific research. The periodic table, in all its incarnations, appears to be a glaring exception to that hope."

How has Elkins prepared his readers for those statements?

What do you think Elkins is hoping his readers will think or do when they have finished this essay, based on these final sentences?

that was rigorously true and could not be shifted and rearranged like the affinity tables. We have settled on a version of Mendeleev's table, but many others continue to be proposed. There are polygonal tables, triangular "scrimshaw" graphs, three-dimensional models, and even old-fashioned-looking schematic trees.

Charles Janet's "helicoidal" classification, proposed in 1928, is a typical elaboration (Fig. 16.4). He imagines the elements all strung together on a single thread. The chain spirals upward as if it were wrapped around a glass tube, and then it leaps to another glass tube, winds around a few more times, and leaps to a third tube. Janet asks us to imagine the three tubes inside one another. At first the helix is confined to the smallest tube, but it spirals out to the middle tube and occasionally the largest tube. The diagram gives the helix in plan, as if the three tubes were squashed flat. Actually, he says, it is very neat because the three imaginary glass tubes all touch on one side (as they would if they were laid on their sides on a table). The problem is that to draw them, he has to cut the chain—hence the confusing dotted lines. In Figure 16.5, the whole thing is spread apart, as if the glass tubes had been removed and the chain were splayed out on a table. That makes it clearer that all the elements are on a single thread wound around three different spools.

It looks odd, but Janet's periodic table has the virtue of being a single piece instead of a stack of blocks like the familiar periodic table. The beginning of Mendeleev's periodic table is at the center of Janet's smallest spool, in Figure 16.4. If you follow the thread, you encounter the elements one after another in the same order as in Mendeleev's table. The middle spool is the middle "block" of the periodic table, separated from the others the way a physicist might do it.

Why don't people adopt schemes like Janet's? Partly from force of habit, because we are all accustomed to Mendeleev's chart. Maybe knots and helices are intrinsically harder for people to imagine. (I certainly have trouble thinking about Janet's helices and trying to picture how they work.) Still, there seems to be an inbuilt notion that something as elemental as the elements should obey some appropriately simple law. It's a hope that animates a great deal of scientific research. The periodic table, in all its incarnations, appears to be a glaring exception to that hope. It seems that when it came to the elements, God created something massively complex and very nearly without any satisfying symmetries at all.

figure 16.5

The same, spread out.

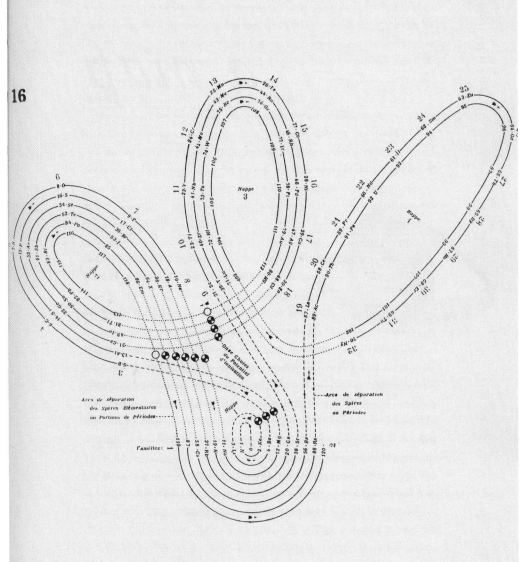

Is this a "satisfying" diagram for you, when you know that it is supposed to represent how all the elements in the universe are related?

The next several pages show the process of thinking one analyzer did as she worked her way through the essay on the periodic table, using the steps for a rhetorical analysis that we described in the opening pages of Section 3.

STEP ONE: What are the piece's purpose, audience, and context? That is, what do you think its maker's statement of purpose is?

When I first read this essay, I thought Elkins just wanted us to learn there is more than one version of the periodic table and to show us a few we might not have seen before. I figured he was speaking not to experts (because he speaks *about* them) but to nonexperts, people who have been to high school and remember a big copy of the periodic table hanging on the wall in chemistry class.

The context for this essay is a book—the essay is part of a book titled *How To Use Your Eyes*—but the context also includes the fact that Elkins knows more about the periodic table and about *seeing* than we do. His relation to us is something like a teacher to a student. I think Elkins wants to expand our nonexpert view of the periodic table.

STEP TWO: List everything about the communication that seems to you to be a choice, especially regarding arrangement, and production.

As I read (and reread) the essay, certain things stood out:

1. Right away, Elkins invoked the image of a periodic table hanging in a high school classroom.

2. He began the essay by pointing out that the periodic table we know—the Mendeleev table—is not the only one.

3. He showed us a German version of the Mendeleev table.

4. He showed us three (actually four!) other versions of the periodic table.

5. He interrupted his discussion of the Mendeleev table by having us turn the page and find, not the rest of his discussion of the Mendeleev table, but two other versions of the periodic table, and we do not get back to his words until we turn the page again (that is, until we are done lingering over the new tables).

6. He spent much time (in such a short essay) discussing the last example, the Janet version.

7. He posed the question, "Why don't people adopt schemes like Janet's?"

8. He titled the essay "How to look at the periodic table"—but his point seems to be that there is not one ideal table but many actual and possible periodic tables.

STEP THREE: How are the choices used strategically?

Here are my observations from step 2, together with my thoughts about why Elkins did what he did.

1. *Right away, Elkins invoked the image of a periodic table hanging in a high school classroom.*

   Why? Perhaps because he wants to pique our interest or get us thinking: "I remember the periodic table being a bunch of squares. What do these other ones look like? Why do we need more than one version? Who is making them? Why are they making them? What can we learn by looking at these other versions?"

2. *He began the essay by pointing out that the periodic table we are familiar with— the Mendeleev table—is not the only one.*

   Why? Perhaps he wants to signal to his readers early on that he assumes we are somewhat familiar with this table—at least with how it looks—and he will be using this fact about his audience to move his essay forward.

3. *He showed us a German version of the Mendeleev table.*

   Why? Here it begins to get interesting. I don't know why. But I do know that Elkins wants us to learn about other versions of the table, and (as we know from the next observation) he criticizes the

Mendeleev table for being asymmetrical and for displaying information in crude blocks. So maybe there's something special about the German version? Is it more symmetrical and less crude? When I look back at the essay to check these ideas out, I don't find Elkins talking about the German vs. the English version at all. It is just there, as asymmetrical and in crude block form as he describes the Mendeleev table being. So—another idea—perhaps he wants us to look at the German Mendeleev table, assume it is the one we are familiar with, then do a double-take and say, *wait a minute, that looks odd—hey, it's in German!* Perhaps he wants the version we are familiar with to suddenly look a little strange. But why?

4 *He showed us three (actually four!) other versions of the periodic table.*

Why three? Why these three, in this order? I assume that for a short essay, three or four would be enough to give us a sense of a range of other versions. The three he shows us are—in order—a detail of one like the Mendeleev table but with more information, an older version called an *affinity table*, and Janet's periodic table—or two versions, one a sort of spiral linking all the elements, and the same idea but flattened out.

I think he chose these three because the first one is similar to but different from the Mendeleev table, the next one looks similar, it has columns, but also includes odd symbols and looks musty and mysterious, and the next one looks very different and is hard to look at and understand.

I think maybe he put them in this order because the tables move from the more familiar to the less familiar, from the easier to look at to the harder to look at (assuming you are someone who has only seen the Mendeleev table).

5 *He interrupted his discussion of the Mendeleev table by having us turn the page and find, not the rest of his discussion of the Mendeleev table, but two other versions of the periodic table, and we do not get back to his words until we turn the page again (that is, until we are done lingering over the new tables).*

Why? I think maybe Elkins thinks that, by this point in the essay, he has put a little distance between us and the version we are familiar with because he's pointed out its flaws and showed us a German rather than an English one, and now he wants to build on that distance by showing us two other, different versions.

The fact that he shows us, first, one that is quite similar (the detail), and then one whose form is familiar (in columns) but whose content is strange suggests that he still thinks we may be a little resistant to these other versions and that we need to be eased into looking at them.

Maybe he arranged them as he did in order to move us gradually into the less familiar—to get us comfortable being uncomfortable, so to speak.

But what's interesting is that he interrupts his own words and leaves us to look at these two versions on our own. This implies he wants us to see for ourselves, that is, to see what we see, not what he tells us to see, or what we have learned to see.

6 *He spent much time (in such a short essay) discussing the last example, the Janet version.*

Why? I think the answer lies in what he goes on to tell us about the other two versions and then about Janet's version. The table with more information than the Mendeleev version is better suited to physicists, we learn, while the Mendeleev version is better suited to chemists. Physicists look at elements in terms of the orbits of electrons, while chemists look at elements in terms of how they react to each other in test tubes. It is about organizing information in ways that are useful, and this is the attraction of the affinity table, according to Elkins: it was a clever way to organize the information people had at that point in time.

Janet's version similarly organizes information about the elements according to his purpose, which is to show that elements form a continuum, as though joined by a single thread. His version is not fanciful, though. It is based on knowledge of modern science. It just invites us to look at the relations between the elements in a different way than the other tables do.

Elkins also tells us that the Mendeleev table took hold at time (the late seventeenth century) when people started to want a single version of the table that captured the truth—the modern scientific truth that was just emerging, as opposed to the partial or mixed truths found in versions like the affinity table.

7 *He posed the question, "Why don't people adopt schemes like Janet's?"*

Why? And why should we care? Again, it looks to me like the beginning of an answer is in what Elkins tells us. He answers his question by saying, "Partly from force of habit." All along we have seen Elkins use strategies that imply he thinks we—his readers—might be stuck in a rut because we've only seen the Mendeleev table. He wondered how—even if—we will look at these other versions. And when he gets to the Janet version, he admits that he himself has trouble looking: it looks complicated, even dizzying.

The other reason people don't adopt schemes like Janet's, Elkins argues, goes back to the seventeenth-century desire for a single straightforward table that presents modern scientific truth. So he tells us that even scientists—who know the difference between chemistry and physics—assume that "something as elemental as the elements should obey some appropriately simple law."

The reason people resist schemes like Janet's, then, is twofold, according to Elkins: we resist out of habit and because we assume there should only be one, true, simple version.

8 *He titled the essay "How to look at the periodic table"—but his point seems to be that there is not one ideal table but many actual and possible periodic tables.*

Why? What gives? I should have begun with this question, since the title is the first thing we see when we read the essay, but now I think I sense why. After answering my other questions, I see that Elkins not only wants us to learn something new about the periodic table, but that, by doing so, he also wants us to learn something about the connection between sight, habit, and assumptions. He wants us to learn that we do not just see; rather, we learn to see, and what we learn affects what and how we see.

STEP FOUR: Test your observations: Are there any anomalies?

I'm noticing two things now.

One, my initial sense of Elkins's purpose—that he just wanted us to see other versions of the periodic table—didn't mention anything about learned habits or assumptions. So my initial statement was based on a partial view of the essay. That is, it was based on the fact that Elkins showed us different versions and invited us to look at them. But it ignored important parts of the essay, for instance, how he ordered the versions he showed us, and his concern that out of habit we might resist looking at new versions. I need a new statement of purpose, audience, and context, taking these details into account.

And, two, I noticed that his title seems odd, given what his purpose is. In the title he refers to **the** periodic table as though there were only one, but any reader ought to realize quickly that Elkins wants us to see that there are many periodic tables, many possible versions, some of which have not even been designed yet.

STEP FIVE: Revise your original statement about the piece.

If we ask now what about his audience most concerns Elkins, I see that it is the way they—we—have learned to see the periodic table and how our habits and assumptions influence how we look at anything new or unfamiliar. The purpose is to make us aware of the role that habits and

compose ▪ design ▪ advocate

assumptions play in how we look at objects. The audience is people who are only familiar with the Mendeleev table, and what is important about the audience is that they have learned to look at the periodic table in a certain way and need some help, some well-crafted strategies, to get them to look—to see—differently. At least, that seems to work for now.

But here's some evidence in my favor. First, the context of the essay supports my statement that Elkins does not just want us to look at the periodic table differently, but from now on to look differently at anything new and unfamiliar. Part of the context is the book title, *How to Use Your Eyes*, which suggests right away that he wants to achieve more than simply changing how we look at the periodic tables. And, second, it just makes more sense to me that Elkins would be concerned more about how we look at things generally than about how we look just at the periodic table (though he cares about that too, and it serves him as a useful example to make his larger argument about how we see and how we understand the world).

STEP SIX: Go back home, and you can start all over again.

But I'm still troubled by why Elkins brought God into the story at the end. Why did he say that it seems "when it came to the elements, God created something massively complex and very nearly without any satisfying symmetries at all"? It is as though all the periodic tables are just fruitless attempts to get at something way more complex than we have models for understanding . . . and maybe that's part of his point, too, that these tables (and other scientific models?) are just attempts, and can never be complete, and we need to use them without thinking that we are getting to the "real" truth . . .?

On the following pages is an essay that takes many of the observations and conclusions from the analysis to the left and builds them into a coherent paper that most composition and rhetoric teachers would like.

A RHETORICAL ANALYSIS OF "HOW TO LOOK AT THE PERIODIC TABLE"

I think James Elkins wrote his essay "How to look at the periodic table" *not* to teach us how to understand the periodic table. Instead, I think he wrote this essay to get us to really *see* the periodic table as a structure that helps us see how we organize the world through charts like these—and that's why there's not just one periodic table, but several (as Elkins shows us), each one giving us a different possible way of seeing, and so understanding, what's out there. By encouraging us to question how charts like these shape how we see, Elkins is asking us to think about our sight in larger ways, too, so that we don't think of it as something that works simply and on its own.

Let me describe some of Elkins's strategies, in the order he gives them to us, to show how I think his strategies support my reading.

Elkins begins by directing us to think about the periodic tables we might have seen in high school because I think high school is the common denominator he assumes his audience will have. This indicates the level of knowledge he presupposes in his audience (and in doing so he also calms any fears the reader like me might have that this essay will be beyond her or him). By reminding us of high school classrooms, he also puts us in a vaguely nostalgic frame of mind because most people look back on their high school days fondly (even if they were, in reality, hell). Elkins also doesn't use abstract scientific language or math, which also indicated he doesn't think his audience is highly-trained scientists. He talks about the elements, something we all learned about in high school, and when he talks about how elements are arranged in the periodic table, he uses expressions like "lightest to heaviest" and "similar chemical properties"—again, language that is easy to follow.

But Elkins seems not to like the more familiar Mendeleev periodic table: Elkins refers to its "unsatisfying lack of symmetry," and he encourages this attitude in the reader by using a German version of the table, in effect also asking a reader to be distant from the familiar version.

Elkins opens the essay with a negative statement, that the periodic table we are most familiar with is not the only version, so from the start the reader is prepared, or being prepared, to consider the merits of other versions. Elkins ends the first page by offering evidence of the "unsatisfying asymmetry" of the familiar version, yet before Elkins has finished with the thought, literally in mid-sentence, the reader turns the page and finds two other versions of the table, and they are intriguing enough to cause one to pause. What Elkins does in this way is interrupt your reading and substitute looking, but he also interrupts consideration of the familiar version of the table and substitutes other versions, just at the point where the asymmetry of the familiar version is being established. The effect can only be (I argue!) to get us not only to look at and see two other versions, but to do so with the question of symmetry in mind. On the surface, each of the two new versions has greater symmetry. The first has two neat rows, without any "big gaps" (such as the one that makes the Mendeleev version "unsatisfying"), and the second runs right to left with thirty-two columns and no gaps between any of them. Some of the columns run longer than others, and the general "look" of the thing is old and funky (kind of "antiquish"), but still it feels more symmetrical, and that is what one has been set up to look for.

For example, were I to have come across the fourth version of the table, Janet's "helicoidal periodic table," I would have thought it look like a complex electrical circuit—or one of those weird Japanese board games like "GO." But having been alerted to the question of symmetry, and having been told by Elkins that different tables capture different interests (the chemist's vs. the physicist's), I am prepared to see right away the relatively satisfying symmetry of this version. It looks at first like a set of about twenty concentric circles, their concentricity clear in the upper portion of the model and broken up with messier dotted lines at the bottom. (Upon closer inspection and with Elkins's help, we learn to see it as "a single piece" that "spirals out.") Again, I might have been put off by the messiness at the bottom—Elkins even admits to it—

but my eye tends to favor the top over the bottom, and that is where the model is cleanest. Elkins later supports this impression by describing Janet's version as "elements strung together on a thread"—certainly an image as satisfying as it is accessible.

Of course the periodic table refers to things that are very complex, and so Elkins's description, beginning so invitingly by talking about a string of beads, becomes more complex. But the effect is clear: messy or not, this model has virtues for Elkins that the Mendeleev model does not because it captures and displays more information and better—and, as Elkins remarks, "It looks odd, but Janet's periodic table has the virtue of being a single piece instead of a stack of blocks like the familiar periodic table" (124). If we did not get his point earlier, that the more familiar Mendeleev periodic table has at best a crude appeal based only on its familiarity, and these other versions have their virtues too, despite being unfamiliar and seemingly complex, we certainly get it at the point at which he contrasts the "blocks" of the Mendeleev table to the "beads" and "single piece" of Janet's table.

At some point during this tour of periodic tables, the reader most likely will ask what the point is. It's not as though Elkins wants us to see one particular table as better than all the rest, even if we understood why we should care which is "best." He makes it clear (as I said above) that different tables serve different interests and purposes, and if value is related to interest or purpose, each will have its value. A reader might then ask, if each has its value, why does Elkins seem intent on trashing the Mendeleev periodic table?

Or *is* this what Elkins is trying to do?

By raising the question, "Why don't people adopt schemes like Janet's?" Elkins responds in a manner that begins to answer our main question regarding his overall point: we don't adopt the other schemes, he writes, "Partly from force of habit, because we are all accustomed to Mendeleev's chart." Besides again circumscribing his audience, Elkins has come full circle (in a satisfying way) back to the opening of the essay, reminding us that, if we are familiar with a periodic table at all, we are probably only familiar with "Mendeleev's chart." Admitting that the other charts have potentially confusing "knots" and "helices," he nevertheless wants us to stretch beyond the familiar chart and try to appreciate the others. The others may be "intrinsically harder for people to imagine," he tells us (and he goes on to make common cause with the reader who feels that way by adding in parentheses "I certainly have trouble thinking about Janet's helices and trying to picture how they work"), but by the end of this short essay, Elkins hopes we are a little more inclined to accept rather than dismiss the twisted "knots" and inscrutable "helices," the stuff of the unfamiliar.

Put otherwise, Elkins hopes we are a little more inclined to accept the idea that not everything obeys simple, easy laws, not everything easy is good, and not everything good is simple. But in case a reader is still wavering on this point, uncertain that there is room for messiness in the world God created, Elkins gently closes the door with his final sentence: "It seems that when it came to elements, God created something massively complex and very nearly without any satisfying symmetries at all" (124). Well, if it is good enough for God, by god, it should be good enough for us, Elkins seems to be saying. And we seem to be buying it.

Learning to see and appreciate requires at the very least that we learn to feel our way beyond the familiar and in the process learn to put up with complexities beyond our initial, easy comprehension. I assume the lesson is supposed to reach beyond our appreciation of periodic tables to all things our eyes happen upon.

"How to look at the periodic table"

▪ **Write:** Write a one- or two- sentence summary of Elkins's essay. Then write several paragraphs in which you use examples of Elkins's words and illustrations to support your summary. Compare your summary and supporting examples with those of two or three other people in your class to see how differently you use Elkins's words and illustrations to support your summaries.

▪ **Discuss with others:** Trace the various strategies Elkins uses in this essay to persuade his readers that they should not accept the familiar periodic table at face value. Are Elkins's strategies relying primarily on *logos* or *pathos*— or a mix? How might his overall purpose shape his choices of strategy?

▪ **Produce a museum . . .:** Using a mix of library and web research, find examples—besides those Elkins uses here—of how the elements are (or have been) represented. (One resource of interesting examples is www. chemicalelements.com). On paper or online, construct a "museum" of the examples for beginning high school chemistry students. You'll need to include commentary to help orient your audience. What do you want them to see and think about as they look at your examples? What strategies will help you focus their attentions on what you think is most important in your collection?

▪ **Make a presentation:** Find other charts or diagrams (besides the periodic table) with which you've grown up or that you see around you frequently. (The food pyramid put out by the U.S. Department of Agriculture [online at www.nal.usda.gov: 8001/py/ pmap.htm] is one possibility; the constellations and a calendar of the months are others.) Using a mix of library and web research, gather together other representations of the same information. Compare the examples, as Elkins does in this essay, to think about how the different configurations of the charts or diagrams ask their audiences to consider the information. Develop an oral presentation in which your examples support an argument about which chart or diagram seems the best or fairest representation to you—or why none of them alone achieves what you think should be represented.

compose ▪ design ▪ advocate

PREPARING TO READ THE NEXT ESSAY, "HIGHER EDUCATION"

About the essay's author

The author of the next essay, Gary Smith, is a senior writer for *Sports Illustrated* magazine and a three-time winner of the National Magazine Award for feature writing; he has also won Excellence in Sports Journalism Awards presented by the organization Sport in Society and Northeastern University's School of Journalism, and he has won a Women's Sports Journalism Award. His works have appeared numerous times in *The Best American Sports Writing* collections. "Higher Education" has been reprinted in *The Best Spiritual Writing of 2002* and *The Best American Nonrequired Reading*, and Jerry Bruckheimer and his production company bought the rights to turn it into a film.

As a writer, Smith takes great care not only to say what he wants to say, but to say it in such a way that he will affect his readers in a thoughtful way. He cares about his readers. And his readers care about his writing—hence all the awards and attention given to him as a writer. But we should be careful not to put him on too high a pedestal, for we can learn much from him that will help us improve our own communication abilities.

What stands out as you read?

In the opening pages to Section 3, when we laid out the steps you can take when reading (listening, or looking) rhetorically, we began by asking you to record your initial sense of what a composer is trying to accomplish, who her audience is, and in what context the author is working. We asked you to treat this initial sense as a hypothesis. Then we asked you to make detailed observations about the piece of communication you are analyzing, and we asked you to turn those observations into questions of the form: "why did she do that? What effects did she want that to have on the reader/audience?" Finally, we asked you to take the answers to your questions, tentative as they may be, test them against your initial sense of what the author is up to, and combine them into a revised understanding of purpose, audience, and context.

Of all those steps, perhaps the most difficult is the second: making detailed observations, especially observations that will lead you to useful questions, takes practice. What if, when you read, nothing stands out? What if the words just sit there on the page flat, mute—maybe even mocking us?

To be able to make detailed observations requires reading something more than once. The first time through, there are certain things you can look for that will help you notice where a composer wants to direct your attentions.

As you read the first time attend to strategies composers can use to make a word or phrase or paragraph stand out, so that you will "hear" it:

- **Titles.** Titles right away give you a sense of the topic as well as (often) the emotional mood.

- **Beginnings.** The first paragraphs are like when you first meet a person: your impressions carry with you through all your experiences of and with that person, coloring how you think about each other.

- **Endings.** This is like a goodbye, the last view you have that lingers, the last view through which you look back on all that preceded.

- **Repetitions.** Anything repeated—a word, a phrase—shows you that a composer wants that word or phrase to stay with you, to shape how you think while reading.

- **Breaks between sections.** Section breaks show you the conceptual chunks through which a composer wants you to think about the essay; the words at the beginning and end of the sections likewise gain importance from being set off.

Read the essay, looking out for these elements (and anything else that sticks out to you). Afterward, we'll show you how and why various things stood out to us, and how we built them into an interpretation.

Indelible Jason Mishler will always carry, on his body and in his heart, the image of his greatest teacher.

(We'll ask questions alongside this essay, to indicate where something stood out to us, using items from the list on the preceding page but also using some other observations we'll explain in more detail after this essay. You might read the first time without paying any attention to our questions, noticing instead what stands out to you; then come back and see where our questions fit with yours or point in other interpretive directions.)

■ What does "higher education"—the title of this piece—make you think the first time you see it? By the end of the essay, do you think Smith is working with a different sense of "higher" than simply that which invokes a college education?

Higher Education

In the unlikeliest of places— Ohio's Amish country—a high school basketball coach changed a community's ideas about race, and about life

BY GARY SMITH PHOTOGRAPHS BY LYNN JOHNSON

THIS IS a story about a man, and a place where magic happened. It was magic so powerful that the people there can't stop going back over it, trying to figure out who the man was and what happened right in front of their eyes, and how it'll change the time left to them on earth.

See them coming into town to work, or for their cup of coffee at Boyd & Wurthmann, or to make a deposit at Killbuck Savings? One mention of his name is all it takes for everything else to stop, for it all to begin tumbling out. . . .

"I'm afraid we can't explain what he meant to us. I'm afraid it's so deep we can't bring it into words."

"It was almost like he was an angel."

"He was looked on as God."

There's Willie Mast. He's the one to start with. It's funny, he'll tell you, his eyes misting, he was so sure they'd all been hoodwinked that he almost did what's unthinkable now—run that man out of town before the magic had a chance.

All Willie had meant to do was bring some buzz to Berlin, Ohio, something to look forward to on a Friday night, for goodness' sake, in a town without high school football or a fast-food restaurant, without a traffic light or even a place to drink a beer, a town dozing in the heart of the largest Amish settlement in the world. Willie had been raised Amish, but he'd walked out on the religion at 24—no, he'd peeled out, in an eight-cylinder roar, when he just couldn't bear it anymore, trying to get somewhere in life without a set of wheels or even a telephone to call for a ride.

He'd jumped the fence, as folks here called it, become a Mennonite and started a trucking company, of all things, his tractor-trailers roaring past all those horses and buggies, moving cattle and cold meat over half the country. But his greatest glory was that day back in 1982 when he hopped into one of his semis and moved a legend, Charlie Huggins, into town. Charlie, the coach who'd won two Ohio state basketball championships with Indian Valley South and one with Strasburg-Franklin, was coming to tiny Hiland High. Willie, one of the school's biggest hoops boosters, had banged the drum for Charlie for months.

And yes, Charlie turned everything around in those winters of '82 and '83, exactly as Willie had promised, and yes, the hoops talk was warmer and stronger than the coffee for the first time in 20 years at Willie's table of regulars in the Berlin House restaurant. They didn't much like it that second year when Charlie brought in an assistant—a man who'd helped him in his summer camps and lost his job when the Catholic school where he coached went belly-up—who was black. But Charlie was the best dang high school coach in three states; he must've

known something that they didn't. Nor were they thrilled by the fact that the black man was a Catholic, in a community whose children grew up reading tales of how their ancestors were burned at the stake by Catholics during the Reformation in Europe more than 400 years ago. But Charlie was a genius. Nor did they cherish the fact that the Catholic black was a loser, 66 times in 83 games with those hapless kids at Guernsey Catholic High near Cambridge. But Charlie. . . .

Charlie quit. Quit in disgust at an administration that wouldn't let players out of their last class 10 minutes early to dress for practice. But he kept the news to himself until right before the '84 school year began, too late to conduct a proper search for a proper coach. Willie Mast swallowed hard. It was almost as if his man, Charlie, had pulled a fast one. Berlin's new basketball coach, the man with the most important position in a community that had dug in its heels against change, was an unmarried black Catholic loser. The *only* black man in eastern Holmes County.

It wasn't that Willie hated black people. He'd hardly known any. "All I'd heard about them," he'll tell you, "was riots and lazy." Few had ever strayed into these parts, and fewer still after that black stuffed dummy got strung up on the town square in Millersburg, just up the road, after the Civil War. Maybe twice a year, back in the

Berlin wall Reese used basketball to bridge the gap between Amish traditions and those of the modern world.

1940s and '50s, a Jewish rag man had come rattling down Route 39 in a rickety truck, scavenging for scrap metal and rags to sell to filling stations 30 miles northeast in Canton or 60 miles north in Cleveland, and brought along a black man for the heavy lifting. People stared at him as if he were green. Kids played Catch the Nigger in their schoolyards without a pang, and when a handful of adults saw the color of a couple of Newcomerstown High's players a few years before, you know what word was ringing in those players' ears as they left the court.

Now, suddenly, this black man in his early 30s was standing in the middle of a gym jammed with a thousand whites, pulling their sons by the jerseys until their nostrils and his were an inch apart, screaming at *them*. Screaming, "Don't wanna hear your shoulda-coulda-wouldas! Get your head outta your butt!" How dare he?

Worse yet, the black man hadn't finished his college education, couldn't even teach at Hiland High. Why, he was working at Berlin Wood Products, the job Charlie had arranged for him, making little red wagons till 2 p.m. each day. "This nigger doesn't

> Berlin's new basketball coach was **an unmarried black Catholic loser. The only black man in eastern Holmes County.**

know how to coach," a regular at the Berlin House growled.

Willie agreed. "If he wins, it's because of what Charlie built here," he said. "What does he know about basketball?"

But what could be done? Plenty of folks in town seemed to treat the man with dignity. Sure, they were insular, but they were some of the most decent and generous people on earth. The man's Amish coworkers at the wood factory loved him, after they finally got done staring holes in the back of his head. They slammed Ping-Pong balls with him on lunch hour, volleyed theology during breaks and dubbed him the Original Black Amishman. The Hiland High players seemed to feel the same way.

He was a strange cat, this black man. He had never said a word when his first apartment in Berlin fell through—the landlord who had agreed to a lease on the telephone saw the man's skin and suddenly remembered that he rented only to families. The man had kept silent about the cars that pulled up to the little white house on South Market Street that he moved into instead, about the screams in the darkness, the voices threatening him on his telephone and the false rumors that he was dating their women. "They might not like us French Canadians here," was all he'd say, with a little smile, when he walked into a place and felt it turn to ice.

Finally, the ice broke. Willie and a few pals invited the man to dinner at a fish joint up in Canton. They had some food and beers and laughs with him, sent him on his merry way and then . . . what a coincidence: The blue lights flashed in the black man's rearview mirror. DUI.

Willie's phone rang the next morning, but instead of it being a caller with news of the school board's action against the new coach, it was *him*. Perry Reese Jr. Just letting Willie know that he knew exactly what had happened the night before. And that he wouldn't go away. The school board, which had caught wind of the plot, never made a peep. Who *was* this man?

Some people honestly believed that the coach was a spy—sent by the feds to keep an eye on the Amish—or the vanguard of a plot to bring blacks into Holmes County. Yet he walked around town looking people in the eyes, smiling and teasing with easy assurance. He never showed a trace of the loneliness he must have felt. When he had a problem with someone, he went straight to its source. Straight to Willie Mast in the school parking lot one night. "So you're not too sure about me because I'm black," he said, and he laid everything out in front of Willie, about

449

Perry Reese Jr.

racism and how the two of them needed to get things straight.

Willie blinked. He couldn't help but ask himself the question folks all over town would soon begin to ask: Could I do, or even dream of doing, what the coach is doing? Willie couldn't help but nod when the black man invited him along to scout an opponent and stop for a bite to eat, and couldn't help but feel good when the man said he appreciated Willie because he didn't double-talk when confronted—because Willie, he said, was real. Couldn't help but howl as the Hiland Hawks kept winning, 49 times in 53 games those first two years, storming to the 1986 Division IV state semifinal.

Winning, that's what bought the black man time, what gave the magic a chance to wisp and curl through town and the rolling fields around it. That's what gave him the lard to live through that frigid winter of '87. That was the school year when he finally had his degree and began teaching history and current events in a way they'd never been taught in eastern Holmes County, the year the Hawks went 3–18 and the vermin came crawling back out of the baseboards. Damn if Willie wasn't the first at the ramparts to defend him, and damn if that black Catholic loser didn't turn things right back around the next season and never knew a losing one again.

How? By pouring Charlie Huggins's molasses offense down the drain. By runnin' and gunnin', chucking up threes, full-court pressing from buzzer to buzzer—with an annual litter of runts,

> The Hawks' Nest, Hiland's old gym, became a **loony bin**, the one place a Mennonite could go to sweat, shriek and squeal.

of spindly, short, close-cropped Mennonites! That's what most of his players were: the children, grandchildren and great-grandchildren of Amish who, like Willie, had jumped the fence and endured the ostracism that went with it. Mennonites believed in many of the same shall-nots as the Amish: A man shall not be baptized until he's old enough to choose it, nor resort to violence even if his government demands it, nor turn his back on community, family, humility, discipline and orderliness. But the Mennonites had decided that unlike the Amish, they could continue schooling past the eighth grade, turn on a light switch or a car ignition, pick up a phone and even, except the most conservative of them, pull on a pair of shorts and beat the pants off an opponent on the hardwood court without drifting into the devil's embrace.

The Hawks' Nest, Hiland's tiny old gym, became what Willie had always dreamed it would be: a loony bin, the one place a Mennonite could go to sweat and shriek and squeal; sold out year after year, with fans jamming the hallway and snaking out the door as they waited for the gym to open, then stampeding for the best seats an hour before the six o'clock jayvee game; reporters and visiting coaches and scouts sardined above them in wooden lofts they had to scale ladders to reach; spillover pouring into the auditorium beside the gym to watch on a video feed as noise thundered through the wall. A few dozen teenage Amish boys, taking

■ Smith comes back to the idea that what happened in the town was "magic," and yet an important part of this story is about religion. What connection does Smith want us to make?

■ Here is where Smith chooses to describe differences between the Mennonites and the Amish. How is the difference important to the essay? How does it shape how you understand the people described in this essay?

Hoops fever A run-and-gun attack—this year including Chris Miller (21, opposite)—and rabid fans are part of Reese's legacy in Berlin.

advantage of the one time in their lives when elders allowed them to behold the modern world, and 16-year-old cheerleaders' legs, would be packed shoulder to shoulder in two corners of the gym at the school they weren't permitted to attend. Even a few Amish men, Lord save their souls, would tie up the horses and buggies across the street at Yoder's Lumber and slink into the Nest. And plenty more at home would tell the missus that they'd just remembered a task in the barn, then click on a radio stashed in the hay and catch the game on WKLM.

Something had dawned on Willie, sitting in his front-row seat, and on everyone else in town. The black man's values were virtually the same as theirs. Humility? No coach ever moved so fast to duck praise or bolt outside the frame of a team picture. Unselfishness? The principal might as well have taken the coach's salary to pep rallies and flung it in the air—most of it ended up in the kids' hands anyway. Reverence? No congregation ever huddled and sang out the Lord's Prayer with the crispness and cadence that the Hawks did before and after every game. Family? When Chester Mullet, Hiland's star guard in '96, only hugged his mom on parents' night, Perry gave him a choice: Kiss her or take a seat on the bench. Work ethic? The day and season never seemed to end, from 6 a.m. practices to 10 p.m. curfews, from puke buckets and running drills in autumn to two-a-days in early winter to camps and leagues and an open gym every summer day. He out-Amished the Amish, out-Mennonited the Mennonites, and everyone, even those who'd never sniffed a locker in their lives, took to calling the black man Coach.

Ask Willie. "Most of the petty divisions around here disappeared because of Coach," he'll tell you. "He pulled us all together. Some folks didn't like me, but I was respected more because he respected me. When my dad died, Coach was right there, kneeling beside the coffin, crossing himself. He put his arm right around my mom—she's Amish—and she couldn't get over that. When she died, he was the first one there. He did that for all sorts of folks. I came to realize that color's not a big deal. I took him for my best friend."

And that man in Willie's coffee clan who'd held out longest, the one given to calling Coach a nigger? By Coach's fifth year, the man's son was a Hawk, the Hawks were on another roll, and the man had seen firsthand the effect Coach had on kids. He cleared his throat one morning at the Berlin House; he had something to say.

"He's not a nigger anymore."

THE MAGIC didn't stop with a nigger turning into a man and a man into a best friend. It kept widening and deepening. Kevin Troyer won't cry when he tells you about it, as the others do. They were brought up to hold that back, but maybe his training was better. He just lays out the story, beginning that autumn day 10 years ago when he was 16, and Coach sat him in the front seat of his Jeep, looked in his eyes and said, "Tell me the truth."

Someone had broken into Candles Hardware and R&R Sports and stolen merchandise. Whispers around town shocked even the whisperers: that the culprits were their heroes, kids who could walk into any restaurant in Berlin and never have to pay. They'd denied it over and over, and Coach had come to their defense . . . but now even he had begun to wonder.

A priest. That's what he'd told a few friends he would be if he

■ Smith tells us that the Amish boys, and "even a few Amish men, Lord save their souls," were drawn to the basketball games. Is he suggesting that they are being led into temptation? Are Perry and the game of basketball undermining the religious values of the community?

■ Are all the values Willie sees Reese sharing with the community religious values? Any? All? Most?

■ Smith tells us that the man in Willie's coffee clan who held out the longest against "Coach" announced one morning, five years after Reese had settled into the town, "He's not a nigger anymore." How is the audience supposed to hear that?

weren't a coach. That's whose eyes Kevin felt boring into him. How could you keep lying to the man who stood in the lobby each morning, greeting the entire student body, searching everyone's eyes to see who needed a headlock, who needed lunch money, who needed love? "Don't know what you did today, princess," he'd sing out to a plump or unpopular girl, "but whatever it is, keep it up. You look great."

He'd show up wearing a cat's grin and the shirt you'd gotten for Christmas—how'd he get into your bedroom closet?—or carrying the pillow he'd snagged right from under your head on one of his Saturday morning sorties, when he slipped like smoke into players' rooms, woke them with a pop on the chest, then ran, cackling, out the door. Sometimes those visits came on the heels of the 1 a.m. raids he called Ninja Runs, when he rang doorbells and cawed "Gotcha!", tumbling one family after another downstairs in pajamas and robes to laugh and talk and relish the privilege of being targeted by Coach. He annihilated what people here had been brought up to keep: the space between each other.

His door was never locked. Everyone, boy or girl, was welcome to wade through those half dozen stray cats on the porch that Coach gruffly denied feeding till his stash of cat food was found, and open the fridge, grab a soda, have a seat, eat some pizza, watch a game, play cards or Ping-Pong or Nintendo . . . and talk. About race and religion and relationships and teenage trouble, about stuff that wouldn't surface at Kevin Troyer's dinner table in a million years. Coach listened the way other folks couldn't, listened clean without jumping ahead in his mind to what he'd say next, or to what the Bible said. When he finally spoke, he might play devil's advocate, or might offer a second or third alternative to a kid who'd seen only one, or might say the very thing Kevin didn't want to hear. But Kevin could bet his mother's savings that the conversations wouldn't leave that house.

Coach's home became the students' hangout, a place where they could sleep over without their parents' thinking twice . . . as long as they didn't mind bolting awake to a blast of AC/DC and a 9 a.m. noogie. There was no more guard to drop. Parents trusted Coach completely, relied on him to sow their values.

He sowed those, and a few more. He took Kevin and the other Hawks to two-room Amish schools to read and shoot hoops with wide-eyed children who might never get to see them play, took the players to one another's churches and then to his own, St. Peter, in Millersburg. He introduced them to Malcolm X, five-alarm chili, Martin Luther King Jr., B.B. King, crawfish, Cajun wings, John Lee Hooker, Tabasco sauce, trash-talk fishing, Muhammad Ali.

And *possibility*. That's what Coach stood

for, just by virtue of his presence in Berlin: possibility, no matter how high the odds were stacked against you, no matter how whittled your options seemed in a community whose beliefs had barely budged in 200 years, whose mailboxes still carried the names of the same Amish families that had come in wagons out of Pennsylvania in the early 1800s—Yoders and Troyers and Stutzmans and Schlabachs and Hostetlers and Millers and Mullets and Masts. A place where kids, for decades, had graduated, married their prom dates and stepped into their daddies' farming or carpentry or lumber businesses without regard for the fact that Hiland High's graduating classes of 60 ranked in the top 10 in Ohio proficiency tests nearly every year. Kevin Troyer's parents didn't seem to care if he went to college. Coach's voice was the one that kept saying, "It's *your* life. There's so much more out there for you to see. Go places. Do things. Get a degree. Reach out. You have to take a chance."

The kids did, more and more, but not before Coach loaded them with laundry baskets full of items they'd need away from home, and they were never out of reach of those 6 a.m. phone calls. "I'm up," he'd say. "Now you are too. Remember, I'm always here for you."

He managed all that without raising red flags. He smuggled it under the warm coat of all that winning, up the sleeve of all that humility and humor. Everyone was too busy bubbling over the 11 conference titles and five state semifinals. Having too much fun volunteering to be henchmen for his latest prank, shoving

Mr. Pratt's desk to the middle of his English classroom, removing the ladder to maroon the radio play-by-play man up in the Hawks' Nest loft, toilet-papering the school superintendent's yard and then watching Coach, the most honest guy in town, lie right through all 32 teeth. He was a bootlegger, that's what he was. A bootlegger priest.

"Kevin . . . tell the truth."

Kevin's insides trembled. How could he cash in his five teammates, bring down the wrath of a community in which the Ten Commandments were still stone, own up to the man whose explosions made the Hawks' Nest shudder? How could he explain something that was full of feeling and empty of logic—that somehow, as decent as his parents were, as warm as it felt to grow up in a place where you could count on a neighbor at any hour, it all felt suffocating? All the restrictions of a Conservative Mennonite church that forbade members to watch TV, to go to movies, to dance. All the emotions he'd choked back in a home ruled by a father and mother who'd been raised to react to problems by saying, "What will people think?" All the expectations of playing for the same team that his All-State brother, Keith, had carried to its first state semi in 24

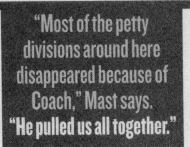

"Most of the petty divisions around here disappeared because of Coach," Mast says. "He pulled us all together."

years, back in 1986. Somehow, busting into those stores in the summer of '91 felt like the fist Kevin could never quite ball up and smash into all that.

"I . . . I did it, Coach. We. . . ."

The sweetest thing eastern Holmes County had ever known was ruined. Teammate Randy Troyer, no relation to Kevin, disappeared when word got out. The community gasped—those six boys could never wear a Hawks uniform again. Coach? He resigned. He'd betrayed the town's trust and failed his responsibility, he told his superiors. His "sons" had turned to crime.

The administration begged him to stay. Who else was respected enough by family court judges, storekeepers, ministers and parents to find resolution and justice? Coach stared across the pond he fished behind his house. He came up with a solution both harder and softer than the town's. He would take Randy Troyer under his own roof, now that the boy had slunk back after two weeks of holing up in Florida motels. He'd be accountable for Randy's behavior. He'd have the six boys locked up in detention centers for two weeks, to know what jail tasted and smelled like. But he would let them back on the team. Let them feel lucky to be playing basketball when they'd really be taking a crash course in accountability.

Kevin found himself staring at the cinder-block wall of his cell, as lonely as a Mennonite boy could be. But there was Coach, making his rounds to all six lost souls. There was that lung-bursting bear hug, and another earful about not following others, about believing in yourself and being a man.

The Berlin Six returned. Randy Troyer lived in Coach's home for four months. Kevin walked to the microphone at the first pep rally, sick with nerves, and apologized to the school and the town.

Redemption isn't easy with a 5' 11" center, but how tight that 1991–92 team became, players piling into Coach's car every Thursday after practice, gathering around a long table at a sports bar a half hour away in Dover and setting upon giant cookie sheets heaped with 500 hot wings. And how those boys could run and shoot. Every time a 20-footer left the hands of Kevin Troyer or one of the Mishler twins, Nevin and Kevin, or the Hawks' star, Jr. Raber, Hiland's students rose, twirling when the ball hit twine and flashing the big red 3's on their T-shirts' backs.

Someday, perhaps in a generation or two, some Berliner might not remember every detail of that postseason march. Against Lakeland in the district championship, the Hawks came out comatose and fell behind 20–5, Coach too stubborn to

What does Smith mean when he calls Reese a "bootlegger Priest"? If that seems an odd description to you, try to explain why Smith might combine those two words.

Smith returns here to the scene of Reese confronting Kevin (with "Kevin . . . Tell me the truth."). What did we learn in the past few pages and what does it add to the story? Why does Smith interrupt Kevin's story?

Smith gives us Kevin's perspective on the break-in. Does he want us to think what Kevin did was okay? Why give us such a compelling view from inside Kevin's head?

Smith shows us that we have now come 180 degrees: Reese quits, and the "administration begged him to stay." Are we supposed to feel that Reese and the town are now fully reconciled? What role does this story (about the break-in) within a story play in the overall story?

call a timeout—the man could never bear to show a wisp of doubt. At halftime he slammed the locker-room door so hard that it came off its hinges, then he kicked a crater in a trash can, sent water bottles flying, grabbed jerseys and screamed so loud that the echoes peeled paint. Kevin and his mates did what all Hawks did: gazed straight into Coach's eyes and nodded. They knew in their bones how small his wrath was, held up against his love. They burst from that locker room like jackals, tore Lakeland to bits and handily won the next two games to reach the state semis. The world came to a halt in Berlin.

How far can a bellyful of hunger and a chestful of mission take a team before reality steps in and stops it? In the state semifinal in Columbus, against a Lima Central Catholic bunch loaded with kids quicker and thicker and taller and darker, led by the rattlesnake-sudden Hutchins brothers, Aaron and all-stater Anthony, the Hawks were cooked. They trailed 62–55 with 38 seconds left as Hiland fans trickled out in despair and Lima's surged to the box-office windows to snatch up tickets for the final. Lima called timeout to dot its *i*'s and cross its *t*'s, and there stood Coach in the Hiland huddle, gazing down at a dozen forlorn boys. He spoke more calmly than they'd ever heard him, and the fear and hopelessness leaked out of them as they stared into his eyes and drank in his plan. What happened next made you know that everything the bootlegger priest stood for—bucking the tide, believing in yourself and possibility—had worked its way from inside him to inside them.

Nevin Mishler, who would sit around the campfire in Coach's backyard talking about life till 2 a.m. on Friday nights, dropped in a rainbow three with 27 seconds left to cut the deficit to four. Timeout, calm words, quick foul. Lima's Anthony Hutchins blew the front end of a one-and-one.

> Something had dawned on everyone in town. The black man's values were **virtually the same as theirs.**

Eleven seconds left. Jr. Raber, whose wish as a boy was to be black, just like Coach, banked in a driving, leaning bucket and was fouled. He drained the free throw. Lima's lead was down to one. Timeout, calm words, quick foul. Aaron Hutchins missed another one-and-one.

Nine ticks left. Kevin Troyer, who would end up going to college and becoming a teacher and coach because of Coach, tore down the rebound and threw the outlet to Nevin Mishler.

Seven seconds left. Nevin turned to dribble, only to be ambushed before half-court by Aaron Hutchins, the wounded rattler, who struck and smacked away the ball.

Five seconds left, the ball and the season and salvation skittering away as Nevin, who cared more about letting down Coach than letting down his parents, hurled his body across the wood and swatted the ball back toward Kevin Troyer. Kevin, who almost never hit the floor, who had been pushed by Coach for years to give more, lunged and collided with Anthony Hutchins, then spun and heaved the ball behind his back to Jr. Raber as Kevin fell to the floor.

Three seconds left. Jr. took three dribbles and heaved up the impossible, an off-balance 35-footer with two defenders in his face, a shot that fell far short at the buzzer . . . *but he was fouled.* He swished all three free throws, and the Hawks won, they *won*—no matter how many times Lima fans waiting outside for tickets insisted to Hiland fans that it couldn't be true—and two days later won the only state title in school history, by three points over Gilmour Academy, on fumes, pure fumes.

In the aisles, people danced who were forbidden to dance. The plaque commemorating the crowning achievement of Coach's life went straight into the hands of Joe Workman, a water and towel boy. Kevin Troyer and his teammates jumped Coach before he could sneak off, hugging him and kissing him and rubbing his head, but he had the last laugh. The 9 a.m. noogies would hurt even more those next nine years, dang that championship ring.

SOMEONE WOULD come and steal the magic. Some big-cheese high school or college would take Coach away—they knew it, they just knew it. It all seems so silly now, Steve Mullet says. It might take Steve the last half of his life to finish that slow, dazed shake of his head.

Berlin, you see, was a secret no more by the mid-1990s. Too much winning by Coach, too many tourists pouring in to peer at the men in black hats and black bug-

Bookworms Reese's players used to read to the Amish children at the Chestnut Ridge elementary school.

- How does Smith create suspense in his description of this state semifinal game? (Look, for example, at his use of time at the beginning of the paragraphs in the second column of this page. What other strategies do you see?)

- There are quite a few paragraphs focused on one particularly exciting basketball game. You might argue that Smith puts this into the article just to keep the interest of his *Sports Illustrated* readers, but how does it also fit into the other rhythms of the story? Why tell about the game here?

World of their fathers At Mullet's auction barn, Berlin's future Amish farmers can get early lessons in the value of horseflesh.

gies. Two traffic lights had gone up, along with a Burger King and a couple dozen gift shops, and God knows how many restaurants and inns with the word *Dutch* on their shingles to reel in the rubberneckers. Even the Berlin House, where Willie Mast and the boys gathered, was now the Dutch Country Kitchen.

Here they came, the city slickers. Offering Coach big raises and the chance to hush that whisper in his head: Why keep working with disciplined, two-parent white kids when children of his own race were being devoured by drugs and despair for want of someone like him? Akron Hoban wanted him. So did Canton McKinley, the biggest school in the city where Coach had grown up, and Canton Timken, the high school he attended. They wanted to take the man who'd transformed Steve Mullet's family, turned it into something a simple and sincere country fellow had never dreamed it might be. His first two sons were in college, thanks to Coach, and his third one, another guard at Hiland, would likely soon be too. Didn't Steve owe it to that third boy, Carlos, to keep Coach here? Didn't he owe it to all the fathers of all the little boys around Berlin?

Coach had a way of stirring Steve's anxiety and the stew of rumors. He would walk slow and wounded through each April after he'd driven another team of runts to a conference crown, won two or three postseason games, and then yielded to the facts of the matter, to some school with nearly twice as many students

and a couple of 6' 5" studs. "It's time for a change," he'd sigh. "You guys don't need me anymore."

Maybe all missionaries are restless souls, one eye on the horizon, looking for who needs them most. Perhaps Coach was trying to smoke out even the slightest trace of misgivings about him, so he could be sure to leave before he was ever asked to. But Steve Mullet and eastern Holmes County couldn't take that chance. They had to act. Steve, a dairy farmer most of his life, knew about fencing. But how do you fence in a man when no one really understands why he's there, or what he came from?

Who was Coach's family? What about his past? Why did praise and attention make him so uneasy? The whole community wondered, but in Berlin it was disrespectful to pry. Canton was only a 45-minute hop away, yet Steve had never seen a parent or a sibling of Coach's, a girlfriend or even a childhood pal. The bootlegger priest was a man of mystery and moods as well as a wide-open door. He'd ask you how your grandma, sister and uncle were every time you met, but you weren't supposed to inquire about his—you just sensed it. His birthday? He wouldn't say. His age? Who knew? It changed every time he was asked. But his loneliness, that at last began to show.

After a successful season, we learn the town is worried Coach may get lured away by another team that wants a good coach and Coach seems to feed their concern. Smith speculates that "[p]erhaps Coach was trying to smoke out even the slightest trace of misgivings about him . . ." Is that a fair speculation? Does it make Coach seem ungrateful, or . . .?

455

Perry Reese Jr.

Tough love Reese's players—and their parents—took his tirades in stride.

▮ Why does Smith spend so much time on the trip to New Orleans? How does he set up this story? That is, what has Smith told us just prior to the New Orleans story that prepares us for the story and its purpose within the overall story?

Coach's teasing and advice, on his cards and flowers and prayers when their loved ones were sick or their children had them at wit's end, and they did what they could to keep him in town. "I wish we could find a way to make you feel this is your family, that this is where you belong," Peg wrote him. "If you leave," she'd say, "who's going to make our kids think?" The women left groceries and gifts on his porch, homemade chocolate-chip cookies on his kitchen table, invited him to their homes on Sundays and holidays no matter how often he begged off, never wanting to impose.

But they all had to do more, Steve decided, picking up his phone to mobilize the men. For God's sake, Coach made only $28,000 a year. In the grand tradition of Mennonites and Amish, they rushed to answer the community call. They paid his rent, one month per donor; it was so easy to find volunteers that they had a waiting list. They replaced his garage when a leaf fire sent it up in flames; it sent him up a wall when he couldn't learn the charity's source. They passed the hat for that sparkling new gym at Hiland, and they didn't stop till the hat was stuffed with 1.6 million bucks. Steve Mullet eventually had Coach move into a big old farmhouse he owned. But first Steve and Willie Mast had another brainstorm: road trip. Why not give Coach a couple of days' escape from their cornfields and his sainthood, and show him how much they cared?

That's how Steve, a Conservative Mennonite in his mid-40s, married to a woman who didn't stick her head out in public unless it was beneath a prayer veil, found himself on Bourbon Street in New Orleans. Standing beside Willie and behind Coach, his heartbeat rising and stomach fluttering as he watched Coach suck down a Hurricane and cock his head outside a string of bars, listening for the chord that would pull him inside.

Coach nodded. This was the one. This blues bar. He pushed open the door. Music and smoke and beer musk belched out. Steve looked at Willie. You could go to hell for this, from everything they'd both been taught. Willie just nodded.

They wedged into a whorl of colors and types of humanity. When Steve was a boy, he'd seen blacks only after his parents jumped the fence, became Mennonites and took the family in their car each summer to a city zoo. Nothing cruel about blacks was ever said. Steve's parents simply pulled him closer when they were near, filled him with a feeling: Our kind and theirs don't mix. Now there were blacks pressed against his shoulders, blacks on microphones screaming lust and heartache into Steve's ears, blacks pounding rhythm through the floorboards and up into his knees. People touching, people gyrating their hips. You could go to hell for this. Steve looked at Willie as Coach headed to the bathroom. "I can't take this," Steve said.

"It's Coach's time, bub," Willie said.

Coach came back, smelled Steve's uneasiness and knew what to do. "Liven up," he barked and grinned. They got some beers, and it was just like the Hawks' radio play-by-play man, Mark Lonsinger, always said: Coach stood out in a room the instant he walked in, even though he did everything to deflect it. Soon Coach had the folks nearby convinced that he was Black Amish, a high-

There were whispers, of course. Some claimed he'd nearly married a flight attendant, then beat a cold-footed retreat. A black woman appeared in the stands once, set the grapevine sizzling, then was never glimpsed again. Steve and his pals loved to tease Coach whenever they all made the 20-mile drive to Dinofo's, a pizza and pasta joint in Dover, and came face to face with that wild black waitress, Rosie. "When you gonna give it up?" she'd yelp at Coach. "When you gonna let me have it?"

He'd grin and shake his head, tell her it would be so good it would spoil her for life. Perhaps it was too scary, for a man who gave so much to so many, to carve it down to one. Maybe Jeff Pratt, the Hiland English teacher, had it right. Loving with detachment, he called it. So many people could be close to him, because no one was allowed too close.

A circle of women in Berlin looked on him almost as a brother—women such as Nancy Mishler, mother of the twins from the '92 title team, and Peg Brand, the school secretary, and Shelly Miller, wife of the booster club's president, Alan. They came to count on

ly obscure sect, and Steve, swallowing his laughter, sealing the deal with a few timely bursts of Pennsylvania Dutch, had them believing the three of them had made it to New Orleans from Ohio in a buggy. Before you knew it, it was nearly midnight, and Steve's head was bobbing, his feet tapping, his funk found deep beneath all those layers of mashed potatoes. You know what, he was telling Willie, this Bourbon Street and this blues music really aren't so bad, and isn't it nice, too, how those folks found out that Mennonites aren't Martians?

When they pulled back into Coach's driveway after days filled with laughter and camaraderie, Steve glanced at Willie and sighed, "Well, now we return to our wives."

"You're the lucky ones," said Coach. "Don't you ever forget that."

Steve realized something when they returned from the road: It wasn't the road to ruin. He felt more space inside himself, plenty enough room for the black friends his sons began bringing home from college for the weekend. He realized it again the next year, when they returned to Bourbon Street, and the next, when they went once more, and the one after that as well. "Some things that I was taught were strictly no-nos . . . they're not sins," Steve will tell you. "All I know is that it all seemed right to do with him."

Funny how far that feeling had fanned, how many old, deep lines had blurred in Berlin, and what occurred in a dry community when Coach overdid it one night four years ago and tried one last time to leave. "I screwed up," he told school superintendent Gary Sterrett after he got that second DUI, 14 miles up the road in Sugar Creek. "You need to take my job."

What happened was sort of like what happened the time the ball rolled toward the Hawks' bench in a game they were fumbling away that year at Garaway High, and Coach pulled back his leg and kicked the ball so hard that it hissed past a referee's ear and slammed off the wall, the gym hushing in anticipation of the technical foul and the ejection. But nothing happened. The two refs had such enormous respect for Coach, they pretended it away.

He apologized to every player and to every player's parents for the DUI. Steve never mentioned it. The community never said a word. It was pretended away.

THEY'VE COMBED through the events a thousand times, lain in bed at night tearing themselves and God to shreds. There were clues, after all, and it was their job to notice things Coach was too stubborn to admit. They thought, when he holed up in his motel room for three days in

> "I wish we could make you feel this is your family," Brand wrote to Reese. "If you leave, who's going to make our kids think?"

Columbus last March, that it was merely one of his postseason moods, darker than ever after falling one game shy, for the third straight year, of playing for the state title. They thought he was still brooding two months later when, preoccupied and suffering from a cold he couldn't shake, he started scrambling names and dates and getting lost on country roads.

It all came to a head one Saturday last June, when he climbed into another rented tux because Phil Mishler, just like 50 or 60 kids before him, had to have Coach in his wedding party. At the reception, Coach offered his hand to Tom Mullet and said, "I'm Perry Reese Jr., Hiland High basketball coach." Tom Mullet had been Hiland's assistant athletic director for 10 years.

Phone lines buzzed that Sunday. People began comparing notes, discovering new oddities. On Monday night two of Coach's best friends, Dave Schlabach and Brian Hummel, headed to Mount Hope and the old farmhouse Coach had moved into just outside Berlin, the only house with lights in a community of Amish. They found him shivering in a blanket, glassy-eyed and mumbling nonsense.

Their worst possible fears . . . well, it went beyond all of them. Brain tumor. Malignant. Inoperable. Four to eight months to live, the doctors at Canton's Aultman Hospital said. You can't bring down a sledgehammer faster than that.

Jason Mishler, Coach's starting point guard the past two years, was the first kid to find out. He stationed himself in the chair beside Coach's bed, wouldn't budge all night and most of the next day. His cousin Kevin Mishler, from the state championship team, dropped his vacation on Hilton Head Island, S.C., and flew back. Dave Jaberg, who had played for Hiland a few years before that, dropped the bonds he was trading in Chicago and drove for six

Spreading the gospel Players on the Hiland bench wear reminders of Reese's teachings on their backs during games.

■ What is the connection between what Smith refers to as the "magic" and this notion of "pretending" things away?

■ Why do you think the essay doesn't end when we learn of Reese's brain tumor, or shortly thereafter?

hours. Jr. Raber was on the first plane from Atlanta. Think a moment. How many teachers or coaches would you do that for?

The nurses and doctors were stupefied—didn't folks know you couldn't fit a town inside a hospital room? Coach's friends filled the lobby, the elevator, the halls and the waiting room. It was like a Hiland basketball game, only everyone was crying. Coach kept fading in and out, blinking up at another set of teary eyes and croaking, "What's new?"

What do people pray for when doctors don't give them a prayer? They swung for the fences. The Big M, a miracle. Some begged for it. Some demanded it. A thousand people attended a prayer vigil in the gym and took turns on the microphone. Never had so much anger and anguish risen from Berlin and gone straight at God.

Steroids shrank the tumor enough for Coach to return home, where another throng of folks waited, each telling the other tales of what Coach had done to change his life, each shocked to find how many considered him their best friend. When he walked through his front door and saw the wheelchair, the portable commode, the hospital bed and the chart Peg Brand had made, dividing the community's 24-hour care for Coach into six-hour shifts, he sobbed. The giving was finished. Now all he could do was take.

Go home, he ordered them. Go back to your families and lives. He called them names. They knew him well enough to know how loathsome it was for him to be the center of attention, the needy one. But they also knew what he would do if one of them were dying. They decided to keep coming anyway. They were family. Even more in his dying than in his living, they were fused.

They cooked for him, planned a trip to New York City he'd always dreamed of making, prayed and cried themselves to sleep. They fired off e-mails to churches across the country, recruited entire congregations who'd never heard of Coach to pray for the Big M. Louise Conway, grandmother of a player named Jared Coblentz, woke up three or four times a night, her heart thumping so hard that she had to drop to her knees and chew God's ear about Coach before she could drop back to sleep. People combed the Internet for little-known treatments. They were going to hoist a three at the buzzer and get fouled.

Coach? He did the strangest thing. He took two radiation treatments and stopped. He refused the alternative treatments, no matter how much people cried and begged and flung his own lessons in his face. Two other doctors had confirmed his fate, and damned if he was going to be helpless for long if he could help it. "Don't you understand?" he told a buddy, Doug Klar. "It's O.K. This is how it's supposed to be."

He finally had a plan, one that would

How much, in the end, was changed by this one man? In Berlin, they're still tallying that one up.

---

make his death like his life, one that would mean the giving wasn't finished. He initiated a foundation, a college scholarship fund for those in need, started it rolling with his $30,000 life savings and, after swallowing hard, allowed it to be named after him on one condition: that it be kept secret until he was dead.

He had no way to keep all the puzzle pieces of his life in boxes now; dying shook them out. Folks found out, for instance, that he turned 48 last August. They were shocked to meet two half sisters they'd never heard of. They were glad finally to see Coach's younger sister, Audrey Johnson, whose picture was on his refrigerator door and who was studying to be a social worker, and his younger brother, Chris, who helps run group homes for people who can't fend for themselves and who took a leave of absence to care for Coach.

It turned out that Audrey had made a couple of quiet visits a year to Coach and that the family had gathered for a few hours on holidays; there were no dark or splintering secrets. He came from two strict parents who'd died in the '80s—his dad had worked in a Canton steel mill—and had a mixed-race aunt on one side of the family and a white grandfather on the other. But there were never quite enough pieces of the puzzle for anyone to put them together on a table and get a clean picture.

Coach's family was shocked to learn a few things too. Like how many conservative rural white folks had taken a black man into their hearts. "Amazing," said Jennifer Bethà, his half sister, a supervisor for Head Start. "And so many loving, respectful, well-mannered children around him. They were like miniature Perrys! Our family was the independent sort, all kind of went our own ways. I never realized how easy it is to get to Berlin from Canton, how close it is. What a waste. Why didn't we come before?"

Coach had two good months, thanks to the steroids. Berlin people spent them believing that God had heard them, and that the miracle had come. Coach spent the months telling hundreds

Coaching change Jordan (right), adopted by the Millers, plays with his brother Cameron as sister McKenzie and mother Shelly look on.

of visitors how much he cared about them, making one last 1 a.m. Ninja Run and packing his life into 10 neat cardboard boxes.

The first week of August, he defied doctors' orders not to drive and slipped into the empty school. Gerald Miller, his buddy and old boss at the wagon factory, found him later that day at home, tears streaming down his cheeks. "Worst day of my life," Coach said. "Worse than finding out about this thing in my head. I cleaned out my desk. I can't believe it. I'm not gonna teach anymore. I'm done."

In early September the tumor finally had its way. He began slurring words, falling down, losing the use of his right hand and leg, then his eyesight. "How are you doing?" he kept asking his visitors, on blind instinct. "Is there anything I can do for *you*?" Till the end he heard the door open and close, open and close, and felt the hands, wrapped around his, doing that too.

On the day he died, Nov. 22, just over a week before the Hawks' first basketball game and 17 years after he first walked through their doors, Hiland looked like one of those schools in the news in which a kid has walked through the halls with an

The mourning season This year's Hawks struggle with their grief in different ways.

automatic weapon. Six ministers and three counselors walked around hugging and whispering to children who were huddled in the hallway crying or staring into space, to teachers sobbing in the bathrooms, to secretaries who couldn't bear it and had to run out the door.

AN OLD nettle digs at most every human heart: the urge to give oneself to the world rather than to only a few close people. In the end, unable to bear the personal cost, most of us find a way to ignore the prickle, comforting ourselves that so little can be changed by one woman or one man anyway.

How much, in the end, was changed by this one man? In Berlin, they're still tallying that one up. Jared Coblentz, who might have been the Hawks' sixth man this year, quit because he couldn't play for anyone other than Coach. Jason Mishler was so furious that he

> Hard to believe, an outsider becoming the **moral compass** of a people with all those rules on how to live right.

quit going to church for months, then figured out that it might be greedy to demand a miracle when you've been looking at one all your life. Tattoo parlors added Mennonites to their clientele. Jr. Raber stares at the R.I.P. with a P beneath it on his chest every morning when he looks into the mirror of his apartment in Atlanta. Jason Mishler rubs the image of Coach's face on the top of his left arm during the national anthem before every game he plays at West Liberty (W.Va.) State.

The scholarship fund has begun to swell. Half the schools Hiland has played this season have chipped in checks of $500 or $600, while refs for the girls' basketball games frequently hand back their $55 checks for the pot.

Then there's the bigger stuff. Kevin Troyer has decided that someday, rather than teach and coach around Berlin, he'll reverse Coach's path and do it with black kids up in Canton. Funny, the question he asked himself that led to his decision was the same one that so many in Berlin ask themselves when they confront a dilemma: What would Coach do? Hard to believe, an outsider becoming the moral compass of a people with all those rules on how to live right.

And the even bigger stuff. Like Shelly and Alan Miller adopting a biracial boy 10 years ago over in Walnut Creek, a boy that Coach had taken under his wing. And the Keims over in Charm adopting two black boys, and the Schrocks in Berlin adopting four black girls, and the Masts just west of town adopting two black girls, and Chris Miller in Walnut Creek adopting a black girl. Who knows? Maybe some of them would have done it had there never been a Perry Reese Jr., but none of them would have been too sure that it was *possible*.

"When refugees came to America," the town psychologist, Elvin Coblentz, says, "the first thing they saw was the Statue of Liberty. It did something to them—became a memory and a goal to strive for your best, to give your all, because everything's possible. That's what Coach is to us."

At the funeral, just before Communion, Father Ron Aubry gazed across St. Peter, Coach's Catholic church in Millersburg. The priest knew that what he wanted to do wasn't allowed, and that he could get in trouble. But he knew Coach too. So he did it: invited everyone up to receive the holy wafer.

Steve Mullet glanced at his wife, in her simple clothing and veil. "Why not?" she whispered. After all, the service wasn't the bizarre ritual they had been led to believe it was, wasn't all that different from their own. Still, Steve hesitated. He glanced at Willie Mast. "Would Coach want us to?" Steve whispered.

"You got 'er, bub," said Willie.

So they rose and joined all the black Baptists and white Catholics pouring toward the altar, all the basketball players, all the Mennonites young and old. Busting laws left and right, busting straight into the kingdom of heaven.   □

Smith tells us in the final pages all the aftereffects Reese had on the town and townspeople. How would you sum up the effects Smith points to?

Smith tells us that Kevin decided after Reese's death to "reverse Coach's path" and teach "black kids up in Canton." Does Smith think this is a simple reversal? Do you?

Smith ends saying "Busting laws right and left, busting straight into the kingdom of heaven." What does he mean? Which laws were being busted?

LOOKING BACK AT "HIGHER EDUCATION": WHAT DID WE NOTICE—AND WHY?

It can sometimes be pretty easy to gather an initial sense of something you've read or seen. In the case of "Higher Education," it is clearly an article written for *Sports Illustrated* about a black, African American high school basketball coach in a small Ohio town mostly populated by people of the Mennonite faith, a Christian sect close-ly related to the Amish. Smith tells the story of the coach's coming to the town, his initial rejection by many of the townspeo-ple, and how the town slowly came to accept, appreciate, and even love the coach. It is a story with a lesson to teach us about how it is possible to learn to live with people who have religious and cultural backgrounds different from our own; Coach already appears to have known, but the townspeople didn't.

So far, so good. But how do we test, extend, qualify, or change this view of Smith's essay? We know we need to start by making more careful observations—by looking more closely at what is said and the way it is written—and then turning those observations into questions about Smith's purpose, audience, and context. We know we need to be able to ask of the moves we see Smith making, *Why did he do that, there? What is it supposed to do to and for the reader? How does it work as a single strategy within Smith's overall plan and purpose?* But how do we know what to

look at, what to observe, in order to start to develop responses to those questions?

Put otherwise, when we get to the sec-ond step in a rhetorical analysis—where we are supposed to make observations about a text in order to test our hypothesis about the purpose, context, and audience of the text—what if nothing really stands out for us? Or what if too many things stand out, and we don't know how to choose what matters to our hypothesis?

Here we go back over what stood out for us in this essay and why; many of the things, as you'll see, come from the list we gave you on page 445.

The essay's title

We noticed that Smith's title draws special attention to what otherwise seems like a small part of the overall story. The story is about—seems to be about—relations between people with different cultural and religious backgrounds. It is also about a high school basketball coach, whose stu-dent athletes may or may not go on to col-lege. Smith mentions that the coach him-self, when he first arrived in town, had not finished his college education (though along the way he does finish). So what?

Go back to the essay and look at how "education" is treated. Who learns what and why? How does the education hap-pen? How is our usual notion of "higher education"—college—changed or modi-fied or turned on its head in the essay?

What is repeated in the essay

Repetition draws special attention to what is repeated—assuming the reader notices the repetition. In Smith's essay a number of things get repeated, and in different ways, and we think they turn out to be important (in different ways) to a better understand-ing of Smith's purpose.

The first repetition we noticed is that Smith keeps referring over and over in the beginning to person we will come to know as "Coach" or "the black man," even before we learn his real name (Perry Reese Jr.). Smith could alternate between that and "the assistant coach," but chooses to emphasize "the black man" at this stage in the story. We wondered why, though not for very long because the story is about the relationship between this black man and a small town that had never experienced having a black man in the community, much less in a prominent position like assistant coach (soon to be coach) of the new and exciting high school basketball team. Referring to him repeatedly as "the black man" keeps front and center the main obstacle between him and fitting into this town. (Notice how in some cases you can move from observation to question to answer rather quickly, and in other cases the process is a little slower. This difference allows you to get started with your analysis by gathering the easier, more obvious pieces first.)

The next repetition we noticed was that in several places Smith calls Reese a "bootlegger priest," without explanation. Given that what Smith calls Reese ("the black man" or "Coach") seems important, it strikes us as important that he calls Reese a "bootlegger priest," but we are not sure why he does it, so we file it away.

Where things are placed in an essay

Once we observe a repetition, for instance, that Smith calls Reese a "bootlegger priest," we then look to see where in the story, exactly, Smith calls him that because placement can be a clue, first, to why he calls Reese that and, second, to what role that strategy has in the overall scheme of things.

In this case, we observe that Smith first calls Reese a "priest" on page 53 of the essay, at the very end of a digression within the story, at the very end of having interrupted the part of the story where Reese confronts Kevin about the break-in. The point of calling him a "bootlegger priest" here seems to be to tell us that the coach is a paradoxical mix of disparate things, part bootlegger (he also calls him a "prankster") and part priest (he also says Reese was like a father to his students). The second time he calls Reese a "bootlegger priest" is on page 54 (not so far away that the reader forgets it), in the middle of the story of one of Reese's biggest wins (at the semi-finals) as a coach, and specifically at the point in the story in which Reese turns a losing game around with a rousing locker-room speech. Here Smith seems to be saying

that Reese was effective in turning the game around both because he had a special relationship with the players, and because, well, he had a certain "magic."

How small changes in repetition call attention to something

The second time Smith calls Reese a "bootlegger priest," Smith seems to imply something a little different from the first time. The second time, it is not so much that Reese embodies paradoxical qualities as that he embodies both natural (or normal) and magical qualities. We don't yet know what to do with this observation, though, so we file it away, too.

Other repetitions

Another instance of repetition is Smith telling us how Reese confronted Kevin, one of his student athletes, about a break-in at the local hardware store, and he says to Kevin, "tell me the truth." After telling us how Reese said this, though, Smith interrupts the story about Kevin to give us more background information about Reese's developing relationship with the town. After a few pages (and immediately after the first time Smith calls Reese a bootlegger priest), Smith returns to the story of Kevin and repeats the line "Kevin . . . tell me the truth." This repetition draws our attention to the fact that Smith somehow feels the need to interrupt the story about Kevin—or he sees an opportunity in doing so—and it led us to wonder why he uses

the repetition in this way, to mark an interruption. Again, we were not immediately sure why Smith does this, but it did cause us to look at what he includes in the interruption that could not wait until later in the story. Put otherwise, we noticed that the suspense created between the two times coach says "Kevin . . . tell me the truth" put a special emphasis on what came between them, on the content of the interruption.

How lists draw our attentions

Another kind of thing we look for is lists. We have learned over time that lists look deceptively straightforward. They are just lists, one thing after another. But what they do is afford a composer the opportunity to order the list to draw your attention to certain things in certain ways. And this works especially well because lists look so innocent. In "Higher Education," Smith, for instance, early on calls Reese an "unmarried, black, Catholic loser." What this list does, clearly, is line up the main things about Reese that the town initially has trouble with, and then focus them on or with the negative word, "loser." This strategy works pretty straightforwardly, we think: it sets up the terms for the big change, that once Reese starts winning games and championships, the word *winner* replaces the word *loser*, and retroactively makes the earlier components of the list ("unmarried, black, Catholic") more tolerable, and (finally) something positive.

We mentioned that our attention had been drawn to what Smith tells us about Reese during the interruption of Kevin's story. Some of what Smith tells us struck us as odd, given the direction the story had been going. Smith seems to go out of his way to describe Reese as a likeable, forthright, honest guy. In the passage Smith inserts into Kevin's story, however, we learn about Reese's antics, such as busting into peoples' houses early in the morning or late at night, waking them up and telling jokes. We learn he pulled a lot of pranks on people, even toilet-papering the superintendent's house. These are relatively harmless revelations about Reese, and they hardly contradict the picture of him as a good, honest guy. But it seems odd that Smith would concentrate his account of the oddest parts of Reese's behavior into one section, and then emphasize that section by placing it in the middle of Kevin's story, which is arguably the most dramatic moment in the overall story, being such a tense moment for the town, with Reese himself feeling responsible because the perpetrators were his student athletes.

We have already mentioned another thing that struck us as odd: calling Reese a bootlegger priest. In this case, not only was the word choice odd—purposefully odd, we felt—but it does not fit with the general direction Smith has been taking us in. Here we are trying to understand Reese and what happened in this town, and then suddenly Smith uses an expression to describe Reese clearly designed to confuse more than to illuminate. What might he be telling us about confusion and its role in stories like this one?

And yet another thing that struck us as odd: Smith spends a long time telling us about a trip Reese took to New Orleans with Willie and a few other townspeople. Why make such a big deal about a vacation? This struck us as odd because it seemed overly emphasized given the circumstances. The focus of the story is on Reese's relation to the town, especially as a basketball coach. We expect attention to be paid to the games and trips to play other teams, but not to a vacation Reese takes with a few guys from town. We quickly understood, though, why Smith does what he does because telling us about the New Orleans trip fits with many other things in the story, such as Reese's odd behavior and his occasional foul-ups (drinking and driving, among them). Taken together, these parts of Reese's personality are the more difficult things the town had to put up with—as they were getting over his being an unmarried, black Catholic. What he had to put up with was obvious: their racism and strict values.

Remember that our initial sense of Smith's purpose was that he wants to offer an inspiring example of people overcoming their differences (of religion, culture, racial background) in order to live well together. Based on what we observed—and the questions brought up by those observations—we now think that Smith's purpose is a little different, though still compatible with our initial idea. As sometimes happens, our initial idea now strikes us as only a part of Smith's overall purpose, though initially it seemed to be the overall purpose.

When we look more carefully at what we noted—at the odd interruption of Kevin's story, at the New Orleans story, at phrases like "bootlegger priest," and at the fact that Smith keeps saying over and over (a repetition we left out here but that we noted alongside the essay) that what happened was "magic"—we began to think that Smith wants not just to show us a shining example. Instead, we think Smith is working to tell us something about what is needed if more such stories are to be told—if what happened in Ohio is to happen again. Two things at least have to happen.

1. People have to find ways of, first, putting up with what seems strange or uncomfortable to them, and then coming to appreciate those very things that felt strange or uncomfortable. The townspeople came to appreciate and indeed truly enjoy some of Reese's antics, and they incorporated them into their daily lives. They not only made room for the

antics, but they built them into what they most looked forward to. According to Smith, then, tolerance is not enough to pull off the magic this town experienced.

2 People have to find gray areas in their values and learn to live in them because the differences they experience are real and uncomfortable—and they become more uncomfortable, more intolerable, the more sharply defined they are. For instance, the townspeople chose to look for overlaps between their values and Reese's rather than use the occasion to make ever sharper distinctions. They said, in effect, "He is hardworking and values family, just as we do" rather than, "The way he values family is different than the way we do, and he works harder at different times and on different things than we do."

The town had been suspicious of higher education and the effects sending their children away to college might have on their values and community, but they also value the discipline that goes along with learning, and so when Reese pushed their kids to go on to college, they embraced it, rather than digging their heels in even more. They also did not approve of drinking, but in order to keep Reese a part of their community, they took him to New Orleans and drank beer with him—at least some did. The others approved of the action, though, even if they did not participate. Such division of labor is a strategy for being flexible and again put the emphasis on living in gray areas as opposed to finding excuses to make ever sharper distinctions.

■ Write: If you have observations about the essay that do not fit with the essay's purpose as we describe on the preceding page—or if you have observations that make our description richer or fuller or more complex—write a short rhetorical analysis of the essay in which you use both our and your observations to support your reading.

■ Write: We purposefully did not write anything about the photographs in this essay. Use what you know from earlier chapters about documentary photography and about how words and photographs or drawings work together to write a rhetorical analysis of the photographs and their relationships to the words of the essay. Be sure to consider why whoever designed the layout for this essay would have put particular photographs where they are. How is this analysis different from an analysis of words alone?

■ Discuss with others: To the right is a scan of a page from the book *The Best American Nonrequired Reading* (edited by Dave Eggers, Boston: Houghton Mifflin, 2002), in which "Higher Education" was reprinted—without any of the photographs. What do the photographs add to (or take away from) how you read, analyze, and understand the essay? You could focus on just the two opening pages of the essay from *Sports Illustrated*: with what sort of thoughts or emotions does the close-up picture of Jason Mishler and his tattoo encourage you to start reading the essay? How does that change when—as in the example to the right—there are no photographs?

GARY SMITH

■

Higher Education

FROM *Sports Illustrated*

THIS IS A STORY about a man, and a place where magic happened. It was magic so powerful that the people there can't stop going back over it, trying to figure out who the man was and what happened right in front of their eyes, and how it'll change the time left to them on earth.

See them coming into town to work, or for their cup of coffee at Boyd & Wurthmann, or to make a deposit at Killbuck Savings? One mention of his name is all it takes for everything else to stop, for it all to begin tumbling out . . .

"I'm afraid we can't explain what he meant to us. I'm afraid it's so deep we can't bring it into words."

"It was almost like he was an angel."

"He was looked on as God."

There's Willie Mast. He's the one to start with. It's funny, he'll tell you, his eyes misting, he was so sure they'd all been hoodwinked that he almost did what's unthinkable now — run that man out of town before the magic had a chance.

All Willie had meant to do was bring some buzz to Berlin, Ohio, something to look forward to on a Friday night, for goodness' sake, in a town without high school football or a fast-food restaurant, without a traffic light or even a place to drink a beer, a town dozing in the heart of the largest Amish settlement in the world. Willie had been raised Amish, but he'd walked out on the religion at

PREPARING TO READ THE NEXT ESSAY, "A MARKETABLE WONDER"

About the essay's author

Julian Dibbell has been an assistant editor at the *Village Voice*, a contributor to *Time* magazine, a contributing editor to the online magazine *Feed* and to the print magazine *Wired*, and a visiting fellow at Stanford University's Center for Internet and Society. In all these positions, he has written on digital culture and hackers, computer viruses, online communities, encryption technologies, music piracy, and gamers. His article "A Rape in Cyberspace: Or How an Evil Clown, a Haitian Trickster, Two Wizards, and a Cast of Dozens Turned a Database into a Society" (1993) has been widely reprinted. His book, *My Tiny Life: Crime and Passion in a Virtual World*, was published in 1999.

To prepare for reading: the contexts of reading . . .

Earlier in this book we discussed reading online and its similarities to and differences from reading print texts. The next essay comes from the online magazine *Topic*, and—as you read—keep in mind how reading this essay is both like and unlike reading in a book (if you have easy access to the web, you can read this essay as it was designed to be read, online, by going to the URL listed at the top of the browser window printed on the next page).

To prepare for reading: asking some questions ahead of time

People who study how we can learn to read with more and easier comprehension and interest recommend that you ask questions about a reading before starting, so that when you read you have ideas you want to look for and questions you want answered.

Here are some questions to prepare you to read the next essay, all based on the title, which is "A Marketable Wonder: Spelunking the American Imagination."

- When you hear the noun "wonder," what do you think?

- Should wonders be marketable? That is, does putting something up for sale take away what makes it wonderful?

- If you don't know what "spelunking" is, know that in Latin *spelunx* means "cave"—which sounds goofy now and nowhere near dark and spooky enough for what caves are. A spelunker is someone who enjoys exploring caves. Why might someone find caves fascinating?

- What do you think when you read "American Imagination"? What might it mean for the country—its combined citizens—to have a shared imagination? Think about how you use your imagination and how it shapes sometimes what you do or think about or dream toward, and then ask how a country's imagination might work in the same way. (Sometimes when people want to speak about the imagination of a country, they'll also use the term "cultural imagination," which we will as we discuss this essay.)

- After responding to the previous two questions, what do you think when you hear "Spelunking the American Imagination"? How might the American Imagination be like a cave? What might you learn by exploring it?

- And (perhaps to pique your interest a little) this essay is about computer gaming, specifically about early adventure games. What do you know about such games? Do you play computer games of any kind? Why? Why do others play these games? Keep these thoughts in mind; Dibbell has a suggestion for why certain adventure computer games matter to us, and it very likely will not match yours.

Based on just those questions and before you read, develop a hypothesis about what you think might be going on in the essay. As with "Higher Education," we'll put marginal questions alongside "A Marketable Wonder" to indicate what stands out to us in the essay and why. As you read, mark places where you think we should have asked questions, but didn't. Now turn the page and start reading . . .

When you first read the opening section of this essay, do you think Dibbell is talking about a "real" place or an imagined place? Do you start thinking one thing and then shift to the other? Why or why not? (After you have read the essay all the way through, come back to this section: why might Dibbell allow there to be some ambiguity here?)

What do you have to know, culturally, to understand the context of the first section of this essay—"You are standing at the end of a road . . ."? Does Dibbell ever explain where these words come from? If so, how far into the essay? What does this tell you about expectations he has of his audience?

TOPIC MAGAZINE

in this issue

2:FANTASY

about us
subscribe
in this issue
past issues
extras
submissions
sponsorships
links

Julian Dibbell

A MARKETABLE WONDER

Spelunking the
American Imagination

You are standing at the end of a road before a small brick building. Around you is a forest. A small stream flows out of the building and down a gully.

You move south, following the stream as it tumbles along a rocky bed through a valley in the forest. At your feet, suddenly, all the water of the stream splashes into a two-inch slit in the rock. Ahead of you, the streambed is bare rock. You follow it down into a twenty-foot depression floored with bare dirt. Set into the dirt is a strong steel grate mounted in concrete. You open the grate and descend into a small rocky chamber. A low crawl over cobbles leads inward to the west. You crawl, dim light coming in through the grate behind you. There is a small wicker cage discarded nearby. You turn on your lamp. You enter a room filled with debris washed in from the surface. A note on the wall says "MAGIC WORD XYZZY," and a three-foot black rod with a rusty star on an end lies nearby. An awkward canyon leads upward and west. You enter it. You come, after a while, to a splendid chamber thirty feet high. The walls are frozen rivers of orange stone.

You pause a moment to take it in.

You are in a splendid chamber thirty feet high. The walls are frozen rivers of orange stone.

A cheerful little bird is sitting here singing.

To speak of fantasy in contemporary American culture is, as any contemporary American adolescent can tell you, to speak of dungeons and dragons.

More precisely, it is to speak of underground labyrinths and the adventures to be had in them. And more precisely still, perhaps, it is to speak of one such labyrinth in particular: Kentucky's Mammoth Cave system, the longest in the world, 350 miles of passageway snaking

Julian Dibbell has been writing about the culture of digital technologies for over a decade. He is the author of *My Tiny Life: Crime and Passion in a Virtual World*, and is currently a visiting fellow at Stanford University's Center for Internet and Society. He can be contacted at jdibbell@yahoo.com.

Topic Magazine is a quarterly non-fiction publication of unparalleled variety of voice. Each issue invites an international collection of writers and photographers to comment on a timely topic. In keeping with its mission, *Topic* respects the original spelling of its authors. Texts written by American authors are edited in American style; texts by British authors in British style. *Topic* is edited in Cambridge and New York.

We accept and welcome unsolicited manuscripts. We prefer receiving all proposals over email. We also accept submissions at either postal address.

system, the longest in the world, 350 miles of passageways snaking intricately beneath some 20 square miles of wooded hill country and surfacing at over a dozen widely scattered holes in the ground, one of which, known as the Bedquilt Entrance, happens to bear a strong resemblance to the small chamber beneath the strong steel grate set in the dirt at the bottom of the depression that rises to the streambed that leads to the small brick building at the end of the road described above.

That description, it turns out, holds a central place in the history of modern fantasy. It comprises the opening moves, quoted more or less verbatim, of the classic mid-'70s computer game Adventure, the world's first computerized role-playing game and the primal ancestor of all those that followed. Today at least a million people live parallel lives in the richly social worlds of multiplayer online role-playing games like Everquest and Ultima Online. Millions more have lost themselves for weeks on end in the lucidly rendered dream worlds of single-player games like Myst and Morrowind. But not many are aware of the debt these vivid, graphics-intensive realms owe to the crude but engrossing text-based world of Adventure -- and fewer still know how much that world owes to the sand- and limestone reality of Mammoth.

What it owes is nothing less than its structure: take away the magic wands, fearsome dragons, axe-wielding dwarves, and other enchantments that populate Adventure's caverns, and what remains is a simulated Bedquilt so topographically correct that experienced Adventure players have been known, on their first visits to the real Bedquilt, to navigate its complex passages more knowledgeably than their guides.

Stephen Bishop was seventeen years old when he first stood amid the poplars outside Mammoth's yawning entrance and felt the chill air of the cavern on his face. The year was 1838, and Bishop was a slave.

His owner was Franklin Gorin, a Glasgow, Kentucky, lawyer who had recently bought the Mammoth Cave tract and planned to build it up as a tourist attraction. He wasn't the first to try. From its discovery by white men in the late 1700s through the end of the War of 1812, Mammoth Cave was exploited primarily for its reserves of calcium nitrate, or niter, a byproduct of bat guano that was easily converted into the saltpeter needed to make gunpowder. During the war, saltpeter prices skyrocketed, and the cave became a subterranean factory for the mining and processing of niter, manned by as many as seventy slaves at a time. But when the war ended, prices collapsed, and the cave's owners shifted into a less labor-intensive business: charging people to come in and take a look.

It wasn't a bad idea. The heavy digging around the niter works had uncovered prehistoric human remains, including a number of "mummies" -- dried-out aboriginal corpses, well-preserved in the cave's mild air, some still dressed in elaborate ceremonial gear. Word of the discoveries spread fast, fascinating a young, culturally insecure nation eager for any signs of ancient civilization in its midst, and the cave owners readied themselves for a flourishing tourist trade. The apex of the mummies' fame, however, was followed swiftly by the financial depression of 1819, and visitor traffic never amounted to much. When Gorin bought the cave two decades later, it had become a steady but hardly impressive moneymaker, and he got it for less than a quarter of what it would have sold for at the height of the saltpeter boom, thirty-five years before.

But Gorin meant business. He started renovating and enlarging the

■ Because this is the end of a section, and because it begins with a slightly dramatic sounding sentence ("What it owes is nothing less . . ."), we pay extra attention to this paragraph. It tells us that there are both "real" and "simulated" Bedquilts——and we wonder why this matters, and how Dibbell will explain why this matters.

■ In preparation for reading this, we asked you what the United States' "cultural imagination" might be, since this is in the title. Here we see Dibbell speaking of a "culturally insecure nation," so we pay attention. What might it mean for a nation to be "culturally insecure"?

▓ What kind of mental image have you developed of Bishop? Look at the words and phrases Dibbell uses to describe him: Does Bishop "come alive" for you? What kind of mental image have you developed of the cave? How have Dibbell's words encouraged you toward that mental image? We ask this because Dibbell is focusing our attentions on Bishop and the cave, and we are curious why and we wonder what Dibbell will do with these characterizations.

▓ Because of the title of this essay—about the cultural imagination of the United States—we also pay extra attention to the paragraph in which Dibbell tells us about how Bishop uses "fancy" (sometimes used as a synonym for "imagination") to strengthen his memory of the caves, memory of its structure but also of its "delights." As with the above questions, we don't find immediate answers in the essay, though, but these questions help us look for and understand what might come in the rest of the essay.

But Gorin meant business. He started renovating and enlarging the cave site's dilapidated inn. He added stables. And in what turned out to be his smartest move, he brought Bishop to the cave to work as a guide.

Small, lithe, and passionately curious, Bishop proved a quick study and an unprecedented caver. Permitted to explore Mammoth's recesses in his off hours, he squeezed through crevices and traversed chasms no man or woman had braved before, pushing on to discover unsuspected marvels: vertical shafts over a hundred feet high, dripping with flowstone; underground lakes and rivers, populated by eyeless albino fish; a chamber thickly blanketed with snowy-looking encrustations and delicate white gypsum "flowers." All through the winter of his first year at Mammoth, Bishop explored, doubling the size of the known cave by spring and securing once and for all its reputation as a natural wonder.

But Bishop did more than that as well: he made the cave a cultural phenomenon. By his second season, visitors arrived asking for him by name, drawn by the fame of his erudite, entertaining tours. "He had a fine genius, a great fund of wit and humor, some little knowledge of Latin and Greek, and much knowledge of geology," Gorin wrote several years later, "but his great talent was his knowledge of man. . . . He knew a gentleman or a lady as if by instinct."

Bishop made the most of this ability to size people up, making sure all comers got the spectacle they felt they'd paid for. Most were easily satisfied; others came hungry to explore uncharted cave. Bishop catered to them all, at times bringing the more adventurous along with him on his discoveries -- at others, apparently, letting them think they were discovering territory he had in fact already surveyed. As expert as he was in exploring, in other words, he was expert, too, in delivering what was then a novel sort of product but is now known familiarly (to students of latemodern marketing culture, anyway) as the commodified experience.

In both areas of expertise, however, his great advantage seems to have been a single insight: that Mammoth wasn't one cave but two, the one embedded in rock and the other in the imagination. Indeed, in at least one sense Bishop dwelled more in the second than the first, since aboveground or below he carried always in his head a nearly perfect image of the cave system. When Gorin sold his property, slaves and all, to Dr. John Croghan in 1839, the new owner asked Bishop to sketch a map of his discoveries and was astonished by the level of detail. Croghan commissioned a more thorough map, and Bishop, holed up at Croghan's Louisville estate, spent two weeks perfecting it, walking through every room and tunnel of the caverns in his mind and ending up with a chart that remained unsurpassed in its accuracy for the next sixty years.

The map documented more than Bishop's keen spatial memory, though. It also recorded the colorful names he'd given his discoveries: Fairy Grotto, Little Bat Room, Snowball Room, Gothic Avenue, Cleaveland's Cabinet, Serena's Arbour, Purgatory, Haunted Chamber, Indian Graves, Giant's Coffin, Dismal Hollow. For Bishop, clearly, it wasn't enough just to map the material structure of the cave's passages and chambers. Its shape, after all, wasn't only topographical. It was fanciful as well, a network of mythic resonances and poetic leaps that had occurred to Bishop and his occasional companions as they'd explored -- and that the names helped keep alive in his mind. They made his memory of the cave more vivid, and they fixed in words and images his delight in the spaces he had found.

Also, of course, they weren't bad for business. Bishop plainly understood that part of his job, maybe even the main part, was to help his guests see more in the cave than what was merely there. The

his guests see more in the cave than what was merely there. The suggestive place names did some of that work. Other bits of underground theater did the rest. The poet and travel writer Nathaniel Parker Willis, who visited Mammoth Cave in 1852, described how Bishop deftly set the mood for fantasy when Willis's tour group came to an empty spot ("not a very attractive-looking place in itself") where once the handsomely attired mummy of an Indian woman had reposed: "Stephen set down his lamp, after showing us the hollow niche in the rock against which the fair one was found sitting, as if, with his sixteen years' experience as guide, he had found this to be a spot where the traveler usually takes time for reverie. It cost me no coaxing to have mine. With the silence of the spot, and all the world shut out, it is impossible that the imagination should not do pretty fair justice to the single idea presented."

For all that his charges sought out such moments of reverie, however, Bishop couldn't have missed the ambivalence that settled around those moments like a fog. What Willis and his like were after was a power Western culture had long imputed to caves -- the power of phantasmatic vision, of oracles and apparitions. But the flipside of this power was an even greater powerlessness -- that of problematic vision, of blindness and delusion -- and Bishop surely knew it. Perhaps his "little knowledge of Latin and Greek" had brought him in contact with Plato's famous "Simile of the Cave." Perhaps he knew therefore that the founding fable of Western philosophy envisioned the cave as a kind of epistemological torture chamber, peopled with prisoners allowed to see nothing of the outside world except its shadows and obliged, in the end, to mistake the shadows for reality. But even if he'd never read the basic texts, Bishop had the basic idea: the first two bodies of water he discovered in Mammoth's depths he named in honor of the ancient mythic links between ghosts, unknowingness, and the underground. He called them the River Styx and Lake Lethe.

Also, there were younger myths afoot in Bishop's day that would have driven the older meanings home in any case. The American mythology of wide open spaces was coming into its own. Outside the cave lay Kentucky, scarcely a generation removed from its frontier days, and further west a continental blanket of unsettled territory rolled on to the Pacific. The ample, welcoming Cartesian plane of the prairie was becoming more and more a symbol of the promised freedom and opportunity at the heart of America's self-image. How un-American, then, the close, crooked, fractal shape of Bishop's cave must have seemed to visitors. How redolent of bondage and limitation, and how fitting to find installed as "chief ruler" and "presiding genius of this territory" a bondsman, his only subjects a handful of dead Indians. For if the open plain had become the defining topology of America's central myth, of prosperous liberty, the cave was necessarily its countermyth, and what better demographics to people it with than those that gave the lie to the official story?

The irony, of course, was that for Bishop the cave was anything but a place of bondage. The guide work was a kind of servitude, certainly, but he didn't seem to mind it. And when he ditched the tourists and went exploring, as he continued to do throughout his life, he could hardly have felt more free. To picture Bishop on his own in the cave's far depths -- striding in awe down some new avenue so vast his lantern barely illuminated the walls, or leading his young wife through the tunnels to admire some piece of subterranean beauty only he had ever seen before -- is to contemplate an image of near-perfect autonomy.

And yet, besotted though he was with this "grand, gloomy, and peculiar place" (as he called it), Bishop recognized that the freedom he enjoyed there was, like so much else about the cave, only partly

■ Dibbell uses Plato's "Simile of the Cave" to talk about Mammoth Cave. In the "Simile," prisoners (in chains with their backs to a large fire) see before them only their shadows cast by the fire—because that is all they can see, they think the shadows are all there is in the world. Dibbell contrasts Plato's "Simile" (which Dibbell speculates Bishop might have known) to the spiritual experience Willis sought in Mammoth Cave.

▥ We think these paragraphs are important because—once again—Dibbell brings up "imagination." Here he shows how imagination can have light and dark sides, and he ties this splitting to "America's self-image" and to Bishop's slavery. Answer for yourself this question: just what are the connections Dibbell seems to be making between the dark and the light, and between slavery and the United States' sense of itself in the mid-nineteenth century?

469

he enjoyed there was, like so much else about the cave, only partly real. One day in 1852, as he and Willis paused to rest on their way down to see the blindfish in the River Styx, the author asked him what he thought of slavery. As it happened, Dr. Croghan had died two years before, and the doctor's will stipulated that Bishop and a number of other slaves were to be set free seven years after his death. As Bishop now confided to Willis, though, that wasn't soon enough for him. He told Willis he meant to buy his freedom -- and his wife and son's -- as soon as possible. He said he was saving the wages he'd been getting since his master's death, and that he planned to take his family to a place far away from Kentucky. They were going to resettle in Liberia, the new African colony for freed American slaves.

Neither Willis nor Bishop could know, of course, that none of this would come to pass. Bishop never would get the money together to buy his way out of slavery; freedom would come to him in 1856, not through his own efforts but in accordance with his master's will; and one year after that, Bishop would die of unrecorded causes, aged thirty-six, his family still in slavery.

For now, though, he had the fantasy, and as sweet as life in Mammoth Cave had been, the fantasy was sweeter. Bishop talked, Willis listened, and then it was time to move on. When they came at last to the River Styx, Bishop dipped a net into the water and brought up a small, wriggling fish, ghostwhite and eyeless. The two men sat by the river a while longer, then headed back to daylight. They took the dying blindfish with them, up, out, and back to the Mammoth Cave Hotel, where it was gutted and placed on public display.

❧   ❧   ❧

Will Crowther was thirty-eight years old when he first gazed into his future as a middle-aged North American white male and felt the chill air of desolation on his face. The year was 1976, and Crowther was going through a rough divorce.

He'd seen better days for sure; much better. Four years earlier, he'd had a wife he loved, two young daughters he adored, a job that pushed his considerable talents to their limit, and an odd but thrilling hobby that both consumed and fulfilled him. Now all he had was the job.

Not that that was anything to sneeze at. To say that Crowther was a computer programmer is, by all accounts, something like saying that Michelangelo was a ceiling painter. By the time Crowther reached his professional stride, sometime in his early thirties, a poll of his peers probably would have ranked him in the top of the top percentile of the world's programmers. His coworkers at the Cambridge, Massachussetts, consulting firm of Bolt Beranek and Newman needed no such confirmation of his brilliance, however. Years later they would still recall his remarkable ability to picture in his head, at every level of detail, the entirety of whatever complex program he was working on -- the equivalent, one said, of "designing a whole city while keeping track of the wiring to each lamp and the plumbing to every toilet."

In 1969, BBN had won the contract to build a new, decentralized kind of computer network for the Defense Department. Called arpanet, the network was the beginning of what would eventually be called the Internet, and while it would be a gross exaggeration to say Crowther invented the thing, it doesn't seem too far off the mark to say he wrote it. Not single-handedly, of course, but if there was one coder on BBN's small programming team who was truly indispensable, Crowther was it. "Most of the rest of us," one teammate later recalled, "made our livings handling the details resulting from Will's use of his brain."

■ Because this is another end of a section, and because the tense of the writing has shifted from the past to the present tense, we think Dibbell is doing something here important to his purpose. Why would Dibbell end this section with Bishop and Willis (who have been contrasted in their attitude toward the cave in the preceding paragraphs) with them bringing to the surface a "small, wriggling fish, ghostwhite and eyeless," a fish that also is dying, that is gutted and put on display? We wonder if the fish could represent something, if it could be something that is supposed to function in our imaginations, too.

livings handling the details resulting from Will's use of his brain."

But if coding was Crowther's gift, his passion lay elsewhere: underground. During the happier years of their marriage, he and his wife, Pat, had spent every vacation they could exploring the network of caves beneath Kentucky's Flint Ridge, adjacent to the Mammoth cave system. They befriended world-class cavers and ultimately joined their ranks, becoming key participants in a concerted quest to conquer "the Everest of world speleology": the discovery of a connection between Flint Ridge and Mammoth, which would confirm the Mammoth system as the longest in the world. When they weren't slogging through the muck and murk on survey trips, Will and Pat contributed to the effort by helping maintain the project's maps. Crucially, Will wangled some room on one of BBN's computers to load in the cartographic data, and for the first time in caving history the shape of the subterranean labyrinth was reduced to the precision of pure numbers. The Crowthers set up a Teletype terminal in a corner of their living room and started keying in cave data, which in turn became cave maps, sharp-lined and schematic, printed out on a plotter at BBN's offices and brought home nightly by Will to clutter up the house.

Somewhere in those pages lay the passage they were seeking. Poring over the maps together in late evenings, after they'd kissed their daughters, Sandy and Laura, good night, Will and Pat must have laid eyes on it a hundred times, never knowing what it was and where it led. In the end it was Pat who found out: the survey party that finally discovered the connection between Flint Ridge and Mammoth, on August 30, 1972, was made up of her and three other veteran cavers, none of them Will. He was thrilled, of course, both for his wife and for the collective effort they had taken part in. But he hadn't been there, and he couldn't feel what Pat felt. She wrote later that when she woke up on the Thursday morning after the discovery, she felt the same way she had after she'd given birth to her children: the whole world seemed new. She put on a Gordon Lightfoot record, she said, and cried.

Was it then that the seed of Will and Pat's eventual breakup was planted? Did Will's absence from the historic trip signal the onset of greater and greater distances between them? Who can say? It's enough to note that by late 1975 their marriage was falling apart, and that by early 1976 it was over.

And here was where Will's own historic moment began. As he later explained to an interviewer, he had lately taken to playing a new kind of game called Dungeons and Dragons, getting together with some of the guys from BBN whenever enough of them had the time. The particular D & D scenario they were playing involved a lot of imaginary traipsing through the woods and caverns of J.R.R. Tolkien's Middle Earth, and in it, Crowther role-played a thief character, called simply Willie the Thief. The game was intensely absorbing, and though he didn't exactly play it to escape from reality, the distraction couldn't have hurt: Will and Pat's divorce was on its way and soon enough arrived.

"And that left me a bit pulled apart in various ways," said Crowther. "In particular I was missing my kids. Also the caving had stopped, because that had become awkward." Between wife, kids, and cave, the divorce had taken from him most of what had given his life its shape, if not its meaning. Faced with such a loss, many men Crowther's age would have turned to desperate consolations -- drinking too much, having affairs with twenty-year-olds, blowing paychecks on high-end audio equipment. Others would have simply despaired. But Crowther, being Crowther, had a different idea: "I decided I would fool around and write a program that was a re-

The shift in Dibbell's writing from the nineteenth century to the twentieth is abrupt, without explanation. We can see it coming, in the layout (see the preceding page and the three dingbats)—but Dibbell says nothing of it. This makes us wonder what Dibbell wants us as readers to take from this shift. How are we to see the relationship between the nineteenth century and the twentieth, in terms of where Dibbell focuses our attentions?

decided I would fool around and write a program that was a re-creation in fantasy of my caving, and also would be a game for the kids, and perhaps [include] some aspects of the Dungeons and Dragons that I had been playing."

The game, of course, was Adventure. What Crowther wrote then was a simple thing compared to what most Adventure players came to know -- a sketch dashed off in three or four bursts of weekend coding. Still, almost everything that mattered was already in place. The lean but vivid cave descriptions, based on Crowther's fondly, fiercely remembered Bedquilt, were mostly all there. The rudimentary puzzles of the opening game -- a few hidden treasures, some difficult beasts, the mysterious magic word XYZZY -- had been installed. Crowther's daughters, then aged seven and five, "thought it was a lot of fun," he determined, and that was enough for him. After a while, having drawn whatever solace he could from the game, Crowther left it on a BBN computer and didn't give it much more thought.

And there it might have remained, had BBN's computers not been attached to the network Crowther helped create. Word of the game began to circulate from network node to network node, as did the game itself. A few months after Crowther wrote it, Don Woods, a grad student at the Stanford Artificial Intelligence Laboratory, found a copy of Adventure on a local computer and was smitten. Frustrated by bugs in the program, though, and by the game's relative simplicity, Woods emailed Crowther asking for a copy of the source code so he could take a shot at improving it. Crowther obliged, and after several months' work, Woods released what has become the game's canonical version. He had added a point system and done a considerable amount of landscaping, putting in an active underground volcano, further complicating the existing mazes, and generally making the game enough of a challenge to suck the average unsuspecting player into a black hole of addiction.

The rest is technological history. As computer culture spread, so spread Adventure, the two so closely intertwining that each became a kind of image of the other. One veteran coder profiled in The Soul of a New Machine, Tracy Kidder's classic inside look at the computer industry circa 1980, could think of no better way to convey the obsessive thrill of programming than to sit the author down and have him lose himself in Adventure's labyrinth of puzzles. "Each 'room' of the adventure was like a computer subroutine, presenting a logical problem you'd have to solve," Steven Levy later explained in Hackers, his epic history of coder culture. "In a sense, Adventure was a metaphor for computer programming itself -- the deep recesses you explored in the Adventure world were akin to the basic, most obscure levels of the machine that you'd be traveling in when you hacked assembly code. You could get dizzy trying to remember where you were in both activities."

By the millennium's end, Adventure had become such an elemental fixture of the computing landscape -- available on every platform from Windows to Linux to Palm and still a common point of reference for computer geeks -- that it seemed always to have been there. Literary critic Espen Aarseth has called it "a mythological urtext, located everywhere and nowhere." For Aarseth, Adventure's mythic dimension derived not only from its sword-and-sorcery ambience but from its privileged place in the technocultural imagination, where it looms as the legendary origin of digital narrative itself. Branching, multilinear, not so much read as explored, the literary mode that theorists have variously called hypertext, cybertext, interactive fiction, ergodic literature, and other, less felicitous names, has as much in common with the structure of caves as with the structure of computing -- and in Adventure, which elegantly conflates the two, it finds not only one of its earliest instances but its most lucid definition.

■ This paragraph calls our attention because Dibbell has used the cave earlier—as an idea—to think about how the United States thought about itself in the nineteenth century. Here the cave is used—as an idea—to describe what computer programming is like. What might be Dibbell's purpose in these various uses of the cave as an idea, as a metaphor? Is the cultural imagination of the United States now shifted to something else?

472

one of its earliest instances but its most lucid definition.

No wonder so many more people have heard of Adventure than have heard of Will Crowther. The game seems so organic an extension of the logic of the digital into the realm of the imaginary that it's easy to forget someone had to invent it. And yes, no doubt it's true that if Crowther hadn't invented Adventure, the nature of computers and of make-believe would sooner or later have compelled someone else to dream up something very much like it.

But the fact remains that Will Crowther did invent Adventure. And if you play it with your mind awake to more than just the challenge of its puzzles, you'll know it wasn't just the nature of computers and of make-believe that compelled him to.

Follow again that path from the small brick building to the steel grate in the ground; go down into the rocky chamber just below it; crawl west, over cobbles. Note the odd, precise details along the way: the debris washed in from the surface, the stream disappearing into a two-inch slit. Note the hint of melancholy in the spare, attentive prose that renders these details, the way it amplifies the loneliness inherent in this solitary quest. Go west again, and then once more. Imagine a man sick with yearning for a place he'll never see again, and for the life he lost when he lost this place. Imagine the care with which he might try to re-create this place in fantasy: how hard he would try not to lose its beauty by remaking it more beautiful than it really was, or on the other hand to sour its memory by reinventing it as anything, finally, but a place of delight. Then look around you:

You are in a splendid chamber thirty feet high. The walls are frozen rivers of orange stone.

A cheerful little bird is sitting here singing.

In his 1995 essay "The Craft of Adventure," game designer Graham Nelson sets out to define an aesthetic of what is generally known as interactive fiction but which he prefers to call adventure games. Addressed to the small but passionate community of amateurs who continue to produce computer games in Adventure's text-only, role-play style (the brief commercial heyday of Infocom's Zork and other shrink-wrapped Adventure knock-offs came and went over two decades ago), Nelson's argument starts with a single principle: "In the beginning of any game is its 'world', physical and imaginary, geography and myth."

It's for this reason, perhaps, that Nelson locates the historical origin of the form not in the creation of Adventure but in the moment Mammoth Cave stopped functioning as a source of well-composted bat shit and started succeeding as a source of marketable wonder. Adventure works as well as it does, Nelson argues, largely because its world is grounded in Crowther's experiences of an actual place -- and that place is Mammoth. Long before Crowther adapted the cave to his purposes, after all, another man had prepared it for him, refashioning the cave as both physical and imaginary, geography and myth. "Perhaps the first adventurer," Nelson suggests, "was a mulatto slave named Stephen Bishop."

It makes more than passing sense. Even at a casual glance the parallels between Bishop and Crowther stand out like signposts. One cave, two men: each man drawn to the cave as a site of both mythic fantasy and arduous exploration; each possessed of an astonishing memory for complex structure and a fascination with the job of mapping the cave's; each, curiously enough, turning finally to the cave in hopes of finding there a kind of domestic redemption --

■ We have noticed by now that, just as the previous section focused on Bishop and the cave, this section focuses on Crowther and the cave. This makes us curious about how Dibbell wants us to understand Bishop and Crowther in their similarities and differences. How is Crowther described? How is he like Bishop, and how different? How is his relationship with the cave similar—and how different?

■ Here we notice that Dibbell is showing Crowther using the cave for the purposes of memory and pleasure, to hold onto good things in sad times—and this takes us back to the place in the essay in which Dibbell described Bishop's use of memory to work the cave into his life. How are Bishop's and Crowther's uses of memory and the cave similar and different?

Once again Dibbell mentions the blind-fish—in the very last sentence, in the very last words; in that sentence he also brings Bishop and Crowther together to state that the two men made their discoveries because they sought dark, not light. (And if you've read *Heart of Darkness*, a novel by Joseph Conrad, you should perhaps be doubly struck by Dibbell's last sentence.) All this makes us very curious, because—even though Dibbell has told us the differences between Bishop and Crowther are more important than the similarities—it seems to show Dibbell arguing, at the very end, that their similar desire for the cave is what is, finally, most important and what we ought to learn from.

Ah, here, finally, is Dibbell telling us why he has told us the parallel narratives of Bishop and Crowther. How are your observations about Dibbell's purpose in the parallel narratives satisfied by his explanation?

mapping the cave's, each, curiously enough, turning finally to the cave in hopes of finding there a kind of domestic redemption -- Crowther grappling in imaginary shadows with the emotions of his divorce, Bishop applying the fruits of his explorations toward the goal of buying his wife and son out of slavery.

Ultimately, though, what interests most about the comparison between Bishop and Crowther isn't the similarities but the differences, and the way they illuminate the shifting cultural contexts the two men inhabited. When Bishop discovered his cave, the American mythos of open space was in ascent, buoyed not only by the expansion of the national frontier but by the burgeoning imperialism of Western civilization generally. By Crowther's day, however, the frontiers had closed (even the "final frontier" explored by the Apollo missions was shutting down), and America was in the market for a new sort of mythic space. And just as Bishop's status as a slave reflected the place of the cave in the cultural imagination of the time, so Crowther's role as an Internet pioneer suggested the cave's new meaning and new centrality: it had become iconic of life in the fast-approaching information age, an epoch in which the occupation of open territory (and the exploitation of its resources) matters less than the knowledge of complex, hidden passageways and what they lead to.

Forking, twisted, and tangled, a topological profusion in which no two points are connected by fewer than two paths -- the shape of caves is, in many ways, the shape we're in these days. It's the shape of the networks we explore now everyday, wanting to or not: communication networks, networks of commerce, of image, of fact. Networks of power, threaded around the world and centered nowhere in particular.

This is not the world Stephen Bishop was born into. For that matter it's not even the world Will Crowther came of age in. But it's a world both showed us how to navigate. Mammoth Cave may not be Plato's, but it's just as dark, and in it Bishop and Crowther learned a new way to seek life's meaning: not by moving toward the light but by descending further into shadow, toward the heart of darkness where the blindfish swim.

Back to Top | Table of Contents | Subscribe to *Topic*

Internet zone

ANALYZING
"A Marketable Wonder"

■ **Discuss with others:** "A Marketable Wonder" starts with a passage from a computer game and has a long section about a man who invented that game—but the title doesn't mention games, and the conclusion doesn't seem to be about games, either. Just what is it that you think Dibbell wants us to take from this essay?

■ **Write:** The title of this essay is "A Marketable Wonder"—but the essay doesn't much discuss markets, commerce, or selling. Look for where in the essay these things are discussed, and see if you can develop a statement of purpose for this essay that explains how and why those things are discussed.

■ **Write:** The medium in which this essay was published is the World Wide Web. Use what you know from the earlier chapters on visual texts and from your own experiences to write a short paper describing how you think the essay has been designed to work on the Web. One approach to such a task is to consider how this text could be designed differently; such an approach offers at least two directions to consider. You could consider a redesign that arranged this text across multiple pages; how might this text's audience understand the text were it to have multiple pages (for example, the introduction, the sections on Stephen Bishop and on Will Crowther, and the conclusion could each be a page)? You could also consider how the text would be read differently were it presented in different colors, or in a different column width, or with different navigational arrangements and information at the top of the page.

■ **Write:** Even though it is easier to make photographs a part of Web compositions than print compositions, "A Marketable Wonder" includes no photographs or other illustrations (such as maps) of the cave or the two men described in the essay. This is not to say that the essay should have them—but how might including photographs or illustrations change how you understand the essay? Write a short paper describing how you might include photographs or illustrations with this essay: describe what you would include, where you would place the photographs or illustrations (would they be on separate pages linked to these pages, or embedded in particular places within the words), and why. What effects would such additions have on this essay? How would they change audience perceptions of the purpose of the essay? Might the designers' decision not to include illustrations with this essay connect in some way with the essay being in some way about imagination?

"THE PLAINTIFF SPEAKS"

"The Plaintiff Speaks" comes from a collection of essays by multiple authors, titled *Picturing Us: African American Identity in Photography*.

We aren't going to tell you here about the author of the essay, Clarissa Sligh, because this essay is about her and her experiences, and so depends completely on how she constructs her *ethos* through her words. We would like for you to attend carefully to how Sligh writes, to watch for how she constructs a particular relation with her readers.

As a reader, you probably look at these photographs before you read anything of the essay. What do you take from these photographs? How do they shape how you read?

Newspaper Clipping, 1956

THE PLAINTIFF SPEAKS

Clarissa T. Sligh

I WAS A TEENAGER WHEN I FIRST SAW THIS GROUP OF PHOTOGRAPHS and the article that they appeared with, on June 1, 1956, in the *Washington Post and Times Herald*, the major daily newspaper in the Washington, D.C., area. Since I was one of the people in the pictures, I knew that they were to be published and had been looking forward to seeing them with great anticipation for several months. Now, as I recall the time when I first saw the photographs and read the words, I remember how I felt very disappointed and let down. I felt that I had been used, although back then, I had no one to whom I could try to articulate why I felt that I had been "wronged."

The difference between right and wrong had been etched in my mind, in large measure at the neighborhood baptist church that we attended. At the Mt. Salvation Baptist Church, you were either on one side of the line or the other; there was never any "maybe" about it. The article appeared during the development of my second great period of cynicism. The first began at the early age of four years old, when it dawned on me that my oldest brother, Clarence Junior, controlled our household. No amount of telling my momma the mean things he did to me could protect me from his wrath.

I did not trust anyone except my brother Stephen, who was three years younger than me. But now that I had begun menstruating, more and more things in my life seemed too complicated and shameful to talk with him about.

I did not know anyone else who would understand me, who would not respond with blank looks or harsh disapproving words. The thoughts that ran through my mind were something like, "Be grateful! What do you expect? You are lucky to get any photograph in the *Washington Post* at all!" It was a newspaper for which we blacks were usually invisible, except as criminals or welfare recipients.

The mingled voices in my head were of my grandma, momma, daddy, the black preacher, and teachers all trying to teach me how to live in the world with a broken heart. As a young black female growing

- How would you characterize the tone of voice Sligh chooses to use in this writing? Does it sound to you as though this piece were written, or does it sound as though she is speaking out loud?

- How do you, as a reader, respond to the last two sentences of Sligh's first paragraph?

- What sense of Sligh do you develop from her choice of talking almost immediately about the sense of right and wrong she learned in church?

- Why might Sligh write about the coming of puberty and how it made her life feel complicated and shameful? How might different readers respond?

up in the American South of the 1940s and '50s, I was taught, in words and by example, how to stand on my own two feet and not expect too much from anybody, no matter how sincere they appeared.

They were trying to teach me how to survive. My grandmother's father and my mother's grandmother had been slaves in this country. They were afraid that if I didn't "get it," I would end up in a madhouse or get myself killed. My father, however, didn't want me to become *too* independent. He would say that nobody would want to marry me.

I loved the out-of-doors, and I learned to do everything my brothers could do and relished the look on their faces when they saw me do it better. But my father's attitude was that doing women's work made a man a "sissy," and he would have no part of it. So I wondered, "Then why should *I* want to do it?" When he sent my brothers out to do chores in the yard, he would look at me and say, "Go help your mother." These words never failed to bring anger and disappointment to my heart. But I thought he would slap me down if I dared to talk back to him. Yet he never put a hand on me, except at my mother's urging, when she felt I was more than she could handle.

My father's only goal for me was to get a husband. He made it pretty clear to me that if I did not remain a virgin, or, worse, if I got pregnant, no man would ever want to touch me. He made it sound like I would spend the rest of my life wandering through hell. Yet I was aware at the same time that he felt that my failing to remain a virgin would be more a matter of another male getting over on him than it being a weakness on my part.

I knew my mother resented the isolated, tedious drudgery of raising babies and doing housework all the time. As the oldest girl, I was the only one who heard her complaints. Neither of us liked her life, and I knew she wanted more for me. So Momma and I were pretty excited when we found out that my picture was to be taken as part of a story about efforts to desegregate schools in Arlington. But Daddy did not want any part of it.

Two years earlier, in 1954, when the Supreme Court ruled that racially segregated schools were unconstitutional, it was like an invisible bomb dropping on our neighborhood. We lived in one of four black communities in the county that was totally surrounded by whites. Since the time when I was about eight my mother had been taking me to state and national NAACP meetings where people gave reports on civil rights

Why might Sligh emphasize her "education" as a woman here?

What sense do you develop of Sligh's parents from how she writes about them? What sense of her do you develop through how she talks about her parents?

What choices do you see Sligh making in how she talks about white people?

work that was going on throughout the South and discussed future strategies and ways to raise money for the legal work.

I did not believe that things would ever change. Momma, however, would quietly sit and listen. She was not one of those people who asked questions or spoke out in public, but I could tell she was intensely interested, because when she wasn't, she would be sound asleep, even while sitting upright in her chair.

Many times, she could not go because no one was available to stay with my three baby sisters, Gloria, Lillian, and Jean. My father refused to do any baby-related tasks. So, on those occasions, she would send me to the meetings with a neighbor or someone from our church. I was supposed to listen and come back and tell her everything that was said, a job I took very seriously.

Prior to the Supreme Court decision, I was "bussed" to the black high school on the south side of the county when I entered the seventh grade. One night while lying awake in bed, I heard my parents talk about how I was not getting much of an education. My bed was against the wall. I could also hear that they were not considering any plans to send me someplace else. I figured that it must have been because I was a girl. My two older brothers, Clarence Junior and Carroll, had been enrolled in the "better" schools of Washington, D.C.

Both of my parents had completed high school. At that time, it was considered the minimum requirement for getting a "decent" job. My mother had come to the D.C. area from Hickory, North Carolina, in order to find work. She had had a dream of going to Howard University, but she had no money to do it. My father grew up in D.C.. He had studied Latin and had read all the classics, but it did not seem to help him get any further than his job as a shipping-room clerk at the Bureau of Engraving. He griped about the stupid white men who were the bosses over his all-black group of workers. He was very bitter about it.

My mother had become a full-time domestic worker, shuttling to different white women's houses every day. She worked for the minimum wage until she was too old to do it anymore. Whenever she wanted to pull me up short, she would scream that if I didn't do well in school I would "end up working in some white woman's kitchen." To her that was as low as you could go. They struggled to make ends meet, and they knew that life would be very hard for us kids if we did not have at least

■ Here is more information about Sligh's parents and their attitudes toward Sligh's being a girl. How is the way Sligh is telling these details of her life shaping your sense of her parents, her world, and her *ethos*?

a high school education. Without that diploma, the most widely available job opportunities for blacks, where we lived, were domestic work for women and ditch digging for men. I saw that my parents were shut out of jobs available to whites with far fewer qualifications. Of course, employment want ads in the *Washington Post* generally began "Whites Only," and that was one qualification they would never have, no matter how much education they got.

My high school was being remodeled, but when I started there two years earlier, the school barely met the state of Virginia's minimum requirements for black students. There had been no gymnasium, cafeteria, science lab, or rooms to take home economics and shop classes in. When it rained, we put buckets around the room in our physical education class to catch the water that poured in. We did not have a library and all our textbooks were used books sent over to us from the local white schools. I remember opening up the books and seeing the names of the white kids who had used them before they were handed down to us. When we complained about it Mrs. Mackley, our math teacher, would say, "Count your blessings. You are lucky to get anything at all."

My mother had thought that the Supreme Court decision would mean that I would begin tenth grade at the white high school that was located near us. I had been pushed by my teachers and I got good grades. However, I felt a little nervous about going, and, I wondered how I would fare. After all, everybody knew that our black school was "not as good." Also, I did not think I was very smart. There were a lot of kids in my neighborhood who I felt were smarter than me but who got lower grades. School was boring; there was no doubt about that. They essentially refused to read or discuss the totally racist materials we were given. It made us feel bad about who we were. They did not believe that it was going to make their lives any different or better. I did not believe it would either, but I was hoping that it might. And I knew, that in going to the white school, we would be expected to prove that we were just as good, which meant doing more work for the same or a lower grade.

Some schools in nearby D.C. and Maryland were desegregated the following fall. In Arlington, however, we were sent back to our segregated schools. In one southern Virginia county, all the schools were shut down in response to the Court's order. I was completely stunned that something like that could happen.

How much emotion does Sligh show as she writes about her schooling? Why might she choose to use emotion as she does, and how does her use of emotion shape your sense of the world in which she lived?

What would someone have to believe if she were then "stunned" by a state government's decision to close schools rather than desegregate?

This, however, did not deter my momma, who wanted more for her children than she had had for herself. I still recall the determination with which she went to meetings with people from the local NAACP and other black parents from our neighborhood to see what they could do about it. This was after being on her feet all day as a domestic worker. All of us kids had to help make dinner, but she saw that we sat down to eat. The following spring, when I was completing tenth grade, she asked me if I was willing to be part of a school integration court case with other kids from the neighborhood, and I agreed to do it. I figured it wouldn't be too bad if we all went together.

This, however, was the summer of 1955, when Emmett Till, a fourteen-year-old black boy, was lynched in Mississippi for "speaking to a white woman." It was in all the papers, but the local black newspaper, and *Ebony* and *Jet* magazines, which we followed carefully for the latest developments on school desegregation, wrote about it in great detail.

Two white men took him from his folk's house in the middle of the night, beat him and lynched him, tied weights to his body, and dropped him in the river. The black publications were the only ones we saw that showed photographs of Emmett Till's body after it came out of the river. Even after the undertaker "fixed up his body," it did not look like the face of a person who had ever been on the earth. I had grown up hearing about whites lynching black men, but because he was so near me in age, the horror of this truly seeped into my bones.

To whom could I turn to express my rage and indignation at the injustices being done? How could the adults around me accept that the white men who killed him would never be punished? Why didn't the major newspapers treat it like the horrible crime it was? I did not know what to do. I felt like a caged animal in a burning house. What was going to happen to me in a white school? How was I going to be able to sit in a classroom without showing how I felt? Whenever I blurted out what was on my mind, my mother would punish me for not behaving myself. At that time I had no idea the price I was paying.

During the fall of 1955, as I returned for eleventh grade to my old school on the south side, the Virginia Legislature passed something called the "massive resistance laws," which gave the governor the power to close down any school system that attempted to desegregate. I tried to talk with my momma about it, but she would say nothing to me

---

- Has Sligh called her mother "momma" before this? Why might she make this word choice here?

- Why tell about Emmett Till here?

- Has Sligh sounded full of rage or indignant?

  Read this whole page aloud: you ought to hear the rhythms change in this paragraph, with this list of questions and short declarative statements. What emotions does Sligh evoke through this? Why?

- What price has Sligh paid? Does she describe the price explicitly? Why, do you think?

about it. Still, she continued going to the NAACP meetings with the other parents from the neighborhood.

Meanwhile, miles away in Montgomery, Alabama, Rosa Parks was being arrested for not moving to the back of a city bus. The bus boycott that followed was exciting news to us. Everybody talked about it. Blacks were fighting back. We saw news photographs of elderly black people walking many miles to work. It inspired us to see that our people, who were further south than us, and in a more hostile environment, were determined not to take it anymore.

At first there was a lot in our local newspapers about it. I read every word of every article I saw. And when the local newspapers stopped reporting what was going on, I went with my mother to some of the meetings where people who had just come from Montgomery told about what was going on, and asked for donations to help out. I would hold my breath as I listened to the accounts of how the city council and the courts were trying to break up the bus boycott by harassing people in so many ways. I could not imagine that they would be able to keep going with the people in power using all their resources against them. After these meetings, I would go home and pray very hard that God would help them hold out. Finally, we heard Dr. Martin Luther King speak on television. Daddy was really impressed. And Daddy was a man who rarely gave anybody any credit at all.

The month after the bus boycott began in Montgomery, whites rioted on the campus of the University of Alabama for three days after Autherine Lucy, a black woman, enrolled there. Because I too was going to be a desegregation plaintiff, I wanted to know everything that was going on. After all, I might find myself in her shoes.

I read every word of every article about it that I saw. She was barred from attending classes. After the rioting ended, she was eventually suspended. I was looking for clues about what I could expect when my time came to enter our local white high school.

A few months later, my mother asked me if I would be willing to be the lead plaintiff in the Arlington school desegregation case. She explained to me that some of the students who had been selected previously were about to graduate and that another student withdrew because her father was going to be fired from his job if she stayed in. I never expected that the court case would take over a year to be put

From the beginning, when she described how she learned about right and wrong, Sligh has been comparing her expectations of the world with what actually happens. For example, here she says that "I could not imagine that they would be able to keep going with the people in power using all their resources against them." How might readers respond to these ways in which Sligh juxtaposes her sense of right and wrong, and human ability, with what happens?

together. And I had definitely never expected to be singled out from what was originally a group of over twenty-five black students. I could only imagine that my life would be in a shambles.

I remember thinking, "Here I am already finishing the eleventh grade. Why would I want to go to a white school for my senior year?"

Although Momma said I didn't have to do it if I didn't want to, I could tell she wanted me to agree. Terrible images flashed through my adolescent mind: of Emmett Till being killed for saying something to a white woman; of Rosa Parks going to jail rather than give up her seat to a white man; of all those elderly black folks walking miles to their jobs in Montgomery; of Autherine Lucy at the University of Alabama. I swallowed hard and told her that I would. Since the age of eight, I had been "in it"; I knew that I was expected to do my part.

On May 17, 1956, the NAACP attorneys filed our lawsuit: *Clarissa Thompson et al. v. the Arlington County School Board et al.* I had no idea what sort of changes it would make in my life. What was happening did not really sink in until the newspaper let us know that they wanted to come out to take our pictures for an article about the case.

The photographs were taken by a newspaper photographer who accompanied the reporter to the home of Mrs. Barbara Marx, a white woman who was vice-president of the local NAACP chapter. Momma could not drive, and Daddy refused to be involved in what was going on. I rode with her in someone else's car to the neighborhood where Mrs. Marx lived. The group had asked my mother beforehand to have me prepare a statement.

During the interview, I was very nervous. I tried to act cool, but the underarms of my blouse were soaking wet. Cold sweat ran down the inside of my clothes. I sat and listened as the newspaper reporter interviewed the adults who were present; they included Edwin Brown, an attorney for the NAACP, and James Browne, the local NAACP chapter president. They talked about the history and background of the court action and about what they wanted to accomplish. When the reporter asked me why I wanted to go to a white school, I remember saying something about wanting equality and an end to being a second-class citizen.

Afterward, the reporter directed the staff photographer to take pictures of us. Then, the reporter, looking at eight-year-old Ann, said,

▧ Do you see Sligh using any strategies to encourage you to empathize with her, to imagine yourself at the age she is describing going through the experiences she is?

▧ We've known from the opening paragraph of this essay that it was to be about the set of photographs shown opposite the title page—and yet it is only here, seven pages in, that Sligh starts speaking about the photographs. What has she done in the preceding paragraphs to prepare readers for her understanding of what the photographs and their accompanying article do?

"Isn't she included in the case too? Let's include her in the photographs!"

The photographer began by taking pictures of Mrs. Marx and her daughter, Ann. He asked her to hold up a piece of paper as though she was reading something. I remember her fumbling around in a drawer until she found an envelope, took out a letter and held it up. It is only now, in looking back, that I realize how nervous she too must have been.

Next, the photographer decided to take photographs of Ann and me outdoors. I felt very stiff; I recall that I was very surprised that Ann and I would be photographed together. As I listened to the adults talk, it was the first time that I heard that her mother had included her and her sister, Claire, who was about to graduate from high school, in the suit. She was one of three white students in the class-action suit of twenty-two students. I was one of nineteen black students. It hardly seemed equal to me.

The photographer shot a number of pictures of Ann and me together. By now she seemed to be enjoying the attention and was very relaxed. I, on the other hand, was freaking out. Here I was, a sixteen-year-old, very self-conscious black female, with these white folks up in this white neighborhood, and I'm supposed to be relaxed? They killed Emmet Till. In addition to trying to keep myself together, I felt very awkward towering above this little girl, in height, as the photographer took shots of us standing together. I was sixteen years old and she was eight, not twelve as stated in the newspaper photo caption. Somehow, it seemed insulting to me to be photographed with an eight-year-old. At the same time, I felt bad that the other black students in the suit were not there. Despite the feelings I had, I tried hard to look agreeable and pleasant. I was hoping that the photographs would come out well, so that people would think I was an "all right" person. After taking several shots, he asked us to walk toward him. Then he asked us to carry a book in our hands as we walked toward him. Finally, he said "Okay, that's it." I was glad when it was over.

When the photographs were published, a picture of Barbara and Ann Marx appeared at the top of the page, just above the headline, which read: SUIT CHARGES BIAS AGAINST WHITE PUPILS. The photograph, which was taken at fairly close range, was shot at just about eye level. Ann is standing next to her mother, who is seated at what appears to be

■ How has Sligh prepared you to understand why she "freaks out"? Why might she choose "freaking out" instead of "confused" or "upset"?

a desk or a table. This makes Ann's head a little higher than her mother's. The edges around both of their heads appear to have been painted in order to make them stand out against the background. The shape of the shadows cast by their heads suggest circular forms, giving the effect of halos behind their heads similar to those in the Christian religious art of the Middle Ages.

The mother and daughter are holding a piece of paper, supposedly a page from the papers filed in the suit; they are both smiling, as if they are happy and satisfied with what they have done. If I am a viewer who is at all sympathetic toward them, I look at this image without thinking how wonderfully honorable and courageous they must be. If I am a viewer who is angered by what they have done, I will be aware that any action I take against them is going to make me look like a "bad guy," so I am not going to express my feelings very publicly.

The second photograph, a closely cropped head shot of me, was placed to the upper right of the picture described above. It was shot from below my eye level, so that I appear to be looking down at the camera. You can tell by the shadow areas under my eyes, nose, and face, that the light source comes from the upper left hand side. This cropped head shot reminds me of the way photographs of "monsters" are lighted and shot. The angle of the lens, pointing up into my nostrils, also suggests to me certain European paintings of horses being ridden into battle. Moreover, the placement of the picture seems to suggest that the mother and daughter are placing themselves at risk by taking the moral action and putting themselves into this position, and that I am their "white man's burden." The caption read: "Clarissa Thompson...asks for equality." The small amount of white background does not give the viewer any clues as to where the picture was taken.

My head was printed larger than that of Barbara or Ann Marx, and the placement of the top of the photograph just above the top of their picture makes it pop off the page more than the other image. Even though the photograph of me is about one third the size of the photograph of Barbara and Ann Marx, the angle of the shot of my dark-skinned face puts my blackness in opposition to their whiteness. The relative placement of the photographs seems to suggest that people who are white are human and nice and that people who are black are threatening to those nice white people.

■ Sligh now gives readers her interpretation of how the photographs advocate an attitude toward the white people shown in them and toward her. Look at the number of details to which she attends: how do they affect your understanding of the photographs you first saw many pages ago?

This meant that whites would only be able to see that generic black face they carried in their minds. They would not have to wonder about the life, the aspirations, the universal humanity hidden behind my dark skin. They would not be forced to examine, in a personal way, the injustice of the life I was forced to live.

The third photograph was printed on a different page. It is a picture of me and Ann walking toward the photographer, and he was crouching down when he shot it. It is close to evening. The photographer has his back to the sun. In the picture, I am on the left, Ann is on the right. We are both smiling and we each carry a book. The image is cropped to show our full bodies, but my right arm is nevertheless cut off. It looks as though I am walking out of the frame. It may even suggest that I am less than a whole person. Portions of the areas around our heads and shoulders have been painted to make us stand out from the background.

This photograph of me and Ann reminds me of similar images of young whites pictured with older, usually adult, blacks. Three references that immediately come to mind are Huckleberry Finn with the slave Jim, various movies of Shirley Temple in which she shows benevolence to an older, black, white-haired male servant/slave, and, of course, images from *Uncle Tom's Cabin*.

The article itself was written about the few whites who worked with us on the school desegregation case. None of the adults from my neighborhood, who had worked on the case for over a year, and who were the parents of the twenty-five black students, were even mentioned. In photographs and words, Barbara Marx and her daughter, a white mother and child, were thus highlighted and elevated to a position of significance over all the black people involved in the case.

If I had not been there on the two occasions when the reporter interviewed us, I would never have known that black adults participated in those meetings. I remember how seriously and carefully they made sure that what they said to the reporter was accurate and correct; how they helped each other find the words to describe exactly what they meant; how they sometimes told jokes to break the tension. Why was none of what they said included?

Except for me, none of the other black students was named in the article. The next to the last sentence in the article states, "The case will be known as Clarissa Thompson et al. vs. the Arlington County School

If you are a non-black person, what authority does Sligh have to interpret these photographs that you do not? What authority does she have as the subject of the photographs for speaking about the photographs?

How do you think Sligh is hoping to shift readers' understanding of the photographs—and the article they illustrate—through giving readers knowledge about the context of the photographs, about who was there?

Board et al. because the 11th grade Negro girl leads the list of plaintiffs."
It was made clear that my photograph was there only because my name
was at the top of a list. Simply by looking at the photographs, both
whites and blacks would think that the suit was initiated and organized
by whites.

Today, I can still remember the safety I felt being surrounded by the
black adults from my community during the interview. I remember all
their faces but only a few of their names. By leaving them out of the
article and photographs, the newspaper made them invisible. If one
reads the article today, it looks like they never existed. Their being left
out also made me feel unprotected and more vulnerable than ever as
time went by. Their courage had been devalued. Their lack of power, of
control over the situation, was magnified before my eyes. Even then, it
was clear to me that readers of the newspaper would get the message
that it was whites, not blacks, who were leading the interracial group to
fight racial segregation in Virginia. It reinforced the stereotype that we
had to be led by whites.

Today, I ask myself how those meetings with the reporter and photographer might have been different. Why were the interviews held at
Barbara Marx's rather than the NAACP president James Browne's
house? Both their homes were equally convenient from the highway. If
the group had not made the decision beforehand to include Barbara
Marx's daughter in the photo session, why didn't they object when the
reporter suggested it? Were the black adults afraid to give the appearance of "slighting" a little white girl? Had they in some way gone along
with their exclusion from the decision-making process? Had we blacks
been excluded from participating in the so-called democratic decision-
making process for so long and in so many ways, that any ordinary
white person took our exclusion for granted—and so, perhaps, did we?

Today, I also ask myself about the motivations of the reporter. I
remember her as being a white woman; yet the reporter's name, as published, appears to be masculine. Was it a pseudonym? As a southern
white, would she have been capable of writing a news article that
included a black person's point of view? Was she able or willing to hear
any of the things we blacks were saying? Did she come there intending
to write a story about white people? Certainly a story about the civil
rights movement that included whites got more attention than one

■ Notice how in the first sentences of this paragraph Sligh calls to our minds how the adults of her community made her feel safe—and how she calls their faces to our minds. Only then does she state that the newspaper article and photographs made them invisible. Why might she order her sentences in this way?

about blacks alone. It later became a tactic which the black leaders in the movement themselves took advantage of. They saw that photographs of whites being beaten up while exercising their civil rights got much more attention; here was something unbelieving American whites could identify with, much more so than with photographs of black protestors being beaten by whites.

When the article was printed I felt betrayed. I had thought that it was really going to be a piece of investigative reporting about our work to win our civil rights under the Supreme Court ruling in *Brown v. Board of Education*. I wanted terribly to believe that I could have rights under the Fourteenth Amendment to the Constitution, which guarantees equal protection under the law. I wanted to believe in the Pledge of Allegiance, the National Anthem, the Bible, and all that other shit I had to regurgitate in school, even though I knew it clearly did not apply to me. I wanted the article to show that black people from my neighborhood were part of the struggle against legalized racial segregation too.

My mother did not say much to me about the article after it appeared. She did mention in passing, that some of the people from the community who had met with the reporter were not happy with the way the article turned out. Still, she seemed happy and satisfied that her daughter's picture was in the *Washington Post*. It was a big thing that would elevate her status in the neighborhood and beyond. She did not seem to fear that she would lose any of her domestic work; on the contrary, she seemed to be looking forward to the reaction of her employers.

The publication of those photographs, however, placed me in a new relationship to both the white and the black worlds. It wrenched me from what I considered to be the safety and security of my anonymous family into the spotlight of the hostile public's scrutiny. People began to notice me. I could no longer be just another black girl, or just myself. I had to mind my *p*'s and *q*'s. My behavior, my grades and test scores, my interests and accomplishments became public information.

I began to be expected to address groups of liberal white people, whose support was being solicited for our case. As a young black person, my personal contact with whites had been minimal before this. In fact, I had heard mostly bad things about them, so I was always scared to be with them. In Arlington, we were barred from the movies, restaurants, white churches, and most other public places. I could check out a

◼ Why "shit"?

Why this indication of anger here?

◼ Why might Sligh write, "I began to be expected to address...," rather than just, "I began to address..."?

book from the public library, but I could not sit down to read it. On my way home from the District of Columbia I often sat alone on the bus, even when it was crowded, because none of the whites would sit beside me. I used to get upset about it, but then tried to act like I didn't see them.

Before I had been invisible. Now I was being scrutinized, not only by whites, but also by the black adults who took me into these new situations. I went along with it, but I tried really hard to hide what I really thought and who I really was.

I felt lucky to have met my boyfriend, Albert, before the photographs were published, because afterward I could not just hang out with my classmates or even slip into some of the places that were considered off-limits for "good girls." Nicknamed "Professor" by some of my classmates, I was never among the more popular girls at a party anyway. Now I could tell I was being seen in an even more distant light.

My teachers did not like my boyfriend, Albert. Considered a street guy, he was not heavy into the books. "Before the photographs," I regularly got good grades and that seemed to be enough; but now they expected me to be outstanding in every way. And even though my teachers were anxious about the future of their jobs if school desegregation were to occur, now I was a representative of their work and they wanted me to look good. They wanted me to succeed. Only one of them came out and said it, but the message from all of them came down to this: Don't you mess up everything by getting pregnant or getting into some other kind of trouble.

To people outside my neighborhood, I was considered a representative not only for black girls but for all young black people. I began to get some understanding of what it must be like to be a Joe Louis or a Jackie Robinson. When they knocked out a white man or hit a home run, it was not just for themselves but for all black people. For whites who did not believe we could do it or who were against us, taking a jab at me was like striking a blow at all blacks. Who I really was and how I really felt was not important. The group was more important. I was a good choice for the role. Because I was a good girl, I tried really hard to be better in every way I could.

This state of tension was the beginning of my learning to live a divided and alienated life. Even as a young person, I knew I had made the decision to allow myself to be used in a way that was unpleasant

Sligh again talks of visibility and invisibility here, about how we do and do not see, about being made visible or invisible to others through actions and events out of your control—or about making decisions to see or not.

What actions or events does Sligh describe that have these effects or encourage such decisions? Why does this matter to her, and how is she trying to make it matter to her readers?

Why might Sligh describe the effects of the photograph and articles on her own life and the way she felt about herself and her place in the world?

and uncomfortable to me. It is true that I had been trained for it, but I could have opted out. I was hoping that it would lead to opportunities that would give me more economic independence and make my life better than my mother's. I learned how to hide myself and my thoughts by keeping my mouth shut, by covering my terror with a smile, and by acting as if everything was going to be all right. In order to get through it, I searched for support, for meaning to my life in the Mt. Salvation Baptist Church. Whenever tough times came, rather than argue or fight, I turned inward and prayed very hard. Later, when the church disappointed me, as it surely had to, I began to smoke and drink. Fortunately for me, stronger drugs were not as available to young people as they are now.

Since those days the nonobjective reporting of newspaper journalism has always been of interest to me. To the average person, news photographs represent reality, but I ask "Whose reality?" and "Why?" As I travel from city to city and from country to country, I see how newspapers vary tremendously in their points of view. I see how photographs are used to reinforce the credibility of stories; and how the same picture is often used to reinforce stories written from opposing points of view. Placing one photograph beside another changes the way the viewer reads it. Adding words to a photograph can make it say almost anything.

It is hard for photographers not to base the photographs they make on pictures they already have in their minds. Even so, their specific intent can easily be altered by an editor's intent, which may be controlled, in turn, by the newspaper's publishers. And then, of course, advertisers often influence what publishers "feel comfortable" including in their pages.

I became a photographer partly in response to the continuous omission and misrepresentation of me and my point of view as a black working-class female who grew up poor. I know I can make a photograph say a lot of different things. However, I hope that the way I make images helps the viewer become better aware of how photographs are really abstracted constructions.

At the end of the essay Sligh explicitly states how the photograph and article affected her, even shaping her career. What do you think she is hoping her readers will learn from her experiences and how she tried to prepare them for this learning?

"The Plaintiff Speaks"—and representing ourselves and others

- **Write with others:** List adjectives that describe for you the *ethos* Sligh constructs in her essay. What strategies does she use to construct that *ethos*?

- **Discuss and write with others:** How emotional is this essay? Does Sligh write as though she is angry and barely controlled, or does she write in a more distanced manner? Try modifying the paragraphs where she names her emotional states, so that the paragraphs make no mention of emotion. How does this change how you understand what is going on?

- **Discuss with others:** What do you take to be Sligh's purpose in writing this essay? How important is her *ethos* in persuading you toward her arguments? How does Sligh's use of *pathos* help her make her arguments?

- **Discuss with others:** The two essays that precede "The Plaintiff Speaks"— "Higher Education" and "A Marketable Wonder"—are by white men writing about a (dead) black man and consider, to varying degrees, the effects of racism on that man's life (and on white people). In "The Plaintiff Speaks," Sligh uses her own experiences to construct arguments about possible effects of being represented by others. Given Sligh's arguments, and that it is a particularly awkward situation for our time and place for a white man to claim to understand how racism shapes the lives of black men, what strategies do you see Smith and Dibbell using to try to persuade us that they are worth heeding? Do you see anything in common among these essays in terms of how these writers each designs his *ethos*? His tone of voice? How does your reading of Sligh shape how you look back on those essays? Write a paper in which you address these questions.

- **Write:** After reading Sligh's essay, what considerations will you now have in mind as you look at newspaper photographs? What considerations will you have in mind as you take photographs of others or write about them?

Based on your reading of the three previous essays, write a set of recommendations you would make to anyone writing about or taking photographs of others.

"A history of empires and regencies, of warfare, injustice, inequality, slavery has shaped the modern vision. Everything one sees, not only what one would leave behind but also what one treasures, has been touched by this inheritance. The whole is like a fresco, appealing in its own way but also disappointing, somehow blunted, and even hopeless in the way the form turns back on itself in irony and despair, but through which here and there one can see a slightly different coloration, places where the paint is peeling, to reveal another, more interesting layer. To see underneath, one must pare away the more recent layer, and perhaps a second and third layer, which obscure the reach of vision."

from *The Eros of Everyday Life*

PREPARING TO READ THE NEXT ESSAY, "RED SHOES"

About the essay's author and why she writes as she does

Susan Griffin is a poet, essayist, lecturer, teacher, playwright, and filmmaker. Her books include *The Book of the Courtesans: A Catalogue of Their Virtues* (2001), *The Eros of Everyday Life* (1996), *A Chorus of Stones: The Private Life of War* (1992) (a finalist for the Pulitzer Prize in nonfiction and nominated for a National Book Critics Circle Award), and *Women and Nature: The Roaring Inside Her* (1978). She has been awarded a MacArthur Grant for Peace and International Cooperation and a fellowship from the National Endowment for the Arts. Her play *Voices* won an Emmy.

Griffin is certainly a writer who has captured the attentions of others—but if you look over the following pages, you'll see that her writing doesn't look like anything else in this chapter. Griffin's work asks readers to stretch beyond their learned expectations of what essays do and how they do it. This is because Griffin is deeply interested in how the ways we compose texts allow us to be. She is interested in how the way we design with words—and, sometimes, representational images—shapes us as people by allowing certain directions for thought and not others, certain kinds of actions and not others.

As we said in the opening pages of this chapter, this writing takes on "the essay itself as an event to consider." Griffin believes—as you will see as you read—that essays have had a rigid structure that aligns with what people have considered to be worthy of being made public; as a consequence, she believes that certain kinds of experience have been hidden away, made to stay private—and that therefore people who have had those experiences have not been able to speak or be heard through the form of the essay. Griffin brings up the matter of the body in this essay, as we also said at the beginning of this chapter: she considers how bodily experiences, especially those of women, have been closed off by the intellectual forms of the essay.

Given those conditions, it ought not to surprise you that Griffin's essay does not look like any of the other essays in this chapter. If she believes that the form of the essay excludes voices and experiences that ought to be heard, then she believes it necessary to find new strategies and new forms for writing.

Griffin also believes that "each solitary story belongs to a larger story" and that "no one acts alone. No one thinks alone." In her writing she thus works to find strategies for seeing how the lives of individuals fit into the larger stories of our time, and how what seems or has been kept private can be made visible—as in the quotation to the left. The shapes of her writing are an effort to make the past visible in such a way that we can see its patterns present here and now.

compose ▪ design ▪ advocate

SUSAN GRIFFIN

Red Shoes

The imprisonment which was at one and the same time understood as the imprisonment of the female mind has a larger boundary, and that is the shape of thought itself within Western civilization.

It is an early memory. Red shoes. Leather straps crisscrossing. The kind any child covets. That color I wanted with the hot desire of a child.

On one level, one thinks simply of the conditions of imprisonment which affected, for instance, the intellectual life of George Sand. How it was necessary for her to dress like a man in order to attend the theater with her friends. She wanted to be in the section just beneath the stage, and women were not allowed in that section. This transgression was a necessary one if she was going to, as she did, enter the realm of public discourse within her mind.

When was it I first heard the title of the film, The Red Shoes? *My older sister had seen it. Did she speak of it with my mother? I must have overheard it. I was often excluded from such conversations. I was too young. And my mother preferred my sister.*

The female world, bounded as it is, contains, as does any world, rich layers of meaning. It is not simply that a woman must stay within this world but that signification itself is kept away from it.

Whatever lies within the confines of the feminine province is defined *sui generis* as either trivial or obscene (as in housework, or lovemaking) and as such not fit for public discourse.

303

Because Griffin's essay is not structured like the previous essays, we're going to supply a little more help for reading in case you need it. This essay is also philosophical, in that it questions how we know things. This essay requires careful reading, but we think the effort is worthwhile because it is through Griffin's careful and planned strategies that she constructs what we believe is a complex but fascinating argument about how we write-and-live-with-others.

Notice (if you haven't already) how Griffin's essay alternates short paragraphs in italics with short paragraphs in what is called Roman type. When you start to read, it may seem the paragraphs are disconnected—but be patient, and watch for repetitions, which build into patterns. Watch for words that repeat, or concepts (like colors, suggested by the title). Don't think that our observations take in everything worth noting.

■ If you do not know the fairy tale of the *Red Shoes*, go find and read it. Reading the story will not necessarily make it easier to read Griffin's essay but will help you understand many of her comments.

■ In the first sentence Griffin announces her concerns: the "shape of thought itself within Western civilization," she believes, sets the bounds that imprison the female mind. She does not try to persuade readers that the female mind is imprisoned; she takes it as a given, providing one example, that of George Sand, a French writer whose birth name was Aurore Dupin. Whether you are ready to agree with Griffin or not, take this as her starting point, and see what logic and what form flow from this belief.

I was, I suppose, shopping with my grandmother in the department store with the X-ray machine that made a green picture of the bones in my feet. I have the vague feeling my grandmother finds red impractical.

In this light it is no wonder that the novel became a literary form so widely practiced by women, a genre in some of its popular manifestations, and in some phases of its development, dominated by women. The novel is allowed to describe what we think of as the private sphere of life, which is also the sphere of life given over to women. And is it any wonder that so many "classic" novels written by men have a heroine at the center of the story? *Anna Karenina. Madame Bovary.*

In my mind, as I remember my grandmother, I can feel the shape of her larger body next to mine. Her elbows are wrinkled in a way that fascinated me. The flesh on her forearms hangs in beautiful white lobes, not so different than the lobes of her breasts.

Why is it the novel can enter the private sphere in a way, for instance, that the essay cannot? One answer presents itself immediately. The novel is fiction. It is not true. It exists in an epistemological category unto itself. Yes, it is lifelike, it evokes or even, as is said metaphorically, creates realities; still the reality of fiction is not to be confused with *reality*.

I cannot remember whether or not my grandmother let me have those shoes. Despite her somberness in my presence, a mouth habitually turned down, and her air of dutiful weariness at having to raise a child at her advanced age, she has another side. I am twenty-one years old when she pulls a black silk robe out of a closet where she has kept it for years and gives it to me.

In the public imagination the feminine world has the same flavor as a fictional world. It is present but not entirely real. Men enter the home in the evening, as darkness descends. They may eat there, play with the children, make love, confess certain feelings hidden during the day to their wives, sleep, dream, but all that fades away into near obscurity with the dawn when they must emerge again into the world of work.

■ Over these pages, watch how Griffin builds (in the paragraphs of Roman type) this list/equation: female = private = fiction = not real = walled-off, unseen, unscrutinized = the body = pain, pleasure, color, taste, sound, smells = sensuality.

■ Meanwhile, the story in italics—of Griffin (at least we think it is Griffin because she is using "I"), her red shoes, and her grandmother—continues on, in parallel narrative (which you've seen in other essays). What is happening with the young Griffin and her shoes?

■ Given the equation Griffin builds in these pages, and the story, and how parallel narratives have worked in earlier essays—with the two stories eventually overlapping or echoing each other in some way—how might the two narratives here eventually come together? (And what is the effect for you, as a reader, in moving back and forth between them? Do you feel like a Ping-Pong ball, or are you withholding your judgment to see what happens, or . . .?)

■ We have red in the title of the essay and in the shoes Griffin is describing, and now we have black. What kinds of associations do you think most readers of this essay will have with those colors?

compose ■ design ■ advocate

Perhaps she did buy me those red shoes. I can see them now in my closet which was also her second closet, the closet of the black silk robe, the place where she kept her rarer treasures, her two fur coats, worn only on the more special occasions . . . and, am I embellishing here, her sweater with the rhinestones on it, or were they pearls? Whenever I wore those red shoes, which was as often as I could, they gave me a secret sustenance, the liberatory feeling of a rebellion conspired between my grandmother and me.

Secrets within the private life are like obscurities within an obscurity. Private life is *private*, walled off, unseen, unscrutinized. To write a history of the private life is a recent departure, an ingenuous idea, and has an erotic edge, not only because of the sexuality which is part of private life, but because in doing so one penetrates a contained world. The secret alcoholism or indiscretion or sexual abuse within a family history is, being an obscurity inside an essentially obscure world, seemingly less real than the rest of private life, and has even more the flavor of fiction. At the same time the novel, being fiction, is congruous with this world. It is formed to the contours of the way we hold the private life in our minds.

When I put the red shoes on it was not only on special occasions. I wore them even on ordinary days. They followed me into a child's world, one that no adult ever saw. If I took them off to play in the sand or the mud, they witnessed me from the sidelines and kept my secrets.

In fiction the whole life of the body, of sensuality, is opened to view. The form of the novel or the short story and even more of the poem allows the reader to enter imagined experience as if within a body. Pain, pleasure, color, taste, sound, smells are evoked. The literary devices of fiction are meant to admit this material world.

I wore them walking the twelve blocks I regularly walked to school. The shoes became so much a part of me that I forgot I was wearing them. I let my mind wander. I looked into the windows of the houses along the way and imagined the lives of the inhabitants.

In depicting the sensuality of the world and our bodily experience of it, fiction is also portraying the mind itself, which always thinks in a sensual

■ You've probably read enough of the two different kinds of paragraphs by now to be able to characterize them. Does it sound fair to you to characterize one kind as private and personal, the other more like the language of an argumentative essay?

Here Griffin gives a reason for why we, as a culture, might want to pull away from our bodies (and, by implication, everything else connected to them in the equation she built on the preceding pages): we want to be free from our bodies—that is, it is implied, we want to be free from death and dying. If we believe that our minds are transcendent—that they are, that is, above or outside or disconnected from the body—then we needn't die. If you accept the equation we claim Griffin has built on the previous pages, then, if we pull away from our bodies (and we use the usual form of the essay to do so) then what else are we pulling away from or forgetting?

context. Without the body, it is impossible to conceive of thought existing. Yet the central trope of our intellectual heritage is of a transcendent, disembodied mind. As the essay moved further away from meditation and reflection, further from what we call "confessions" and closer to science, with its claim of objectivity, it began more and more to resemble this celestially detached brain. At a fairly recent point in the history of the essay it became a radical act to use the pronoun "I."

Perhaps she did not buy me the red shoes. But even if that were true, the fact is she might have.

The idea of an entirely autonomous mind has a subtext, and that is the desire for unlimited freedom from natural limitations.

In the lay and ken of her soul, this was a possibility. As I imagine that she gave me the shoes, which perhaps she did, am I bringing part of her soul into being?

And yet limitations are a necessary predisposition for any existence, including the existence of something we suppose to be abstract and cerebral, like the essay. And when the essay is built on the purposeful "forgetting" of the body, these limitations paradoxically grow greater. The form of the essay circumscribes imagination. At its edges many other imagined possibilities are hovering.

Was this the reason for her attachment to the peach-colored bedspreads? They covered the single beds where she and my grandfather slept. They had a luxuriant feel, suggesting an erotic dimension that otherwise was absent in her house.

Add "peach" to the list of colors at work. What associations do you have with this color? What associations is Griffin making by having peach be the color of bedspreads? (Notice also how the colors have been showing up only in the italicized sections so far. Why might that be, given the equation Griffin has set up and given the kinds of things she is writing in the paragraphs of Roman type?)

To speak of housework, or childbirth, or sexuality, or rape in the form of the essay represents, in each instance, a crumbling of the fortifications erected by a masculine world against the feminine world. But still, in each instance, the sensual reality of these phenomena is stripped away so that they may enter public discourse. And when these subjects are made into sciences, they gain a certain legitimacy. Though it is often marginal, as in Home Economics.

Or perhaps not entirely absent, but never more open, never so frank, as in those bedspreads. They were luminously sexual, the sort of bedcover Mae West might have had. Of course we never spoke of this quality. It could never be spoken, only suggested.

One might think that, because fiction brings one into a fully sensual world, the subject matter would be more rigidly policed. But this is not the case. The idea that fiction is untrue allows it a greater radius. I am thinking of Virginia Woolf's *Orlando*. At the time of its publication, it was her most popular novel. What she suggested about the malleability of gender was far more palatable in this form than in her essays, which treated the subject, by comparison, more conservatively.

The bedspreads were symbolic of many aspirations. She cosseted a desire to be socially elevated. In her mind we were finer than all our neighbors, though I, with the working-class language of my father, and my childish ignorance of manners, constantly endangered our superiority.

Just as the reader is protected by the supposition that fiction is not true, so too the author of fiction is shielded by this idea. Stories can be told that otherwise could not. But what is even more interesting is that, because fiction evokes particular social and natural worlds in their entirety, many possible stories exist inside the narrative world implicitly, without being explicitly described. They exist as possibilities or even likelihoods. A door to a barn is described. The narrator does not open that door. But it exists. And therefore the reader can imagine what is behind the door. The shape of circumstances in both *Jane Eyre* and *Wuthering Heights* suggest sexual abuse. One knows a racist political history has preceded *Their Eyes Were Watching God*. Neither writer nor reader needs to have delineated these events. The experience is part of the reality that is conjured.

I was fascinated by my grandparents' bedroom. The family story was that they slept in a double bed until one day my grandmother woke to find my grandfather's hands around her neck. He was having a dream. I am certain the significance of the dream was never discussed. Only thereafter they slept in single beds. I can't remember when I heard that story. Now it is as if I've always known it.

In Virginia Woolf's *Orlando*, a person shifts from female to male and has many different lives over the course of several centuries.

But unless one knows the history of racism or the configurations of sexual abuse, one does not see them in the narrative. They are felt perhaps, sensed, but not delineated, unnamed.

In this bedroom, they lived as if in separate worlds. I liked to watch my grandmother at her dressing table, trying on her earrings, her perfumes; I felt privileged to catch a glimpse of her fleshy body, her long pendulous breasts emerging from her corset. I preferred to look at my grandfather's desk when he was absent. What I loved best was his collection of fountain pens.

Reading a book about the documentation of torture in Brazil, I come across this distinction made by Thomas Nagel: ". . . the difference between knowledge and acknowledgment." He defines "acknowledgment" as "what happens to knowledge . . . when it becomes officially sanctioned, when it is made part of the public, cognitive scene." The essay, is a forum for the "public cognitive scene."

One evening when my grandparents went out and I was alone in the house I was pulled as if by a magnet to my grandfather's desk. I wanted to write with his fountain pen, which he never let me use in his presence. But the ink was heavy in it. Many times I had seen him shake it down to the nib, and so I did this, but not with the same experienced gesture. The ink sailed across the room in a sure trajectory toward my grandmother's satin bedspreads. Both covers were evenly spattered.

The integration of knowledge into public consciousness is more than a simple act of education. Perception itself in human consciousness is a social act. It is not only that knowledge and language are socially derived, but the moment of perception itself is prismatic. A single viewer will react differently when part of an audience. Certain responses are amplified. A small gesture made on the stage, whose meaning otherwise might be ignored or even forgotten, brings the whole theater to laughter. In the assembly of others, perception becomes a demarcated event. And, as it is said in the same book about torture in Brazil, the process of transforming knowledge into public acknowledgment is also "sacramental."

> From this paragraph, look back over the preceding pages and make a list of the characteristics that Griffin gives to essays. How does this list play against the list/equation we made several pages back, the one that starts "female = private . . ."? Are the lists opposites, or some other relation?

> What emotion comes to you as you read this paragraph about Griffin staining her grandparents' bedspread with the grandfather's ink?

I tried to wash the spots out but only made them worse. I can feel the terror of discovery now. It is hot under my skin. I would have preferred the discovery to be private, between my grandmother and me. I was rarely physically punished. But she beat me this once, with a belt. My father and grandfather were in the next room, and I was angry at them, not because they failed to intervene but because they were witnesses at all.

Sitting in the public gardens that are close to my house, I hear a white-haired woman exclaim to her friend, "The color is so intense!" Their bent bodies are as if curled together around a rosebush. The gardens are tiered and shaped like an amphitheater and so her voice travels easily. It is an extraordinary moment. All at once I am pulled into her passion and the brightness of the roses, and I begin to think how closely twinned in human consciousness are experience and the expression of experience. Something happens, indefinable yet palpable, as all of us in the garden are pulled simultaneously toward the sound of this old woman's voice and the color of the rose.

What was it I did not want them to know? That I had committed a crime and been found out? Or that I had become abject, shamed by the pain itself of my punishment? I had been in such abject states before, when, through the neglect of my mother, I was cold, frightened, perhaps hungry. Afterward I would feel a profound embarrassment. Writing of his experience of torture, Jean Amery recalls that "one never ceases to be amazed that all those things one may . . . call his soul, or his mind, or his consciousness, or his identity are destroyed when there is that cracking and splintering in the shoulder joints." It is this that is humiliating and, as Amery writes, "The shame of destruction cannot be erased."

After a time I leave my bench and walk up the tiers of the amphitheater. I hope to catch a glimpse of these two women. In my imagination I have already given the speaker a rich mystical life. But they are gone.

Such a memory is perhaps more easily recalled when it is only an abstraction of itself. One says, "I was tortured," or "I had a difficult childhood," without entering the experience in any concrete way, and thus also without reliving the feeling of destruction. But sensuality and abstraction are mutually dependent. In the mind, the capacities are inseparable.

◾ Here Griffin tells how her punishment was public—and watch how the next paragraph, which the patterns of the previous pages has led us to expect would be abstract and about how we know things, comes to be a story in which color appears. Are public and private starting to blend in this essay? Given the logic Griffin has been establishing, what allows or causes that to happen—if you think it is happening? Does this shift continue over the next pages?

◾ Does it take you a second to figure out who the "them" are in the first sentence of this paragraph? When we first read this, we thought Griffin was talking about the women in the garden—and then we thought she meant her grandparents and her father. Why might Griffin allow this ambiguity here, where it looks as though the two separate threads of this essay are starting to overlap?

◾ Why do you think Griffin has started on these pages to pull in torture and what torture—or a difficult childhood—do to a person?

What associations and connections are made with colors on these two pages? How does this fit—or not—with the equation from several pages back that included color?

I had wanted to see the old woman's face. There was something in the tone of her voice which led me to believe she had crossed that barrier which we so often erect against what is seen. Did she fall into the color of the rose?

Fiction, as opposed to the essay, is often viewed as an escape from reality. The storyteller can make up a world and has no moral reason to stay loyal to this one. Shame and suffering can be left at the boundaries of this imagined world.

I imagined the color of the rose to be red. As I entered the garden I saw a rose whose deep burgundy color drew me. This red is replete with associations. Some of them wonderful. Some terrible.

But any really good story includes both pain and pleasure, sorrow and joy, in infinite complexities. And any imagined world, if it is to be believed, will soon be replete with its own requirements, consequences, and limitations, just like this world.

Falling into that color, was she not also falling into herself, as I fall into myself now, my own memories of red, and my own redness? For me this is still a color heavy with menses and childbirth, with violence and loss. But in her voice I hear something different. All that, yes, but an added dimension, a kind of lightness, an aspect of this color that comes to one perhaps only in old age.

Is Griffin defining fiction differently here than she has earlier, or adding new characteristics to her definition and list/equation?

The freedom that fiction affords is a freedom not from concrete limitations but from the limitations on the mind imposed by ideas. This is a secret liberation, the same liberation given by direct experience. For the limits of physical reality are not the same, nor as distinct in experience as the limitations described in abstraction. As John Berger writes in his long work on the peasants of Alpine France, those who live on the land "never suppose that the advance of knowledge reduces the extent of the unknown."

It is easy for me to imagine beginning to perceive another dimension of color in old age. Imagining this, I am pulled toward a future I have never until now predicted.

The extent of the unknown borders all language. One's relationship with it is erotic. One has a passion to know. But one can never entirely know what is other. Telling a story, no matter how much you know, you are very soon pulled into unexplored territory. Even the familiar is filled with unexpected blank spaces. The usual Sunday drive is all of a sudden a wild ride into terra incognita. You are glad to be going, but there is a vague feeling of discomfort. Where are you?

This is not a dimension of color acknowledged in our culture. Still, it exists within the culture. It has been painted. I am thinking of the work of Helen Frankenthaler. Color as she paints it takes a different place in the mind. Or rather one might say the mind takes place in the color. One is infused with it, the same way one is taken in by water, swallowed.

I am thinking of a Sunday drive with my grandparents. We went to the country place of friends. They had an orchard filled with peach trees. I have remembered it all of my life. The vividness of the peaches I pulled from the trees. The sharply sweet taste in my mouth, nothing like store-bought fruit.

Is this experience of color had by some in old age, and others who are artists, a return to an earlier state of mind, the beginner's mind of infancy? To a perception untutored, not yet muted by the mediating presence of language?

Now as I remember that peach, it is a taste indistinguishable from the shapes of trees, the tall grass surrounding them, the summer heat, the breeze blowing, the sight of my grandmother in a white blouse standing on the ladder. And was there a kitten, or am I confusing the memory of my great-grandmother's garden, and her kitten, with this one?

There are of course two experiences of the red color of that rose. One is acknowledged. It is the social red, the historical red, the red, as Merleau Ponty writes, "that is a punctuation in the field of red things." The other red is unacknowledged, it exists in an exiled region of consciousness. But can they be separated, these two reds? And what of the tension one feels between experience and the forms experience assumes in the imagination? One feels it while writing. The words are not quite right. They betray. Lie a

▨ To see the paintings of Helen Frankenthaler, go to www.nmwa.org/collection/profile.asp?LinkID=249 or www.artcyclopedia.com/artists/frankenthaler_helen.html.

▨ What do you understand by "the mind takes place in color"? To say "color takes place in the mind" is to say, perhaps, that color occurs only because we have a mind. If you were to entertain the possibility of the shift Griffin suggests, what might be some consequences? What does this imply about "reality" or about what is public or about how we know things?

▨ Maurice Merleau Ponty was a French philosopher of the mid-twentieth century who was interested in how we experience the world because we have or are bodies.

In the paragraphs in Roman type, Griffin has been speaking philosophically about how we know things (in philosophy, the area of study devoted to how we know anything is called *epistemology*)—and questioning if we can ever know anything absolutely. In the paragraphs in italics, she is questioning if she remembers her past correctly . . .

little. Fail to make a perfect fit. Take off in another direction entirely on their own.

Of course I am embellishing. I doubt that my grandmother wore white. It is the color one is supposed to wear if one is a woman in a pastoral setting.

In recent critical discourse, the awareness that in the mind experience is replaced by a construction of experience has led to a despair of the possibility of describing reality. But in the sway of this despair, how do you point out a lie? How do you answer the contention that torture in Brazil never took place?

That day in the country I breathed in a certain state of mind. One that I never had before with such force. Later, when I encountered the same mood in certain paintings, certain myths, I mixed not only my memory but also my hope with these images.

. . . but here, when she speaks of what happens when she writes and it seems as though language isn't adequate to describe something, "a larger body" starts to help out. What might this mean? She describes how this body—and new patterns—start to appear as she works with words and tries new forms. What is implied about the "traditional" essay here?

I love that moment in writing when I know that language falls short. There is something more there. A larger body. Even by the failure of words I begin to detect its dimensions. As I work the prose, shift the verbs, look for new adjectives, a different rhythm, syntax, something new begins to come to the surface.

Looking back, I see a maze of associations I must have had with the color red. I know my mother also loved the color red. That she would have bought me those shoes unhesitatingly. That she wore bright red lipstick. That she used red henna on her dark brown hair. But I cannot remember if I thought of her that day I chose red shoes.

. . . and here she implies that perhaps what allows us to think that something never happened—that we can't know it— is when we stop speaking of it.

The manner of telling lies in public life is seldom direct any longer. Far more pervasive is the habit of ignoring an event of great significance. No official need argue that torture never existed. The torture is just never mentioned. No one goes to trial. No torturer is ever named. A general, vague reference is made to troubling events of the past which must be changed. The actuality of the torture begins to fade from public consciousness.

She had faded away from my life. I could not remember her at all as my mother, but only as a woman I would visit, and whom I liked. Liked her in a way unaccountable even to myself.

Among those who were tortured or those who lost a loved one to torture there are two reactions. Some wish to evade the memory at all costs. Even though the memory is always there in some form, the pain of recall is too excruciating. Others live to tell the truth, or hear it told, and never tire of the telling. Of course, this is also too simple. For most of us, who have not been tortured, but experienced lesser pains and fears, the two impulses, to remember and tell, or to deny and forget, are side by side, and mixed together.

She was not easy to remember. It was not only neglect but abuse I suffered from her, a nastiness when she drank that came from her, as if from a demon, and which she herself would forget the next day.

I underline this passage in a recent issue of the *Paris Review,* in which Nathalie Sarraute is being interviewed. ". . . it seemed impossible to me," she said, "to write in the traditional forms. They seemed to have no access to what we experienced."

It seems possible to me then that even as a child I would be drawn to the color red, and yet also welcome my grandmother's common interdiction. It is certainly not a practical color. It won't get you anywhere.

Form can be transgressed for transgression's sake, but it can also be transgressed in an attempt to lean in a certain direction. It is a tropism toward the light and heat of another knowledge. And is this knowledge a memory?

Even so I cannot forget my desire to wear red. Even if my grandmother failed to buy me those shoes, years later as an adult woman I make up another story. I investigate the possibility that she did buy them. This is not an escape from my desire. It is instead an instigator of grief. I learn more fully what it is I have lost.

■ How, for you, does the echoing of the word "fade" link this paragraph to the one that precedes it? What could Griffin possibly be trying to do by linking the fading of her mother from her life with the fading of torture from public memory?

■ Do you think this tension between remembering-and-telling and denying-and-forgetting is the same tension as Griffin described on the bottom of page 311 of her essay?

■ Griffin seems to be arguing in the last two paragraphs on this page that knowledge can be memory, and that form (which, given what Griffin has written about form and writing on the last two pages, we take to mean the form of writing, and specifically the form of writing the essay), when transgressed, can lead one toward that memory—or vice versa, that memory, even when unsure, can lead one to new knowledge. Does this fit for you what has happened in the writing?

■ Here again we return to the list/equation of private = female = body of several pages ago, and to forgetting or trying to avoid the various parts of the equation. In the italics section, Griffin writes that she wants to make public what had been private: her memory of red, her associations with red. In the paragraph that begins "There is then . . .," Griffin writes that when we bring what is private (and hence what is equated with it) together with what is public, and try not to move back and forth between them (like moving back and forth between forgetting and remembering, on the previous page) but rather to have both at once, "someone in us awakens." Who might this someone be? Is this essay an example of trying to have the public and the private held together at the same time?

■ In these paragraphs, it sounds to us as though Griffin is responding to those who might say there are good reasons for keeping the public and the private, the real and the fictional, separate. List Griffin's responses—do they persuade you enough (has this essay persuaded you enough) to think these responses might be worth attending to?

What we would wish to remember and what we might wish to forget are so intricately woven. Would we perhaps like to forget the life of the body, of the inner self, the private world, the world of children and childhood, of sucking and orgasm and death? This world which is a privacy within a privacy, protected by the double walls of house and skin, the conventional forms of expression and silence.

It is not the inner place of red I am seeking but the right to wear it outwardly. To wear it brazenly. Like a sequined dress. Or a scarlet letter.

There is then a hypnotic movement of the mind. We are used to it. We move back and forth from fiction to essay. From private to public. The arc of the pendulum has put us to sleep. But when the two poles meet, and the swaying stops, someone in us awakens.

It is one thing to love the color red and quite another to wear it openly. For my mother, wearing red was an act of defiance, a flag of another kind. Despite everything, she has won some territory for me, her daughter. I am like the daughter of Madame Bovary. The daughter of the fallen woman.

Bringing the public world of the essay and the inner world of fiction together, is something sacrificed? The high ground? Perspective? Distance? Or is it instead a posture of detachment that is renounced, a position of superiority? The position of one who is not immersed, who is unaffected, untouched? (This is, of course, the ultimate "fiction.")

And she, my mother, was the daughter of a respectable woman. But that is not the whole story. My grandmother had her own rebellion. She was a club woman. In the organization that was defined as auxiliary to my grandfather's club, she was made president. The proceedings of the club were secret. It was a secret realm of power, a fictional world, closed from that other world described as real life.

But there is always the other side of the coin. Behind the "superior" stance of the essay a quality of fragility is concealed. Theory pales when faced with the complex world of experience. Almost as soon as any idea reaches the page, another argument comes to mind. And while it is true that in the realm of ideas one can diminish the reality of everything outside these ideas, this is at best a temporary diminishment and one that always rebounds upon the self. For ultimately this diminishment requires a lessening of one's own knowledge, one's perceptual experience and, even, existence.

It was to these clubs that my grandmother wore her best finery. Treasures sequestered from her closet, the closet of the fur coats and the black silk robe, which was also my closet.

On the other hand, the realm of experience longs for more than knowledge. What goes on in the private body, in the inner quarters of the mind, cannot fully be redeemed, or even understood, without public acknowledgment. I am thinking of the tears of the victim who has finally heard her assailant convicted. In this case, paradoxically, it is not an imprisonment which takes place so much as a liberation from the imprisonment of an enforced privacy.

On the nights when the family could attend dinners or occasions given by my grandmother's club we were given little party favors and corsages. These had been made by the women in their secret sessions together. They contained bits of plastic fruit, sprays of pine, sparkles, all tied together with a bit of ribbon, most often red.

Is it possible to write in a form that is both immersed and distant, farseeing and swallowed? I am thinking now that this is what women have been attempting in the last decades. Not simply to enter the world of masculine discourse but to transform it with another kind of knowledge.

My grandmother has been dead for nearly two decades, and now my mother, who is old herself, has become respectable. Yet it is an astonishing moment for me, now, to recall these two women, and myself as a child, my red shoes, my mother's rebellion, my grandmother's secret wardrobe, the inner meanings of these, and the threads of meaning that reach out like tendrils in the larger landscape of mind.

■ Here we return to "imprisonment"—with which Griffin began this essay—but now Griffin writes of being liberated from imprisonment. How do you explain, given what Griffin has written about privacy and what is associated with it, what she means by "imprisonment of an enforced privacy"?

This essay has discussed Griffin's past life and her thinking about the public and the private and women's relationships with traditional forms of writing. Why do you think, then, that Griffin ends by pulling us into the present, into what sounds like the moment in which she stopped writing the essay and got up to move out from being alone with herself into the world?

If I rise from my desk, leave my pen and paper behind, walk to the door, the play of life before me and inside is suddenly dazzling in its intensity. Is it because I am thinking about consciousness that suddenly my experience sharpens? And when I return to write will I be able to reshape the form so that more of this world falls on the page? One can spend a whole life writing, I think to myself, and still hardly begin.

There are examples of online essays that use unexpected formats in the online chapter 14 resources at www.ablongman.com/wysocki

ANALYZING
"Red Shoes" and the form of essays

■ Discuss with others: It is quite possible that you've not encountered an essay like Griffin's before, or that in all the years you spent being taught to write you were never taught how to go about constructing an essay like hers. Why might that be?

■ Discuss with others: In this essay, Griffin seems to be arguing that a part of her purpose—which we think might be stated, quickly, as something like persuading us that "Women have been kept silent and out of the public by the form of the essay"—can only be achieved if she mixes public and private forms of writing. Her arguments, therefore, support her in shaping her essay as she does. How would her argument be changed if she had to present the essay in a more traditional shape?

■ Write: Using a "traditional" form, write a rhetorical analysis of "Red Shoes." Try to answer why Griffin chooses to use an unfamiliar form for making her arguments. You could focus on how color works in the essay to think through what is going on, or you could focus on the alternation between italics and Roman type and between the personal writing and the more public writing, or you could focus on another larger-scale strategy you see.

■ Write: Using a "non-traditional" form, write a rhetorical analysis of this essay. This is hard, for at least two reasons. First, your audience is at ease with and generally expects forms with which they are accustomed; they might need some help from you (by way of an introduction or a postscript, or another strategy) to understand how to read what you present. Second—and this is perhaps even harder—you too are probably most familiar and comfortable with customary forms, to the extent that you might even think within those forms and not realize it (and this may be part of what Griffin is trying to show us in her essay); it is hard to come up with new forms, and hard to understand what new forms can help us express and argue. If you use an unexpected form, and do not see that explaining yourself explicitly within what you write itself fits your purpose, then be sure to write at least a paragraph describing your purpose, and how your purpose supports your strategies. (Teachers are like other people in that they too have grown up into traditional forms that just plain feel like how things ought to be; if you turn in a separate page explaining why you did what you did, this often makes teachers feel more at ease.)

thinking through production

■ Douglas Hesse, a writer and teacher, has written that, "Form in an essay is not dictated by conventions of deductive logic or formal convention but rather by the author's attempt to create a satisfying and finished verbal artifact out of the materials at hand." Use this criterion of "a satisfying and finished verbal artifact" to write a comparison and evaluation of two of the essays in this chapter. You will have to define what "satisfying" and "finished" mean when it comes to a piece of writing.

■ Susan Griffin's purpose in her essay might be stated, quickly, as persuading us that "Women, and bodily experiences, have been kept silent and out of the public eye by the form of the essay." Hers is an argument, then, for mixing public and private forms of writing. Look over all the various examples of photographs, magazine articles, webpages, and other kinds of pages in Section 3 of this book. Because these are media to which many of us have become accustomed simply by being educated in our schools and through what we read and see, it is hard to think about what the expected structures of the examples encourage us to think or do or feel. (And maybe the very distinctions among thinking, acting, and feeling are tied to these examples?) Pick an example from this book—or another text that intrigues you—and restructure it as Griffin restructures the essay, to explore what other kinds of thinking, feeling, or doing can be encouraged by different structures, by trying unexpected strategies. Try making a tiny poster, for example, or

interviewing yourself or your arm or your mind. Produce an interview using only photographs and no words, or use a webpage to make an essay that is as wide across as five sheets of paper, or . . .

You could also try mixing examples: can you make an interview that is an essay or an instruction set? What does experimenting with an example in these ways show you about what the genre allows, or not? What other kinds of arguments are possible with your experimentations? And what kinds of audiences might be able to understand—or begin to understand—what you've done?

▢ There are more "Thinking Through Production" activities in the online chapter 14 resources at www.ablongman.com/wysocki

compose ▪ design ▪ advocate

analyzing comics

What counts as comics—and as a history of comics—is debatable. Some researchers say comics started in the nineteenth century, with "Penny Dreadfuls," teaching tools (that look like present-day Sunday comics) for poor people. Others see the origins of comics in Egyptian painting and Mayan folding books.

The comics with which we are most familiar—those in the Sunday papers, comic books, or graphic novels—depend on particular technologies and audiences. Prior to computers, comics were drawn by hand; print comics couldn't exist until there was an easy way to mass-produce hand-drawn illustrations. That technology is the same as for posters, and—like posters—comics require there to be a large enough literate audience for comic reproduction and selling to make sense to those who finance this work.

Because comics are sequences of pictures with captions, they have been considered less serious than books without pictures. As we noted in the first paragraph, some believe them to have been first produced for the working class; in the United States in the 1950s, Congress heard from experts on child behavior about how comic books were corrupting youth. In the 1960s, comics underwent a renaissance; in the social and political upheaval, cultural assumptions were questioned, and comic books were seen as one way for those who were—or considered themselves to be—outside the mainstream to express or question what couldn't be expressed or questioned in "traditional" formats. As a result, comic books can now be artform as well as children's entertainment, and can be a structure for serious thinking in combined words and drawings.

HOW WE ANALYZE COMICS

HOW WE UNDERSTAND COMICS BECAUSE WE HAVE BODIES . . .

Until the digital age, print comics were almost always reproductions of drawings made by hand. Our bodies link us in two ways to such comics.

First, because almost all of us know what it is to draw, we know something of the bodily gestures of producing the drawings in comics: when we look at such drawings we therefore have a sense of physical closeness to the drawings that we do not have with photographs, for example, which are not produced directly by hand.

The other bodily link we have to comics (and now we can discuss comics that are made from photographs or digital reproduction as well as those that are drawn) is to the objects and bodies in the comics. When we look at comics—just as when we look at posters and photographs—it is in no small part because we have bodies that move in the world that we understand what the objects and bodies are doing and why.

HOW WE UNDERSTAND COMICS BECAUSE WE LIVE IN PARTICULAR TIMES AND PLACES

The Leviathan was an immense sea creature in the Bible, and is the name of the baby in the comic to the right, written and drawn by a man from the United States but published weekly during the early 1990s in the *British Independent on Sunday*. The composer, Peter Blegvad, says he named the baby because of his own children: they're "born, you bring them home, and they're bigger than anything else in your life." In the strip, the baby Leviathan, his stuffed Rabbit, and the Cat interact with others as though babies and cats were capable of complex intellectual observations—without being able to express them to adults.

Leviathan is very self-aware, full of verbal and visual puns. In the panel to the right, the audience is asked to pretend (as with all comics and many paintings and drawings) that what is captured on the page is four-dimensional: there is a moving train about to run over a baby and stuffed animal. At the same time, however, the audience is asked to step out of that pretense to be aware that this is just ink on paper.

This panel uses conventions that we've had to learn. "Chugga chugga" is supposed to mean there's sound, and all the lines moving across the train are supposed to mean the train is moving. The flat white balloons coming out of the characters' mouths are supposed to mean they are

talking. There are also conventions about how drawings represent our experiences, such that we understand that a faceless big head on a little body in a green suit is supposed to be a baby. (Think of all the various cartoon and comic characters you've seen in your life, and how many of those characters look like people only in the sketchiest ways—and yet you accept that they talk and behave like people.)

We've used just one panel of a comic here to get started, but think about the conventions of multipanel comics. You've learned how to read comics so that you can make connections among the panels of a page, understanding how (for example) the passage of time or a shift in location is shown by changes between panels.

Finally, we couldn't understand any of these drawn elements without having grown up in a culture where it's perfectly normal to think flat drawn pictures some-how have movement, sound, and life in them.

Mix into all of this how many conventions we have for using words (and think here about how many years you had to spend learning to read and write) and you have a sense of how complex comics are.

▢ There are examples of more comics in the online chapter 15 resources at www.ablongman.com/wysocki

A MULTIPANEL COMIC

This strip is produced by Joey Comeau and Emily Home; Comeau writes the strips and Home arranges the photographs and words. You can learn more about Comeau and Home by reading their blogs, which are linked to the website. (There is another example of their work in chapter 9.) Comeau and Home have been putting out a new strip every Friday since early 2003.

Comeau and Home's strips draw on ideas that started engaging comic book artists in the 1960s, when comics were seen as one way for those who were—or considered themselves to be—outside the mainstream to express or question what couldn't be expressed or questioned in "traditional" formats. Comic book artists started integrating painting and photographs into their panels, and experimented with how time could be shown across panels.

"A Softer World" has the multiple panels with pictures and captions that we associate with comics, but the relationship it establishes with its audience seems to us very different from superhero comics. "A Softer World" often uses one photograph (broken into several panels or repeated with different framing) with overlaying strips of typewriting. The effect can suggest how we think while we scan a scene around us: the scene doesn't change, but the words in our heads do.

The photographs Comeau and Home use rarely have much implied action in them, and are sometimes out of the ordinary (flying horses) or of overlooked details (the lights around a carnival game or small ornaments on a Christmas tree). The strips of type seem to be the thoughts of the person (or in this case, the cat) in the photograph or of the person taking the photograph.

What conventions about comics do you have to know to make sense of this strip? What conventions from outside the world of comics help you understand?

A MULTIPANEL, MULTIPAGE COMIC

Lynda Barry—who produced the strip above—is primarily known as a cartoonist: her work has been syndicated in more than 100 alternative papers and published in many books. Barry also paints, writes essays, welds, and provides commentary on National Public Radio.

It will help you in reading the comic above—which presents itself as autobiographical—if you know that Barry is one-quarter Filipino and grew up in a working-class Seattle neighborhood (she now lives in the Midwest).

Look for Barry's subtle strategies as you read. She uses self-deprecation and indirection to bring up and consider an issue we don't talk about too much: smell.

I HAVE ALWAYS NOTICED THE SMELL OF OTHER PEOPLE'S HOUSES, BUT WHEN I WAS A KID I WAS FASCINATED BY IT. NO TWO HOUSES EVER SMELLED ALIKE, EVEN IF THE PEOPLE USED THE SAME AIR FRESHENER.

WHAT'S THAT KIND AGAIN?

FRESH EVERGREEN GLEN.

YEAH. AT THE BIDMAN'S THEY GOT THE SAME KIND BUT HERE IT SMELLS LIKE A FRESH, UM, BUS BATHROOM.

SOME OF THE SMELLS WERE UNCOMPLICATED, LIKE THE CAT PEE SMELL OF THE HOUSE NEXT DOOR. THE LADY HAD 14 CATS. IT WAS HARD TO STAY AND VISIT. SHE SOMETIMES BURNED INCENSE WHICH ALSO SMELLED LIKE CAT PEE.

(BREATHING THROUGH MY MOUTH)

HAVE SOME PEANUT BRITTLE, DEAR. JUST PICK THE FUR OFF IF YOU'RE FUSSY, BUT IT WON'T HURT YOU NONE.

52

■ "Common Scents" is the fourth story in the book *One Hundred Demons*, and in the earlier stories we learn that Barry represents her younger self in her drawings by the speckled, red-haired girl. What is the effect on her *ethos* of her visually representing herself in this less-than-flattering way?

■ The captions represent Barry's thinking in the present. What *ethos* does she develop through the words (including how the words are drawn)?

BUT THERE WERE BAD MYS-
TERIES TOO, LIKE THE MYSTERY
OF THE BLEACH PEOPLE WHOSE
HOUSE GAVE OFF FUMES YOU
COULD SMELL FROM THE STREET.
WE KEPT WAITING FOR THAT
HOUSE TO EXPLODE. THE BUGS
DIDN'T EVEN GO IN THEIR YARD.

ALSO GIVING OFF BLEACH FUMES

HEYA, JANINA.

HEYA.

'N I ASK YOU A PERSONAL THING?

POSSIBLY.

HOW COME YOUR HOUSE SMELLS LIKE THAT?

SMELLS LIKE WHAT?

SOME SMELLS WERE MYS-
TERIOUSLY WONDERFUL LIKE
AT THE PALINKI'S WHERE IT WAS
A COMBINATION OF MINT, TAN-
GERINES, AND LIBRARY BOOKS.
BUT HOW? I NEVER SAW ANY
OF THOSE THINGS THERE.

WHAT'S YOUR KIND OF AIR FRESHENER, BECAUSE THAT'S THE KIND I WANT MY MOM TO GET.

I DON'T USE AIR FRESHENER, DEAR.

WELL, THAT'S WEIRD BECAUSE YOUR HOUSE SMELLS PERFECT.

53

■ As you read, compare the written words
in the captions to the drawings and
what the characters say in the drawings.
What do you learn from the captions
that you don't learn from the drawings
and word balloons——and vice versa?

What attitude does Barry encourage you to take toward her family and her family home? What strategies does she use to shape this attitude?

This panel shows the third time someone hasn't noticed the smells of their own homes. Why do you think Barry doesn't just simply write, "People don't notice their own smells"? Why might she leave it up to her audience to notice the repetition and the argument it is making?

The colors here are bright and saturated. Notice how there is very little black—except for the outlines—and no gray. This means that in many cases we would describe the colors Barry uses as cheerful. If you were to read only the words in the captions, would you imagine the colors Barry uses? Why?

What conventions of drawing do you have to know to understand what is going on in this panel? How did you learn those conventions?

The comic panels contain the following text:

Panel 1 (narration): SHE HAD THOSE CAR FRESHENER CHRISTMAS TREE THINGS HANGING EVERYWHERE. EVEN THE MARSHMALLOW TREATS SHE MADE HAD A FRESH PINE-SPRAY FLAVOR. SHE WAS FREE WITH HER OBSERVATIONS ABOUT THE SMELL OF OTHERS.

Panel 1 (speech): YOUR ORIENTALS HAVE AN ARRAY, WITH YOUR CHINESE SMELLING STRONGER THAN YOUR JAPANESE AND YOUR KOREANS FALLING SOMEWHERES IN THE MIDDLE AND DON'T GET ME STARTED ON YOUR FILIPINOS.

Panel 2 (narration): SHE DETAILED THE SMELLS OF BLACKS, MEXICANS, ITALIANS, SOME PEOPLE I NEVER HEARD OF CALLED "BO-HUNKS" AND THE DIFFERENCE IT MADE IF THEY WERE WET OR DRY, FAT OR SKINNY. NATURALLY I BROUGHT THIS INFORMATION HOME.

Panel 2 (speech): AIE N'AKO! WHITE LADIES SMELL BAD TOO, NAMAN! SHE NEVER WASH HER POOKIE! HER KILI-KILI ALWAYS SWEAT-SWEATING! THE OLD ONES SMELL LIKE E-HEE! THAT LADY IS TUNG-AH!

56

This is Barry's grandmother with the black hair, using words from a language most of us probably don't know—although you might feel you can make a good guess about what the words are. Why do you think Barry chooses to use the non-English words?

57

What emotions do you think Barry is working to shape for her audience? What attitudes to their pasts, and to others, is she trying to shape? What strategies has she chosen for evoking these emotions and attitudes?

58

Why might Barry choose to bring us into the present in this frame?

compose ▪ design ▪ advocate

I'VE NEVER HEARD A SINGLE PERSON EVER SAY THEY LOVED THE SMELL OF AIR FRESHENER AND YET THERE ARE SO MANY PEOPLE WHO FILL THEIR HOMES WITH IT.

PLUG-INS

POP UPS

LIGHT BULB SCENT RINGS

POTPOURRI MIXES

AIR WICKS

DANGLERS

STICK ONS

SPRAYS

SCENTED CANDLE NIGHTMARE

CAT PEE INCENSE

WHEN COMBINED WITH NATURAL BUT POWER-FILLED SMELLS, THE RESULTS CAN BE TRAUMATIC.

CHERRY POP-UP FRIED LIVER

TROPICAL PASSION AROMA THERAPY CAT BOX

VANILLA-SPICE DIAPER PAIL

STRAWBERRY-DREAMSCAPE PLUG-IN FRIED FLOUNDER

PINEY WOODS PIG'S BLOOD STEW BREAK DOWN

59

Why do you think Barry ends with this note of nostalgia, saying that she'd like a can of this improbably-smelling air freshener? How are smells connected with memory and with our relations to those closest to us?

compose ▪ *design* ▪ *advocate*

ANALYZING
"Common Scents"

■ **Write:** In this textbook we've focused on sight and hearing: these are the senses addressed by writing, drawings, photographs, and oral communication. Barry asks us to consider smell.

Because smells are tied to bodies and personal spaces, Barry shows how they work both to hold us together and to set us apart. If people smell different from us—or have smells at all (Barry argues that we don't notice our home smells, only those of others)—then we can judge them as different and therefore bad. Those who smell like us (or who don't seem to have smells because they smell like us) we recognize as close, as our family or our culture.

Smells are thus very much tied to emotion—but Barry seems to believe that if we can see how smells both bind and separate us then we can make more thoughtful and generous decisions about our lives with others.

In writing, discuss how persuasive you find her arguments. What strategies does Barry use to pull you into the experiences of smell, families, and neighborhoods so that you will consider smell as she presents it?

■ **Discuss with others:** Like us and like Barry, you probably have had experiences in which others (or their cooking) smelled very strange, if not offensive. Smells can have surprising intensity in shaping how we think about others.

And so Barry's argument is very serious, about the intensity and complexity of relations among different people—and yet Barry's ways of drawing and writing her letters is cartoonish. Her ways of drawing and writing her letters can suggest a childish approach to interpreting the past and our relations with others. Why might she choose such visual approaches to considering relations among people, both adults and children?

How do you think adult audiences—made up of people like you—will respond to such a "childish" approach? Is this a way to "sneak up" on audiences, to present them something serious by leading them to think it's not? Or do you think that this is a way to use emotion in ways hard to do with writing, so that Barry can more easily make us feel what is at stake in how we use smells?

"THE VEIL," FROM *Persepolis: The Story of a Childhood* BY WRITER AND ILLUSTRATOR MARJANE SATRAPI

"I believe that an entire nation should not be judged by the wrongdoings of a few extremists. I do not want those Iranians who lost their lives in prisons defending freedom, who died in the war against Iraq, who suffered under various repressive regimes, or who were forced to leave their families and flee their homeland to be forgotten. One can forgive but one should never forget."

Marjane Satrapi was born in Rasht, Iran, in 1969 and grew up in Iran during the Islamic Revolution and subsequent war with Iraq. She now lives in Paris. *Persepolis* is the comic-story of her childhood years, age six to fourteen. The words above are from the introduction to the book, and give Satrapi's overall purpose for writing the book, to remember.

As you read "The Veil," which is the first chapter of *Persepolis*, watch to see what relationship with her story and ideas Satrapi is asking you to develop through how she draws, the words she puts in the captions and bubbles, and the ordering of the panels.

The questions column:

How would you describe the style of drawing? Does it look sophisticated and elegant to you, or more like the work of a child? Do the drawings show a lot of detail, or do they give you a general idea of how people and places looked? Can you tell people apart?

How would you describe the style of writing? Is it sophisticated and elegant, incredibly detailed, or . . .?

Given the three categories of how words and drawings can interact (which we described in chapter 9), how would you say the words and drawings are interacting here? Could the words exist alone, and still have the same effect?

Why might Satrapi choose to start with a panel of herself, alone, at 10? What sort of *ethos* does this start to establish? What kind of *pathos* is being developed?

By the end of this first page, what conception of Iran has Satrapi constructed for her readers?

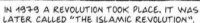

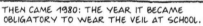

AND ALSO BECAUSE THE YEAR BEFORE, IN 1979, WE WERE IN A FRENCH NON-RELIGIOUS SCHOOL.

WHERE BOYS AND GIRLS WERE TOGETHER.

AND THEN SUDDENLY IN 1980...

ALL BILINGUAL SCHOOLS MUST BE CLOSED DOWN.

THEY ARE SYMBOLS OF CAPITALISM.

BRAVO!

WHAT WISDOM!

OF DECADENCE.

THIS IS CALLED A "CULTURAL REVOLUTION."

WE FOUND OURSELVES VEILED AND SEPARATED FROM OUR FRIENDS.

AND THAT WAS THAT...

■ Notice how some of the panels have white backgrounds, and some black. What is going on in the panels with the black backgrounds? Why do you think Satrapi chose to use the black backgrounds where she has?

■ Why might Satrapi choose to show us the man's face in this row of panels first from close up, then from a distance, and then extremely close up?

525

You've read far enough to have a sense of the tone of voice in the writing. Is it highly emotional, or completely neutral, or . . . ? How does Satrapi show us emotion in this strip? Why might she have chosen to show emotion as she does?

Why do you think the drawing in the panel showing Satrapi's mother dyeing her hair is at an angle?

526

I REALLY DIDN'T KNOW WHAT TO THINK ABOUT THE VEIL. DEEP DOWN I WAS VERY RELIGIOUS BUT AS A FAMILY WE WERE VERY MODERN AND AVANT-GARDE.

I WAS BORN WITH RELIGION.

AT THE AGE OF SIX I WAS ALREADY SURE I WAS THE LAST PROPHET. THIS WAS A FEW YEARS BEFORE THE REVOLUTION.

O' Celestial light!

BEFORE ME THERE HAD BEEN A FEW OTHERS.

A WOMAN?

I AM THE LAST PROPHET.

I WANTED TO BE A PROPHET...

BECAUSE OUR MAID DID NOT EAT WITH US.

BECAUSE MY FATHER HAD A CADILLAC.

AND, ABOVE ALL, BECAUSE MY GRANDMOTHER'S KNEES ALWAYS ACHED.

COME HERE MARJI! HELP ME TO STAND UP.

DON'T WORRY. SOON YOU WON'T HAVE ANY MORE PAIN. YOU'LL SEE.

■ Why do you think Satrapi tells us about her own religious feelings several pages into her story, rather than at the very beginning?

■ How does Satrapi represent the tensions she was feeling at the time? How do you understand those tensions?

527

How would these pages be different if they were in the bright colors of the Lynda Barry comic strip?

Is Satrapi using strategies that ask you to identify with the young girl, or is she making the girl seem too distant or mature or strange for a reader to feel any such emotion for the girl?

7

EVERY NIGHT I HAD A BIG DISCUSSION WITH GOD.

GOD, GIVE ME SOME MORE TIME. I AM NOT QUITE READY YET.

YES YOU ARE, CELESTIAL LIGHT, YOU ARE MY CHOICE, MY LAST AND MY BEST CHOICE.

EXCEPT FOR MY GRANDMOTHER I WAS OBVIOUSLY THE ONLY ONE WHO BELIEVED IN MYSELF.

WHAT DO YOU WANT TO BE WHEN YOU GROW UP?

I'LL BE A PROPHET.

HAHA! HAHA! HAHA!

SHE'S CRAZY.

MY PARENTS WERE CALLED IN BY THE TEACHER.

YOUR CHILD IS DISTURBED. SHE WANTS TO BECOME A PROPHET.

WHAT ABOUT IT?

DOESN'T THIS WORRY YOU?

NO! NOT AT ALL!

?

■ On these pages Satrapi is showing us she had a childhood desire that worried people around her. Do you think Satrapi has tried to develop this narrative so that her readers will not think she was odd? If so, what strategies has she used to do this?

529

8

In our short introduction to Satrapi's story, we quoted some of her words about how one reason she produced *Persepolis* was to keep in our memories those who have suffered or died because of events in Iran. If she is interested in keeping in mind others besides herself, why do you think she keeps this chapter so focused on herself and her religious inclinations?

ANALYZING
"The Veil"

■ Discuss with others: Read the captions in "The Veil" to several friends who haven't seen the book—and when you read, do not show your friends the pictures. Ask your friends to describe what they learn from the words. How does this differ from what you think you learned from reading the comic with the drawings?

■ Discuss with others: In the remaining chapters of *Persepolis*, Satrapi describes how political changes in Iran over the years, the Iranian revolution, and the war with Iraq affected the lives of her extended family, of friends— and of all Iranians. There are bombings and exiles, torture and death—as well as births and parties and vacations abroad. Given the seriousness of these matters, why do you think Satrapi chose to tell her story as a comic book? What various purposes might she be trying to achieve?

■ Write with others: Compare how Satrapi and Barry use captions in their comics. List for yourself how comic producers can use captions as strategies. As you make your list, consider how the captions interact— support, or add information to, or work together with or against—the drawings.

thinking through production

■ Choose a text you've already produced, such as a paper for a class, a brochure, or an informational website. Using the technologies available to you, reproduce the text as a paper or online comic book. (Use the various strategies you see in this chapter or in examples you know from elsewhere to make choices about your arrangements, media, and other strategies.) Test the two different texts with similar audiences: How do audience responses differ? How do you account for the differences?

Write a short paper (or make another comic) in which you analyze the differences between the original text and the comic. What different kinds of relationships can you develop with your audience in your different texts? What differing kinds of *ethos*, *pathos*, and *logos* can you develop in the different texts?

■ The examples of this chapter suggest to us that there is a tremendous amount of untapped potential in comics for making arguments we've not seen in comics.

Choose a topic you've not seen addressed in comics, and use the rhetorical design process from chapters 2–4 to plan, produce, and test a comic on that topic.

■ As we produced this chapter about comics, we realized that at least two of our examples show how emotions are complexly woven within our lives. Both Satrapi and Barry use what some might characterize as childish drawings to engage us in considering the strong and rich emotional lives we have and how those lives are shaped by what goes on around us.

Choose a complex emotional event from your experiences, and develop it as a comic. Use the rhetorical design process from chapters 2–4 to plan, produce, and test your comic. (Use the various strategies you see in this chapter or in examples you know from elsewhere to make choices about your arrangements, media, and other strategies.)

☐ There are more "Thinking Through Production" activities in the online chapter 15 resources at www.ablongman.com/wysocki

compose ▪ design ▪ advocate

CREDITS

IMAGE CREDITS

Page 7, Timothy Hursley (l), Copyright ©2002 Guerrilla Girls, Inc., courtesy of www.guerrillagirls.com (c), Courtesy of the Occupational Therapy Department, Columbia University (r); page 9, Vatican Pool/CORBIS SYGMA; page 22, Getty Images; page 23, Getty Images; page 39, Getty Images; page 40, Getty Images; page 42, Getty Images; page 50, CORBIS; page 57, Getty Images; page 76, Getty Images; page 89, Courtesy of Kaplan Gaunt DeSantis Architects (t), Subliminal Projects (b); page 93, Library of Congress, cph 3b52087; page 95, Library of Congress, LC-USZC2-936 (c), Library of Congress, LC-USZC2-926 (r); page 96, Josef Koudelka/Magnum Photos (t), Josef Koudelka/Magnum Photos (b); page 106, Getty Images; page 121, Schomburg Center for Research in Black Culture / General Research and Reference Division, New York Public Library, Astor, Lenox, and Tilden Foundations; page 123, Photography Collection, Miriam and Ira D. Wallach Division of Art, Prints and Photographs, New York Public Library, Astor, Lenox, and Tilden Foundations; page 125, Schomburg Center for Research in Black Culture / Photographs and Prints Division, New York Public Library, Astor, Lenox, and Tilden Foundations; page 126, Photography Collection, Miriam and Ira D. Wallach Division of Art, Prints and Photographs, New York Public Library, Astor, Lenox, and Tilden Foundations; page 128, Photography Collection, Miriam and Ira D. Wallach Division of Art, Prints and Photographs, New York Public Library, Astor, Lenox, and Tilden Foundations; page 129, Photography Collection, Miriam and Ira D. Wallach Division of Art, Prints and Photographs, New York Public Library, Astor, Lenox, and Tilden Foundations; page 130, Photography Collection, Miriam and Ira D. Wallach Division of Art, Prints and Photographs, New York Public Library, Astor, Lenox, and Tilden Foundations; page 131, Photography Collection, Miriam and Ira D. Wallach Division of Art, Prints and Photographs, New York Public Library, Astor, Lenox, and Tilden Foundations; page 134, Library of Congress ; pages 136–137, Library of Congress, cph 3b27563; page 138, Library of Congress, cph 3g11368; page 139, Library of Congress, cph 3b08296; page 147, Getty Images; page 152, Getty Images; page 159, Getty Images; page 177, Getty Images; page 269, Library of Congress, var 0515; page 269, Library of Congress, ppmsca 02512; page 294, Rare Book and Manuscripts, Library of Congress; page 304b, Joey Corneau and Emily Horne; page 306, Minneapolis Public Library, Special Collections Department; page 307, National Archives; page 308, Helen Hughes; page 310, Chris Jordan; page 312, David Lance Goines; page 318, Archives and Special Collections, RIT Library, Rochester Institute of Technology (l), Library of Congress (c); page 319, "Common Scents" taken from *One! Hundred! Demons!* by Lynda Barry, reprinted courtesy of Darhansoff, Verrill, Feldman Literary Agents (rc); page 324, Courtesy Everett Collection; page 324, Courtesy Everett Collection; page 325, Courtesy Everett Collection (l), Kobal Collection (r); page 331, Courtesy Everett Collection; page 332, Courtesy Everett Collection; page 333, Courtesy Everett Collection; page 334, Courtesy Everett Collection; page 335, Courtesy Everett Collection; page 335, Courtesy Everett Collection; page 336, Reel Poster Archive Company (l); Courtesy Everett Collection (r); page 338, Library of Congress, LC-USZC4-2736 (l), Library of Congress, cph 3g03858 (c), National Archives (tr); Library of Congress (br); page 339, Trustees of the Imperial War Museum (tl), International Poster Gallery, Boston, MA (tr), Library of Congress, LC-USZC4-2010 (bl), National Archives (bc), Library of Congress, cph 3g11317 (br); page 340, Library of Congress, LC-USZC4-2736, page 342, Yolanda M. Lopez; page 345, Reel Poster Archive Company; page 346, Reel Poster Archive Company; page 349, Library of Congress, LC-USZ62-103851; page 350, Library of Congress, LC-USZ62-98125; 351 Library of Congress, LC-USZ62-99609 (tl), Library of Congress, LC-USZ62-112235 (bl), Library of Congress, LC-USZ62-89992 (r); Page 355, Library of Congress, LC-USZ62-69913; page 356, Library of Congress, LC-USZ62-69913; page 358, Library of Congress, LC-USZ62-116204 (t), Library of Congress, LC-USZ62-98125 (bl), Library of Congress, LC-USZ62-103851 (br); page 359, Library of Congress, LC-USZ62-45843 (t), Library of Congress, LC-USZ62-69913 (b); page 364, Guergui Pinkhassov/Magnum Photos; page 365, Guergui Pinkhassov/Magnum Photos; pages 366–367, Guergui Pinkhassov/Magnum Photos; pages 368–369, Guergui Pinkhassov/Magnum Photos; pages 372–373, Josef Koudelka/Magnum Photos; pages 374–375, Josef Koudelka/Magnum Photos; pages 376–377, Josef Koudelka/Magnum Photos; page 394, Kidde Safety; pages 418–419, The Trustees of the Ansel Adams Publishing Rights Trust/CORBIS; page 421, The Trustees of the Ansel Adams Publishing Rights Trust/CORBIS; pages 446–447, Lynn Johnson/Aurora; pages 448–449, Lynn Johnson/Aurora; page 450, Lynn Johnson/Aurora; page 451, Lynn Johnson/Aurora; pages 452–453, Lynn Johnson/Aurora; page 454, Lynn Johnson/Aurora; page 455, Lynn Johnson/Aurora; page 456, Lynn Johnson/Aurora; page 457, Lynn Johnson/Aurora; page 458, Lynn Johnson/Aurora; page 459, Lynn Johnson/Aurora; page 476, © The Washington Post, reprinted with permission (C), 476R © The Washington Post, reprinted with permission (R); page 511, Peter Blegvad, from "The Book of Leviathan," 2001; page 512, Joey Corneau and Emily Horne; pages 513–522, "Common Scents" taken from One! Hundred! Demons! by Lynda Barry, reprinted courtesy of Darhansoff, Verrill, Feldman Literary Agents; pages 524–530, "The Veil", from PERSEPOLIS: THE STORY OF A CHILDHOOD by Marjane Satrapi, translated by Mattias Ripa & Black Ferris, Translation copyright ©2003 by L'Asociation, Paris, France. Used by permission of Pantheon Books, a division of Random House, Inc.; All others courtesy of the author.

TEXT CREDITS

page 6: *Multiliteracies: Literacy Learning and the Design of Social Futures* by Bill Cope and Mary Kalantzis. London: Routledge, 2000.

page 14, 183: Excerpt from "Race and the Public Intellectual: A Conversation with Michael Dyson" in *Race, Rhetoric and the Postcolonial,* eds. Gary Olson and Lynn Worsham, State University of New York Press, 1999. Used by permission of the State University of New York Press.

page 15: From *Sunday, Monday and Always* by Dawn Powell, published by Steerforth Press of Hanover, New Hampshire. Steerforth Press Edition Copyright © 1999 by The Estate of Dawn Powell. Used by permission.

page 50: From "Back Talk," an interview with Steven Heller by Don Norman from PRINT Magazine, March/April 2001. Used by permission of PRINT Magazine.

page 56: Excerpts from *A Smile in the Mind: Witty Thinking in Graphic Design* by Beryl McAlhone and David Stuart. Copyright © 1996 Phaidon Press Limited. Used by permission.

page 60: *Multiliteracies: Literacy Learning and the Design of Social Futures* by Bill Cope and Mary Kalantzis. London: Routledge, 2000.

page 64: The New Yorker Online, The Meaning of Coincidence—An Interview with the writer W. G. Sebald by Joe Cuomo, 2001.

page 80: From "Moonrise" by Penny Wolfson. *The Atlantic Monthly*, December 2001.

page 80: From "Notes from the Country Club" by Kimberly Wozencraft. *Witness*, 1987.

page 95: Lyrics from "Don't Drink the Water," written by David J. Matthews. Copyright 1998 Colden Grey, Ltd. Used by permission.

page 81: From *Political Crumbs* by Hans Magnus Enzensberger, translated by Martin Chalmers. Verso, 1990.

page 81: From foreword by Mary Pipher to *Real Boys* by William Pollack. Henry Holt, 1999.

Page 82: Excerpt from "Reading Philosophy at Night" from *Wonderful Words, Silent Truth* by Charles Simic. Ann Arbor: The University of Michigan Press, 1990. Used by permission.

Page 83: Excerpt from "Who We Are" by David Halberstam, originally published in *Vanity Fair*, November 2001. Used by permission of the author.

Page 83: Ehrenreich, Barbara, from "Welcome to Cancerland" by Barbara Ehrenreich. Copyright © 2001 by Barbara Ehrenreich. Originally appeared in *Harper's*. Reprinted by permission of International Creative Management, Inc.

Page 85: From "One Violent Crime" by Bruce Shapiro. *The Nation*, 1995.

Page 91: From "Out of the Ordinary" by Cullen Murphy. *The Atlantic Monthly*, October 2001.

Page 91: From *Dispatches from the Tenth Circle: The Best of the Onion* by Robert Siegel. *The Onion*, Inc. 2001.

Page 94: Thomson, David. From *The New Biographical Dictionary of Film* by David Thomson. Alfred A. Knopf, 2002.

Page 94: From "Gettysburg" by Arthur C. Danto. Grand Street, 1987.

Pages 116–119: Screen shots courtesy of AVODAH, www.avodah.net.

Pages 120–131: "After Seattle: Anarchists Get Organized" by William Finnegan in *The New Yorker*, April 17, 2000. Used by permission of the author.

Pages 145–140: Reprinted with the permission of Simon & Schuster Adult Publishing Group from *Partly Cloudy Patriot* by Sarah Vowell. Copyright © 2002 by Sarah Vowell.

Pages 182 and 213: Selection from page 7 "You write it all...delicate as a worm" and from page 46 "How appalled...hands like a gardener." from *The Writing Life* by Annie Dillard. Copyright © 1989 by Annie Dillard. Reprinted by permission of HarperCollins Publishers.

Page 202: From *First You Build a Cloud* by K. C. Cole. Harcourt, 1999.

Page 207: From *Life As We Know It* by Michael Bérubé. Random House, 1996

Page 212: From "Save the Whales, Screw the Shrimp" by Joy Williams. Copyright © 1989 by Joy Williams. Originally appeared in *Esquire*. Reprinted by permission of International Creative Management, Inc.

Page 218 (Churchill): From *20,000 Quips & Quotes*, Evan Esar editor. Copyright © 1968 Evan Esar. Barnes & Noble Books, 1995.

Page 218 (Nietzsche): From *20,000 Quips & Quotes*, Evan Esar editor. Copyright © 1968 Evan Esar. Barnes & Noble Books, 1995.

Pages 234–237: Reprinted by permission of Waveland Press, Inc. from Sonja K. Foss and Karen A. Foss, *Inviting Transformation: Presentational Speaking for a Changing World*. (Long Grove, IL: Waveland Press, Inc., 2003). All rights reserved.

Page 239 (Freud): From *20,000 Quips & Quotes*, Evan Esar editor. Copyright © 1968 Evan Esar. Barnes & Noble Books, 1995.

Pages 246–249: Reprinted by permission of Waveland Press, Inc. from Sonja K. Foss and Karen A. Foss, *Inviting Transformation: Presentational Speaking for a Changing*

World. (Long Grove, IL: Waveland Press, Inc., 2003). All rights reserved.

Page 240: From *A Room of One's Own* by Virginia Woolf. Harcourt, 1929.

Page 245 (Locke): From *20,000 Quips & Quotes*, Evan Esar editor. Copyright © 1968 Evan Esar. Barnes & Noble Books, 1995.

Page 245 (Nietzsche): From *20,000 Quips & Quotes*, Evan Esar editor. Copyright © 1968 Evan Esar. Barnes & Noble Books, 1995.

Page 245 (Shaw): From *20,000 Quips & Quotes*, Evan Esar editor. Copyright © 1968 Evan Esar. Barnes & Noble Books, 1995.

Page 245 (Wilco, Wings, Doors): Acknowledged in text of book.

Page 261: From *The Collected Poems of Langston Hughes* by Langston Hughes, copyright © 1994 by The Estate of Langston Hughes. Used by permission of Alfred A. Knopf, a division of Random House, Inc.

Page 265: From "Wrong Turn" by Malcolm Gladwell from *The New Yorker*, June 11, 2001. Used by permission of the author.

Page 276: Brochure used by permission of PETA, People for the Ethical Treatment of Animals.

Page 294: Screen shot from 360 Degrees website. Used by permission.

Page 299: From "To Li Po" from *Monsoon History* by Shirley Geok-lin Lim. Copyright © 1994 by Shirley Geok-lin Lim. Used by permission of the author.

Page 300: "How to Write a Protest Letter" by Jennifer L. Pozner, founder and executive director of Women in Media & News (WIMN). Used by permission of the author.

Pages 383–385: Excerpt from *An Illustrated Dictionary of Japanese Onomatopoetic Expressions*, with illustrations by Taro Gomi, published by *The Japan Times*, 1989. Used with permission of *The Japan Times*.

compose ▪ design ▪ advocate

INDEX

compose ▪ design ▪ advocate

technical details of, 48–49
Productus typeface, 284
Professional quality to visual text, 272
Proofreading, 214, 215
Protest letter, 300
Public speaking, 234
  anxiety of, 252–253
Public writing, 400, 429, 508
Purpose. *See also* Statement of purpose
  analysis of, 320, 321
  of communication, 25
  of essay, 438
  planning speech and, 232–233
  sample design plan description of, 53
  sense of, 67–68
    for instruction sets, 383, 385, 386, 388
  of speech, 251
  of visual communication, 268
  of writing, 190

Q
Questionnaire, for audience, 230
Questions
  generating, 64
  interview, 258
  in introduction to speech, 240
  research
    of consequence, 147, 148, 149
    of definition, 147, 148
    developing initial, 147–149
    of fact, 147, 148
    of interpretation, 147, 148, 149
    of policy, 147, 148, 149
    researching, 152–153
    using to determine what need to research, 150
    of value, 147, 148
Quotation
  in introduction, 194
    to speech, 240
  as support material, 255

R
Racism, essays on, 194, 446–464
Read-aloud tests, 103

Readers, transitions and, 205. *See also* Audience
Recordings, 88
Reference librarian, preparing to get help from, 155
Relationships, communication and creation of, 27, 30
Relaxation exercises, 253
Repeating alignment, 293
Repetition, 95–96
  in essay, 445, 460–461
  in visual communication, 287–294
    creating visual hierarchy using, 288–290
    creating visual unity using, 291–294
  in writing, 203
Research
  advocacy and, 144
  into audience, 150
  carrying out, 151–160
  choosing sources, 153
  citation of, 169, 171
  in community, 154, 158
  contexts of visual communication, 266
  deciding what to, 152
  defined, 144
  designing rhetorical, 146–147
  to develop and test design plan, 161–163
  documentation, 160
  ethics of, 145
  evaluating, 159–160
  interviewing and, 256
  motivations for, 145
  of not so obvious topic, 150
  of obvious topic, 150
  online, 154, 156
  in organizations, 154, 157
  preliminary, 63
  producing and testing communication, 164–174
  purpose of, 143
  questions
    to ask sources, 160
    to determine what to research, 150
    developing initial, 147–149
  as social action, 145
  sources of, 153–158
  stages of, 151
Research paper, 59

argumentative, 144
  design plan for, 161–163
  draft, 164–166
  feedback form for, 220
  final draft, 168–172
  testing, 173
Research writing, qualities of polished, 173–174
Respect, establishing in interview, 258
Revision, of writing, 213–217
  example, 216–217
Rewriting, 214
Rhetoric
  composition and, 3
  design and, 29–30
  design *vs.*, 5
  effects of color, 276
  grammar and spelling and, 218
  origin of, 29
  revising and editing and, 214
  visual communication and, 263
Rhetoric, The (Aristotle), 80
Rhetorical analysis, 189, 320–327
  of editorial, 422–423
  of essay, 438–443
  of visual essay, 360–362
  writing up, 323–326
Rhetorical research, designing, 146–147
Rogerian organizational pattern, 248–249

S
Safety, transformation and, 236
Sans serif typeface, 280, 281, 282
Saturation, 275
School desegregation cases, essay on personal effect of, 476–491
Screen visual arguments, 95
Script typeface, 281, 283
Secondary audience, 71
Section breaks, in essay, 445
Seeing, selectivity of, 265
Self-change, 236
Self-identity, audience and, 69
Selfish advocacy, 133
Self-test for writing draft, 219